MONSON
Free Library and Reading Room
ASSOCIATION
Monson, MA 01057

No. 65338

RULES AND REGULATIONS

Assessed fines shall be paid by every person keeping library materials beyond the specified time.

Every person who borrows library materials shall be responsible for all loss or damage to same while they are out in his/her name.

All library materials shall be returned to the Library on the call of the Librarian or Directors.

SEE ALSO
General Laws of Mass.
Chapter 266:
Sections 99, 99A and 100

Tales of New England Past

Edited by
Frank Oppel

CASTLE

65338

Tales of New England Past

Copyright © 1987 CASTLE
a division of Book Sales, Inc.
110 Enterrpise Avenue
Secaucus, NJ 07094

Manufactured in the United States of America.

ISBN: 1-55521-229-8

Contents

Huntsmen of the Sea
(1874)

HUNTSMEN OF THE SEA.

A NIMROD OF THE SEA.

WITHIN the memory of most of us there was a time when we sought some quiet spot at home to read, undisturbed, a romance of the American whale-fisheries. The subject has charms that commend it to all young readers, since it comprehends at the same time both hunting adventures and the wonders of the deep. We are not surprised, then, at the great number of writers for boys who have chosen this field for the scene of their books. But we are surprised and regretful that none of them ever trusted in the riches it contains, and that they preferred to follow their own imaginations into the wildest impossibilities rather than to gather truths infinitely more interesting. More scientific writers have scarcely done better. Perhaps we should say they have done worse, for they have stated as facts things as flimsy as the flimsiest yarns of the story-tellers. Heretofore there have been no trustworthy authorities on the subject, and for the first time a writer appears with credentials that entitle him to the widest consideration.*

He is not a romancer who fabricates his thrilling stories of the sea on dry land, nor a learned Dryasdust, who comes with fresh and sprightly theories from the dissecting-room, but a man from before the mast, who saw and heard with his own eyes and ears all the things that he has written about. His narrative is the unvarnished story of a forecastle hand, and its chief merits are its veracity and its picturesque simplicity. In some chapters it is rollicking and brimful of adventure; in others it is sad, and weighted down with the miseries of forecastle life. The descriptions of scenery and the phenomena of the ocean are often so very *naïve* that if we were not told of their author's busi-

* *Nimrod of the Sea; or, the American Whaleman.* By W. Morris Davis. New York: Harper and Brothers.

ness, we could easily guess it. The work is eminently one for popular entertainment and instruction; and in one of its most absorbing chapters it shows the brilliant development of the American whale trade. Furthermore we have nothing to add, save to reiterate that the whole subject is one of intense interest to old and young, as, we think, the material gathered in the succeeding pages will prove. The historical part properly comes first. Some of the adventures will be told later on.

"THERE SHE BLOWS

In the reign of King Alfred, it is said, there appeared in England a gallant old Northman, who told his majesty wondrous stories about the whales captured by the Finns off the coast of Lapland. Alfred was so impressed with the advantages of the enterprise that he caused the information to be spread through his kingdom, hoping that his people would engage in it. But they did not, and until 1598 there is no further record on the subject. In that year, according to Hakluyt's *Voyages and Discoveries*, an honest London merchant wrote to a friend of his, requesting "to be advised and directed in the course of killing a whale." The answer conveyed the information that competent whalemen and tools were to be obtained in Biscay, where the people had been engaged in the hazardous business since 1390. The correspondence resulted in the equipment of a whaling fleet, which met with great success, and was increased until the English were unrivaled in the Greenland fisheries. Things might have gone happily, but the Dutch intruded on English ground, and met with a hearty English welcome. Their tackle and oil were seized, and they were told to depart, under the penalty of losing their vessels also. They submitted, but only until some war vessels arrived to protect them, when they resumed the business, and continued it unmolested.

Soon afterward the English relinquished the fishery, and did not again occupy it until the time of Charles the Second. In 1618 it is recorded that the whale-fisheries of Holland employed 12,000 men. This is considered an exaggeration; but in a work called *Discourses upon Trade*, published in 1670, the statement occurs that "the Greenland whale-fisheries of the Dutch and Hamburgers have annually 400 or 500 ships, while the English have only one." It is also said that in forty-six years, ending with 1721, the Dutch made 5886 voyages, and captured 32,906 whales, valued at £16,000,000.

Emulous of so prosperous a traffic, the English again made determined efforts to recover what they had lost, the government granting bounties to whalemen, and allowing them exemption from the press-gang. But for some hidden reason the capitalists and tars alike avoided the service, and refused the bait held out to them. The amount of the bounty offered was again increased, and Protestant foreigners were invited to immigrate and avail themselves of all the privileges extended to natural-born subjects; but England, though so grand a naval power, was still unable to muster a whaling fleet or find the stalwart men to man it.

The service required strength, pluck, and enterprise. In these things Americans would suit it, and in 1672 the fruit of their toil in the whale-fisheries first appeared in the markets. We believe there is yet extant the first agreement ever made in America on the subject. In it "James Loper doth ingage to carry on a design of whale catching on the island of Nantucket. That is to say, James ingages to be a third in all respects, and some of the town ingages on the other two-thirds in a like manner."

This little spark, Captain Davis observes, kindled a great flame that burned around the world.

Work was begun on the smallest scale in boats from the shore by thrifty, industrious, and courageous men. It attracted the Americans almost as much as it repelled the English, and in 1761 the small island of Nantucket employed ten vessels of 100 tons each. In the year following the number had increased to fifteen vessels, and within twelve months more a magnificent fleet of eighty vessels, all hailing from Nantucket, were afloat in search of whales on the nearest and most distant waters.

The whalebone exported from America to Great Britain reduced the price of that material one-third. The British government had thus far expended the extraordinary sum of £1,687,902 in bounties, and were content a while to watch the progress of their colonial subjects in the whale-fisheries; but after the Declaration of Independence they were no longer interested in them, and renewed and added to their offers of bounties. They offered a premium of £600 to the vessel proceeding to the Pacific, continuing four months on the ground, and, after being sixteen months out, having the greatest quantity of sperm-oil on board. Five hundred pounds more were promised to any of the seven vessels having the next greatest quantity. A second invitation was also issued to foreigners, who were allowed to import their goods free of duty and to compete for all the premiums. The pertinacity of the government appears as strange as the aversion of the sailors to an exciting service in which they might be expected to glory.

The Americans were never assisted by their government, and depended on their own resources alone. Their success elicited a brilliant eulogy from Burke in the English Parliament; and on the Arctic and Antarctic, the Pacific and the Atlantic, they were unrivaled as hunters of the grandest game in the world. In 1840 the whaling fleet numbered 675 vessels, most of them measuring over 400 tons each, and their total capacity was 200,000 tons. They were manned by 1700 of the hardiest, pluckiest, and most indomitable seamen. Their value was $25,000,000, and they carried on an annual business of $5,000,000.

The secret of the success of the Nantucket whalemen is strikingly stated in *Nimrod of the Sea*. They practiced co-operation to perfection. "From the first," says Captain Davis, "the people clubbed their means to build or buy a vessel, and many branches of the labor were conducted by those immediately interested in the voyage. The cooper while employed in making casks took good care that they were of sound and seasoned wood, lest they might leak his oil in the long voyage; the blacksmith forged the choicest iron in the shank of the harpoon, which he knew, perhaps from actual experience, would be put to the severest test in wrenching and twisting as the whale, in which he had a one-hundredth interest, was secured; the rope-maker faithfully tested each yarn of the tow-line to make certain that it would carry 200 pounds of strain, for he well knew that one weak inch in his work might cause the loss of a fighting monster; the very women and girls who made the clothing remembered in their toil that father, brother, or one dearer yet might wear the garment, and extra stitches were lovingly thrown in to save the loss of a button or the ripping of a seam." Thus it was that the profits of the labor were directly enjoyed by those engaged in it, and the workman's interest was the master's, and the master's the workman's.

The English capitalists could not compete with such a hive of co-operationists, although their government aided them with a premium of ten dollars per ton burden of the vessels, protected them by excessive duties on American oil, and granted unprecedented immunities to their seamen. They were compelled to relinquish the honor and the glory and the profit, and to simply watch how others could excel them. For many years to come the commoners of Nantucket, New Bedford, and New London were destined to be masters of the whale-fisheries.

No doubt those of you who are young are impatient for a glimpse of life on board a whaling ship, and now that we have shown you how the Americans came to be renowned in the profession, this desire shall be gratified. The excitement, the adventures, the perils, and the prizes of the service very naturally allure many boys of a roving disposition away from home. If you happen to stroll along the docks to-morrow,

STRUCK ON A BREACH.

you will see outside some of the shipping-offices such unflattering advertisements as, "Greenhorns wanted for whaling voyages." And not far off there will likely be an uncouth lad contemplating it with a wistful eye, ready to obey the first beck of the agent within, and to sign articles for a long three years' cruise. The lad is fearful that the agent will reject him; but usually the agent is as anxious to ship him as he is to be shipped. Captain Davis had the charms of a whaling voyage most eloquently described to him as he stood, fresh from a Pennsylvania farm-house, in a New London shipping-office: "There's fresh beef in plenty; the porpoise is to be had for the catching, and there's muscle in porpoise—it'll stiffen you up, porpoise will. Then there's albatross as big as geese—a little oily, but you'll get used to that, and it makes a man waterproof to eat albatross." And so the lad, who needs no cajolery, willingly writes his name in a sprawling hand to the articles, and with a pat on the back is sent to the outfitter's store, where he is rigged in kerseys, canvas, and tarpaulin.

The whale-fishery is considered one of the best schools for seamen that we have. But the relations between officers and men were as brutal on the vessel in which Captain Davis sailed his first voyage as on most ships in other services. The captain and officers were tyrannical masters, and the men vindictive slaves. The rope's-end and, on one occasion, the revolver were the arguments used to bring refractory sinners to their senses. The officers swore at the men aloud, and cheated them to their faces. The men swore at the officers in an under-breath, and were treacherous in dark corners. Once there was a revolt, the men protecting a lad from the captain's cat-o'-nine-tails. The mutineers were imprisoned without a trial by an ignorant consul of the United States in one of the Hawaiian ports, and were released after many months by a war vessel. Quarrels, threats, blows, and desertions were of frequent occurrence, and out of the large crew that sailed from New London only four or five returned home in the same ship.

The good days of co-operation were waning, we should think, when Captain Davis went to sea. But there was never a time when the crew refused to work, or allowed a whale to pass without lowering the boats and cheerfully risking their lives in its capture; and a can of grog was never sent to the forecastle nor a kind word said that did not awaken manifest gratitude in these poor sons of the sea. Considering all things, we think that the sailors were to be blamed least. A pathetic incident is related of the illness of a boy named Beers. He was left alone and unattended, without nourishment or medicines, on a narrow shelf in a foul-smelling, vermin-infested pantry. When one of the forecastle hands found him he was delirious, murmuring the words over and over again, "Oh, how lonely to die so far away from home and friends!—how lonely! how lonely!" And when he recovered consciousness he stroked the hand of his comrade and continued in the same strain, "I should not mind dying near the shore in the track of other vessels; but here, so far at sea, how lonely! how lonely!" His spirit was not released until after many hours of suffering, and he died "babbling of green fields."

All ills on shipboard were treated by one formula. A powerful dose of Epsom salts was first administered to the patient, and if that effected no improvement, a still more powerful dose of jalap followed, with the object of neutralizing the salts. But if neither medicine produced a favorable change, they were supplemented by a potion of calomel that either killed or cured.

In the long voyage around Cape Horn to the sperm-whale ground there are few incidents that have not been often described before. The vessel is followed by the flying-fish, the pilot-fish, and the albatross, and in smooth weather the crews are drilled in capturing a dummy whale. A spar is towed astern, and the greenhorns in the boats manœuvre around it with a great deal of earnestness, and are taught some of the tricks of the trade. But as soon as they reach the Banks of Brazil actual service is due, and each man is alert for the stirring cry from the mast-head, "There she blows!" The ship is under sail during the day only, and in the night she stands by under close-reefed canvas, an arrangement which allows the crew long watches below, and prepares them for hard toil during the day. The captain and mates strain their eyes across the waters, and the humblest deck hand is not less zealous and anxious. When at last the word is heard from aloft, and is repeated quick and oft, the boats are manned with such alacrity and precision as are seldom seen elsewhere.

The American whale-boats, by-the-way, are unexcelled in beauty, speed, and durability. They are twenty-eight feet long, swelling amid-ships to six feet in breadth. The gunwale is twenty-two inches above the keel amid-ships, and rises with an accelerated curve to thirty-seven inches at each end. The elevation of bow and stern, and a clipper-like upper form, give them a duck-like capacity to ride advancing waves that would fill and sink ordinary boats. The gunwale and keel are of the very best timber, and are the heaviest parts, giving a firmness to the rest of the structure. The planking is of half-inch white cedar. We scarcely hope that these specifications will interest the landsman, but by them the quality of the boats shall be known to watermen. Let us add that one of these boats can be lifted by two men, and that it will make ten miles an hour in a dead chase by oars alone.

The equipment of each consists of a line tub, in which are coiled 300 fathoms of the best hempen cord; a mast and sprit-sail; oars, harpoons, and lances; a small apparatus to extinguish the fires that might be ignited by the friction of the cord drawn from the reel; a water keg, lantern, candles, compass, waif flags on poles, and bandages for wounds. The harpoon is a barbed triangular iron, very sharp on the edges, and the lance is a somewhat similar instrument. There is a modern invention, called a bomb-lance, which is not often found in American boats. It is an iron tube about eighteen inches long, sharp at one end, and provided with elastic wings at the other, which serve as the feathers of an arrow. The tube contains six ounces of powder and a fuse, and is aimed at the whale's vital parts. Sometimes it kills instantly, but it is considered uncertain in fastening, and, as we have said, American whalemen generally avoid it.

In boats of such lightness as we have described the royal game of the seas is chased and attacked. His moods are variable, his courage is always the same. Sometimes he is killed by the first dart of the harpoon, and dies a quiet death; at other times he fights for hours at a time, destroys boat after boat, mangles the men, and even charges at the ship itself. Such a vicious customer was one of the first Captain Davis had to encounter.

As soon as the harpoon had struck him he swiftly ran a short distance under water, carrying a line with him. Then turning in his course, he rose to the surface, and rushed at full speed, with his head out of water, for one of the boats, which he stove in and rolled over. The captain's boat, in which Davis was bow-oar, came to the rescue; but as the captain saw that the men were not in immediate danger, and that a third boat was approaching, he left them swimming, and attempted to coax the whale away from the wreck, which the enraged monster was threshing with his terrible jaw. Just then the whale noticed the swimmers, however, and rushed toward them, with his jaw at right angles with his body. But before he could reach them a second harpoon was hurled into him, and with that to accelerate his speed, he ran away to the windward, towing the captain's boat in the wake.

It was then the duty of the bow oarsman to grasp the fastening line and haul the boat alongside the enemy, so that the lance might be used upon the huge body. But it was impossible, owing to the increasing speed of the whale, and the savage manner in which he tossed his flukes. The captain used an implement called a spade, with the hope of severing the tendons of his tail, and so bringing him to; but the operation was unsuccessful, and he ran with undiminished speed, often rolling as he went, so as to give the flukes

IN THE WHALE'S JAWS.

a side-cutting power, with the intention of crushing his little antagonist. Under similar circumstances the ordinary manœuvre of the hunters is to sheer the boat to one side of the whale by taking a bight of the line over one side of the boat.

"In this instance," Davis tells us, "the bow oarsman had been tugging at the line for an hour, but was utterly unable to get the boat in advance of the flukes of the whale. A little line might be gained for a short time, but it would soon be torn through the clinging hands, almost taking the flesh with it. This was certainly very aggravating to the excited captain, who was a religious man, and under his own vine and fig-tree, with none to rile him, I guess he would average well in the patience line. But with all our troubles on this day, I believe he wished there had been no sin in a ripping oath.

"He was a little hard on his bow oarsman, and rather more than hinted at somebody's cowardice. This was too much for my hot Welsh blood, and with the aid of two others I brought the boat right up to the iron in the whale's body, and coolly passed a bight around the thwart and made all fast. The captain was delighted to be held up to his work so well, and plied his lance thrust after thrust; but the brute seemed to bear a charmed life. He would not spout blood, and the little jets that came from the lance holes would not bleed a whale to death in a month. Our boat buried her nose in the waves, and the bloody spray leaped over her sides as we swept right royally onward. Now our majestic race-horse grew impatient of the captain's prodding. He *milled* [turned] across our course, and we ran plump against his head. 'Slack line!' roared the captain. 'Starn all! slack line, and starn!' He turned in his tracks to step aft of the bow oarsman, fearing the upward cut of the whale's jaw, when he saw that the line was fast to the thwart. 'For God's sake cut that line!' he shouted, as he sprang forward for the hatchet; but the loosened bight went over the side, as the whale came up under the forward part of the boat, and carried the bow clear out of the water as he rounded slowly forward.

"At this moment the captain and old Ben [the harpooner] occupied the stern of the boat, and in the perilous moment I was just mad enough to enjoy the expectant look with which the two old whalemen awaited the arrival of the on-coming flukes. Fortunately for all of us, the blow was delayed a moment, and when the thundering concussion came it cleared our boat by a few feet. The other boats were out of sight, and the ship's hull could be dimly seen to the leeward. For two hours more the whale ran and fought with redoubled energy. The captain got long darts with the lance, but with no good effect. The iron drew, and the victorious whale passed from us."

It was night-fall when the worn-out crew reached the vessel, and found that their comrades, whose boat had been wrecked, were all safe on board. On the next day the green but plucky bow oarsman was told that in fastening the line to the boat he had placed six men within an inch of death. If the whale had gone down, the frail craft and her crew would have been a quarter of a mile under water in less than a minute.

More pages than one number of this magazine contains could easily be filled with instances of the heroic daring of whalemen, and the prowess of the game which they seek. An infuriated whale is a vastly more terrible antagonist than the wildest and mightiest of land animals. His courage is equal to his power, and instances are on record in which a sperm-whale, after defeating the men in the boats, has actually rushed upon the ship, stove in her bow, and sunk her. A boat or two lost is usually the smallest cost of an encounter, and often the crew are tossed high in the air by his monstrous flukes, with a bristling shower of harpoons, lances, and splinters following after. Coming to the water bruised and lacerated, the men are still pursued by the enemy, and have to avoid his jaws by diving under or crawling over him, until one of the other boats has an opportunity to dispatch him. Whale ships do not carry surgeons, and the most horrible wounds are dressed unskillfully by the captain, who, in all probability, knows less of surgery than of Latin or Greek. Amputations are performed with carpenter's saws and butcher's knives, and wounds bandaged with canvas. If you should ever meet an old whaleman you may read in his patches and scars the evidence of the manifold perils of his profession.

In the pretty cemetery at Sag Harbor, Long Island, there is a marble monument bearing a touching record. It is in the form of a broken ship's mast, with an unstranded hawser twisted around the foot, and engraved upon it are the names of six captains of whale ships belonging to the town, all of them under thirty years of age, who died, within ten years of each other, in actual encounter with the monsters of the deep. An old whaleman who had escaped death several times used to declare that he only lived "on borrowed time, a monument of God's infinite mercy." We may also mention here the case of Captain James Huntling as an example of a whaleman's endurance. His boat was upset and rolled over him by a large sperm-whale. When he rose to the surface he was entangled in the line, and struggled hard to free himself, but before he could succeed he was jerked out of the sight of his horrified shipmates. A bight of line yet attached to the whale was around his ankle. Drawing himself nearer the retreating animal, he drew a sheath-knife and managed to cut the cord. When he again came to the surface a boat rescued him and con-

"CUTTING IN."

veyed him to the ship. His ankle was broken, and in the presence of his men he set it himself, and then resumed his usual duties.

CARCASS ADRIFT.

Captain Davis mentions a sperm-whale which first wrecked two boats and afterward charged at the ship, tearing away the cut-water and the copper sheathing around the bow. Several harpoons, lances, and bomb-lances were fired into him without effect. During the night he remained on the surface in the vicinity of the wrecked boats, and was frequently heard fighting the fragments. On the following day thirty-one bomb-lances more, each containing half a pound of gunpowder, were exploded in him before he yielded. The monster produced 115 barrels of oil, half of it head-matter, the value of which will be explained anon. Finback whales are even more dangerous than sperm. They are occasionally 120 feet long, and extremely swift and powerful in their motions. But their blubber is thin and the whalebone scant, and they are considered less valuable than others of the species.

When the whale has been killed and is hauled alongside the vessel, the "cutting in" process is begun. This is surgery on the largest scale known. The immense carcass is brought underneath some elaborate tackle rigged on board. From the head of the mast two great sheave blocks depend, a rope about eight inches in circumference running through them. The rope also passes through a corresponding traveling block, to which, in the beginning of the operation, a heavy iron hook is attached by a clevis and bolt. The fall leads to the windlass, near which a number of men stand ready to lend a hand. The rail and side planks above the deck of the vessel are all removed, and two platforms, or gangways, are erected over the side in front of the opening thus formed. The whale is next brought directly underneath the hoisting tackle, which swings above the platforms. On these, secured by ropes around the waist, the officers are stationed, and provided with broad-edged tools called spades, which are mounted on sixteen-foot poles. A circular flap is cut from around the whale's eye. One of the boat-steerers now appears, dressed in a rough woolen suit. Secured by a rope fastened around his waist, he is lowered on to the whale's back, and inserts the hook of the tackle in the eye. This is a dangerous duty in a heavy sea, the smooth skin of the whale affording but a poor footing, while a score of sharks are nibbling around, and the ponderous hook and block are swaying with the roll of the ship.

When the hook is inserted the order is given to "haul taut" and "heave away," and the flap, technically the blanket, or blubber, slowly ascends beyond the deck until it reaches three-fourths of the height of the mainmast. A second boat-steerer then cuts an oval plug from it, which is secured by other tackle, both parts being afterward lowered into the blubber-room. The first cut is extended to other parts of the body, the head excepted, which is reserved for the last, and the windlass is constantly working until five hundred or more feet of the blanket have been brought on board. When every bit of the carcass has been stripped of blubber, it is turned adrift and floats away, coloring the water by its oozing blood, and attracting a shoal of sharks and a flock of albatrosses, which hold carnival in the sea and air over the fallen majesty.

The head is one-third the entire length of a sperm-whale, and in obtaining the valuable spermaceti which it contains the whalemen divide it into three parts—the "case," the "junk," and the bone. The "junk" is first hauled on board and stowed away, and then the "case" is bailed. You will find an illustration of this operation below. The "case" is a massive part of the head, cellular in the interior, the walls of the cells running vertically and transversely. It is filled with an oily substance of a faint yellow tint, translucent when warm. The oil-bearing flesh forms about one-third of the mass, and in a large whale it has yielded three and a half tons. The case also contains the respiratory canal, and a cavity of extraordinary depth filled with oil. An opening is made at one end for the purposes of bailing, and it is next hauled to a vertical position beyond the reach of the water. A deep and narrow bucket attached to a line and pulley is then lowered, and brought up full of transparent spermaceti, mixed with silky integuments having the odor of freshly drawn milk. The sore hands of the crew, bathed in this rich substance, are relieved and healed, and the greenhorns dabble in it with the ineffable satisfaction displayed by city youngsters in a mud puddle.

As soon as the case has been emptied it is abandoned, and the "try-works" are brought into use. The "try-works" are one of the disfigurements that cause merchantmen and man-of-war's men to laugh at whaling vessels. They are boilers set in a foundation of brick on the deck, and are used for reducing the blubber to oil. The mainyard is taken aback, the mainsail and top-sails are furled, and, while the vessel drifts in her course, the fires are lighted. "Trying out," as the work is called, is one of the most wearisome and offensive of the whaleman's toils. Captain Davis states that he never experienced six hours of greater wretchedness than those during which this operation was performed on his first whale. The scene on board is weird in the extreme. Red flame and smoke issue from the flues and shoot into the black night, bringing the outlines of the masts and rigging into strange relief. The feet of the men slide over the wet and slippery deck at every roll of the ship, and their clothes are wet, sooty, and greasy. If the greenhorn has not yet repented, the words of penitence will surely come to his lips in the "trying out." The orders of the officers are harsher than ever, and the men swear sullenly in rejoinder. In fact, the ship becomes for the time "a little hell on earth," and we can scarcely wonder that English sailors avoided so unpleasant an occupation. With every whale caught the drudgery is repeated, and sometimes the decks have been no sooner holy-stoned and the brass-work polished than the furnaces are again lighted. The chase is magnificent

BAILING THE "CASE."

sport, but the "cutting in" and the "trying out" have an opposite equivalent in horrors.

"TRYING OUT."

The cruise after sperm and right whales in the Pacific is a long and dreary one. It generally lasts for three or four years, and there are few incidents to vary its monotony except the excitement of the chase. Calls are made occasionally at South American ports, where the sailors find dirt and debauchery in abundance, and frequently manage to get into conflict with the petty authorities; at the volcanic Galapagos, where delicious terrapin are more plentiful than clams on Long Island, and afford a welcome change in the vessel's dietary, which ordinarily consists of salt pork and mouldy biscuit; at the evergreen Cocos Island, a land of leaf and flowers, where the purest water is found; and at Sandwich Island ports, where the smooth-tempered Hawaiians exchange innocent hospitalities with the sailors, and even extend them so far as to also exchange names and clothing during the vessel's stay in port.

But it is time that we said something about the form and habits of the whale itself. A great diversity of opinion exists on the subject, and an old tar once averred the number of tails a whale carries depends altogether on the quantity of grog the looker-on has drunk. Such authorities as we have had differ most widely, but Captain Davis's observations were submitted to an assemblage of old whalemen at New London, who unanimously indorsed their accuracy in all except two or three minor points. One of the most interesting peculiarities of the whale is its immense loss of blood in death. It is presumed to have a large supply arterialized in a reservoir, which is brought into use when that in general circulation becomes vitiated during a prolonged submergence. This reservoir is what whalemen term the "life" of the whale, and is the spot sought by the harpoon and lance. When touched, Captain Davis states, the bloody torrent surcharges the lungs, and is expelled through the spout-hole. Suffocation and death follow, but when the wound is only slight the agonies of the dying beast are considerably prolonged. The poor creature will lie on the surface feebly propelling itself onward, and, with quick-repeated sobs, will pour out its life by slow degrees, coloring the surface of the ocean with a deep crimson. From this stupor it is aroused to its last struggle. The head rises and falls, and the flukes thrash the water rapidly. With great speed it will swim in a large circle two or three times, and then fall on its side dead, with "fin out."

The length of time a whale can remain below the surface is probably much greater than has hitherto been allowed. Sometimes, notably during the full of the moon, the whales abound over the feeding ground, and many are taken. But the busy season is followed by a period of two weeks or more during which none will be visible. Vessels will be spoken from all points of the compass, and to the question, "Have you seen whales?" the answer will be, "Not for a week or ten days." The busy and dull seasons alternate uniformly over an area of six hundred miles north and south by nine hundred miles east and west. Bull whales often appear as though they have been reposing on a muddy bottom, and off the coast of New Zealand they have been seen with such barnacles on their lower jaws as are found on a ship's bottom.

In the same connection Captain Davis states an ingenious theory, which we will quote in his own words as nearly as we can remember them. "The 'case' and 'junk' of the largest spermaceti may attain a length of twenty-five feet, a depth of eleven feet, and a breadth of nine feet, with a total weight of sixty thousand pounds. There is nothing to break the alabaster color of the interior, nor any tubular structure, save the breathing pipe. Yet the animal heat of this part is as great as though the circulation was perfect. Now blood is generally regarded as the common carrier of animal economy; but in this case the building and wasting processes are conducted twenty-five feet from the presence of blood, with which the other parts of the whale's body are proportionately more highly charged than land animals. What are the uses of this immense mass? Most writers believe that it acts as a buoy to lift the nostril above water. But, in truth, the head is much less buoyant than the body, owing to the heavy casing of 'white horse;' and when the whale dies the head turns spout-hole down and bony jaw upward, showing the part containing the fatty matter is the heaviest." With these facts as a basis, Captain Davis believes that the sack of oil has a use in the whale's submergence.

It is commonly conceded that whales have a mysterious power of communicating with each other, and instances are mentioned which, if trustworthy, afford the strongest proof possible. Stationed at the mast-heads of their vessels, captains have observed that when their boats were attacking a whale to the leeward, a school several miles to the windward, and out of sight of the combatants, would show signs of alarm, and retreat the moment the first blow of the harpoon was struck. Sound was not the means of communication, as the distance was too great, and furthermore it is a well-ascertained fact that whales only signal by sound in the practice of "lob-tailing." In "lob-tailing" the whale rises perpendicularly in the water, with its head downward. Thus poised, it will swing from side to side, sweeping a radius of thirty feet with awful violence. The concussions of its body with the water may be heard for many miles, while the sea is a mass of foam and the air is filled with spray. The practice is supposed to be intended for amusement, but it is also a tocsin.

"Breaching" is another strange habit common in all varieties of the whale. It consists in the whale's elevating three-fourths of its body out of water, and then falling heavily on its side. In "sounding" the whale raises its head a few feet out of the water, gives a long spout, rounds its back, and revolves as on an axis. Rounding higher by degrees, it gently lifts its massive flukes without the least spray to a surprising height, and the next moment it smoothly disappears beneath the surface in a perpendicular descent. Considering the size and the apparently unwieldy proportions of the monster, the litheness with which it executes these movements is extraordinary. The sea is not disturbed, and not the least sound is heard. "Sounding" is a certain indication of sperm-whale on a cruising ground, as the right-whale is never found in water so deep that the act is possible, and as the humpback and sulphur-bottom whales do not intrude on sperm-whale ground. Unless it is disturbed by the hunters, the sperm-whale always descends in this manner.

Another manœuvre is "settling," which is often a means of safety to the whale when diving or running will not avail. From a position of inaction the whale can suddenly sink without a stroke of the tail or fins, and without any apparent effort. It is as a mass of lead, and sinks from the head of a pursuing boat so rapidly that the harpoon may be darted but not delivered. Many whales thus escape.

The speed of the sperm-whale and the regularity of its movements are scarcely less wonderful. A vessel once gave chase to a whale, and ran after it at the rate of ten knots, with yards squared and every stitch of canvas stretched. But during twelve hours of daylight she did not gain one knot on the whale, which passed from sight. In other instances captains of vessels have carefully ascertained the course of a fleeing whale in an afternoon's chase, and have followed it during the night. At the return of daylight the same whale has still been in sight ahead or astern, having stood through the dark on the course in which it started. On one other occasion a whale began a chase to the windward as soon as he was struck, towing the boat after him. The ship followed with a full top-sail breeze, but in four hours the whale and the boat in tow were lost to sight.

A large sperm-whale will produce about one hundred and seven barrels of oil. Its length is about seventy-nine feet, its height at the forehead eleven feet, and its width nine or ten feet. It has about fifty teeth, the heaviest of them weighing about one pound and a half.

According to Captain Davis the skin is not naked. Beneath what is called "the black skin" a curdy deposit is found, which is easily scraped away after the death of the animal, and reveals a close fur one-eighth of an inch in thickness. This fur envelops the entire surface, and has root in the true skin or blubber. The flesh is a dark red, very firm, and of the texture of rope-yarn. It is fit for food in an emergency, but is not sought by epicures. The average temperature of the blood is 104° Fahrenheit.

The whales are gregarious in their habits, but the old males are often found alone. Their ordinary rate of travel is about five miles an hour, although they far exceed that when urged by the hunters. The young are said to measure fourteen feet in length at their birth. How long they remain with their mother is unknown, but the herd watches them until they attain a considerable size. The milk is white and fatty. They are supposed to live to a great age; and, apropos, a story is told of a sailor whose boat was wrecked, while he and his messmates were tossed high into the air, by a mad whale's flukes. As he came down, after half an hour had elapsed, the whale awaited him with open mouth, and instead of sinking as deeply into the sea as he had been high in the air, he slid smoothly into the whale's interior. As soon as he recovered breath he drew out his tobacco-box and helped himself to a liberal "quid," which he rolled over and over in his mouth as he laughed at his adventure. Presently he arose from the soft but moist couch on which he had been thrown, and surveyed the apartment, which contained many wonders, you may be sure. Some writing on one of the walls attracted his attention, and on examination it proved to be the words, "Jonah, B.C. 862." This amused him so much that the "quid" fell out of his mouth, and the whale at once began to writhe and show a violent dislike to the nicotine. A happy idea occurred to him, and he cut his plug of tobacco into small pieces, which he distributed over the floor. The whale then heaved more violently than ever, and while Jack was holding his sides at the joke, he was shot into the water and almost on board one of the ship's boats. Some of his comrades doubted his wondrous story, but, for the benefit of unbelievers, he had brought back with him a pocket-knife with a buckhorn handle on which were stamped Jonah's initials and an American eagle.

The whale's mouth is out of proportion to its other parts, and is so narrow, comparatively speaking, that one might suppose the animal would have difficulty in entrapping its prey. But its food is the voracious cuttle-fish, or "squid," which is found at great depths, and is allured by a white and shining object. The jaw and tongue of the sperm-whale are of silvery whiteness, and thus nature enables the creature to overcome the defect. The sperm-whale only frequents deep water; the male is much larger than the female; the upper jaw, the "case," and the "junk" form the greater portion of the head; and the under jaw is supplied with ivory teeth. The right-whale is found only in soundings off the coast; the female is larger than the male; the lower jaw, with its lips and tongue, is much larger than the upper jaw; neither the upper nor the lower jaw is supplied with teeth, the upper jaw having great slabs of whalebone instead. The sperm-whale is the more combative of the two, and no large bull whale of its species is taken that has not been scarred by the teeth of its rivals. The sperm-whale is dangerous to the huntsmen at each end. The motions of its flukes are limited; but, to compensate for this, it is possessed of admirable skill in fencing with the jaw. The right-whale's jaw is not dangerous; but it is more active and powerful with its flukes than the sperm-whale; and there is a spot on the upper jaw which is seemingly as sensitive as the antennæ of an insect. However swiftly a right-whale may be advancing on a boat, a slight prick on this point will suddenly arrest his movements, and he will not advance a yard farther, but will either descend, back, or turn to the right or left.

A large-sized right-whale will afford three hundred barrels of inferior oil and three thousand pounds of bone.

The golden days of American whaling are over. In the Revolutionary war Nantucket alone lost by capture 134 vessels, and the war of 1812 was also disastrous. But from both of these calamities the whalers recovered, and, as we have already shown, the whaling fleet of the United States consisted, in 1840, of over 670 vessels, with a capacity of 220,000 tons. The introduction of petroleum materially reduced the demand for and the consumption of whale-oil, however, and the trade received a serious blow when the rebel cruiser *Shenandoah* destroyed thirty-four United States vessels on the arctic ground.

At present the fleet numbers 203 vessels, showing a decrease of fifteen per cent. per annum for the past two years. Our entire import of sperm and whale oil in 1872 was about three-fourths of our import of sperm alone in 1853, and one-fourth of our import of whale-oil alone in 1851. Our import of whalebone in 1872 was only one-twenty-eighth of the import of 1853. No whaling grounds have been abandoned, and every sea and ocean are still explored by American whalemen. But it is believed that the arctic fishery will be discontinued soon, as the perils that attend vessels visiting it have caused the demand of an increased rate of insurance. Nevertheless the arctic fleet in 1873 numbered about thirty-two vessels, although the disasters of the previous year were numerous. The profits of whaling are exceedingly small, and the wealthiest capitalists engaged in it are seeking other employments for their ships.

Running the Rips
(1907)

RUNNING THE RIPS

BY THOMAS FLEMING DAY

DRAWINGS BY WARREN SHEPARD

I CAN remember when one night lying to the southward of the Vineyard some forty miles, it fell calm and left us rolling about until, growing disgusted with the slatting of the cloth and the clattering of the sheet-blocks, I lowered everything and tied all fast. Then, rousing out my mate, who had turned in after supper, I went below to sleep. At half-past three, just as dawn was showing, the watch came below and woke me.

"It looks dirty," he said, "and the glass is falling rapidly."

"Any wind?" I asked.

"Light air, 'bout south; we are just moving with it. What are you going to do?"

Having turned in all standing, that is, with everything on except my hat, I was quickly on deck. Rubbing the gravy out of my eyes, I cast a squint around the circle. The mate was right; it did look dirty. The whole horizon from northeast clear round to northwest was stuffed full of muddy-gray, greasy-looking vapors, over the ruffled heads of which the faint light of dawn was shivering up. The sea was gray, oily and moving uneasily, the swell pushing in, not rolling. This movement is the sure sign of a coming and not of a passing gale. Distinctly heard, and yet unheard, undefinable, unlocateable, yet unquestionably existing, was that ghostly sound, the sea-warn, the moan of the gale-dreading waters. It is a sound that once heard is never forgotten. They say men hear the same in the great deserts. It is the expression of disturbed vastness; perhaps the faint echo of that ghostly cry which haunts the hopeless stretches of the universe.

One glance round the horizon was enough. It was going to blow; already the clouds were spitting a scattering of fine drops, and the wind was cat's-pawing in irregular streaks. There was no perceptible movement to the higher clouds, but it could be seen the mass was growing from below, and that it would soon fill the whole vault. Forty miles from port, eight hours with a good breeze, with all she could carry, say six hours. The gale would come in gradually and be a laster, probably thirty-six hours before its back was broken. Would it pay to lay-to and ride it out, or run for port? Question, how is the tide?

But why the tide, you will ask. What has that to do with it? Listen. In order to get shelter we had to pass between the islands through comparatively narrow fairways, having to run past Gay Head and into Vineyard Sound, or through Muskeget Channel and into Nantucket Sound. Through these passages the tide runs with a high velocity, especially when ebbing. If when rushing out it meets the wind and swell coming in, charging against it, it makes up a high and confused sea or rip, impassable at times for a small boat. If you have ever been in a rip, it is unnecessary for me to say more; if you haven't, make for yourself a mental picture out of the expression, a "hell of water." But more of this anon.

It was now close on four o'clock; the tide made ebb at one hour and thirty-four minutes P.M. at Cross Rip Light vessel, so allowing for difference of distance it would change in the channel mouth at one. Therefore, if we could get there at or before one, we would have comparatively smooth water, nothing worse than the natural nastiness of the sea going in over shoaling stretches; but if delayed and caught by the ebb, well, I hated to think of it. With a gale behind, there would be no turning back; it would be either the channel or the beach—a throw with death either place. But no danger, no fun, so head her north a half east, my boy, while I go below and get some breakfast ready before it begins to blow. Breakfast eaten, the next move is to make all snug below. Everything that can possibly get adrift is lashed or wedged, so as to stay put no matter how she cuts up; then the bilge is dried out to keep the water from splashing about, and the ports looked to and locked fast. This done, all hands on deck. The wind is now blowing a fresh breeze and the sea rising. The mate is standing with one eye on the card and the other on his mainsail, helming her carefully, with everything drawing except the jib, which only gets a draught when she yaws and rolls. His slicker and sou'wester are shining with wet, and a stream of drops runs off his sleeves and trickles from the tips of the fingers of his tiller hand to the floor of the cockpit.

"If I could hold her up another point, she'd do better," he says, taking his eye off the compass for a quick glance at the sail. "The wind is right on the end of the main boom."

"Where is it?"

"South by east, and seems to be easting slowly."

"Well, let her come up. How's the sheet?"

"Might get a little aft, she'll steer easier."

"How's that?"

"All right."

"I think I'd better stick a reef in the mizzen in case we need it; not doing much good now, and by and by if it keeps on breezing, we'll reef the main."

The mate nods his assent to the plan, and with a steady eye ahead keeps working his helm up and down as she ascends and shoots the following seas.

Now if you have never reefed a mizzen or jigger, as we generally call it, on a small boat running off under a press of sail in a seaway, you have never done an acrobatic stunt that knocks out the most thrilling feats of the arena. It is not so bad as laying out on the headspar to shift a jib, because the wet is left out, and therefore it is a job not so detested by seamen. Working on the bowsprit is most dreaded of all sea jobs. More men lose their lives off that spar than from all other parts of the ship together. Driving along she takes a plunge into it, at the same time the heavy foot of the sail bangs across, knocking off your hold, and overboard you go, to be swept under and trodden upon by the swift rushing forefoot. A dark night on a jib-boom, with a half-muzzled sail storming about, and the spar end pitching, bucking, and forking the brine at every plunge—there may be nastier places; if so, they have never crossed my hawse. A yacht's bowsprit is worse than a merchantman's, because it has little or no steeve, consequently it dives oftener, goes deeper, and stays under longer. All seagoing yachts with head spars over six feet outboard should have them made so as to reef. A reefing bowsprit is one made to haul in and out. On the lee side of the western ocean, where they have heavier water than we do, most of their boats are rigged in this way. But the modern practice on all classes of sailing vessels is to so arrange the sail as to curtail the bowsprit, and on many yachts the whole head-rig is abaft the stem head.

One thing you have to learn before you can write sailor after your name, and that is to master a sail. Brute force is of no account. To use brute force with a sail is like employing it to capture an elephant or run down an untamed steed. Mastering a sail is a game of strategy, fineness, diplomacy, flattery, persuasion, and perseverance, with fierce energy flashed in at the right instant. You must know your sail. Sails are not all alike. What will work with a jib will fail if applied to a mainsail or topsail. When once a man has become skilled at this game he can do more at it than three lubbers. I've seen three men tackle a jib and come back on the head baffled and beaten after a fifteen minute fight, and then a fellow not a quarter their combined weight go out and conquer the sail, binding it captive in ten minutes. A sail master has five hands—two on his arms, two on his legs, and his teeth. Besides, he has knees, his elbows, the grip of his thighs, his neck, and his whole body. He must be an octopus, a boa-constrictor, and a monkey, combining with their qualities the patience of an ox, the quickness of a tiger, and the subtlety of a fox.

Sometimes a sail is only playful, and willful at the worst, and after a slight show of resistance will succumb to your arts, but at times they get malignant and cruel. They will fight you fiercely, hitting back viciously, spitefully battling for every inch, taking most treacherous advantage of any relapse of alertness or looseness of clutch. When a canvas has got that devil in it, look out for yourself. That is when it fights to kill. That is when it hurls men off yard and boom to their death. At times you can only conquer after a steady and well-generaled fight. At other times a bit of trickery will succeed. I have cursed a sail and turned away pretendingly beaten, when, thrown for a moment off guard by my apparent carelessness, it has opened its defense. A tiger spring, a turn of rope, and the victory is won. But I tell you it makes a man of you, a fight to the finish with a sail. Every nerve tingling, every vein flushed with blood, you take the last turn, and with a "damn you, you're fast now," go aft and report all snug. But to reef the mizzen.

Drawing by Warren Shepard.

Cape Cod Fishermen off Highland Light—Twilight.

This, except for the unsteadiness of the hull is comparatively an easy job. To be sure she throws her tail here, there, and everywhere, but with the sheet fast and a good leglock you can use both hands. But first slip off your long oil coat. You will work twice as quickly without it. Oilers and seaboots are fine things, but out of ten men lost at sea, they drown seven. You might better go over with a millstone round your neck than a pair of seaboots on your feet. A fisherman isn't happy out of his seaboots, and they take him to Davy Jones. But what's the odds, there are more boots and more men. I never wear boots in bad weather on a small vessel.

Having reefed the mizzen I pulled on my coat and relieved the mate at the helm.

"North," he says, as he hands over the stick, and turns to go below, shaking off his sou'wester before opening the slide. Soon through the half-drawn door I see him peering over the chart. "What's she doing?" he asks.

I glance over the side, watching the

flakes of foam swirl by. "About six," I call back.

"That gives her fifteen, and it's nine o'clock; twenty-five more to do in four hours; six and a quarter, she ought to do that."

"I should think so," I reply. "How does this course bring her?"

"'Bout half a mile west of the point of Tuckeruuck. The flood ought to carry us up enough."

"Well, if it don't, the leeway will. Let us hope we get a sight of something before too close in."

"Hope so; I'm going to lie down. Call me if you want anything," and the mate takes to his bunk.

Now while we are hurrying inshore, racing with the tide for a safe passage over the shoals, let me explain to you what a rip is.

If, let us say, six inches of water is flowing through a sluice, and the bottom of the sluice is perfectly level, it will stream through with a smooth surface, but if you drop in the sluice a flat stone three inches thick, what will happen? Why, when the six inches of water gets to the stone, it can pass only the upper three inches, but the lower three can't stop, so they crowd up and force the upper layer over the stone, making a wave or ripple. That is what a rip is. The tide running out thirty feet deep meets a ten-foot shoal, and the twenty feet of water is obliged to crowd up and over. If the sea be calm, this movement simply forms three waves. These waves are not like ordinary waves, progressive. They remain in the same place, their bases moving with the tide and their heads against it, consequently they stand still, uplifting on their hind legs and pawing the air like savage horses. At such times they are harmless. You see the same waves in rivers, where they are called rapids. Another form of rip is made by two currents meeting or crossing, or by rough water coming against calm. This latter form is frequently seen on the leeward side of high islands, especially those lying in the track of the trade winds.

Drawing by Warren Shepard.

Monomy Point—A welcome sight to the mariner.

Shovelful Light Ship—Foggy morning.

Drawing by Warren Shepard.

The border of the calm space is fringed with breakers, into which a ship plunges and dives, at the same time losing the wind, and is knocked about helpless until she drifts clear. Another form of rip is found at the mouths of rivers, where the outpouring fresh water meets and breasts the salt flood.

When the sea is calm, these rips are disagreeable but harmless, but let the wind blow, and a sea or swell make and they become, next to breakers, the most fearful thing a small boat can face. If the tide is going with the wind and swell the rip is rough but not dangerous, but let those forces be arrayed against it and all hell is afling in its fury. The swell rolls in and, crowding over the shoal, is brought to a standstill by the tide's rush. Maddened by this check it rears up and throws its length into the air, then topples and thunders into a host of broken, leaping, pyramid-shaped masses, hurling their forms against each other. No words can picture the result—a hissing, roaring, leaping, tumbling, boiling, swirling acre of liquid madness.

To a steam vessel these rips are not so dangerous, as she can be driven through them, and as they are never wide, the ordeal is soon over; but a sailing vessel is often forced to remain in their clutches until a happy chance delivers her. The motion is so violent and directless that the wind is completely shaken out of the canvas, and losing way she is held by the tide, or, worse still, driven stern foremost against the inrushing swell. If a small vessel is caught in this way, unless she is decked in she is likely to be swamped and sunk. No open boat has any business in the rips, except in light weather.

While there are lots of stories knocking round of boats having been lost in these rips, I never could nail one of them to the doorpost of the man who saw or suffered it. I've been into them myself, in all kinds of summer weather, going in purposely to see what they would do, and only once did I, with the exception of this time, come near a catastrophe. One time the boat was badly pooped, the rip falling on her stern and sweeping clear over from end to end. If she had been an undecked boat she would have surely sunk.

The "rubes" who navigate around the islands, fishing and sailing parties, have a wholesome fear of these rips, and if they can possibly help will never go near one in bad weather. For this you can't blame them, their craft are not suitable for the performance, being shoal-draught, broad centerboard cats, with an open cockpit that takes up the after half of the boat. If they once shipped a sea and filled the pit, they would go down like a shell-loaded oysterman.

At ten I called the crew and ordered the mainsail reefed, as it was blowing harder and harder, and when the job was done passed over the helm to the mate and went below to prepare a meal. By eleven this was ready, consisting of soup, bread and butter, and hot cocoa.

This being securely stowed away, the fire was put out, the pipe removed, the lid screwed on and everything battened down and locked fast. The next thing was to ascertain as near as possible our position. The wind at this time had hauled south-east, and we were running on a north by east course.

At 11:30 we slowed up for a sounding. I didn't care to round her up to the wind, as the sea was running nasty, so the mizzen being furled kept her about two-thirds off and spilled the mainsail. The mate hove the lead. The lead is a chunk of that metal weighing ten pounds, made fast to the end of a line on which six feet or fathom lengths are marked. You cast it by throwing it ahead as far as possible, and then the line runs through your hand. When the weight hits bottom, the line stops and slacks. If it hits directly under where you stand, you get what sailors call an up-and-down or proper cast. When all is ready I shout: "Let her go, my boy!"

The mate gives the chunk a couple of swings around his head and lets go. Too much way on, and the boat moves over the spot before the lead gets to bottom.

"No bottom!" says the mate, hauling in. I slack off more sheet and check her all I dare. Away goes the lead again. This time he gets a feel.

"All right!" he sings out, hauling in, and at last, almost breathless, announces, "twenty-one fathoms."

"Now jump below," I say, "and see where that puts us."

While the mate is going over the chart let me explain to you what a sounding is, and how it gives you your position. Let us suppose that we have a pond shaped exactly like a wash hand-basin, that is deepest in the middle and gradually sloping up at the sides. Now if we start from the edge and sail toward the middle, we shall find the water deepens as we go out. At say 200 feet from the edge it is five feet deep, at 300 feet ten feet, and so on. The ocean is built on a plan similar to this supposed pond, its bottom sloping off gradually, the water getting deeper as you go out, until you get to what is called "off soundings." But, unlike this supposed pond, the slope is not regular, being sometimes ridged and other times full of holes more or less deep. All these depths of water are marked in on a chart, which is a map of the sea bed. Let us suppose at a particular place the sea at five miles from the shore is ten fathoms deep, at ten miles twenty, and at twenty miles forty. These distances are marked on the chart by drawing a line through all the ten-fathom places, and this line is known as the ten-fathom curve. Inside it, and nearer to the land, the water is less than sixty feet deep; outside, it is more than sixty feet deep. Consequently, if I take a cast of the lead and find that there is only nine fathoms, fifty-four feet, at the spot, I know my vessel is less than five miles from the land. Taking the chart, I look at it at a place about five miles from shore and find a spot marked nine fathoms, but there are several places marked with the same number, and my boat may be over any one of them. But close to the nine fathoms and in the direction I am sailing is a spot marked six, so when the boat has sailed far enough I take a second cast and get six fathoms. By this second cast I know where my boat is, or her position, as we say at sea, the second cast confirming the first.

After a close inspection the mate sings out: "Right on the course fifteen miles from Skiff Island. There's several twenty-ones together right here; three miles north is a nineteen."

"Right you are; come on deck; we'll run another hour and then try again."

Fifteen miles and two hours to do it in, is cutting things pretty close, but still we were undoubtedly doing six through the water, and would have the last of the flood tide. We might be a half-hour late, by that time the tide would not be ebbing very strong. Anyhow it was push her, so I ordered the mizzen set. The wind was getting vicious. So long as it pushes you with its fingers or shoves you with its fist it is all right, but look out when it begins to slap with the flat of its hand. When it hauls back and lets you have it in quick, vixen-like slaps, that is a nasty time, and makes the helmsman sweat to keep his course. The sea under the rushes of air was beginning to act dirty. It was breaking and throwing its heads. Altogether I did not like the look of things.

After running an hour I tried to get another cast, but the sea being heavy and dangerous I did not like to check her, so we failed to get a sound, but from the drag estimated it to be about seventeen fathoms. If this was so, we were close to the ten-fathom curve, which runs close in here about five miles off land. Now came the anxious time, the most anxious of all times to a man in charge of a vessel—running in on a lee shore, with a gale of wind behind and a narrow opening to make, with almost certain disaster if he misses it. If we could get our bearing in time we could haul up if not dead on the channel; but if we saw the land late, when too close in to haul off, the jig would be up. I had hopes from the first sound confirming our supposed track that we would make the channel mouth exactly, but the next thirty minutes were about as cruel a thirty as I ever spent.

The land hereabouts on both sides of the channel is low, and there are only one or two buildings that show above it, so that in good weather it can be seen not more than six miles off. One of these buildings is an abandoned hotel with a peculiar tower. For this I searched diligently and anxiously, but through the thickness nothing could be seen. Our time was running out fast, and we were driving rapidly in. At ten minutes to one I estimated her to be about three miles off Skiff Island. At this time it was blowing so hard that in order to steer we dropped the mizzen.

At one o'clock, much to our disgust and dread, a rain squall blew in and hid everything for a few minutes; then, like it often does, it got quite clear for a short spell in its wake, and we sighted a mass of breakers off the port bow, and at the same time a

Drawing by Warren Shepard.

In the very jaws of the Rip.

buoy. A cry of joy broke from both our lips at this sight—the outer channel buoy almost dead ahead. I felt like doing a jig. The gale and sea were forgotten, we no longer had any dread of them; four miles more and smooth water.

It is nonsense to say that men do not know fear when placed in danger. A man absolutely devoid of fear never existed, unless he was an idiot or insane. Certainly no person with a normal intellect is without fear. When a man tells you that in a situation facing bodily harm or death he felt no fear he lies. Of course there are times when a man is close to death and does not realize it, and at such times he feels no fear because he has no dread.

But nothing becomes so quickly familiar as danger. The horror that appalled you Monday you will nurse in your lap Tuesday. A threatened death that sent chills along your spine one day is the source of jest the next. That is a thing I believe peculiar to our race, the habit of jesting in the face of danger. Like the Jacobite lords, we must crack a joke at the foot of the scaffold. At sea to grow lachrymose over danger is considered a gross breach of ocean etiquette.

One day we got becalmed and tide-bound and anchored off the shore, with a stony bar between us and the beach. At night, suddenly, a heavy northerly wind broke on us. The chain on the heavy anchor snapped, and we hung to about sixty fathoms of good hawser and our second hook. If the hawser parted we went on the bar, she having dragged too close for any chance of working off. One of the boys on board I could see was sick to faintness with fright, so to pull him out we began joking about our appearances as objects of interest for the coroner. The next day I heard him telling somebody that he thought we were in great danger until he heard us guying and jollying each other. Well, that lad that night was about as near death as he probably will ever be until his watch gets the call. Nothing but three inches of good manila stood between him and a watery grave.

My stock subject to relieve my anxiety at such times is solicitude for my spare pair of socks. When I begin to worry as to their situation and prospects of keeping dry, you may know I am anxious. I will go anywhere or do anything if assured of a pair of dry socks after the battle. I don't mind being drowned, but object to catching cold. My companion's worry this day was over a new straw hat which he unintentionally brought on board, and which had narrowly escaped several shipwrecks. As we dashed into the sea at the mouth of the channel we discussed the probable condition of the hat and socks after we had run the rips.

Over Skiff Island the sea was breaking heavily, and across from it as far as you could see toward Nantucket the channel was a mass of seething white water. I shall never forget those next few minutes. They seemed like hours. Lashed fast to a cleat, I stood at the helm, but it was nearly useless in my hands. The movements of the boat are indescribable. She seemed to leap ten different directions at once. She was thrown, pitched, heeled, reared, and knocked about. The water came in over the bow, sides, and stern. She would start to rise the sea ahead, when suddenly the one under her stern pulled out and she fell ino a pit of lashing, broken heads that buffeted and flooded her. The drift and spume blew over and thrashed the sails and deck. You could see nothing. Twice she nearly pitch-poled, and once rolled right down so the mainsail lay on the seas. These more dangerous moves were left impressed on my mind, but the rest is a turmoil, the one principal retention being the ceaseless roar. A roar without variation, a toneless, boundless sound, a bath of liquid thunder. It haunted the alleys of my brain for days after.

What a blessed release when she pulled clear and drove into the smooth. We both turned and looked silently back, then began to shake ourselves like dogs come out of the sea. I saw my companion's lips move as he turned from contemplating the hell of water astern. I don't know what he said, but I said "Thank God!"

A New England Village
(1871)

A NEW ENGLAND VILLAGE.

THE "STOCKBRIDGE BOWL," OR MOUNTAIN MIRROR.—COTTAGE IN WHICH HAWTHORNE WROTE THE "HOUSE OF SEVEN GABLES."

A PROPER New England village is a thing unique, the product of a new and peculiar type of civilization. As such, the history of hardly any one can be sketched without unfolding much that is of general interest. Some of these villages, however, stand out by themselves, and eminent above the rest, on account of certain marked peculiarities which have characterized their origin or their subsequent development. Among such, and yielding to none in features calculated to interest general readers, is one near the centre of Berkshire County, Massachusetts.

The tide of summer tourists sets strongly every year through this westernmost portion of the State, and many a denizen of the crowded and sultry city has learned that there is new life to be found in an abode of even a few weeks among its picturesque hills and valleys. But as the traveler, threading his way among them, comes upon the wide plain which had been made by Housatonic in its almost vain effort to pass the mountain barriers that seem here to hem it in, and say, "Hitherto shalt thou come, and no farther," obliging it to turn and double upon itself for a distance of nearly six miles without gaining as many rods in its general course toward the south; and as he passes along the noble street, level as the meadow whose course it follows, and of proportionate width, bordered on either side by stately elms, such as are found only in the valleys of New England, and from beneath their emerald arches looks out upon the gleaming river and the graceful slopes which stretch away in every direction, save where their gentle beauty is contrasted and heightened by the bare and rugged cliffs of Monument Mountain on the south, whose touching legend Bryant has sung in his own sweet verse; and as all around him, on every house, and in every field and door-yard, and even in the nicely graveled foot-paths by the road-side, he sees the marks of care and culture—he seems to have found the most admirable blending of nature with art and taste, and altering only a little the verse of Goldsmith, is disposed to exclaim,

"Sweet *Stockbridge!* loveliest village of the plain!"

But how few of those who from year to year are surprised by this scene of loveliness are aware that this most beautifully set jewel of Berkshire was only a little while ago the wild hunting-ground of the Indian, kept as such long after the surrounding region had come under the ownership of the whites! It is but a step from this bright scene of civilization back to the midst of heathen barbarism. There are those alive to-day in Stockbridge who were living there when the Indian tribe who owned its whole territory had not yet parted with it nor removed to their new home nearer the setting sun. Such is the change wrought within a human lifetime. The later settlements of the West, aided by our modern appliances of railroads and telegraphs, may show greater changes in a briefer period of time, but for New England the change here wrought is little less than a marvel. The growth of our country during the first century and a half, if we may not say two centuries, was comparatively slow. The day of railroads and steamships had not come. It was a hundred years after the settlement at Plymouth before Massachusetts had any white inhabitants west of the Connecticut River valley, or the region properly included in it. Westfield, as its name tells us, was then the westernmost settlement, the very outpost of civilization. All beyond to the Mississippi, and to the Canadian line on the north, was a wilderness. But in the year 1722 the wave of migration, which had rested for sixty years in the fertile meadows of the Connecticut, rolled forward to the valley of the Housatonic. Upon the petition of Joseph Parsons and nearly two hundred other inhabitants of Hampshire County—which then embraced almost all the western half of Massachusetts—for the grant of two townships of land upon the Housatonic River, a committee was appointed for the purpose of purchasing the Indian title to the designated tract, and dividing the same properly among the settlers. The committee was instructed also to reserve a suitable portion of the lands for the first minister, for the subsequent maintenance of the ordinance of the Gospel, and for the support of schools. Thus the new settlements were begun in the true Puritan style, with scrupulous regard to the rights of the aborigines, and with a zealous interest in behalf of education and religion.

The townships thus granted and opened to settlement embraced all the lower part of the present county of Berkshire, with the reservation of a small portion on the southern border, and another larger portion (including nearly all of the present town of Stockbridge), which were then occupied by Indians. These Indians, the sole inhabitants of this whole region, were a small band of the Mu-he-ka-ne-ok, or River Indians, as they were called, from their residence being on and near the Hudson River. Their name signifies "the people of the continually flowing water." That portion of the tribe who resided in Berkshire came to be known as the Housatonic Indians, from the name they gave to the river on whose borders they lived. They had a tradition that their tribe came originally from a country northwest of their present home, having, as they said, "crossed the great water at a place where this and the other country are nearly connected." They said, also, that in coming from the west "they found many great waters, but none of them flowing and ebbing like Muhekaneok until they came to Hudson River." Then they said, one to another, "This is like Muhekaneok, our nativity." Here, then, we have a tradition which, if to be relied upon, indicates that one tribe of Indians at least found its way hither from Eastern Asia by way of Behring Strait—an origin which agrees, it is well known, with the theory of some of the best ethnologists.

The committee charged with the duty of laying out the new townships set about their work at once. In a few months they had received the names of fifty-five proposed settlers; and in April, 1724, the Indians gave a deed of the land, signed by Koukapot, their king, or chief, and twenty others. The consideration in the case is somewhat peculiar, but indicates strongly the change, in some respects, which has taken place in the usages of society. The land was given, as the deed says, "in consideration of £450, three barrels of cider, and thirty quarts of rum."

As the settlers occupied their newly granted lands, and thus came into contact with the Indians, they were surprised to find them well disposed and of good moral character, and that Koukapot, their chief, was even favorably inclined toward the Christian religion. This coming to the knowledge of Rev. Samuel Hopkins, of Springfield, he became very desirous that the Indians should have the Gospel preached to them. After conferring with some others, he made his wishes known to the Commissioners of Indian Affairs at Boston. This board, embracing among others the Governor of the colony, was an agency of the London Society for Propagating the Gospel in Foreign Parts. The Commissioners approved the plan of Hopkins, and requested him, in conjunction with Rev. Stephen Williams, who in his youth had been carried away as a captive from Deerfield by the Indians in their fa-

SOLDIERS' MONUMENT AT STOCKBRIDGE.

mous attack upon that place, and who, by residence among them, knew their character and habits, to procure a suitable person to act as missionary to the Housatonic tribe, or, as they were afterward called, the Stockbridge Indians, and authorized the pledge of £100 a year for his support.

They were fortunate in finding very soon a man eminently fitted for the proposed work. This was John Sergeant, a native of New Jersey, and at that time a tutor in Yale College. He had been heard to say that he would prefer the life of a missionary to the Indians rather than any other. Accordingly, when applied to on behalf of the Commissioners, he engaged at once, if the college authorities would consent, to spend half the year with the Indians and half the year at the college, until he should have carried the class he was instructing through their course, which he was anxious to do, and then, if his missionary efforts gave promise of success, to devote his life to the Indians.

He was soon on his way to his new field of labor. A company of twenty adults was gathered to meet him almost as soon as he reached the Housatonic, and he began at once to preach the Gospel to them by means of an interpreter. The name of this interpreter was Poohpoonuc. He had lived among the whites, and those of the better character, and had gained from them a knowledge of the Christian religion. Under the preaching of Sergeant he was disposed to avow his faith openly, and, after a proper examination, was publicly baptized, assuming the English name Ebenezer. With this Indian convert began the church in Stockbridge as it exists to-day. It is surprising and interesting as one looks into the catalogue of that church, as it is printed most recently, to find standing second on the list of its officers the name of Peter Pau-qua-nau-peet; while Ebenezer Poohpoonuc heads the roll of members, followed by such a succession as this: Captain John Koukapot, Mary Koukapot (wife), Catharine Koukapot (daughter), Lieutenant Aaron Umpachenee,* Hannah Umpachenee (wife), Isaac Wuaumpee. And so the roll goes on for more than fifty years, the names of whites and Indians mingled; the latter, however, gradually losing their predominance as the white population becomes relatively more numerous, and finally, with the removal of the Indians to their new home in New York, their names disappear; the church ceases to be a mission church, and takes its place with the other churches of the commonwealth.

The peculiar growth of this New England village is shown also in the fact that for many years the town offices, as well as those of the church, were shared by the Indians. Thus in 1761 we find Johannes Mthoksin and Captain Jacob Cheek-sou-kun were selectmen, Frederick Poh-pou-seet constable, Peter Nau-nee-wau-nau-koot tithingman, and King Benjamin Kau-ke-we-naunaunt and Captain Cheek-sou-kun on the committee for seating the church. In the year 1765 a constable's return reads thus: "By virtue of the foregoing order I have warned all the Indian inhabitants within said town, as within described, to meet at time and place within mentioned. Per me, Joseph Quinsquaunt, Constable."

When Sergeant came to Stockbridge he found the Indians living in two villages several miles apart. Divided thus into two bands, and of roving habits at the best, it was felt that it would be difficult to reach them in the most effective manner. This difficulty was in part removed by the agreement of the Indians to take up their residence in the winter at a point midway between their two villages, building there a school-house, and pitching their huts or lodges around it. Here the missionary taught a school during the week-days, and on the Sabbath preached to his dusky auditors. But no sooner had the spring begun to return than he found his parishioners forsaking him and going into the woods for the purpose of making maple sugar. It seems we are indebted to these Housatonic Indians for the discovery of that delightful sweet, so universally relished; for in the history of the

* Governor Belcher had conferred the commission of captain and lieutenant upon Koukapot and Umpachenee.

mission by Hopkins, published soon after Sergeant's death, he not only describes the process of making maple sugar, but the article itself, and gives its name, as though something previously unknown. He speaks thus, also, of the sirup: "The molasses that is made of this sap is exceeding good, and considerably resembles honey. Three, or at most four, barrels of this sap, reduced to one by boiling, will ferment and make a very pleasant drink, which is sufficiently *spirituous*, and, I suppose, by being distilled, would make excellent rum, though the experiment has not, that I know of, been yet made." He suggests also that if the business were to be properly taken up, maple-trees are so abundant that the whole country might be supplied with sugar from this source.

As the Indians would go to the woods to make sugar, the faithful missionary resolved to go with them. Night and morning he led their devotions, and, when the daily work was done, taught them to sing. When the sugar-making season was ended the Indians returned to their central camp for a little while, but soon went to their separate settlements, as the planting season came on, that they might engage in their rude agriculture and follow the chase. This scattered and unsettled condition of the natives was so unfavorable to the work of instruction that, after the experiment of a year or two, an effort was made to induce them to settle permanently in one place. This was favored by the General Court, as the government of Massachusetts was called, and a tract of land six miles square was set apart and given to the Indians. This tract included the upper and larger settlement of the Indians and a considerable portion besides, and embraced the present township of Stockbridge, with that of West Stockbridge, and some land in addition. There were already a few Dutch and English settlers on this land, but their titles were purchased by the colony. The Indians were pleased with this action on their behalf, and almost immediately gave up their lower village, and settled together on the Great Meadow, or W-nahk-ta-kook, which afterward was incorporated as a town by the name of Stockbridge. The work of preaching and teaching was now prosecuted with increasing interest and success by Sergeant and his worthy assistant, Mr. Timothy Woodbridge.

It was part of the plan, in gathering the Indians together in one place, to introduce into the settlement a few white families of the best character for the sake of their influence both in civilizing and Christianizing the natives. By consent of the Indians one-sixtieth part of the land assigned them was reserved for each of four such families, as well as for Sergeant and Woodbridge. These families were carefully selected by a committee appointed for the purpose by the Legislature. The result of this arrangement was that a choice society of whites was formed at Stockbridge from the beginning. Men and women of Puritan descent laid its foundations. Begun thus with families of the highest respectability and the best character, rather than by any company of adventurers or speculators, and pains being taken at the same time to remove the few of doubtful character who had previously gained a foot-hold, such as may always be found in or near new settlements, it was only a natural consequence that, in subsequent years, the spot which came into notice as the seat of a mission to heathen savages should be distinguished for the high-toned character of its people and the many persons of eminence who have had their abode there.

The formal ordination of Sergeant to his missionary work was a peculiar scene, and is eminently a fit subject for the canvas of the artist. It shows the remoteness and difficulty of access of the Housatonic region that this installation took place at Deerfield, fifty miles from Stockbridge. It shows, too, the connection of the colonial government at that time with the religious affairs of the people, and especially with this mission to the Indians, that it took place by direction of the Governor and Council, and with their personal presence and participation. The scene is thus described by our historian: "August 25, the Governor and a large committee from the Council and House of Representatives arrived, and the week was spent in forming a treaty, ratifying the peace and friendship which existed, and exchanging pledges. On the evening of Friday, the 29th, Mr. Sergeant reached Deerfield, and the morning of the Sabbath, August 31, was set apart for the services of the ordination. The neighboring ministers attended, the usual congregation worshiping in the church assembled, many of the Indian delegates were grave spectators of the scene, the Governor and Council were in their places, and the Housatonic Indians, seated by themselves, completed the motley and interesting group. As an introduction to the ordination, the Rev. William Williams, of Hatfield, addressed the Governor, and humbly asked if it were his Excellency's pleasure that the pastors there convened should proceed to set apart Mr. Sergeant for the work to which he had been appointed. The Governor manifested his approbation. Mr. Williams then asked Mr. Sergeant if he were willing to devote himself to that work; Mr. Sergeant gave his assent, and the ordination services were performed. After the fellowship of the elders had been given, Rev. Dr. Williams, of Longmeadow, asked the Indians, through an interpreter, if they were willing to receive Mr. Sergeant, thus solemnly set apart to the work of teacher, among them. The Indians signified their assent by rising."

When Sergeant came to his missionary field he found a greater obstacle to his success in the lawless and immoral conduct of some whites from the Dutch plantations on the Hudson than from the paganism of the Indians. As one has said, "the trials incident to other missionaries were to be encountered—perils among the heathen, perils in the wilderness—and one peril which the apostle does not mention—peril among the Dutch." It is the old story which runs through all our Indian history. Even in those early times there were to be found those who, for their selfish purposes, were ready to make victims of the aborigines. Rum was then, as it has been ever since, the grand instrument of their success. Happily the influence of the missionary was so great, and such the good sense and moral principle of a portion of the red men, that they were led early to take strong measures against the threatening evil. It was not a year after Sergeant came among them when they passed a resolution "to have no trading in rum." The General Court also came to their assistance with its law, antedating the "Maine Law" by more than a century, making it a criminal offense for any private person to sell strong drink to an Indian. The Dutch traders, fearing, like those of old who made silver images of Diana, that the hope of their gains would disappear in proportion as the Gospel should produce its effect upon the Indians, endeavored to excite their opposition to the missionary and to the colonial government, telling them that the latter was unfriendly to them, and seeking to deprive them of their liberty in not allowing liquor to be freely sold them. But their confidence in their pastor enabled him to convince them that the law was enacted for their welfare, and that the traffickers in rum were their real enemies.

In 1734, when the mission was begun, the number of Housatonic Indians within its reach was not more than fifty. In two years this number had increased to ninety, and it was not long before the faithful labors of Sergeant and those associated with him had made such an impression upon the Indians of the vicinity that the settlement at Stockbridge embraced more than four hundred of the children of the forest. Sergeant was not content, however, with the endeavor to enlighten and Christianize the few families he found residing upon the Housatonic. He designed, rather, the mission here to be a focal point of influence which should make itself felt through a wide region. Early in the history of his labors here he formed the plan of a manual-labor school. In this school he hoped to gather not only the children of the Indians living in the vicinity of Stockbridge, but those of more distant tribes, who might be induced to avail themselves of its benefits. Here he proposed, in addition to the common education of the school and the instructions of religion, that the boys should be taught the arts of agriculture, and the girls those of domestic economy. It was an intelligent and far-sighted plan, worthy of the apostolic zeal and love of such a man as Sergeant. It enlisted much interest, also, not only among the ministers and churches of New England, but among the people of Great Britain. The mission to the Housatonic Indians had, indeed, derived the main portion of its pecuniary as well as moral support from abroad ever since its beginning. The Commissioners of Indian Affairs at Boston were the agents of the Society in London for Publishing the Gospel in Foreign Parts, and Sergeant, as well as Edwards and West, his successors, received their salary largely from that source. The plan of the boarding-school was formed in consultation with gentlemen of piety and distinction abroad, and had their encouragement from the first. Rev. Isaac Hollis, of London, a nephew of Hollis, the distinguished benefactor of Harvard College, had been interested in the mission from its start, and had offered to support twenty of the Stockbridge Indians at an annual charge of £500. When the larger scheme was proposed he was quite ready to second the plan. Rev. Dr. Watts also took up a collection among his friends in its behalf, and sent Sergeant £70, together with a copy of his treatise on the "Improvement of the Mind," a little volume which is cherished as a memorial among the descendants of Sergeant to this day. Other English clergymen took hold of the matter with interest. The Prince of Wales, also, and the Dukes of Cumberland and Dorset, and Lord Gower, with others, became liberal subscribers to the mission and to the school. Dr. Francis Ayscough, of London, clerk of the closet and first chaplain to the Prince of Wales, also made a donation of a copy of the Scriptures in two large folio volumes, gilt and embellished with engravings. Upon the fly-leaf was written, "Presented by Dr. Ayscough to Rev. John Sergeant, missionary to the Stockbridge Indians, in that vast wilderness called New England." It is creditable to the catholicity of Dr. A. that, when he was informed that Mr. Sergeant was a Dissenter, he replied, "What if he be a Dissenter? It is time those distinctions were laid aside...... I love all good men alike, let them be Churchmen or Dissenters."

The Indians cherished these volumes of the Scriptures with great regard, and took them with them in their several migrations after they removed from their old Stockbridge home.

But the plan of the boarding-school, though in itself so generous and so generously helped, was not altogether successful.

SERGEANT'S HOME, STOCKBRIDGE.

maker of all things, though some believed the sun to be God, or, at least, his body. He also gave him one of their beautiful traditions, which was that the seven stars are so many Indians translated to heaven in a dance; that the stars in Charles's Wain are so many men hunting a bear; that they begin the chase in spring, and hold it all summer; by the fall they have wounded it, and that the blood turns the leaves red; by the winter they have killed it, and the snow is made of its fat, which, being melted by the heat of the summer, makes the sap of the trees. A beautiful legend, certainly.

The Stockbridge Indians, as they were eminent for their good morals, were also distinguished for their peaceable character. So far as we know, they never had any hostile encounter with the whites living near them, and when the French war, so called, broke out, they endeavored to prevent the other tribes from engaging in the threatening conflict, urging upon them a position of neutrality. The superior influence of the French prevented the success of their endeavors. But if they did not succeed in holding others apart from the conflict, they became a very great protection to the whites in the region of Western Massachusetts and Connecticut, below them. These people lay directly in the natural pathway of the Indians coming down with the French from Canada; but so great seems to have been their dread of meeting the Stockbridges, in alliance with the whites among whom they were living, that the hostile tide swept on either side of them, and left the people of this region unharmed. And to the last, through all their history in connection with the whites, whether at Stockbridge or in their subsequent settlements elsewhere, the Housatonic Indians have sustained the most amicable relations with their pale-faced neighbors. Hardly any thing of the traditional character of the savage is found among them.

At the solicitation of the Indians, soon after their settlement on the tract assigned them, the Legislature of the colony appropriated funds for the erection of a church at Stockbridge and a suitable school-house.

The Stockbridge Indians did their part, not only by sending their own children to the missionaries, but by offering a portion of their lands to the Mohawks and Oneidas, if they would come and settle with them, and receive the benefits of the school; and at one time there were as many as ninety of these New York Indians resident on the Housatonic. But the outbreak of the war between England and France created great disturbance among the red men, and other causes combined to defeat the plan. The Indians from the other tribes returned to their homes after a while, and left the Stockbridge tribe as the only direct subjects of the missionary work begun in Berkshire.

It is much to be regretted that Sergeant has not left behind him such an account of the Indians as his rare knowledge of them so well fitted him to give. From the brief memoranda he has left, however, we are led to ascribe a high character to the Stockbridge Indians as compared with many others. President Dwight, writing near the close of the last century, speaks of them, also, in a commendatory way, and says that "this tribe was, both by itself and the other tribes, acknowledged to be the eldest branch of their nation, and as such regularly had the precedency in their councils." Ebenezer, his interpreter, told Sergeant, as they were on their way to attend a religious ceremony of the Indians, that the latter now generally believed in one supreme invisible being, the

This church stood on the ample "Green" on which the present house of worship stands, and its oaken timbers—though, after the removal of the Indians to New York, they were put to a different use from their original one—have been in a good state of preservation until within a few years; and quite recently the remains of them have been wrought into various articles of ornament and use, which may still serve as mementoes of the history of a century and a half ago, and of life in the wilderness.

No bell rang out its call to worship through the primeval forests. But the people of Boston gave the little Indian church what was deemed a very handsome substitute for one, in the shape of a conch shell, then recently imported from the tropics. This was blown lustily at the hour of worship, and usually by an Indian. Hence, perhaps, the tradition that it was of such size that no ordinary man could even lift it. The shell, however, is now to be seen in the museum of the Stockbridge Library, and though somewhat worn by its long use, is of the usual dimensions. The office of blowing the conch seems to have been an important one, as we find the town at various times voting to make contributions for the purpose of paying David Nau-nau-nee-ka-nuk for this service. Under the labors of Sergeant and those associated with him, the rude aborigines were constantly growing in enlightenment and virtue. At the time of his death in 1749, fourteen years after his missionary work began, one hundred and eighty-two of the Indians had been baptized by him, and forty-two were then professed Christians. Forsaking the society of scholars that he might instruct a heathen race, enduring poverty and the many privations incident to a life in the wilderness, incessant in labors in behalf of his adopted people, his death was felt by them as a sore bereavement; and the stone which still marks his resting-place in the cemetery at Stockbridge bears this quaint inscription, composed by one of his Indian pupils, a token at the same time of their regard for him, and of the civilizing and religious work he had wrought upon them:

"Where is that pleasing form? I ask: thou canst not show;
He's not within, false stone; there's naught but death below.
And where's that pious soul, that thinking, conscious mind?
Wilt thou pretend, vain cipher, that's with thee enshrined?
Alas, my friend, not here with thee that I can find;
Here's not a Sergeant's body or a Sergeant's mind.
I'll seek him hence, for all's alike deception here;
I'll go to heaven, and I shall find my Sergeant there."

After the death of Sergeant the Indians and the few whites at Stockbridge were without any pastor for nearly two years. Then there succeeded to that vacant office in the wild woods one whose name is not only highly honored throughout this land, but better known and more honored abroad, perhaps, than that of any of our countrymen except Washington. As a preacher, a philosopher, and a person of devoted piety he is unsurpassed. In his days of boyhood he found his enjoyment in the study of natural science and mathematics, and was an acute observer both of objects in the outward world and in the world of mind. Locke "On the Understanding" was his source of youthful recreation. When hardly beyond his majority he had been called to the pastorship of one of the most important parishes of New England, and had soon become distinguished as an eloquent and effective preacher. His fame had crossed the Atlantic, and eminent men in Europe were his friendly correspondents. But now, after a most successful ministry of more than twenty years, a controversy had arisen between him and his people, and they had thrust him out from them rudely and almost in disgrace. The subsequent adoption of his views, not only

SERGEANT'S GRAVE.

EDWARDS'S HOME AT STOCKBRIDGE.

at Northampton but throughout the churches of New England, has abundantly vindicated his position in that lamentable controversy. But at the time it was a sore trial to him. Driven from his place of labor, unpopular by reason of his well-known views on the qualifications for church membership, with a large family dependent upon him, even his strong faith was hardly sufficient to sustain him as he thought how little likely the churches were to employ him in their service. It was at this time and in such circumstances that he received an invitation from the little church in the village of Stockbridge, then containing but twelve white families, to become the successor of Sergeant. And this was Jonathan Edwards, whose descendants, from Minnesota to Maine, have lately collected at Stockbridge to rehearse together the story of the life and virtues of their great ancestor, and to erect an abiding monument to his memory.

But he was not too great in his own estimation to accept the place now offered him. Without any sense of wounded pride or mortified self-esteem, he stepped down from his high and conspicuous position at Northampton and became a missionary to the Indians in the wilderness. He gave himself at once with earnestness to the work before him. In his preaching, however, he made use of an interpreter. He deemed himself too old, perhaps, and was too much occupied with metaphysical and theological studies, to give the necessary time for mastering the difficult language of the Indians. Besides, that language was very deficient in words expressive of moral and religious ideas. Edwards therefore thought it desirable for the Indians to learn the English tongue, and through it receive their instruction.

Allusion has been made to the studies in which Edwards was engaged while prosecuting his work as a missionary. It would be leaving out a most important item in the history of Stockbridge not to speak of these. When the Indians and the mission to them are forgotten, this quiet village among the mountains will be memorable on account of the work which this eminent man wrought there at the time almost in secrecy and silence. Edwards, on coming to Stockbridge, purchased the house which Sergeant had erected, but which the latter soon left for another he had built half a mile northward, upon a hill which overlooks the village. The house he first built still stands, and until quite recently was little changed from its original appearance. It is the oldest house in Stockbridge, having been built in 1737. It stands near the centre of the village, fronting the south, and commanding a fine view of the beautiful meadows, and of Monument Mountain, and other elevations in that direction. The room on the left hand, as one enters the door-way, is pointed to as the library, perhaps serving also as parlor. On either side of the ample chimney there was, until quite lately, a closet, in dimensions about four feet by six. Tradition had it that the closet in the southwest corner of this room, with its one little window looking toward the west, was Edwards's study—his intellectual workshop—where he wrote his world-famous treatise on the "Freedom of the Will," as well as those other treatises on "Original Sin," "God's Last End in Creation," and the "Nature of True Virtue," which are hardly less celebrated. It is one of the finest moral and intellectual pictures which the history of the race affords—that of this man, who ranks with Plato and other greatest masters

JONATHAN EDWARDS.

of thought, sitting down in that little closet in the wilderness, and amidst a flock of rude savages, to compose in the space of not more than four or five years those essays which have moulded and modified the thinking of a large part of the world, and which will always be referred to by students of the human mind with the utmost respect.

The private life and personal habits of such a man become a matter of interest. Edwards was pre-eminently a student. Tall in person, and having even a womanly look, he was of delicate constitution. He was, however, so temperate and methodical in his living that he was usually in good health, and able to give more time to study than most men. Twelve or thirteen hours of every day were commonly allotted to this. So devoted was he to his work as a student that he was most unwilling to allow any thing to disturb it. Though he was careful to eat regularly and at certain fixed hours, yet he would postpone his meals for a time if he was so engaged in study that the interruption of eating would interfere with the success of his thinking. He was so miserly also in his craving for time that he would leave the table before the rest of the family and retire to his room, they waiting for him to return again when they had finished their meal, and dismiss them from the table with the customary grace.

Edwards was almost a thinking machine. Wherever he was, wherever he went, his pen was with him as the means of preserving his thoughts, and if by chance he failed to have it with him in his walks or rides, he would fasten pieces of paper to various parts of his clothing by means of pins, and associate with each some train of thought or some important conclusion, to be thus preserved until he could get to his ink and paper. So, also, at night he would fasten pins into his bed curtains as the mementoes of his thoughts during his wakeful hours.

That a man thus thoughtful should yet be indifferent to many things of practical importance would not be strange. Accordingly we are told that the care of his domestic and secular affairs was devolved almost entirely upon his wife, who happily, while of kindred spirit with him in many respects, and fitted to be his companion, was also capable of assuming the cares which were thus laid upon her. It is said that Edwards did not know his own cows, nor even how many belonged to him. About all the connection he had with them seems to have been involved in the act of driving them to and from pasture occasionally, which he was willing to do for the sake of needful exercise. A story is told, in this connection, which illustrates his obliviousness of small matters. As he was going for the cows once, a boy opened the gate for him with a respectful bow. Edwards acknowledged the kindness, and asked the boy whose son he was. "Noah Clark's boy," was the reply. A short time afterward, on his return, the same boy was at hand and opened the gate for him again. Edwards again asked, "Whose boy are you?" The reply was, "The same man's boy I was a quarter of an hour ago, Sir."

Stockbridge, as a mission station, and in connection with the Indians, reached the height of its importance, perhaps, under the ministry and care of Sergeant. At the time

MRS. JONATHAN EDWARDS.

of Edwards's dismission to take the presidency of the college at Princeton, about six years after he came to Stockbridge, the Indians numbered but forty-two families, while the white families had increased to eighteen. Stockbridge was no longer the Indian settlement it had been. The Indians seem to have felt the growing preponderance of the whites, and though the latter were entirely friendly, and even devoted to the interests of the red men, the latter were soon ready to accept an invitation from the Oneidas, and relinquish their home in Berkshire for one in the neighborhood of their brethren in New York.

Still, while the Indians remained, the missionary work in their behalf was unremitted. Soon after Edwards's removal to Princeton, the Commissioners joined with the people of Stockbridge in inviting Rev. Stephen West to become his successor. For several years he preached, as his predecessors had done, both to the whites and the natives. But as it became difficult to secure a proper interpreter, and the white population was rapidly increasing, so as to be able to support a pastor independently of the colony and the Commissioners, by whom Sergeant and Edwards had been chiefly supported, in the year 1775, Dr. West, sixteen years after his settlement, gave up the instruction of the Indians to Rev. John Sergeant, son of the first missionary, who perfectly understood the Indian language, and who continued to be the minister and teacher of the natives, both at Stockbridge and after their removal to their new home in New York, until the time of his death in 1824, at the age of seventy-seven.

With this relinquishment of his care of the Indians by Dr. West, about the time of the declaration of our national independence, Stockbridge may be said to have become a white settlement. The Indians remained at Stockbridge ten years after this period, but their church was removed from the centre of the village to a place a mile westward, and they were gradually selling their lands to the whites, thus in every way admitting the ascendency of the latter. And thus gradually, with little that was known to the world at large, a great change was wrought in the character and relations of that beautiful spot upon the Housatonic. One race silently gives way to another, barbarism to civilization, and the foundations are seen to be laid already for one of our most prosperous, influential, and distinguished New England villages.

Dr. West, the successor of Sergeant and Edwards, was, like them, a man of mark, and must ever stand forth as a central figure among the people of Stockbridge. Like Edwards, he was fitted to be the teacher and the influential leader of the most cultivated and the best educated. And he found himself among such at Stockbridge. Though comparatively small in numbers when he came to it, his parish comprised those choice families which had been called in from various parts of the colony at the beginning of the mission to be the companions and, in an important sense, the helpers of Sergeant. To them had been added from time to time others of like character. Joseph Woodbridge, brother of Timothy, the early assistant of Sergeant in the school, had come in. Brigadier-General Dwight, a graduate of Harvard College, and subsequently judge of the Berkshire courts, was now a citizen of Stockbridge. Here were also Colonel Thomas and Ephraim Williams, relatives of that other Colonel Williams, afterward founder of Williams College, who was also one of the earliest white inhabitants of Stockbridge. Here, also, was Judge John Bacon, in early life pastor of the Old South Church in Boston, and in later life member of Congress, and judge of the Common Pleas. Here was Hon. Theodore Dwight, a brother of President Dwight, of Yale College. Here, also, were Henry W. Dwight, a son of Brigadier-General Dwight, and his eminent sons after him. And here, also, was Theodore Sedgwick, long so eminent as Representative and Senator in the State and national councils, and as judge of the Supreme Court of Massachusetts. He was often said to "govern Congress," and his name as judge is honorably connected with one of the earliest decisions in our country against slavery. His own eminence, and that of his children, especially that of Catharine, the authoress of "Hope Leslie," have associated the name of Sedgwick abidingly with Stockbridge as with no other place.

Such, not to speak of other distinguished residents, was Stockbridge when Dr. West became its minister, or during his pastorate there. A society in which such names were found could not be other than marked among surrounding communities. In this society Dr. West held his position as a leader during the long period of sixty years. He commanded the respect of all by his superior abilities of mind and excellences of heart. In social life he was gentle and tender as a woman, and no one was more welcome to every house. The children were attracted to him, and regarded him as at the same time their friend and protector. The story is told, even, of a boy in a neighboring town who, having to pass through a dark and lonely wood at dusk with his cows, solaced his fears by saying constantly, "Old Dr. West, old Dr. West," feeling sure that with such a charm no harm would come to him.

The doctor wore the three-cornered hat, the bands at the neck, and the small-clothes of the olden time, and, being small in stature at the best, his bodily presence was

MISS SEDGWICK'S GRAVE.

somewhat weak. But his face beamed with the unmistakable signs of character, and his speech was far from being contemptible. In the pulpit he was a very thunderer. No one listened to him without being impressed by the strength of his reasoning, and as an expositor of the Scriptures few have equaled him. The late Dr. Emmons, himself regarded as one of our acutest reasoners, said that Dr. West was the only man he was ever afraid of, and pronounced him the greatest divine whom he knew.

Dr. West was the most methodical of men. His boots and shoes, it is said, stood in the same place from year to year, and his hat, whip, and overcoat were always hung on the same nails. He was in the habit of visiting his friend Dr. Hopkins, of Newport, and so exactly did he plan his long journeys thither, though dependent upon his private conveyance, that his wife used to say that she knew as well when to have his tea ready for his return as though he had only gone down to the village for the afternoon.

His place of residence was, on the whole, the most charming spot in all Stockbridge. It was on the point of the high ground which overlooks the village and the valley of the Housatonic from the north, and commands an unusually wide range of view and a combination of mountain, valley, and river scenery seldom equaled. The house he occupied was built by Colonel Ephraim Williams, the founder of Williams College, and honorably distinguished in the French and English war as the commander of Fort Massachusetts, in the northern part of Berkshire County. The site he occupied so overlooked both the northern and eastern valleys of Stockbridge that his house was made a fortification in the early and exposed times. The old well which was then dug in the cellar still remains, but the house was torn down a few years since. What was available of its materials was used, however, in building another house almost on the same site, which is now owned and occupied by Rev. Dr. H. M. Field, editor of the *Evangelist.*

The high reputation of Dr. West as a reasoner and preacher, and especially the fame of his treatise on "Moral Agency," made his house for many years the resort of students preparing for the sacred ministry, and he may be said to have converted Stockbridge from a place for the instruction of rude savages into a place for the training of the most cultivated for the highest and most difficult office known among men. For a period of thirty-five years he was thus engaged. Among his pupils were Dr. Kirkland, afterward president of Harvard University, and Samuel Spring, who, more, perhaps, than any other man, was the founder of the Theological Seminary at Andover, which may thus be traced in its roots to Stockbridge.

Dr. West died in the year 1818, at the age of eighty-four. He was born in 1735, the very year that the Indians were gathered upon the Great Meadow, and the history of Stockbridge began. His one life, therefore, measured the growth of the place from its beginning, when a missionary, without a house and with only one white associate, stood up amidst their rude huts to teach the few Indian families living here in the wilderness, until it had become one of the most enlightened and distinguished towns of New England. The change thus wrought in a single lifetime was marvelous. Even when Dr. West was ordained at Stockbridge there were only about twenty log-huts at what is now the important place of Pittsfield. The whole country north of that point as far as the Canada line was a wilderness; and toward the west, while there were a few Dutch residents on the Hudson and the Mohawk, there were no English settlements between Stockbridge and the Pacific Ocean. When Dr. West closed his ministry Stockbridge was in the midst of a garden of civilization and cultivated beauty, and was known far and wide through the names of those of her residents already mentioned. About this time also the name of Sedgwick, now one of the peculiar names of Stockbridge, and which had been distinguished by the judicial and Congressional services of the Hon. Theodore Sedgwick, was getting an additional importance and renown from the writings of Catharine, his daughter, who was then beginning that career of authorship which has classed her, with Irving, among those who first created an American literature worthy the name, and who has endeared herself by the pure and beautiful tone of her writings to a great multitude of her countrymen and to many abroad. The name of Hopkins also, one of the early and honorable names of Stockbridge, has more recently taken an additional lustre from the character and writings of the distinguished president of Williams College, and his hardly less eminent brother, Albert, who for forty years has occupied the chair of Natural Philosophy and Astronomy in that institution, and whose character seems to have borrowed its peculiar sereneness and saintliness from his converse with the stars.

Nor would the mention of Stockbridge, in its later days, be complete without allusion to another name which has reflected its light upon this village from different walks of life and literature. As with the Sedgwicks, so with the Fields, Stockbridge has become their historic home. Rev. David Dudley Field became the pastor of the church here only about a year after the death of Dr. West, and proved himself the worthy successor of that eminent man. He was the pastor of the church eighteen years, and after filling the like office in another place fourteen years returned to Stockbridge as his chosen home, where, only recently, he has died at an advanced age. Distinguished as a preacher and as a devoted student of history, his sons have been even more widely distinguished in various callings and professions. They have clung also to the old village home. Two of them, and the family of a third one, recently deceased, have their residences

CYRUS W. FIELD.

there. The old Dr. West estate, as has been mentioned already, is now owned by Dr. H. M. Field. The Hon. David Dudley Field, while owning his father's homestead, also owns and occupies, as his summer residence, the beautiful estate which formerly belonged to Sergeant, the missionary. Mr. Cyrus W. Field, more widely known than the others, though not a resident now of Stockbridge, is counted as one of her sons. When his long and persistent but often baffled efforts to link the continents with electric bands had been finally crowned with success, and he had more than realized the promise to "put a girdle round about the earth in forty minutes," no place was more ready to participate in the general rejoicing and congratulation, and no place felt more honored by the event, than Stockbridge; and now she feels that instead of being in the midst of the wilderness, and shut out from light and civilization, as she was a hundred years ago, one of her sons has placed her in the very centre of the world's thought and movement.

Nathaniel Hawthorne resided in Stockbridge for some time. It was here that he wrote "The House of Seven Gables." There is still to be seen on a window-pane in the room which he used as his study this inscription, "*Nathaniel Hawthorne, February* 9, 1851." This little room could only be reached through the kitchen, and had a single window overlooking the "Stockbridge Bowl," as the beautiful lake in the background was named by Miss Sedgwick. Fanny Kemble Butler called it the "Mountain Mirror." From Hawthorne's retreat he could see visitors approach on the road from Lenox, and on such occasions he frequently made good his escape by passing out unnoticed into the woods by the lake side. The house in which Hawthorne lived at Stockbridge is every year visited by hundreds of people from all parts of the world—from England especially. Herman Melville had a residence within an easy drive of Hawthorne. In 1851 Henry James, the novelist, purchased a residence in Stockbridge.

We spoke, at the outset of this article, of the combined attractions of nature and art which Stockbridge presents. The old Indian designation of the place as the "Great Meadow" indicates its characteristic feature as being an unusually wide expanse of river bottom in the midst of surrounding mountains. The peculiar conformation of the mountain ranges in this vicinity compels the Housatonic to change at Lee its southerly course for an eastern, and to keep this general direction through almost the entire breadth of the town of Stockbridge. There are indications also that what are now the meadows were once the bed of a lake, which, by some convulsion of nature, has since been drained off. However this may be, hardly

MONUMENT MOUNTAIN, WITH GRAYLOCK IN THE DISTANCE.

any meadow scenery can be more beautiful than that which one beholds as he looks down from Sergeant Hill and traces the Housatonic as, with many a graceful turn, it winds lingeringly and lovingly along between its enameled banks. Certainly there needs only to be added to this lovely picture of tranquil beauty the setting which is given by the background of encircling mountains wreathed around it in various shapes, like some boldly carved frame of oak around a delicate water-color, to fill the eye and soul of the beholder with a feast of beauty.

And then the individual mountains them-

ICE GLEN.

again. Giant hemlocks and other trees have now grown upon and among these rocks, and covered the sides of the great rift to the very top. The place is wild and impressive in the extreme. You step at once from the warm, sunny pasture-ground without into a cool, dark grotto or labyrinth. The transition is sudden and complete. You go now over and now under the great masses of rock piled, as by the hands of Titans, one upon another. Now you cross from side to side upon a bridge made by some fallen hemlock, so beautifully matted with its enveloping mosses that you hesitate to touch it with the foot

selves have each their several and special attractions. Monument Mountain, which lifts itself on the southern border of the town as the grand mountain feature of the place, with its eastern wall of bare perpendicular rock to which not a tree can cling—how many know something of it since Bryant has enshrined it in his verse! From its summit one looks off upon the Catskills, and his eye sweeps from old Graylock on the north to the Litchfield hills in Connecticut, while around and beneath him the land lies like a garden of beauty.

"It is a fearful thing
To stand upon the beetling verge, and see
Where storm and lightning, from that huge gray wall,
Have tumbled down vast blocks, and at the base
Dashed them in fragments, and to lay thine ear
Over the dizzy depth, and hear the sound
Of winds, that struggle with the woods below,
Come up like ocean murmurs. But the scene
Is lovely round; a beautiful river there
Wanders amid the fresh and fertile meads,
The paradise he made unto himself,
Mining the soil for ages. On each side
The fields swell upward to the hills; beyond,
Above the hills, in the blue distance, rise
The mountain columns with which earth props heaven."

On the east, and quite near the village, is the high range of Bear Mountain, and a walk of less than a mile brings one to Ice Glen, so called, a rift in this mountain nearly half a mile in length. The whole side of the mountain seems to have been rent asunder and tilted over, and then huge boulders as large as houses thrown into the cleft to keep the sundered parts from coming together

lest tne wood-nymphs cry out at your invasion and pollution of their halls. Now you are fain to slide down the smooth face of a rock, steadied by your climbing-staff, and occasionally you pause to look up from some depth, and catch, as from a well, a glimpse of the blue sky, never more "deeply, darkly, beautifully blue" than from such a point of view. To go through this glen, so wildly beautiful, is an event long to be remembered. Its grand rocks can not be forgotten. Its ferns and mosses will keep their greenness and grow in memory for a lifetime.

It is but the walk of a few minutes from the northern opening of the glen to a beautiful eminence which the Housatonic seems to have cut off from Bear Mountain, and left right in the midst of the village as a little bit of wildness and natural beauty furnished for the convenience of invalids and little children. This is Laurel Hill—so called from the abundance of the kalmia, which grows upon its sides in great beauty. The hill is, perhaps, a hundred feet in height, and separated from the main street of the town only by an intervening meadow of an acre or two in extent, upon which, with an unusual felicity of position, stands the village academy. Half-way up the hill, on its western side, is a plateau large enough to accommodate two thousand people. This plateau is backed on the east by a perpendicular wall of rock thirty feet or more in height. And here, amidst the tall trees kept free from underbrush, the villagers are accustomed to meet on occasions of public and social interest. Especially it is used by the Laurel Hill Association, which takes its name from the hill, and has for its object the beautifying of the town by causing art and taste to lend a helping hand to nature. This it does by keeping the village streets in good condition, bordering them with nicely graveled walks, kept clean and well graded; by planting rows of trees for shade along all the highways of the town; by keeping the village cemetery in proper order; and, in general, by encouraging a spirit of taste among all the inhabitants. It spends hundreds of dollars annually in this work, and every year, in August, it holds its anniversary upon the hill itself. A rostrum of earth, covered with turf, is built against the wall of rock of which we have spoken, and which acts as a sounding-board for the help of the speaker. From this rostrum the secretary of the Association reads the record of its doings for the past year. The election of officers then takes place. An oration, and usually a poem, are then recited to the listening auditors. Afterward impromptu speeches are made by one and another, and the good work is thus encouraged for another year. It is the great day of the year in this New England village.

Closely allied to the Laurel Hill Association, though not such a peculiarity of Stockbridge, is another institution, which ought, at least, to be mentioned. This is the public library. A village library, to be sure, is no new thing; and yet a truly successful library is somewhat rare. The history of too many has been somewhat like this: one or two hundred dollars expended in the purchase of a few books, so few that they were not worth the care of a special custodian or a building specially adapted to their preservation, and so were thrust into the corner of some post-office or grocery store, where, after a little interest and attention on the part of the public, and a little gratuitous service on the part of the postmaster or grocer, the books were neglected, forgotten, and lost. A good village library, especially in these days, when books of some sort are found in every family, in order to live and do the proper work of a library, must be of considerable size, in most cases, at the outset. It must be large enough to make a decided impression upon the public by the variety and richness of its contents. It must be large enough to have a value which shall make all feel that it is worth caring for, worth preserving, and worth making constant additions to. In such a case a proper building will be likely to be provided, a librarian will be secured, who will make the care of the books not secondary to that of groceries or dry-goods; and, what is more, the sight of such a feast will stimulate the mental appetite of the community, and the taste of the feast will cause them to secure its continuance.

Such was the start of the library at Stockbridge only half a dozen years ago. A purchase of two thousand volumes was made at the outset. A beautiful stone building was erected for them. When its doors were opened the public saw and felt that they had a treasure in their possession. The town at once assumed the payment of a librarian's services, and enabled the managers to open the library to the public every day, instead of but once a week, as had been expected, and as is so often the case with village libraries; and so almost at once the library became a manifest power in that community. The town would not be willing now to give it up for ten times what it has cost. It is the crowning embellishment of the most beautiful of Berkshire villages.

THE PUBLIC LIBRARY, STOCKBRIDGE.

Boston Light and the Brewsters (1895)

THE

NEW ENGLAND MAGAZINE.

OCTOBER, 1895.

BOSTON LIGHT AND THE BREWSTERS.

By R. G. F. Candage.

EVIDENCE is not wanting that beacon lights fed by wood or coal existed upon the shores and headlands of the Mediterranean for the guidance of mariners earlier than the Christian era, and later in Spain, France and England; yet the light-house as known to us is comparatively modern. The Pharos of Alexandria, erected 300 B. C., was regarded as one of the wonders of the world, and it gave its name to its successors. Light-house in Latin is *pharus;* in Italian and Spanish, *faros;* in French, *phare;* and *pharo* was once used in English, though now obsolete. The pharos of Meloria was built by the Pisans in 1154; the light-house at Leghorn, which still exists, was built in 1304; that at Genoa, called Torre del Capo, was originally built in 1139, and first lighted in 1326.* The Cordouan, at the mouth of the Gironde, France, one hundred and sixty-nine feet in height, begun in 1584 and completed in 1610, is first in importance of modern light-houses. The first light-house in Great Britain, at Lowestoft, was erected in 1609. The next were Hunstanton, in 1665; then Bailey, 1671; Scilly, 1680; Old Head,

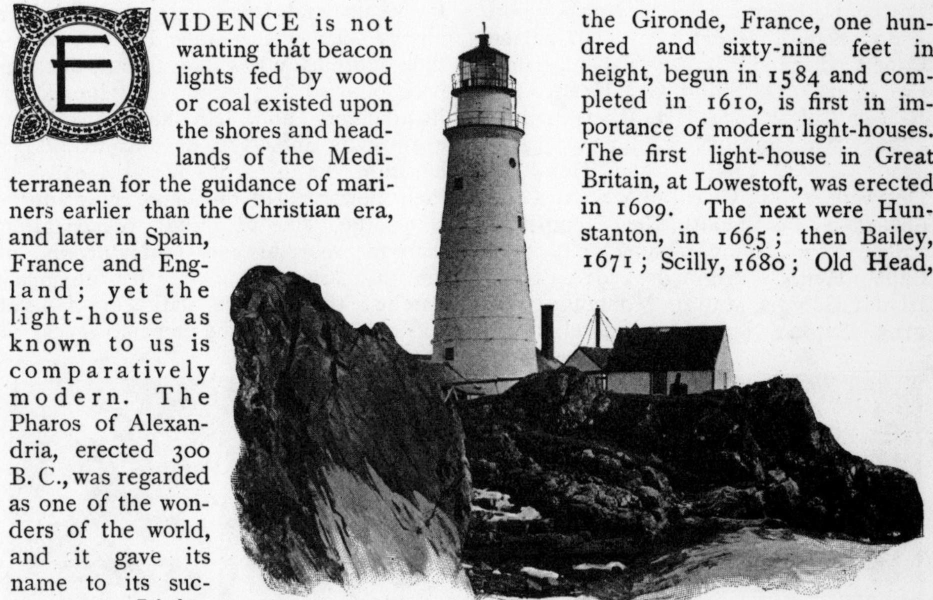

Kinsale, 1683; Eddystone, 1703; St. Ann's Point, 1714; and the Skerries, 1714,—eight before the erection of Boston Light in 1716, the first in America.† These light-houses, as probably those on the American coast until the Revolutionary War, were lighted by candles. The Eddystone was lighted by twenty-four candles, weighing two and a half pounds each.

* "Ancient and Modern Light-Houses," by Major D. P. Heap, 1889.

† Adams's "Light-Houses and Light Ships," 1870.

Of the eight hundred and sixty-three light-stations on the Atlantic and Gulf coasts of the United States in 1894, twenty-seven were erected previous to the year 1800; and of the twenty-seven, thirteen were erected in the province and state of Massachusetts. They were: Boston Light, 1716; Brant Point, Nantucket, 1746; Gurnet, Plymouth, 1769; Nantucket Great Point, 1784; Thatcher's Island, two lights, 1790; Portland Head, 1790; Newburyport, 1790; Sequin Island, 1795; Highland, Cape Cod, 1797; Baker's Island, Salem, two lights, 1797; and Gay Head, 1799. Beaver Tail, Rhode Island, was built in 1761; Navesink, New Jersey, 1762; Sandy Hook, 1764; Cape Henlopen, Delaware, 1764; Charleston, South Carolina, 1767; Portsmouth, New Hampshire, 1789; New London, Connecticut, 1790; Cape Henry, Virginia, 1791; Tybee Island, Georgia, 1793; Montauk Point, 1795; Eaton's Neck, Long Island, 1798; and Cape Hatteras in 1798.

AN EARLY CUT OF BOSTON LIGHT.

From a commercial and maritime point of view, Massachusetts at the beginning of the eighteenth century was the most prosperous, progressive and important of the American colonies. Boston, her largest seaport, had a trade with the other colonies and with foreign ports more important and lucrative than that enjoyed by any other American port. Her merchants and shipowners were bold, enterprising and far-seeing; and to their energy and perseverance Boston's maritime supremacy was due. Many of them had followed the sea in early life, knew its dangers and hardships, and were ever ready and even anxious to aid in lessening its hazards by all means in their power. No one more fully appreciates the value of guides to navigation than the mariner and navigator who in the discharge of his duty has anxiously watched through the darkness of night and has waited for the dawn to reveal to

BOSTON LIGHT IN 1789.

FROM THE MASSACHUSETTS MAGAZINE, FEBRUARY, 1789.

him the entrance to his desired haven. Many of Boston's energetic citizens had had that experience; in their enthusiastic efforts others joined, and as a result the first light-house on the American continent was erected at the entrance of Boston harbor. Forty-four years — nearly half a century — afterward, New York succeeded in having a light-house established as a guide to ships seeking her harbor. We cannot understand why she lagged so many years behind her then great rival, Boston, in this improvement; but so it was. The inhabitants of Boston early in the last century agitated the subject of erecting a light-house at the entrance of the harbor, believing that their large coasting and foreign trade would prosper and be made more safe thereby.

"There is no doubt," says Shurtleff, "but that early in the settlement of the colony a beacon and watch-house were erected on Beacon Island, — hence its name, — as well as on Point Allerton Hill, by the town of Nantasket (Hull), to look out for and warn an enemy's approach." The Massachusetts Archives contain the following: "Hull, March 9, 1673–74 A true copy of the charges of the town of Hull hath been at about the Beacon, with the persons that warded the said Beacon, with an account of corne that was spoyled by carting over the said corne, and what was pluct up to set up the Beacon. The ward was first, Benj. Bosworth, Sen'r, 17 days, and other names, 66 days. In the name of Towne Serg't Bosworth, Nathaniel Bosworth, etc."

THE PRESENT BOSTON LIGHT.

At a meeting of the inhabitants qualified to act in town affairs, called and held the ninth of March, 1712 or 1713, among other business questions introduced was that of providing for a light-house; and it was "Voted: That the consideration of what is proper for the town to do ab't a Light Hous, be referred to the select men." Later the subject was introduced into the meetings of the General Court, the town of Boston proposing to erect the building and maintain the light, by levying rates or light-money upon shipping. In a town meeting held May 13, 1713, it was "Voted: That in case the Gen'll Court shall see cause to proceed to the establishment of a Light-House for the accommodation of vessels passing in and out of this harbour, — that then the selectmen or the Representatives of the town be desired to move to the s'd Court that the Town of Boston may have the preference before any perticuler persons in being concerned in the charge of erecting & maintaining the same, and being Intitled to the Proffits and Income there-of."

The General Court on June 9, 1715, "Ordered: That a Light-House be erected at the charge of the Province, at the Entrance of the Harbour of Boston, on the same Place and Rates proposed in a Bill projected for the Town of Boston's doing it, accompanying this vote, and that a Bill be drawn accordingly." On the fourteenth of the same month the

House of Representatives "Ordered: That Mr. William Payne, Col. Samuel Thaxter, Col. Adam Winthrop, with such as the Honorable Board shall joyn, be a Committee to Build a Light House at the Entrance of the Harbour of Boston pursuant to the Votes of this Court." The order was sent to the Council for concurrence; Hon. William Tailer and Addington Davenport were added from that body, and the order was then approved by Governor Joseph Dudley. A bill was introduced into the House on the seventeenth day of the same month, entitled "An act for Building and Maintaining a Light-house upon the Great Brewster, called Beacon Island, at the entrance of the Harbour of Boston;" and this was passed through its various stages to its final enactment in July, 1715. The preamble and act were as follows:

BUG LIGHT.

"Whereas, the want of a Light-house at the entrance to the Harbour of Boston hath been a great discouragement to navigation, by the loss of the lives and estates of several of His Majesty's subjects, — for prevention whereof: Be it enacted by His Excellency the Governor, Council and Representatives in General Court assembled, and by authority of the same, that there be a light-house erected at the Charge of the Province, on the southermost part of the Great Brewster, called Beacon Island, to be kept lighted from sun-setting to sun-rising. That from and after the building of the said light-house, and kindling a light in it, useful for shipping coming into or going out of the Harbour of Boston, or any other Harbour within the Massachusetts Bay, there shall be paid to the receiver of impost, by the master of all ships and vessels, except coasters, the duty of one penny per tun, inwards, and also one penny per tun, outwards, and no more, for every tun of the burthen of the said vessel, before they load or unload the goods therein."

Coasters under that act were to be "vessels which imported provisions, tar, pitch, turpentine and lumber, belonging to Rhode Island, Connecticut, New York, Jerseys, Pennsylvania, Maryland, Virginia, North Carolina and Nova Scotia," and that were "bound *bona fide* to some of the forementioned governments;" all such to pay two shillings each time they clear out. "All fishing vessels, wood sloops, &c. imployed in bringing of fish, wood, stones, sand, lime or lumber, from any of the parts within this Province coming into said Harbour of Boston, &c. pay five shillings at their first coming in or going out, and no further payment to be demanded of them by the space of one year next following. And no ships or vessels shall be cleared by the Naval Officer

NIX'S MATE.

until a certificate be produced that the duty of the Light-house be paid.” The act further states how vessels shall be measured for their light dues, and that the keeper of the light should be appointed by the General Court, — “who should carefully and diligently attend to this duty at all times in kindling the lights, from sun-setting to sun-rising, and placing them so as they may be most seen by vessels coming in or going out.”

This act was passed July 23, 1715, the first year of the reign of George the First. “In consequence of the determination to build the light-house,” says Shurtleff, “application was made to the proprietors of the undivided lands of Hull, for a grant of the Little Brewster (or Beacon Island) for the purpose.” The result of the request may be seen in the following extracts from the Hull Proprietary Records, as determined upon on the first of August, 1715, and entered upon the records by Mr. Joseph Benson, the clerk:

“At a legal meeting of the proprietors of the undivided land in Township of Hull held on munday the first day of August; Lieutenant Goold Seenior was chosen Moderator for the work of the daye. At ye s’d meeting Co’ll Samuel Thaxter applied himself to the s’d proprietors in the name of the Committee appointed by the great and ganarall corte in their session in June 1715, for the building of a light house on Beacken Island so caled adioyning to the greate Brewsters northerly from the town of Hull and being part of theire township the s’d proprietors being censable that it will be a ganarall benifit to Trade and that thay in perticuler shall rape a greate benifite thereby have at the s’d meeting Unanimus voate given and granted the s’d Becan Island to the province of the Massachusetts Bay for the use of a light house forever; To be disposed of as the government shall see meet; provided that the s’d proprietors of the greate Brewsters be keept harmless.”

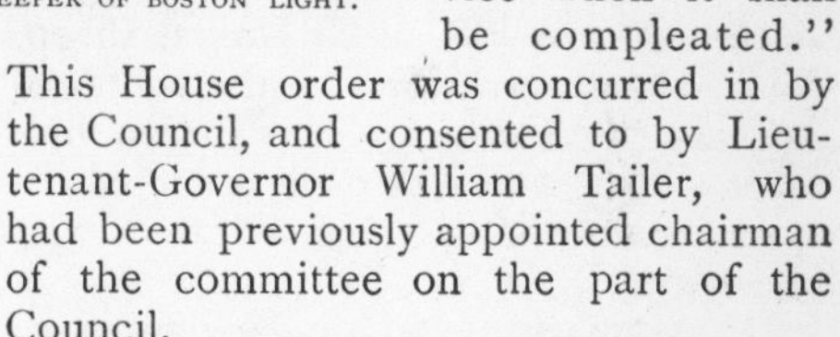

CAPTAIN THOMAS BATES.

FOR TWENTY-NINE YEARS KEEPER OF BOSTON LIGHT.

“The committee appointed to take care of the building of the light-house” not having leisure (as the General Court records state on the twenty-fifth of December, 1715) to oversee and direct the work, it was “Ordered, that the oversight of that work be committed to Mr. William Payne, and Capt. Zachariah Tuthill, to carry on and finish the same agreeable to the Advice and Direction they shall from Time to Time receive from the said Committee, and that the sum of Sixty Pounds be allowed them for the whole of that service when it shall be compleated.”

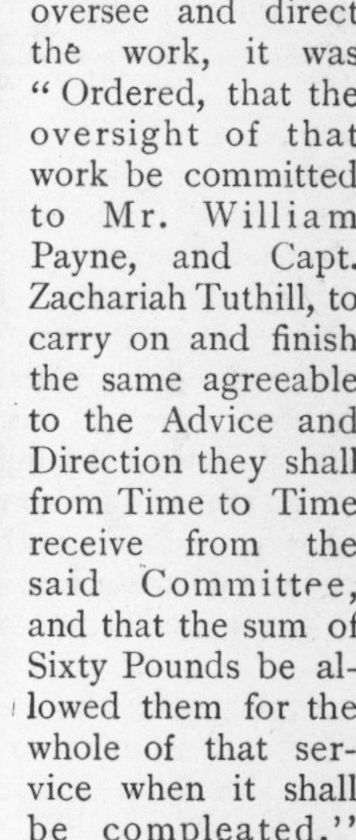

This House order was concurred in by the Council, and consented to by Lieutenant-Governor William Tailer, who had been previously appointed chairman of the committee on the part of the Council.

A competent keeper of the light-house was found in the person of Mr. George Worthylake, whom, on June 25, 1716, the commissioners were empowered to employ at a salary of fifty pounds per year, “to begin when the lights are set up.” Drake says that Hayes was the first light-keeper, but that is an error; Hayes was the second keeper, as we shall see later. Shurtleff says: “George Worthylake, the first keeper of Boston Light-House, was a husbandman, forty-three years of age, who had been brought up in the harbor; for his father, who bore the same name, had been for many years previous a resident of Pemberton Island, now called George’s Island. He himself appears to have dwelt upon Lovell’s Island at the time, where

THE GRAVES.

his farm was, and where his son resided after his death."

This statement is not very clear, and it is necessary to state that George Worthylake, Sr., died in 1693. An engrossed copy of his will, mistaken for that of his son, the light-keeper, who died in 1718, hangs upon the walls of the Certificate Room of the Bostonian Society at the Old State House.

The light-keeper was to receive for his first year's salary, as already stated, fifty pounds; but the second year seventy pounds, the increase having been made on his petition to the General Court, "on account of the loss of fifty-nine sheep, which were drowned during the winter of 1716–17, they having been driven into the sea by a storm through want of his care of them when obliged to attend the light-house."

The commissioners, on November 7, 1716, presented to the General Court an account of money expended in building the light-house, "£2385 17*s.* 8*d.* half penny, whereof £1900 had been paid." The report was referred to a committee, who reported favorably thereon on the seventeenth of the same month, and the account was allowed and the balance ordered to be paid.

Mr. Worthylake kept the light for two years, up to the time of his death. He and his wife and daughter were unfortunately drowned on November 3, 1718, while sailing from the light-house to Noddle's Island. Their bodies were recovered and buried in Copp's Hill burying-ground, in the centre, a few feet south of the tool-house. Over their graves was placed a triple stone marked, "George, in his forty-fifth year, Ann in her fortieth, and Ruth, their daughter." This incident was the origin of the ballad called "The Light-House Tragedy," which Benjamin Franklin, then twelve years of age, was induced by his brother to write, print and sell about the streets, and which he said "sold prodigiously, though it was wretched stuff." This was said to be Franklin's earliest poetic effusion; but not a word of it has been handed down to our time.

The body of Mr. Worthylake had scarcely been placed in the grave before petitions were presented to the General Court requesting the appointment of his successor. The petition of John Hayes, a mariner, recommended by the merchants of Boston, on November 6, 1718, as an experienced mariner and pilot in the harbor and an able-bodied and discreet person, prevailed, and he was appointed on the eighteenth of the same month.

The duties of a light-house keeper were arduous, as, in addition to his attention to the lights, he was to pilot vessels in and out of the harbor, act as health officer in case of sickness on board of incoming

THREE-MASTER PASSING POINT ALLERTON IN MIDWINTER.

vessels and order them into quarantine, and as an entertainer at his house of such persons from town or elsewhere as sought his hospitality; answer by signal gun signals from vessels in the offing in distress or otherwise, etc.

Keal, in 1719, says: "The Light-house was built on a rock above water, 2 leagues from Boston, where, in time of war, a signal is made to the castle & by the castle to the town, by hoisting and lowering the Union flag so many times as there are ships approaching. If they exceed a certain number, the castle fires 3 guns to warn the town of Boston, & the Gov'r if needs be, orders the Beacon fires, which alarms the adjacent country, and gives 6 or more hours to prepare for their reception."

LOOKING UP THE HARBOR FROM THE MIDDLE BREWSTER.

Shaw's "History of Boston" (Pemberton's account), 1817, says: "Light-House Island is a high rock of 2 or 3 acres, ¾ of an acre of it good soil; a bar, dry at low water, connects it with Great Brewster; a stone light-house shows one light; it is 8¼ miles from Long Wharf, Boston, and was formerly known as Beacon Island, &c. Pilots here have a piece of artillery to answer signal guns." This island and all the islands, as well as Nantasket, including its beaches, were on the settlement of the colony covered with dense woods. In 1676–77 the proprietors of Hull divided the wood on the Lesser Brewster, as they afterward did on the other Brewsters, to clear them for planting and grass, to be done by May 1, 1679, — the land and lots to be divided by lot.

The light-house burned down and was rebuilt in 1720. The following account was inserted in the Boston *News Letter* at the time: "On Wednesday night last, the 13 Instant, an unhappy accident fell out that the Light-House was burned and the Government has Ordered the following advertisement:

"'At a Council held at the Council Chamber in Boston on Friday the 15 day of January, 1720. That an advertisement be put in the Newspaper giving notice of the fire lately happening at the Light-House, and that care will be taken to refit the same with all possible Expedition; and that in the mean time there will be set up at the said Light-House as good a light as conveniently can be projected to serve for the Present. J. Willard, Secr.'"

This was in the issue for January 18. In the issue for February 22 there followed another notice: "Whereas the Light-House by an Unhappy Accident was burnt down the 13 of Jan. past, and

HOUSES ON MIDDLE BREWSTER.

the Government then gave Publick Notice thereof several times by this Print, that forth-with all due Care would be taken to refit the same, And they do therefore now Also Order the like Publick Notice to be given, that on Wednesday last the 17 instant the Lights were lighted and are burning as they did before they were burned down; and all vessels coming in may depend of seeing the Light to the full height from the surface, as they did the former." *

A petition from John Hayes, keeper of the light-house on Beacon Island, was sent to the General Court, November 22, 1720, "showing that he is necessitated for the faithful Discharge of his office to Hire two men constantly to attend that Service as well as himself, So that after Men's wages are paid & Provisions are supplied them the Petitioner's allowance is not sufficient to give himself and family a support, and in-as-much as it may have been Represented that his Profits are considerable by Giving Entertainment for the last Twelve Months, And that for the Affair of Pilotage, In the Summer Season almost every Fisher-Man or Boat Man they meet with in the Bay, Pilot the Ships in, And that his Benefit by Pilotage is by that means very inconsiderable, and therefore Praying that some sufficient addition may be made to his salary." In answer to this petition, the House of Representatives, on November 24, 1720, "Resolved — That the sum of Seventy Pounds be allowed and paid out of the Publick Treasury to the petitioner for his services the year coming. To be paid quarterly as it becomes due. In Council Read and concurred."

I find no further mention of Captain Hayes in the Province records until August 22, 1733, when he sent in his resignation, "on account of age and infirmities," to take effect on the eighth of November following. The merchants of Boston recommended for the vacancy Mr. Robert Ball, an Englishman, a mariner and pilot, who was selected for the place on August 23, 1733, the day following the receipt of Captain Hayes's resignation. Captain Ball married Mrs. Martha King of Charlestown, whose daughter married Adam Knox, a pilot. The Boston Committee of Correspondence gave Mr. Knox a certificate of "friendly behavior" on June 18, 1776, as follows: "Mr. Adam Knox, of this Town having applied to this committee, for a certificate of his friendly behavior, with respects to the Rights and Liberties of his country — the following was given him signed by nine of the Committee. 'This may certify whom it

* I am indebted to Colonel William R. Livermore, Corps of Light-House Engineers, for this item, — he having received it in a letter from Dr. Samuel A. Green of the Massachusetts Historical Society.

may concern, that Mr. Adam Knox who has long been improved in this Town as a Pilot, has ever appeared to us as a person friendly to the Rights and Liberties of Americans.' " *

Captain Ball, in the early years of his keepership of Beacon Light-House, requested appropriations to be made for repairs upon the light-house, and also upon the dwelling-house, — and these were granted. The following singular account rendered by John Fayerweather, a Boston merchant, for hospitality at the light-house in June, 1746, under Captain Ball's administration, explains itself: "Charged to the Town of Boston 50*s*. cash paid ye Light-House Tavern for meetings held there with ye Committee to measure ye rocks from ye lower middle ground, for order to sink hulks, if occasion, & 8*s*. 6*d*, more for drink for the boat's crew in April — total £5-19-8. Henry King to receive it. King credited with having paid over £2-19-8."

In 1751 Boston Light-House was again destroyed by fire, and on June 22 of that year an act to repair it was passed, as follows:

"An Act In Addition To An Act Made And Passed In The First Year Of The Reign Of His Majesty King George The First, Intitled An Act For Building And Maintaining A Light House Upon The Great Brewster (Called Beacon Island) At The Entrance Of The Harbour Of Boston.

"Whereas the light-house at the entrance to the harbour of Boston hath been greatly damaged by fire, and it hath been

"RUFFIANS" FISHING, MIDDLE BREWSTER.

ordered by this Court that it should be repaired; and it being reasonable that the Charge of such repairs should be born by those who receive the immediate benefit thereof: —

"Be it therefore enacted by the Lieutenant Governour, Council, and House of Representatives: That the Commissioner of import be and hereby is directed, by himself and his deputies, to demand and receive of the master of every vessel (which within the space of two years from the publication of this act, shall clear out from any port within this province, being bound to any port within this province) over and above what is already by law provided the following rates at each time of clearance: For every vessel of less than one hundred tons, two shillings; for every vessel of above one hundred tons and not exceeding two hundred tons, three shillings; and for every vessel of above two hundred tons, four shillings."

Robert Ball, Sr., was light-

MIDDLE BREWSTER, LOOKING TOWARD OUTER BREWSTER.

*New England Historical Genealogical Register, July, 1876.

MINOT'S LIGHT.

house keeper from 1733, under the Royal Government, up to or after 1766, and one account thinks until after the British fleet left Boston harbor in the Revolution. Captain Ball's son, Robert Ball, a sea captain, willed, in 1772 or 1782, Calf Island, Boston harbor, and Green Island in Hull, to his son John; and to his daughter Sarah, the Outer Brewster, which in 1794 was sold for £50.

"The light-house standing at the entrance to the harbor," says Shurtleff, "was the original structure of 1716, modified somewhat by repairs after the fire of 1751. It became early in the siege [of Boston] an object of concern for both sides; and more than one expedition conducted by the Provincials destroyed the destructible parts of it; the tower being of brick was allowed to stand. While it was in possession of the British, a party under Major Vose, of Heath's regiment, in whale-boats, landed on Nantasket Point, before day, and set fire to the light-house. At daylight the men-of-war discovered them, and fired upon them. An eye-witness says, 'I ascended an eminence at a distance, and saw the flames of the light-house ascending up to Heaven, like grateful incense, and the ships waisting their powder.'" Major Vose returned the next day, burnt the wooden portions of the light-house, brought off its furniture, lamps, etc., and the boats. The enemy had commenced rebuilding the light-house, and on July 31, 1775, Major Tupper, with three hundred men, was despatched to disperse the working party. The enemy prepared to receive them in a hostile manner. Major Tupper landed in good order on the island, marched to the works, killed ten or twelve men on the spot, and took the remainder prisoners. Having demolished the work, the party were ready to embark; but the tide leaving them, they were obliged to remain until its return. Meantime a number of boats came up from the men-of-war to re-enforce those at the island, and a smart firing from both parties took

GREAT BREWSTER.

place. A field-piece under charge of Major Crane, planted on Nantasket Point to cover a retreat, sunk one of the boats and killed several of the crew. Major Tupper brought his party off with the loss

GREAT BREWSTER IN WINTER.

of one man killed and two or three wounded. He killed and captured fifty-three of the enemy. Washington, in general orders, August 1, 1775, thanked Major Tupper and his men "for gallant and soldier-like behavior in possessing themselves of the enemy's post at the light-house."

The British were compelled to evacuate Boston in March, 1776, but did not immediately leave the harbor, contenting themselves for a time in doing all the mischief they could upon the several islands within it. On the thirteenth of June, three months after they took refuge on board their ships, the Continentals brought their guns to bear upon them, and on the fourteenth the cannon from Long Island began to play upon the ships, which obliged them to weigh their anchors and make the best of their way out of the harbor. As they passed Nantasket and the light-house, they sent their boats on shore and brought off a party of regulars and blew up the light-house; and then the fleet made all sail and went to sea, steering their course easterly for Halifax.

"The commander of the ship *Renown*, Captain Bangs," says Shurtleff, "who sent his boats to the light-house to take his men from the island, left powder so arranged that it took fire an hour afterward and blew up the brick tower. The Light-House Island, was therefore the last stop occupied by a hostile force in Boston harbor."

On November 8, 1780, Governor Hancock sent a message to the Massachusetts legislature, recommending the building of a light-house at the entrance of Boston harbor, upon the site of the old one, which had been in ruins more than four years. The legislature appointed a committee, which reported upon the subject, the result of which was the building and completion of the new light-house in November, 1783, and the passage of an act relating to light-houses. This new building was made of stone, seventy-five feet in height, including the lantern, fifteen feet. The diameter at its base was twenty-five feet, and at the top fifteen feet. The wall at the bottom was seven and a half feet in thickness, and at the top two and a half feet, with a cylindrical opening in the centre of ten feet for stairs, etc. The lantern was octagonal, fifteen feet high, and eight and a half feet in diameter. It had four lamps, holding each a gallon of oil, with four burners to each lamp.

On November 28, 1783, Captain Thomas Knox, a pilot, was appointed keeper of the light by Governor Hancock. Captain Knox's father, Adam, who has been mentioned, and his mother, Martha

Knox, resided at the light-house with him. The latter died there in January, 1790, and Adam died there in December of the same year, aged eighty-one.

ON THE OUTER BREWSTER.

On June 10, 1790, under an act of Congress passed August 7, 1789, the island and light-house were ceded to the United States. When the United States government assumed control of the light-house stations of the country, Massachusetts ceded three, Boston Light, the Gurnet at Plymouth and Brant Point at Nantucket; New Jersey ceded two, Navesink and Sandy Hook; New Hampshire, Portsmouth Light; Rhode Island, the Beaver Tail; Delaware, Cape Henlopen; and South Carolina, Charleston.

Until the United States assumed jurisdiction of the light-houses on the coast, Boston Light was under the control of the Governor and Council, and its expenses were defrayed by a duty on vessels, called "light money," which was a shilling a ton on all foreign vessels and twopence halfpenny on American vessels clearing from the custom house.

On March 23, 1797, Thomas Knox (the light-keeper), Charles Cole and Robert Knox, probably a brother of Thomas, were recommended to the Governor and Council by the Boston Marine Society to be pilots, — the former doubtless for reappointment, as he was a pilot when appointed light-house keeper in 1783. In 1803 Thomas Knox was owner of the island in the harbor called Nix's Mate, "once of more than three miles in circumference, but now reduced to a small heap of sand with a few rods of the original surface continually decreasing and undermined by the sea, which he is willing to cede to the United States for the purpose, if Congress in its wisdom shall think fit to appropriate a sum of money adequate for the building a sufficiently strong stone wall round the remains of said island and for placing thereon a beacon." *

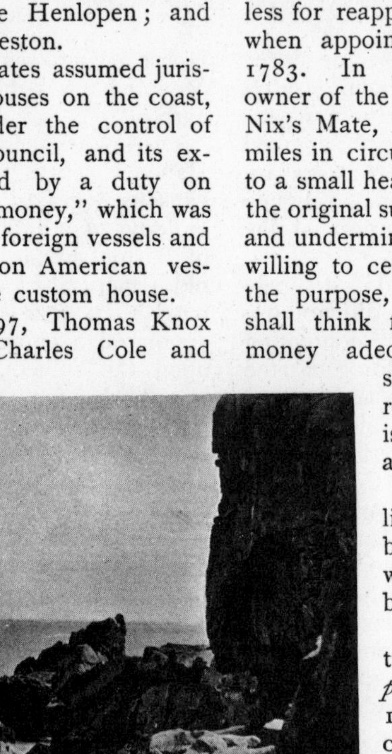

OUTER BREWSTER.

Thomas Knox was the light-keeper for many years; but when he resigned, or who was his successor, I have not been able to ascertain.

The naval encounter between the frigates *Chesapeake* and *Shannon*, June 1, 1813, which resulted in the capture of the *Chesapeake* with the loss of forty-seven of her crew killed, including Lawrence, her commander, — the *Shannon* losing twenty-

* Petition of the Boston Marine Society to Congress in 1803, on "the necessity of preserving an ancient Landmark of the greatest importance to the navigation of Boston."

three killed and over fifty wounded, including Broke, her commander,— an engagement which lasted but fifteen minutes, took place twelve miles outside of Boston Light.

In 1815 the Boston Marine Society petitioned the government "to have the light-house lit." It had probably been closed during the War of 1812. In 1829 Jonathan H. Bruce, a pilot, was keeper of the light, he having been recommended for the place by the Boston Marine Society. The same year he was recommended by the Marine Society to the Governor and Council as a pilot, probably a reappointment. He held the office of light-keeper for many years. He died in Boston, February 15, 1868, aged seventy-six. His son Jonathan, brought up on the island when his father was light-keeper, was for many years a Boston pilot. He died a few years ago, aged seventy-two.

The light-keepers succeeding Bruce were David Tower of Cohasset, Captain Cook, Captain Long of Charlestown, Mr. Small, Mr. Douglass of Swampscott, Captain Babson of Gloucester, and Captain Thomas Bates of Cohasset. Captain Bates was appointed July 18, 1864, and served until April 6, 1893, dying in office. Mr. Albert M. Harte was the successor of Captain Bates, serving one year. On May 1, 1894, the present incumbent, Mr. Henry L. Pingree, was appointed to succeed Mr. Harte.

Since the erection of Boston Light-House in 1783 the present building has been altered and refitted. In 1856 the lighting apparatus was renewed, the new apparatus consisting of fourteen twenty-one-inch reflectors, fitted in the best manner to illumine when lighted an area of sixteen square miles at each revolution; and the light was considered by ship-masters one of the best lights on the American coast. In January, 1860, the tower was raised in height to ninety-eight feet, and the lantern was newly equipped with revolving illuminating apparatus. The light can be seen in clear weather at a distance of sixteen nautical miles. The tall white tower surmounted with the black lantern is an imposing object when seen from vessels entering or leaving the harbor.

BEACH OF GREAT BREWSTER IN WINTER.

Life at Boston Light is tame and commonplace as compared with that at more exposed places on our coast and on the light-ships far out from land. It has more or less of the character of a long sea voyage, each succeeding day entailing duties exactly like those of the days which have passed. The thrilling experiences met with by the keepers at Minot's, Boon Island, Wooden Ball, Mount Desert Rock, and on the light-ships at Pollock Rip and Nantucket South Shoal, are unknown here; and yet there are many incidents which give variety to and enrich the life of the light-keeper on Little Brewster.

His duty is to tend carefully the light, keep it burning brightly and steadily from sunset to sunrise, and in thick weather to sound the fog whistle. He must keep the lenses of his lamps and the glass of the lantern scrupulously clean in order to throw the utmost power of the light over the sea. He must, with diligent care, watch it through the night to see that it does not grow dim or go out.

When a heavy storm comes on, and the drift strikes the lantern, and the waves dash with fury against the rocks below, with anxious gaze he peers out into the darkness for the sail of the tempest-tossed mariner, and listens intently for the cry of the shipwrecked ones. These are anxious and trying times for

the light-keeper, and the nerve tension is so great as oftentimes to seem unendurable. After a storm he finds sea-fowl, which in bewilderment have dashed themselves against the lantern and fallen dead at the foot of the tower.

Although not of frequent occurrence, there have been wrecks near the light-house, and of course at such times the keeper's aid is invaluable, having often been the means of saving lives.

There is also a cheerful and pleasant side to life at the light-house. The steamers with their human freight, the coasting and fishing schooners, the tug boats and yachts with their gay flags, and all manner of craft pass under the keeper's eyes by day, and their lights often make the harbor a veritable fairy-land by night. Ships bound for all parts of the world he sees as he stands at the gateway of Boston harbor. The drudgery and sense of imprisonment are forgotten as he feels the responsibility of a calling which makes him of service to all who "go down to the sea in ships and do business in great waters." These owe a debt of gratitude to the light-keeper who faithfully performs his duties, whose name is perhaps almost unknown, but who is nevertheless an important factor in their lives.

Boston Light, the first in America, erected in 1716, as stated in the preamble to the act of its establishment, for "the prevention of the loss of lives and estates," has been of incalculable service, notwithstanding many "lives and estates" have been lost near it, in thick and stormy weather, against which it could not avail. Let us hope that in the future, as in the past, Boston Light may shine on to illumine at night the channel entrance to our harbor, a "protection to lives and estates," until ships shall cease to enter and depart, and "the sea shall be no more."

As one approaches Boston from the sea through Light-House Channel, one of the first objects that meets his eye on the left is the projecting promontory of Point Allerton. It was named in honor of Isaac Allerton, one of the passengers in the *Mayflower*. Tradition informs us that a company of the Plymouth Pilgrims, on one of their voyages northward, put into Boston harbor, landed upon the islands at the entrance and upon the headland opposite, naming the headland Point Allerton, and the islands the "Brewsters," in respect for Allerton's wife's brothers and sisters, the children of Elder Brewster.

The Brewsters were granted to Hull in 1641, and in 1652 to Captain John Leverett, afterward Governor of Massachusetts, in return for money his father put "into the common stocke in the beginning of the plantation, for which he neuer had any consideration." Later the General Court gave Captain Leverett a better domain, and restored the islands to the town of Hull. In 1686 Mr. Coomes of Hull, a mariner, sold the group to John Loring for £4.

The Great Brewster, the innermost island, is a high bluff, containing some twenty-five acres, a considerable part of which has been eaten away by the sea,— further encroachment upon it having been checked by a massive sea-wall, built by the United States government at great expense. The projection, Little Hill, has been so worn away by the sea that it now contains but an acre and a half. The view from the crest is grand, and presents a pleasant prospect of the whole group. A curving ridge of gravelly beach, a mile and a half in length, covered at high tide, stretches away to the Bug Light, and a short bar, bare at low water, leads to Light-House or Little Brewster Island. The Great Brewster was purchased by the city of Boston in 1848 for $4,000, except the part of it adjoining the sea-walls, which is owned by the United States. Some years ago Hon. Benjamin Dean leased the island from the city, and there erected a dwelling in which he has spent a part of his summers. A family lives upon the island the year through.

The Middle Brewster is high, with rocky shores, with some ten acres of soil hidden behind its cliffs. Twenty odd years ago it was owned by three fishermen; but the greater part of it was purchased, leaving to them a corner, by Mr. Augustus Russ, a prominent Boston lawyer. He built upon its highest part a large summer house, in sight of all who sail in and out of the harbor, where he entertained his friends. Since his death a few years ago it has been owned by Mr. Melvin O. Adams, also a well-known lawyer and a warm personal friend of the former owner. Here yachtsmen, painters, photographers and other friends of the proprietors have spent cool and comfortable dog-days, far removed from the din and heat of the city, where the sea and the whole scenery are truly enchanting. On the southerly side of the island is a fairly good landing, made good by the removal of the surface rocks, and leaving a part of the beach sheltered by an outlying reef. The view from the highest point on the island takes in a great sweep of the horizon seaward, the adjacent islands rugged and grand, the inland hills of Saugus and the Middlesex Fells, and the channels leading to and from the city, the highway of nations, dotted with a hundred vessels passing and repassing. The geological structure of the islands is of great interest to scientific persons, as it has little in common with the mainland; its dark granites and porphyries represent a different epoch in the history of the world.

Between the Middle and Outer Brewster there is a narrow and difficult passage called the Flying Place, which boils and foams like a caldron when the sea is high. The brig *Jachin*, bound in from Santa Martha, in 1828, was forced among these rocks in winter, and was wrecked on the Middle Brewster, with the loss of part of her crew.

The Outer Brewster is a frowning pile of rocks, upon which are several acres of fertile soil and a spring of fine, fresh water. Shurtleff says: "This island is one of the most romantic places near Boston, far surpassing Nahant in its wild rocks, chasms, caves and overhanging cliffs. Attempts have been made to use the stone from the Outer Brewster for building purposes; and the walls of an edifice erected on City Square, Charlestown, were of this stone. About the year 1840, General Austin owned this island, and took from it the stone used for macadamizing Warren Bridge. There is a pond upon the island, which in rainy weather is said to attain to very respectable dimensions. On the right-hand side of the western cove there is a singular rock formation, called the pulpit, from which the Reverend East Wind delivers powerful addresses. In the northern cove are the remains of an unfinished canal, cut through the rock by General Austin, with the idea of forming an artificial harbor. It once had a gate at its entrance, and made quite a secure dock. In 1840 there were two or three inhabitants on the island, with six head of cattle and fifty sheep. The house was afterward burned by rowdies from the city. In 1861 a fisherman named Jeffers, with his wife and children, came to the island, and built a dwelling near Rocky Beach. On a stormy night in November, with two men from the Middle Brewster, in trying to get home in a dory, he was wrecked near the mouth of the canal, and he and one of his companions were drowned. The grief-stricken widow soon after left the island, and the house was burned down. This is the most inaccessible of the Brewsters, and many lives have been lost in trying to land upon it. It has no shelter nor anchorage. The lonely island has been called the home of the east wind, a scourge in winter and spring, but delightful in summer.

The Shag Rocks are a group of rocks south of the Brewsters, dangerous to mariners, upon which many lives have been lost. In December, 1861, the ship *Maritana*, laden with a cargo of rice, struck at midnight upon Shag Rocks, and held fast, her stern being in deep water. There was a severe snow-storm, and it was very cold. In the morning the vessel went to pieces, and twenty-five persons of her crew and passengers, women and children among them, were drowned. Thirteen persons clung to the rocks until the next day, when they were rescued by Samuel James of Hull, who put off to them in a dory and placed them on board a Boston pilot-boat. Other vessels and other lives have been lost upon Shag Rocks.

Calf Island, once known as the Northern Brewster, lies north of the Great Brewster, and contains ten acres and some small houses. Among the rugged ledges which front the sea. there are several bits of beach where landings can be made. In former years this was a favorite spot for Sunday tourists from the city; and it is thought by some that the art of pugilism had here a shrine. The island is inhabited by lobstermen and fishermen. A hundred feet or so northward, and connected at low tide, is Little Calf Island, a barren rock surrounded by ledges covered with sea-weed. North of this is Hypocrite Passage, a narrow strait through which boats and small vessels pass.

Green Island is the most northerly of the group. It has a small area of grassy earth upon it, in a bowl of rock, and a long gravelly point extending southward. In 1841 an ancient mariner, fifty years of age, Samuel Choate by name, settled upon this islet, built a rude hut, and there resided alone for twenty or more years, subsisting upon fish, mussels, and what he gathered about its shores. During the famous storm in 1851, which destroyed Minot's Ledge Light-House, this marine hermit was taken off by one of the pilot-boats, his house being submerged by the unusually high tide; and in 1865, when old and feeble, he was removed to a charitable home, where he ended his days in peace.

Northeast of the Brewsters lie the black and frowning ledges known as the Graves, over which the sea surges in heavy weather with terrible effect. Off their eastern end is a large whistling buoy, automatically worked by the waves to warn mariners of their approach to this dangerous point at night or in thick weather. The wild moan it sends over the water can be heard for miles when the air is still. Shurtleff says the Graves were named for the British Admiral Graves, who made himself so disagreeable to Americans during the Revolution and is said to have touched his ship upon these rocks. This cannot be correct, however, for upon a chart published in 1689, a century earlier, they bore their present name. The fishermen and residents upon the adjacent islands believe that the resemblance of the rocks to tombstones, rising in irregular form from the sea, and whitened by bird-lime, gave rise to the name. It is said also that they were named in honor of

Thomas Graves, who came over in command of the *Talbot*, the vice-admiral of Winthrop's fleet. This is more likely to have been the origin of the name. In 1643–44 Thomas Graves commanded the *Trial*, the first large vessel built in Boston, in her voyages to Bilboa and Malaga. The *Trial* was built by Nehemiah Bourne, who, after some years' residence at Boston, returned to England and became rear-admiral in the Parliament's navy.

The islands in and about Boston harbor are not only of historic interest, but they reveal to the gaze of those who sail out and in among them delightful bits of natural scenery adorning the waters of one of the most superb and picturesque ports in America.

Knocking About Cape Cod (1905)

KNOCKING ABOUT CAPE COD

BY THOMAS FLEMING DAY

DRAWINGS BY WARREN SHEPPARD

AH, those Corners! All the world has balked at them. From Matapan to the Pillars the ancients crept round one by one. For fifty years the Portuguese lay on this side of Non, until a favorable or unfavorable slant drove them past the forbidding promontory, and into a career of discovery and life of glory as made them a real nation for a space. Again they grew cold at the Hope and returned, leaving it for a later and pluckier man to win immortality by putting Agulhas astern.

Don't you recall how when a child you were afraid to pass the corner; how readily you toddled up to it, constantly looking back to see if home was still there? The curiosity of the beyond balanced by your fear of losing sight of your point of departure kept you from rounding. Then one day in a sudden burst of courage you passed the edge and the world on the other side was yours. You found it almost the same thing, very much like the world you had left on the other side, and beyond about an equal distance another corner. After rounding two, corners cease to inspire fear, and you developed the corner mania. Your only aim for days being to put yourself on the other side of as many as possible.

Maritime people in their early days had just the same experience; they at first dreaded the corner, but once around found that there was nothing very different or very fearful on the other side, and they from then on thirsted for capes to double. Besides they were points in the voyage. Master milestones, before and beyond which something was different. A place of change; fair wind one side, foul the other. Hardship and suffering, round she went, ease and plenty. Generally half the voyage was over with this or that cape under the lee. "Now, then, boys, square the yards!" or "lee main braces, sharpen her up!" It either meant more work or less work, better or worse weather, perhaps death or life.

Thus at sea, capes have come to be the subject of constant reference. Half the yarns begin with when we rounded Cape Hard or doubled Cape Soft. You may be an old, brave and skillful seaman, but you are not of the aristocracy unless you have weathered either the Hope or Horn. In the presence of these gale-defying veterans you sit with all humility, feeling as felt a home-detained knight in mediæval days when his more fortunate brothers who had followed Richard and Louis to Palestine made the castle rafters noisy with their yarns of Acre and Jerusalem. But all this is running off the course, so let's take a new departure and hold up for Cape Cod.

That's the trouble with me, when I get to spinning a yarn you can't hold me down to the subject proper. I yaw about like a head-loaded vessel in a breeze of wind, but have patience and you'll get where you belong before we let go the hook and furl all. When I think, I think like a starfish, my brain pushing out ideas in five different directions at once, consequently, instead of following a subject in a straight line, I am continually making a circular traverse, fetching up after a couple of boards within a ship's length of where I started from. Sometimes I get so fouled in my own gear, that to save going aloft and rendering through the block swallow I have to cut away everything. But back to the Cape.

Cape Cod, renowned in history, song and story is about as poor a piece of real estate as ever man took title to. When I speak of the Cape I don't mean all that chunk, but the Cape real; the part from Barnstable east, that lies in the sea, not the miles of mosquito-haunted brush that stretch from Woods Hole to Plymouth. A lot of those hamlets claim to be on Cape Cod, but they are not; a real Cape man resents their assumption of this right. Those born to the manor proper look upon themselves as aristocrats, and all others are as dirt compared with clean, white sand. The genuine Cape Cod man proclaims his origin with all the pride of a Spartan or Devonian. He believes the Yankee to be the top crust of the human pie, and himself the gloss on the top crust.

Now, I'm not going to bother you with precise dimensions, and will trust to my memory for miles, so if it don't exactly agree with the chart you will understand that I have forgotten some things. The length of this sand bank along its ocean face from what is called Monomoy to Race Point is forty miles. It varies in breadth from a quarter to five miles, the bay known as Cape Cod Bay being back of it, and in height from nothing to about one hundred and fifty feet, the highest part being up at the north end, where what is called the Highland Light stands. It is chiefly made of sand. What isn't sand has been brought there by man and dumped, the ice delivered the sand ages ago.

Like all the banks and islands hereabouts, Cape Cod is a relic of the ice age, a portion of the terminal moraine. The weight of drift lying on a bed of clay tilted it up, and made the Highlands just as the same force did the Gay Head Cliffs on the Vineyard. I don't know which theory you are lashed to, but despite my bringing up as a geologist I kind of have one sound foot over in the astronomers' camp. The geologists sadly stretch things to masthead some of their theories, but it is a little too much of a tautness, this having to sink the Isthmus and pour the Gulf Stream into the Pacific in order to have skating around Monomoy in July. Nor do I believe that what we see is the effect of one icy visitation. There have been repeated ages of ice. Nor do I believe that the last occurred so lately as twenty-five thousand years back.

The cause of the ice age and its heel marks are one of my favorite subjects, a subject upon which I pour forth at every opportunity. One voyage we were off Gay Head, and in my usual happy manner I began to descant on the causes that produced that headland, at the same time I was valeting a pot of cocoa on an oil-stove between my legs, I standing in the companion. In a moment of extra profundity I raised one foot, and on its reobeying the force of gravity placed it a mite too far aft, and it landed right in the boil. My audience consisting of two in the cockpit were suddenly frightened by the lecture breaking off into a howl, and the lecturer wildly diving for the side to get his foot in the water. This was the worst thing I could do, but the emergency directions did not just then happen to occur to me. Ever since the word glacier is associated in my mind with hot cocoa, and I invariably hop on one leg when the ice age is mentioned. But to get back to the Cape.

As I said, the Cape is sand, and like everything of a desert nature is nomadic. Like the Arab, it is always silently stealing away, so that the appearance of the peninsula constantly changes. The prevailing winds in the winter being from the north, the sand is blown south; in summer it is blown t'other way, but the winter winds being stronger, the land is gradually working south. Monomoy at the lower end used to be an island, its extremity being called Cape Malabar, a name not used now. Why, I cannot say. This island of Monomoy is rapidly growing toward Nantucket, it having advanced some five miles in the last fifty years. One of the Rubes told me that his father used to fish where the light is now. Of course you can always strain Rube talk and pick out about fifty per cent. sediment, but the old charts show that the point is working south fast.

Just back of Monomoy there used to be in the early days a fine anchorage known as the Powder Hole and Jackknife Harbor. The Hole is there yet, but the beaches that sheltered it have completely gone, and the Harbor is sanded full. This used to be a favorite anchorage for coasters in days gone by, when the average coasting vessel was comparatively a small craft. I've laid in the Powder Hole many nights. It's all right with a northeast wind, bearable in a sou'wester, but not for me in a nor'wester. There is a good channel leading up to it from the end, between the island and the Handkerchief. The fishermen have their cats moored in the Hole, and when one of them is absent you can pick up a mooring.

I asked one of the Rubes how the harbor came to sand-up, and this is what I got.

First, you must know there are three grades of coasters—Down-Easters, Others and Jerseymen. The Down-East skipper looks down on all others, and has nothing but contempt and bad words for the Jerseyman. He treats him with just about as much courtesy as a British admiral could show to the commander of the Haytian Navy. Just as the monks in their stories, when they wanted a character half-knave and half-fool to deride, took the devil, so the Down-East coaster or fisherman always takes a Jerseyman. This comparison is not at all complimentary to the devil, but it is just now the only one I can think of! Well, for the Rube's yarn:

"One time there was a Jersey coasting skipper living down in Egg Harbor, who had his vessel laid up for a long time. He was anxious to get a cargo, so when a fellow came along and told him what to get and where to take it, he bit like a bluefish. This fellow, who hailed from Cape Cod, told the Jerseyman that they had run out of sand down his way, and that if he would load his schooner with some of the Jersey beach, and sail down to the Cape, he would find a ready market for it. The Jerseyman did. The first harbor he made was Jackknife, and when he found how he had been tricked he dumped the whole load right there and spoiled the place."

Just off the point there is a deep hole close to the beach, made by the tide whirling round. It was here that the lifeboat capsized and drowned her crew a few winters ago. There is a very nasty sea running there with a heavy easterly. A barge had taken the bottom on the Stone Horse, a big shoal south and east of the point, and a wrecking crew was on board. A storm came up and the life-savers took part of the men off and started back, the boat upset and drowned all but one, if I remember rightly. The barge weathered the gale, and those who remained on board were saved.

There have been a lot of wrecks on and about this point. Here the channel crooks out to sea past Shovelful and between the Stone Horse and Pollocks. It is very narrow, and vessels working through frequently take bottom. One evening about sunset I anchored on Bearces Shoal, just opposite the light, to wait for the west tide, being bound home across the Shoals. About midnight it shifted and we stood down past Shovelful to get southing enough to cross the Handkerchief. A big steamer came up and passed close to us, and pretty soon he ported his helm and ran smack upon one of the detached lumps. I saw in the paper the next day that he got off at high water, after twenty-four hours of pulling and hauling. It was a fine, clear night, and what her pilot was up to I cannot imagine. But that is what brings tears to the eyes of the underwriters. Another time a barkentine struck the remains of a wreck and tore her bottom out. She was grounded off Chatham, and went to pieces in the winter storms.

These shoals are the remains of islands that have had their tops washed off. In every one of these islands you will find ponds, so in these shoals you will find a deep hole surrounded by a shallow ring; this hole is the bottom of the old pond. There is such a hole in the middle of the Stone Horse, one in the Handkerchief, and the Horse Shoe. It is these shoals that are responsible for the rips, a species of wave that is about the worst thing a small boat has to tackle. Rip waves are not waves of progression, they stay right in one place and jump up and down, just like those in a river at the foot of a rapids. When the regular sea comes in and makes with them, then there is Hades. I've been through most every rip on the shoals, and have rather grown to like the sensation; but you want a good boat under you, a very good boat.

I remember once getting a dose of rip that nearly finished my career, and if you're not getting tired, why I'll tell you how it happened. You must know that while the big craft always go out 'round Pollocks, there is a channel for small boats close along the beach, between Bearces Shoal and the island. In it there is a rip, it shallowing to about eight or ten feet in one place. I was coming south with a strong northeast wind, that was growing all the time, and a tidy bit of a sea running. Off Chatham I very foolishly decided that rather than go out round the light-vessel I would risk going through this channel, so as to get into shelter the quicker. I figured that the tide would be about slack, and the rip robbed of its nastiness. When I got into the pocket between the shoal and the shore, and it was too late to haul my wind, I saw a sight that made my hair raise. The rip was laboring overtime, and making a grand display of water works. The boat was one

Small fishing boats—Race Point.

of those regular Cape cats, with a big open cockpit.

We closed the cabin up tight, loaded an anchor and some other weight on the cockpit hatch, lashed ourselves fast, breathed a prayer and went into the first wave. She covered the two first all right, but the third and last was a regular six-foot fence. The first two having killed her way, she balked this one, and it broke right over as she stood still in the trough between them. What a smash; right up the mast for six hoops. When we drifted clear the pit was nearly full up, and the boat almost flush with the water astern. Another fifty gallons and we would have sunk. No more short cuts for me, with a northeast wind blowing, round that shoal.

But with a properly constructed and full-decked boat, having a small and well-scuppered cockpit, there is not much danger in running rips in any reasonable weather. The greatest danger is that of taking bottom and being rolled over. But in partly open boats a man has no business in the rips; that is, if he can keep out of them. Sometimes he can't, but if we keep on monkeying round these rips we will never finish the story, so let's up stick and head north abouts.

From Monomoy the shore runs a little east or north until you get to Wellfleet, then it trends away again. There is a shallow sand off Chatham, but above it you can hug the beach all along, there being plenty of water close in. With a sou'wester such as you generally get in summer, it is fine sailing; smooth water and a strong, puffy breeze. There's something peculiar about the behavior of these sou'westers hereabouts, so if you don't mind a slight deviation from the course, just listen. All winds, as you probably know, blowing offshore, when they reach the edge and tumble off, either veer or back, as the case may be. This is because wind, like every other thing in nature, except some men, takes the path of the least resistance. For example, if the wind is sou'west and it blows off a coast running north and south, it will come off more westerly. This is because it is in a hurry to get to sea, and takes the shortest course. The sou'westers do this off Cape Cod. But a wind blow ing across an island or piece of land having water on back and front, is during sun-up always stronger on the lee than on the weather side. The friction of the land and its obstructing objects retards the lower layers of current, causing it to roll up and accumulate strength, thus forming waves or puffs, as we generally call them. For instance, you will have on the south or ocean side of the Vineyard a nice whole-sail breeze, but on rounding Pogue and crossing the north or Sound side, this same breeze will be a two-reefer, and nasty at that.

When the sou'west wind hits the rear side of the Cape, it is a steady, ladylike breeze, but after spending a few minutes waltzing over the hot sands, it gets a fit of crazy whirls and disports like a dancing dervish. In hot, black puffs it sweeps over the sandhills and drops with a rush down on the sea. This pouring over the edge of the bluff causes a vacuum above, and to fill this hole a counter-current is formed, which flows back again from the north and east. In this current can be seen small bunches of scud seemingly serenely streaming like Byron's banner of freedom against the wind. In such a way is the wind freed over and over again, and it blows, blows hard, under these bluffs. But, man, it makes grand sailing.

I think I told you that the land gets higher as you go north, steep sand bluffs topped with a sparse herbage. The beach is fairly broad and hard, and generally steep, too, so that there is no danger in lining it close. Here and there are breaks in the bluff. These the natives call hollows, and through them you get back into the interior. They also shelter the life-saving stations and houses of the Rubes. Why people ever chose to live in such places beats me. If it were the only spot; but with millions of acres of good land farther west, why did or do they stop there? I suppose the ease of getting a living caught and kept the first settlers. Fish were plentiful, and they were unmolested by Indians, who were joyfully scalping their sour-faced, canting brethren over on the mainland.

After the Cape gets by the Highlands it trends away northwesterly and begins to shrink down into a series of broken mounds, until it flattens out completely, turns south, then east and rolls its end up in a fishhook barbed with a sandspit. Off the most northerly part, are what are called the

Peaked Hill bars. This place has the reputation of being a ship's graveyard. They are really not bars, being simply shoal pieces of bottom made up of soft sand.

You will always find along a coast certain spots that are particularly fatal to vessels, where they perish not singly but in bunches. Such a place is the south side of the Elizabeth Islands, which is known to coasters as the graveyard. If you go into the reason for the fatalness of these spots you will always find there is a natural cause intensified in its action by human carelessness. The cause that has piled up wrecks on the Elizabeth Isles is an oblique tidal current setting across the axis of the channel and against these shores both on the flood and ebb. This with man's neglect to properly ascertain his position before shaping a course either up or down the Sound has knocked the bottom out of many a good craft. But the season of wrecking on Peaked Hill bars is different. One night when working out past the bars I reasoned it out. The course from Thatchers Island, the point of departure on the north side of the bay, to Race Point is S. by E., and the course to Highland is S. S. E., leaving between the two only a point difference. In this difference lie the bars. Now the majority of coasting vessels do not have entirely reliable compasses; in fact many of them are very poor instruments, and a deviation of a point or two is not exceptional. I have known coasters after running a course of one hundred and sixty miles to be twenty miles out in their landfall. So it is not impossible that on a run of forty miles they would be out three miles. In fact with compasses corrected and steering most carefully I have often done worse than that in a fifty-mile passage. Running off in a strong wind and high-following seas it is almost impossible to steer a fine course with a sailing vessel.

Moonlight off Cape Cod.

This is the cause of the wrecking on these bars. A vessel running in the winter time with a heavy north or northeasterly wind takes her departure from off Cape Ann. The weather getting worse and thick, the skipper decides to haul in behind Race Point for shelter. He will generally make up his mind to do this halfway across, consequently would steer southwest or southwest-by-south, thus bringing the wind over the stern. Now, a vessel running with the wind on the end of the mainboom will always weather out, and yet it is natural for a navigator to suppose she will sag off to leeward of her course. Afraid of passing Race Point in the thickness the skipper cuts it too fine and goes plunk on the bars. These bars have done some cruel work in their time, that is, since man took to knocking about the cape. But the horrible part in the old days was played by the shelterless shore after the poor devils got out of the sea's maw and reached the beach. Here they circled around blinded by drifting snow and driving sand until cold killed them. About 1802 a ship called the *Brutus* struck on the bars, and the crew all reached shore but froze to death; twenty-seven hardy men perished miserably among those sand hills. Think of it, their elation when, after a fierce struggle with the breaking seas, they felt the land beneath their feet. Death behind roaring and beating the bars, cheated of his prey, so they thought. Better had they drunk of the sea and gone down out there with their battered vessel.

This catastrophe aroused the merchants and seamen of all New England to do something to prevent another such. A society was formed to place shelter huts along the coast. This was the foundation of the present Humane Society, whose red buildings you will see from one end of Massachusetts to the other. The Life Saving Service has made their work largely unnecessary, but years back they saved hundreds of lives through this means. There were scattered huts some years before the wreck of the *Brutus,* but there was no organized effort to keep them up, and vandals and accidents frequently destroyed them.

The man-of-war *Somerset* was wrecked on this piece of the Cape, and what is left of her bones lie covered up in the sands. She was one of the vessels that covered the crossing of troops the morning of Bunker Hill battle. She was cast ashore while watching the French fleet, sheltered in Boston Harbor. Her guns were taken out by the Yankees and used to defend different ports. Sir George Collier, in one of his raids, recaptured several of them. There is a man whose name is almost forgotten, and yet he was the only British admiral except Rodney who at that time was worth a tarred gasket. He was a man of the Nelson and Cochrane stripe, and had he been properly backed up would have swept the French off the seas. He left Sandy Hook with a fleet and in forty-eight hours had Portsmouth, Va., in flames. It took that old fool, Graves, six weeks to make the same passage, and after he got there he let DeGrasse slip through his fingers. Graves, like Howe, was one of the old maneuvering school, who would jockey away for a month trying to get the weather gauge, and who had an idea that ships ought to be marshaled and moved like a body of infantry. The French admiral very kindly assisted them in keeping up this farce of fighting, his object being to escape a decisive action and cover the enemy's movements on shore. If Byng deserved shooting for his mistake off Majorca, Graves deserves to be drawn and quartered for the foolishness of that day on the Middle Grounds. There is no question that the pre-revolutionary flag-officers of the French Navy were superior in education and skill to their British opponents, and their ultimate defeat was the result of operating under a defective system and to the physical inferiority of the French seaman. Under the Republic and Empire, the Gallic admirals and captains with an exception or two were a poor lot, bad seamen and worse gunners. But what's all this got to do with the lay of our yarn! Mind your helm, my lad, and back to the course.

Round Race Point the tide ebbs and flows like the devil, and it takes a good breeze to put a boat on the other side, if the current be running foul. Once around, you can find good anchorage from northerly or easterly winds. Further along, round the Hook is Provincetown; this has an excellent harbor, and that's about all it has. Of the inside shore of the Cape I know nothing; it's a stretch of sand flats and shallows; a place to be shunned and

The old-timer.

feared by all humans without webs between their toes. A few bunches of Rubes inhabit it, hanging on here and there like tufts of beach grass, getting a small living out of the sea, and raising crops of future coasting skippers and tug-boat pilots. Summer people are beginning to frequent the Cape more generally, and the Rubes are rapidly losing their good, old-fashioned ways of doing business, and are becoming first-class resort pirates. I can remember when they used to hate to take pay for a few lobsters or scup, but things are not as they used to be. But take 'em all through, males and females, they are not a bad lot, and sometimes are very accommodating, so the boys tell me; anyhow the girls are the best looking in New England, which—just lean over this way and I'll whisper in your ear.

The ancient name of Cape Cod peninsula was Namset, but evidently after the settlers began to frequent it to get their breakfast food, they called it after the chief delicacy its waters afforded. It must have been a great cod ground in those days, but the fishing has gone to the dogs, being ruined by the use of nets. It is one of the biggest errors that our state and national government has made, that of allowing these fish destroyers to be set in the sea or anywhere else. Some day we shall pass drastic laws to prevent net fishing; it will be when the fish are all gone. We are rapidly earning the curses of posterity by our hoggishness. What right have we to destroy this food supply, depriving future generations forever of fish-balls and broiled lobsters. But to return to names. The Highland Light was originally known as Clay Ponds. The light was erected in 1797, one of the first lights put up by the United States Government; the Race Light was built I think in 1815, and the other beacons lower down about 1830. Now, the whole south end is beset with lights, too many of them in fact, so that they confuse by their superfluity. It has made navigation hereabouts a question not of knowledge and skill, but simply a matter of eyesight. Any man who can see a light and steer for it or by it, can pass safely anywhere around the Cape. The good old days of leading and ranges are gone forever, and the pilot is a man almost without an occupation.

The shoals used to be famous for their pilots. These chaps harbored in Holmes Hole and could take a vessel across the shallows with their eyes shut. It took some daring in those days, with few buoys or marks to guide, but to-day, unless the vessel draws big water it is child's play. I've headed over the shoals many times in a thick fog and surprised myself by the good navigation it is possible to perform. It's all right leading in the summer time, but in winter excuse me.

But talking about names, many of these have been sadly altered in the last hundred years. Whether it was that the old navigators spelled them wrong and we have corrected them or the other way, I can't say, but somehow they are badly twisted. I have a lot of old books on coast navigation in which the names are spelled very differently from the way we spell them to-day. But years agone every man was his own dictionary, much the better, and spelled as he darn pleased. What right has any man to sit up and say that we must spell a name his way? Does he know how it was originally pronounced by the Indian or settler who christened the spot? I have often smiled at the Rubes calling Nobska Point, *Nobskee*, but they are right. It was originally spelled Nobskee, and that is the proper pronunciation.

About the upper end of Cape Cod, and in the Bay, was a hanging-out place for the frigates and privateers blocking the port of Boston during the 1812 war. The frigates maintained a constant patrol from Cape Cod to Cape Ann, the inner squadron keeping within about ten miles of Boston Light, while the rest of the vessels lay farther outside. In bad weather, when they were driven off, the Yankee ships outward bound made a run for it, and generally got clear. It was off here the celebrated fight between the *Shannon* and the *Chesapeake* took place. Many of the villages and towns hereabouts made secret treaties with the blockading fleet, allowing the vessels' crews to provision and water on condition they left their boats alone and allowed them to fish. The island of Nantucket made such a treaty, but the Government heard of it and jumped on the village fathers. There seems to have been considerable traffic carried on between the enemy's ships and the shore, the Rubes of those days not being averse to earning a dollar by aiding and abetting their country's foe. But the biggest rascals of all were the privateers.

Of all business that man ever legitimatized, barring slave-trading, privateering was certainly the worst. To license men to murder for money, to give the privilege of plundering to any rascal who applied for it, to make a business out of war, was a disgraceful practice. Nothing can palliate or excuse such conduct on the part of a civilized government. Yet scarcely a hundred years ago all civilized governments did it. While our privateers were not so bad as those of Spain, France and other Latin powers, refraining from cutting the passengers' throats and wronging women, they were none the less a pack of robbers. History has in measure glorified them, but history in order to do so has altered much and hidden more. Let any man read the logs of these vessels; let him peruse the chronicles of the time, and he will turn away amazed that such atrocity should have been not only permitted, but encouraged by civilized nations. There seems to have been both in Britain and the United

States among the more decent people a strong feeling against privateering; it was not considered to be an altogether respectable business, and many men engaged in backing it up endeavored to conceal their connection. Privateers were particularly disliked by men-o'-warsmen, for reasons that are obvious, but at the same time the naval officers were largely responsible for their existence, as they gained more by permitting them to remain at work than they did by capturing.

There was neither glory or money to be gained by taking a privateer. If she happened to be a notorious customer, the captor might receive the thanks of the Station admiral and perhaps a piece of plate from Lloyds, but if only an ordinary vessel, he got nothing but a mere mention in the *Gazette*. But if instead of taking the privateer he recaptured one of her captures, all hands received a good whack of prize money. Enormous fortunes were made in this way. One frigate stationed off Sandy Hook made captures and recaptures that brought to her crew over $4,000,000. That's nothing nowadays, when one ship is worth as much, but it took a deal of catching in those times. This was why naval men frequently could not see a privateer until the privateer had made a capture, when they promptly pounced down on her prey. It was the same performance as you have seen played between the pirate-gull, the loon and the unfortunate mackerel.

Off Highland Light.

Along toward the close of the 1812 war, when the American merchant vessel had been pretty nearly swept off the sea, and there was nothing much for the British privateers to pick up but their own captured ships, they made a practice of hanging about outside our harbors. Most of these privateers hailed from the provinces, some from Bermuda, and the West Indies. Among them was a very fast schooner out of St. Johns, New Brunswick, which was currently reported to be the fastest vessel of her class afloat. She cruised constantly off the New England coast. During the years 1813 and 1814 she sent in many prizes for condemnation to either Halifax or Bermuda, where the prize courts sat. Nearly all these vessels were recaptures, British merchantmen that had been taken by American privateers. Her success was so phenomenal that it at last attracted the attention of the Admiral of the Station. Anyhow, the story leaked out, either somebody got drunk and gave away the snap, or who knows—but it led to an investigation. She was boarded and her log thoroughly overhauled; and this was what had been going on. Some American privateers, two or three, if I remember rightly, finding it difficult to get their prizes in past the block frigates, put up a job with the St. Johns man. They sent their prizes to an agreed locality, where the St. Johns man promptly recaptured them, sent them in, recovered salvage, and whacked up the proceeds with the original captor. The admiral stopped the game, but what became of the foxy skipper the chronicle does not mention.

To a great many yachtsmen Cape Cod is a fearsome place. It is to them what Cape Horn is to the merchant seaman. Yet most of this fear is groundless. Like all capes, it has its gales, but they are in summer few and far between. Nine days out of ten it is passable. Even in a small boat, you can always get around it in comfort and safety by picking your weather. A man who cannot tell what the weather is going to be at least forty-eight hours ahead, has no business to be in charge of a vessel of any sort.

I have a genuine affection for Cape Cod. I delight to coast its shore and to hover about its beaches. There is something expansive in its atmosphere, so that every day spent rollicking there is like two days lived in the space of one. It never inspires the least fear; some coasts do—one of those dark, dismal, rocky, repulsive shores, that you dread to approach. But Cape Cod, white and pure, sun-lighted and breeze-swept, draws you to it as the face of a good and beautiful woman draws you. It may be very different in winter, but I never saw it then. Every memory I have of the peninsula is a warm and bright one. But my most happy time is when I run it by night, making the Highlands just at midnight and coasting south in the moonlight, with a fine southwester, a smooth sea, and a long, slow swell. That is sailing.

Fifty miles away lies a city and a mass of men, wretched beings, contented that night brings sleep and forgetfulness; but for me these hours bring unexplainable delight. Go below, boys, turn in; leave me the deck and the watch to keep. I want, I crave no company but the good beach to windward, the sea and the heavens. My scepter the tiller, my crown an old sou'wester, and my robe an oilskin to keep out the cold, now I reign monarch of a fairy realm, with a council of three of man's best friends, a contented mind, a full stomach and unmortgaged conscience. Add to this a pipe, and you have described the happiest kingdom in existence.

Look, sou'west; just clear of the bluffs drops the half-spent moon; east-southeast well risen is Jupiter, and Venus, red as a rose, lifts close to the horizon. Soon will the magnificent Orion, with all its glories, follow her. What a marvelous collection of stars that is: Procyon, Betelguese, Rigel, Bellatrix and the splendid twin orb Sirius. Farther to the west is my old favorite Aldebaran, flashing, flickering, and showing color like a driftwood fire.

Away go my thoughts, leaping over space. What a wonderful, amazingly wonderful thing is thought, even outstripping light, as light outstripped sound. In less than a second I can send my thoughts to the farther visible orb. They leap from star to star across unmeasurable distances. Puny sea; puny world! I float on the great water of which you boast, a stretch over which man voyages for months, aye and for days, never meeting craft or fellow being; a great flood that belts you, that washes and absolves all your lands. What is it, compared with that which to-night engages my thoughts? A drop, a miserable drop on a grain of dust. Yon star, yon fiery speck, blinking and reddening in the lower layers of the atmosphere, could eat you up a thousand times, and scarce spot its glowing surface.

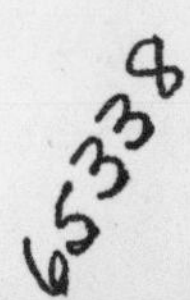

The Fishermen of Gloucester (1903)

Gloucester Harbor.

THE FISHERMEN OF GLOUCESTER

By VICTOR J. SLOCUM

PHOTOGRAPHS BY ARTHUR HEWITT

THERE are two Gloucesters. One is the Gloucester that has forgotten the rigor of its traditions, when hardy men from England made fishing voyages to the coast of Maine, and cruised as far South as Cape Ann, in 1623. She is ashamed of the smell of gurry, grown into a false estheticism, and generated into cheap politics like many another city.

The other Gloucester is an honor to manhood, and crowned by a galaxy of beautiful vessels, America's famous fishing fleet. There

Figuring Out the Profits of the Catch.

Old Hulks, High on the Shore.

"The big fellows come swinging out of the hold by the tail."

From the Sea to a Barrel.

are three or four hundred sail in this fleet. The most modern of them are modeled somewhat after the type of the Burgess idea when yachts were yet healthy. In fact, Edward Burgess designed several "fishermen" besides defending the *America* Cup three times, and it was quickly discovered that the innovation brought in fares ahead of the old-timers. The vessels are superior to yachts as real ships, and in point of beauty are above comparison.

Many yachtsmen with real sailor blood in their veins have felt proud to beat one of these flyers under a cloud of canvas, and one was even known to build a vessel just to hold his own in general sailing qualities when he met a certain fisherman off shore.

See a fleet in the open harbor ready for sea! The topmasts that float so much coquettish muslin to the amorous summer air are stowed ashore, and their absence gives the vessel a long, rakish look. These vessels are "bankers" and sail for cod and halibut, to be found where icebergs tell them to go no farther north, and where the ice floe may catch them on the coasts of Labrador or Newfoundland. The sharp, high bow is not yet covered by ice, as it soon will be while the ship is riding at anchor on the fishing grounds, to her immense manilla cable, now coiled down abaft the windlass. They wait for their crew. Some dark forms are seen crossing to her in a boat, and, although the wind is strong enough to blow down fish-houses, they peak up the white sail without thinking of a reef, set the head sails, and stand out with lee rails awash, out by Norman's Woe and around the whistling buoy that makes its faithful moan off Eastern Point. The seagulls scream a warning that speak of frozen rigging, and of the stark corpse adrift in the dory. But what care they for warnings! There are mouths ashore to feed, and bread must be gotten out of the sea.

* * * * *

All the fishing is done in dories, flat bottomed boats, peculiar to Gloucester, about eighteen to twenty feet long. A good-sized schooner carries ten or twelve dories, lashed down to the deck in two nests, piled upon each other like saucers.

When the fishing grounds are reached and the weather is suitable, the crew are told off in pairs to man the dories and lay out the trawls. This is the French way of fishing, and before its general introduction each man would go on his own hook and fish over the side, account being taken of the exact number of fish caught by each. Now, the fare is lumped together and shares are taken from the general stock. A trawl is a long warp fastened at either end to the ground and to it, at short intervals, are attached cod lines about a fathom long, each ganged with a hook. The dory starts out at one end of the warp that runs over a roller at the bow, and the men simply haul ahead, pick off the fish, and rebait the hooks as they go along. When the end of the line is reached they haul back again, and repeat the process until the dory is full to the gunwales. No danger arises from filling a dory this way, for the mucus that envelopes

Long Lines of Fish Drying.

On Shore—Between Cruises.

Sometimes a voyage of despair brings them to some rocky coast, and their little world is startled by a tale of exposure; again they may be picked up when it is too late and the sea tragedy is complete; but most often they are never heard of again. A greater percentage of men are lost in this calling than in any other, not excepting the profession of arms; so there is truth in the saying that the history of Gloucester fisheries is written in tears.

Next to fog fishermen fear the liner. It is bad enough when the weather is clear, but when it is so thick that the end of the bowsprit is out of sight, the lone lookout keeps an anxious ear open for the throbbing machinery, and the rush of water hurled from a thirty thousand horsepower machine on its flying mission. According to international law, ships must slow down to moderate speed in a fog, but fishermen know too well how this is evaded, for they can tell a twenty-knot from a ten-knot gait in spite of all the log-book red tape. But they sleep soundly in their bunks and, if the steel cutwater sends them to an icy death, no one is the wiser except the officer on the bridge and a few others who know how to keep their mouths shut. The sea *is* cruel when one has n't the upper hand.

The men who sail out of Gloucester are sure that a third of their lost vessels go in this way.

In early times, on the shores of Europe from France to Italy, people went down on the quay to chant a vesper for their toilers on the sea. This custom was, no doubt, brought over by the early fishermen who first found cod near the shores of Newfoundland; so now we find the tradition exemplified in Gloucester when once a year little orphans scatter flowers on the sea for the unburied dead.

When men leave their port to go to sea there is no demonstration on the part of mothers, sisters, or wives. That is all done in the little home and is not to be seen. These

the fish causes them to form a jelly-like mass, and the sea rolls right over them without interfering with the stability of the load, so the fishermen sit in the center of their catch and load until they are practically in a decked boat. Perhaps this is the reason why they don't eat much fish at the table. They go a whole cruise without so much as seeing one on the bill of fare; and yet people ashore who cannot get fresh fish even for money, will envy them.

Men working together are called dory mates, and peril breeds the attachment common to all men who face danger together, whether on land or sea. In the little boats they see some of the greatest perils of their calling. They are seldom capsized; but a sudden fog bank sometimes shuts off the schooner. Then there is a long, hopeless drift about, until by mere chance some other vessel picks them up and brings them into port. Sometimes men have been on the wharf to see their own schooner come in with flag at half mast for them. Thus they would literally attend their own funeral.

Straight to Market.

homes are never squalid, though their tastes may be a little crude. In many homes you will see an upright piano of the very latest garnish, but never a token of the dangerous calling, no models of fishing craft or festoons of netting, and seldom any painting of them on the walls, but rather a characterless chromo of no particular subject.

It is strange to see so little mark of character amid the surroundings of men who have

In From a Cruise.

"While the vessel is being fitted up again."

so much of the real thing. In the crooked streets along the water front, where the real Gloucester breathes, one meets these men, dressed in oilskins and sou'wester', hands encased in huge white mittens (blue ones bring bad luck), wet with gurry. They may have just landed the fare, have the sea noises yet in their heads, and still a contempt for the solid soil, that the strong, clumsy gait denotes. It does one good to meet men so perfectly in touch with the elemental forces. They throw around them such an atmosphere of delightful freshness. Their eyes look straight to yours with the beautiful honesty they learn from being prime producers. They need none of the garnish of culture to make them men, and if the page of knowledge that is so rich with the spoils of time is seldom unrolled before them, the secrets of real life and nature are focused on them stronger than they know, and they reap an unconscious benefit from her teachings. It is one of the glories of the sea that she has always a page that is still unread. The advancements of science and the encroachments of heroism make this page more of a mystery instead of less, for it is a secret that grows the more by the very forces we use to unlock it. Men brought close to it by the prosaic demands of mere bread and butter are strangely loth to leave it, and many never can. They often swear by all the prongs of the Trident of Neptune, and by his Nereids to boot, never to face it again; but a few weeks of shore monotony tells them that their resolution was a mere sophistry.

Fishermen often perform feats of heroism

Laying Up Alongside the Wharf.

and self-sacrifice without just compensation. One was known some time ago to render aid to a steamer on the Newfoundland coast and gave up a five-thousand dollar fare to do it. Another case called to my attention was the rescue of the crew of a British steamer. The skipper told me that neither he nor his men got the customary allowance of gold awarded for these occasions; "But they sent me a letter!" "It was writ on a kind of paper that was thick as the fore staysail, big enough to make trouser seats for all hands, and there was a lion and a unicorn on it. Yes, sir, I kept it five years and then burnt it up, for it was a regular nuisance looking at it."

"Yes, sir; I was out in the gale of '62, off Prince Edward Island, and there was a slew of vessels lost then. It was my first year master. I was twenty-two then. Fifteen sail lost at one clip. One hundred and twenty lives lost, and there were seventy widows and a hundred and forty orphans made in just that one blow. No, we don't mind a flag at half mast any more than that it is part of the business; that one you see over there had the captain and one man washed overboard. Never saw them after she shipped a heavy sea. These craft they have nowadays never lift the lee rail, and they just smother her down into it when they have a fare, and don't think much of reefing either.

"I'll tell you how many of them are lost," said he, drawing a diagram on a sail that was hauled over some fish casks. "They often sink each other when they drag their anchors. You see, on the grounds one vessel will anchor about here, and another about there, and another one there, and so on, about three cable lengths apart. Now, when it comes on to blow and kicks up a rip we all try to hold on as long as we can, and if this one drags why she will drift into that one, and they will both sink, and sometimes that happens to almost a whole fleet. The proper thing to do is to cut and set a jib and risk it; that is your only chance.

"I had a close shave once," he continued. "We started to drag on another fellow, and I got the ax out to cut, and there I was between those men and their lives, and the owner's interest, for a cable costs about four hundred dollars, and I hated to cut it. The sea was standing right on end, and we came closer and closer, and I got the fore staystail on and hauled it over, and, by gracious, we dragged by without even touching him, and I saved the crew, the vessel, and the cable."

The most interesting vessels of the fleet in the winter are the halibut trawlers. As some halibut weigh three hundred pounds, it is regarded as quite a feat to get one of them over the side of the little dory without capsizing her. They are killed by a few good whacks with a club before being hauled aboard, and I heard one amusing account of a halibut that "came to" after being hauled. The man got right down and held it flat in his arms in the bottom of the dory to prevent its leaping overboard, The arrival of one of these vessels at the wharf is the signal for a gathering of the people who know about fish, and who like to see the big fellows come swinging out of the hold by the tail.

The crew unload their own fare in about two hours—it took a month to get it—and then rig up in shore togs to look at the town and recreate for a week or ten days, while the vessel is being fitted up again. All of this work is done by the owners, who engage professional riggers and mechanics to put the craft in perfect shape and to bend the sails, so that all the crew have to do is to set sail, bait the trawls, and be off for the fishing banks. In the summer these halibuters make voyages to Iceland, where they find larger fish than on the home grounds.

Gloucester has many nationalities, but they are all one type, honest, strong, manly fellows; untutored in the wiles of general civilization. Most of them are from the British Provinces. A large percentage are Scandinavians; there are many Portuguese from the Western Islands, Italians and Greeks; there is even a Japanese on record from this port.

As a general thing fishermen are quite prosperous, and most of them have snug bank accounts as soon as they get over the little debt at the outfit store that started them out with proper clothes, oilskins, and sea boots.

One of the Fleet.

The Isle of Peace
(1881)

MIDSUMMER HOLIDAY NUMBER

OF

SCRIBNER'S MONTHLY.

AUGUST, 1881.

THE ISLE OF PEACE.

THE Isle of Peace lies cradled in the wide arms of a noble bay. Fifteen miles long and from four to five miles in width, its shape is not unlike that of an heraldic dragon, laid at ease in the blue waters, with head pointed to the south-west. From this head to the jutting cape which does duty as the left claw of the beast, the shore is a succession of bold cliffs, broken by coves and stretches of rocky shingle, and in two places by magnificent curving beaches, upon which a perpetual surf foams and thunders. Parallel ridges or low hills run back from the sea. Between these lie ferny valleys, where wild roses grow in thickets, and such shy flowers as love solitude and a sheltered situation spread a carpet for the spring and early summer. On the farther uplands are thrifty farms, set amid orchards of wind-blown trees. Ravines, each with its thread of brook, cut their way from these higher levels to the water-line. Fleets of lilies whiten the ponds, of which there are many on the island; and over all the scene, softening every outline, tinging and changing the sunlight, and creating a thousand beautiful effects forever unexpected and forever renewed, hangs a thin veil of shifting mist. This the sea-wind, as it journeys to and fro, lifts and drops, and lifts again, as one raises a curtain to look in at the slumber of a child, and, having looked, noiselessly lets it fall.

The Indians, with that fine occasional instinct which is in such odd contrast to other of their characteristics, gave the place its pretty name. Aquidneck, the Isle of Peace, they called it. To modern men it is known as the Island of Rhode Island, made famous the land over by the town built on its seaward extremity—the town of Newport.

It is an old town, and its history dates back to the early days of the New England colony. City it calls itself, but one loves better to think of it as a town, just as the word "avenue," now so popular, is in some minds forever translated into the simpler equivalent, "street." As the veiling mists gather and shift, and then, caught by the outgoing breeze, float seaward again, we catch glimpses, framed, as it were, between the centuries, quaint, oddly differing from each other, but full of interest. The earliest of these glimpses dates back to an April morning in 1524. There is the cliff line, the surf, the grassy capes tinged with sun, and in the sheltered bay, a strange little vessel is dropping her anchor. It is the caravel of Vezzerano, pioneer of French explorers in these northern waters, and first of that great tide of "summer visitors," which has since followed in his wake. How he was received and by whom, Mr. Parkman tells us:

"Following the shores of Long Island, they came first to Block Island, and thence to the harbor of Newport. Here they staid fifteen days, most courteously received by the inhabitants. Among others, appeared two chiefs, gorgeously arrayed in painted deer-skins; kings, as Vezzerano calls them, with attendant gentlemen; while a party of squaws in a canoe, kept by their jealous lords at a safe distance, figure in the narrative as the queen and her maids. The Indian wardrobe had been taxed to its utmost to do the strangers honor,—coffee bracelets and wampum collars, lynx-skins, raccoon-skins, and faces bedaubed with gaudy colors.

"Again they spread their sails, and on the fifth of May bade farewell to the primitive hospitalities of Newport." *

Wampum and coffee bracelets are gone out of fashion since then, the application

* "Pioneers of France in the New World."

of "gaudy color" to faces, though not altogether done away with, is differently practiced and to better effect, and squaws are no longer relegated by their jealous lords to separate and distant canoes; but the repu-

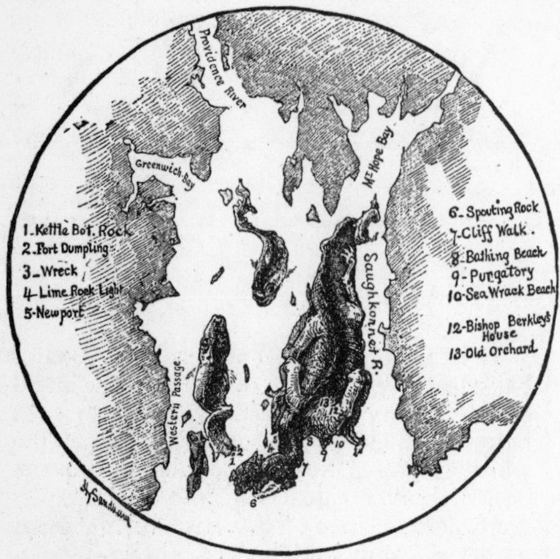

SOME CURIOUS THINGS TO BE SEEN IN NARRAGANSET BAY.

tation for hospitality so early won, Newport still retains, as many a traveler since Vezzerano has had occasion to testify. And still, when the early summer-tide announces the approach of strangers, her inhabitants, decking themselves in their best and bravest, go forth to welcome and to "courteously entreat" all new arrivals.

Again the mist lifts and reveals another picture. Two centuries have passed. The sachems and their squaws have vanished, and on the hill-slope where once their lodges stood a town has sprung up. Warehouses line the shores and wharves, at which lie whalers and merchantmen loading and discharging their cargoes. A large proportion of black faces appear among the passers-by in the streets, and many straight-skirted coats, broad-brimmed hats, gowns of sober hue, and poke-bonnets of drab. Friends abound, as well as negroes, not to mention Jews, Moravians, Presbyterians, and "Six Principle" and "Seven Principle" Baptists; for, under the mild fostering of Roger Williams, Newport has become a city of refuge to religious malcontents of every persuasion. All the population, however, is not of like sobriety. A "rage for finery" distinguishes the aristocracy of the island, and silk-stockinged gentlemen, with scarlet coats and swords, silver-buckled shoes and lace ruffles, may be seen in abundance, exchanging stately greetings with ladies in brocades and hoops, as they pass to and fro between the decorous gambrel-roofed houses or lift the brazen knockers of the street-doors. It is a Saint's-Day, and on the hill above, in a quaint edifice of white-painted wood, with Queen Anne's royal crown and a gilded pennon on its spire, the Rev. Mr. Honeyman, missionary of the English Society for the Propagation of the Gospel, is conducting the service in Trinity Church. The sermon begins, but is interrupted by a messenger who hurries in with a letter, which he hands to the divine in the pulpit. The clergyman reads it aloud to his audience, pronounces a rapid benediction, and "wardens, vestry, church, and congregation" crowd to the ferry-wharf, off which lies a "pretty large ship," just come to anchor. A boat rows to the shore, from which alights a gentleman "of middle stature, and an agreeable, pleasant, and erect aspect," wearing the canonicals of an English dean. He leads by the hand a lady; three other gentlemen follow in their company. The new arrival is George Berkeley, Dean of Derry, philosopher and scholar, who, on his way to Bermuda with the project of there planting an ideally perfect university, "for the instruction of the youth of America" (!) has chosen Rhode Island as a suitable vantage-point from which to organize and direct the new undertaking. His companions are his newly married wife and three "learned and elegant friends," Sir John James, Richard Dalton, and the artist Smibert. Not every Saint's-Day brings such voyagers to Newport from over the sea. No wonder that Trinity Church services are interrupted, and that preacher and congregation crowd to the wharf to do the strangers honor!

The Berkeley party spent the first few months of their stay in the town of Newport, whence the Dean made short excursions to what Mrs. Berkeley terms "the Continent," meaning the main-land opposite. Toward the close of their first summer, James, Dalton, and Smibert removed to Boston, and the Berkeley family to a farm in the interior of the island, which the Dean had purchased and on which he had built a house. This house still exists, and is still known by the name of Whitehall, given it by its loyal owner in remembrance of the ancient palace of the kings of England.

The estate, which comprised less than a

hundred acres, lies in a grassy valley to the south of Honeyman's Hill, and about two miles back from what is now known as "The Second Beach." It commands no "view" whatever. Dean Berkeley, when asked why he did not choose a site from which more could be seen, is said to have replied that "if a prospect were continually in view it would lose its charm." His favorite walk was toward the sea, and he is supposed to have made an outdoor study of a rocky shelf, overhung by a cliff cornice, on the face of a hill-ridge fronting the beach, which shelf is still known as "Bishop Berkeley's Rock."

Three years the peaceful life of Whitehall continued. Two children were born to the Bishop, one of whom died in infancy. The house was a place of meeting for all the missionaries of the island, as well as for the more thoughtful and cultivated of the Newport society. At last, in the winter of 1730, came the crisis of the Bermuda scheme. Land had been purchased, the grant of money half promised by the English Government was due. But the persuasive charm of the founder of the enterprise was no longer at hand to influence those who had the power to make or mar the project; and Sir Robert Walpole, with that sturdy indifference to pledge, or to other people's convenience, which distinguished him, intimated with fatal clearness of meaning, that if Dean Berkeley was waiting in Rhode Island for twenty thousand pounds of the public money to be got out of *his* exchequer, he might as well return to Europe without further loss of time. The bubble was indeed broken, and Berkeley, brave still and resolutely patient under this heavy blow, prepared for departure. His books he left as a gift to the library of Yale College, and his farm of Whitehall was made over to the same institution, to found three scholarships for the encouragement of Greek and Latin study. These bequests arranged, his wife and their one remaining child sailed for Ireland. There, a bishopric, and twenty years of useful and honorable labor, awaited him, and the brief dream of Rhode Island must soon have seemed a dream indeed. Few vestiges remain now of his residence,—the shabby farm-house once his home, the chair in which he sat to write, a few books and papers, the organ presented by him to Trinity Church, a big family portrait by Smibert, and, appealing more strongly to the imagination than these, the memory of his distinguished name as a friend of American letters, still preserved by scholarship or foundation in many institutions of learning—and the little grave in Trinity churchyard, where, on the south side of the Kay Monument, sleeps "Lucia Berkeley, daugh-

WHITEHALL, BISHOP BERKELEY'S RESIDENCE.

PURGATORY.

ter of Dean Berkeley, *obiit* the fifth of September, 1731."

The traveler who to-day is desirous of visiting Whitehall may reach it by the delightful way of the beaches. Rounding the long curve of the First Beach, with its dressing-houses and tents, its crowd of carriages and swarms of gayly clad bathers, and climbing the hill at the far end, he will find himself directly above the lonely but far more beautiful Second Beach. Immediately before him, to the left, he will see Bishop Berkeley's Rock, with its cliff-hung shelf, and beyond, the soft outlines of Sachuest Point, the narrow blue of the East Passage, and a strip of sunlit main-land. The breezy perch where "Alciphron" was written is on the sea-face of one of the parallel rock-formations which, with their intervening valleys, make up the region known as "Paradise Rocks." Near by, in the line of low cliffs which bounds the beach to the southward, is the chasm called "Purgatory," a vertical fissure some fifty feet in depth, into which, under certain conditions of wind and tide, the water rushes with great force and is sucked out with a hollow boom, which is sufficiently frightful to explain the name selected for the spot. The rocks which make up the cliffs are in great part conglomerate of soft shades of purple and reddish gray. Beyond, the white beach glistens in the sun. The sand-dunes which bound it are yellow, the salt marshes behind them stretch in fields of umber and vivid glances of green. The stillness of utter peace seems to rest over the spot, broken only by the dash of surf and the calling sea-birds; it is difficult to realize that only a mile or two distant is one of the gayest watering-places in America, and a throng of pleasure-seekers to whom quiet is a distasteful and undesired thing.

GATHERING SEA-WEED.

But the Second Beach is not always so quiet. It may easily happen that the pilgrim to Whitehall, topping the hill on a brilliant autumn morning, shall come upon a scene in which quiet plays no part. The sea-weed, that harvest which, ripening without labor, is neither bought nor sold, is setting inshore under the urgings of wind and tide, and scores of farmers have crowded to the spot to gather it. An artist could hardly wish a better subject for his pencil than one of these wild harvestings. The plunging horses, forced far out into the surf, their slow return, half swimming, half wading, dragging the heavily loaded rakes

AN ISLAND WINDMILL.

which leave behind them a long furrow of foam, the heaped-up kelp glistening in the sunshine, the oxen, yoked by fours, waiting for their load, the shouts of the men, the dash, the excitement, and beyond and above all, the wonderful blues and iridescent greens which are the peculiar property of Newport waters and the Newport sky. To the left, the white road curves on past farm-houses and "cottages of gentility." Farther away on the valley slope, the slow sails of a windmill revolve and flash, casting a flying shadow over the grass. A mile farther, and the road, making a turn, is joined to the right by what seems to be a farm-lane shut off by gates. This is the entrance to Whitehall. The house can be dimly made out from the road—a low, square building with a lean-to and a long steep-pitch of roof, fronting on a small garden overgrown with fruit-trees. The present owner holds it from the college under what may truly be called a long lease, as it has still some eight hundred and odd years to run. He has built a house near by, for his own occupation, and alas! has removed thither the last bit that remained of the decorative art of the old Whitehall, namely, the band of quaint Dutch tiles which once surrounded the chimney-piece of the parlor. But the parlor remains unchanged, with its low ceiling and uneven floor; the old staircase is there, the old trees, and, spite of the tooth of time and the worse spoliation of man, enough is left to hint at the days of its early repute and to make the place worth a visit.

One more glimpse through the mist before we come to the new times of this our Isle of Peace. It is just half a century since Berkeley, his baffled scheme heavy at his heart, set sail for Ireland. The fog is unusually thick, and lies like a fleece of wool over the sea. Absolutely nothing can be seen, but strange sounds come borne on the wind from the direction of Block Island—dull reports as of cannon signals; and the inhabitants of Newport prick up their ears and strain their eyes with a mixture of hope and terror; for the French fleet is looked for; English cruisers have been seen or suspected hovering round the coast, and who knows but a naval engagement is taking place at that very moment. By and by the fog lifts, with that fantastic deliberation which distinguishes its movements, and presently stately shapes whiten the blue, and, gradually nearing, reveal themselves as the frigates *Surveillante*, *Amazone*, and *Guêpe*, *The Duke of Burgundy*, and *The Neptune*, "doubly sheathed with copper"; *The Conquerant*, *The Provence*, *The Eveillé*, also "doubly sheathed with copper"; *The Lazon* and *The Ardent*, convoying a host of transports and store-ships; with General Rochambeau and his officers on board, besides the regiments of Bourbonnais, Soissonais, Saintonge, and Royal Deux Ponts, five hundred artillerists and six hundred of Lauzan's Legion, all come to aid the infant United States, then in the fourth year of their struggle for independence. Never was reënforcement more timely or more ardently desired. We may be sure that all Newport ran out to greet the new arrivals. Among the other officers who landed on that eventful eleventh of July, was Claude Blanchard, commissary-in-chief of the French forces—an important man enough to the expedition, but very little important now, except for the lucky fact that he kept a journal,—which journal, recently published, gives a better and more detailed account of affairs at that time and place than any one else has afforded us.

It is from Blanchard that we learn of the three months' voyage: of sighting now and again the vessels of the English squadron; of the Chevalier de Fernay's refusal to engage them, he being intent on the safe conduct of his convoy; of the consequent heart-burnings and reproaches of his captains, which, together with the stings of his own wounded pride, resulted in a fever, and subsequently in his death, recorded on the tablet which now adorns the vestibule of Trinity Church. The town was illuminated in honor of the fleet. "A small but handsome town," says Blanchard, "and the houses, though mostly of wood, are of an agreeable shape."

The first work of the newly arrived allies was to restore the redoubts which the English had dismantled and in great part destroyed. It was at this time that the first fort on the Dumplings, and the original Fort Adams, on Brenton's Reef, were built. The excellent Blanchard meanwhile continues his observations on climate, society, and local customs.

One of his criticisms on the national characteristics strikes us oddly now, yet has its interest as denoting the natural drift and result of the employment of a debased currency.

"The Americans are slow, and do not decide promptly in matters of business," he observes. "It is not easy for us to rely upon their promises. They love money, and *hard* money; it is thus they designate specie to distinguish it from paper money, which loses prodigiously. This loss varies according to circumstances and according to the provinces."

Later, we hear of dinners and diners:

"They do not eat soups, and do not serve up ragouts at their dinners, but boiled and roast, and much vegetables. They drink nothing but cider and Madeira wine with water. The dessert is composed of preserved quinces and pickled sorrel. The Americans eat the latter with the meat. They do not take coffee immediately after dinner, but it is served three or four hours afterward with tea; this coffee is weak, and four or five cups are not equal to one of ours; so that they take many of them. The tea, on the contrary, is very strong. Breakfast is an important affair with them. Besides tea and coffee, they put on table roasted meats, with butter, pies and ham; nevertheless they sup, and in the afternoon they again take tea. Thus the Americans are almost always at table; and as they have little to occupy them, as they go out little in winter, and spend whole days alongside their fires and their wives, without reading and without doing anything, going to table is a relief and a preventive of *ennui*. Yet they are not great eaters."

On the 5th of March, 1781, General Washington arrived in Newport. Blanchard

FORT DUMPLING.

thus records his first impressions of the commander-in-chief:

"His face is handsome, noble, and mild. He is tall—at the least, five feet eight inches (French measure). In the evening, I was at supper with him. I mark, as a fortunate day, that in which I have been able to behold a man so truly great."

OLD FARM-HOUSE, NEWPORT ISLAND.

Following the close of the war came a period of great business depression, in which Newport heavily shared. The British, during their occupation of the town, had done much to injure it. Nearly a thousand buildings were destroyed by them on the island; fruit and shade trees were cut down, the churches were used as barracks, and the Redwood Library was despoiled of its more valuable books. Commerce was dead; the suppression of the slave-trade reduced many to poverty, and the curse of paper money—to which Rhode Island clung after other States had abandoned it—poisoned the very springs of public credit. Brissot de Warville, in the record of his journey "performed" through the United States in 1788, draws this melancholy picture of Newport at that time:

"Since the peace, everything is changed. The reign of solitude is only interrupted by groups of idle men standing, with folded arms, at the corners of the streets: houses falling to ruin; miserable shops, which present nothing but a few coarse stuffs, or baskets of apples, and other articles of little value; grass growing in the public square, in front of the court of justice; rags stuffed in the windows, or hung upon hideous women and lean, unquiet children.

Count Rochefoucauld-Liancourt, writing ten years later, calls the place "*cette ville triste et basse*," and further ventures on this remarkable criticism of its salubrity:

"The healthfulness of the city of Newport and its environs is doubtless the result of the brilliancy and coolness of its climate, but this coolness proves fatal to its younger inhabitants, and the number of young men, and, above all, of young women, who die yearly of consumption is considerable. It is noteworthy that the inscriptions on the tombstones in the cemetery indicate in almost all cases that the person interred is either very young or very old—either less than twenty years of age or more than seventy."

Whether this statement of Count Rochefoucauld's bears the test of examination would be impossible now to determine, for the century since his visit has made changes in the city of the dead as marked as those effected in the city of the living. But the "cool and brilliant air" with which he finds fault has since been proved by many invalids to be full of health-giving properties. Consumptives are more often sent to Newport for cure, nowadays, than away from it. Asthma, diseases of the chest and throat, nervous disorders, insomnia, excitability of brain, are in many cases sensibly benefited by the island climate, which, however, is less "brilliant" than sedative. This is attributed to the relaxing effects of the Gulf Stream, which is popularly supposed to make an opportune bend toward the shore and to produce a quality of air quite different from that of other New England sea-side climates. Whatever may be the truth as to the bend of this obliging current, it is certain that something has given to the place an exceptional climate, pure, free from malaria, and exempt equally from the fiercer heats of summer and the severer colds of winter. Much has been done during the past twenty years to counterbalance these great advantages. The drainage of the place is in an inchoate and primitive condition, population has increased with no adequate increase of sanitary provision, and there is an almost amusingly strong distaste and disbelief in the necessity of improvement. But, spite of these drawbacks, the town is so happy in its situation and in the torrent of splendid sea-wind which blows continually over it, that it still retains and deserves its reputation as a healthful place, and the next decade will doubtless see it put beyond danger or suspicion of danger.

It was not till about the year 1830 that the true source of Newport's prosperity was realized to be her climate. Since then she has become more and more the Mecca of pilgrims from all parts of the country. Year by year, the town has spread and broadened, stretching out wide arms to include distant coigns of vantage, until now the summer city covers some miles in extent, and land, unsalable in the early part of the century, and but twenty years ago commanding little more than the price of a Western farmstead, is now valued at from ten to fourteen thousand dollars an acre! Every year adds to the number of cottages and villas and to the provision made for the accommodation of strangers. The census, which in winter counts up to less than seventeen thousand, is, during the four months of "the season," swelled by the addition of thousands of strangers, many of whom are, in a manner, residents of the place, owning property and paying taxes. A large number of these partial residents make their season a long one, giving nearly or quite half the year to their sea-side homes, and every winter brings an increasingly greater number of new-comers to replace the summer absentees; so that, taking the year through, society in Newport possesses an unique variety and charm. With much of the freedom and simplicity of the country in its out-of-season habits, there is nothing of the narrow dullness inevitable to most small communities, and the fact that its members, in great part, belong to and are in alliance with the larger cities, gives a vivacity and range of interest to their occupations and amusements which it would be hard to match in any other American town of the same size.

Newport, as it appears to its crowd of summer visitors, is so well known as hardly to require description. The most famous, perhaps, of American watering-places, it is distinctly the most elegant. There is very little of the hotel life which is so prominent a feature of Saratoga, and our other springs and spas. It was tried, but it failed. One by one, the big caravansaries, with their piazzas and bands, their "hops" and crowds of dressy idlers, have been taken down piecemeal, to make part and parcel of smaller houses, or, in some cases, ignomin-

CLOCK-TOWER OF THE CASINO.

THE MEET.

iously sold for fire-wood. The Ocean House alone remains to represent this phase of accommodation. For differing tastes, there are lodgings of every grade of comfort and elegance—apartments, houses, half-houses—to be had on the terms of home-like seclusion, with everything from cook to candles furnished from the outside, besides scores of cottages and villas of all sizes, situations, and prices to be let furnished. In this way, Newport, even in the height of the season, is a congregation of homes, and a large proportion of visitors preserve their domestic privacy, living in their own hired houses, dispensing and receiving hospitalities. It is this fact, perhaps, more than any other, which makes her personality so distinct and so unlike that of the customary "resort," with its crowd, and noise, and glare, its impossibility of separateness, its unrefined display, and absolute discomfort.

The amusements of Newport, in the season, are many and various. First and foremost should be named the Casino, a new feature, but already a most important one. This charming place, which is both like and unlike the conversation halls which, in Europe, bear the same name, is built on the Avenue not far from the Ocean House. Its aspect from the street is that of a low, picturesque façade, two stories in height, in the old English style, of brick and olive-painted wood, quaintly shingled and oddly carved, with wide casement windows, and here and there a touch of gilding. A single year has toned its color down to a delightful oldness, which would do no discredit to a street in Chester or Coventry. A broad entrance-hall in the middle of the building leads to an inner quadrangle, turfed and set with flower-beds, in the midst of which rises a splashing fountain. Above and below, on the street side of this quadrangle, are club-rooms and offices, broken by a picturesque clock-tower. To right and left are more club-rooms, a restaurant, reading, dining, and smoking rooms; dressing-rooms for ladies and gentlemen; smaller saloons, where entertainments may be given; and kitchens, wisely ordered on the second floors, where their noises and smells can annoy no one.

The fourth side of the quadrangle is filled with a double curve of roofed galleries, two stories in height, where ladies sit the morning long, work in hand, chatting with their friends, enjoying the smell of the spray-freshened flowers, and listening to the music of the band. Beyond this first quadrangle lies another and wider one, edged with trees and shrubberies, past which winds the carriage-drive from an entrance at the back. This lawn is devoted to open-air tennis. At its far end is another long building, in which are racket-courts, bowling-alleys, and a beautiful ball-room, fitted up with a stage and all appurtenances for private theatricals. It will be seen how many and how various tastes may be served by a building of this sort.

Polo play, and sitting by to see polo played, are among the other favorite Newport amusements. Still another is to ride or drive to the meets of the Queen's County Hunt, which, in the latter part of the season, has a run about twice a week. Foxes are not too plentiful in the island, and there are days when the hounds are forced—*faute de mieux*—to follow a trail of anise-seed, instead of their more legitimate scent. But the pace, the jumping, and the chance of broken bones are equally good; and, as Reynard does not complain, and no baby in act of being soothed of its infant ailment by the mild infusion which does duty as scent, has as yet fallen a prey to the mistaken ferocity of the pack, there seems no reason to cavil. Ladies often join in the sport.

The Fort music is another bi-weekly pleasure, involving as it does the pretty drive round the southernmost curve of the bay, with the villa-crowned slopes of Halidon Hill on one hand, and on the other the wide outlook of blue water, broken by many islands. Close by is the tiny rock with its time-washed light-house, where dwells the brave Ida Lewis, heroine of so much daring adventure, and beyond stretches the long point of Brenton's Reef, surmounted by the

LIME-ROCK LIGHT—THE HOME OF IDA LEWIS.

casemates and smooth glacis of Fort Adams. In the deep point of the inner cove lie the wrecks of two ships, one of them an abandoned slaver, drifted many years since into this quiet harbor, and gradually breaking to

WRECK OF A SLAVER.

pieces under the slow, untiring touches of wind and tide. Only the ribs now remain; they lie, black, skeleton-like shapes, reflected in the tranquil waters of the cove—a perpetual pleasure to such artist eyes as take pleasure in contrast and happy accidents.

Besides the fashionable Bellevue Avenue, and the celebrated ocean drive, which for nine miles follows the sinuosities of the shore from Bailey's Beach to Brenton's Cove, there are others less famous, but no less enjoyable: the drive over the two beaches, for example, and out to the long end of Sachuest Point, through gaps in stone-walls and across fields of grain, by overgrown tracks, where wild flowers and tall, nodding grass half bury the wheels; or the drives to Coddington's Cove, to the Glen, to Lawton's Valley, or along the shore

OLD ORCHARD.

of the eastern passage. These inland drives afford constant characteristic glimpses. Many of the farms are old. Now and again you come upon country-seats dating back to the last century, and embowered amid historic elms or lindens. There is always good chance of catching glimpses of a windmill, that inevitably picturesque shape, and the certainty of old apple-orchards. The apple-orchards of the Isle of Peace have an unusual character of their own. Low, thickly growing, with densely interlaced branches and gnarled trunks, twisted into strange shapes by the scourging winds, they are as solemn of aspect, as full of intense and passionate expression, as groves of olive. Contrast is one of the charms of Newport Island, and every turn affords it: on one side the repose and the quaint peace of old stability and habitual simplicity; on the other the whirl and dazzle and directed movement of modern life and modern luxury in its most splendid and pronounced development.

For those who prefer sailing to driving, the beautiful harbor of Newport affords a daily delight. At the close of a summer's day, when sky and water and shore are bathed in a soft mist of radiance, which is more like magic than reality, nothing can be more charming than to flit with a favoring wind past the shores of Canonicut, and so out to Beaver Tail. The water in the little inlets and fiords of the rocky coast lies still and blue—blue as ultramarine; but farther out in the glancing tideway, all other jewels, opal and tourmaline, and sapphire and diamond, seem melted and fusing, and running a race together. Above, on the rocky headland, is the ruin of the Dumplings' Fort. Yachts come sailing in from the sea—proud, beautiful shapes, their sails shining against the sunset. As the dusk deepens, light-houses flash into view

THE KETTLE BOTTOM.

on distant points, their revolving lamps throwing a beam, now red, now gold,—

> "Petal by petal each fiery rose,
> Out of the darkness buds and grows,"—

while, noiseless as white-winged moths, the fishing-boats flit in for the night. And, perhaps, just where the sunset lies on the water with loveliest pink, you may come upon a huge rock-table, set in a wild confusion of waves and spray, on and about which innumerable black forms of sea-birds perch and flap, flecking the surf with their wings, and filling the air with strange, wild cries. "Cormorants," the old fishermen call these birds, and their favorite rock, the "Kettle Bottom" by name, is rarely found without them.

The Cliff-walk, with its four miles right of way through carefully kept private grounds, and its fine effects of rocks, and surf, and precipice, is another of the pleasures of Newport. It ends at the boat-house close to Bailey's Beach, and opposite the point on which lies the Spouting Rock, whose chief attraction seems to be a certain coy indisposition to spout.

A walk in the older and more thickly settled parts of the town is not without its rewards. There are to be found well-known objects of interest,—the Jewish burial-ground, with its luxurious screen of carefully tended flowers; the Redwood Library, rich in old books and the possession of the finest cut-leaved beech on the island; and the old Stone Mill, on which so much speculative reasoning in prose and verse has been lavished. Those ruthless civic hands which know nor taste nor mercy, have, within a year or two, despoiled the mill of the vines which made it picturesque, but even thus denuded it is an interesting object. There is old Trinity, with its square pews and burial tablets, and a last-century "three-decker" pulpit, with clerk's desk, reading-desk, and preaching-desk, all overhung by a conical sounding-board of extinguisher pattern—a sounding-board on which whole generations of little boys have fixed fascinated eyes, wondering in case of fall what would become of the clergyman underneath it. And, besides these, each westward-leading street gives pretty glimpses of bay and islands and shipping, and there is always the chance of lighting on a bit of the past,—some quaint roof or wall or door-way, left over from Revolutionary times and holding up a protesting face from among more modern buildings.

Newport is famous for its lawns, which rival those of England in freshness and verdure, being fed by a like perennial humidity. Nowhere are geraniums so splendid a red, roses so fair and sweet, or foliage-beds so magnificent, as here. There is a universal love and culture of flowers. The smallest house has its strip of garden, its window boxes, or basket-hung piazza.

Very little can be said in praise of the architecture of modern Newport. There are many costly houses, but few whose exteriors are beautiful. Of tasteful interiors there are many, and in many varieties of style, from the grand château to the Queen Anne cottage. Among the more lately built houses are some pretty examples of Jacobean and seventeenth-century styles, and two or three really old houses have been restored with admirable effect.

Many hundreds of people can be found to testify to the charms of the Newport summer, but only a chosen few know how delightful are its winters. After the crowd takes its flight; after four-in-hands have ceased to roll and key-bugles to sound in the streets, and one by one the big houses on the cliffs and along the Avenue have certified their emptiness by shuttered windows and nailed-up doors; and the bric-à-brac dealers have folded their rugs like the Arabs and silently stolen away,—the real Newport comes out of the corner where all summer long she has lain hidden, and stands on the shore to watch the flight of her gay-plumed birds of passage. Presently a sense of peace begins to fill the place. Roses go on blossoming, the geranium-beds grow redder and more riotous, frosts delay; day after day brings such noonshine, such sun-settings, and such sweet air as August never dreams of. People return from their summerings, scattered circles are reunited, winter plans are made and carried out with that zest and enjoyment which only small and intimate communities can know. Autumn lingers on till Christmas, and, when winter comes, he seems like autumn's twin-brother, only to be distinguished from him by an occasional burst of temper, soon repented of;—or if, as may chance once in six or seven years, the winter prove a severe one, with weeks of ice and snow, even then, Newport, sharing the common fate of New England, contrives to temper and modify the harshness of it by her own friendliness, so that cold seems less cruel and less hurtful than it is anywhere else. Nothing in the way of air can be imagined more delicious than the wind which sometimes breathes in from the ocean on a bright winter's noon. It has positive fragrance, as if blown from invisible spice-islands immeasurably distant, and winnowed from all suspicion of impurities by its passage over a thousand leagues of salt sea. The days go by happily and swiftly. There are pleasant things to do,

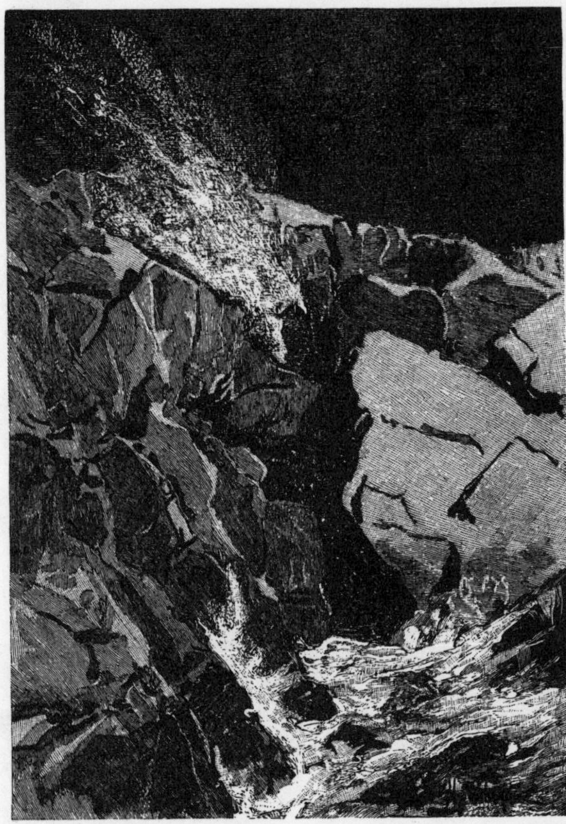

SPOUTING ROCK.

and leisure in which to do them—leisure to study, to enjoy, to be lazy, to form friendships. There are music, acting, gay little reunions, and entertainments with bright, novel features to quicken them; people have time to be original. And suddenly, one day, spring peeps in at the window, not unwelcome exactly,—for how should spring lack welcome?—but unexpected and disturbing. The best, the choicest of the year is over, and Newport, with a furtive sigh, girds herself afresh for the agreeable toils of the near summer.

But, winter or summer, the charm which most endears Newport to the imaginative mind is, and must continue to be, the odd mingling of old and new which meets you on every hand. A large portion of the place belongs and can belong to no other day but our own, but touching it everywhere, apart from it but of it, is the past. It meets you at every turn, in legend or relic or quaint traditionary custom still kept up and observed. Many farm-hands and servants on the island still date and renew their contracts of service from "Lady-Day." The "nine-o'clock bell," which seems derived in some dim way from the ancient curfew, is regularly rung. The election parade, dear to little boys and pea-nut venders, continues to be a chief event every spring, with its procession, its drums, its crowd of country visitors, and small booths for the sale of edibles and non-edibles pitched on either side the State-house Square, which, in honor of this yearly observance, is called familiarly, "The Parade." One of the oldest militia companies in New England is the Newport Artillery, and "The Mercury," established in 1758 by a brother of Benjamin Franklin, is the oldest surviving newspaper in the United States. Newport also possesses a town-crier. He may be met with any day, tinkling his bell at street corners and rehearsing, in a loud, melancholy chant, facts regarding auction-sales, or town-meetings, or lost property. And, turning aside from the polo-play or the change of the day, you may chance on an old salt spinning yarns of pirates and privateers, phantom ships, or buried treasure, or an antiquary full of well-remembered stories whose actors belong to the far-gone past, —stories of the extinct glories of the place, of family romance and family tragedy, or tragedy just escaped. What could be finer contrast than tales like these, told on a street-

VIEW IN THAMES STREET.

Avenue crowded with brilliant equipages, a few rods carries you to the quiet loneliness of a secluded burial-place, with the name of an ancient family carved on its locked gate, in which, beneath gray head-stones and long, flowering grasses, repose the hushed secrets of a century ago. Or, fresh from the buzz and chatter, the gay inter-corner where, just before, perhaps, the question had been about Wall street or the Casino, if the French frigate were still in the bay, or when would be the next meeting of the Town and County Club! Indeed, it is not so many years since visitors to Newport might have held speech with a dear old lady whose memory carried her back clearly and distinctly to the day when, a child six years old, she sat on Washington's knee. The little girl had a sweet voice. She sang a song to the great man, in recompense for which he honored her with a salute. "It was here, my dear, and here, that General Washington kissed me," she would say to her grandchildren, touching first one and then the other wrinkled cheek; and to the end of her life, no other lips were suffered to profane with a touch the spots thus made sacred.

In a country whose charm and whose reproach alike is its newness, and to a society whose roots are forever being uprooted and freshly planted to be again uprooted, there is real education and advantage in the tangible neighborhood of the past; and the Newport past is neither an unlovely nor a reproachful shape. There is dignity in her calm mien; she looks on stately and untroubled, and compares and measures. The dazzle and glitter of modern luxury do not daunt her: she has seen splendor before in a different generation and different forms, she has shared it, she has watched it fade and fail. Out of her mute, critical regard, a voice seems to sound in tones like the rustle of falling leaves in an autumn day, and to utter that ancient and melancholy truth, *Vanitas, vanitorum!* "The fashion of this world passeth away." We listen, awed for a moment, and then we smile again,—for brightness near at hand has a more potent spell than melancholy gone by,—and turning to our modern lives with their movement and sunshine, their hope and growth, we are content to accept and enjoy such brief day as is granted us, nor "prate nor hint of change till change shall come."

DOOR-WAY OF HOUSE ON THAMES STREET.

The Story of Portland (1895)

THE STORY OF PORTLAND.

By James P. Baxter.

A THOUGHTFUL Gallic penman wrote that "there is nothing beautiful, sweet or grand in life but its mysteries;" and we may well agree with him that those things which lie beyond the scope of sense and reveal themselves only to the eye of sentiment give life and meaning to everything about us. What are the crowding tenement and lofty mansions, the massive towers and cloud-kissing spires of a great city, if the mind contemplating them does not feel behind them the varied forces which have contributed to the city's construction, from the time when its last building was completed, back to the pioneers who fixed upon its site in the wilderness, or among the ruins of aboriginal camps?

Here on the shores of Casco Bay, by shelly beach and bowlder-strewn headland, or under the dark pines which shade its verdant slopes, we may picture to ourselves scenes which have taken place, now visible but to the eye of imagination, but as real as any which lie within the compass of bodily sight. Here the ice age reigned, holding the land with relentless grasp and crushing out every vestige of life which it sustained. Glaciers from the north, resistless save by the sea, which devoured them as they advanced, tore the mountain crags from their foundations and strewed them along their way; forces of hidden origin, amid terrors too appalling for human vision to behold, moulded the peninsula known by the red man as Machegonne, outlining valley, and cove, and waterway, lifting crag and hill to place, and making them things of beauty to delight forever the eyes of man.

Thus this beautiful peninsula, rising above the blue sea, adorned with sheltering groves and verdant glades kept fresh by perennial springs, in due time became the abode of men, of wild men whose tastes were simple and wants such as sea and forest could amply supply. Generation after generation of these people came into existence and passed out of it as the seasons rolled by, cherishing with childish delight the mysteries of a past of which they knew little, until a time came when a greater wonder than any of which they had before dreamed appeared to their awe-stricken vision. In from the mysterious sea, whose boundless waters somewhere in space washed the shores of dreamland, came a ship — a white-winged monster it seemed to their eyes — bearing visitants whose aspect and speech were to them alike strange: indeed superior beings. Along the shores which the red men had ever regarded as their own, these white-faced men erected their habitations; and Machegonne began to be the abode of civilization.

Who were these early comers? Some have supposed them adventurers from the sterile shores of Greenland, the kin of the Norse sea-kings, whose dragon prows were the terror of those who dwelt by the sea; but no remains exist on the shores of Maine to give support to this supposition. The Venetian Cabots may have looked into the harbor palisaded by wooded islands, or the Spanish Cortereals, or the weather-beaten toilers of the sea from the rocky shores of Brittany, or Verrazzano, or Pring, or Gosnold; but this is uncertain. Providence seems to have jealously preserved this jewel for the Anglo-Saxon; for even that noble man, the brave and pious Champlain, when in the spring of 1606, after a winter of suffering at Saint Croix, he searched the coast for a site upon which to plant his colony, was not permitted to look upon it. Passing outside the islands at its mouth, he skirted the shores of Cape Elizabeth, not suspecting that he had passed the noblest haven to shelter the ships of his beloved France to be found on the coast. And what a Providence was this! — for Champlain, noble as he was, represented a power which was a menace to human liberty and progress; and had Gallic government been set up here, the history of the continent might have been widely different from what it is.

Two years after this, Ralegh Gilbert, exploring the coast from Sagadahoc, probably looked into the harbor of Machegonne, and perhaps drank of the spring at Clay Cove; and in 1614 the ship of Captain John Smith anchored here, seeking fish and furs. Thomas Dermer, too, in 1619, — the agent of Sir Ferdinando Gorges, the father of American colonization, — must have been here when exploring the coast, and have taken account of the advantages which the harbor afforded for a maritime settlement. Still we have no definite description of the locality from any of these.

In 1623 Christopher Levett, the son of an innkeeper of York, in the native county of Frobisher, inspired with a zeal for adventure, conceived the plan of founding a city in New England. In furtherance of this project he obtained, May 5, 1623, from the council established at Plymouth for governing New England, a grant of six thousand acres of land to be located by him upon any territory belonging to the council. Levett well understood the advantage of official patronage, and he at once undertook to enlist the interest of Lord Conway, then Secretary of State, Lord Scrope, and even royalty itself in his enterprise. To gain the support of his Yorkshire friends, as well as to gratify his patriotic pride, he proposed to name this projected city in the New World, York, in honor of the stately city of his nativity. His efforts in obtaining financial support for his enterprise do not appear to have been attended with much success; but his energy attracted the attention of Sir Ferdinando Gorges, who was about to send his younger son Robert to the New World to represent the council of which Sir Ferdinando was the moving spirit, as Governor and Lieutenant General of New England, — and Levett received the appointment of councillor in the new government.

Thus equipped, Levett set out on his voyage, and in early autumn reached the mouth of the Piscataqua, where he met Gorges, and assisted him in setting up the forms of government within the domain of the council. This duty accomplished, he set out on a voyage of exploration eastward, being joined on the way by men whom he had engaged to accompany him. The season was late for exploration, and Levett possessed only open boats with which to coast along the wild shores of Maine, bleak and dangerous in winter; but with a bold heart and cheerful spirit he pushed on, lightening hunger and hardships with a quaint tale or pleasant joke. At night Levett and his men encamped on the seashore, protecting themselves from the wintry storms which swept around them as best they could by such rude structures as they were able to hastily erect. After several days of severe toil and exposure, the islands at the mouth of Portland harbor were reached. Levett examined the harbor and passed up Fore River, which he was told by the Indians abounded in salmon in their season. Upon this pleasant stream he bestowed his own name; and wishing to continue his explorations farther east, he passed around Munjoy to the mouth of the Presumpscot. The shores of this charming river and the lofty island at its mouth, dividing its waters as they mingle with the sea, were the haunt of the red man. To an Indian town located near the first fall of the Presumpscot, which Levett declared to be "bigger than the fall at London Bridge," he proceeded, and was received in friendly fashion by the chief residing there, Skitterygusset by name, who gave him comfortable shelter in the royal wigwam. The town was a convenient rendezvous for the eastern Indians on their way west to barter their furs with the English traders, who were now becoming numerous on the coast; and while sojourning with the friendly chief of the Presumpscot, Levett became acquainted with a number of the friends of his host, both from the east and west. With these rude people he was soon on friendly terms; and when he started to pursue his explorations eastward, Sadamoyt, the sagamore of the Penobscots, pressed upon him a beaver skin, then the savage's most coveted treasure, as a token of his esteem for the Yorkshire adventurer.

Though Levett had probably determined already to locate his grant from the council for New England about Portland harbor, he extended his explorations to the neighborhood of Sagadahoc, where his patron Gorges, always confident of retrieving his failure under Popham and Gilbert, cherished the idea of founding a "state county" and building a city which should have the honor of being christened by the king.

Levett, in his exploration of the Maine coast, found the natives hospitable; and although he saw sites suitable for settlement at many points along the coast, his heart was fixed on the region about Portland harbor, which experience told him afforded a site of unsurpassed advantages for a maritime city. After a brief exploration of the coast to the east, he returned there and selected the site for his proposed city of York. With conspicuous wisdom, instead of seizing upon the land by virtue of his English patent, as others had usually done in the New World, in disregard of the natives' rights, he proceeded to obtain from Cogawesco, the sagamore of Casco, and his wife, to whom the land belonged by inheritance, the right of occupation. He accomplished this in an amicable manner, and then, to afford shelter and protection for his men, erected a fortified dwelling upon one of the islands at the mouth of the harbor. Here he placed a garrison of ten men; and in the summer of 1624, greatly to the grief of the Indians, whose friendship he had won by his unselfish course, he set sail for England, in order to obtain men and means to enlarge his enterprise. The friendly savages, who stood on the shore regretting his departure, and saw the ship which bore him vanish from sight, looked upon him no more. He had promised them that he would return after some moons, and they talked of his coming, and speculated upon the cause of his delay; yet he returned no more than the friends who had passed to those realms of mystery where dwelt their shadowy gods.

When Levett reached England he found affairs there unpropitious for advancing his colonial projects. The charter of the council for New England was on trial, and had been pronounced a monopoly dangerous to the public weal. There was also threatened trouble with Spain, and France was claiming the territory where he had located his prospective colony. Men who under favorable circumstances would have listened to his enthusiastic description of the new country over the sea were not disposed to risk their lives and money in a scheme likely to be overthrown by foreign power; and, baffled but not disheartened, he was obliged to wait for happier times.

Over two years passed away. What had in this time become of his fortified dwelling in Portland harbor, and the men he had left there, we know not. The pretensions of the French king had just been put to rest, and interest in colonial enterprises began to revive. Levett seized the occasion to press his design upon the attention of the king, and with the aid of powerful friends succeeded in obtaining a proclamation directed to the ecclesiastical authorities, requiring the churches of York to take up a contribution in aid of the colonial enterprise in Casco Bay. The king's reasons for this extraordinary order were that, his colonial plans in New England having been interrupted by his difficulties with France and Spain, it had become necessary, in order to secure English interests in the new land, to render assistance to those who had entered upon such enterprises, and that, as his "well-beloved subject, Christopher Levett," was willing to risk to the utmost both life and estate in order to establish a colony in New England, and was well acquainted with the Indians, he had thought best not only to make him Governor of New England, but to order churchmen to contribute means to aid him in his undertaking, the success of which would enable the

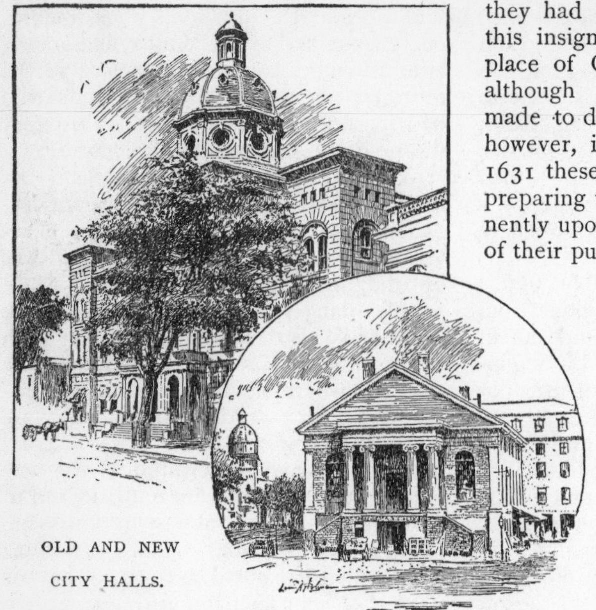

OLD AND NEW CITY HALLS.

they had dropped from the skies upon this insignificant spot. Even the birthplace of Cleeve is involved in mystery, although persistent efforts have been made to discover it. For most readers, however, it is sufficient to know that in 1631 these pioneers were here, evidently preparing to establish themselves permanently upon these unpeopled shores, one of their purposes being traffic with the natives and fishermen frequenting the coast. Cleeve had received from Sir Ferdinando Gorges a promise of land to be located by him on territory not already granted to any person, and had taken possession of territory which had been granted by the council for New England to one Bradshaw, of whose claim he had possessed himself. He therefore felt his tenure of the land he occupied fairly secure, although to make it really so would have required a confirmation of the title to him by the council.

poor and ignorant savages to acquire a knowledge of the true faith, a work which especially commended itself to the king's affection. This scheme, promising as it seemed to be, failed of result. Levett, however, to bring his plans more prominently before the public, prepared and published an account of his voyage to New England and his explorations of its coasts. Shortly after, Buckingham, upon whom he largely relied for support, fell by the knife of an assassin, and troubles with France and Spain recommenced. Three more years passed, during which time we know little of Levett's motions; but in 1630 we find him at Salem welcoming John Endicott to the New World. Shortly after, he sailed for home, and died on the voyage. His patent passed into the hands of Plymouth merchants, to whom he was probably indebted, and the city of York in Casco Bay proved truly to be but the insubstantial fabric of a vision.

In 1631 George Cleeve and his associate, Richard Tucker, had erected a rude habitation at the mouth of the Spurwink River, opposite Richmond's Island. The exact date when they landed here has never been revealed, and from what port they came is still as unknown as if

A few straggling adventurers had begun to make their appearance in the vicinity of their place of settlement: Bagnall at Richmond's Island, Stratton on another island near by, Bonython, Lewis and Vines on the Saco, and Mackworth on the point which still bears his name, at the mouth of the Presumpscot. These were their only neighbors within a radius of a dozen miles or more, unless a few fishermen were plying their toilsome vocation at one or two points in the vicinity which are still the haunts of those who gather their harvest from the sea. All about these pioneers of civilization reigned a silence unbroken save by the voice of bird and beast. On one side, an illimitable expanse of ocean, with no sail to suggest the proximity of human life; on the other, an equally boundless extent of forest. From contemporary accounts we have some knowledge of the incidents common to the daily life of our pioneers. Something new and strange was before their eyes from morn when they were awakened by the clamor of innumerable sea-fowl which crowded the shores of bay, cove

SITE OF THE FIRST HOUSE, RICHMOND'S ISLAND.

and inlet, until nightfall, when the strident notes of these wild choristers gave place to the harsher voices of the wolves, whose sharp barks re-echoed through the gloomy woods. The deer, the moose and the caribou came out into the clearing to browse upon the new grass; wild pigeons settled down upon the tall pines in myriads, bending and breaking the branches with their weight; shoals of seals at flood-tide sought the shore to bask in the sun; and at ebb clumsy bears clambered over the rocks in search of shell-fish.

But Cleeve and Tucker were not to plant themselves permanently upon the banks of the Spurwink. Other work more important, although they did not know it to be so, was to be assigned them. One day a sail appeared in the offing, and was doubtless watched by them with deep interest as it drew near. It proved to be a vessel from home, sent out by Robert Trelawny, a Plymouth merchant, and was in charge of an agent commissioned to take possession of Richmond's Island and the opposite shores, where they had settled. While they were busy building their new home, the enterprising merchant had procured of Gorges a patent of the territory; and they were peremptorily ordered by his agent, John Winter, to vacate the premises, or to become tenants of his master. It would seem as if the generous air from ocean and mountain inspired those who breathed it with the spirit of independence as soon as they landed upon the shores of New England. Cleeve, who had grown to manhood under a government where prerogative was still potent, replied to Winter that "he would be tenant to never a man in New England."

Five days after Winter's arrival, a second vessel arrived with another colonist, Captain Thomas Cammock, who had a patent for land west of the Spurwink, comprising what is now known as Prout's Neck.

The position of Cleeve and Tucker was humiliating. They were but interlopers, and Winter having procured the official aid of Captain Walter Neale, who was in the vicinity, they were promptly served with a notice to quit. It was but a paper notice, however, and Winter was not in a position to employ force. He had come here only to make arrangements for a future settlement, and was to return to England immediately for men and materials to effect this purpose. Needing men to leave in possession until his return, he engaged three fishermen, who were living "in a house at Casko," probably the one erected several years before by Levett, and, placing them in charge of his patron's property, set sail for England in July, leaving Cleeve and Tucker to harvest the crop which they had planted. They, however, well knew that he would return the next

THE CLEEVE MONUMENT.

season with a force sufficient to drive them out; hence they began looking about for a new place of settlement.

Several miles northerly from their present habitation was a neck of land which seemed well adapted to their purpose; and when John Winter returned, March 2, 1633, they were ready to leave the Spurwink and begin again the foundations of a home on the shores of Casco Bay. Leaving Winter in undisputed possession of his employer's rights, Cleeve, with his wife and daughter, his partner and a servant, set out in an open boat for the neck known to the Indians as Machegonne. This neck terminated in a rounded hill crowned with a forest, to the west of which rose another hill, and between them lay a valley, through which coursed a brook to the sea. Near the mouth of this brook the little party landed, and here again began a habitation. A finer site for settlement could not have been found on the entire coast. Between the place where they had broken ground and the opposite shore of Cape Elizabeth was a broad and deep harbor, so shut in from the sea as to afford a safe anchorage for the royal navy. Cleeve's simple dwelling was soon erected, on the southerly slope of the cove, protected by the wooded hill in its rear from the north winds, and looking out upon the harbor and the green shores of Cape Elizabeth.

REV. THOMAS SMITH.

Although Cleeve had again a shelter for his family, with a garden and cornfield about it, he must have been troubled with many anxious thoughts. Like others, he had emigrated to the New World under a promise from the council for New England, or its moving spirit, Gorges, of a grant of land to be selected after arrival in the country from any land not already occupied; besides, a proclamation of the king entitled every man to one hundred and fifty acres of land for himself and for each person whom he should transport thither. He had secured Levett's grant of 1623; but this was a title of doubtful value at that time, and he must have realized that he was liable at any minute to be supplanted by some one with a patent fresh from the seal of the council.

MEETING-HOUSE OF THE FIRST PARISH, 1740–1825.

The details of the disputes concerning his title in which Cleeve became involved, of his difficult trips to England to confer with Gorges, and of his quarrels with Winter and Trelawny it is impossible to give here.

He succeeded, in January, 1636, in procuring from Gorges a patent for fifteen hundred acres of land, comprising the entire neck, which bore the Indian name of Machegonne, but which was changed to Stogomor, in honor of Stogumber, the little village where Tucker was born.

His first act was to obtain the services of Arthur Mackworth, who as the agent of Gorges was to complete his title by delivering him possession of the terri-

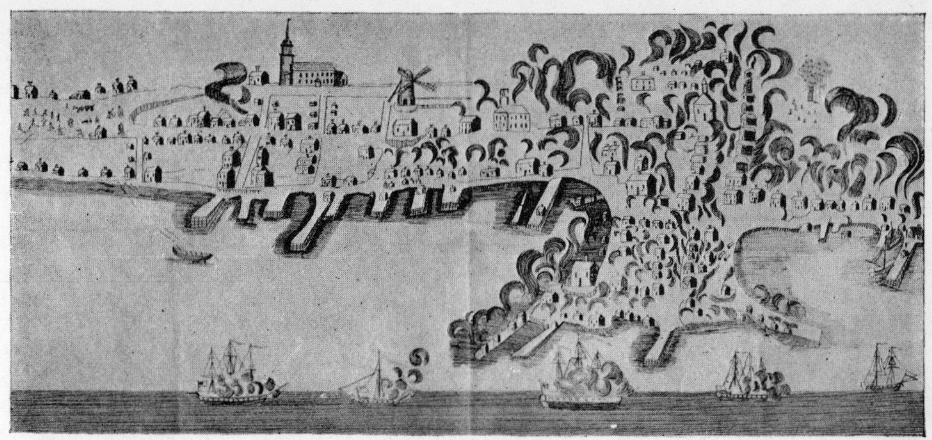

"THE TOWN OF FALMOUTH, BURNT BY CAPTAIN MOET, OCTOBER 18, 1775."

FROM "IMPARTIAL HISTORY OF THE WAR," BOSTON, 1781.

tory. This formal act was accomplished in the presence of several of Cleeve's neighbors on the eighth of June.

Cleeve had other enemies than Winter and Trelawny, who were active in placing him before the eyes of Gorges in unfavorable light; and in this they so far succeeded as to call forth a letter from the Lord Proprietor to Henry Vane, Winthrop and other magistrates, requesting them to interfere in the controversy. But Vane had already sailed for England, and Winthrop with his usual sagacity refrained from involving himself in the affairs of his neighbors. Cleeve, however, must have felt that his position, which had appeared so strong upon his first return from England, had become insecure, for his enemies were influential, and he well knew what such influence could accomplish.

The year following that in which Cleeve reached home was marked by many events. Emigration was active, and new settlers were rapidly finding their way to Stogomor, where they received a warm welcome from the patentees, who were glad to grant lands to them upon almost any terms. Among those who came into the vicinity was John Josselyn, the genial author, then fresh from his studies, who accompanied his aged father, Sir Thomas, to visit his brother Henry at Black Point. From him we get many interesting glimpses into the life of that period, which, in spite of the hard conditions surrounding the people, was often spiced with conviviality. Josselyn describes to us a merry evening passed at Cammock's house, at which Michael Mitton, who had recently married Elizabeth Cleeve, was present. Josselyn, was in western parlance, a "tender-foot," and Mitton and Cammock imposed upon the credulity of the new-comer by the relation of marvellous tales, which were evidently taken seriously by the verdant young Englishman.

PORTLAND, FROM THE HARBOR.

Intoxicating liquors formed one of the chief articles of import; and Richmond's Island became the centre of the traffic. Trelawny's ships brought, in exchange for the furs, fish and other products of the vicinity, Spanish wines and various more powerful intoxicants, greatly to the demoralization of the colonists, and especially to the injury of the Indians, who would part with all they possessed to obtain the coveted fire-water. Although this traffic did not touch the public conscience, in fact as a moral question received no consideration whatever even with the best men among the colonists, its deadly effects could not fail to arouse attention, and it was deemed necessary for the preservation of society to pass laws regulating it as soon as courts were established in the country.

PORTLAND HEAD LIGHT.

Religion, although not regarded as the mainspring of social order to the degree that it was in Boston, was nevertheless not neglected in Maine; and the early comers to Stogomor could, if they chose, occasionally receive religious instruction from Richard Gibson, a young Episcopal clergyman, whom Trelawny had sent in 1635 to minister to the spiritual needs of his colony at Richmond's Island and Cape Elizabeth. There was no settled religious feeling among the new settlers. Nominally the principal portion of them belonged to the Church of England; and this fact, with the natural feeling always entertained toward a strong rival, kept alive a sentiment of opposition to Puritan Massachusetts, whose influence, owing to the wise management of Winthrop and his able associates, was rapidly making itself felt among the little settlements along the coast. Massachusetts realized its growing strength and the necessity as well as the duty of establishing as widely as possible its authority and discipline, if it would permanently maintain its supremacy. Its northeastern boundary was still undetermined, but it was evident that a strict legal interpretation of its charter would carry it far enough to include a considerable portion of the province of Maine.

Gorges had been censured by impracticable zealots for making his province the asylum of dissenters, and to quiet their clamor he undertook to set up the forms of ecclesiastical government in his possessions. An elaborate plan was formulated, and numerous officers chosen to put it into operation, a proceeding which he doubtless feared Massachusetts would not regard with favor. At the first court set up under the new government, Vines, Godfrey and Winter appeared as litigants against Cleeve, who in turn pressed claims against his inveterate enemy Winter for dispossessing him of his property on the Spurwink and disturbing him in his possession of Stogomor. Cleeve's position, without money or influential friends in England, grew desperate, and he would soon have succumbed but for political troubles in England. In 1642 came the

FORT PREBLE.

FORT SCAMMEL.

FORT GORGES.

great Civil War, and Trelawny, Winter's powerful protector, was thrown into prison, where he soon died.

Seeing now an opportunity to strengthen his position, Cleeve again set out for England, where he succeeded in gaining the attention of Sir Alexander Rigby, a powerful parliamentarian, whom he induced to purchase a dormant title to the province of Ligonia, which comprised territory forty miles square between and including Cape Elizabeth and Cape Porpoise; and in the early autumn of 1643, with his commission of deputy governor of the province in his hand, he appeared, to the consternation of his enemies, at Stogomor, or Casco, as it was familiarly called. The royal or Gorges party were not disposed to yield gracefully to the new order; and Richard Vines, the founder of Biddeford, was chosen by them deputy governor. For three years there was a conflict of authority between Cleeve and Vines, when it was brought to an end by the decision of the Commissioners of Plantations in England, which sustained the claim of Rigby, and Cleeve assumed full sway in the province. Trelawny had died, Gorges and Winter soon followed, and it seemed for a few years as if the troubles of Cleeve were ended. Under his management the town of Casco began to assume importance, when in the summer of 1650 Rigby, his patron, died. Again Cleeve took the long journey across the ocean, and the affairs of the town were thrown into confusion.

At this juncture, Massachusetts having defined her eastern boundary, Casco was brought within the jurisdiction of that colony, and Cleeve upon his return found new troubles awaiting him. A conflict of authority ensued, which continued until 1658, when Massachusetts triumphed and Casco with adjoining territory was organized into a new town under the name of Falmouth. From this time we hear little of the original proprietor of the thriving settlement on "the neck." His brief power had passed away, and death soon found him, a broken-down and poverty-stricken man. But Falmouth continued to thrive, in spite of the rival claim of Massachusetts and the heirs of the former Lord Proprietor, Gorges. Its greatest danger was from the savages, who regarded the settlers with distrust and aversion, which were encouraged by French emissaries; indeed so threatening was this danger that Massachusetts

THE DRAW. MARINE HOSPITAL IN THE DISTANCE.

felt obliged to pass a law that every man should "take to meeting on Lord's days his arms with him with at least five charges of powder and shot." In 1676 the fears of the people of Falmouth were realized by an attack of the savages upon the town, destroying it and dispersing those of its inhabitants who were happy enough to escape their fury.

THE UNION STATION, FROM THE WESTERN PROMENADE.

With the establishment of peace the scattered inhabitants returned one by one, and with the aid of new settlers began relaying the foundations of Falmouth. The growth, however, was slow. The savages were feared, and their frequent outbreaks rendered life and property insecure; hence most of the dwellings were clustered about Fort Loyal, which was near the site of the present Grand Trunk Railroad station. In the autumn of 1689 the savages made an attack upon Brackett's farm, and killed a number of persons. The next spring, with their French allies, they attacked the fort and captured it, making prisoners of the people in it, and again destroyed the settlement.

In 1716 there were but fifteen men on the neck; but its superior position soon began to attract settlers, and in 1718 the town was incorporated under its former title of Falmouth. The savages, however, instigated by the French, continued to threaten the stability of Maine settlements. This retarded the growth of the place. But in 1725 a treaty of peace was ratified at Falmouth, the result of a vigorous war, in which Norridgewock was destroyed and the savages of Pequawket driven to take refuge with the French in Canada. At this time the town numbered fifty-six families, according to the Rev. Thomas Smith, upon whose invaluable journal we are obliged to rely for particulars of the history of the time. It presents to us most vividly the most notable persons of the period; the visits of the royal governors to the town;

CUSTOM HOUSE.

AMONG THE WHARVES.

the sessions of the courts; the conferences with the savages; wars and rumors of wars; in fact a most satisfactory picture of the town, its people and their fortunes, for a period of more than a half a century, — a picture which cannot be better painted, and which all should study who are interested in New England history.

In 1740 the church known as the First Parish Church was erected for Parson Smith; and in this he labored through a

THE PUBLIC LIBRARY AND HISTORICAL SOCIETY ROOMS.

long life to improve the spiritual condition of the people. His life was passed amid stirring scenes. Wars and rumors of wars kept the people in a constant state of agitation. The siege and capture of Louisburg in 1745, its surrender to France and subsequent recapture, and the fall of Quebec in 1759 were some of the incidents of the period; and Smith was preaching when, in October, 1775, Captain Mowat's fleet appeared in the harbor and bombarded the town, causing its destruction for the third time. The Rev. Jacob Bailey, who was an eye-witness of this affair, gives the following graphic account of it:

"The morning was clear, calm and pleasant, without a breath of wind, and the town was crowded with people and carts from the country to assist in removing the goods and furniture of the inhabitants. . . . At length the fatal hour arrived. At exactly half an hour after nine the flag was hoisted to the top of the mast, and the cannon began to roar with incessant and tremendous fury. The streets were full of people, oxen and horses. The oxen, terrified at the smoke and report of the guns, ran with precipitation over the rocks, dashing everything to pieces and scattering large quantities of goods about the streets. And now a scene inexpressibly grand and terrible was exhibited in view of thousands of spectators. Bombs and carcasses, armed with destruction and streaming with fire, blazed dreadfully through the air and descended with flaming vengeance on the defenceless buildings. It was impossible for persons of sensibility and reflection to behold the mingled multitude without emotion, — to see the necessitous and affluent, the gentleman and mechanic, the master and servant, the mistress and maid, reduced to the same undistinguished level. Those ladies who had been educated in all the softness of ease and indulgence, who had been used to the most delicate treatment, and never ventured out of town without an equipage and proper attendants, were now constrained to travel several miles on foot to seek a shelter from the cold and tempest. About three quarters of the town was consumed, and between two and three hundred families, who twenty-four hours before enjoyed in tranquillity their commodious habitations, were now in many instances destitute of shelter for themselves and families; and as a tedious winter was approaching, they had before them a most gloomy and distressing prospect."

THE LONGFELLOW STATUE.

Though Mowat may have acted under orders from his superior, Admiral Graves, it will be a long time before he will be forgiven by Portland people for his share in this wanton destruction of the town. Parson Smith himself found shelter in Gorham, where some of his descendants still live. Many relics of this notable man are still in existence, and are carefully treasured by their fortunate possessors.

But the town was again to arise from its ashes; and a few years after peace was declared it began to assume an air of importance. Parson Smith's old church escaped destruction, and had become a somewhat venerable structure when, in 1787, a second parish was organized, and a church erected on the corner of Middle and Deer Streets. In the same year an Episcopal church was erected, called St. Paul's, on the corner of Middle and Church Streets; all of which made the good Parson Smith exclaim: "Poor Portland is plunging into ruinous confusion." Only the year before he had presided at the christening of Portland, that part of Falmouth known as the Neck having had that name bestowed upon it in 1786.

From this time the business of Portland began to increase, until troubles with England resulted in the Embargo, which gave a death blow to foreign commerce. The vessels which had brought wealth to Portland merchants tugged at their rusty chains in the harbor or chafed their weather-stained timbers against the deserted wharves, and many an opulent citizen saw the savings of a lifetime rapidly disappear.

In 1812 came the war with England, and Portland became a theatre of activity. Military companies were formed, fortifications for defence erected, and privateers armed and sent forth to make reprisals upon the enemy. These privateers wrought great havoc among British merchantmen, and when they came into port with their prizes, the victors were welcomed vociferously and feted to their hearts' content by the enthusiastic citizens.

THE POST OFFICE.

The most noted event, however, which occurred was the battle between the *Enterprise* and *Boxer*, which was fought September 5, 1813, inside of the island of Monhegan. The vessels, although nearly forty miles distant, could be seen from the observatory with a spy-glass, and the keeper when he saw the battle going on communicated the news to the excited crowd below. Although no one could see the vessels from the observatory with the naked eye, an aged gentleman, who was a lad at the time of the battle and in the crowd on Munjoy, gave an account of the event a few years ago in a manner to convey to the hearer the idea that he heard the guns and saw the vessels engaged, so deep an impression did the repetition of what the lookout saw from the observatory make upon his youthful imagination.

In this battle both commanders exhibited heroic qualities, and both were killed. Blyth, the British commander, nailed his colors to the mast, and Burrows, while lying mortally wounded upon the deck of the *Enterprise*, ordered that his flag should never be struck. The vessels were brought into Portland harbor with their dead commanders, who were buried side by side in the old cemetery, where their tombs are objects of ever increasing interest to those who visit the Forest City.

Although Portland did not suffer directly from the war, her business was almost annihilated; yet she slowly recovered from its effects. In 1819, when the separation between Maine and Massachusetts took place, Portland was regarded as the proper capital of the new state. A state house was erected where the city building now stands; and here the state legislature held its annual sessions until 1831, when it removed to Augusta, somewhat to the chagrin of the citizens of Portland, who still feel that their beautiful city, from her commanding position and ease of access from all parts of the state by rail and water, should be the capital of the state.

MIDDLE STREET.

CONGRESS STREET.

One of the most noteworthy enterprises of the

LONGFELLOW'S BIRTHPLACE.

people of Portland was the building of the Atlantic and St. Lawrence Railroad. It was a great undertaking, and but for the energy and ability of Portland men would not have been built. The building too of the Portland and Ogdensburg Railroad, through the notch of the White Mountains, was a Portland enterprise. The men who labored with heroic zeal to open these grand avenues of traffic between the seaboard and the producing centres of the West should ever be held in grateful remembrance by the people of Portland.

Among those who led in the construction of the Atlantic and St. Lawrence Railroad were John A. Poor, William Pitt Preble and Josiah P. Little, who made themselves conspicuous in the enterprise by their untiring efforts in its behalf. The first was a man of great breadth of intellect, a genius whose dreams were all too splendid for complete realization. Such men are, however, among the world's benefactors. It may not be possible for clumsy hands to reproduce the airy fabrics which they so deftly construct, but they may imitate them in some degree and so make practical what else might never have been attempted. The breaking of ground at the Atlantic end of the line was a great event to Portland citizens.

PORTLAND YACHT CLUB HOUSE.

Preble, with a shovel especially made for the purpose, which was the admiration of the town for several days before, threw up the first clod of earth amid the enthusiastic plaudits of the thousands assembled to witness the beginning of the work. He was a prominent lawyer, and lived to an advanced age. Little, who was as able, but of less conspicuous talents, died comparatively young.

THE LONGFELLOW MANSION.

Every great enterprise has its leader; and as the Atlantic and St. Lawrence Railroad had its Poor, so the Portland and Ogdensburg had its Anderson. But for General Samuel J. Anderson, assisted by his brother, the late John F. Anderson, by whose engineering skill the road was carried through the notch of the White Mountains, Portland would not to-day possess this valuable avenue of traffic.

Portland has been prolific of men conspicuous for ability in every walk of life, men who would have made themselves leaders in any community and under any conditions. Though not a native of Portland, Chief Justice Mellen resided here during the better part of his life. His brilliant son, Grenville Mellen, whose early promise of poetic fame failed of fulfilment, is still held in pleasant remembrance by the older citizens. Portland was also the native home of that erratic genius, John Neal, an American of Americans, whose "fierce gray bird with a startling shriek" made his name famous for a season the world over. Although exceedingly passionate, he was a most polished gentleman, and prided himself in the gentle accomplishment of fencing. The surprising dexterity with which he delivered flanconade and carte over the arm cannot be forgotten by any one who witnessed it. N. P. Willis was also born here, and some of his best work was done amid the congenial surroundings of Casco Bay. Here, too, resided William Willis, the historian, and his successor, William Goold, Seba and Elizabeth Oaks Smith, and Henry W. Longfellow, whose name is immortal.

EVERGREEN CEMETERY.

Longfellow loved Portland beyond any spot on earth, and never tired of her shady streets, her old wharves, and Deering's Woods, of which he so pleasantly sang. The house on Fore Street, where he was born, is visited every year by throngs of tourists. It is still in a fair state of preservation, but the locality where it stands in severe dignity has deteriorated since Longfellow's father lived in it, and now looks unkempt and slovenly. Longfellow, when in Portland, lived in the house known as the Longfellow house, on Congress Street, which is often mistaken for his birthplace. Here it was that he passed his youth, and the house is more intimately associated with him than the one in which he was born. This house, it is understood, will eventually come into the possession of the Maine Historical Society and be preserved as a memorial of the poet.

No citizen of Portland, excepting Longfellow, has a wider celebrity than William Pitt Fessenden. Not only was he eminent as a lawyer, but as a statesman he achieved well-merited fame. No one ever hated shams more than Fessenden. He never learned the arts of the politician, and achieved political success by sheer force of intellect. In debate he was the opposite of Charles Sumner, his *confrère* in the United States Senate, whose ornate oratory was distasteful to him. Nor did Sumner sympathize with the Portland statesman, whose trenchant logic made him shiver; hence there was not that friendship between them which ought to have existed between such noble men. Sumner regarded Fessenden as cold and cynical, while Fessenden regarded Sumner as a literary coxcomb, who would have found a more appropriate field for the exercise of his talents in Utopia than in the United States Senate. As a matter of fact, both were mistaken in their estimate of each other. Fessenden, in spite of his cold exterior, was kindly and sympathetic, a close student, and honest to the core. Sumner possessed the same admirable qualities; and had the men known each other more intimately, they might have been warm friends, as they should have been.

WILLISTON CHURCH.

Although it is not intended to speak here of living citizens of Portland, two exceptions may be permitted. Everybody is familiar with the name of Neal Dow, the author of the Maine Law, so called. General Dow is now upwards of ninety years of age, but is still hale and hearty, and apparently as capable of delivering telling blows at the monster Intemperance as ever. He is a most aggressive man, but only aggressive against wrong. Socially no man is more genial and sympathetic. He is an admirable story-teller and full of interesting reminiscences, which he relates with a charming simplicity and directness.

Of Thomas B. Reed, who is the other living citizen in whose favor an exception is here made, it may be truly said that he is a Portlander *a capite ad calcem*. Mr. Reed is a descendant of George

THE DEERING OAKS.

ON THE WESTERN PROMENADE. THE MAINE GENERAL HOSPITAL.

Cleeve, the founder of Portland; he played in Portland's streets when a child, in youth was educated in her public schools, and almost upon attaining manhood was her chosen representative in the legislature of the state, and later in the councils of the nation. He is as loyal to Portland as Portland is to him, and both are proud of each other.

In 1866 occurred the great fire, which laid a large portion of the city again in ashes. The loss wrought by this terrible conflagration can never be wholly repaired. Ancient documents, invaluable to the historian, priceless heirlooms, which had come down through many generations, rare books, the spoil of patient book hunters, all were swept away, with the ancestral homes of many happy families. But the people of Portland were not discouraged, and under the exhilaration which great loss often occasions they sprang to the task of rebuilding the town before the fires had died out, and within two years the city was practically rebuilt and the wheels of business were again prosperously revolving.

Up to this time the principal trade of Portland had been with the West Indies. Longfellow has sung how, standing on the wharves of the old town, he saw

> "The Spanish sailors with bearded lips,
> And the beauty and mystery of the ships,
> And the magic of the sea."

The West India trade of Portland, however, like the East India trade of Salem, has dwindled away, until now it is but one among many kinds of business carried on by her enterprising merchants.

While Portland is well situated for many kinds of manufacturing industries requiring small plants, it can never become a large manufacturing centre. A commercial and residential city, however, is the best kind of a city, and this is what Portland is to be. Hence to extend her commerce and to make her attractive for residents will be the aim of her citizens. The latter can be accomplished by beautifying and adorning her streets and by enlarging and im-

VIEW FROM THE OTTAWA.
THE OTTAWA, CUSHING'S ISLAND.

FIRST PARISH CHURCH.

proving her park system as far as possible.

That we have entered upon an era of park building in America there can be no doubt, for we see evidences of it on every side; indeed it is generally admitted that no city with any claim to enterprise is worthy of existence which does not provide its inhabitants with generous park privileges. It has been well said that a man may as well do without lungs as a city without parks. Nor are parks now built for the rich alone, as in bygone times, but for the poor also, who are confined a large portion of their lives within narrow limits, and to whom an opportunity, however brief, to breathe pure air and enjoy the beauty of green lawns and umbrageous walks is a boon of incalculable value. Hence parks are built in the poorest localities, like the Charles River Embankment in Boston. Here a few years ago for nearly half a mile extended a dilapidated row of old buildings in the midst of heaps of filth alike offensive and dangerous to all who had to be near them. Could this polluted piece of earth ever be converted into verdant lawns and umbrageous paths — this hades of ash heaps and tin cans and innumerable forms of dirtiness, into a paradise of bloom and beauty? It demanded the vision of a seer to forecast for it such a bright destiny; but inspired with something akin to faith the work was begun, — and, presto! an Eden where before was a desert waste. On her park system Boston has already expended over ten millions, and probably it will require as much more to complete it. A wiser expenditure of money was never made by any American city, and she is already reaping the benefit of her enterprise and liberality. Portland will be wise to follow her example; and as she possesses great natural advantages, she can do so with a good prospect of success.

DIAMOND ISLAND.

LINCOLN PARK.

Up to the fire of 1866 Portland possessed no park; but then, during a period of great suffering, when the demands upon her citizens were all too great to be satisfied, the city council was wise enough and broad enough to purchase and set apart for public use a park in the midst of the burnt district. It was a commendable undertaking, and furnished one of the best exhibitions of wise enterprise which Portland has ever made. This park was named for our martyred President, Lincoln. The benefit which the public derived from the opening of Lincoln Park awakened popular interest in public grounds. Deering's Woods, the haunt of Portland's youth for generations, whose beauties Longfellow had embalmed in poetic memories, were regarded by all as most suitable for park purposes. These extensive grounds, so near the best residential portion of the city, were valuable for building purposes; and the severe loss which the people had sustained from the great fire rendered the immediate acquisition of the woods impracticable. This was fully realized by the Deering heirs, who with commendable generosity conveyed them to the city. Under the wise administration of the Park Commission, whose chairman, Mr. A. W. Smith, has devoted himself personally to their development, Deering's Woods have become a park in which the citizens of Portland take a commendable pride. Here they take the strangers who visit the city, and in the shadows of the ancient oaks repeat to them the familiar lines of Longfellow's "My Lost Youth:"

"And Deering's Woods are fresh and fair,
And with joy that is almost pain
My heart goes back to wander there,

STATE STREET.

And among the dreams of the days that were
I find my lost youth again.
And the strange and beautiful song,
The groves are repeating it still:
'A boy's will is the wind's will,
And the thoughts of youth are long, long thoughts.'"

That no one may forget these lines they have been inscribed upon a table of stone

A FOREGLIMPSE OF THE ENTRANCE TO THE NEW PARK.

over the fireplace in the picturesque shelter near the entrance.

The city of Portland, occupying as it does a point of land extending into the waters of Casco Bay, would, if the land were level and but slightly elevated, be favorably situated for residence; but with a considerable eminence at either extremity, from which extensive views may be had of the country and White Mountains to the west and north, and the island-dotted waters of Casco Bay and the Cape Elizabeth shore to the east and south, it is more beautifully situated for a residential city than any other on the Atlantic coast. The people of Portland have not been slow to recognize the beauties of their surroundings and the capabilities which they afford for improvement; they have therefore begun a

AS IT MAY BE IN THE PROPOSED PARK.

system of improvements upon the two hills, Munjoy and Bramhall's, over whose summits and slopes, with the intervening valley, their city has spread itself. Partially encircling each of these hills a broad driveway has been laid out, which when adorned with trees and shrubbery will be extremely attractive.

Although much has been done in improving these two promenades, much remains to be accomplished. Adjoining lands are to be acquired, and arbor ways and outlooks created, such as landscape architects now so artistically fashion. From the Bramhall promenade, upon which the landscape gardener has done some modest but commendable work, a beautiful strip of country is spread before the visitor. Not only does the eye rest delightedly upon outlying hamlets and villages, green fields, wide woodlands and gleaming waters; but when the atmosphere is clear, upon the White Mountains, nearly a hundred miles distant, whose lofty slopes beaming in the sunlight reveal the reason why the savages so aptly named them the crystal hills and believed them to be the abode of spirits, the happy hunting grounds which they hoped finally to attain.

From the eastern promenade an entirely different view is obtained. From Fort Allen Park, a small park laid out on the southern extremity of Munjoy, we may look out over the waters of Casco Bay to the gleaming waters of the Atlantic dotted with innumerable sails, or may glance directly down upon the harbor, where "commerce plies its busy trade," and watch the ships unloading at the wharves and steamers and vessels with outspread sails moving here and there; or may follow the Cape Elizabeth shore, taking in the forts and lighthouses and ever increasing lines of summer cottages, around to the islands which Christopher Levett, nearly two and three quarters centuries agone, looked upon and thought worthy to describe to his noble patrons in England, — namely, House, Cushing's, Peak's and Diamond, now adorned with summer cottages, as alluring to those who draw near their charming shores as the Hesperides of which the poets have sung so persistently, but which were not a whit more beautiful than these "gems of Casco Bay." Or one may pass round toward the north and delightedly follow the panorama of sea and island to the cove-indented shores of old Falmouth, as beautiful a scene as may be found in this world of beauty.

On the side of Munjoy looking down upon the city is another small park called Fort Sumner Park, which affords a bird's-eye view of the city, of great beauty. Standing here and looking over the scene, one is impressed more than anywhere else with the wonderful beauty of situation possessed by Portland. To the south and east lies Casco Bay with its

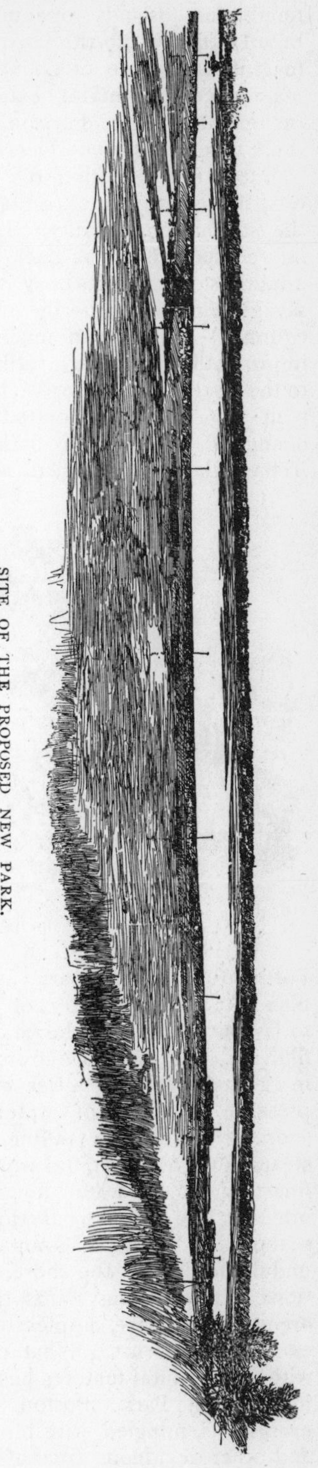

SITE OF THE PROPOSED NEW PARK.

numberless islands opening into the broad Atlantic; to the north and west, a magnificent sweep of country walled by magnificent mountains extending along the entire western horizon. Nearer lie the "breezy domes of Deering's woods."

But in this direction the eye encounters, if the tide be out, a blot which mars the surrounding beauty. It is the ill-odored spot known as Back Bay. It was doubtless owing to its oozy waste that the savages came to name the neck "Machegonne" — a place of much slime. To improve this foul place, alike dangerous to the health and offensive to the eye, a plan has been elaborated which will change it into a water park, and which, if the scheme is carried out, will give Portland a unique park system. The plan is to dam the waters of the bay and to lay out around its shores a park. By filling a short distance from high-water mark and building a sea-wall so as to preserve a depth of water about the shores sufficient for sailing yachts and steam launches, Portland will possess the finest sheet of water for regattas and other marine sports to be found on the seaboard. Taking advantage of the undulating line of the shore, its indentations and projecting points, the landscape architect will have ample scope for the exercise of his art. What can be done with such natural features has been shown in Franklin Park, Boston. Groups of evergreens, mingled with birches, willows and other deciduous trees of light foliage, intermingled with clumps of flowering shrubbery, will change one of these points, now covered with rank grass, into a paradise. Here rustic shelters may be erected and refectories maintained for the convenience and pleasure of visitors, and mazy paths amid sheltering shrubbery take the place of muddy creeks. Back a short distance from the water line, a broad corso for carriages may be laid out, commanding an uninterrupted view of the water from all points around the shore. Separated from this carriage road by trees and shrubbery, amid which paths and arbor ways for pedestrians may be constructed similar to those in the arboretum and other parts of the Franklin Park system, it is proposed to lay out an equestrian way, which can be made one of the most attractive features of the park.

BASIN, NEW PARK.

The high ground which surrounds the Back Bay, and which is now of insignificant value, will afford hundreds of fine building sites and make this the most attractive portion of the Back Bay region. With this park completed and connected with the promenades and Deering's Oaks, Portland and its suburbs will offer advantages for residence unequalled by any city in New England. Indeed, it is becoming every year more and more sought by summer tourists on account of its situation on the sea. A fleet of pleasure steamers afford the summer resident water excursions in every direction. One may skirt the rockbound shores of Cape Elizabeth, visit the numerous islands in the bay, trace the romantic coves and headlands of old Falmouth, or take a farther flight to Harpswell or the storied Orr's Island, within the compass of a few hours. When Portland shall have completed her park system, adorning herself within as she is already adorned without, no city on the continent will match her as a residential city.

A Summer in Nantucket (1860)

A SUMMER IN NANTUCKET

Illustrated by Porte Crayon

DISMANTLED.

It is an Ancient Mariner,
And he stoppeth one of three:
"By thy long gray beard and glittering eye
Now wherefore stopp'st thou me?"
* * * * * * *
He holds him with his skinny hand:—
"There was a ship," quoth he.

COLERIDGE.

ON entering the harbor of Nantucket one is impressed on every hand by the signs of decadence. A few battered and dismantled hulks of whale ships sleep alongside the lethargic old wharves; quiet, listless seeming people saunter about with an aimless air very uncommon in New England; grass-grown streets and dingy warehouses all combine to complete the picture of departed glory.—No, not of departed glory: I mean, simply, "of decadent commercial prosperity;" for the fame of Nantucket is historic, and the glory of having given birth to the boldest and most enterprising mariners that ever furrowed the seas is hers, imperishable and forever.

Of all the attributes of man that which should always command our most unreserved regard is simple manhood; and I must confess that, when I entered the precincts of this island-city, I experienced very much the same sort of feeling as when for the first time I passed the gates of

Imperial Rome. Here, I thought, are the familiar haunts of men who have hunted over the aqueous globe and despoiled the deep of its living wealth, who have striven face to face with mighty leviathans and driven them from sea to sea, and from pole to pole, smiting and destroying, enriching commerce, illuminating the darkness of the world. Before Nantucket we had pine knots and tallow; since Nantucket we have camphene and kerosene: representatives of lusty barbarism and an overstrained and diseased civilization. For the golden age of reason, the true and healthful light of convenience and common sense, commend me to the days of the great *Physeter macrocephalus*.

A rapid sail over salt-water, if it does not prove an emetic, is a famous stomachic tonic; and so we made no unreasonable delay sentimentalizing over the homes of the Vikings, but made our way to the Ocean House, where we dined and reposed. Later in the afternoon we went a strolling at our leisure to see whatever was to be seen. The town of Nantucket contains near seven thousand inhabitants, and in its general features resembles New Bedford, being at the same time smaller, older, more quiet, and less wealthy. Of her ancient mariners, indeed, we saw few; but their wives and children seemed numerous enough. One can not but remark the great preponderance of women and children in the visible population of the place; and this circumstance gives to the streets and thoroughfares in the interior of the town a more cheerful and home-like air. Inquiring for the cause of this disparity in the sexes, your response is found in the old song of The Sea:

"The sea has one and all,
Fathers, brothers, sons, and lovers."

In addition, a few years since, the California fever swept the island with a virulence more fatal than war and pestilence combined. It is estimated that Nantucket lost some six or eight hundred men by that epidemic. At night there was music in the Public Place, and observing the crowd collected to hear it, I judged that at least four-fifths were women.

A STRANGE GENTLEMAN.

As the morning after our arrival was delightfully fair and fresh, we, by the advice of an acquaintance at the hotel, determined to drive over to Siasconsett, the Newport of the Nantuckoise. Our buggy appeared like all the other craft we saw, a little the worse for time and use; but by the judicious adaptation of some straps, buckles, and a silk handkerchief, we managed to make her sea-worthy—sand-worthy I should have said, for having cleared the town we found our road a plain track of loose sand, through an open country, scantily clothed with grass, weeds, and low shrubs, and totally destitute both of trees and inclosures. Some browsing cattle, sheep, and horses—to say nothing of sand-flies—gave life to this dreary landscape; and several lonely and poor-looking farm-houses in the distance showed that agriculture was not altogether ignored.

A drive of eight miles brought us to Siasconsett, situated on the southeast part of the island. The old town, which resembles a group of hen-houses, about fifty in number and compactly built, occupies a level grass-plot, immediately on the brink of a sand cliff facing the open ocean. Formerly the cod fishery was actively prosecuted here; but of late years the trade has dwindled into insignificance, and consequently the place retains but a very small permanent population. In recompense, it has become a favorite summer resort for the town folks and strangers who visit the country. For the accommodation of these seekers of health and relaxation a new suburb has arisen which totally eclipses the fishing hamlet in size and appearance. There are a number of pretty private cottages and a neat hotel, none of which, however, were occupied at the time of our visit.

As we saw no one of whom to inquire concerning the premises, we drove on slowly until the road seemed to run out; and we turned into a narrow grass-covered way, which, like the streets of Genoa, seemed to have been laid off without any reference to horses and carriages. Dick remarked that we would get tangled up among these blasted turkey-houses, and would not be able to get out without driving over some of them. I persevered, notwithstanding, until we were presently brought up against the village pump. Our shouts opened the door of a tenement near at hand, from whence an old cripple issued, and, shuffling toward us with great eagerness, offered to take our horse. We yielded the reins readily, and inquired if there was a house of entertainment in the place.

"Certainly," said he; "jist you go in there (indicating the low door from which he had sallied), and Mistress Cary will entertain you as nice as need be."

We entered and found ourselves in a cuddy, measuring about eight by ten, which, in addition to its capacity as public reception room of the hotel, seemed to serve also as a general storehouse of groceries, provisions, and fancy goods of varied character. By a cursory glance I was enabled to inventory a portion of the contents, as follows: Dried codfish, bottled beer, sugar-candy, fishing lines and hooks, eggs, whisky, ginger-cakes, opodeldoc, pork, cigars, cheese, Radway's Ready Relief, tobacco, ship biscuit, Pain Killer, jack-knives, lucifer-matches, and jewelry.

The prospect was not so bad. The house was well provisioned at least; as tidy as could be expected under the circumstances; and, besides, the most delicate olfactories could not have detected the slightest smell of any kind, except dried codfish: but if folks are squeamish on this or other subjects, they had better stay at home, and be content to do their traveling through *Harper's Magazine*. As no one appeared to receive us, Dick thumped upon the glass case that contained the fancy goods, jewelry, and ginger-cakes, and forthwith from a side door entered a little old woman with a mothery vinegar aspect, who saluted us sharply with,

"Well, what have ye got to sell?"

"Nothing at all," replied Dick, depositing upon a chair the knapsack which contained our baggage.

"Then," quoth she, "take your traps and tramp."

"Madam," said I, with mildness, yet assuming some dignity of manner, "we are strangers who have come a-pleasuring to this famous place, and have been informed that you could entertain us for the day, perhaps."

MOTHER CARY.

"Oh, that's it, is it? That's quite another thing. Set down, Sirs, and rest yourselves, and we'll see what we can do for you."

The old woman looked mollified; but to remove the disadvantageous impression that we were pedestrians, I continued,

"Our horse and carriage, Madam, has been attended to by your husband."

"My husband!" exclaimed Mother Cary. "My husband?"

"Madam, I allude to the lame gentleman who took our horse and promised to have him fed."

Our hostess stood for a moment speechless, as if undecided whether she should put me to death *à la basilisk*, or annihilate me with a package of codfish which lay near at hand. At length she shrieked out, like an angered sea-gull,

"My *husband*, did you say? *gentleman*, did you call him?—that creature that I hired from the alms-house to attend to people's horses! I guess your eye-sight is not very good, Sir, or you must be strangers in this country. I am Mistress Elizabeth Cary, at your service. My husband! faugh! I thank God I'm not that low yet!"

And in high disdain she flounced out of the room.

"Cousin Bob," said Dick, in a cautious whisper, "I think it quite lucky for the poor old hostler that he is only her hireling."

"True, Dick. Old, a cripple, and a pauper—yet he is not her husband. God tempers the wind to the shorn lamb."

Presently Mother Cary re-entered, clothed in calm dignity and severe politeness, with the addition of a high white turban and a glistering black silk gown.

We bowed until our heads nearly touched the floor. "Madam," I said, "excuse the absurd and awkward mistake I made just now."

"It's of no consequence," she answered, with the slightest trace of acrimony. "I mistook you for a couple of gimcrack peddlers; but it seems neither of us was very sharp-sighted. I hope we'll get better acquainted. What's your orders?"

Having ascertained that we could procure a fishing-boat, the hostler was sent to call the boatman, and we proceeded to order liberally; bottles of porter, ship biscuit, cheese, boiled eggs, and divers articles of fishing tackle, until our bill amounted to a round sum. The clink of the solid coin upon the counter effectually smoothed the wrinkles from the amiable mother's countenance, and just then the boatman entered, accompanied by an assistant.

Bluefishing was to be the sport, and the big boat was to be launched. Where every body is willing, arrangements are soon made. Our boatman's name was Coffin too, and to sail in company with one of the Coffins of Nantucket is something for a landsman; consequently drinks were proposed. In a twinkling Madam produced a bottle of her best whisky—I don't drink whisky myself, but shammed for politeness' sake; but Dick, who scorns all humbug in such matters, pronounced the liquor good, ordered a repetition, and pressed a glass on our worthy hostess.

By this time she had become radiant.

"I like to deal with liberal-minded, polite gentlemen," quoth she.

"Then," said Dick, "your visitors during the summer are not always of that stamp?"

"I guess not," she replied, with a scornful toss. "Why, there are people that come here who would spend the day skinning a clam rather than pay five cents for a good dinner."

"It's abominable that people should be so stingy," cried Dick, slapping the old woman on the back.

She returned the salute with a confidential poke in the ribs. "To be sure, young man, they're your half-cut people—trash; but for a gentleman, I can tell one as far as I can see him."

Dick helped Mother Cary a second time.

"Young man," quoth she, "I don't know where you came from nor who you are, but it's plain to see you've been bred a gentleman."

"Come," said I, "the bluefish are waiting for us; let's be off." And so we started for the beach.

"I wish ye good sport, gentlemen," screeched Mother Cary. "Your horse shall be well attended to, and any thing I have in the house is at your service."

With the assistance of half a dozen fishermen the sail-boat was launched, and we started on our cruise. Unfortunately for our anticipated sport, the breeze failed us entirely. To remedy this we tried the oars; but so stout a craft, with but two oarsmen, made so little progress that we were obliged to abandon the hope of trailing, and forced to adopt another mode of fishing practiced here. This is done by throwing the leaded hook to as great a distance as possible, and then drawing it home with sufficient rapidity to keep the bait afloat. A skillful hand will throw out two hundred feet of line, by whirling the lead rapidly round the fore finger and letting go at the proper time; and in drawing it home will lay his line in a clean coil, ready to repeat the throw the instant that he boats his fish or draws his hook from the water. A green hand plumps his lead alternately into the deck and among the rigging, hooks his finger or his breeches, and tangles his line into the most extraordinary loops and knots that can be imagined. In all these performances Dick and myself had some experience. In addition, we caught nothing, and without the excitement of taking the fish the process soon became intolerably fatiguing. So after rowing and floating about for an hour or more without any success we anchored, and knocking the necks off the porter bottles, solaced ourselves with Mother Cary's provisions. While the lunch was in progress the fisherman's son pointed out a group of black points dimpling the surface of the water about a hundred feet from us. "There," said he, "goes a shoal of bluefish!" Down went the cheese and beer, and out went the lines. Throwing the lead beyond the shoal, we drew it rapidly through, and each hook was followed by half a dozen or more ravenous fish, snapping, darting, and leaping up to the gunwale of the boat. A noble pair were hooked on our first cast, and presently fresh shoals appeared to the right and left of us, driving by with the tide. Many thousands must have passed us in the course of the next hour, sometimes showing their fins at distances beyond our reach, sometimes passing directly under the boat. The sight of our game aroused the sporting fervor to the highest degree, and for an hour we whirled our leads so industriously and effectively that the bottom of our boat was all a-flutter with the spoils.

With the turn of the tide the fish disappeared, and, satisfied with our success, we rowed back to the Siasconsett landing. When we got ashore we straightway repaired, with our ship's company, to the hospitable store-room of Mother Cary, where drinks again went round and all fatigues were for the time forgotten.

"Mr. Coffin," inquired Dick, "you have storms on this coast sometimes, don't you?"

The sailor gave a solemn wink at the venerable mother, whose back was turned at the time, and replied in a manner savoring of reverential facetiousness:

"We have, Sir, some devilish hard blows; dangerous for them as happen to be outside of the breakers; but once get inside and it's smoother sailing."

"This whisky," observed the hostess, "is none of your common stuff. I've got mean whisky for sich as it suits; but this I keep for them that know what's what. Shall I open another bottle, Sirs?"

"Certainly, Madam, another bottle. Friends, here's good sport and a full season for Siasconsett; pour out for yourselves."

"Mister," whispered Coffin, "I guess you're all safe inside the breakers."

The lame hostler now brought out the buggy, and taking leave of this queer, quizzical, humorsome, jolly little place, we drove back to the city of Nantucket.

"How do you like Siasconsett?" asked our acquaintance.

"We had a pleasant day," I answered; "but I should like to see it during the full season."

"It would be worth your while," said he; "they have lively times then, and I can tell you some good stories."

"Then tell us one, by all means."

At all places where men and women congregate for social pleasure and recreation, no pie can be opened that Love don't stick his finger in, and Siasconsett, like all summer retreats, great and small, has its spice of gossip and romance.

Something less than a thousand years ago—said our narrator—Miss Mehetabel Fizgig was the beauty and belle of our island. I won't waste time in attempting to describe her loveliness; but just let every man fancy the sort of girl he would wish his sweet-heart to be, and then I'll wager she would have surpassed them all. Nor were her good looks her only recommendation. She was considered uncommonly clever with her books, and no girl of her age was comparable to her in handiness with her needle and smartness in housekeeping. After going over this catalogue of her perfections, it may seem superfluous to add that Hetty was an heiress. Being a married man, I never took the trouble to remember how many houses, shares in whale-ships, and certificates of bank stock her father had left her, but have heard it said frequently that "it was enough to give a clever and industrious young man a very good start in the world."

Although Nantucket is not overrun with young men of any kind, Hetty's charms were not suffered to go a-begging; and before she was eighteen she had had offers that most girls would have jumped at; but she seemed to have no mind for any of them. Not that she was by any means indifferent to admiration and attention. On the contrary, she exhibited a fondness for such worldly vanities that set numerous old-fashioned, plaited bonnets and divers unguarded tongues to wagging at her. In fact, she treated her admirers with as much tact and as little remorse as her ancestors had shown to the poor whales; giving a puffing swain the *coup de grace*, and laughing at his death-flurry; or when the game became troublesome, cutting the line, and sending the animal plunging away into unknown and unheard-of seas, where four years of salt junk and bilge water generally cured his wounds effectually.

From such doings as these it came to be currently reported and believed that the little beauty had no heart; and this serious defect set all the old ladies who had marriageable daughters very much against her; and all the old maids who hadn't given up yet agreed that her behavior was any thing but prudent. Now it was somewhat singular that one very significant fact had thus far escaped the observation of our heroine's female acquaintance, which was, that for two years or more Hetty had been receiving letters from remote parts of the globe, and oftentimes so moulded and faded that she could scarcely decipher them; and that said letters, although by no means cased in filigree and perfumed envelopes, were oftentimes honored with a welcome the very thought of which would have made a crack harpooner miss his throw.

Yet true it was, that, besides the lady herself, no one in all Nantucket knew of these things, except an old jolly wag of a sea-captain, with one leg spliced with whalebone; and what this old joker knew of the subject we can not explain at this time, because it would spoil the dramatic surprise we have in store for those who have not yet guessed that our heroine's true lover would turn up presently.

Well, sure enough, one day the good ship *Three Brothers* came into port, returning from a long and successful cruise; and among her crew was a stout, ruddy, tight-built young sailor, who, on landing, steered directly for the widow Fizgig's cottage, and entering unannounced, surprised Hetty into a scene before some of the neighbors. In an hour after it was known all over town that Hetty's beau had come in earnest. In two hours after it was known when they were to be married, who the bridemaids were to be, and how the bride was to be dressed.

Here the story should have ended. I wish it had. But there were certain old ones who shook their heads at all this news. Abijah Bowline needn't be too sure of his fish until he had it moored alongside. Hadn't she fooled young Folger and Mayhew in the same way? And how did she treat Tommy Coffin, the promising grand nephew of the famous Long Tom Coffin that was lost on the *Ariel*, as Mr. Fenimore Cooper tells us? Bless the old folks! they know too much by half; so our story must go on.

The season at Siasconsett was in full blast; all the wealthy residents and idle sojourners of the city were there; and there were reported to be at least half a dozen strangers from Boston and elsewhere at the hotel. Although the sea view and sea air had no especial attraction for the newly arrived sailor, yet a feeling of vanity, pardonable enough under the circumstances, engendered a wish to show off his prize before the gay and elegant society there assembled. So he hired a buggy wagon and drove his sweet-heart over, taking a kiss or two by the way, and setting her down, very properly, at the cottage of her aunt, who was keeping house over there.

Young man, if you have a sweet-heart and are well with her, never let her go to a watering-place, especially if she is pretty. I have not time to give reasons at present, but if ever you should find yourself in the supposed circumstances you'll probably remember this caveat.

Now there was at Siasconsett at this time a proper, tall, and handsome young fellow who sported a superb black mustache and whiskers, and who dressed in the highest style of lace cravat, gold chain, and brocade vest that a very liberal public opinion could tolerate. Dr. Flugens, besides these merely personal advantages, was an affluent conversationalist, and had the enviable art of impressing those who listened to him with an amazing idea of his travels, accomplishments, knowledge of society, and general importance in the world. The Doctor was a professor in one department of the noble art of surgery, and in fact, on his arrival at the Ocean House in this city, he stuck up his card:

Professor Flugens,
OF BOSTON,
CHIROPODIST,
OFFERS HIS PROFESSIONAL SERVICES.

Finding that all the fun was going on at Siasconsett, he withdrew this tender of service, and appeared on the new theatre as a gentleman of elegant leisure traveling for health and diversion. In this capacity he took famously with the ladies, and soon became the standard beau of the society. It is true that an over-nice observer might have remarked some discrepancies between his manners and pretensions. At table he was an unreserved eructator, and picked his teeth with his penknife between courses, which seemed a little odd in one accustomed to the best society in Boston, and, when "het up" in conversation, he "wanted to know," and "admired to see," and alluded to "Bosting" and the "White Mountings" with a twang that did not do much credit to Harvard University, where he was educated. But it is only our great watering-places that folks visit for the purpose of criticising each other's manners and pretensions. To Siasconsett folks go for enjoyment, and they find it, without bothering themselves about each other's little peculiarities.

But to make a long story short, our Professor met Miss Hetty Fizgig in the dance, sought an introduction, and from that moment a flirtation commenced which progressed so rapidly that, in twenty-four hours from date, poor Abijah was gasping and staring like a fish thrown high and dry upon the sandy beach, and felt for all the world like a certain mariner who went to sleep with his vessel riding at anchor in a cozy harbor and woke up next morning to find himself blown out of sight of land.

The public was presently divided into two parties on the subject. Some favored the Doctor's pretensions, while those who sided with the young sailor thought he had been shamefully treated. Uncle Billy Bowline—the old Captain with a whalebone leg—so swelled with indignation that he looked like a fresh-caught sculpin, at what he considered an insult put upon himself first, and his nephew in the second place.

"Hadn't the little baggage often kissed him for bringing her letters from Bijah, and thanked him so sweetly for keeping her secret, and rejoiced with him at the prospect of his nephew's return, and promised him that she would be true as the needle? etc. Ay, ay, so it is: the needle gets bewitched sometimes, and when you see a craft with more sail than ballast there's no counting on her in any kind of a blow. But, Abijah, my boy," continued the Captain, in answer to some desperate suggestions of his nephew, "don't harpoon him just yet, for the sake of conveniency. The sarpent would be worth nothing at the Tryworks, and it might bring you trouble. Moreover, if you was to perforate him, how would that mend matters in regard to her? It's the gal that has done you the foul turn, not that blower. So if you'll mind me, boy, you'll act the man, cut her adrift, and say no more about it."

Abijah Bowline promised he would follow his uncle's counsel, and part of the promise he fulfilled. He acted the man, and held his peace —the more easily, perhaps, because he therein exhibited the native characteristics of his race. But when he came to fulfill the order to cut adrift, he found the wide difference between a simple manilla line and the web of tough and tender heart-strings in which he was entangled.

On the other side, Hetty tossed, flirted, and enjoyed her triumph to her silly little heart's content. She walked on the beach at low tide, went fishing, drove to Sancoty Head to see the fine view, danced, and sat on the cottage porch with the Doctor, where they talked about Boston and New York, Nahant and Newport, until she felt quite bewildered in her mind, and wondered how it was possible that she had been content to pass her life thus far, cut off from the splendors and delights of the great world; or that she should have so lately purposed to fix her destiny beyond the pale of repentance on this secluded little sand bank, Nantucket.

Then Aunt Noddy highly approved of Hetty's conquest. "To marry a sailor," quoth she, "is to pass one's life in drudgery and hopeless widowhood. Ah me!" she sighed, "for the best half of my life I haven't been able to tell whether I was a married woman or a widow. But patience, we must all submit; yet wouldn't it be mighty pleasant to have Hetty settled in Boston, where a body might pay her a visit between times? Then he, such an agreeable sort of person, a great professor in the colleges—a—a—chiro— Bless the mighty word—I can't exactly call it—but I'll be bound it means something great!"

So things went on, until one evening the teacher of the Grammar School came over from town and stepped in at the cottage to pay his respects. The young lady was walking out as usual; but Aunt Noddy was especially glad to see him, and intimated that she had some particular confidential inquiries to make.

Mehetabel, my niece, you know, has got a sweet-heart.

"Yes," replied the teacher, "I know, young Bowline."

"Not him, by any means," said Mrs. Noddy, a little confused.

"The gentleman she's got now is a Professor in the colleges, and a mighty learned scholar like yourself. A Doctor they call him, and a something which I don't understand, and which I can't find in the dictionary. Here's a card he dropped one night when he pulled out his gold watch to see what time it was."

The master took the card and read "CHIROPODIST," and then burst into a long and loud fit of laughter. Mrs. Noddy knitted her brows and scanned his face with a look of dumb but searching inquiry.

"*Chiropodist*, madam, means a professional manipulator of corns and bunions—a corn-doctor, in plain English."

Mrs. Noddy's countenance at this information looked as if her gaiter-boots might have contained all the corns, bunions, and hang nails that have tormented humanity since the invention of shoe leather.

That evening the wind freshened, and it was thought too damp for the young folks to sit on the porch as usual. Hetty retired early for some reason, and the Doctor also retired to the hotel, troubled with a sense of benumbing chillness which he could not quite explain, and which numerous glasses of brandy failed to overcome. He asked to see his bill; but that was the clerk's business, not ours.

That night the rest of the villagers was broken by the howlings of the most terrific storm that ever burst upon that stormy coast. The lightning blazed, the thunder roared, the rain poured in torrents, and the very earth trembled with the shock of the surf as it burst upon the beach.

Soon after daylight a little knot of men was gathered on the sand cliff, whose excited movements and vehement gestures showed that something of uncommon interest and importance was on hand, and it presently became noised abroad that a vessel had struck upon the shoals and was going to pieces. In a short time all the population of the place, residents and sojourners, men, women, and children, were gathered upon the shore, where, regardless of wind and weather, they strained their eyes in the direction of the perishing vessel with that eager and absorbing interest which such a scene is always sure to awaken in the breasts of a people whose lives and fortunes are continually exposed to similar dangers.

Chief among the breathless and excited spectators stood Uncle Billy Bowline, balancing himself upon his sound leg, viewing with his glass alternately the wrecked schooner, and what had now become an object of still greater interest, the boat with five men which had put out from Siasconsett to their relief.

"Stand back!" cried the one-legged Captain, fiercely; "let go my arm: she'll go to pieces before the boat reaches her. It was a desperate venture, a sinful temptation of Providence. I told him so. Let go my arm, I say!"

It was a young girl's hand that plucked the old sailor's jacket sleeve, and a girl's voice, tremulous and husky with emotion, that whispered,

"Tell me, is it Abijah Bowline that's gone in the boat?"

The Captain looked down. "Woman," said he, in a harsh and bitter tone, "go home; what business have you here in the rain?" and immediately he hobbled away to another place, and again pointed his glass seaward.

Hetty cast a despairing look around, when an old woman, with a basket of refreshments on her arm, having overheard the inquiry, approached and hissed into her ear,

"Who but Abijah Bowline would fling away his life on sich a fool's errand? And the lives of the four men he shamed and bullied into going with him, Studley, and the Coffins, and Pollard, they'll leave widows and orphans behind; but for him—a desperate man—it's no great matter."

A skipper, wrapped in a pea-jacket, said: "They're brave lads anyhow, and it was nobly done; but I fear it's of no use: I pity 'em."

"Would ye like a drop of whisky, Sir, this wet morning?"

"Thank ye, mother, I don't care if I do."

Hetty stood the while unnoticed and alone. Her silken hair hung wet and matted about her

STUDLEY.

face and neck. Her handsome features white and clammy like a fair chisled statue, all but the convulsive, heaving breast, and the restless eye wandered eagerly and anxiously over the raging expanse of ocean. There and then she stood until it was all over.

As the old skipper had said, the vessel went to pieces before the boat reached her, and her crew, ten in number, clinging to a floating portion of the wreck, were picked up by young Bowline's boat. Thus laden, it was doubtful whether she could land in the surf. They made the dash, and, as was feared, the boat swamped; but both the crew and passengers were hardy and practiced watermen, and a hundred hands stood by with boat-hooks, oars, and lines to help the failing. All were saved; and with the rejoicings there were shouts and oaths, thanksgivings and tears.

In the long procession that marched up the bank and along the street of Siasconsett the leading man was Abijah Bowline. Hatless and shoeless, his woolen shirt and sailor pants drenched and dripping with brine, he looked like a handsome merman just landed. His right arm was supported by proud old Uncle William, who marched with all the state and dignity his whalebone leg permitted. The hero's left arm was clasped tightly by the white hands and burning cheek of that marble statuette we left standing on the shore a short time since. His gait was unsteady, his face had a listless and half-bewildered expression, and from a cut on the side of his head a slender stream of blood trickled down mingled with the salt-water. When the boat turned over in the surf he had got a heavy blow which cut and stunned him considerably; but that to a strong man was no great matter. Uncle Bowline cast occasional grievous looks at the girl but said nothing, and once or twice Abijah noticed her and made a motion as if to shake her off; but the grasp upon his arm was like the grasp of one overwhelmed and perishing in the deep waters, and the generous sailor had not the heart to loosen it. These three said never a word as they walked along, while behind the crowd was loud and clamorous in their joy.

At length they reached the gate of Aunt Noddy's cottage, which was open, and beside it stood the old lady with a smiling face.

"You'll come in with us, won't you, my brave boy? I've a warm coat and a cup of hot coffee for ye; and Hetty and I will make you all comfortable in a jiffy."

In his indignant astonishment Uncle Bowline let go his nephew's hand; and as we have seen a tall man of war with flaccid sails and drooping pennants yield to the guidance of a diminutive steam-tug whose chimney-stack scarcely reached to her bulwarks, so did our stout sailor heel and veer from his course through the gate, around the grass-plots, between the rose-bushes, and, finally, disappear within the cottage.

"Captain Bowline," said the dame, "will you walk in and take breakfast with us?"

"Madam, I'll see ye d——d first," replied the Captain, as he limped hastily away toward his own quarters.

"And so would I," exclaimed Dick Dashaway, "if any girl had treated me in that way!"

"Young man," said our narrator, "every body knows precisely what he would do beforehand, but he very rarely does it. As for Captain Bowline, he reconsidered that last observation of his and formally withdrew it, supplying its place with cogitations somewhat in this vein: 'The needle is our main dependence after all. Sometimes she varies a point or two. Do we cuss her? No! we take observations, and calculate. I've been told that in thunder-storms, at times and places, she gets clean reversed. I never see it, but I've seen things quite as singular. Shall we throw her overboard then? No! we let her right herself, and travel on. I don't see that a man can do any better with his present lights.'"

BIRD EGGING AT MUSKEGEET.

As our programme allowed us another day at Nantucket, we had choice of a cruise on the Sound for scup fishing, or a bird-egging frolic to Muskegeet. This Muskegeet is a small sandy island lying to the westward, uninhabited, and a favorite resort for sea-fowl during their egging season. The people of the neighboring coasts frequently visit it, and make a frolic of gathering the spoils. But as our information in regard to the means of getting there was somewhat obscure, and, for my part, influenced by conscientious scruples on the subject of robbing birds' nests, we concluded in favor of the scup fishing.

In pursuance of this determination we called on Watson Burgess, our ex-whaleman and present owner of a first-class fishing-boat called the *Naiad Queen*. We are continually checked and disappointed at finding the choicest virtues and capabilities of our race bestowed in mean and unworthy cases; but occasionally Nature treats us to a combination, as it were, to show us what she can do. Painter or poet who would look upon the perfect model of a Nantucket whaleman, I commend you to Watson Burgess.

"Our boat was cheered,
The harbor cleared,"

WATSON BURGESS.

and away we dashed before a spanking breeze, the white caps leaping half-mast high and drenching us with showers of spray. At the helm sat our stalwart mariner, trimming his lively and graceful craft to the breeze with a quiet fatherly pride lighting his face, as one might imagine an Arab chieftain affectionately smoothing the mane and patting the shoulders of his favorite mare, while they scoured the sand waves of the desert. Well, our Captain had a right to be proud of his equipage, for from keel to pennant he had built her with his own hands, and her crew was his own son.

Arrived at the fishing-ground, we cast anchor

and spent two hours or more in pulling out scuppaug. This is a species of perch, plump and white, weighing from one to three pounds, and when first taken from the water it is extremely beautiful, its scales glittering with iridescent hues like a fretwork of silver and diamonds. As the sport was not particularly exciting, and our anchorage very rough, we returned to port, and landed with true sharkish appetites and bodies thoroughly wet and salted.

These healthful inconveniences being remedied in due time, I spent the remainder of the afternoon and evening in looking over Obed Macy's History of Nantucket, from which I extract some interesting information concerning its first settlement, trade, manners, and customs.

The island was discovered by Gosnold during his voyage of exploration in 1602. It is situated about thirty miles south of the main land of Massachusetts, is fourteen miles long from east to west, and has an average breadth of three and a half miles from north to south, and contains about thirty thousand acres of land. Tradition says that it was formerly wooded, and that the soil was moderately fertile. At present it seems but a demi-lune of sand, only kept from blowing away by a scanty growth of grass and shrubs. The first white man settled on its shores in 1659. One Thomas Macy, a worthy citizen of the colony, having offended against the laws then in force, by giving shelter to four Quakers during a storm, sought refuge among the savages of this island. As the savages were not sufficiently enlightened to abhor his crime, the dispenser of unlawful hospitality was kindly received and permitted to live in peace. At that time the island contained about fifteen hundred inhabitants, and was divided, after the manner of civilized countries, into two antagonistic and discordant sections, the east and west. The cause of the quarrel is supposed to have been because the island divided conveniently in that way. If the territory had stretched toward the other points of the compass, it can not be doubted that there would have been a northern and southern party. In time more white people began to come in, the aboriginal disputes were settled by a royal marriage between the east and the west, and every thing went on with Christian love and harmony until (as usual) the Indians disappeared. The last of the race died in 1822. So adroitly were the natives supplanted and devoured, that the historian felicitates himself upon the fact that, in their whole intercourse, the white man never drew a sword nor violated a Christian law.

The first whaling expedition undertaken by the settlers is thus described:

"A whale of the kind called a *scragg* came into the harbor and continued there three days. This excited the curiosity of the people, and led them to devise measures to prevent his return out of the harbor. They accordingly invented, and caused to be wrought for them, a harpoon with which they attacked and killed the whale. This first success encouraged them to undertake whaling as a permanent business—whales being at that time numerous in the vicinity of their shores. In furtherance of their design they made a contract with James Lopar to settle on the island and engage in the business. The agreement was as follows, copied verbatim from the original record:

CONTRACT.

"'5th 4th mo. 1672 James Lopar doth Ingage to carry on a design of Whale Citching on the Island of Nantucket, that is the said James, Ingage to be a third in all respeekes, and som of the town Ingage also to carrey on the other two-thirds with him in like manner, the Town doth also consent that first one company shal begin and afterward the rest of the freeholders or any of them, have liberty to set up another company Provided that they make a tender to those freeholders that have no share in the first company and if any refuse, the Rest may go on themselves and the Town do also Ingage that no other Company shal be allowed hereafter, Also whoever Kil any whale of the Company or Companys aforesaid they ar to pay to the town for every such whale five shillings. And for the Incorragement of the said James Lopar the Town doth grant him Ten Acres of Land in som convenant place, that he may chuse in (Wood Land exceped) and also Liberty for the Commonge of thre Cows and twenty sheep and one horse with necessary wood and water for his use on Conditions that he follow the Trade of Whaleing on the Island two years in all the season therof beginning the first of March next insuing. Also is to build upon his land, and when he leaves inhabiting upon the Island then he is first to ofer his land to the town at a Valluable price, and if the town do not buy it—then he may Sel it to whome he please—the commonage is granted only for the time he stays here.'"

In addition, they sent a man to Cape Cod to learn something more of whale-fishing and the art of trying out the oil from a people who had already made great proficiency therein. Thus the business went on increasing from year to year until it became the principal occupation of the islanders. The Indians, whom neither force nor persuasion could ever bring to follow the ordinary pursuits of civilized men, readily joined in this congenial business, cheerfully taking any place that was assigned them, and by their activity and skill rendering invaluable service to their employers.

In these days the fishing was carried on by boats from the shore, the oil boiled out and fitted for market in Tryworks on land, and the species captured the Greenland or Right whale. The first spermaceti whale known to the inhabitants was washed ashore, dead, on the southwest part of the island. The same historian we have quoted gives the following naïve account of its division:

"There were so many claimants to the prize that it was difficult to determine to whom it should belong. The natives claimed the whale because they found it; the whites, to whom the natives made known their discovery, claimed it by a right comprehended, as they affirmed, in the purchase of the island by the original patent. An officer of the crown made his claim, and pretended to seize the fish in the name of his Majesty, as being property without any particular owner. After considerable discussion between the contending parties, it was finally settled that the *white* inhabitants who first found the whale should share the prize equally among themselves. The teeth, which were considered very valuable, had been extracted by a white man and an Indian before any others had knowledge of the whale. *All difficulty being now settled*, a company was formed who commenced cutting the whale in pieces convenient for transportation to their Try-works."

"Lo, the poor Indian! whose untutored mind"

ALL DIFFICULTY SETTLED.

was not yet sufficiently elevated by education to discern upon what principles of equity the difficulty was settled, doubtless, however, acquiesced in the decision, wondering and admiring at the advantages of such a civilization, especially exhibited in questions concerning the rights of property. They went to work, of course, as they were ordered, to assist in saving the valuable carcass. Yet one may easily imagine how Prince Kadooda, Nickanoose, Kuttashamaquat, and other wiseacres among them, looked first into each other's blank faces, and then at the whale, muttering in the best English they could command, "Injin find 'em fust—tell white man—white man never say whale to Injin no time. Say, Go to work, lazy cuss—help save 'um oil. Ha! ha! Masaquat, pass that bottle, ugh! Praise the Lord!"

Furthermore, although it is not related in the history, I'll warrant that the lively native who got a share of the teeth was eventually prosecuted before a squire, and whipped for stealing.

About the year 1712 one Christopher Hussey was blown out to sea by a northerly gale, and falling in with a school of spermaceti whales, killed one and brought it home. This event gave new life to the business. With such rich prizes in view, the fishermen became more adventurous, and small vessels of thirty tons were fitted out for a six weeks' cruise, returning to port whenever they had killed a whale, delivering the blubber, and immediately putting out to sea again.

Thus did this brave and hardy people progress from year to year, increasing in wealth and enterprise until their ships had explored all known and unknown seas, and their fame was established in every land. Statesmen lauded their success, and foreign Governments, covetous of their skill, sought to win their friendship. Yet the tide of their prosperity had by no means been uninterrupted. During the French war of 1755, the Revolutionary struggle, and the war of 1812, they had their seasons of mourning and tribulation. From wealth and plenty they were reduced to the brink of starvation. Trade annihilated, their ports closed, their vessels captured, and many strong men that went out full of life and hope returned no more

Such was the condition of Nantucket, especially during the two wars we have waged with the greatest maritime power in the world.

Nevertheless, these dreary seasons past, like a vigorous and hardy plant, she sprung again with renewed life and power. It was near the

TOWING THE WHALE.

south shore of the island that the fight took place between the American privateer *Neufchatel* and the boats of the British frigate *Endymion*. The privateer schooner, with a prize ship from Jamaica richly freighted, was at anchor near the shore, while wide in the offing appeared a vessel supposed to be a British man-of-war. Seeing a number of boats leaving the ship and heading toward him, the Captain of the privateer cleared his ship for action, and prepared to give them a proper reception.

It was not until nine o'clock in the evening that the five barges got up to the *Neufchatel*. They were permitted to approach within musket-shot, when the action commenced with such terrible effect on the part of the American that in thirty-five minutes the attacking flotilla was nearly annihilated. Of the five barges and one hundred and forty-six men that composed the expedition, only two barges and sixteen men escaped. The privateer lost but five men. Says the worthy Obed Macy: "The action took place within five miles of the town; and while the work of death was going on, the reports of the cannon and muskets were distinctly heard by the inhabitants. Such a scene, almost under the eye of a large community, one of whose distinguishing and, we think, noblest traits is a strong aversion to war, could not fail to bring a solemn gloom over their minds."

TARRING ROPES.

"A solemn gloom," did you say, my venerable friend? Can the "Ethiopian change his skin, or the leopard his spots?" Can a strait-breasted coat smother out the fire of the human heart, or a vain theory of right or wrong stifle the glorious joy of a victory? Think you that a people whose wealth had perished; whose husbands, sons, and brothers had mouldered in loathsome prisons; who had been robbed, starved, and humiliated, could look on with indifference when the pride of the strong was humbled and the bow of the mighty broken? Go to, old friend! There is not a heart in Nantucket which has not thrilled with the story of that gallant and terrible combat.

The palmy days of Nantucket, judging from statistics, began about 1820, after the place had recovered from the effects of the war, and continued until 1835 or thereabout; since when, owing to the successful rivalry of New Bedford and other places on the main land, and, more than all probably, to the general declension of the whaling business, her prosperity has been on the wane.

To give activity to the unemployed labor and capital of the town, a number of public-spirited citizens have formed a company for the manufacture of boots and shoes. The ancient mariners shake their heads, and thoughtful citizens doubt of its success. The hand which has wielded the harpoon and steering oar will hardly condescend to the pegging awl, and the lass that has loved a sailor won't be bound to bind shoes. I was myself invited to look at the establishment, but declined. I am pleased sometimes to take the poetic view of life, and did not wish to see Samson in the tread-mill.

Consciousness of power and familiarity with great deeds tend marvelously to simplify a man's speech and chasten his manner. In social life, on shore, your true whalemen is courteous, good-humored, manly, quiet, and unaffected, not easily distinguished in dress, manner, or conversation from any other citizen of his condition. Mark that fellow with the rolling gait, swaggering speech larded with sea phrases, the flash sailor costume, tipped with a huge brass anchor breast-pin. That fellow, perhaps, has served on the raging canal as mule-driver, or as cabin-boy on a ferry-boat, has caught eels and cat-fish from the wharf with a hand line; but order him to mount the main truck in a gale, or put a harpoon in his hand and send him against an enraged sperm whale—you will then learn the true value of all those airs and frippery.

Would you hear the ring of true mettle? Read the following characteristic autobiographies from Macy's history:

CAPTAIN BENJAMIN WORTH'S LIFE AND ADVENTURES.

"I began to follow the sea in 1783, being then fifteen years of age, and continued until 1824. During this period of forty-one years I was shipmaster twenty-nine years. From the time when I commenced going to sea until I quitted the business, I was at home only seven

THE HARPOONER.

years. At the rate of four miles an hour while at sea, I have sailed more than 1,191,000 miles. I have visited more than forty islands in the Atlantic and Pacific oceans, some of them many times, and traversed the west coasts of North and South America from Baldivia, lat. 40° S. to 59° N. on the northwest coast, and up Christian Sound to Lymn Canal. I have assisted in obtaining 20,000 barrels of oil. During the last war I was taken by the English in the ship *George*, and lost all I had on board. While I commanded a vessel not one of my crew was killed, or even had a limb broken by a whale, nor have any died of the scurvy."

A GROVE.

CAPTAIN GEORGE W. GARDNER'S LIFE.

"I began to follow the sea at thirteen years of age, and continued in that service thirty-seven years. I was a shipmaster twenty-one years. I performed three voyages to the coast of Brazil, twelve to the Pacific Ocean, three to Europe, and three to the West Indies. During thirty-seven years I was at home but four years and eight months. There were 23,000 barrels of oil obtained by vessels which I sailed in. During my following the sea, from the best estimate I can make, I have traveled more than 1,000,000 miles. I was taken by the English in the late war, and lost all the property I had with me."

What years of stirring adventure are condensed in these terse paragraphs! What concentrated and suggestive sentences, each of which would furnish a writer like Alexandre Dumas with material for three volumes octavo.

But time presses—wherefore I can not tell. I commenced this journey with no other limit to my free-will than my own phantasy; yet, driven by an irresistible and mysterious impulse, I find myself continually hastening. Though this island were more delightsome than the realm of Calypso, old Mentor points to the boat, and says it is high time we were steering toward the main land. Who ever traveled that did not presently perceive this old bore at his elbow? "Ducunt volentem fata, nolentem trahunt." Yet the idea is a terrible one. Are we then all wandering Jews by nature? Pilgrim of life, passing through the dark valley of the shadow of death, you can not hasten your steps, nor yet may you turn aside to rest your weary feet in the pleasant land of Beulah. From the cradle to the grave the eternal cry is—Onward!

It was raining next day when we took passage on the steamer *Island Home* for Hyannis on the Barnstable coast. The water was rough, and the passage of the Sound might have passed with a lubber for a sea voyage. On the forward deck some waggish fellows were tormenting a raw youth by passing jokes upon his birth-place. "On Cape Cod," said one, "greens are so scarce that if a man finds three mullein stalks and a huckleberry bush growing near together, he incloses it for a grove, and warns the neighbors not to trespass." Said another: "They sweeten their tea with molasses over there. So once, when they got a new preacher, he was asked home to tea with old Mother Stebbins. The old soul was saving enough when she sweetened other people's tea; but when it came to the preacher's cup, she kept on pouring in. As he didn't admire to have his tea oversweet, he got nervous, thanked her over and over again, and at last begged her to leave off sweetening. The old lady rolled up her eyes in a loving, sanctimonious way. 'Ah, Sir,' said she, 'if it was all molasses it wouldn't be too good for you.'"

The youngster seemed to be wanting in the gift of free speech, and slow at repartee; and,

TOO SWEET.

in attempting to reply, he stammered and got red in the face; so I volunteered to help him out.

"A sandy soil," said I, "if not good for raising great cabbage-heads, produces the best quality of men. An Admiral of the Blue of the Royal Navy was asked by George IV. who was the bravest man he ever saw. He replied, 'A Cape Cod trader whom I met at Port Mahon, the commander of a thirty-ton schooner. He assisted in two duels between American midshipmen, thrashed five English sailors on the quay for calling his flag a gridiron, took in cargo, and set sail, all between sunrise and sunset.'"

We landed at Hyannis, and, on taking our seats in the cars for Boston, my companion and myself commenced a retrospect of our adventures for the past month. Dick seemed to have entirely forgotten his misadventure in love, and to have so far gratified his maritime yearnings that he no longer alluded to his intention of shipping before the mast; indeed, he seemed rather to hail with pleasure the anticipated change from salt-water to city life. Among other things, he expressed his surprise that, although we had been in New England more than a month, we had seen no Yankees yet. I had myself begun to doubt whether the stage Yankee of the Sam Slick school might not be altogether a myth, or a gross exaggeration of dramatic and artistic humorists; for up to this point our travels had made us acquainted with a people totally different in appearance, manners, and character from what we had expected. Yet the islanders and sea-faring population, with whom we had chiefly associated, and who had impressed us so agreeably, are a people "sui generis" amphibia—in many traits, physical and moral, very nearly resembling the English, yet with more vivacity

VILLAGE LAWYER.

and intelligence than the Englishman, and generally with better manners; and, for the rest, exhibiting greater breadth, both of body and soul, than we had hoped to find in these latitudes.

But it seemed, as our train hurried on toward Boston, partially changing its living freight at every station, that the type of man began to change; and we could recognize among the physiognomies around us characteristic marks of that great whittling, guessing, speculating, moralizing race whose destiny is—still a matter of guess-work.

This dapper gentleman, with a smirk on his face, which he thinks is a smile, a shining, high-

RAILROAD PRESIDENT

AGENT OF HUMANE SOCIETY.

crowned hat, and a silk umbrella, I should take to be the president of some railroad or manufacturing company, a prince of button-makers, or principal stock-owner in a wooden bucket-mill.

That quiet, inscrutable little man, who reads the newspaper, we would guess might be a village lawyer, with a legal mind, which, if united with a thoroughly legal morality, might entitle him to a seat in the State Legislature.

This prim, tallow-faced individual, with a white cravat and puckered mouth, is unmistakable—the traveling agent of some great moral reform, or humanitarian society, whose plans, if universally adopted, promise incalculable benefits to the human race. The specialty of this person may be, perhaps, the propagation of vegetarian principles among the Esquimaux, or a grand union movement for the abolition of polygamy among the Turks, and the enforcement of monogamy among the Roman clergy. The celebrated Cardinal de Retz advises us "so to lay our plans that even their failure may be productive of some benefit to us;" and our great reformer does not usually forget so to make his arrangements that, if the original object of the society should fail, he will make his living out of it, at least.

FROM MAINE.

These chaps immediately in front of us seem cast in a harder mould. The eye of the elder has a metallic glitter, as if it had frequently been whetted against the edge of an axe, and the firm, resolute lip, as of a man accustomed to strive with mighty pine-trees. From Maine, I'll warrant you—high up on the Kennebec or Penobscot.

But we are near enough to overhear something of their conversation.

"Peleg has quit business, you tell me?" inquires No. 1.

"Yas—yas. He quit airly last fall, I guess, and took himself off to the Mountings."

"What is he thought to be a-doing of?"

"Wa'al, he's got an idee, and he's a-workin' at that."

This information appeared satisfactory, and the subject was dropped; but Peleg's idee may possibly be heard of again at the next World's Fair, held at San Francisco or Pekin.

By dinner-time we were in Boston, and roomed at the Parker House, in School Street; and without pretending to dogmatize upon a mere matter of taste, we would only suggest that we never saw a finer hotel. Finding a hack

HACK-DRIVER.

at the door, we prevailed upon the driver to forego his literary labors for a short time, and show us 'round.

POVERTY AND RICHES.

About the water all our large Atlantic towns are alike, and Boston is no exception to the rule; but the interior of the old town has something decidedly characteristic in its appearance. What could be more conceited and pragmatical than that State House dome, rising like the phrenological bump of self-esteem inordinately developed? What more crooked, devious, incomprehensible, mystical, narrow, and absurd than her labyrinthian streets? What more liberal and enlightened than her noble Common? What more expressive of educated refinement and domestic elegance than her beautiful suburban towns and villages?

After the blaze, bustle, and hurry of New York, Boston appears provincial, quiet, and slow. Yet, on the other hand, the absence of tawdry and misplaced finery from the streets—the prompt, systematic, and effective manner of transacting business—with the best-bred and best-fed dray-horses in America—give her an air of solidity and gentility more characteristic of an English town. Boston likes to be thought English, and affects to be a little more so than she is in fact.

ORGAN-GRINDER.

That apparent equality of conditions which we remarked in New Haven, and many other smaller New England towns, entirely disappears in Boston. Here haughty and exclusive wealth may be contrasted with the "want" that "cometh like an armed man." He that is meagre with starvation, and he that is heavy with surfeiting, pass on the streets, mutually envying or pitying each other, as the case may be. Here we may see poverty meanly jealous of the rich man's state, and splendid ennui that covets, but dare not enjoy, the jolly insouciance of the poor.

Here the Italian organ-grinder shares public favor with his more ambitious compatriot, the Italian Opera. And this reminds me that, after we had dined and coffeed, a friend called and offered us tickets to the Opera. The Opera-house was well enough, and the audience most decidedly English in manners and appearance. The entertainment was *Lucrezia Borgia*—the most exquisite of Donizetti's compositions; and the piece (as well as the Borgia's guests) was most inhumanly murdered. Supposing that the audience was not stolidly indifferent on the subject of bad music, they behaved with praiseworthy forbearance during the performance. A female personating Gennaro sung Il Segreto tolerably well, I believe; for the piece was not followed, but interrupted, by thunders of applause—always in the wrong place. The song was encored, and its repetition greeted by an enthusiasm that bordered on extravagance.

"Your formal and frigid Bostonians seem to be thoroughly warmed. Il Segreto must be immensely popular here," I remarked to my friend.

"The singer," he replied, "is a Boston lady."

"Oh!"

But in truth I was in no condition to appreciate the Opera this evening, and may have shown a disposition to be hypercritical. I have understood that the atmosphere of Boston engenders hypercriticism in all matters pertaining to literature and the fine arts; but I was affected by another cause. The shifting of the scene from Nantucket to the Italian Opera was too sudden and striking not to excite reflection and suggest comparison. The twittering and squeaking of fiddles, and grunting of bassoons, fell strangely on ears so lately filled with the solemn roar of ocean. The clap-trap and tinsel of the stage stood, as it were, face to face with the Quaker simplicity and stern reality of life on the Islands; the affected strut and bombastic periods of the players with the undramatic manners and hard, terse speech of the whalemen. From the true grandeur of nature one can not descend thus suddenly to unskillful mimicry.

After all (and in spite of Shakspeare), the English are not a theatrical people. Music and the drama have always existed with them as unacclimated exotics. More sweepingly may the same observation be applied to their descendants in the New World; for here we not only import the raw material for the stage but the consumers. Among a people whose days are passed in ceaseless activity—whose common experiences continually surpass the ordinary limits of credulity—whose lives of wild vicissitude and adventure eclipse all dramatized fiction—it may be doubted whether a taste for these scenic entertainments will ever obtain a strong foothold. But should the drama ever prosper here, it is essential that its inspiration shall be drawn from American scenes — that the chords shall be wakened by the touch of native minstrels. For the present I have my doubts whether the majority of our Opera-goers (barring full dress and bouquets) would not sincerely prefer Yankee Doodle at the Circus.

But we are in Boston, and must remember the advice of Pliny:

"C'est a Athénes que vous allez, respectez les dieux."

ON THE WHARF.

Casco Bay
(1896)

CASCO BAY.

By Holman Douglas Waldron.

A HUNDRED nautical miles or more alongshore from Boston, or reached by rail in three hours and a half, lies beautiful Casco Bay. Its shores are not so deeply indented as those of bays farther east upon the coast of Maine, for no great rivers like the St. Croix, Penobscot and Kennebec help form broad estuaries to expand its waters. Its shores circle in one regular sweep from Portland Head on Cape Elizabeth to the long peninsulas of Harpswell, which two points of the crescent, approaching each other to within twenty miles, with an extreme depth of ten miles from the main, enclose two hundred square miles, corresponding in size to Moosehead Lake. A great part of the bay is occupied by the numerous and famous islands. A majority of the writers upon Casco Bay have strengthened the popular error that there are 365 of these islands, one for each day in the year. In truth, there are 122, great and small, ranging from a mammoth of two thousand acres, to "Punkin Nub."

Casco is a deep-water bay. Its tides rise and fall ten feet between ebb and flood, yet at their lowest mark expose no reeking mud-flats. The island shores are chiefly precipitous rock, interspersed by pebbled beaches; above the water-line they are covered with verdure, and in most cases are heavily wooded. A bountiful nature has bestowed matchless favors upon the region, to which man has added civilization's adorning touches; no element of natural beauty, summer comfort, seaside sport or historical interest is lacking. The legends of Captain Kidd and buccaneers of his ilk, without which no New England coast town can hope to appeal to the public, have been carefully sorted and none but the best retained; while the sea serpent is seen here as often as anywhere.

There are three epochs in the history of Casco Bay. The story of the first is told in the more or less vague records and traditions which have come down from the time of discovery and the early settlement of its shores; the second is that period when its waters were troubled by the ever-increasing keels of merchantmen, and its coast towns were building; while the third covers Casco's growth in popularity as a summer resort.

One cannot approach, as a histor-

PHOTO. BY GEORGE LEWIS STONE.

ical student, any one of the prominent bays which indent the coast of Maine, without meeting some of those picturesque characters from the Old World, whose names are so stamped upon that romantic page of the New,—the period of early settlement. Thus Passamaquoddy has its Des Monts and Champlain; Penobscot, its D'Aulnay and Castine; while Casco, modestly retiring behind its threefold screen of islands, evaded discovery by adventurers from Catholic France and remained to form part of Puritan New England. For this it forfeited from its history that spice of romance and chivalry which characterized the Gallic adventurers farther east; French dominion, guided by the powerful hand of Richelieu, reached no farther than Penobscot Bay, with Pantegoet (Castine) as its extreme outpost.

The earliest recorded mention of Casco Bay, which also shows the derivation of its name, is taken from the log-book of a voyage undertaken in the time of James the First. After the failure of the Popham colony at the mouth of the Kennebec, within one year after its commencement, the prejudices against the northern coast raised at home by the disheartened adventurers, who branded the country as "over-cold and not habitable by our natives," checked the spirit of colonization; but in the following year (1614) an expedition was fitted out under command of Captain John Smith "to take whales" and also "to make trials for a mine of gold and silver." The first quest seems to have proven of the fox and the grapes order, for Smith says in his log: "Of whales we saw many and spent much time chasing them, but could not kill any, they being a kind of 'jubartes' and not the whale that yields fins [bone?] and oil as we expected." The mines also were disappointing; so, leaving his vessel, with eight men in a boat, Smith ranged the entire coast from Penobscot to Cape Cod. He says: "Westward of Kennebeke is the country of Aucocisco, in the bottom of a long, deep bay full of many great isles, which divide it into many great harbors." Aucocisco expresses the aboriginal name of the bay as nearly as it could be pronounced by the English tongue; and Casco is its natural curtailment. The same name is given to the bay by Jocelyn in his voyages, and its na-

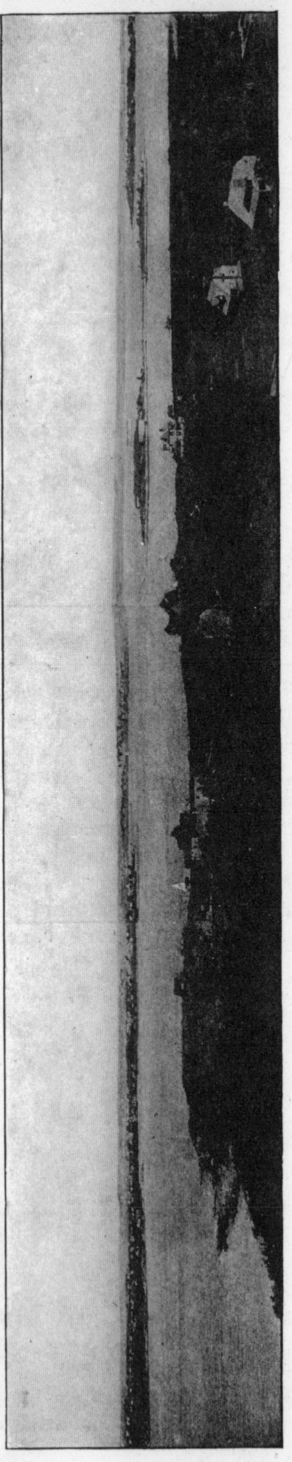

PORTLAND HARBOR FROM CUSHING'S ISLAND.

STEAM PACKET PORTLAND, J. HOWES *Commander.*

tives are given the same as a tribal name by Georges in his "America Painted to the Life." The meaning of the Indian word, according to the best interpretation, is "the place of the heron," a bird which to this day much frequents its shores and islands.

Many incidents of historical interest occurred in the mid-period; for Portland early became noted for its West India fleet, as much its specialty as the East India trade was that of Salem, or the whaling industry that of New Bedford. In the year 1826, the tonnage of vessels entering the port of Havana alone from the United States was 117,776, of which 11,619 was from Portland. Boston could boast but 10,930 tons, New York 8,516, and Philadelphia 4,936. In 1832, the registered vessels belonging to this port were twenty-eight ships, ninety brigs and twelve schooners, in addition to which there were vessels enrolled and licensed from Portland, bringing the number up to 412, all told, employing in their navigation 2,700 seamen. Even fifty years earlier than these dates show the commerce of Casco Bay active and enlarging, and the Yankee sailor a power in the land.

This commerce received a stinging blow from the embargo act of President Jefferson in 1807, from which it did not recover until after the peace of 1815. The shipping before the embargo was valued at a million and a half of dollars. In the two years following 1807, the navigation of Portland fell off nine thousand tons, and the amount received for duties, which

PHOTO. BY GEORGE LEWIS STONE.

DEVIL'S BACKBONE, ORR'S ISLAND.

in 1806 was $342,909, declined in 1808 to $41,369.

During this epoch, busy scenes were being enacted about Casco Bay, in numerous coves and at advantageous points upon the mainland, from Portland to Harpswell, rose the ways from which floated many of the commerce carriers of that day. The booming stroke of the shipwright's adze and maul, and the ring of the hammer upon the anvil, as the ship's irons were forged, merrily broke the stillness of the shore. Still standing to-day are many examples of the great square-framed "cook-house," where "Master" this and that boarded his crew of builders; while veterans of that day love to point out the spots where ships of large tonnage were built and launched, where to-day a modest sloop would scarcely float. From within some obscure cove has sailed many a noble ship, officered by men of the stamp of "Zephaniah Pennell," that lovable character in Mrs. Stowe's "Pearl of Orr's Island."

"He had read many wild leaves of God's great book of Nature, for, like most Maine sea captains, he had been wherever ship can go, — to all usual and unusual ports. His hard, shrewd, weather-beaten visage had been seen looking over the railings of his brig in the port of Genoa, swept round by its splendid crescent of palaces and its snow-crested Apennines; it had looked out in the lagoons of Venice at that wavy flood, which in evening seems a sea of glass mingled with fire, and out of which rise temples, and palaces, and churches, and distant, silvery Alps, like so many fabrics of a day-dream. He had been through the Skagerrack and

THE "COTTAGE CITY."

Cattegat, into the Baltic and away round to Archangel, and there chewed a bit of chip and considered and calculated what bargains it was best to make. He had walked the streets of Calcutta in his shirt-sleeves, with his best Sunday vest, backed with black glazed cambric; and in all these places he was just Zephaniah Pennell — a chip of old Maine — thrifty, careful, shrewd, honest, God-fearing, and carrying an instinctive knowledge of men and things under a face of rustic simplicity."

PHOTO. BY GEORGE LEWIS STONE.

ORR'S ISLAND FROM BAILEY'S ISLAND.

In addition to the great sea-rovers, nondescript home-built craft, so admirably described and sailed by the Rev. Elijah Kellogg in the healthy pages of his Elm Island stories, carried the lumber, masts and spars from Casco's forests to the Spanish markets. For no longer was the King's reservation placed upon the best of the forest product, to be used in the construction of English ships; America was free, and each freeman alongshore saw the wealth that surrounded him. As master-builder or master's man, sailor or farmer, the sea was made to pay him tribute. Small wonder, then, that the coast-wise people of Maine are sailors. From just such an obscure port as I have described came in 1895 the entire crew of the yacht "Defender"; while it is claimed for Maine, that the state furnishes commanders for fully one-third of our entire merchant marine.

Having named the Elm Island stories of Kellogg and the "Pearl of Orr's Island"

PORTLAND HEAD LIGHT.

WHITE HEAD, CUSHING'S ISLAND.

A TYPICAL SUMMER COTTAGE.

Casco's summer coterie of guests is more democratic than that of any other Maine resort. Near neighbors all must be, perforce; yet the narrow separating water-ways form barriers which prevent a social clash. The uproarious fun of Peak's, which is visited daily by hundreds of Portland people, cannot affront the more decorous Cushing's, nor disturb the quiet home life of the brilliant Diamonds. It is as if each island was a feudal castle, with its deep surrounding moat always flooded. It is wrong, however, to suggest caste here; call it, rather, diversity of tastes. The visitors to Peak's are every whit as companionable as their neighbors, and the entire *ensemble* of the bay is necessary to the full enjoyment of the scene. The life which gay Peak's adds relieves any sense of solitude, and affords always the possibility of fun; if a party from the quiet islands wishes to join the merry-making at Peak's, there is always the steamboat service or the row boat, and it is a matter of but a few moments' pull. This must not be construed into an

by Mrs. Stowe, let us approach their scenes through the Casco Bay of to-day, which has advanced less than two decades into the rediscovery period; for it was again discovered by the advance guard of the annual tourist throng, in the same sense that Saratoga, the White Mountains and Bar Harbor were discovered. A handbook of Portland and Casco Bay, published in 1876, says, with reference to summer sojourning: "It is estimated that 500 people are camping out on the islands; the building of cottages has begun, — already five are completed." Such was the small beginning of this resort.

LOBSTER POUND, HOUSE ISLAND.

VIEW FROM THE EASTERN PROMENADE, PORTLAND.

apology for Peak's. It needs none. Of all the islands, barring Mt. Desert, it is the bright and shining light of the Maine coast, and would be more generally mourned than any should it drop out of the galaxy of Maine resorts. My purpose is to show that within five miles from Portland, Casco Bay can offer surroundings to suit any taste; and, if the taste be for quiet, none will be disturbed therein, though the neighboring isles abound with fun.

Portland and Casco Bay form the Utopia of those of moderate means; nowhere will a dollar procure more of enjoyment. The city itself has abundant hotel accommodations and boarding-house facilities. Stronger and stronger each season grows the practice of selecting Portland as the base of summer campaigning. The Portland citizen has long predicted that his precious town was ultimately to become a second Newport. Seldom indeed is a city blessed by such surroundings as Portland, a non-manufacturing trade centre, with well-stocked stores, pleasant homes, many points of historical as well as scenic interest and a perfect electric car service, connecting all important points in the city and its suburbs.

The steamboat service of Casco Bay is remarkable. No large steamboats are required, for in the land-locked waters danger and sea-sickness are unknown quantities. A fleet of trim screw steamers plies the waters of the bay with a frequency suggesting ferries, making it possible to visit its farther confines, take dinner and return to the city before evening.

The visitor to Portland seeks first the remarkable Eastern Promenade, which is to Portland what the citadel is to Quebec. From its heights, o'erlooking the tranquil bay, he sees a clear water expanse of three miles to the shores of its most populous islands. So closely do these islands

PHOTO. BY GEORGE LEWIS STONE.

THE BRIDGE, ORR'S ISLAND.

approach each other, in regular military order, that the harbor of Portland resembles a broad inland lake, an illusion only dispelled when the eye seeks the horizon and encounters "the sheen of the far-surrounding sea."

Voyaging upon the surface of the bay, threading the narrow channels between its numerous islands, the matter-of-fact observer concludes that these water-ways were first plowed out of the mainland and then the furrows filled in by the sea. Whatever the plowshare that grooved these passages, its work seems to have been systematically performed. The long, irregular peninsulas, mere ridges of hard granite, islands almost, which extend from the mainland at the northeast extremity of the bay thrust themselves into the sea for many miles, in a uniform southwest direction; and beyond, like broken-off fragments, extend the outer islands of Casco Bay, preserving the same general trend as the peninsulas, until they meet the mainland again at Cape Elizabeth, that stupendous bulwark, bold enough to stop even the ice cap of the glacial period; that Cape Elizabeth named in honor of the virgin queen by the young adventurer, Raleigh Gilbert. Three groups of these islands are thus formed, called the outer, middle and inner group. Of these, the islands comprising the inner group are much the largest and are the ones most resorted to for recreation and health.

But it is a mistake to approach Casco Bay in any other direction than from the west, by Portland Head, that noble promontory, the sea-wall of Cape Elizabeth, which gave the name to the city of Portland. Portland Head bore its present name as long ago as 1750, while it was not until 1786 that that part of Falmouth known as the "Neck" was separated from the rest and reincorporated with the name of Portland. Upon the seaward extremity of this headland was displayed the first beacon-light upon the New England coast by the United

States government, lighted for the first time January 10, 1791, from a tower erected by the government upon a beginning made by the city, to mark the entrance to the narrow ship channel, not more than one mile from mainland to island shore, which allows passage for the largest ships from the open sea to that safe haven within the shelter of the inner islands. In vain the northeast gales incite the sea to struggle for an entrance; island barriers beat back every effort, until no more angry, baffled waves are to be seen upon any coast than, in times of storm, break along the seaward ledges of the islands.

A CAPE ELIZABETH FISHERMAN.

Upon the mainland of the Cape, but a short distance west of Portland Head light, have stood since 1828 the "Two Lights" of Cape Elizabeth, on each extremity of a long and narrow granite ledge which rises fifty feet or more above the low ground surrounding it, giving an elevation of 150 feet to the beacons which they bear. Very brilliant lights of the first order they are, one a fixed white, its mate a flashing white, raised upon dark cylindrical towers, exactly alike, not so picturesque, either in position or outline, as the spotless white tower upon Portland Head, but so large that seventeen persons have stood together within the lantern of one tower, when lens and lamp were both in position. The three form the harbor lights of Casco Bay.

THE WATER CARNIVAL.

Under the shadow of the "Two Lights" nestle the little gray cabins of the life-saving station, with its paraphernalia of life-boats, bombs, signals and beacons. The duties of the crew at this point are no sinecure, for the reefs and rocks now and then claim a victim in the laboring coaster or fisherman; but since the wreck of the *Bohemian*, no disaster attended with loss of life has befallen a passenger steamer in Casco Bay. The ill-fated *Bohemian* was an iron British mail steamer of the Allan Line, which in attempting to enter the harbor of Portland through the ship channel one stormy spring morning in the year 1864 struck upon the outer ledges, passed over, and was torn to pieces by the waves in one of the coves near the "Two Lights." Twenty lives were lost, and the shores were strewn with wreckage from Casco to Cape Ann.

All about these shores are jagged reefs and rugged masses of sea-worn rock, with narrow water-ways between, through which the ocean billows incessantly plunge and recede

SHORE DRIVE, CUSHING'S ISLAND.

with booming chorus. It seems improbable to a witness of the scene that, but a short distance beyond, one descends from crag and cliff to the silvery-sanded shore of that continuous line of beaches which, beginning with Scarboro, terminates in Old Orchard and extends to the mouth of the Saco River.

Much resorted to are the rocks of the Cape, about the lights, by fishing parties, for here the cunner is at his best, and from the ledges a line may be thrown into deep water. A common sight in summer to the people of the Cape are the passing teams, each with its long bamboo poles trailing out behind. By these signs they may be recognized as fishing parties bound for "The Lights." But even this pastime, like the camping at the islands, is falling into disuse. The hotels and road-houses at the Cape, with their specialties of shore cuisine, are claim-

CAIRN, ERECTED BY THE CUNNER CLUB.*

ing more and more of the outing throng each year. Where the past generation was content to catch its own fish from the rocks and cook the chowder and the fry over a driftwood fire, their children demand a more luxurious feast. The chowder is passing. No more will poets sing its praises, nor men like Daniel Webster boast of their skill in its preparation, nor men like N. P. Willis leave recipes for it:—

"O, chowder! monarch of the stews—
With onion tinctured,—I am fain,
By aid of my enraptured muse,
To sound thy virtues in a strain:
The nation's glory, greatest dish
By art conceived and born of fish."

Even the "Cunner Club" has abandoned its old-time tryst, erected a

* At the annual meets since 1845, each member has placed one stone upon this pile.

THE HOME OF "THE PEARL OF ORR'S ISLAND."

club-house further alongshore, and employed a caterer. This organization of twenty-five choice spirits, no more, no less, have, since 1845, enjoyed an annual outing on the Cape, always in one spot on Portland Head, where they each year prepared and ate their cunners, with all the detail which the "State in Schuylkill" devoted to their planked shad, or the famous "Beefsteak Club" of London bestowed upon their choicest cuts.

All along the Cape shore, which is picturesquely wooded a few hundred yards inland and rejoices in good roads, are summer villas and cottages, from the little lean-to to the turreted "Queen Anne." One source of congratulation have the happy summer colony upon the mainland—the Cape Shore and Falmouth Foreside; the matchless water supply of Portland, drawn from the clear depths of Sebago Lake, is conducted to their cottages, a blessing denied the denizens of the islands. During the season of 1895, another pleasing feature was added, in an electric car line, which promises to make the Cape shore more popular than ever. From the centre of the city it now threads the roads of the Cape as far as Simonton's Cove, a pleasing bit of beach just beyond the ramparts of Fort Preble, where a Casino is in process of erection for 1896, while the rails will be extended to the "Two Lights." Such activity will possibly make a break in the

END OF ORR'S ISLAND.

personnel of the "Jordan neighborhood," a Cape locality covering a wide area where it is said every mother's son glories in the surname of Jordan, save one,—and his name is Jordan Larrabee.

Hearty, saline types of humanity are the majority of the dwellers upon Cape Elizabeth, half farmer, half fisherman, dipping their lines occasionally into that great grab-bag of Nature, the Atlantic, in the intervals permitted by the great growth of cabbages, which is the vegetable specialty of the Cape. There are localities peculiarly adapted to various vegetable growths. It is so with the potatoes of Aroostook, the turnips of Passamaquoddy, and the cabbages of Cape Elizabeth. Some combination of the soil with the sea air imparts a growth and flavor which has won for the Cape cabbage a marketable distinction. Tons upon tons, carload after carload, of the well-favored, humble vegetable are shipped from the Cape each winter, a sequel to the long rows of green which in summer have stretched shoreward from the roads which skirt the ocean. Their cabbages are as sure a crop as their fishing ventures are uncertain.

EVERGREEN LANDING, PEAK'S ISLAND.

The islands at the entrance of Portland harbor crowd in toward the Cape, and fortifications upon either hand guard the entrance. The first island off the Cape shore to demand attention, the outermost one of importance, is Cushing's, one of the most exclusive of Casco's isles, crowned by its large hotel, and with its not numerous, but imposing, cottages. There is not much picnicking at Cushing's, in comparison with gay Peak's, yet the abundance of wild raspberries draws many a frugal housewife from the city thither during the fruit-canning period. Its hotel is thronged each season by a happy coterie of guests, many artists among them, drawn by the rare opportunities for marine studies which the island affords. The seaward side of Cushing's is particularly rugged and precipitous, culminating in that colossal cliff—White Head—which rises directly from the sea to an elevation of one hundred and fifty feet.

BEACH, CUSHING'S ISLAND.

Cushing's was the island refuge for the little band of men, women and children who fled from "The Neck" (Portland) during the Indian raid of 1676. Led by their pastor, the Rev. George Burroughs, they held the savages at bay with patient fortitude and great bravery, until rescued by a vessel providentially sent from Boston by order of Governor Leverett in aid of the eastern colonists. This Parson

DIAMOND ISLAND, FROM PEAK'S.

Burroughs is the same whom we find later suffering the extreme penalty of the law at Salem, condemned for witchcraft.

Next inside of Cushing's, toward the city, is House Island, recognized by the gray granite walls and green ramparts of Fort Scammel, which lies almost directly opposite the Cape shore fortification, Fort Preble. Between these narrowly separated barriers, an invading force must pass to approach the city nearer than five miles, while but a short distance within the harbor, in another commanding position, Fort Gorges stands upon its isolated ledge of rocks, its numerous ports sweeping all points of the compass. But in these days of heavy armament and long-distance-firing guns, a five-mile limit would be no greater barrier than the forts themselves, which are chiefly notable for their picturesqueness and the interest they add to "the altogether" of Casco Bay. Fort Preble is the only one of the three which is at present garrisoned by troops and floats "Old Glory." The government has recognized their unsuitability for defence, and shore batteries which shall mount modern guns are being erected on Portland Head and Cushing's Island.

The channel forts were built about the time of President Jefferson's unpopular embargo act; therefore the structures were derisively called "embargo forts," and their purpose declared to be to keep the Yankee shipping in rather than the enemy out. As originally constructed, Fort Preble held but eleven and Fort Scammel but nine guns. In 1864, thorough repairs

PHOTO. BY GEORGE LEWIS STONE.

UNLOADING FISH, BAILEY'S ISLAND.

PORTLAND AND HOUSE ISLAND FROM GREENWOOD GARDEN.

and extensions were made, giving to Preble seventy-two pieces, to Scammel seventy-one. At this time, also, Fort Gorges was built, designed to hold two hundred guns.

Although these harbor defences are placed about but one approach to Portland, it must not be inferred that there is no other entrance to Casco Bay. White Head passage — between Peak's and Cushing's islands — allows vessels of moderate draft to enter or depart, when the tide serves, and one of the most absorbing marine pictures imaginable may be caught at night from the shores of either island, as the trim schooners of the fishing fleet pass silently through the phosphorescent water. Farther down the bay toward Harpswell are two other passages to the sea — Hussey's Sound and Broad Sound, neither of them, however, feasible for vessels of large tonnage. It was through Hussey's Sound that the cutting-out party took the captured cutter *Caleb Cushing;* but — to use Kipling's word — "that's another story." It must not be omitted, however.

Notwithstanding the numerous de-

THE LONG PENINSULAS OF HARPSWELL.

fences about its harbor, Portland was the only Northern port to be entered by an armed Confederate force during the Civil War, a period in which its citizens were in continual anxiety, owing to the fact that during a part of the time gunboats were building here for the Federal service, while but a short distance out were powder mills where, it is claimed, two-thirds of all the powder used by the Northern forces was manufactured, for which Portland formed the shipping point. It was with the purpose of destroying the gunboats that an incendiary party entered the harbor on June 27, 1863, in the schooner *Archer*, passing the forts as a fisherman about six o'clock in the evening.

ON CUSHING'S ISLAND.

The *Archer* was manned by a prize crew originally from the *Florida,* the first commerce-destroyer of English origin owned by the Confederacy. With eight guns and commanded by a lieutenant bearing a commission from the Confederate government, they were placed on board a prize taken by the *Florida* on the Brazilian coast; and immediately this new broom started North to sweep the sea. Between May 6, 1863, and the date of their appearance at Portland, the party had taken and destroyed fourteen prizes; the last of these, the *Archer,* became the privateer that entered Casco Bay. Fortune favored Portland in the events which followed. The breeze proved so light that the scheme of firing the gunboats was abandoned, and a plan was laid for the cutting-out of the revenue cutter *Caleb Cushing* from her anchorage very near the city's wharves. It was well into the night before the attempt could be made, for a dancing party had gone to the islands early in the evening, and until their return the invaders dared not move. Finally the coast was clear, the capture was successfully made, the crew confined below, and the cutter got to sea; but so light was the wind that the captors were obliged to tow their prize, and when morning dawned the missing craft was seen from the observatory at Portland, not more than five miles at sea. The pursuit was active, the breeze light, the pursuers using steam, the pursued dependent upon their sails; consequently, ten miles off the Cape an exchange of shots was possible.

DIAMOND COVE, CROW ISLAND.

ON CAPE ELIZABETH.

shrapnel from the cheese-shotted guns. Eventually, the cutter was abandoned by her captors, who first fired the magazine, blowing the *Cushing* skyward in view of a vast concourse of spectators, who had hurried to the Cape to watch the pursuit.

House Island is credited with having given a home to the first white inhabitant of the bay, though to-day it is far from populous. Although nearest to the city, it is not one of the island resorts. No pleasure steamers land at House, which is given over to the deserted fortifications, the flakes which surround the fishing station at the opposite end of the island, and a hermit fisherman who plays the jew's-harp in fine and a fog-horn in foul weather, one for the amusement, the other for the protection, of the steamboat passengers as their bark speeds past his shores. Here also is a

Then it was discovered that something was radically wrong on board the *Cushing;* they could find no shot for the guns,—powder in plenty, but no shot. Supplies and ammunition had been taken on that day and, there being no opportunity to distribute them, still lay in a confused mass between decks, the supplies covering and entirely concealing the shot. Not one of the captured crew would reveal the secret. It is said that what the captors did find was several round Dutch cheeses of available calibre. In lieu of more effective ammunition, they loaded these upon the blank cartridges; and, if we may believe the story, many a man among the pursuers that day was driven below by the scattering

VIEW FROM HOUSE ISLAND.

fine example of the fisherman's low, white house that is so common upon the Maine coast, always occupying the highest point of land, always overlooking the sea, apparently brooding, like the women who call it home, over the fearsome changes of the treacherous deep. It is rumored that the New York Yacht Club proposes to purchase a site on House Island and erect a club-house as a rendezvous for its members in eastern waters.

Rounding House Island, we come in sight of Portland, at the farther shore of the bay,—sea-surrounded, throned on hills, tree-embowered. The citizens of Portland are extremely

OLD REVENUE CUTTER "CALEB CUSHING." *

proud of their harbor. They love to hear it designated "The Natural Seaport," and are fond of the extravagant saying that its waters would float the combined navies of the world. For this sentiment, which is still rampant, they paid roundly in the year 1859, when the Victoria wharf was built to accommodate that stupendous marine failure, the "Great Eastern." It was in the year 1853 that the first British steamship sought a winter port in Portland and found her citizens then, as now, possessed of unbounded faith in the city's future. Therefore, when the announcement was made that the *Great Eastern* was to make port here, at the earnest solicitation of the Grand Trunk Railway, Portland, its seaport terminus, appropriated $60,000, to which the railroad added $25,000, and the wharf was built. It consisted of two piers extending into deep water, across the ends of which the mammoth was to lie. Down each pier the railroad extended its tracks, to facilitate loading and discharging. Everything was in readiness, enthusiasm ran high, thousands of tickets of admission to view the ship were printed and distributed to the eager citizens; but the steamship which they longed for never came. To this day, the wharf is known as the Great Eastern wharf to many who are unacquainted with its story.

Nevertheless, other notable ships have since visited Casco Bay and allayed the chagrin of its people. To Portland harbor came, in 1869, H. M. S. S. *Monarch,* then the pride of the British navy, with a convoy of American men-o'-war, bearing the remains of George Peabody. It was in the city hall of Portland, tastefully decorated for the occasion, that the body lay in state prior to that last stage of the journey toward its Massachusetts resting-place.

Portland harbor is a favorite summer rendezvous for the North Atlantic squadron of the American navy; and twice since the establishment of the "White Squadron" have the citizens been afforded an opportunity to contrast those glorious ships with such types of the old wooden navy as the *Tennessee, Kearsarge, Vandalia* and *Ossipee,* which were frequent visitors. Hither came the cruiser *New York,* fresh from her triumphs at Kiel, and in November, 1895, followed the U. S. battleship *Maine,* to receive the silver plate given by the state to its proud namesake.

Portland harbor forms the winter port for two lines of ocean steamships, the Allan and the Dominion Lines. Wharf facilities are abundant, and the huge grain elevator of the Grand Trunk Railway discharges the products of the great Northwestern grain

* Re-drawn from a pencil sketch made by a member of the crew of the *Cushing*, just previous to the cutting-out, and presented to Howard D. Waldron of Portland, father of the author. This is without doubt the only picture of the cutter now extant.

belt direct into their capacious holds. These steamships are a never-failing source of interest to the citizens of Portland,—"Down to the English steamers" being with them a favorite Sunday promenade. Beginning with the earliest days of steamboat navigation, the waters of Casco Bay have witnessed the advance from the most crude to the most modern type. When one compares the steamer *Portland* of 1835 with the *Bay State* of 1895, it will be admitted that the advance in sixty years has been rapid. The steamboat *Portland* carried the engines from Robert Fulton's *Chancellor Livingstone,* the largest craft ever attempted by the father of steamboat building. Built at New York in 1816, under the superintendence of Fulton himself, and designed to run on the Hudson, the *Livingstone* was purchased, in 1832, by Commodore Vanderbilt and placed upon the route between Boston and Portland as an opposition boat. The *Livingstone* was finally broken up at Portland in 1834, and her engines used in the steamer *Portland,* launched in 1835. During the Mexican war, the *Portland* was chartered by the United States government, and was lost on the gulf coast of Mexico.

In 1895, the writer accompanied three hundred members of the International Ticket Agents' Association upon a cruise in Casco Bay upon the last acquisition to the Portland-Boston fleet, the steamer *Bay State.* Representatives from every state in the American Union were in the party. What pleasure for a man loyal to his state to point to our splendid type of steamship as entirely of Maine construction and equipment! Her hull was built at Bath, her engines and furnishings were supplied by Portland.

In addition to the line of steamers between Portland and Boston, there is the outside line between Portland and New York. Then, too, the steamers between Boston and the British Provinces make Portland a port of call. These, with the pleasure steamers al-

ways on the move, the merchant sailing craft of every degree, the many yachts of the home club with their numerous visitors, and last, but not least, the fishermen, make up a lively harbor scene. This brilliant scene is never seen to greater advantage than at late afternoon. Then the host of cottagers from the city are returning from the day's occupation to their summer homes. A half-dozen boats steam out from the wharves at this hour to take the cottage contingent down the bay. They will return for the larger party who go down after tea each evening for the theatre, the dance, or the skating rink at Peak's. Down from the city, as if pursuing the pleasure fleet, there comes the regular evening boat to Boston, a spotlessly white side-wheeled steamer, of the type conspicuous on Long Island Sound. Less frequently appears the dark-hulled screw steamer of the Portland-New York Line. These majestically round the buoy which marks the channel and pass out beyond the Light; now the boom of the sunset gun is heard from Fort Preble; down come the colors from the flagstaff; and, as the electric lights begin to kindle, we land at Peak's, after twenty minutes from the city, with the summer evening for enjoyment.

Sea bathing is both a delightful and a healthful pastime in Casco Bay, as a visit to the bathing-beaches will show. There are none of the crowded bathing-hour scenes one witnesses at Old Orchard, for those who visit the islands for the day do not bathe,—that is, in public; yet each island and each cottage colony has its bathing-beach, where all participate in the sport.

Peak's, although not the largest of Casco's isles, is by far the most populous, and is the only one which may be called an all-the-year-round suburb of Portland. It is not a heavily-wooded isle, and upon its western side, where are located its pastimes and its largest cottage colony, it is a grassy plain. Stately oaks, however, shade the approach to the steamboat landing, and a towering hard-wood grove utilized as a summer garden occupies one extremity of the island. In addition to this, its principal landing, there are two others upon the harbor side of Peak's, about each of which are hotels and large cottage colonies. To reach these landings, one must steam down through the narrow roads, with the evergreen-clad shores of Peak's upon the right and the heavily wooded heights of Great Diamond upon the opposite hand.

There are no hotels upon the Diamonds—the land, in the portion not covered by the magnificent timber growth, being occupied by cottages of architectural beauty and abounding in home comforts. Here the professional man and the unostentatious man of means have their summer homes. Their cottages are most systematically arranged upon the gently-rising greensward, from the shore to the apex of the island, in company-front alignment, overlooking the inner bay toward Portland and the mainland shore. Great Diamond possesses a pretty little casino of its own, where hops, musicales and private theatricals are indulged in by the cottagers *en famille.* The background to the cottage colony of Great Diamond Island is the "Salvage Woods," whose ancient beeches, oaks and maples it must have been which inspired Whittier's lines on Casco Bay:

> "Where hillside oaks and beeches
> Overlook the long blue reaches,
> Silver coves and pebbled beaches
> And green isles of Casco Bay."

Nowhere are the fir and the hemlock more green or fragrant than those which line the shaded wood-roads through the miniature forest of this gem of Casco Bay. The wood extends to the farther verge of Great Diamond and there borders the shores of Diamond Cove, a spot more in favor with chowder parties than any other upon the islands during the sail-boat period of their popularity. At that time, Diamond Cove was about the limit of picnicking in Casco Bay, though occasional excursionists visited Chebeague, the largest of the islands lying on the direct route to Harpswell. On their route, they passed Long Island, which has since leaped into favor, as have also the islands off Harpswell and the peninsulas of Harpswell themselves. Still it will be many years ere the farther islands present the populous appearance of the favorites that are in close touch with the city.

No better introduction can be had to the farther end of Casco Bay than the opening words of Mrs. Stowe's "Pearl of Orr's Island":

> "Sunday morning rose clear and bright on Harpswell Bay. The whole sea was a waveless, blue looking-glass, streaked with bands of white and flecked with sailing cloud shadows from the skies above. Orr's Island, with its blue-black spruces, its silver firs, its scarlet sumachs, lay on the bosom of the deep like a great, many-colored gem on an enchanted mirror. A vague, dream-like sense of rest and Sabbath stillness seemed to brood in the air. The very spruce trees seemed to know that it was Sunday and to point solemnly upward with their dusky fingers; and the small tide waves that chased each other up on the shelly beaches, or broke against projecting rocks, seemed to do so with a chastened decorum, as if each blue-haired wave whispered to his brother, Be still — be still."

The habitant of the lower bay forms a type as quaint and as interesting as the people of the Cumberland Mountains, though still wanting a modern writer to idealize him. Like his neighbor of the cape, he is a semi-marine, for a sailor or fisherman he issues from his cradle. It is he and his ilk, dwellers upon the shores of Casco Bay, who have won for Portland the distinction of being the third fishing-port of America in size of fleet and value of catch, when food fish alone are considered and the whaling industries are left out; Gloucester and Boston alone exceed it. The United States Fish Commission credits Portland with a fishing fleet of ninety-six sail, and Boston with but fifty-nine. Boston's tonnage, however (3,231), slightly exceeds Portland's (3,224), and the value of Boston's annual catch ($350,000) exceeds Portland's ($280,000). This shows that the Boston craft are larger than the "down-easters," and that a large part of the Portland fleet are shore-fishermen, making short trips in and out of Casco Bay to assist in keeping the New York and New England market supplied with fresh fish; for Maine's shore fisheries are of much greater consequence than those of any other New England state.

Leaving the outer islands and following the mainland shore of Casco Bay, off which lie the islands of the inner range, from Portland eastward towards its confines, we find several towns abutting the bay, their shores known as "The Foreside," to distinguish them from other parts of Falmouth, Cumberland and Yarmouth, each of which presents a foreside to the sea. Of these, Falmouth Foreside is most populous. From Mussel Cove to Broad Cove, there is one long-drawn-out line of handsome villas and substantial old farm-houses, with Madocawando Landing in the centre, commemorative of the meeting here, in 1703, between Governor Dudley of Massachusetts and ten sagamores of Maine, supported by two hundred and fifty well-armed warriors. Some of the establishments on Falmouth and Cumberland Foreside are the most pretentious about Casco Bay. All along these foresides, safely anchored beside their orchards and corn fields, are many retired seamen still attracted by the ocean, as typified by Casco Bay, still also with their weather eye open upon its ventures. Past Cumberland, Yarmouth and Freeport, the shores extend to the head of Maquoit Bay and there, turning, begin the formation of the Harpswell peninsulas. It is this Maquoit Bay, an arm of Casco, which penetrates farthest the mainland of Maine; and it was from the head of Maquoit Bay that the Indians chose their carrying-place between the sea and the Androscoggin River. A bee-line from the head of the bay, authentically vouched for as the old carrying-place, extends for five miles to the falls of the Androscoggin at Brunswick, forms the broad main street of that charming university town, and passes the buildings of Bowdoin College. No carrying-place in Maine was in so common use as this, owing to the peculiarity of the Androscoggin not finding the sea itself, but joining forces with the Kennebec. The whole region teems with stories of Indian warfare, in which a hardy lot of settlers struggled with the aborigines for the possession of one of the fairest spots upon the continent; for such surely is the region about Casco Bay.

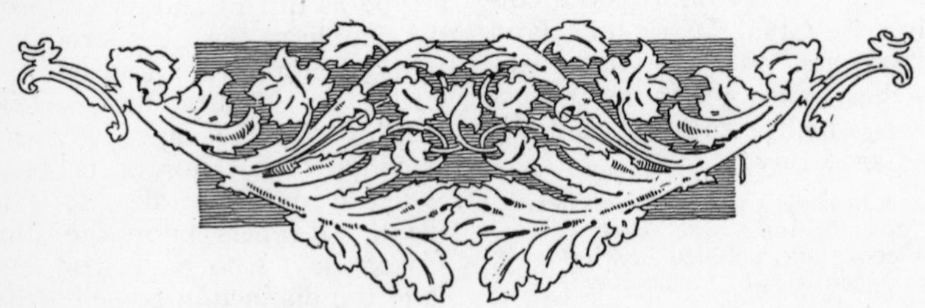

Coos and the Magalloway (1860)

HARPER'S
NEW MONTHLY MAGAZINE.

FEBRUARY, 1860.

COOS AND THE MAGALLOWAY.

VALLEY OF THE ANDROSCOGGIN.

THE tourist who has in summer time stood upon the top of Mount Washington can not forget the view which stretches away to the northern horizon. Immediately below him winds the Androscoggin; near it coils the Grand Trunk Railroad; and beyond rise the successive peaks of mountains, some bald and glittering in the sun, and others clothed in deep foliage, until

Entered according to Act of Congress, in the year 1860, by Harper and Brothers, in the Clerk's Office of the District Court for the Southern District of New York.

they become blue and shadowy in the distance. The Percy range lifts its snow-white tops toward the northwest; and beyond them the green Monadnock guards the west bank of the Connecticut. In the northeast the mountains of Northern Maine are seen, with the naked top of Escohos on their left; while the ragged spurs of Camel's Rump rise directly at the north, higher even than those shattered crags which form the jaws of Dixville Notch. Lifting up against the northern horizon, blue and misty, stretching eastward and westward, are the peaks of the Canadian Highlands—that wind-swept range which forms the boundary between the United States and Canada. Sections of the Connecticut valley on the west, and the valleys of the Androscoggin and Magalloway on the east, appear between the mountains; while, sparkling like mirrors set in the deep green of the forests, the Umbagog chain of lakes repose far up in their wood-encircled basin.

Over nearly the whole of this broad and wild region is thrown the gloomy mantle of the forest. A few farms and villages are visible near by, and then comes the dense and unbroken wilderness. Who that has gazed upon this wild panorama has not desired to penetrate the secrets of those gloomy solitudes, or conjectured what legends peopled those gorges and ravines, or what deeds of adventure those dusky valleys might reveal?

Lancaster, the shire town of the famous County of Coos, in New Hampshire, was the starting-point of our party. This charming town is one hundred and eighty-five miles from Boston by railroad and stage, and is at the outlet of one of those streams which rise among the White Mountains and flow westward into the Connecticut. The village is spread out upon those broad meadows which even here border that noble stream. A broad and shaded street, intersected by a few cross avenues, rows of neat cottages with a few elegant residences, three churches, an academy, a court-house, a jail, three hotels, one of which is very large and elegant, with stores, shops, and a bank, make up the village.

On a cloudy morning in September the long two-horse wagon was drawn up in front of the Lancaster House. Mount Washington was capped, and slight drops came down slowly through the humid air. It was circus day in the shire town. Joe Pentland was coming, and all was bustle and excitement. Already strange-looking vehicles, loaded with passengers, were driving in from the adjacent country. A crowd of the curious had gathered upon the piazza of the hotel as we came down, in thick boots, gray pants, red flannel shirts, and slouched hats.

COME TO SEE THE CIRCUS.

Here was the fellow who had come, with his wife and children, twenty miles to see the circus. He had left his "burned-piece" just in the nick of time, and his oats in the stook, and some stone wall which he was in a hurry to build, and his house that was to be shingled anew, and was bent on seeing "them chaps" ride six horses, and laying up a store of clown's jokes. He wore his best blue coat and gray pants, and high collar, and boots rubbed with tallow, and had brought with him his dinner and provender for his horse. Already he had invested in a stick of candy, and stood surveying our wagon with that cool, thin, sharp visage which is the type of a thorough-bred Yankee, at whom the whole world laughs, but whose owner outwits the whole world.

Near by stood quite a different individual, whose off-hand manner, easy motion, erect figure, and confident eye showed him to be a man of the world. He was the proprietor of a meadow farm, and lived in the same large house which his grandfather had built in the early days of Coos. He had been a member of the Legislature; owned the eighth of a township, from which he took lumber to the markets below; and that very morning had ridden over to the village, behind a spanking black colt, in a new Concord wagon. You may some day see him dash up to the Crawford House with a span

OWNS A MEADOW FARM.

of bays which he is breaking, dine, talk a few moments with Joe Gibbs, light a cigar, crack his whip, and roll away again. He is a type of the young men who are seen in all this upper country.

We were all seated in the wagon. There were two barrels of pilot bread and half a barrel of pork. There was a Champagne basket, in which was a medley of articles. There were fry-pans and kettles, a huge coffee-pot and a bag of sugar. There was a tent, a tripod, a compass, and a transit. There were guns, pistols, powder-flasks, and long knives. In short, we were completely prepared for a month's camping in the woods. The stars and stripes—an old tattered flag, which had seen several expeditions

GOOD-BYE TO LANCASTER.

of this kind—waved from a corner of the wagon, and all was ready.

"All ready!" called out the Colonel, the leader of the expedition, as he climbed into the wagon. Dan drew up the reins, flourished the whip, and we rolled slowly away. Three cheers burst spontaneously from the crowd as we drove off, bright eyes and smiling faces appeared at the windows, occasionally a white handkerchief waved an adieu, and the village was behind us.

Onward we went up the Connecticut. First came Northumberland, then Stratford, and at last, in the dusk of the evening, Colebrook, forty miles from Lancaster. Cheerily the lights of the little village shone as we rose over the hill and brought them into view. Right merrily, and with a prodigious clatter of wheels, did we drive up to the door of the only tavern.

A dozen individuals or so stepped out of the two stores and the tavern to inspect the new arrival, and gathered curiously about the wagon. Among them we were gratified to meet again our old friend, "The Squire," whose acquaintance we had made on the Umbagog years ago. His locks were whiter than when we had seen him, his voice slightly more tremulous as he gave us his hand, but he was still vigorous in mind and body, active and vigilant in business as when he first pioneered his way to this region of mountains. The Squire was a native-born gentleman, well educated, and a splendid specimen of an old mountaineer and lumberman. After supper we talked long before the wood fire. Captain Jones had come in; he was anxious to know about the Atlantic cable, and his surprise was unbounded when he learned that it was not an inch in diameter. Jim Sturtevant protested that he had seen trout in the Magalloway which would bite it off the first time. Bill Wright, "an old true-blue Isaac Hill Democrat," gave it as his opinion that it was a Federal trick to bind this country to England.

"I go agin' havin' any thing to dew with them British," persisted Bill.

Enter Major Eleazer Archibald. A chair for Major Archibald; and Major Archibald saluted each individual patronizingly. The Major proceeded to rub his hands before the fire and to assert, with caution and dignity, that there had been some prospect of rain; and then advanced the opinion that the nights would begin to grow cool before the end of September. Assented to by the whole company. The Major soon struck upon the universal theme of politics, and after descanting oracularly upon the tariff, Kansas, Cuba, and the whole list of topics, he came to the question of the removal of the shire town of Coos county from Lancaster. Here a fierce dispute arose between him and the Colonel, waxing warmer and warmer, until Bill Wright broke off the discussion by declaring that he was "agin' havin' any county seat at all."

"No county seat?" vociferated the Major.

"None at all," reiterated Bill; "courts are a humbug, got up to feed a lazy set of lawyers and cheat us poor devils."

The Major was commencing an argument with Bill on the propriety of courts of justice, when the Squire lighted his pipe, which he had been filling, rose, and wishing us a pleasant trip, walked out. We accompanied him along the short street of the now silent little hamlet. The lights in the two stores were blown out, and the loungers had scattered. Echoing musically upon the air came the murmur of the Connecticut and its more noisy tributaries, while as we looked out the giant hills, shooting far up into the starry sky, stood grimly, like mighty and silent Titans, sentinels of the night.

Never was a lovelier morning than that upon which we started to cross over the ridge of land which separates the Connecticut from the Umbagog. Our route lay in a southeasterly direction: first, up the valley of a small stream, called the Mohawk; then through a gap in the mountain ridge, which is only less famous than the White Mountain Notch because more remote from traveled routes; thence down the opposite slope to the valley of the Androscoggin and the basin of Lake Umbagog.

Now the road wound along the valley; now it coursed along the sides and over the very tops of high hills, from which we looked down upon farms, and around upon the crowded groups of mountains clothed with the magnificent foliage of autumn. The road becomes rougher, the farms disappear; we plunge down, down into a deep ravine through which foams a torrent. A few strokes of the axe repair the trembling pole bridge, and we rattle across it; up we clamber on the other side, over rocks, roots of trees, and stumps; down again and up again. The forest becomes dense and gloomy, and the branches interlock over our heads. We emerge into a little meadow, and before us suddenly stand the shattered and ragged walls of Dixville Notch.

Not more than a hundred feet in width, the walls of mica slate rise to the height of a thousand feet on either side, and overhang the path like gloomy and broken battlements. The frosts and storms, in their action of ages, have chipped these dark walls into all fantastical shapes—sometimes like the massive angles of some impregnable fortress — sometimes leaving ragged columns like the ruins of old towers. The path, just wide enough for one wagon-track, is hewn into the side of the chasm. On one side rises the threatening cliff, while below yawns the gulf.

Dan gave the Colonel the reins, leaving him to drive through; while the rest of us dismounted. Blowing a tin horn which we carried—the same which afterward disturbed the solitudes among the crags of the Canadian highlands—it gave out a blast like a war-trumpet; then dying away a moment, as if concealed among the broken rocks, it leaped out in a thousand commingling tones, clashing, contending, echoing, until they died away in varying cadences of melody. We discharged our fowling-piece at an eagle hovering over a cliff, when from behind every rock came a discharge as if guerrillas were

DIXVILLE NOTCH.

hidden there. Altogether this notch is a most remarkable natural curiosity, rarely seen by tourists, never by the languid summerers on the luxurious couches of the Glen House or the Profile House, but only by those who are ready to diet a week on salt pork—to be shaken beyond the reach of dyspepsia over roads rougher than the passage down Ararat—or to face swarms of black flies and mosquitoes.

The sun rose brilliantly, and a sky of cloudless blue hung over the mountains and forests, before the large batteau had swung from the shore above Erroll Falls, and turned its prow up the Androscoggin. The barrels and boxes and bags and packs and baskets were piled into the elegant craft, and from the prow floated the old tattered flag. In the stern, with paddle in hand, sat the Colonel. At the oars sat two of our party—a round, portly, muscular fellow, and a slender, but nervous and active, native of Coos. The narrator found a seat in the bow; while at other convenient places were stowed the mail-carrier for the Magalloway settlement —a sharp-visaged frontiersman—and a still smaller, but keen-eyed and wiry hunter, who was bound for Parmachene Lake, to spend three months in trapping.

Dan stood upon the bank near his horses and wagon as we were ready to push off.

"Yes, *Sir*," said Dan, "I should like to go on with ye." But just then his horses started, the batteau swung into the dark stream, the oars dipped, the wheels of Dan's wagon rattled across the rough bridge, a blast from the tin horn echoed along the shore, and we glided merrily up the Androscoggin.

Durkee's Landing, on the Magalloway, was the first point made. This Magalloway settlement, of about thirty families, is the last on the borders of Maine and New Hampshire, lying along the Magalloway River for about eight miles. No road connects it with the rest of the world, but the only avenue is the river and the Umbagog Lake. The river, starting in the Canadian highlands, is nearly a hundred miles in length; and the meadows which border it at this point are broad and very fertile. Loading our baggage upon a hay-cart, and sending it forward, the company amused themselves during the heat of the day by smoking their pipes under the awning of the rough wood-shed, telling stories, shooting the rifle, and collecting from Durkee information respecting the region.

Toward sunset we started for a walk of eight miles—to Captain Wilson's, the last house on the frontier. It was hot and sultry, and we sweltered along under the weight of our packs, guns, and axes. The long shadows came on speedily, and soon the sun, after resting a moment in a gorge of the mountains, sunk amidst a flood of golden light, leaving us to darkness and swarms of mosquitoes.

The woods through which the road led was musical with their hum. If we stopped a moment, myriads of the blood-thirsty wretches assailed us, ensconcing themselves in our hair and necks, until some tough-billed fellow would bore through our shirts and transfix our backs. As a last resort we lit our pipes, after which the whole swarm, evidently becoming delirious under the influence of tobacco-smoke, screeched with indignation, but kept aloof. In four miles we began to apprehend something of the pleasures of a summer tour in the backwoods, or, at least, that part of it which consists of traveling on foot over rocks and among stumps with packs lashed to our backs. Walking brought perspiration; perspiration produced thirst; thirst, heat, and fatigue combined produced faintness. There were stumblings against rocks; there were splashings through water and mud; there were imprecations on the whole race of mosquitoes; there were remarks deprecatory of the general nature of hot weather; and mutterings about the length of miles on the Magalloway River.

"What's that?" said John, resting a moment against an old stub.

We heard the sound of wheels echoing into the woods, and presently a horse and wagon came slowly and noisily on through the darkness.

"How far to Captain Wilson's?" all inquired at once.

"Are you goin' to Cap'n Wilson's?" returned the driver.

It was Captain Wilson's wagon sent out to meet us.

"Hawkum, for this is the best goin' you'll have," said the driver, and the wagon jolted on.

We emerged into open land, passed one or two cottages, then a school-house in which was a cheerful light: then the roar of a cataract fell upon our ears: we crossed a bridge hung above the foam, went up a gentle slope, and were at the door of Captain Wilson, the last settler on the frontier.

The Captain was a native of the vicinity of Portland, and was allured to this region just in the dawn of the great Eastern land speculation. He came to this spot by the Escohos Falls, surrounded on all sides by lofty mountains, twenty-five years ago, and settled in the expectation that the country would become populous, and consequently bring him wealth. But he has lived here twenty-five years, and still finds himself on the frontier, with no settler beyond him nearer than the Megantic Lake in Canada. He has led the life of a woodsman, a farmer, a surveyor, and an explorer. Many are the adventures he has met in this wild region. Often has he coursed through the trackless woods, between his house and Quebec, camping on a winter's night under the shelter of a few fir boughs, or

GOING UP THE ANDROSCOGGIN.

SETTLEMENT ON THE MAGALLOWAY.

living for days on moose meat. Time and exposure have now bowed his form, and furrowed his brow, and silvered his hair; but he is still active and enterprising, and enthusiastic in regard to the development and prosperity of this region where he has spent his life. He has been a member of the Maine Legislature, has a respectable law library, and is the Justice of the Peace and the legal adviser of the whole settlement.

We now prepared for the woods. A party of eleven were collected, consisting, in addition to that already mentioned, of the Captain and six experienced woodsmen. The object was an exploration and re-marking of lines. The party divided, and six started through the woods on a straight line, and five followed up the river in boats, carrying the stores. The two squads filed slowly into the woods at two different points, and each disappeared.

Two days the boats sped up the Magalloway, between the silent banks overhung with fir, pine, birch, and maple. The river winds among the mountains in all directions. The Rio Grande is not more crooked. Over the tops of the trees bald mountains are constantly seen, but otherwise nothing relieves the monotonous pathway, excepting where a crane soars clumsily into the air, or a flock of ducks start up ahead, or we discover where a moose has just scrambled up the soft bank, or when a fugitive trout is taken as we drop our hook into the water.

At night of the second day we encamped at the mouth of the Magalloway. Finding a level spot near the bank of the river, at the mouth of a little brook which came over the hill the tent was pitched. Soon the fir boughs were spread down for the bed, and a big fire blazed in front. We took an abundance of trout, some of them weighing nearly four pounds, and that night there was a banquet of roasted trout and frizzled pork, while stories were told around the camp fire.

When morning dawned the rain was coming down in torrents. All through the day it poured constantly. The wind rose and swept over the forest with a continuous roar. Clouds hurried swiftly through the heavens, and the old trees

IN CAMP.

other woodsman, and both were still again.

How much are we creatures of education and habit! To us few things could have been more startling than the weird tones which in that solitude were detected in the howlings of the storm. But the hunters had camped too many times on the snow, and too often following the moose up that valley had been overtaken by night in the dead of winter, to attach much importance to the occurrence. So they slept. Black as Erebus was the night; and as the fire, hissing and spluttering, threw its flickering light out into the darkness, making the spectral shadows of the huge trees dance to the music of the gale, we slept the sleep of neophyte woodsmen.

Not long after the sun had come out and the clouds scattered, an elderly man—a woodsman—came to the camp. He was drenched with water shaken from the bushes, and wore an anxious face. Two of his sons, he said, had started from a camp a few miles above to search in the woods for a "logging chance," and had not returned. We told him of the sounds we had heard in the night. He raised his gun and discharged it; then listened a moment; but hearing nothing, walked slowly into the forest. A few hours later voices were heard in the woods, and Captain Wilson, with another of the men, arrived at the camp, having started from the other party the day before. Being caught by the storm, they had found quarters in the woods overnight, and had been twenty-three hours without food. Toward night three more of the party, who had gone in with the stores, arrived. They also slept out in the storm under a little covering of birch bark.

Another day brought three of us—the rest having gone in with stores—to the "carry" at Parmachene Falls. The boat was taken out of the water, yokes hewn out with the axes, and carried by the rapids. Imagine the delights of a "carry!" A path led by the falls, but across it were big logs blown down in some hurricane, and it wound up the sides of hills and through tangled thickets.

Even here the lumbermen have penetrated, and at these falls have built a dam to facilitate

writhed and groaned as their tops bowed and swayed together. It was that terrific storm which swept over the North about the middle of September of that year.

As night again came on the Magalloway rose wildly within its banks and lifted our boat from its moorings. The little brook became a torrent, and roared close by our tent. The water streamed through our cloth roof. Settling down to sleep as best we might, we heard the excited Magalloway lashing its banks and the roar of the winds, while occasionally the dull, heavy sound of a falling tree announced the mastery of the gale. Hark! there was a crash, and an old dry tree plunged into the whirling water.

"Do you hear that noise?" said one of the men, starting up suddenly from under his blanket, and turning his ear up to catch the sound. His quick sense had detected the sound of a human voice mingled with the howling of the storm and the creaking of the old forest trees.

"That was a man's voice, sure," said he, starting up to his feet.

Again it was heard, like a long, low, tremulous halloo, and answered promptly by the woodsman. Again fainter, and again answered. The woodsman listened long, but not catching the sound again, at last slowly rolled himself in his blanket.

"A wet night they'll have of it!—most likely somebody from Joe York's camp," muttered the

the running of logs down the river. At a lumberman's camp near by—a unique specimen of architecture—we found lodging overnight. These camps are built entirely of logs, roofed with shingles rived from the pine-trees. They have one room, which is the cook-room, sleeping-room, and lounging-room; a large fire in the centre, from which the smoke escapes through a hole in the roof; a bunk on one side for sleeping, and a rude table made of split shingles at one end. A barn of similar architecture stands near. Here the lumbermen coming up from the settlements live during the long months of these Northern winters, going out in the morning as soon as it is light, cutting the logs and drawing them upon the ice of the river, to await the spring freshet which is to float them down, and not returning until dark. At night, after supper, pipe-smoking, and story-telling, they turn into their bunks. When the ice clears out of the river all hands commence driving the logs down the stream, until, through the tortuous channel of the Magalloway and Androscoggin, they arrive at Bath, where they are cut into boards and distributed to Boston, New York, and other ports, ultimately to line the palaces of Fifth Avenue or the residences on Brooklyn Heights.

The little skiff launched, the stores loaded into it, bringing it down to the water's edge by the slow and sturdy stroke of the paddle, the party followed up the Magalloway and swung out into Parmachene Lake, beyond reach even of the lumbermen, and opening to a region undisturbed save by the hunter.

Parmachene is a charmingly wild sheet of water, four or five miles in length, and one or two miles wide. As the little skiff dashed over the wave a solitary hunter's camp on the north side was the only evidence that man had ever trod its shores. First forest-covered hills, and then more distant and more lofty blue mountains lifted their tops all around us, wild and precipitous. This is a famous hunting-place, and is the resort of the woodsmen down the river as well as of the Indians.

Again the tent was pitched at "Little Boy's Falls"—three miles up a stream which enters the Parmachene, which is still called the Magalloway. Here we remained two days, waiting for the arrival of two of the other party, who were coming for provisions. They having arrived, three of us started early one morning for a walk of ten miles through the woods, following only the directions of the compass, to join our friends, who had been all this while sojourning in the depths of the wilderness.

"THE CARRY."

Nay Bennett led the way—a voluble, jolly woodsman, with a face, written all over with humor, protruding under the narrow rim of an old felt hat, with the tin trumpet slung under his arm, thirty pounds of provisions lashed to his back, and a hatchet in his hands. Then we followed, with only our blanket, gun, and ammunition. Behind came Linnell—a woodsman as quiet as Nay was voluble—one of the best hunters on the Magalloway, his cautious eye constantly out noting the forest trees, the brooks, and the elevations, and occasionally giving advice to Nay as to the direction to be taken. Both had trapped and followed moose through these wilds,

LUMBERMAN'S CAMP ON THE MAGALLOWAY.

and kept their course in the woods with as much ease as one bred in the city finds his way along the avenues and squares. Up and down heights, through snarled thickets of undergrowth, along mossy swamps, darkened by the boughs of the fir, we paced steadily. Some time after the sun had passed the meridian all three were lying upon the leaves, resting at the foot of a steep hill before ascending.

"There's thunder, and we shall get wet," said Linnell, quietly getting up, lashing his pack, and starting.

"It'll make it very pleasant for us," replied Nay, jumping up, looking at his pocket-compass, and giving a blast on his trumpet.

There had not been a cloud in the sky; but as we came over the height the gray and bald top of Cam-

PARMACHENE LAKE.

ON CAMEL'S RUMP.

el's Rump stood up right before us, and beyond it hung the cloud.

"That makes out to be Camel's Rump," said Nay,

Our course lay across the northern spurs of the mountain. We hurried on, the thunder muttering louder every instant, and occasionally the wind swaying the forest. At last, far up on the mountain spur, whence we looked down upon miles of dark forests and illimitable ranges of mountain peaks, the charged cloud enveloped the height and broke upon us. We had never been *in* a thunder-storm before; but here it was all around us. Now a tree was twisted from its slight rooting and hurled headlong down the steep. Now another was shivered by the bolt as the thunder bellowed around us.

"'T makes it very pleasant for us," said Nay, as we crouched under the leaning trunk of an old tree, endeavoring to get clear of the drenching torrents of rain.

We thought Nay's assertion was to be taken in inversion, and then and there so declared. So dense was the cloud that the lightning glared as in the deeper twilight. When the violence of the storm had passed over the rain still continued, and the only alternative was to advance. It was the same succession of gulches, gaps, and thick masses of witch-hazel bushes. Nay occasionally looked at his compass, took the direction, and went straight on, whether the way led over the top of a dizzy and tottering cliff or down the cavernous gulch.

After clambering up to the top of one of these spurs we were upon an immense bald and naked rock, which seemed to hang like a great excrescence upon the mountain side. The giant peak above us was wrapped in cloud, and far northward, westward, and eastward other summits pillared the vapory roof. All stood gazing down into the shadowy valleys, hundreds of feet below, arrested, seemingly, by the wild and solitary grandeur of the view. Our attention was attracted by the report of a pistol, coming dull upon the ear, as if from a long-distant height. Another, and then another, followed, more distinctly, and our own fowling-piece answered back. We took the direction of the sound, and started. Night was rapidly approaching. We stood at last at the base of an almost inaccessible steep.

"That's the way," said Nay, consulting his compass and pointing up among the jutting rocks.

"Can't go over that to-night," we protested, now thoroughly tired out.

"Give me your gun and take my hatchet," replied Nay; and we started again, dragging ourselves slowly and wearily up. Nay was creeping up in a fissure of an almost perpendicular rock, and we after him.

"'T makes it very pleasant for us," he ejaculated, in long pauses, just as he got his head above the edge of a table-rock.

We were denying it, *ab imo pectore*, as we hung to a small shrub which had rooted to the rock, when Nay commenced a series of exclamations and expletives, not unfit for that occasion, but not appropriate to print, and closing with a blast on his horn, stood pointing to some fresh spots upon a tree which stood upon the edge of the precipice. We had struck the line which our friends had spotted as they passed along, and we hastened over the crags. It was not until the darkness had enveloped us that the sound of an axe was heard ahead. A shout—a response—three cheers from the whole party, and we bounded on toward the light of a fire.

"'T makes it very pleasant for us," asserted Nay, throwing off his pack, sitting down upon a log, and giving a final blast upon his horn.

All hands were at work pitching the tent, some breaking wet fir boughs and shaking off the water, others leveling the ground and spreading the canvas, and others piling logs upon the fire. The rain still poured, but when the canvas was spread, the fir boughs laid down thick, the fire blazing up hot and drying our saturated clothes, things began to wear an air of comfort. The pork was frizzled upon the ends of long sticks, the hot tea poured into the tin dippers, the hard bread thrown out, and there was not a more jolly festival in the land than beneath that roof of canvas, high up on the mountain side, in the black night and the driving storm.

As we lay smoking our pipes, dry and comfortable in contrast with the dreary desolation outside our tent, the Colonel narrated the incidents of their trip; of the solitary and sombre glens, of the wild mountains, of the gentle streams, beautiful with none to admire; of the glorious sunrise and magnificent sunset, of ravishing landscapes, of the storm and the hurricane gamboling among the giant trees. They had ascended the highest peak of Camel's Rump and encamped overnight 4000 feet above the level of the sea, scaling, for miles, the steep precipices by the aid of lichens and shrubs, and coming down had discharged a small revolver from different peaks, hoping to attract our attention.

Then one of the woodsmen, who declared that they had "seen some proper bad pizgys" on the way, sang a song, one of the rude madrigals of the frontier. It was of a fair maid and a brave hunter, and an obstinate father. In vain the hunter busied himself in the woods and brought back rich burdens of furs. In vain he was the smartest chopper and best wrestler. So one night when the moon was full, John and the loving Julia started to cross the lake. But the obstinate father pursued, overtook them, was knocked overboard by John; after which himself and Julia, with great coolness and good judgment, embraced and jumped overboard also.

"'T made it very pleasant for 'em," said Nay, as the song ended.

But half the company had already rolled themselves in their blankets, and the camp was still.

Another day of mingled hail, rain, and snow kept the party in camp; but the next morning, while the trees were white with frost and the ground slippery, they took their course for the Canada line. Late in the afternoon they came upon the ruins of an old birch-tree, which was

CAMP ON CAMEL'S RUMP.

long the corner between the States of Maine and New Hampshire. It was covered with hieroglyphics, the initials of names once famous in the two States who had visited the spot long years before. Twenty rods beyond stood an iron monument, now the real boundary between the United States and Canada, as well as the corner of the two States. The line established by the Ashburton treaty runs from peak to peak of those Highlands which separate the waters which flow into the St. Lawrence from those which flow into the Atlantic.

IN THREE DOMINIONS.

This was the end of the trip. Nay sat himself down in Canada, hugging the iron monument, with one foot in Maine and one in New Hampshire, but declared that he felt no better in three dominions than he did in one. Now, nearly eighty miles from Captain Wilson's by the route we had come, the party, cutting their names upon trees and rocks, turned back.

Northward were seen the lower hills which border the St. Lawrence, and southward mountains piled one upon another, and gorges and deep dark valleys. But all was wilderness. Up the mountain sides the bright tinge of autumn had commenced; but down in the deep valleys, where the dark and changeless fir covers the ground, hung dusky shadows, and as we looked down it seemed as if we could not see the bottom. No sable drapery can be more solemn than these forests of fir. They seem to make the silence more still and the solitude more funereal. Seen from the heights, it is as if a vast pall were wound around the base of the mountains and stretched down the narrow valleys.

From this summit could be seen the sources of five large streams of the continent. The tortuous St. Francis, and the Chaudière, whose banks the terrible expedition of Arnold made at once sad and glorious, find their way hence to the St. Lawrence. Hence the Connecticut starts southward, and within sight of one of the hills which our party ascended were to be seen at the same time the head waters of Dead River, which feeds the Kennebec, and the Magalloway, which feeds the Androscoggin.

Nay was ahead, and the whole party, on the second day of their return, were treading along wearily, following each other like Indians in trail. It had rained all day, and now, nearly dark, more than fifteen miles lay between us and the camp of the night before.

"That makes out to be Little Boy's Falls," said Nay, listening, then giving a blast on his trumpet.

The crack of a revolver answered down the river. "Crack" answered the Colonel's revolver. "Crack" again down the valley. "Crack"—"crack"—"crack"—"crack"—from both sides, until the woods echoed and shouts rang out from both parties, and Nay's trumpet doubled its volume, while the cataract chimed in with a voice like Minnehaha.

"Nay, do you remember the catamount we saw over yonder once?" said the Captain, as all were at their rude supper.

"I make out to," responded Nay, just as he was putting to his mouth a heavy piece of fried trout, "What a cussed Babylonian he was, Cap'n: 't made it very pleasant for us; didn't it, Cap'n?"

Forthwith Nay commenced with the story.

"The Cap'n and I were spot'n' a line one spring before the snow was off. 'Long in the afternoon we heard what we thought was a man's voice a long ways off in the woods. Wa'al, I hooted, and it hooted back. 'T kept comin' nearer and yelpin' louder. 'Look 'ere, Cap'n Wilson,' says I, 'I've been in the woods a good deal, but I never heard that sound before.' By'm-by we set down on the snow to rest, and when we had got about twenty rods along the fellow gave such an ungodly screech as made my hair stand on end. Says I, 'Cap'n, that makes out to be a cussed Babylonian.' We had only an axe and a small shot-gun, not enough to make a dust in the eyes of the critter. 'Cap'n, didn't we take long steps?' After a while the critter lagged behind, and we heard him screech off in the woods. Wa'al, 't came night, 'nd we built a fire, 'nd made a camp, 'nd after a while got to sleep. I waked up some time in the night. The fust thing I see, when my eyes opened, was a couple of glaring balls right t'other side of the fire. There that cussed whelp set, on a log, not ten feet off, starin' right at us 'nd switchin' his tail jest like a cat afore she grabs a mouse. I didn't dare to start up the Cap'n, so I got up my shot-gun easy, and pinted it right into his face 'n' eyes. I tell ye he was a savage-lookin' devil, 'nd I reckon he liked the looks o' me about as well as I did o' him. Purty soon he turned his head round one side, and seemed to look at somethin' else. Then he turned clear round, and curled down close to the log, and kept on switchin' his tail, and lookin' off in another direction.

All of a sudden, as quick as a wink, he bounded off into the darkness, and then there was such a yellin' as I never heard. The Cap'n screamed and jumped up, and began to hunt for his axe. 'Get your gun, Nay!' yells the Cap'n; 'the cussed thing is after us.' 'Keep still, Cap'n,' says I, 'he's after that lucive: I've been watchin' him for a half hour.' 'Twas a short fight, and the lucive had the worst of it. Away went the cussed Babylonian into the woods, with the lucive in his mouth, growlin' as he went. He had pounced right into him, and took him for his breakfast instead of the Cap'n or me. If ever I meet a Babylonian again, I'll tell him to wait till I send for a lucive."

When the party arrived at Cap'n Wilson's, a few days afterward, the little settlement seemed great to them, and when they made the beautiful town of Bethel, Maine, it appeared to them as Rome did to the dwellers on the banks of the Mincius.

The author, having arrived at home, walked into his hotel, gun in hand, wearing still his woodsman's dress, but the clerk was in doubt about accommodating him, and intimated that they were *very* full that night. All stared as he took his accustomed seat at the table, and one inquired if that was the "Lumbermen's Hotel." He walked down through the lighted street, in the evening, passing his most intimate friends unrecognized.

CIVILIZATION.

In the night dreams of the Magalloway haunted his sleep. He traveled alone through interminable woods, and camped at night in a howling storm. Then he was on Parmachene Lake, and the little skiff swamped and sunk down unfathomably, until at last he was going up Camel's Rump, in the thunder-storm. Suddenly he heard Nay iterate that "'t made it very pleasant for us," and looked up. There was a catamount, having Nay's face, and with his trumpet hung to his neck, and his narrow-rimmed hat on his head. The Colonel was breaking great trout off from fir-trees, and spreading them down for a bed, and the rest of the party were coming over a rock in a boat. Suddenly the catamount showed his teeth, growled, and pounced upon Captain Wilson, who took a "lucive" from his pocket and gave him, which he swallowed at once and then growled more furiously than before. He seized his gun—such unearthly yells!—and he awoke in time to catch the last roll of the gong as it was announcing breakfast.

The Charter Oak City (1876)

SCRIBNER'S MONTHLY.

NOVEMBER, 1876.

THE CHARTER OAK CITY.

THE NEW CAPITOL.—VIEWS ON BUSHNELL PARK.

THE last census of the United States gave Hartford a population of considerably less than 40,000 inhabitants, ranking it as the thirty-fourth city in size in the country. Midway between two enumerations, as is the present date, it is possible only to guess as to the increase, and to surmise what now is its position numerically in the roll of cities. But if the number of its citizens cannot give it a higher place, still in many other respects it is one of the very foremost. The traditions of its history lead back to the first beginnings of New England settlement, and come down to the present time full of patriotic recollections. Its people have always been active in whatever they have undertaken, and whether in historical association, in the range and magnitude of its business undertakings, or in the culture and comfort that the success of these has brought, Hartford has come to be known, not only very widely through the country, but by the universal use of certain of its products, almost around the world.

SHIP-YARD AT DUTCH POINT.

Relatively to the number of its inhabitants, it is the richest city in the United States. Its savings banks have deposits of about $12,000,000; its banks of discount have capital and surplus of nearly $12,000,000, and deposits of more than $9,000,000; the capital of its other joint-stock companies is $18,000,000; the assets of its insurance companies are more than $113,000,000, and after the taxable portion of what has been mentioned is taken from the city tax list, the assessed value (not more than one-third the real worth probably) of the rest is more than $40,000,000. Of course, besides these evidences of wealth, there is a great deal, as in every city, which never finds its way into the tax list, and can only be estimated. Some of the manufacturing companies included in the aggregate are only organized, not operating; but others have surpluses more than doubling their capital, so that the figures given are certainly low enough; and if some of the assets of the insurance companies are not in Hartford, they are still all tributary to it, and pour their income regularly into the city. The total amount of the list is very much more than $200,000,000, and undoubtedly that estimate of the wealth of Hartford is less than facts would justify.

This attitude of Hartford as a rich city, though comparatively a new one, and to the historian probably not its most interesting, nevertheless is that which, in a mercenary age, is likely to attract for it the first attention. Permanently settled in 1635, it was until some time after the Revolution very far from being the richest town even in poor Connecticut, and the whole colony has not left a barrowful of prerevolutionary plate. Its increase has come chiefly through its railroad communications, the late successes of its manufacturing companies, and the vast development of its insurance interests. It is as a sort of City of Refuge that it is to-day most generally thought of. There is authority to believe that fire will ultimately destroy the world, and death the body; but, meanwhile, the Hartford insurance companies are ready to take risks on the realization of either certainty, and, thus far, in spite of some hard blows, they seem well in advance of fate. By the last official report, it appears that 212,467 people have their lives insured in Hartford. If each of these represents a family of five, then more than a million people are looking to the city as their refuge in the time which the insurance agent, himself a Hartford product, can so pathetically describe as certain to be, for the uninsured, of acute financial as well as domestic distress. These lives are insured for $450,000,000 altogether, and the property insured in the fire companies is $645,646,000 more, so that the total risk which Hartford carries is in round numbers $1,100,000,000. But the business of insurance has reached such a scientific basis that the probable losses admit of close calculation, and the amount of assets necessary to a certain payment is definitely fixed. The Hartford companies, having $113,000,000, have large surpluses above the amount required. Yet nearly all of this accumulation

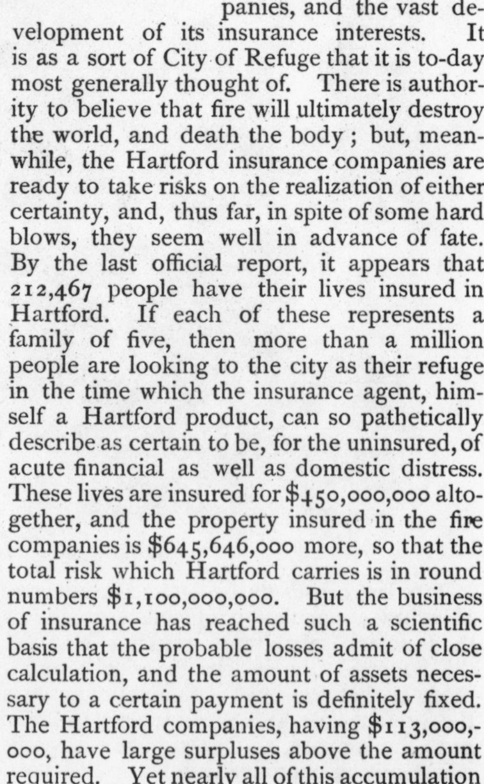

has come within a short time. The life insurance business began about 1850, and but three fire companies antedate the exceptional disaster of the Chicago fire.

No important life company has ever failed in the city. Although death seems so much more certain than fire, it is also so much more methodical that it is easier to calculate upon its ways. Fire companies, on the other hand, have failed. The Chicago fire put between the writing and the reading of this, some new great fire may have made fresh havoc with them, although the lessons of recent years have taught the managers to scatter their risks, and not to take whole city blocks together as they used. That one affair of Chicago, which marks Hartford's black day, took about ten millions of dollars away from the city, and, eight hundred miles distant from the fire, impoverished men who,

INSURANCE BUILDINGS.

1. Conn. Mutual Life Building, containing also Phœnix Mutual Life Ins. Co. 2. Travelers Ins. Building, with Railway Passenger's Ins. Co.'s Office. 3. Phœnix Fire Ins. Building, containing also Conn. Fire Ins. Co. 4. Hartford Fire Ins. Building, with Offices of State Insurance Commissioner, Atlas Fire and Continental Life. 5. Ætna Ins. Building (Life and Fire Co.'s). 6. Charter Oak Life Co. Building, containing also Office of Hartford Steam Boiler Ins. Co.

out six at once. But the oldest company,—probably the oldest in America,—the Hartford, which was insuring in 1794, is still flourishing. It, the Ætna, and the Phœnix, have paid in full every loss in every fire since they began business, and they are old, while the rest, revived or created since 1871, though young, are thriving under prudent administration. At best, however, they all are engaged in a truly risky business, and, the day before were rich. A singular freak of fate made the loss seem even a bit worse than if it had come on any other date. In Hartford, insurance stock is taxed at its market value, and the tax lists are sworn to, October 1st each year. The fire came on the ninth of the month, and so the holders of the worthless or fallen stocks had for that year to pay taxes on the highest valuations the stocks had ever known. If the fire had occurred ten days earlier, the difference in favor of the individual losers would have been very considerable. It was only by securing large amounts of new capital, and

RESIDENCE OF MRS. COLT.* (PORTE COCHÈRE.)

sacrificing all the accumulations of years, that the three great companies at that time saved themselves. Under the present official supervision of the business, the companies do not run risks after their early fashion; yet, even then their apparent recklessness often ended in complete success. For an instance: the great New York fire in 1835 which broke every New York company, came upon one of the largest in Hartford just as, after a series of poor years, it was about to pay a liberal dividend. The loss was complete; capital, surplus, dividend, all the assets, went to ashes. But instead of despairing, the President, Mr. Nathaniel Terry, a well-known citizen, who died years ago, borrowed the then considerable sum of $10,000 on his own personal credit, and instantly sent an agent to the city with the money. As soon as he arrived, he paid one loser, a prominent merchant, the whole of his loss, and, with his card of acknowledgment, printed a notice in the newspapers, promising to pay every loss within the sixty days allowed by the contract. This announcement took panic-struck New York by surprise, and everybody who had anything to save rushed at once to insure in a company so evidently sound. A round rate was charged for the privilege, and, before the sixty days had passed, the agent had taken in in New York alone enough money to fulfill his promise to pay all losers, and he did do it. This sort of venture would not now be either attempted or allowed; but it suggests the "enterprise" that in the beginning pushed the Hartford companies toward their present high rank. Their losses paid in 1875, when there was no great fire, were $4,913,217. One company has paid $45,000,000, and another $20,000,000, in losses since organization.

Three of the life companies—the Connecticut Mutual, Ætna, and Charter Oak—and two of the fire companies—the Hartford and the Phœnix—have put up fine buildings in the city. These, and three or four other comparatively new, or yet unfinished, structures, are the most noticeable business blocks in Hartford. A half dozen of them tower over the rest of the city in a way to give the spectator, at first sight, the perplexing doubt as to whether the architecture of the town has had a little too much,

* By kind permission we have here made use of several engravings from the beautiful Colt Memorial Volume.—Editor.

or much too little, leaven in it to produce such startling inequalities of elevation. But, after several seeings, the odd effect is lost, and there are found significance, utility, and no little beauty in things as they are. The successive levels reached mark the steady rise of the city in importance; first, low brick or wood buildings; then, more pretentious of brick, or brick and stone; then, stone generally from the Portland quarries near by; and now great granite piles, rising six or eight stories high, with, too, a revival of the use of brick in some of the finest works. The upper floors of some of the insurance buildings are occupied as residences on the "flat" plan, and are light and cool by reason of their height, and command beautiful views of the city and the country about.

FOUNTAIN AT ARMSMEAR.

Hartford's situation, though probably chosen by accident, is admirable for its beauty and for its business advantages. It lies on the west bank of the Connecticut River, about fifty miles from Long Island sound, and has the Little, or Park River, flowing about and through it. This empties into the Connecticut at Dutch Point, the place where the Dutch, the first settlers, built a fort in 1633. The high ground of the city affords at various places a fine sweep of scenery up and down the Connecticut Valley. Outlying manufacturing villages, grown up beside every tributary stream, are here and there visible; the river comes into sight at intervals among its curves; fields and foliage fill the valley, and parallel mountain ranges bound it on the east and west, about twenty miles apart. These, continuing south to tide-water, mark the course of the river as nature first arranged it,

CONSERVATORY AT ARMSMEAR.

when it flowed into the sound at New Haven, and before the stream was turned off toward Saybrook at Middletown, a little below here, by a recent convulsion, only a few hundred decades ago. The soil of the valley is made fertile by annual freshets, and its tobacco, of which large crops are raised, is the most expensive American product of the plant. There is an important trade in that and in other agricultural staples here. For a large district around it, Hartford is the base of supplies, and its local business of all sorts is extensive. Five railroads center here, and the river bears an important commerce, so that the city is made a point of general distribution. All about it are manufacturing communities, mainly created by Hartford capital, among which are Collinsville, with its famous axes and other edged tools, and agricultural implements; New Britain, with its hardware; Thompsonville, with its carpet-works; Rockville, with its woolen-mills; Willimantic, with its immense spool-cotton factories; and South Manchester, the model manufacturing village of America, where the most of the Cheney Brothers' silk-works are situated.

PINERY AT ARMSMEAR.

For a long time the city has been noted for its inventive skill. Before the present century began, Hartford and its vicinity were operating printing-presses, paper-mills, powder-mills, glass-works, tinware factories, —from which the first Yankee peddlers set out,—the first Connecticut clock factories, and woolen-mills. Many of these industries have remained until now. The first printing-press, set up in 1764, printed the "Courant," and that journal, now 112 years old, has ever since been regularly issued, save for one brief delay during the Revolution, when the supply of paper failed. To meet this emergency, the proprietors hastily built a paper-mill of their own, and that was the founding of the since important East Hartford paper-making interests. The Hartford woolen-mill was in operation in 1788, when General Washington visited it, and his admiration of its work was such that he wrote home to say he should use its best fabrics for himself, and its cheaper stuffs for his slaves, thereafter. The next year, when he was made President, he wore a complete Hartford suit, everything about it, even the buttons, being made in the city, as a present for him, and it was in this Hartford dress that the first President of the United States made the first inaugural speech. There is not space here to enumerate all the manufactures now carried on in Hartford. Connecticut's products are more varied than those of any other State in the Union, and nearly all its varieties are represented about or in the city. A single factory,—perhaps the most famous in the country,—that of the Colt's Arms Manufacturing Company, will have to suffice; and it is worth a note how much Hartford, a city where a battle never was distinctly heard, has had to do with war. The East Hartford Powder Works, the Colt arms, and the Sharp's rifles, of especial Kansas notoriety, are to be considered; and

CHURCH OF THE GOOD SHEPHERD.

VIEW IN "COLT'S MEADOWS."

also the fact that two secretaries of the navy, and at least five prominent generals, have been, or are of the city. Everybody has heard of—almost everybody, indeed, has heard—the Colt revolver. No modern invention has come into more nearly worldwide use, nor has any other so universally carried with it its inventor's name. It is a safe assertion that no modern name is more familiar around the globe to-day than Colonel Colt's.

In choosing Hartford for his manufactory, he made a wise selection of a site for his works, and laid out one of the most important parts of the city. The Connecticut River has its spring freshets with all the regularity of nature. Each year it washes out the lower part of the city, and produces trouble all along the line for the residents in the water-wards, who are each year, as regularly as the freshet comes, freshly surprised at its advent. It was a lot of low land, just below Dutch Point, that Colonel Colt selected. He built a solid dike about three hundred acres of land there, and that district has known the spring flood no more. Then the factories, operatives' homes, and other necessary buildings, were put up, which, with their constant increase, have become now almost a city by themselves, and include mills, store-houses, a large public school, the finest church in the city, dwellings, and many other establishments, besides the Colt factories. The first set of these was burned during the war, but new and large fire-proof buildings were erected at once in their place. Now, besides the Colt revolvers, there are made in the factories, steam-engines, printing-presses, and various other machines, and the Gatling guns, large revolving weapons that can be used on land, at sea, or on horseback, and that at the turn of a crank pour out bullets at the rate of four hundred a minute, making them one of the most formidable of recently invented arms. The willow basket-works that utilized the osiers with which the dike is planted and strengthened have lately been burned, and are not rebuilt; but the first purpose of the osier-planting is still met in the hold their roots have upon the dike.

STATE-HOUSE SQUARE, DAY BEFORE "THANKSGIVING"

"Armsmear," with the residence which

Colonel Colt built on the high ground that slopes back from the meadows, is a beautiful place, nearly two-thirds of a mile deep by one-third in its street frontage on Wethersfield Avenue. The prospect from the house and grounds is magnificent, and the premises are laid out with all the beauty that skilled landscape gardening could add to a naturally graceful situation. The place has its lakes, its deer park, its graperies and groves and gardens; and

THE CHARTER OAK.

through the grounds are set a number of fine works of statuary. Within the diked district is the Church of the Good Shepherd, built by Mrs. Colt as a memorial of her husband and children. It is a remarkable piece of church architecture, the work of Mr. E. T. Potter of New York. Its design is exquisite, and the plans, even to their minutest detail, have been executed with a scrupulous fidelity that makes of it an almost faultless structure, symmetrical in every line, and rich and appropriate in its ornamentation. Its large memorial window, imported from England, and its singularly graceful baptismal font, are among its first-noticed beauties. It is considered one of the finest churches in the country; many say that it has no equal in America.

On the same hill-side, but a little north of Armsmear, is the site of the Charter Oak, the venerable tree, whose familiar tradition has for years reflected glory on Hartford, often called the Charter Oak City.

GRAVE-STONES IN OLD CEMETERY.

It stood on the Wyllys place, and the illustration, specially copied from a painting, made for the late Isaac W. Stuart before the tree fell, shows the oak and the old and now departed Wyllys mansion, the frame of which was brought over from England and set up

THE REV. DR. HORACE BUSHNELL.

about 1636. The tree was, so goes the story, spared when the clearing for the house was made, because the Indians had so long used it for a landmark that they had a deep veneration for it, and begged for its preservation. However old it then was, it lasted two hundred and twenty years longer, and only fell in 1856. The current version of the story of the Charter Oak is as well known as that of William Tell or Pocahontas. On the last day of October, 1687, Sir Edmund Andros came to demand back the liberal charter that Charles II. had granted, and to set up a new rule. There was a meeting of the general court, a charter was produced at his demand, suddenly the lights went out in a general confusion, and on the resumption of order and candles, the document was gone, Colonel Jeremiah Wadsworth having rushed with it off to the oak, and hidden it in the hollow trunk. This act saved the liberty of the colony then, and made Wadsworth and the oak famous now. That is the gist of the story. That there was a meeting with Andros, and that there was a charter and a tree, are admitted still by all; but the more careful historians in this day of reversing "the verdicts of history," are not inclined to go much further in support of the old tradition. Certainly there were two charters, the original and its duplicate. In May, six months before Andros came, the original was put out of the way. One definite account says it was kept in Guilford, Connecticut; and again there are reasons to think it may have gone into the oak. At best, there is nothing certain about it. Whatever disturbance occurred with Andros was over the duplicate, not the original charter; and until some time after the affair, the oak is not heard of in connection with it. A tradition of the Wadsworth family had it that the charter was hidden in the cellar of the Wadsworth house. Years afterward the Connecticut Assembly refused to give Colonel Wadsworth four pounds as a reward for his services, but voted him twenty shillings, suggesting that our fathers did not prize liberty very highly, or else failed to view this deed just as the school-books now record it. Moreover, Mr. C. J. Hoadly, the Connecticut State Librarian, an authority in antiquarian subjects, has, in a recent note to a work he edited, pointed out what seemed to him proof that Andros's visit did put an end to the colonial government, so that if the charter went into the oak, it still went out of legal existence. To retain it, annual elections had to be held. But after Andros came, one election was omitted, and this, he says, terminated the government. A singular proof is offered as evidence that later administrations knew the illegality of their tenure of office, in the fact that Connecticut had no witchcraft craze, although so near to crazy Massachusetts. People were aroused enough to try several witches, and a few were sentenced to death, but all were reprieved by order from Hartford, showing that the administration did not dare to exercise the death penalty, being conscious of its own imperfect hold upon the government, and so of its personal accountability for such deaths. On the other hand, even if the government was not legal, it was all there was; and it is one of the proudest facts in Connecticut history that the charter was preserved, whether in the oak or not, and that the colony never was governed by officers appointed by the crown, but has always, from the beginning, chosen its own rulers by popular election. The original charter reappeared in 1689, and hangs now in the Capitol in the custody of the Secretary of State. The duplicate disappeared, and was found in Hartford in 1818 by the late Hon. John Boyd in a curious way. He was a student preparing for college, having a fancy for odd papers and an antiquarian taste.

He saw the lady with whom he boarded about to cut up into a bonnet-frame an old piece of parchment. By replacing it with pasteboard, he secured the document, and, on subsequent examination, found he had saved the duplicate charter. It now is held by the Connecticut Historical Society out of the range of all the votaries of fashion

All that marks the place to-day where the Charter Oak stood is a white slab set in the sidewalk. Not even a railing fences in the sacred spot, which is daily trodden under foot. But the name cannot be forgotten; for, from high to low, the title Charter Oak is emblazoned upon sign-boards all over the city. These and the chips of Charter Oak that may be found in the home of every "son and daughter of Connecticut" are its chief and its steadily increasing mementoes. Not the gloomiest iconoclast expects ever to see the supply of wood from the old tree give out.

After the Charter Oak Place, the most historic ground in Hartford is the State-house Square, originally much larger than now, very near the middle of the city, where State street, running back several blocks from the river, meets at right angles Main street, the great north and south thoroughfare. The present State-house, about to be vacated for the new Capitol, stands in the Square, and the new post-office is begun there. The two previous State-houses, the first church (which was half church, half State-house, and, later, was made into a barn), the first tavern, first jail, and first burying-ground, were all in the Square. But these have entirely disappeared, the graveyard being more easily forgotten, because, as is said, an economical generation used the grave-stones for the foundations of new buildings. It may have been from the Square that Wadsworth took the charter, perhaps to the oak. It was on this ground that Washington and Rochambeau first met each other, an event of great importance in the Revolution. It was there that Lafayette was publicly received. Indeed, the story of the events of the spot is almost the history of Hartford. A vestige of the old-time market day is found now at Thanksgiving Day and Christmas, when the Square is filled with farm-wagons, from which poultry is sold in the open street. Hotels, eight banks, and a number of the finest business blocks, stand about the present limits of the Square. Near by, on Main street, is the Center Congregational Church, that of the oldest society in the city; and back of this church is the old town cemetery, full of queer grave-stones and graves of the early settlers.

WARD'S STATUE OF ISRAEL PUTNAM.*

Churches are abundant in Hartford. The first English colony of settlers came with their religious organization all perfected, and the pulpit of the city has been always influential. Stone and Hooker, the first ministers, were both men of note. It was for Stone that Hartford was named from Hertford, England, which had been his home; and Hooker, the master-spirit of the colony, has left a name and memory that will survive as long as Hartford is. From them down to the present time there has been a

* See SCRIBNER'S MONTHLY; Vol. VI., p. 500.

BARTLETT'S STATUE OF WELLS, "DISCOVERER OF ANÆSTHESIA."

succession of strong minds in the ministry here. Of late years was Dr. Joel Hawes, who died in 1867 after a settlement of nearly fifty years, over the Center Church. One of his published works, "Lectures to Young Men," reached a circulation of 100,000 copies, and he was known and felt very widely. Dr. Horace Bushnell, who died this year, was one of the foremost thinkers in the American pulpit. He was a pastor in Hartford for twenty-three years, and a resident for twenty more. His power through his pulpit was felt deeply at home, as well as all through the theological world; but it was as a citizen, as much almost as it was as a minister, that he was known and loved here. He was interested in all the projects for the city's welfare that have matured, and was the source of many of them, and of many others that would have been of great benefit had they been undertaken. The Bushnell Park, recently named in his memory, which is one of the finest of its size in the country, was designed by him, and his energy carried through against great opposition the scheme for its creation. What was one of the worst and most desolate parts of the city has been transformed into a complete garden, a pleasure-ground, and a breathing-spot, that is now of inestimable value, and one of Hartford's chief ornaments. The new Connecticut Capitol, a fine marble structure, is approaching completion on the high ground of the west side, a site selected by Dr. Bushnell, from which Trinity College is being removed. Mr. J. Q. A. Ward's statue of Israel Putnam, erected by the late Hon. Joseph P. Allyn, is on the west park too; and back of it, beyond the river and the railroad are seen, on the left, the High School, on the right, the residence of ex-Lieutenant-Governor Julius Catlin, where Mrs. Sigourney, the poetess, lived for more than twenty years. On the east park, by the fountain, is T. H. Bartlett's statue of Dr. Horace Wells, erected by the city to honor the discoverer of anæsthesia, who was a resident of Hartford, and performed here the experiments by which he made his discovery. A bitter dispute, for which there seems to be no anæsthesia, prevails as to whose the credit of this really is; but, without arguing the point, it may be said that in Hartford there is, and seems possible, only one opinion,—that Dr. Wells was the first to introduce to the human race this grateful gift, for which men owe him most, just when they are most unconscious of all their obligations.

Returning to the subject of the Hartford pulpit, at least eleven Episcopal bishops—Coxe, Doane, Potter, and Wainwright of New York; Chase of Illinois, Clarke of Rhode Island, Burgess of Maine, Doane of New Jersey, Niles of New Hampshire, and

FORMER RESIDENCE OF MRS. SIGOURNEY.

YUNG WING.

Brownell and Williams of Connecticut—have been residents of the city; while four other Episcopal bishops are graduates of Trinity College, and one Roman Catholic archbishop, Bailey of Baltimore. The Congregational Theological Institute, formerly the East Windsor Hill Seminary, is now in Hartford, and is in excellent condition. The Hartford churches, the buildings themselves, are of all types and of all materials,—wood, brick, and the various sorts of stone. The dark sandstone is perhaps the most frequently chosen. The variety of styles is noticeably agreeable to the eye, and many are very graceful works; several spires, in particular that of the Pearl street Congregational Church, next to the Phœnix Fire Insurance building, being really admirable. Yet, church spires are rather a delicate subject to allude to, for perhaps to signify their faith in the future, an unusual number of the societies have built their churches steepleless, leaving these ornaments to be added in the hereafter; and, meanwhile, the lack of the spires, for which the bases have so long stood waiting in their unfinished rudeness, is the most serious flaw in the appearance of the city.

The Hartford school buildings are said to be the finest in the State. There are nine large public schools, including the public High School, with about nine thousand pupils altogether. The High School, under Professor Joseph Hall, in which is practically merged the old Hopkins Grammar School, established in 1657, has about four hundred and fifty scholars, and has a reputation with all the leading colleges as one of the best of all the preparatory schools. Some of its scholars now are Japanese. It is a singular feature of Hartford that it has a really considerable Oriental population. A dozen or so of Japanese boys—very bright ones too—have been studying in the city for some time. They dress in simple European style, and are distinguished only by their Japanese stamp of countenance, and by being at the head of the classes they enter in the schools. There is also a Chinese settlement, the most important in the country, and one of the most interesting elements of Hartford life to-day. Under the charge of Mr. Yung Wing, the Imperial Commissioner, who has been lately made LL. D. by Yale College, the Chinese Educational Mission has been established, with head-quarters in the city of Hartford. Chinese boys are brought over, and given by this Mission as liberal and useful educations as can be had; and they are to go back eventually cultivated men, familiar with the world, and able to maintain for China its independence and increase its influence among nations. This educational work, conceived years ago by Mr. Wing, and now at last being put into practice, bids fair to

CHINESE PUPIL RECITING.

be one of the great facts of our time, and factors of the future. The pupils and attachés of the mission retain their Chinese manners, dress, and speech, though they learn English, and it is no longer a matter of any remark to see the full Chinese costume on the street, with the queer shoes, bright-colored clothes, white sun umbrellas, and the round caps with a long "pig-tail" flowing out from each, and to hear the strange jargon of their almost unutterable language. The work of the mission is being very thoroughly done; it has an ample fund, and a building for its use is now being put up on Collins street. The intelligent and attractive young people are put among careful families in various places, but each has to spend a certain time every year at the central establishment, to revive in Hartford the ways and tastes of China, his home. A single incident of their school customs will show how thoroughly the reverse of our ways are theirs of the reverse side of the globe. In studying, each scholar is required to repeat his lesson constantly to himself out loud, and the teacher detects the shirker by missing his voice in the general Babel; and again, at recitation, the scholar stands in front of the teacher, but with his back turned toward him, and repeats his lesson in that attitude. Mr. Wing's work, and his remarkable personal history, were made the subject of a special article in SCRIBNER for May, 1875. Nor is it necessary to write here of Trinity College among Hartford educational institutions, for that was fully described in the number of this magazine for March, 1876.

Besides the actual schools of the city

THE WADSWORTH ATHENÆUM.

there is a powerful educating influence in its libraries. The Watkinson Library of Reference, established by will of Mr. Robert Watkinson, a member of one of the old Hartford families, who left $100,000 for the purpose in 1857, has about 27,000 volumes, selected under the excellent judgment of

HARTFORD PUBLIC HIGH SCHOOL.

Dr. J. Hammond Trumbull, its librarian, who has made it an exceedingly useful and valuable consulting library, since he took charge of it in 1862. The Connecticut Historical Society has about 15,000 volumes, the most of which are rare works; while, besides its innumerable and very curious relics, it holds in trust all sorts of old correspondences of great historic importance, as well as interest. These libraries are in or added to the Wadsworth Athenæum building. In this is also the Wadsworth Art Gallery, where, besides works by Trumbull, the early historical painter, and Mr. F. E. Church, a native of Hartford, may be seen a full-length portrait of Benjamin West by Sir Joshua Reynolds. In the statuary is a large collection of the pieces by the sculptor Bartholomew, of Hartford, who, though an early death cut him off from the greatest fame, left behind him works full not only of promise but of merit. The Young Men's Institute, in the same building, has a circulating library of about 25,000 volumes; and in the Capitol is the State Library, with a full collection of English, American and Irish law and also other books and manuscripts. On removal to the new Capitol, it is proposed to add to the State Library a copy of every book by a Connecticut author. This list, leaving out the Historical Society, which is private, presents pretty fully the fund of information open to the public. Then there are private libraries known by name at least to all book-collectors. Of these the finest, as it is one of the finest in America, is that of the late Mr. George Brinley, who spent many years and a deal of money in getting it together. It contains a perfect Mazarine Bible, really the first important work ever printed in the world with movable type. A copy advertised in England this year is priced at $15,000 gold. It has also two or three copies of each of the two editions of the rare old Eliot Indian Bible, and these copies are respectively the finest in existence. There is, too, a "Bay State Psalm-book," and of works of the early American press, between the psalm-book (1640) and the year 1700 there is a collection absolutely unequaled. These are only a part of the many volumes, and are its rarities, not its especial elegancies, but the superlatives used in description are fully justified by the facts. Few people know the library except by name, because Mr. Brinley guarded it most zealously as long as he lived. Dr. J. Hammond Trumbull also is the owner of a fine collection of books, manuscripts, and literary valuables, among which are at least two Eliot Bibles, and he is the only person living who can read the book.

Publishing began to assume visible proportions in Hartford early in the century, and, after the issuing of a series of school books, became, as it still is, a thriving industry of the place. The influential volumes in establishing the business were Smith's Geography and Arithmetic, by the late Roswell C. Smith, of Hartford; Olney's Geography; Comstock's Philosophy and Chemistry, and Mrs. Lincoln's Botany. Schoolboys of fifty years ago will remember some of these better than more recent scholars can. The first Connecticut Bible was printed in Hartford in 1809, called the "standing Bible," because the types were brought over from abroad all set up, and were kept standing to print from. Between 1809 and 1861 there were eighty editions of the Bible printed in the city. Of late years the most of the Hartford books have been "sold by subscription," and the book agent may, perhaps, be put beside the insurance agent among the products of the city.

The prominence of the city in literature dates back to the first of this and last of the previous century, to the period of Joel Barlow, John Trumbull, Dr. Cogswell, Theodore Dwight, Dr. Hopkins and Richard Alsop, known as the "Hartford wits." These brilliant men, who earned their title mainly by their contributions to a number of papers that were occasionally printed, may properly be called the founders of the literature of the place. Trumbull, the author of "McFingal" (who was admitted to Yale College when seven years old, and who, settling as a lawyer in Hartford in 1781,

GENERAL JOSEPH R. HAWLEY.

lived to be eighty-one), and Theodore Dwight, were probably the best known of these. Dwight was an editor, and was offered, but declined, the editorship of the New York "Evening Post," before it was given to Mr. Coleman in 1801. He was in Congress in 1806, and shortly afterward established the "Connecticut Mirror," a brilliant Federalist sheet, intended to be more pronounced than the "Courant" that he had edited. Dwight was secretary of the Hartford Convention, and after it left Hartford. Near to these in time was S. G. Goodrich, the familiar "Peter Parley," who was a publisher before he began to write, and brought out Trumbull's poems in 1820 in Hartford, and afterward, moving to Boston, established there the "Token," in which he introduced Hawthorne and others to the public. His work in American literature was something like Knight's in England. He popularized and, either in his own name or as Peter Parley, he was the writer of one hundred and seventy books, of which his compends of information—history, geography, travel—are still remembered and used. His "Recollections," in two volumes, are full of Hartford stories. The poets Percival and J. G. C. Brainard, the latter one of Connecticut's favorites, were his friends and contemporaries. Of Brainard, whose theme was mainly nature, he says that he wrote his "Ode to

Niagara," admitted to be the finest ever written on the subject, in a hurried half hour, at a call for copy in the office of the "Mirror," which he edited, and when he wrote it he had never been within five hundred miles of the Falls! A story of the Hartford pulpit, told in the "Recollections," illustrates the simple customs of the days gone by. Dr. Strong, after his Revolutionary chaplaincy, was a pastor for many years in the city, where he was universally loved and respected. On week days, the Doctor was interested in the sale of rum as member of a firm who distilled and sold the liquor. This may seem strange, yet it is worth remark that the liquor business appears to have been better in the time when ministers managed it than now; but that is not all the story. The firm failed, and the sheriff followed up the minister with a writ. The latter retired to his house and shut himself up there to escape, but as writs could not be served on Sundays, he would come out of exile on those days, and, making his way to the sanctuary, would in safety lead his flock in their religious duties, nor did anybody then comment on the affair as peculiar. Another version of the tradition has it that the sheriff did arrest the minister but he was released "within limits" as the custom then was, and the legal "limits" had to be especially extended for the benefit of this culprit in order that he might be able to reach the church where he preached. Mr. Goodrich tells of a "literary club" forming in 1818, and there have been such clubs almost always since then. One of the present time, of limited membership, has in its number General Hawley, Dr. J. Hammond Trumbull, Charles Dudley Warner, General W. B. Franklin, Mark Twain, the Hon. H. C. Robinson, the present Republican candidate for Governor of Connecticut, U. S. Judge Nathaniel Shipman, Professor C. E. Stowe, and several others of the leading members of the various professions. Dr. Bushnell and the late President Jackson of Trinity College, were also members.

RESIDENCE OF "MARK TWAIN."

George D. Prentice, who, in 1828, took charge of the "New England Review" here, and John G. Whittier, who succeeded him in 1830, and published his first volume of poems while in Hartford; Lewis Gaylord Clark, who edited the "Mirror," and William L. Stone, another of its editors, afterward founder of the "New York Commercial Advertiser," and author of numerous volumes, were at some time busy in literary life in the

RESIDENCE OF CHARLES DUDLEY WARNER.

city, and, of later date, are to be named Dr. Trumbull, the late Dr. Bushnell, President Barnard, now of Columbia College, Mr. Warner, the late Henry Howard Brownell, the poet, Mr. Clemens ("Mark Twain"), and the Hon. Henry Barnard, at one time United States Commissioner of Education. Noah Webster, compiler of the Dictionary, was born in Hartford. Among women, either now or formerly of the city, who have acquired prominence in letters, are Mrs. Sigourney, whose first volume appeared in 1822; Miss Catharine Beecher, Mrs. Stowe, Mrs. Rose

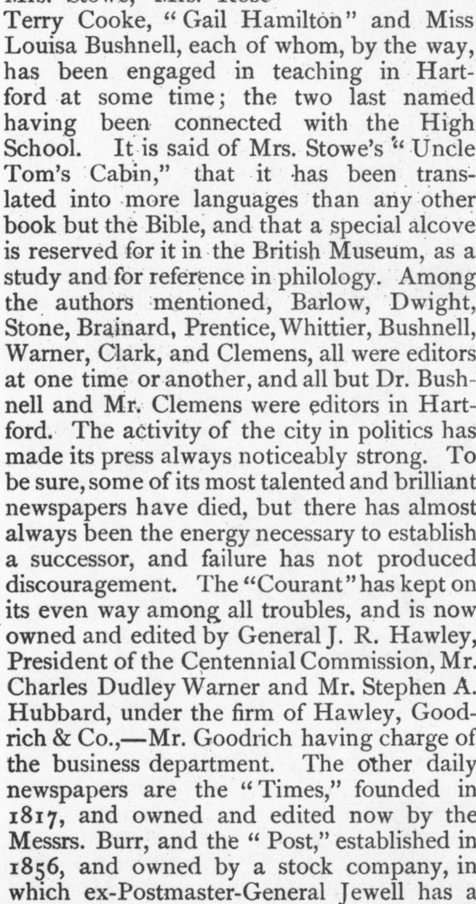

Terry Cooke, "Gail Hamilton" and Miss Louisa Bushnell, each of whom, by the way, has been engaged in teaching in Hartford at some time; the two last named having been connected with the High School. It is said of Mrs. Stowe's "Uncle Tom's Cabin," that it has been translated into more languages than any other book but the Bible, and that a special alcove is reserved for it in the British Museum, as a study and for reference in philology. Among the authors mentioned, Barlow, Dwight, Stone, Brainard, Prentice, Whittier, Bushnell, Warner, Clark, and Clemens, all were editors at one time or another, and all but Dr. Bushnell and Mr. Clemens were editors in Hartford. The activity of the city in politics has made its press always noticeably strong. To be sure, some of its most talented and brilliant newspapers have died, but there has almost always been the energy necessary to establish a successor, and failure has not produced discouragement. The "Courant" has kept on its even way among all troubles, and is now owned and edited by General J. R. Hawley, President of the Centennial Commission, Mr. Charles Dudley Warner and Mr. Stephen A. Hubbard, under the firm of Hawley, Goodrich & Co.,—Mr. Goodrich having charge of the business department. The other daily newspapers are the "Times," founded in 1817, and owned and edited now by the Messrs. Burr, and the "Post," established in 1856, and owned by a stock company, in which ex-Postmaster-General Jewell has a large share. The "Churchman," the very prominent Episcopal weekly journal, is published in Hartford, as are other denominational "weeklies," and several Sunday papers, advertising sheets, insurance journals, and so on.

Political activity is a habit inherited from the old Hartford. The colony of Connecticut formed about Hartford, and the first written constitution in the world was drawn up in Hartford, and adopted for Connecticut in 1639. The word "king" does not occur in it, and the liberality of its whole spirit is historic. Under the famous charter, Hartford, that is Connecticut, acquired New Haven colony in 1662, and, after a long opposition, New Haven yielded and consented to be taken in. Hartford was the capital until 1701, then it and New Haven nearly all the time had each the legislature once a year till 1818; then each had it on alternate years, and now, since 1874, Hartford has been the sole capital of the State, and a long dispute is quieted. In national affairs, the place has been honorably conspicuous. Its recruits have been ready always when needed for service. The capture of Ticonderoga by Ethan Allen was the result of an expedition organized in Hartford. Its Revolutionary record is good. The Hartford Convention of 1814, was certainly an important event. It was held in the Senate Chamber of the present State-house. In the Mexican war, Thomas H. Seymour, afterward Minister to Russia, won his fame, and among high officers of the late war, who are, or were of

"LOVE LANE."

Hartford, are Generals Alfred H. Terry of the regular army, J. R. Hawley of the "Courant;" W. B. Franklin of the Colt Arms Company, and the late R. O. Tyler. In civil life, Hartford has had the second Chief-Justice of the nation, Oliver Ellsworth, a native of Windsor, near by, but often resident in the city; Joel Barlow, Minister to France; Seymour and Jewell, Ministers to Russia; Oliver Wolcott, Secretary of the Treasury under John Adams; J. M. Niles under Van Buren, and Jewell under Grant, Postmaster-Generals; Isaac Toucey under Buchanan, and Gideon Welles through both of Lincoln's administrations, Secretaries of the Navy; and Toucey, Attorney-General under Polk. Postmaster-General Niles founded the Hartford "Times," and Mr. Welles was at one time one of its editors.

This is only an imperfect review, after all, of some of the characteristic features of the city, its wealth, how earned and used, and its literary and political importance. With regard to the first of these, something should be said of the Hartford banks. The history of these institutions yields in itself material for a long work. To-day, the National Banks here have more than a third of all the deposits in Connecticut; more than a quarter of the capital, and surpluses averaging forty-three per cent.; while, through the rest of the State, the average surplus is thirty-two per cent. The wholesale dry goods business of the city, built up by sheer perseverance, began about forty years ago in a small way, but developed to great importance; and, a few years ago, every important town in the West had business relations with Hartford through the dry goods trade; yet, there was not in the city a single cotton or woolen mill. The sales of prints, last year, were more than $6,000,000, and of all dry goods between $10,000,000 and $12,000,000. In connection with business, it should be added, that the city pays about one-third of all the taxes of Connecticut.

Of the general appearance of the city, it is not imprudent even for a resident to say that it is remarkably attractive. Its reputation is already established in that respect, and is aided by the fact that the railroads pass along the edge of the park, affording a full view of this charming spot, of the imposing Capitol upon it, and of the pretentious buildings on Main street which are seen beyond. The position of the city is picturesque; it seems to rest naturally and easily where it is put; its macadamized streets are many, and are generally clean, and not yet altogether stripped of fine trees, although many have been "improved" out of existence in the past twenty years. Its residences are home-like and tasteful, and it is noticeable how generally a bit of land is owned with the house Blocks are few. There has

MAIN STREET TO CEDAR HILL CEMETERY.

been a wide spreading out from the center in recent years, and where some of the finest places now are, not long ago there were only outlying groves or pastures. "Armsmear," Mrs. Colt's home, has already been described. Another remarkable place is "Mark Twain's," on Farmington avenue. The house is made entirely of brick, with wood trimmings. Some very unique but excellent effects have been given by setting the bricks at different angles in various colors of mortar, and by using different colored bricks. The house within is not noticeable at all for its peculiarity, as it is outside, but is admirably planned. The fine hall and staircase, and the wood-work of the library, which is antique and a foreign importation, are models of beauty. And yet with all that there is to admire in the house owing to the skill of the architect and the taste of its occupants, it remains a fact that Mr. Clemens does most of his writing in his barn,—a habit which, to avert some wretched punster, ought to be cited as one reason why among humorists of the day, his works are stable while others perish; indeed, his "Innocents Abroad" has still a steady and constant sale, and, especially at the West, is a household word, where it ranks as chief among Old Testament commentaries. All of his books are published in Hartford. Close by his house is Mrs. Stowe's, and not far off is Mr. Warner's, gracefully set among fine chestnut-trees, with his "garden" sunning itself back of the house for summer exercise and instruction, and in the winter the "back-log" burns in a grand open fireplace in the drawing-room, which is lighted by south, east and north windows. These are in the west part of the city. Toward the north, the visitor sees the State Arsenal and several of the older cemeteries, and at the far south, after passing the new Trinity College site and several conspicuous residences, there is reached a comparatively new cemetery at Cedar Hill, well laid out on high ground, from which the prospect includes all the city and a long range up and across the valley. A favorite drive is to Cedar Hill; and Hartford people are, next to base-ball, notoriously fond of horses and driving. The Hartford base-ball grounds and the Charter Oak trotting park are regarded as models among public works of that sort. Another drive, renowned for years for its sentimental associaciations, which have given it the name of Love

THE RETREAT FOR THE INSANE.

THE AMERICAN ASYLUM FOR THE DEAF AND DUMB.

IN THE BOYS' READING-ROOM.

Lane, is just about disappearing, its rich woods going down to make way for buildings. Wethersfield, with its State prison and its onions, is but a few miles south of the city; and the Tower, about eight miles west of the city, on Talcott Mountain, is a place of constant resort all summer long. Its views are unequaled anywhere else in the State. The Farmington and Connecticut Valleys lie under it west and east. North, appear Springfield, Mass., and Mounts Tom and Holyoke; the Catskills show themselves at the west in clear days; and south, the East Rock at New Haven is visible.

There is no fitter or pleasanter conclusion to the statements of the city's wealth than the fact that it is a place of many charities. The Hartford Hospital has a very liberal endowment, and is one of the largest buildings in Hartford. Near it is the Retreat for the Insane, a private asylum, founded in 1824, which has treated six thousand patients, more than three thousand of whom have been discharged recovered. There is, near the railway station, on Asylum avenue, on Asylum Hill (both named from it), the American Asylum for the Deaf and Dumb, established in 1817 by Thomas Gallaudet, assisted by Laurent Clerc, a French deaf-mute gentleman, a pupil of the Abbé Sicard. This was the first institution of its kind in the country. Until it was opened, the deaf and dumb had been held incapable of relief. Now they are not only taught useful industries, but learn to read with perfect ease, and to communicate ideas by signs, often more rapidly than others can by words, and sometimes they actually acquire speech. A bust of Mr. Clerc which was designed by a graduate of the institution, stands in the Asylum grounds. There are also among the charities, the Orphan Asylum, the various institutions of the Roman Catholic Church, which, besides several large churches,

THE COFFEE-HOUSE OF THE UNION FOR HOME WORK.

has a convent, schools, and asylums in the city; the Women's Home of the Women's Christian Association, the Widows' Homes, several especial funds held in trust for the poor, and the Union for Home Work, the latest of the Hartford charities, the fullest realization of well-wishing in well-doing that has yet been developed. It is an association of ladies, the payment of a small fee being the only qualification demanded of members. The lady managers consult with a board of gentlemen about important matters of finance; but practically it is all woman's work. A visitor employed by the Union is constantly among the sick and needy. There is a coffee-house, on the Holly Tree Inn plan, in Market street, where thoroughly good food is sold without profit, and where, in a soup-kitchen department, meal-tickets, sold to any purchaser for distribution among beggars, are redeemed on presentation. The coffee-house has a meat-market attached, where meats are sold to any purchaser at rates to cover in profit what is consumed in the restaurant, the market being in no sense a charity, but rather a means of sustaining one. Next door to the coffee-house, still a Union department, is the building used for a day nursery, or *crèche*, where young children are given good care and food all day while their mothers are away at work; and in the same building are lodging-rooms, and the reading-room for girls, who are taught sewing and music, and are read to and furnished with books. On certain days some of the ladies open a sewing-school for children, and at the coffee-house work is furnished to those who really need it, and food and clothes are provided at cost, much also being given away. The aim is not to help poor people to stay poor, but to show them how to earn, and to help themselves; it is scarcely necessary to say that professional and profitable beggary is the greatest obstacle the society meets. In connection with the Union, there is also a newsboys' reading-room, open winter evenings, which is a useful thing, and a very lively place. Books, baths, checkers, and other luxuries are allowed to every boy who wants to come in, the washing being not only allowed, but, if necessary, enforced. This outlines the plan of the Union for Home Work. It is no longer an experiment, but seems to be an established institution, living upon members' fees, the income from occasional entertainments, and voluntary contributions given whenever they are wanted,—for the Union is thoroughly appreciated. Its buildings are utterly plain old houses; there is no show about it; its funds have not gone into a monumental building, and it into debt as a consequence. Its only advertisement is the great work it is quietly doing. Already, kind-hearted people of other cities, who have been looking for some practical scheme to reach just the results the Union reaches, are taking it for their model.

The existence and maintenance of all these charities, the presence of societies of every religious creed, the peaceful blending of as many nationalities as any city in the country contains, are all indications of the liberal spirit which prevails in and characterizes Hartford, whose wealth, culture, business enterprise, and philanthropy are each a reason for its fame among American cities. As to its future, there is room for speculation. Just now, like every city in the country, it suffers serious depression in business, and prophets are not lacking to say that it has reached its growth, and that, having spread out too much, it must steady itself to remain even of its present size and importance under the confessedly heavy taxes that are levied on its citizens; but against these are the known energy of the people, the evidences of how past opportunities have been improved, the traditions of success which attach to the city, and the power of increase that belongs to capital already acquired.

ANDIRONS IN HISTORICAL ROOMS.

Ridgefield, The Connecticut Lenox (1895)

RIDGEFIELD, THE CONNECTICUT LENOX.

By Harry E. Miller.

CALLED BY THE Indians Candatowa or Caudatowa, meaning "high land," the town of Ridgefield, Connecticut, lies along the New York state line, in Fairfield County.

Up to 1708, the small tribe of Ramapoo Indians occupying this territory seem to have been little disturbed by the colonial settlers, who were gradually absorbing and populating all the land. In May of that year, the General Assembly was petitioned by a number of the inhabitants of Norwalk for "libertie to purchase of the Indians a certain tract of land bounded south on Norwalk bounds, northeast in Danbury, and west upon York line." Then followed the transfer of the land from Catoonah, chief of the Ramapoos, who executed the deed on September 30, 1708, upon receiving the sum of one hundred pounds. A year later, the General Assembly appointed Major Peter Burr of Fairfield, John Copp of Norwalk, and Joseph Starr of Danbury, a committee to survey the newly acquired territory, for which the patent was granted in 1714.

Immediately following the purchase, the twenty-five original settlers moved upon the home lots, which faced on the present Main Street in the village of Ridgefield. Near the western corner of the Ridgefield cemetery, and about opposite the schoolhouse at Titicus, is a large flat-topped bowlder, upon which, tradition records, the five earliest white men to arrive in the new territory passed the first night, building a fire around the base of the rock for protection against forest marauders.

These early settlers possessed the same spirit of thrift and perseverance for which the world has honored the company who came in the *Mayflower*. Like those voyagers of 1620, these twenty-five settlers, and the pioneers who soon followed them to Ridgefield, encountered the many obstacles found in developing a new dominion. They did not have, however, warlike Pequods to subjugate, as did their near neighbors; the Ramapoos were most friendly and respectful toward their white brothers, who, with the justice of William Penn, recognized the prior rights of the aborigines to American territory. As the colonial population increased it became necessary to make other purchases of land from the Ramapoos, which purchases were made in 1715, 1721, 1727 and 1729. That some of the Indians had already felt the contact with civilization is apparent from such names signed to the deeds as Jacob Turkey, Ah Toppeer, Moses Crow and Wett Hams. In Bedford, Westchester County, New York, hardly a dozen miles from Ridgefield, a grave is pointed out as the burial place of the sachem Catoonah and his favorite wife. The village of Katonah, in the same county, is named in his memory, as is also the street in Ridgefield called Catoonah.

The new village was hardly established before Queen Anne's war was terminated by the Treaty of Utrecht in 1713. Thirty years later New England was again under excitement at the beginning of King George's war. Although they spread to the colonies, Ridgefield seems to have had no active part in these conflicts between the English and French. James Resseguie and Vivus Dauchy, two residents of the village, were killed in the French and Indian war.

Like many American towns, Ridgefield was not hasty to engage in the Revolutionary conflict; but once the plain alternative was fully comprehended, she acted with promptness and energy. In 1776 Captain Gamaliel Northrop's company of sixty-four men was organized in the town. From this village also came Colonel Philip B. Bradley, commander of the Fifth Connecticut Regiment, who afterward became marshal of the district of Connecticut in Washington's first administration, as well as during the term of John Adams. The old Bradley home at a later period was the property of Dr. D. L. Adams, and is now the summer residence of Mr. Lucius H. Bigelow, of the New York publishing house of Bigelow & Main. Lieutenant, afterward General Joshua King, who had the unfortunate Major John André in his charge at the Colonial headquarters in South Salem, was a resident of Ridgefield.

SETTLERS' ROCK.

It was not until the spring of 1777 that southern Connecticut realized the terrors of an invading army. No opposing troops sufficient to prevent the raiders from carrying destruction through the villages were to be easily gathered. Sir William Howe, having learned that the Americans had extensive stores in and near Danbury, to be used for the support of the Continental army, directed Governor William Tryon of New York to sail up Long Island Sound with two thousand picked men and, landing at a convenient point, make a quick march through Connecticut, for the purpose of burning the American supplies, the secret places of which would be disclosed by the Tories. With General Tryon came Sir William Erskine and General Agnew; and at four o'clock in the afternoon of April 25 the British convoy of twenty-five vessels anchored in Saugatuck harbor, four miles east of Norwalk. The detachment of two thousand men landed at once and proceeded on the twenty-mile march toward Danbury, halting for the night in Weston township, after covering nearly eight miles of the journey. At an early hour of the following day the troops were again in motion, arriving in Danbury at two o'clock in the afternoon, there to begin immediate destruction of all the accessible provisions and other necessaries gathered for the provincial army, amounting to "eighteen hundred barrels of pork and beef, seven hundred barrels of flour, two thousand bushels of wheat, rye, oats and Indian corn, clothing for a regiment of troops, and seventeen hundred and ninety tents." The British soldiers had not continued long about their work of plunder before unearthing among the stores a supply of liquor with which they at once regaled themselves; and when darkness fell the camp presented a bacchanalian scene such as the people of Danbury had never witnessed. General Tryon was not a little annoyed by this debauch of nearly his whole army. Through Tory informers he was made aware that the patriots of the adjoining country were rapidly gathering. What if under the darkness of night they should suddenly attack his drunken troops? On the day after, which was Sunday, before Tryon departed from Danbury, he burned "the Congregational meeting-house, nineteen dwelling-houses, twenty-two stores and barns, and great quantities of hay and grain." His soldiers having recovered from their dissipation, the march was resumed over the ten-mile road leading to Ridgefield, which was hidden from sight by the southern hills.

SKIRMISH GROUND NEAR RIDGEFIELD.

Meanwhile the American General Silliman had hurriedly collected a body of five hundred youths, aged men and such farmers as were not already supporting Washington, and with these he started on April 26 to resist the British march. He was joined within a few hours by Generals Benedict Arnold, Parsons, Huntington and David Wooster, who was the commanding officer. The provincial army in pursuit of Tryon now numbered seven hundred poorly trained and armed men and boys, not disciplined soldiers, but men praying for the deliverance of their country from the British chain. While General Wooster harassed the rear of the English with two hundred of his militia, he directed Arnold and Silliman to make a forced march to intercept the enemy's front.

At nine o'clock this pleasant Sabbath morning Wooster overtook Tryon where his troops had breakfasted, nearly opposite the schoolhouse, just north of the present residence of Mr. Samuel Scott, above Ridgefield, and on the ground shown in one of the accompanying illustrations he made a furious assault upon the rear British regiment, throwing it into such disorder that he quickly secured forty prisoners, a number equal to a fifth of his whole force. Tryon pressed onward in the direction of Ridgefield, with Wooster in close pursuit continuing his galling fire. Upon reaching the flat lined with maples directly above the present home of Mr. James L. Hunt, Wooster again made a fierce attack, when the British rear guard faced about, using their small arms and artillery to such advantage that the Continentals soon began to fall back. Seeing their disorder, Wooster, who was on horseback, immediately turned to his men and, waving his sword, shouted: "Come on, my boys; never mind such random shots!" Hardly had he given the command before a musket ball from a Tory rifleman shattered his spine, and he fell from the saddle into the arms of his men, who stripped from him his sash and removed him some distance up the road, where a flat rock offered a suitable place to attend to his wound. From this point he was carried to the house of Nehemiah Dibble, in Danbury, where, attended by his faithful wife, he died on the second of May, a warrior whom his country could ill afford to lose. Over his burial-place in the Wooster cemetery in Danbury is erected a shaft honoring his memory. The house in which he died is no longer standing; it was also famous as being the headquarters of General Tryon during his stay in Danbury.

The loss of the commanding general was seriously felt by the Americans, and it is doubtful whether Tryon would have easily reached his ships had not this misfortune occurred to the Continental forces. Mr. James L. Hunt, whose grandmother, with her people, witnessed this engagement from an adjacent hill, says that Wooster was informed by some of the Provincials that a platoon had withdrawn from the British army and, using the commanding position of a slight elevation, were endeavoring to shoot the American

WHERE GENERAL WOOSTER WAS SHOT.

commanding officer; and upon being urged by his men to shield himself, Wooster was riding behind a tree, when the fatal musket ball overtook him. The blood stains remained for years on the rock where his wounds were dressed; but the stone, which should have been sacred to every resident, was afterward destroyed merely that the road might be straightened.

With their detachment of five hundred Arnold and Silliman entered Ridgefield at eleven o'clock, and hastily erected a barricade at the head of Main Street, across the slight ridge upon which stands the house known as the William Lee place. At noon the British reached the obstruction, and Generals Agnew and Erskine advanced to attack the fortification, soon gaining the commanding ledge; and, after an engagement of ten minutes, by their superior numbers, forced the Americans to withdraw from the field. Sixteen British and eight Continentals were killed during this battle of Ridgefield, and were buried in two graves in a field just southeast of the battle-ground. This would be a suitable place for the village to erect a monument to its heroes, who fought as valiantly as ever soldiers did to uphold the cause of independence.

In the engagement Benedict Arnold behaved with the same daring bravery which he showed less than six months later at the battle of Saratoga, when the black horse and rider were everywhere in the midst of the conflict. At Ridgefield he was nearly the last American to desert the field; and although a platoon of the enemy fired upon him at a distance of not a hundred feet, his only misfortune was in having his horse fall, shot by nine bullets. The exact ground as tradition has it is marked by a large tamarack tree inside of the fence of the Lee place.

General Tryon's army passed this Sunday night, April 27, 1777, in Ridgefield, encamping on the grounds of Samuel Olmstead. The British attempted without success to burn the old meeting-house. They did destroy, as reported by the selectmen to the General Assembly, "a grist mill and saw mill of Isaac Keeler, and six dwellings." The houses fired on High Ridge, in the village, were probably intended as signals to the fleet on the Sound.

The morning after, Tryon continued his raid beyond the boundaries of Ridgefield, followed by the Americans, who made the march so miserable for his soldiers that they had no rest until the last man was safely embarked on the ships and the fleet had sailed away from the shores of Connecticut.

On the battle-ground of Ridgefield there stood until recently an old house, the grounds around which were lately purchased by Mr. George M. Olcott. In this weather-stained building was a cannon ball, a relic of the conflict; and in a room where wounded soldiers were carried, the dark blood stains were held in such tender regard that as long as the house remained they were never washed from the floor.

Another house of historical importance is situated on South Main Street, bearing on its brass door plate the inscription:

A. RESSEGUIE.

In the early history of Ridgefield this was the building occupied by Timothy Keeler, whose tavern was a celebrated stopping-place for travellers on their route from New York to Boston. To-day this old white house seems more than quaint standing among the homes of modern architecture. Knowing that Mr. Keeler was loyal to the Federal cause, and hearing that cartridges were being manufactured in this old tavern, the British planted a cannon near the Episcopal church and shot a number of balls into the building, one of which, lodging in a timber at the north side of the house, is still to be seen by drawing out the shingle concealing it. At the time that the house was being bombarded, a cannon ball whistled between the feet of a man who was climbing the stairs, which so frightened him that he tumbled down backwards, yelling, "I'm a dead man! I'm a dead man!" It required some time for his friends to convince him that he was not a dead man.

Another incident of the Revolution is that related about Jeremiah Keeler, a young man of seventeen, who became so zealous from witnessing the battle of Ridgefield that he immediately enlisted in the Continental army, presently to become a sergeant. He was among the first to scale the English breastworks at Yorktown; and as a token of esteem from General Lafayette, who was his commanding officer, he was presented with a sword which is still in the Keeler family. When Lafayette came as America's guest in 1824, he visited the old Keeler tavern for the purpose of seeing Jeremiah Keeler; and while he was in Ridgefield a grand ball was given in the tavern to celebrate the event.

BATTLE-GROUND OF RIDGEFIELD.

GENERAL ARNOLD'S TREE NEAREST TO THE STEPS.

The wounded British who died in the village were buried, it is reported, in the upper part of Flat Rock woods. During their stay the British, for some reason unknown, filled a well with stones on the grounds afterward belonging to the Ridgefield Agricultural Society.

In the autumn of 1778 General Putnam was ordered to take his army for winter encampment from White Plains and Peekskill, New York, to Redding, Connecticut, eight miles northeast of Ridgefield. The situation was advantageous, as, lying midway between the Sound and West Point, he could throw his support in either direction, while at the same time his presence lessened the fear of further British invasion in this section.

At Ridgebury, in the township of Ridgefield, Washington passed a night at Ensign Samuel Keeler's hotel, while on a journey to Hartford to consult with Count de Rochambeau, the French commander. At Weathersfield he held a second interview with Rochambeau, to make more particular arrangements as to the disposal of our French allies in the last campaigns of the war. In June, 1781, the forces of Rochambeau and the Duke de Lauzun marched from Newport for quarters at Ridgebury, where they settled, bringing under guard over eight hundred carts of supplies. The presence of an army in Ridgebury gave it the same prominence which Putnam's winter camp had given Redding. The Duke de Lauzun departed from Ridgebury on the second of July, followed two days after by Rochambeau. Their troops were moving toward the battlefield of Yorktown.

THE KEELER TAVERN.

In the days of the Revolution there was a small country store at Yerk's Corners, now Bogtown, just across the New York state line, some eight miles from Ridgefield village. From this store, in the township of North Salem, went the three captors of Major André, on that memorable September day in 1780. After these three young men, who were hardly more than boys, had taken André under their escort, he was hurried directly away from the Hudson, and on the morning following was placed in charge of General Joshua King of Ridgefield, then a lieutenant in Colonel Sheldon's second regiment of light dragoons, stationed at South Salem, within four miles of Yerk's Corners. The headquarters of Lieutenant King were in a house which stood about a mile north of the South Salem Presbyterian church, to which house André was brought a little before King's breakfast. A friend of King's wrote to him in 1817 for details concerning the capture of Major André; and the following letter, which was first published in the "History of Ridgefield," by the Rev. Daniel W. Teller, issued in 1878, repeats the story of the capture as related by Major André to Lieutenant King:

"RIDGEFIELD, June 17, 1817.

"*Dear Sir:* — Yours of the 9th is before me. I have noted the contents, and am sorry to express the indignation I feel at the idea of being obliged to translate a foreign language to obtain a true history of any part of our Revolution. The facts, so far as I am acquainted with them, I will state to the best of my ability or recollection. Paulding, Williams and Van Wart I never saw before or since that event; I know nothing about them. The time and place where they stopped Major André seems to justify the character you have drawn of them. The truth is, to the imprudence of the man, and not the patriotism of any one, is to be ascribed the capture of Major André. I was the first and only officer who had charge of him whilst at the headquarters of the second regiment of light dragoons, which was then at Esquire Gilbert's in South Salem. He was brought up by an adjutant and four men belonging to the Connecticut militia under the command of Lieutenant Colonel Jamison, from the lines near Tarrytown, a character under the disguised name of John Anderson. He looked somewhat like a reduced gentleman. His small clothes were nankin, with long white top boots, in part, his undress military suit; his coat purple, with gold lace, worn somewhat threadbare, with a small-brimmed tarnished beaver on his head. He wore his hair in a *quieu* with long, black band, and his clothes somewhat dirty. In this garb I took charge of him. After breakfast my barber came in to dress me — after which I requested him to undergo the same operation, which he did. When the ribbon was taken from his hair, I observed it full of powder. This circumstance, with others that occurred, induced me to believe I had no ordinary person in charge.

"He requested permission to take the bed, whilst his shirt and small clothes could be washed. I told him that was needless, for a change was at his service, — which he accepted. We were close pent up in a bedroom with a guard at the door and window. There was a spacious yard before the door, which he desired he might be permitted to walk in with me. I accordingly disposed of my guard in such a manner as to prevent an escape. While walking together, he observed he must make a confidant of somebody, and he knew not a more proper person than myself, as I had appeared to befriend a stranger in distress. After settling the point between ourselves, he told me who he was, and gave me a short account of himself from the time that he was taken at St. John's in 1775 to that time. He requested pen and ink, and wrote immediately to General Washington, declaring who he was. About midnight the express returned

MAJOR ANDRÉ'S CHAIR.

"PETER PARLEY" PLACE.

with orders from General Washington to Colonel Sheldon to send Major André immediately to headquarters. I started with him, and before I got to North Salem Meeting-house met another express with a letter directed to the officer who had Major André in charge, and which letter directed a circuitous route to headquarters for fear of recapture, and gave an account of Arnold's desertion, etc., — with directions to forward the letter to Colonel Sheldon. I did so, and before I got to the end of my journey I was joined by Captain Hoodgers first, and after by Major Talmadge and Captain Rogers. Having given you this clue, I proceed with the major's own story. He said he came up the North River in the sloop-of-war *Vulture*, for the purpose of seeing a person by flag of truce. That was not, however, accomplished. Of course he had to come ashore in a skiff, and after he had done his business, the wind was so high the Dutchman who took him ashore dared not venture to return him on board. The night following, the militia had lined the shore, so that no attempt could be made with safety; consequently he was furnished, after changing his clothes, with a Continental horse and General Arnold's pass, and was to take a route by Peekskill, Crumpound, Pinesbridge, Sing Sing, Tarrytown, etc., to New York.

"Nothing occurred to disturb him on his route until he arrived at the last place, except at Crumpound. He told me his hair stood erect and his heart was in his mouth on meeting Colonel Samuel B. Webb of our army plump in the face. An acquaintance of his said that Colonel Stoddert knew him, and he thought that he was gone, but they kept moving along and soon passed each other; he then thought himself past all danger, and while ruminating on his good luck and hairbreadth escapes, he was assailed by three bushmen near Tarrytown, who ordered him to stand. He said to them, 'I hope, gentlemen, you belong to the lower party.' 'We do,' says one. 'So do I,' says he, 'and by the token of this ring and key you will let me pass. I am a British officer on business of importance, and must not be detained.' One of them took his watch from him and then ordered him to dismount. The moment that was done, he said he found he was mistaken; he must shift his tone. He says, 'I am happy, gentlemen, to find I am mistaken — you belong to the upper party and so do I, and to convince you of it here is General Arnold's pass,' handing it to them. 'Damn Arnold's pass,' said they. 'You said you were a British officer; where is your money?' 'Gentlemen, I have none about me,' he replied. 'You a British officer with a gold watch and no money! Let us search him.' They did so, but found none. Says one, 'He has got his money in his boots; let's have them off and see.' They took off his boots, and there they found his papers, but no money. Then they examined his saddle, but found none. He said that he saw that they had such a thirst for money, he would put them in the way to get it, if they would be directed by him. He asked them to name their sum to deliver him at Kingsbridge. They answered him in this way, 'If we deliver you at Kingsbridge, we shall be sent to the sugar-house and you will save your money.' He says, 'If you will not trust my honor, two of you may stay with me, and one shall go with the letter I will write; name your sum.' The sum was agreed upon, but I cannot recollect whether it was five hundred or one thousand guineas, but the latter, I think, was the sum. They held a consultation a considerable time, and finally they told him if he wrote a party would be sent out and take them, and then they should all be prisoners. They said they had concluded to take him to the commanding officer on the lines. They did so, and retained the watch until General Washington sent for them to Tappan, when the watch was restored to Major André.

"Thus, you see, had money been at command, after the imprudent confession of Major André, or any security given that the British would have put confidence in, he might have passed on to Sir Henry Clinton's headquarters with all his papers and Arnold's pass in the bargain. I do not recollect to have seen a true statement of this business in any history that has fallen into my hands. If my memory serves me, Arnold solicited and obtained the command of West Point in consequence of his being an invalid; as to the reason why his negotiation was not completed by flag of truce, I will state what General Washington told the French ambassador, Lucerne. He stated, on his route to Hartford, that he dined with General Arnold at Haverstraw, at Joshua Smith's, where Arnold and André met. General Arnold showed him a letter from General Robinson directed to General Israel Putnam or the officer commanding West Point, requesting an interview by flag on business of the first importance to the United States. General Arnold asked General Washington if he should go and hear what he had to say. General Washington replied that it would be very improper for the commander-in-chief of a post to meet anybody himself — he could send a trusty hand if he thought proper. 'But,' he added, 'I had no more suspicion of Arnold than I had of myself.' This accounts for Major André's failure to negotiate by flag, and his subsequent movements. I have thus complied with your request, giving you such facts, viz., what I had from the mouth of Major André and what I heard General Washington tell the French minister soon after the execution of André."

GEORGE WASHINGTON GILBERT AND HIS HOUSE.

TITICUS RIVER.

Major André's statement to General King — which is given here at length because it will be new to most — and the account accepted by American historians are at variance; for the British officer represents Paulding, Williams and Van Wart as having mercenary desires, and as regardless of what might happen to their country if they had released the spy with his papers. Not the slightest charge of dishonor has ever been proven against these three Americans in all the thorough investigation of this historical event. Probably no one ascertained more of the details than did Washington himself, who in his letter written at Paramus, October 7, 1780, to the President of Congress, said: "I have now the pleasure to communicate the names of the three persons who captured Major André, and who refused to release him, notwithstanding the most earnest importunities and assurances of a liberal reward on his part. Their conduct merits our warmest esteem; and I beg leave to add, that I think the public will do well to make them a handsome gratuity. They have prevented in all probability our suffering one of the severest strokes that could have been meditated against us." Such words would never have been written by the first of Americans had the three patriots acted in a dishonorable manner. André's audacious charge is about as reasonable as the famous letter he wrote to Washington from South Salem, in which he pretended that Arnold had betrayed him, or that he had been unknowingly duped into being a spy. There is no doubt about this message being written in South Salem; and through the courtesy of Mr. J. Howard King, grandson of General King, a photograph has been made of the identical chair in which André sat, utilizing a swinging desk formerly borne on one of its arms to inscribe his appeal to the American commander. On the back of the chair is found the following inscription:

"IN THIS CHAIR SAT MAJ. ANDRÉ, ADJ. GEN. BRITISH ARMY, WHEN HE WROTE, AT THE HEADQUARTERS OF LIEUT. JOSHUA KING, THE LETTER TO GEN. WASHINGTON REVEALING THE TREASON OF GEN. ARNOLD."

General King remained with André until the morning of October second, when at Tappan he accompanied the British soldier to the gallows.

Ridgefield also had a part in the second war with Great Britain. To the Civil War the town forwarded one hundred and sixty soldiers.

Rev. Samuel Goodrich, pastor of the Congregational church, writes that all but one Indian had disappeared from the town by 1800. In remarking upon the mineral and other resources of the township, he writes that iron and sulphur had been found in small quantities at that early date, and that while no freestone was known, limestone and grayish-blue stone for building were not uncommon. He speaks, likewise, about the beautiful rose quartz, which until lately was shipped from Ridgefield to be made into table ware. The watercourses rising around Ridgefield, as Mr. Goodrich then reported, do not furnish sufficient power for factories, and consequently few foreign mechanics have found their way to the place. It is to-day, as in 1800, as pure an American town as, probably, can be named in any section of New England. At one time there were some tanneries and shoe and hat factories, and coarse ducking was prepared here for the southern market, but the place has never become a business centre. The early settlers found their new territory tenanted by deer, bears, wolves, panthers, wild cats and beavers, while as late as 1800, rattlesnakes were not uncommon in "the Cliffs."

THE DEPOT.

THE TOWN HOUSE.

RIDGEFIELD CLUB-HOUSE.

In the Congregational parsonage at Ridgefield, August 19, 1793, was born S. G. Goodrich, a son of the Rev. Samuel Goodrich, whom the world has long known by the name of "Peter Parley." In his interesting "Recollections of a Lifetime" Mr. Goodrich has included much concerning the early Ridgefield life. He gives an account of his first day at school, when the teacher, pointing to a letter, insisted that he should tell its name. He replied that he did not go to school to teach the teacher, and thought that she should tell him the letter. "Peter Parley" remembers old Granther Baldwin, who lived close to the school, guarding well his apples from the lads of the village. Baldwin was a man somewhat noted for his propensity for long prayers. A young man who was courting Granther Baldwin's daughter came one evening to visit the maiden, and had not been long in the house before Granther prepared for one of his extended invocations, which usually began with the creation of the world, and wound slowly down through the course of history. The young man was in deep slumber at about the time Granther Baldwin arrived at the fall of Rome, and tottering in his chair, suddenly tumbled over the elder, upsetting him and violently interrupting the devotional proceedings. As he finally married the damsel, however, it may be inferred that he was forgiven. "Peter Parley" tells another story showing that Baldwin had a true respect for the laws of his state. A carpenter who had been at work for a considerable time on Baldwin's premises presented a bill for thirty dollars when the work was finished. Granther, having considered the amount of debt, remarked that a certain statute imposed a penalty of a dollar upon every person who used a profane word, and according to the account he had kept the carpenter uttered twenty-five such while about his work, so that he was really entitled to but five dollars. Granther asked the workman if he would receive the balance due in "his way"—meaning pork and vegetables.

"No," said the man, "I'll take it out in my way"—which he did by using more profanity than was ever heard in Ridgefield before or since its settlement.

Goodrich remembers his hunting and rambling about the fields and woods near his birthplace, which developed in him a deep love of nature; and when moving through the salons of Europe his thoughts turned often to the village whose hills were dearest to his memory. In Goodrich's boyhood Colonel Philip Bradley was the most distinguished man in Ridgefield, besides being leader of the Federalists, while his rival, General Joshua King, who later became the prominent man of the town, was the recognized chief of the Democrats, or Republicans as they then called themselves. Ezekiel Sanford, a schoolmate of Goodrich, was afterward editor of the *Eclectic Magazine*, and wrote a history of the United States covering the period prior to the Revolution.

About the summer of 1804, writes Goodrich, an unusual sensation was caused in Ridgefield by Napoleon's youngest brother Jerome stopping at Keeler's Tavern with his young American wife, lately Miss Elizabeth Patterson of Baltimore. At nearly the same time the town was honored by a visit from Oliver Wolcott, recently a member of Washington's cabinet, and again by the entrance of Timothy Pickering.

In Boston, whither he went, Goodrich engaged in the publishing business, issuing his *Boston Token* and *Atlantic Souvenir*, to which the leading American writers of the period were contributors. Hawthorne's "Sights from a Steeple," "Sketches Beneath an Umbrella," "Wives of the Dead," and "Prophetic Pictures" appeared in the *Token*, but excited so little comment that Goodrich felt chagrined. He wrote several articles calling the attention of his readers to these remarkable productions. Hawthorne's remarkable genius was appreciated by "Peter Parley" long before the advent of "The Scarlet Letter." He writes that "Hawthorne was, in fact, a kind of Wordsworth in prose—less kindly, less genial toward mankind, but deeper and more philosophical. His fate was similar: at first he was neglected, at last he had worshippers." While in the employ of Goodrich, Hawthorne helped edit the "American Magazine of Useful and Entertaining Knowledge," and also "Parley's Universal History," which

SOUTH MAIN STREET.

became one of the standard text-books for schools, and now on account of its rarity it brings a good price at the auctions. With another friend of Hawthorne's, Horatio Bridges, Goodrich aided the author to issue his first volume of "Twice Told Tales," of which he says: "It was deemed a failure for more than a year, when a breeze seemed to rise and fill its sails, and with it the author was carried on to fame and fortune." Hawthorne's memory is connected with Lenox through his residence at the little red house in that place. By his acquaintance with Goodrich he seems to be associated with the Connecticut Lenox.

METHODIST EPISCOPAL CHURCH.

FIRST CONGREGATIONAL CHURCH.

ST. STEPHEN'S EPISCOPAL CHURCH.

"Peter Parley" revisited his native village after an absence of many years, writing an account of the same to his brother in 1855. In this letter of forty years ago he becomes enthusiastic over the natural attractions of the village, saying: "The main street, on the whole, is one of the most beautiful I know of. It is more than a mile in length and a hundred and twenty feet in width, ornamented with two continuous lines of trees, — elms, sycamores, and sugar-maples, — save only here and there a brief interval." The view from the crest of High Ridge "equals the fairest scenes in Italy," and from this elevation can be witnessed sunsets which to him far surpassed any of a foreign clime. "Where is the landscape more smiling?" he asks, "the earth more cheering? One thing is clear, — that there are in continental Europe no such country towns and villages as those of New England and some other portions of this country. Daniel Webster once said, jocosely, that New Hampshire is a good place to come from; it seems to me, in all sincerity, that Ridgefield is a good place to go to. Should I ever return there to end my days, this may be my epitaph:

"'My faults forgotten, and my sins forgiven,
Let this, my tranquil birth-place, be my grave:
As in my youth I deem'd it nearest heaven,
So here I give to God the breath he gave.'"

He revisited the old Keeler Tavern, and was greatly elated that the culinary arts, which had made the inn celebrated, had not been forgotten in the years of his absence; he asserts that nowhere else has he known the science of cookery to reach the perfection attained at the Keeler hostelry. While he was visiting again his old home on High Ridge, a young man volunteered an explanation concerning the property to the supposed stranger, telling him that the house was quite famous, since it had been built and occupied for several years by "Peter Parley."

His mood is sorrowful when he hears a new bell ringing from the church of his boyhood. From the church he missed the patriarchs of his boyhood, especially the reserved deacons and Granther Baldwin, Squire Keeler and General King; and instead of the commanding person

RESIDENCE OF EX-GOV. LOUNSBURY.

RESIDENCE OF GEORGE M. OLCOTT.

RESIDENCE OF HENRY E. HAWLEY.

RESIDENCE OF LUCIUS H. BIGELOW.

RESIDENCE OF J. HOWARD KING.

of the Revolutionary officer, he found his son Joshua.

While Goodrich was ruminating about the churches, no doubt the humorous conflict between the Stove and Anti-Stove parties, of which he has preserved the record in the "Recollections," recurred to him. At the time of the new invention an effort was made to introduce a stove in a Ridgefield church, when one part of the congregation bitterly objected to the innovation; foot-stoves, they said, would answer the requirements in severe weather for women and children, while religious devotion should be sufficient for warming the men. Was not this late thought of man a mockery in the sacred place? The warfare between the Stovites and Anti-Stovites increased to such warmth, that the pastor of the church, trying to be neutral, feared to select a text for his sermon, as both factions would draw from it arguments to substantiate their opposite positions.

"Parley" recollects a quiet summer Sabbath, when a parson from the neighboring village of South Salem was discoursing from a Ridgefield pulpit to the morning congregation. He was in the midst of a long prayer, when far up Main Street could be heard the clatter of a horse galloping in the direction of the church with that reckless speed with which the Headless Horseman pursued brave Ichabod Crane through Sleepy Hollow.

Now if there was anything in the country for which the pastor from South Salem had an uncontrollable love, it was good horseflesh; and he was so good a judge that a horse's footbeats revealed to him its merits. The horse and rider dashed nearer, the sounds coming through the open doors and windows. A suspense hung over every person in the congregation, augmented from the pulpit, and when the profane galloper was speeding by the door, the pastor halted abruptly in his prayer, exclaiming in a distinct voice: "That's a real smart critter,"—and then continued his supplication.

There is an unmarked grave in the Episcopal burying-ground at North Salem, near Ridgefield, in which during the winter of 1810 was interred a hermitess, known in all the neighboring villages as Sarah Bishop. Hers was a gaunt figure, not seldom seen on the streets of Ridgefield; and the first poem ever printed by "Peter Parley" had this solitary creature for a theme; a single verse describing her in this manner:

"Her face was wrinkled, and passionless seemed
  As her bosom, all blasted and dead,
And her colorless eye like an icicle gleamed,
  Yet no sorrow or sympathy shed."

Her residence was four miles west of Ridgefield, in a lonely cavern on the southern slope of West Mountain, overlooking Lake Waccabuc beneath, and in the distance the Sound with the hills of Long Island outlined against the horizon. It is told that her father's home on Long Island was burned during the Revolution, and that she suffered cruelties from a British officer, which may account for the strangeness of her subsequent life. Yet notwithstanding her peculiar mode of existence, some visitors to the cave of the hermitess in 1804 "found her to be of a sound mind, a religious turn of thought, and entirely happy in her situation." The cavern was formerly quite inaccessible, but now, since a path has been built to it, visitors each year seek the wild place, once the lonely resort of Sarah Bishop.

In a hundred ways Ridgefield is suggestive of Lenox, though its fertile undulating surface is not broken by so great a number of picturesque hills as please the rambler in the Berkshires. Not only the beauty of the surrounding country, but the beautiful trees, lawns, streets and palatial mansions, remind one of Lenox. It is doubtful whether any American village street surpasses in beauty the main street in Ridgefield. The mammoth old trees on the street have attained a remarkable age; those around some of the homes, forming most attractive parks, are of the same gigantic size. In front of each residence is a well-kept lawn, and between the sidewalk and the highway still another green. Main Street is not an unbroken level; it is far more pleasing on account of its undulations, with occasionally a graceful bend, shutting out a further view. Close to Main Street lies High Ridge, at an altitude of eight hundred feet above sea level. Not only have the splendid summer homes across its summit made this a point of interest, but the panoramic view from the Ridge has caused it to be widely known. Fourteen miles away stretches Long Island Sound spreading before the sight for more than sixty miles, with the shores of the island plainly visible; and farther away still is to be seen West Rock, near New Haven. In the west one sees the mountains along the Hudson. Between these points are hills, woods, valleys and watercourses, with an occasional little mountain rising abruptly, and in the hazy distance seeming to touch the sky.

The interesting drives in and about the village have gained the admiration of thousands, which again makes us think of Lenox. The road to Danbury is much travelled. One is carried past historic Ridgebury, and farther on through Sugar Hollow, with its dark mountains, once the resort of highwaymen, looming up on either side of the highway and throwing a shadow over the lonely road.

Driving from Ridgefield in the opposite direction from High Ridge, another part of the village is reached, known as East Ridge. One of the elegant mansions on this elevation is Hawk's Nest, being the property of Mr. W. S. Hawk, one of the two proprietors of the Windsor Hotel in New York. East Ridge is yearly becoming a more popular building place. Leaving this eminence, a short drive through the woods carries us to a very old house, close to the road, which is occupied by George Washington Gilbert, widely noted through the region as the Ivy Hill hermit and weather prophet. Every summer visitors drive through the picturesque woods to the old domicile, said to have been standing for one hundred and thirty years, to have a chat with the hermit, as well as to examine his big kitchen fireplace. Scattered through the rooms of the house are antiquities dating from a time when spinning-wheels and powder-horns were not considered useless. In our illustration the hermit weather prophet has an old sword across his breast, which his grandfather brought from the battle of Trenton, and in the other hand he holds a highly prized warming pan from among his antiquities.

Another pleasant journey leads one through Titicus, across the river over which the British passed into Ridgefield in 1777, thence onward to the battlefield where Wooster fell, and continuing a mile to the northwest, where on the skirmish ground by the schoolhouse the provincial troops secured the forty British prisoners. Turning to one side of the main road, we arrive at "the Cliffs," or "Aspen Ledges," and to the other to Lake Mamanasco, with its curious floating island. Some distance beyond is a low stone post marking the New York and Connecticut state line; and in the town of North Salem is to be seen the Titicus storage reservoir for New York City, named after the river supplying the artificial lake. Not far from the reservoir is the Episcopal cemetery, in which Sarah Bishop slumbers, with her life secrets locked forever in the grave. One of the houses near by is the summer residence of Mr. U.S. Grant, the youngest son of the General, and another a plain old dwelling once occupied by Horace Greeley for the summer months, during which he remained among the hills of Westchester County. Passing into South Salem, near which is the elegant home of Robert Hoe, of printing press fame, the traveller has a view of beautiful Lake Waccabuc, lying in a picturesque basin, with West Mountain, the old home of Sarah Bishop, rearing its massive bulk on the north shore. Without forgetting Major André, we depart from South Salem, until Round Lake, deep and cool, and the summit of West Mountain are attained — from which commanding height a vast panorama is spread before us. Through the summer homes constructed around West Mountain the locality has been redeemed from a once unattractive wilderness. The residences especially noticeable belong to Mr. Theodore H. Mead, Mr. Dexter L. Stone, Dr. Bache McEvers Emmet and Dr. John G. Perry.

Putnam's headquarters at Redding may be reached by an easy drive from Ridgefield; and in another direction, Elmsford Avenue, where General Garfield visited while on a furlough during the Civil War. Not far from this avenue are New Caanan, Norwalk and Long Island Sound.

No visitor can fail to be attracted by the homes in Ridgefield, which, either from their historic associations or their own beauty and taste, are among the important objects of the town. Upon passing the extensive grounds of the Ridgefield cemetery, and entering Main Street from the north, one sees the palatial residence of Mr. George M. Olcott, built at a cost of more than $125,000. Just opposite is the house owned and occupied until her recent death by Mrs. Youmans, wife of Edward L. Youmans, founder of the *Popular Science Monthly*. Near the Youmans or William Lee place, as it is now better known, is that of Mr. Lucius H. Bigelow, of which mention has already been made. Mr. Sylvester Main of the same publishing firm was for many years a resident of Ridgefield. The fine residence of ex-Governor Lounsbury, with its park-like grounds, is on the east side of the street, and a little above on the west side the summer home of Mr. J. Howard King, president of the New York State National Bank at Albany. Mr. King has reproduced the colonial mansion of his grandfather, General Joshua King, which with its valuable contents was destroyed by fire not long ago. Excepting the north and south enclosed verandas, both the interior and exterior of the house, even to the door-plate, have been made to conform as nearly as possible to the original condition. Adjoining the King grounds is the castle-like home of Mr. Henry E. Hawley, surrounded by some of the noblest trees in Ridgefield. The old Keeler Tavern is a conspicuous building on south Main Street. Near it is the road to High Ridge and the "Peter Parley" home, now belonging to Mr. John A. King. In the row of summer mansions beyond is recognized that of Mr. E. P. Dutton, the well-known publisher. Among the prominent families in and near the village, we find the names of Hawley, Olcott, Morris, Dutton, King, Schenck, Bigelow, Hawk, Starr, Bailey, Egleston, Emmet, Stone, Lounsbury, Scott, Mead and Perry.

The village has four churches. The Jesse Lee Memorial Methodist Episcopal Church, St. Stephen's Episcopal, and the First Congregational are on Main Street, while St. Mary's Roman Catholic Church is on Catoonah Street. The first church of the Episcopal society, by which the British planted a cannon to fire upon the Keeler Tavern, was built in 1740, and rebuilt soon after the Revolution; while the church on its present site was finished in 1842. The old Congregational church stood on a green with the highway running on each side; and the handsome new stone edifice is but a little below the site of the first building. The Methodist church, the third belonging to that sect erected in New England, would certainly be appreciated by the early Methodists of the village, who about the year 1800 worshipped in Dr. Baker's kitchen.

The first town-house was built in 1743, and the present one in 1876. In 1875, the weekly Ridgefield *Press* was established, with the title of "Baxter's Monthly." It is to-day a flourishing country newspaper under the editorial management of Mr. E. C. Bross. There is in the village a savings bank, and a club with its club-house, the rooms of which will soon be adapted for lectures and dramatic entertainments.

The schools are quite different from what they were when in "Peter Parley's" boyhood they taught "reading, writing, arithmetic and grammar, some catechising, and a little manners," making the best use of that now rare book, the "New England Primer." The interesting history of the town should be taught in all of its schools. If every town would present local history for the children to study, a wider sympathy would be developed for the history of the world. As early as 1795 a small library was established in Ridgefield, containing in 1800 one hundred and fifty titles, and now possessing over three thousand volumes. A society known as the Indian Territory Association of Ridgefield was organized, mainly through the efforts of Mr. Theodore H. Mead, in the spring of the present year. A large company assembled at Mr. Mead's home on West Mountain, where they were addressed by John Gilmer Speed, the well-known authority on road-making and village-improvement societies. The association has for its objects the general improvement of town roads, sidewalks, fences, grounds and residences, and also legislation for better roads throughout the state.

Ridgefield has a population of about twenty-five hundred, increased by more than one thousand in summer. Probably no village in America of equal population represents a greater amount of wealth.

It has not the society nor the activity of Lenox, although the summer residence of many society people. It is their desire that the place shall not become too much of a society town; it is already too popular to please some of them.

The popularity is attested by the long visits made each year by those who have found the restful landscape and healthful atmosphere to be so helpful in ministering to reawakening a love of quiet life and a true appreciation of nature.

LOOKING FROM HIGH RIDGE.

New London, Connecticut (1896)

New London, Conn.

BY HENRY ROBINSON PALMER.

ONE of the most notable anniversary observances of the year in New England is set for the sixth of May at New London, when the historic town at the mouth of the Thames will celebrate its two hundred and fiftieth birthday. On the preceding evening, Mr. Walter Learned will deliver a retrospective address and Mr. George Parsons Lathrop will read an appropriate poem; and these literary features of the celebration will be followed the next day by an elaborate spectacular commemoration of the first permanent settlement in the Pequot country by John Winthrop the younger in the spring of 1646. In the morning there will be a historical parade, several hundred children from the public schools will sing patriotic choruses, the pastor of the First Congregational church will eulogize the Congregational founder of the town, and the corner-stone of a Winthrop memorial will be laid. Later in the day there will be a parade of civic and military organizations, several thousand strong; and a soldiers and sailors' monument, presented to the city by Mr. Sebastian D. Lawrence of New London, will be unveiled. This memorial is a granite shaft surmounted by a statue of Peace, and flanked by figures of an American sailor and infantryman. The monument is composed of alternate layers of red and blue stone, and at its base are polished panels and emblems carved in high relief, commemorating the four branches of the national service. It rises to the height of fifty feet, and its location on the Parade at the foot of State Street will make it one of the most conspicuous objects of interest in the city.

THE SHORE NEAR THE PEQUOT.

JOHN WINTHROP, THE YOUNGER.

It is fit that New London should thus observe the anniversary of its establishment; for few American towns have had a more inspiring past or have contributed in more generous measure to the annals of American history. We find epitomized in its record the record of New England. The struggles of the early colonists on these "stern and rock-bound coasts," the preponderating influence of the church in public affairs, the intermittent warfare with the aborigines, the gradually increasing sense of political importance, the stirring of the revolutionary spirit in the latter half of the eighteenth century, the commercial prosperity of the early days of the nineteenth—all these New London experienced in common with those other communities which may properly be called representative New England towns. The Puritan life-blood has pulsed in her veins through all the years of her honorable history, and what was best in Puritan faith and teaching survives in her to-day.

Since the interest in New London must be at present so largely of a historical character, let us glance backward for a moment to that far-away time when John Winthrop, Jr., son of the Governor of Massachusetts, first made his habitation in the Pequot country. Already the spirit of unrest had manifested itself in the colony on the shores of Massachusetts Bay. Already adventurous settlers were pushing out into the wilderness to found new homes by quiet streams, with only the unsocial red man for company. The towns on the Connecticut had been established more than a decade, and the community at Saybrook was nine years old, when Winthrop availed himself of the Massachusetts grant

HOUSE IN WHICH NATHAN HALE TAUGHT.

PERKINS HOUSE, WASHINGTON'S HEADQUARTERS.

which gave him possession of Fisher's Island, and laid the foundations of what may fittingly be called the Pequot Commonwealth. For it was not at New London that the first English settlement within the hunting-grounds of Sassacus was made, but on the surf-beaten shores of "Fysher's Island," now a portion of the State of New York.

The younger Winthrop is one of the most attractive figures in early New England history. We find ourselves drawn strangely to him, though more than two centuries have rested upon his tomb. He was courtly and dignified, yet gentle and winsome, compelling the respect which his austere father commanded, but inspiring a greater degree of intimate friendship and love. He has been called the flower of New England Puritanism, and there is something in his bearing to remind us of Sir Philip Sidney, the "flower of English chivalry." He was born at Groton, England, in 1606, was educated at Bury St. Edmunds school and Trinity College, Dublin, began the study of law, but abandoned it for the naval service, accompanied the expedition to Rochelle to relieve the Huguenots, travelled extensively in the far East, and in 1631 married Martha Fones of London, with whom he emigrated to Massachusetts in the same year. He founded the town of Ipswich, Mass., where Mrs. Winthrop died in 1634, and afterward returned to England, marrying, in 1635, Elizabeth Read of Wickford in Essex. In the latter part of that year he made a second pilgrimage to America, this time bringing with him a commission from Lord Say-and-Seal and Lord Brooke to build a fort and begin a plantation within their grant at the mouth of the Connecticut River. With twenty followers he executed this commission, which was for a single year and does not seem to have been renewed. In 1638 and 1639 he was living at Ipswich, and in 1640 the General Court of Massachusetts ceded him Fisher's Island, a tract of land some nine miles in extent, separated from the westernmost limits of Rhode Island territory by some two miles of ocean, and reaching westward to the mouth of the river Thames. It was not certain whether the island lay within the jurisdiction of Massachusetts or not, so a proviso was in-

THE GOVERNOR WINTHROP HOMESTEAD.

serted in the deed of gift; but Winthrop applied to Connecticut for a clear title, which was granted to him under date of April 9, 1641, in these words: "Upon Mr. Winthrop's motion to the Court for Fysher's Island, it is the mind of the Court that so far as it hinders not the public good of the country, either for fortifying for defence or setting up a trade for fishing or salt, and such like, he shall have liberty to proceed therein." The island was ultimately included in the grant to the Duke of York, but Winthrop secured a new title from the government at Manhattan, thus fortifying his possession by deeds from three colonies.

HEMPSTEAD HOUSE, THE OLDEST HOUSE IN NEW LONDON.

MONUMENT AT FORT GRISWOLD.

Fisher's Island as seen from the mainland to-day is a bleak and treeless stretch, with little to attract the eye. But in the days of Winthrop it was a favorite resort for the Indians, its extensive woodlands sheltered deer and other game, and its great ponds furnished abundant sport for the fisherman. The famous gale of 1815, which worked such havoc throughout New England, stripped it of its forests, and at the present time almost its only trees are the inconsiderable groves on the shores of the ponds. So fierce was the fury of this memorable tempest, that the salt spray from Fisher's Island Sound is said to have been carried a dozen miles inland, where it crystallized on the window-panes of the astonished inhabitants. But shorn as it is of its glory of foliage, the island is still a pleasant spot. The winding lanes at West Harbor, the fields of grain and rolling meadows, the glimpses here and there of water in all the variety that ocean, land-locked haven and inland pond afford, give it a charming rural aspect, while the many cottages of its summer colony add a modern and picturesque element to the view. It was here that Winthrop lived from 1644 to 1646. Here he built the first white man's dwelling-house in the Pequot country and reaped the first harvest gathered by English hands between the Connecticut River and Narragansett Bay. The island remained in the possession of the Winthrop family

THE RIVER SIDE.

until 1862; and there may still be seen at East Harbor the Winthrop homestead, built, it is said, by Francis Bayard Winthrop, who lived in the eighteenth century.

During the latter part of his residence at Fisher's Island, John Winthrop appears to have been engaged in preparing a settlement on the west bank of the Thames. In 1644 the General Court of Massachusetts had granted to him "a plantation at or near Pequod for iron works," and as early as 1645 he was on the site of the future city of New London with a few associates. We are told by the elder Winthrop that the actual beginning of the town was made in 1646, on the sixth of May of which year this act of the Court was entered on the records at Boston: "Whereas Mr. John Winthrop, Jun., and some others, have by allowance of this Court begun a plantation in the Pequot country, which appertains to this jurisdiction, as part of our proportion of the conquered country, and whereas this Court is informed that some Indians who are now planted upon the place, where the said plantation is begun, are willing to remove from their planting ground for the more quiet and convenient settling of the English there, so that they may have another convenient place appointed,—it is therefore ordered that Mr. John Winthrop may appoint unto such Indians as are willing to remove, their lands on the other side, that is, on the east side of the Great River of the Pequot country, or some other place for their convenient planting and subsistence, which may be to the good liking and satisfaction of the said Indians, and

THE PEQUOT HOUSE.

OCEAN BEACH.

likewise to such of the Pequot Indians as shall desire to live there, submitting themselves to the English government. And whereas Mr. Thomas Peters is intended to inhabit in the same plantation,—this Court doth think fit to join him to assist the said Mr. Winthrop for the better carrying on the work of said plantation."

New London, as may be gathered from these facts, is the daughter of Massachusetts, rather than of Connecticut. It was emigration from the colony on Massachusetts Bay, not a movement of population from the river towns at that time composing the colony of Connecticut, that resulted in the settlement of the Pequot country. Saybrook at the mouth of the Connecticut withstood for several years the offers of political union advanced from Hartford; New Haven and her sister towns relinquished their separate existence only after a protracted and bitter struggle for autonomy; and for some time succeeding the establishment of Winthrop and his followers on the banks of the Thames it was uncertain whether Massachusetts or Connecticut would finally administer the affairs of the settlement. The Commissioners of the United Colonies were appealed to, to decide the question, Mr. Winthrop's own preference at this time seeming to be for Massachusetts. Massachusetts argued that the region round about the mouth of the Thames was hers by right of conquest; Connecticut claimed the district by virtue of royal patent as well as conquest. "Jurisdiction," affirmed the Commissioners, "goeth constantly with the Patent," but although the hold of Massachusetts upon the territory became gradually weaker, it was some time before the authority of Connecticut was firmly established. In some portions of the Pequot country, indeed, the Bay Colony long continued to exercise her

FIRST CONGREGATIONAL CHURCH.

sway. According to the testimony of certain Pequot Indians, examined by Rev. James Noyes and Mr. Amos Richardson of Stonington during the long-protracted dispute between Connecticut and Rhode Island as to the jurisdiction over the lands immediately east of the Pawcatuck, the possessions of that tribe extended some four or five miles beyond the present boundaries of Connecticut. From this point on the east, near the present village of Niantic, R. I., to the Mystic River on the west, Massachusetts asserted her authority for years after the inclusion of New London within the jurisdiction of Hartford. In 1658 the Commissioners of the United Colonies decided that the Mystic River, the name of which recalls to-day the Massachusetts origin of the neighboring settlers, should be the boundary between the colonies, "soe far as the Pond by Lanthorne Hill, and thence from the middle of said pond, to run away upon a north line"; and in the succeeding year this decision was confirmed by the same authority. It was not until 1662, eighteen years after the first settlement of the Pequot country, that the royal charter obtained by Winthrop from King Charles put it permanently under the jurisdiction of Connecticut; so it is only fair to say that New London and the towns of the surrounding region owed their initial impulse to Massachusetts and were thus the offshoot of the chief colony of New England.

SOLDIERS AND SAILORS' MONUMENT.

Nor did any of the daughter colonies of Massachusetts receive from her a more vigorous or valuable vitality. To the towns on the Connecticut she gave Haynes, Hopkins and Ludlow, to Rhode Island Williams and Coddington; New Haven, though owing much of its early vigor to a direct English emigration, received from her a grateful impetus; and some of her best sons found new homes north of the Piscataqua. But to New London she gave likewise a distinguished coterie of citizens, foremost among them the younger Winthrop, the travelled gentleman, enthusiastic scientist and courtly diplomat,—

a personage less heroic perhaps than the stern and serious founders of New Haven, less impressive than the seer of Rhode Island, whose name is forever joined with the watchwords of human freedom, but more lovable than they, and no less worthy our remembrance and esteem. He is said to have been the best educated man of his day; his library contained a thousand choice volumes, and he was an eminent member of the Royal Society. His name is perpetuated in much of the local nomenclature of the present generation; and perhaps some competent historian will be inspired by the contemporary celebration at New London to write his biography in appropriate form.

OLD BURYING GROUND.

JOHN MASON MONUMENT, PEQUOT HILL.

While the soil at New London proved to its early tillers less fertile than that of the Connecticut valley, the situation of the place offered them the best possible facilities for commercial activity, and the varied scenery of river, valley and forest afforded them a perpetual inspiration. The town is set on the west bank of the river Thames, and overlooks one of the finest harbors in the United States. From the hills on which it is built, distant views of the Sound and ocean may be caught, and on unclouded days the white cliffs of Long Island come clearly into view. So attractive is the situation, that the General Court of Connecticut wished the first inhabitants to give up the ancient Indian name of Nameaug, which had been derived from the tribe of the neighborhood, and adopt that of Faire Harbour, a picturesque and appropriate designation; but the love of the country they had left across the sea was still strong in their breasts, and they determined to establish a new London on this side of the Atlantic. Finally, in 1658, the General Court at Hartford approved this choice, de-

THE THAMES BRIDGE.

THE YALE CREW OF 1895 ON THE THAMES.

claring: "Whereas, it hath been a commendable practice of the inhabitants of all the colonies of these parts, that as this country hath its denomination from our dear native country of England, and thence is called New England; so the planters, in their first settling of most new plantations, have given names to those plantations of some cities and towns in England, thereby intending to keep up and leave to posterity the memorial of several places of note there. . . . This court considering that there hath yet no place in any of the colonies been named in memory of the city of London, there being a new plantation within this jurisdiction of Connecticut, settled upon the fair river of Monhegin, in the Pequot country, it being an excellent harbour and a fit and convenient place for future trade, it being also the only place which the English of these parts have possessed by conquest, and that by a very just war, upon that great and warlike people, the Pequots, that therefore they might thereby leave to posterity the memory of that renowned city of London, from thence we had our transportation, have thought fit, in honor to that famous city, to call the said plantation NEW LONDON."

For similar reasons, the "fair river Monhegin" became the Thames.

In 1650, four years after the original settlement, the village had increased so considerably that a public grinding-mill was found to be a necessity. A substantial structure was therefore erected under the supervision of Winthrop; and so well was the work done that the building remains to the present day, a monument to the sterling carpentry of our colonial forefathers. It is regarded as one of the most interesting landmarks of the present city, and will attract general attention at the celebration in May. The Winthrop homestead, which stood near by

THE OLD AND THE NEW — OLD MILL (BUILT 1650) AND WINTHROP SCHOOL.

PEQUOT CASINO AND NEW LONDON LIGHT.

and is shown in an illustration accompanying this paper, was demolished some years ago, but in its place has risen a Winthrop school, which affords a marked contrast to the colonial architecture of the old mill beside it.

The records of the town during the first years of its existence give us here and there pleasant glimpses of the peaceful life of its inhabitants, but nothing is more picturesque than an incident related by Winthrop at Hartford, some years after its occurrence, when he had been called upon to testify to the correct boundary between the towns of New London and Lyme. In order to show that the original limits of the former extended as far west as Bride Brook, near the present village of Niantic, he recalled this episode: While deriving authority as magistrate at New London from the General Court of Massachusetts, he was requested to marry a youth and maiden at Saybrook. A Connecticut magistrate had been engaged for the ceremony, but "there falling out at that time a great snow," travel from the interior was blocked, and application was made to Winthrop as the most accessible official. He could not perform the ceremony in Connecticut territory, and a journey from Saybrook to New London would have been irksome for the bridal party; but a compromise was made, and a meeting effected at the boundary line of the two colonies, where Bride Brook, receiving its name from this incident, flows into the Sound. "Romantic lovers," says Miss Caulkins, the historian of New London, "have sometimes pledged their faith by joining hands over a narrow streamlet; but never, perhaps, before or since, was the legal rite performed in a situation so wild and solitary, and

THE NAMEAUG SCHOOL.

THE WILLIAMS MEMORIAL INSTITUTE.

under circumstances so interesting and peculiar."

Another important influx of Massachusetts settlers occurred in 1651. In that or the preceding year, Rev. Richard Blinman, formerly of Chepstowe in Monmouthshire, England, removed from Gloucester to New London, becoming the first minister of the town, at a salary of sixty pounds per annum in addition to the gift of six acres of land on Meeting-House Hill; and he was followed in the spring of 1651 by many of his Gloucester parishioners, after the contemporary fashion of many congregations. House-lots for the new-comers were platted "beyond the brook and the ministry lot," and the thoroughfare adjoining received the name of Cape Ann Lane. Thus another tie between Massachusetts and the plantation on the "Great River of the Pequot country" was created.

Eleven years after the founding of New London, Winthrop was elected governor, and compelled to remove to Hartford; but the connection of the family with the place survived this event. The governor's sons returned in 1662, and at the present time some of his descendants are to be found in New London. One of his sons, Fitz-John Winthrop, became the second governor of the colony contributed by New London; and subsequently a third executive was supplied by the town in the person of Rev. Gurdon Saltonstall, the Congregational minister. In recent years the city has given the state another governor, Hon. Thomas M. Waller, who was also first vice-president of the World's Fair Commission at Chicago. Gov-

STATE STREET.

ernor Saltonstall was chief justice of Connecticut for a single term, and Richard Law, the first mayor of New London, occupied the same office; while among the members of the Continental Congress in the eighteenth century were Law and William Hillhouse; and on the lists of the United States House of Representatives have appeared the names of Amasa Learned, Joshua Coit, Elias Perkins, Lyman Law, Thomas W. Williams, Nathan Belcher and Augustus Brandegee, all of New London. But this is necessarily a resumé of significant events, not of individual achievements.

The situation of New London made it an important centre in many colonial enterprises. Here the Connecticut troops rendezvoused in preparation for the Great Swamp Fight of 1675, when the powerful Narragansett nation received its death-blow; here as early as 1658 a customs-officer was appointed, probably the first in the colony; and an act of Parliament in 1710 made the town the chief postal station in Connecticut. In the French and Indian wars it had an honorable part, and in 1745 the Connecticut troops en route for Louisburg assembled here to embark. Possessing the best harbor between Newport and New York, the town saw many warlike enterprises undertaken, as in 1776, when the first naval expedition under the authority of the Continental Congress was fitted out in the Thames, with Commodore Hopkins in command.

THE PUBLIC LIBRARY.

No survey of the history of New London would be complete without at least a passing reference to its long commercial record. In 1665 the Colonial authorities sent a communication to the king, reminding him that New London had received its name from the hope entertained for it as a future important place of commerce and trade, and petitioning His Majesty to make it a free port for a space of years. In 1680 they wrote to the lords of the Privy Council, praying the same favor, and pointing out that the harbor was so capacious that a "ship of 500 tunns may go up to the Town and come so near the shoar, that they may toss a biskitt on shoar." These requests of the colonial officials were not granted; but commerce flourished and the trade of the town increased year by year. The New London customs district included

SECOND CONGREGATIONAL CHURCH.

ST. JAMES'S EPISCOPAL CHURCH, BURIAL PLACE OF BISHOP SEABURY.

all Connecticut, as is noted by Douglas, in his History of the British Settlements: "In Connecticut are eight convenient shipping ports for small crafts, but all masters enter and clear at New London, a good harbor five miles within land and deep water; here they build large ships, but their timber is spongy and not durable." Commerce and ship-building naturally went hand in hand. The records show an immense total number of crafts launched in the river, among them Jeffrey's "great ship" of 700 tons, which was floated in 1725 in the presence of a throng of spectators. Trade was opened at an early date with the ports of Newfoundland, and New London vessels were familiar objects at the Barbadoes. From March 25, 1748, to March 25, 1749, the whole number of vessels clearing for foreign ports was 62, while 37 arrived from foreign harbors; but this distant trade formed a small share only of the total commerce of New London. The historian Douglas, writing at about this period, says: "Connecticut uses scarce any foreign trade; lately they send some small craft to the W. Indies; they vent their produce in the neighboring colonies, viz., wheat, Indian corn, beaver, pork, butter, horses and flax." A few years before the opening of the Revolution a considerable trade with Great Britain and Spain had indeed sprung up, but as the commerce of the town had suffered previously on account of the Canada wars, during which French vessels preyed upon it, so the outbreak of the greater struggle put an end to whatever hopes the New London merchants may have indulged for a profitable commercial intercourse with Europe. It was years after the independence of the Colonies had been secured before the marine trade of the place approached its former proportions.

No other American town was more deeply affected than New London by the stirring events of the Revolution. Lying at the mouth of the Sound, it was constantly exposed to the designs of the British fleets, and while the actual attack did not occur until the

THE COURT HOUSE, ERECTED 1784.

naval expeditions embarking in the harbor. British ships patrolled the Sound from one end to the other, and once the inhabitants of New London were thrown into dire alarm by the spectacle of no less than a hundred of the enemy's vessels in the offing. On such occasions the sound of bells and the blaze of beacon fires mingled with the booming of signal guns along

latter part of the year 1781, it was for months at a time almost daily and hourly expected. When Lexington was fought and the news reached Connecticut, two companies were formed at New London, both of which participated in the battle of Bunker Hill. A New London seaman, in command of the ship *Harrison,* is said to have taken the first British prize into port. Patriotism burned brightly in the town, and was fanned by the constant sight of militia gathering on the green, or

the coast. The hastily prepared earthworks on either side of the river were manned with excited troops, the women and children scurried inland to places of safety, and the sloops and smacks of the port were hauled up the river toward Norwich. Prisoners released by the English on exchange frequently thronged the wharves and brought filth and disease into the town. Privateers, coming into the harbor to refit, set their crews adrift in the streets and added a lax and noisy

THE THAMES ON REGATTA DAY.

element to the population. It was in Long Island Sound more than anywhere else that the American and British privateers waged their guerilla warfare against each other and gave a new and thrilling chapter to marine adventure. Some really fine vessels were fitted out at New London for this hazardous business, of which Miss Caulkins says, with a good deal of truth: "It has been customary to make a distinction between the regular navy of the country and those private armed vessels, called letters-of-marque or privateers, as if the former were an honorable service and the latter but little removed from piracy. The distinction is unjust; one was as fair and lawful as the other. Both were sanctioned by the custom of nations; the object of each was the same. The Continental vessels no less than the privateers seized upon peaceable merchantmen; and as much historical credit should be awarded to the brave privateersman, as to the commissioned officer."

THE THAMES NEAR THE PEQUOT HOUSE.

Many were the rich prizes brought into New London during this stirring period, and many the disasters which befell the daring seamen who risked their lives and liberty for the cause of the Colonies. Toward the close of the war men available for the service became scarce, and advertisements like the following were frequent in the Connecticut *Gazette:* "The ship *Oliver Cromwell,* Timothy Parker, commander, ready for a cruise against the enemies of the United Independent States. All gentlemen volunteers that have a mind to make their fortunes, are desired to repair immediately on board said ship in the port of New London, where they will meet good encouragement." "Gentlemen volunteers" is an obvious euphemism; but it sounds well in cold print and in the early days of the war it abundantly justified itself.

New London furnished to history the one figure of the Revolutionary struggle around whom clusters its chief pathetic interest, the gallant schoolmaster and captain, Nathan Hale, executed as a spy by the British and glorified in his untimely death by the familiar words which have been put on his monument in New York city: "I only regret that I have but one life to give for my country." The schoolhouse in which he taught at

New London is still preserved, and will doubtless remain as a silent teacher of patriotism for years to come. As Dr. Leonard Bacon said at the Sons of the American Revolution dinner in New London, in 1892: "Let it stand like the Whitefield house at Guilford and the old meeting-house at Hingham, amid the sumptuous edifices of our thriving and booming times, the monument of a simpler age; but more than a monument—the shrine of a heroic memory. Save the old schoolhouse. It has not done teaching yet. There may be therein no word of teacher nor murmur of children's voices,—'there shall be no speech nor language, its voice shall not be heard'; but, standing dumb upon these busy streets, 'its line shall go out into all the land,' to teach the youth of the future generations how to live for their country and how to die for it."

In tragic contrast to the figure of Hale, whose brief career of nineteen years has appealed so deeply to the imagination of the American youth of every later period, stands that of Benedict Arnold, who was born in New London county, and who returned toward the close of the war to wreak his disappointment and vengeance upon his former neighbors and friends. The story is too familiar to be retold in detail, but may be recalled in its main features. The constant annoyance experienced by the British from the New London privateers culminated in 1781 in the loss of a particularly valuable prize, which in spite of their best endeavors had been piloted safe out of reach into the Thames River. An expedition against the town was determined on at New York, and on the fifth of September a fleet of thirty-two vessels under command of Arnold made its appearance off the mouth of the harbor. On the morning of the sixth, the feeble battery south of New London, known as Fort Trumbull, was attacked by the enemy in force and deserted by its garrison of twenty-three men, who had received orders to retreat to Fort Griswold across the river in the event of a direct assault, but did not obey until they had delivered a well-aimed volley at the invaders. The British took possession of the town in force, resistance on the part of the inhabitants being hopeless, and proceeded to destroy the shops, stores and public buildings in the vicinity of the water. Arnold himself occupied an elevated position near the centre of the town and directed the progress of events in person, being by reason of his familiarity with the place well qualified for his peculiar service on this occasion. It is supposed that his original intention was to destroy not the private residences of the town, except in a few particular instances; but whether on account of the explosion of powder in the storehouses set ablaze, or because the rapacity of the soldiers increased with the sight of the flames, perhaps for both reasons, the fall of night saw sixty-five dwelling-houses burned, together with thirty-seven mercantile stores and warehouses, eighteen mechanics' shops, twenty barns, and nine public or semi-public structures, including the Episcopal church. The wharves and shipping met a similar fate, and so great was the blow to commerce that years were required for its revival.

Meanwhile eight hundred troops had disembarked on the Groton side of the river, under command of Lieutenant-Colonel Eyre. A flag of truce was sent to Col. William Ledyard, the commandant at Fort Griswold, calling for the unconditional surrender of the garrison. Colonel Ledyard had but 150 men all told, but he returned a gallant refusal. A second time a British flag of truce was sent forward, this time with the information that if the works should be carried martial law would be enforced. "We shall not surrender," was the brave reply, "let the consequences be what they may!" Over the awful struggle which ensued between the eight hundred British regulars and the one hundred and fifty Continental volunteers who opposed them a veil may well be drawn. No annals recite a more desperate resistance on the one hand or a more determined onslaught on the other. Englishmen contested with the descendants of Englishmen, and both fought as alien foes might never have battled. By sheer force of numbers the British won the day, swarming over the ramparts like madmen when the garrison, absolutely powerless, flung down their arms. This token of surrender, however, did not avail. The enraged redcoats poured a terrible fire upon their defenceless enemy, and Colonel Ledyard, presenting his sword to the British commander, was run through the heart. Infuriated by their fierce struggle up the crest of the hill, their wrath intensified, as they afterward declared, by the continued resistance of some of the garrison after the majority had surrendered, they swept across the narrow confines of the fort like a pestilence which leaves only hideous corpses in its wake. When their fury had subsided, eighty-five of the original one hundred and fifty defenders of the hill lay stark dead within the ramparts; almost every one of the remainder was wounded, the majority mortally; the loss of the British was itself considerable; and the sun went down on a scene so dreadful that we of a later time who read the record must pray for the peace of the Anglo-Saxon nations. Whenever one of our Congressional jingoes takes it into his head to deliver a warlike harangue he ought first to read anew the story of Fort Griswold as a preventive. "Stop! stop!" cried a British officer at the height of the massacre. "In the name of heaven, I say, stop! my soul cannot bear it." Blood flowed in streams on every side; the crazed victors plunged their swords and bayonets into dead and wounded alike, till some of the bodies on the morrow showed a score or thirty life-thrusts; the wounded were dragged outside the works, that the torch might be applied to the magazine, and some of them were placed in a rough cart and drawn down the hill toward the landing. When the descent had been but partially accomplished the impetus proved too great for those in charge of the wagon, and to save themselves they dashed aside and left it to find its way to the foot of the declivity. Near the end of its journey it crashed against a tree, and the shock to the maimed and groaning occupants, heaped brutally upon each other, was so fearful that the noise of their cries was heard far across the river. Some of them were killed outright; and thus, amid the burning of dwellings and shops on both sides of the river, the saddest chapter in the history of the Revolution came to a close.*

Nothing better marks the rise of New London during the first half of the nineteenth century than the increasing importance of the whaling industry. Year by year the capital invested in this business expanded, till in 1846 it amounted to nearly two million dollars. New Bedford's share in the industry was much larger than this; but no other American port equalled it. In 1846, no less than seventy-eight vessels, the complete list of which, with names, may be found in Daboll's Almanac for 1847, hailed from New London, while the neighboring towns of Stonington and Mystic had a combined fleet of nearly fifty more. The New London crafts aggregated 26,200 tons, and together with the ninety or a hundred fishing vessels of the port employed a small army of some three thousand men. Mr. George T. Marshall of New London relates in a recent issue of the *Day* of that city, that more than one hundred thousand barrels of oil were brought into port in 1844–45. A barrel held thirty-one and one-half gallons, and sold for about $6.30. The wharves were the scene of incessant activity, one hundred and fifty ship-carpenters, a hundred caulkers and three hundred riggers, stevedores

* See article, "The Smitten Village," in the *New England Magazine*, August, 1895.

and sailors, together with a host of painters, lending life and color to the water-front. All the available space about the wharves was crowded with oil-casks brought, full of oil, from the vessels to be tested; great piles of empty casks, yellow pine lumber and iron hooping might be seen in every direction; money was plenty; and the evidences of prosperity abounded. But with 1847 the tide turned, the industry slackened, and the town, in common with New Bedford and the other whaling ports of New England and Long Island, experienced a long period of commercial depression. It is only in the last few years that it has taken on new life and begun to cherish wider ambitions for itself. The last whale-ship sailed out of New London harbor years ago, and now the port is not represented by even one of the vessels still engaged in the perilous industry. Some of the fortunes made in the halcyon forties remain, however, and a new spirit of progress has manifested itself in the ancient town. Its growth in recent years has been substantial, and it is gradually becoming again one of the commercial centres of New England.

The population of New London at the present time is approximately 16,000. The evidences of the antiquity of the town are still many; but it is all the time taking on a more modern appearance. So far as ornamental edifices are concerned, it is equal to any other city of the same size east of the Hudson, and every year sees a substantial increase in the number of its handsome public or semi-public structures. The latest noteworthy addition is that of the brick building at State and Meridian streets, the future home of *Munsey's Magazine,* which is said to be the most extensively circulated monthly magazine in the world. The structure is one of the largest in the state, and within its walls a million copies of this magazine may soon be printed, bound and prepared for shipment every month. Another magazine, the *Cosmopolitan,* has built for itself a home at Irvington, N. Y.; and who knows but a general exodus of the monthly periodicals from the metropolis will follow? Towns like New London, with excellent shipping facilities, are peculiarly adapted to the material production of such publications. Land is naturally cheaper in a city of sixteen thousand inhabitants than it is in New York, and other requisite facilities are obtainable at lower rates.

Among the elements contributing to the recent prosperity of New London must be reckoned the drift of summer population toward it. Situated as it is near the mouth of one of the most charming streams of New England, with the blue waters and cool breezes of the Sound close at hand, the dwellers in the larger cities of the country have flocked to it in ever increasing numbers, until the vicinity of the Pequot House, two miles south of the centre of the town, is now comparable in its artificial beauty, as it is also in its natural attractiveness, to the famous cottage colony of Newport. On both sides of the river handsome villas are being erected every year, good stone roads are branching out in all directions, well kept lawns and hedges are multiplying, and within a few seasons the shore for miles east and west will be graced with pleasant summer homes. Every August the New York Yacht Club, with its hundred white-winged cruisers, sails majestically up the Sound and into the river, where the vessels remain at anchor over night and illuminate the surrounding country with their vari-colored pyrotechnics. Each year until the present, the Yale and Harvard crews have contested with each other on the Thames, and thousands of spectators have been drawn to the town to see the battle of the Crimson and the Blue. Race-day was long the festal occasion of the year in New London. Long trains of crowded coaches drew into the station at the foot of State Street on the morning of the regatta, and the streets were gay all day with pretty girls appropriately decked in the colors of the contestants, enthusiastic collegians armed with tin horns and partisan emblems, folk from the neighboring towns attracted quite as much by the incidental features of the occasion as by the race itself, excited graduates who seemed to have sipped from the Fountain of Youth, and various other people who had evidently discovered some ruddier fountain. But this year there will be no college regatta on the American Thames. The Cornell, Harvard, Columbia and Pennsylvania eights, erstwhile visitors to New London, will row over a New York course, and the Yale crew is to try its fortune at Henley; so there will be no eager watching at Winthrop Point for the rival boats as they sweep down the four-mile course to its conclusion at the big bridge, no long excursion train following the slender craft from start to finish, no crowded steamers or gaily decked pleasure boats, no fusillade of cannon and whistles as the victors, big and brawny, stripped to the skin and wet as so many seals, glide between the final flag-posts. But it cannot be long before the excellence of the course attracts, if not the Yale and Harvard crews again, the oarsmen of other universities.

New London is now a modern city in all its essential aspects. It has a handsome public library; a group of ornamental schoolhouses, including the Bulkeley High School for young men and the Williams Memorial Institute for young women; a commodious brick railway station and good hotel accommodations, the latter being augmented in the summer by two large hotels on either side of the river near its junction with the Sound; and many handsome churches, among them St. James's Episcopal church, where Samuel Seabury, the first American Episcopal bishop, and a long-time resident of New London, lies buried, and where the other day the one hundredth anniversary of his death was fittingly commemorated by a great company of laymen, clergy and bishops, with the venerable Presiding Bishop at their head. It has been selected as the dividing point between the New Haven and Old Colony railroad systems, and plans are now in progress which will make it one of the most important railway centres in the New England states. The Norwich line of steamers to New York has its headquarters here, and from this port, not from the city which bears the name of the line, the fine vessels of the fleet take their departure. Among these steamers is the *City of Lowell*, one of the fastest two steamboats on Long Island Sound, and perhaps the fastest—it will not do to say anything to the contrary in New London. She has made the trip from New York to her wharf in New London in five hours, which is proof that she is an extremely able craft.

New London has also a substantial new armory for its militia, a theatre with modern equipment and decorations, electric cars, smooth boulevards along the river shore, a casino for its summer guests at the Pequot, electric lights and an excellent water supply, prosperous banking and commercial institutions, well-stocked shops, extensive manufactories of a great variety of things from sewing-silk to printing-presses, ship-yards, marine railways, and the longest drawbridge in the world, a mighty structure with a draw of 503 feet. The soldiers and sailors' monument, to be dedicated on the sixth of May, makes one more of a group of local historical memorials already notable—the impressive granite shaft which rises a hundred and fifty feet above the ramparts of Fort Griswold and commemorates the gallant defence of 1781, the recently erected monument marking the site of the ancient Avery homestead at Poquonnoc, and the John Mason memorial near Mystic, where the warlike Pequot tribe was destroyed in a night. To these the Winthrop monument at Bulkeley Square is to be added in the immediate future.

How Swordfish are Caught (1893)

HOW SWORDFISH ARE CAUGHT.

BY PELEG'S GUEST.

IT was on the quay at Stonington, Conn., that I met my sea friend, Peleg S. Chawner, early on a September morning. The rain was pelting down. I was catching eels, which were biting well; and moored to the dock was the fishing schooner *Saucy Sall*, a craft about fifty feet long, old and weather-beaten, with grimy, greasy decks, and an ancient fishlike smell exuding from her hull generally. Of this gallant craft Peleg was skipper. We had formed a nodding acquaintance with each other through meeting on the water front, and his picturesque appearance had many charms for me.

He had long, shaggy hair and resplendent whiskers of auburn hue, that finely fringed his sun-tanned face. He had the regular "shell back" of the sailor. If you had peeled off his garments and fitted him out with a trident, he might well have posed for Neptune, being so physically constituted as to be able to give points to the ordinary professional nautical model.

And there he stood on the quay, a sou'wester on his thickly thatched pate, from which the heavy morning shower dripped over his yellow oilers and his great sea-boots of horsehide. Presently he jumped on the deck of his boat, and, after looking at me with much interest, as if I were some queer fishy specimen he had never seen before, he hailed me with a voice thick and hoarse as a fog-horn:

"Ahoy there! you pale-faced New Yorker, jump aboard and come with me for a cruise. We're bound out after swordfish."

I gladly accepted Captain Peleg's invitation, and, after buying a few cabin stores at a neighboring ship-chandler's, I embarked on the old craft; and under a double-reefed mainsail and storm foresail we sailed out of the harbor, passed by the breakwater and out by Watch Hill to sea. Our destination was along the shore of Block Island, a favorite resort or rendezvous of swordfish during July, August and September.

Before we had been out an hour the wind shifted from southeast to southwest, the rain ceased and the sun shone, drying the wet decks and soaking sails. We shook out our reefs to the merry little breeze and bowled along speedily through the sparkling water.

The ship's company consisted of Skipper Peleg, the mate, Theodore, and Toby, a boy of fourteen, who acted as cook and general factotum. The cabin was a comfortable snuggery, with four bunks; and the forward bulkhead contained shelves and lockers, in which were neatly stowed the modest provisions for the crew, salt pork, beans, hard tack, molasses and coffee, also a kettle, frying pan and other kitchen utensils. Whether it was the skilled cookery of Toby or the salt strong air that gave us an appetite, I know not, but we dined well on a big bluefish, caught, half an hour before he was eaten, by the skipper, who never failed to troll a line astern when under way, thus combining thrift and sport.

While enjoying a hearty meal, that old sea-dog, Peleg, discoursed knowingly of the habits of the swordfish, which he had observed carefully for more than a quarter of a century. He had never seen a young fish of the species, nor had he ever fallen in with anybody who had. The swordfish appears in large numbers in the waters near Block Island about July 1st, and disappears suddenly in the last week in September. Where does he come from, and whither does he go? This is a problem that has puzzled many fish experts as well as fishermen.

Peleg told of dories pierced by the fish's sharp, formidable weapon, of the sides of seagoing vessels that its keen point had penetrated, but he declared that the fish never uses its sword in the pursuit of its prey, as so many naturalists avow.

"I was down to Boston oncet," he said, "and I went to hear a lecture on swordfish by a white-headed old chap in specs and a clawhammer coat. He was old enough to know better, but he up and told a room full of 'spectable people that swordfishes uses thar weepons to go on the ram-page among schools of herrin', mack'rel, and bluefish. Now, that's all tommyrot. If so be as wot he says is true, how is it we never finds any pieces of herrin' or other fish in 'em when we comes to cut 'em open ? Now, I've been killin' swordfish ever since I was knee-high to a dory, and I never found anything but jellyfish, squid, and small fry in their innards."

After dinner the shaggy old skipper lighted his pipe, and going on deck exhibited the tools of his trade. The apparatus for capturing swordfish is rude but effective. Out at the end of the bowsprit an iron framework is erected called the "pulpit," from which is suspended a boatswain's chair. In this sits the harpooner with his "iron" in his hand. The harpoon proper is made fast to a small but strong line one hundred fathoms long, neatly coiled down in a tub so as to be clear for running. The other end of this line is secured to a small barrel. A lookout is stationed in the crow's-nest at the foremast head.

When a fish is struck the pole of the harpoon, which is usually ten or twelve feet long, becomes detached from the iron. The fish, as soon as it feels the sting of the point, darts off at double-quick time. The line flies rapidly out of the tub, and the barrel to which the end of the line is attached is thrown overboard. It acts as a float, and the man at the masthead keeps his eye on it, and directs the helmsman how to steer in its wake. The schooner follows it. If the fish is badly wounded it soon succumbs. This is indicated by the barrel resting almost motionless on the surface of the sea. Then is the time to run up to the barrel, heave the dory over the side, man it with two hands, haul the barrel aboard and pull in on the line.

As the line tautens, the fish often indulges in vigorous contortions and struggles, and has been known to tow a dory a considerable distance; but, as a rule, the capture is not difficult, for your New Englander is both muscular and expert, and his iron generally reaches a vital spot.

After the fish is hauled up to the dory he is dispatched with a sharp lance. Then he is towed alongside the schooner and is hoisted on deck.

For several hours the *Saucy Sall* cruised about, but never a fish was sighted, although Theodore kept a bright lookout from aloft. Captain Peleg Chawner ever and anon glanced somewhat reproachfully at me, as I thought, as though I was responsible for his bad luck. At one time I thought my name was Jonah, and cast my eye to windward and to leeward in search of a hospitable whale, but there wasn't one in sight.

Presently I was aroused from my contemplation of the horizon by the hoarse and excited cry of Theodore, the mate, from his lofty perch :

"Fish broad on the lee beam, and a big one at that!"

"Keep her away!" shouted the skipper, as he let go the mainsheet by the run ; "hard up with the helm, you young lubber, or I'll bring you up with a round turn." This to the boy Toby, who was steering.

In an instant Captain Peleg was out at the bowsprit end, hanging on by nothing in particular and firmly gripping his harpoon.

"I see him!" he yelled; "he's right ahead ; steady as you go, Toby, you beauty."

By this time I, too, could see the fish plainly, with its large dorsal fin above the water. It was motionless, apparently taking an afternoon nap, probably after a huge meal of jellyfish Theodore jumped down from aloft and stood by the barrel. Slowly and deliberately the schooner approached her prey. The skipper clenched his teeth and got a new grip on his weapon.

"Starboard your helm a bit!" cried he to Toby, and just as the end of the bowsprit got over the fish he drove his dart with great force into the back of the basking monster. With a jump and a splash the stricken fish sped away, the line flying out of the tub with amazing velocity. Theodore hove the barrel overboard just in the nick of time, and then climbed aloft to his perch at the masthead.

"Keep your weather eye on the barrel, Theodore!" shouted Peleg.

"Aye, aye, Cap! I've got her," was the cheery response.

The *Saucy Sall* followed the barrel for perhaps a quarter of an hour, though to me it seemed much longer. At length the tugging on the line grew feebler. The fish was evidently exhausted. Theodore hopped down from aloft. In the twinkling of an eye the dory was overboard, Peleg and Theodore were in it, and a few strokes of the oars brought the barrel alongside. It was taken into the boat, and then the skipper and the mate hauled away vigorously on the line, and pulled the fish to the dory. He was indeed a big fellow, and when he was towed to the schooner he was dead as mutton.

"I SEE HIM! HE'S RIGHT AHEAD!"

A tackle was hooked onto a strap round his tail, and he was hoisted inboard in triumph. The iron was cut out of his flesh. He was disemboweled, his head cut off, and his carcass lowered into the hold, where it was covered with ice. When got ashore he was weighed, and he tipped the beam at 500 pounds.

I examined his mouth. It was as free from teeth as that of an unweaned babe. Naturalists will tell you that the whole dental arrangement exists there in rudimentary form, but so far as I can learn no swordfish has ever yet been harpooned that had attained to the dignity of cutting its teeth.

The Passing of the New England Fisherman (1896)

THE

NEW ENGLAND MAGAZINE.

FEBRUARY, 1896.

THE PASSING OF THE NEW ENGLAND FISHERMAN.

By Winfield M. Thompson.

GO down to the New England coast, wherever you will, from Nantucket to Quoddy Head, and you will witness the passing of the New England deep-sea fisherman. Not many years ago he was on a practical equality in respect to the importance of his craft, with the farmer, and, with his sturdy qualities, he was a force among his fellows. Much has been written about the New England farmer's changes of fortune; the gathering of statistics regarding abandoned farms has been dignified by the state of Massachusetts through being made a function of the Commonwealth. But the deserted fish-wharves of New England have not been made objects of solicitude on the part of economists; and the fisherman of the old stock has been allowed to wither and pass out of the industrial field, unobserved and unlamented. He sees the old order of things passing away. Concentration of the fishing business has crowded him out, just as the gradual concentration of mining interests in the hands of corporations has crowded out the individual gold digger of the sort pictured in California annals and Bret Harte's stories.

With this concentration of the fishing business at a few ports, a new type of fisherman, of foreign birth, less citizen and more laborer than his predecessor, has come in; and the small fishing villages, deprived of the business that was their main support, have retrograded. The old fisherman finds the vessels which at different times he sailed in scattered. Some lie at wharves, falling apart from disuse; others have been pressed into service as coasting craft, carrying freight of lime, bricks or lumber, their hulls appearing in their old age like worn-out bodies, almost ready to lay down the

"THE DESERTED FISH WHARVES . . . HAVE NOT BEEN MADE OBJECTS OF SOLICITUDE."

over-heavy burden; others still are broken on some barren shore, or thrown high above the tide-line on a bleak waste of sand, to bleach in sun and rain. More modern vessels have taken their places in the fishing business; but these hail from the central ports, and are manned by strangely assorted crews.

The old-time fleet, owned in the villages, depended on the Grand and Western Banks fishery to keep them busy. It cannot be said that since the disintegration of the fleet the volume of the New England fisheries has decreased. A statistical article from the pen of Mr. George A. Rich, printed in the *New England Magazine* for April, 1894, showed that the fisheries were more important in the last decade, both in tonnage and the number of men employed, than ever before. The fact remains, however, that the bank fishery has diminished in volume, and that the native New Englander has ceased to figure in any large degree in the business which he built up, and for many decades, before manufacturing reached its present stage of development, made the leading industry of the New England States.

While the interior of New England was yet a wilderness unscarred by axe and undisturbed by plow, the fisherman followed his ancient calling off the rocky coast, founded villages at sheltered points on cove and bay, and went far to lay the foundation of future states and promote their commercial welfare. Antedating the farmer, he was for a long period of our history a greater factor in the development of the community. His bravery and skill made him virtual master of the seas. From the stern school of the New England fisheries the American merchant marine drew its hardiest men, and the American navy the most valiant defenders of the flag.

The typical New England fisherman was a sturdy, wholesome citizen, as hardy as good blood and tough labor could make him, clean-minded, blunt in speech, open-handed, generous and confiding. He tried to rear his children to become as honest in purpose as himself. He saved what he could from his earnings after all the mouths dependent on him were fed, and paid his taxes without questioning the theory which might underlie the system by which he was taxed. He exercised the right of suffrage as a sacred function established by a wise plan of government, and he voted for the best interests of his community according to his light. His mind worked within narrow limits, and never strayed far from the serious problem of how to cause there were a good many little ones to feed and clothe at home, and nobody to do it but himself. He had his life task allotted him; as fishing was the most natural thing for him to do, his father having done it, he accepted the situation, and fished. He felt himself there to stay, and he left his post only when there was nothing more to be had by staying.

FROM A PHOTO. BY E. W. LUNDAHL.

"CARRYING FREIGHT OF LIME, BRICKS OR LUMBER."

live uprightly in the struggle between men for gain. He saw the workings of nature in its most awful moods, and respected the power that controlled them. The constant presence of danger in his labors, when only the thin plank lay between himself and the depths, robbed his nature of frivolity. Living was too serious a task to be gone through lightly. Yet within his rough breast beat a warm heart, and the light in his clear eye showed his appreciation of the amenities of life. He was no dullard, this Yankee fisherman, and he was no visionary. He went fishing and braved danger be-

The causes which have led up to the New England fisherman's loss of identity seem to have developed naturally enough. In the leading fishing ports of New England,—Gloucester, Boston, Portland, and Provincetown,—his place has been taken by the thrifty sons of England's North American possessions, by the blonde and frugal Swede, and the swarthy Portuguese. Where twenty years ago there were fifteen Yankees to one man of foreign birth in a vessel's crew, there are now more likely to be fifteen men of foreign extraction to one Yankee, or possible none. Data compiled

DRAWN, AFTER A PHOTO. BY FREDERICK A. MAC NEAL.

"BROKEN ON SOME BARREN SHORE."

from recent reports of casualties among fishermen sailing out of Gloucester bear this statement out. One hundred and twenty-two of the men engaged in the Gloucester fisheries were drowned in the twelve months of 1894 and the first month of 1895. Of this number only three, or less than two and one-half per cent of the whole, were of American birth and parentage,—according to a record kept by the Gloucester Relief Association, an organization whose object it is to distribute funds among needy widows and orphans of fishermen. A list of the men lost in the thirteen months was read at a memorial service held in Gloucester on February 9, 1895. The nationality of each man was given, except in a few cases in which it was unmistakably indicated by his name. The table of unfortunates was made up as follows: From Nova Scotia 35, Newfoundland 21, Sweden 15, Cape Breton 14, Portugal 9, St. Pierre, Miq., 8, Ireland 6, Norway 4, United States 3, Finland 3, Iceland 2, Germany 1, Italy 1. Total, 122. A dispatch from Provincetown, printed in a Boston paper on February 27, 1895, giving details of a Provincetown fishing schooner's narrow escape from foundering on the Grand Banks, stated: "Of the twenty men comprising the vessel's crew all were of Portuguese extraction. Nineteen were natives of Fayal, in the Azores, while one was born in this town."

In a country as new as ours no newcomer can with consistency be called a foreigner, if it is his intention to become a citizen. The original Americans died sorry that they ever saw a white man, and the remnants of the people whom our forefathers dispossessed are still nursing their resentment against the intruders on the reservations of the plains. We are not ancients, and the situation bespeaks charity and brotherly love for all. If the New Englanders feel any resentment against the new men who have secured a footing in the fisheries, it is perhaps directed more toward their Provincial cousins, who make their money here and spend a large part of it at home, than against the new comers from beyond the Atlantic who become citizens and spend their money where they make it. But the Nova Scotian or Newfoundlander has a right of course

"HIGH ABOVE THE TIDE LINE . . . TO BLEACH IN SUN AND RAIN."

to spend his earnings where he pleases. The change in blood and personnel in the New England fisheries therefore becomes interesting mainly from the economic and pathetic features it presents, in the decay of coast villages and the disappearance of a sturdy type of American citizen.

Visit the fishing villages with tablet and pencil, and the facts which may be compiled there will form an instructive chapter in the industrial statistics of New England. Everywhere signs of decay are found in once prosperous places. Especially is this true along the Maine coast. As the same conditions prevail in all these sea-shore Auburns, a description of the scenes and former customs in one may be taken as applying in large degree to the whole. The typical place which I choose, because I happen to have seen much of it, is Southport, in Lincoln County, Maine, where vessels were fitted out which once gave employment to 300 men in the aggregate, the town's population then being about

900. The wharves are now in condition to drop down, or have disappeared altogether, and the fish-houses on the shore stand like skeletons, the boards dropping from their aged frames. There are several of these former centres of activity in the town, each on some navigable cove; and in the county there are probably a hundred. In the vicinity of each wharf are a number of houses, and at some of the larger settlements are stores, silent and weatherbeaten now, with no goods upon their shelves.

"THE TYPICAL NEW ENGLAND FISHERMAN, — A STURDY, WHOLESOME CITIZEN."

Here in the prosperous days of Bank fishing, before the government took away the tonnage bounty, men came by the score in the spring, from near and far, to "ship." As soon as the sun of early March had melted the snow on the south roofs of the fish-houses, they appeared, as true harbingers of spring as the first robin. The winter was an irksome time to them, when chopping spruce trees in the woods and preparing the cord-wood for the stove at home was their chief occupation. The thrifty man, who could be called a "good provider," was known by the size and neatness of his spring wood pile. This task of wood gathering being over in February, the fisherman watched the sun's rays grow stronger day by day, eager to construe its faintest smile into a promise of spring; and no sooner had March come in than the old family dory was cleared of ice and snow and fitted with fresh thole-pins, ready to take a little party to "get a chance." Usually the nearest fish firm was visited, but not always, for the quality of the vessels fitted out and the reputation of the firm for fairness in settling with the men were matters of prior consideration.

There was no question of wages, for the business was conducted "on shares," the nearest approach to a purely coöperative basis of profit-sharing in a successful business ever attained in this country, and a system which always has been and is now free from dissension and anything like "labor" troubles. As a rule, the fisherman of to-day, like the fisherman formerly, is satisfied with what he gets, providing Fortune favors him in his catch. In the Bank fishery, the owners supplied the vessel, equipment, salt and provisions. The crew paid the cook's wages and half the bait bill. The gross proceeds of the trip were divided equally between owners and crew, each man being assessed his part of the expense for bait and cook's wages, and then given his share of the net balance according to the number of fish he caught. Thus, if the high line caught 20,000 fish and earned $200, and the low line caught 10,000, he earned but $100. The captain was usually allowed an average share and given a percentage, from three to five per cent, of the gross receipts for the voyage. This percentage was paid by the firm. The cook was allowed to fish in return for caring

"THE FISH-HOUSES ON THE SHORE STAND LIKE SKELETONS."

for the vessel while the men were out in the dories, and he received a share of the receipts in proportion to his catch, besides his wages, which ranged from $40 to $60 a month. If he was a smart fisherman and capable of doing a great deal of work, he could make more than the captain himself. The cook was shipped at the same time as the crew; and while the crew were at work painting the vessel, scraping spars and mending sails, he was cleaning up the fo'c's'le, and getting the range and cooking utensils into shape.

In the old days, the owners kept open house during fitting-out time, every man in their employ being welcome to their board in the big house, which stood only a little way back from the fish-houses and store. This custom waned as time went on, and finally died out. With it was dissolved one of the strongest ties that bound employer and employed,—or, more properly, the parties in a mutual venture; for while the owners put capital into the enterprise and could be guarded by insurance against loss, the fisherman contributed skill and daring, and hazarded his life. In return for this the owner assumed the rôle of creditor and supplied the wants of the fisherman's family in his absence, taking chances on the season's returns being sufficient to balance accounts, and the honesty of the debtor in case they were not. As soon as a man shipped in the spring he was entitled to open an account at the store, to which account everything supplied himself or his family until autumn was charged. The first entry on the day book almost invariably included a pair of "buck," (red leather) or rubber boots, from five to ten pounds of tobacco, some clay pipes, a jackknife, a sou'wester, oil-

"A FORMER CENTRE OF ACTIVITY IN THE TOWN . . . SILENT AND WEATHERBEATEN NOW."

"FLAKE YARD," STORE AND FISH-HOUSES OF A TYPICAL FISH-CURING ESTABLISHMENT.

clothes, and at the end a list of groceries,—pork, beans, corned beef, flour and saleratus, to help the family "up March hill" and through the spring. After the vessel had sailed away, which was usually before April was very old, the purchasers at the store included brown-faced boys in jumpers and overalls, who timidly ordered what "mother said" was wanting, and stern-visaged women, who spoke without inflection of the voice and bought sparingly of such luxuries as rice and dried apples, and ordered only small quantities of necessaries like lard and molasses.

When the time for "settling up" came in the fall, the balance was not always on the right side. It was a hard pull at the heartstrings of the husband and father to be told that he had no money coming to him; for the winters were long and hard, his family was large, and no money meant more work and the suffering of fishing in winter. Sometimes the account would almost balance, and a few cents would be coming. Then the fisherman's face hardened a little, his jaw became more firmly set as his fingers closed over the few coppers placed on his calloused palm by the owner. He went out of the store slowly, and around the first corner. Only a few cents. He looked at them, now that he was alone. There was all he had to show for eight months' hard work and privation. As he looked, a word formed in his mind. It was "Georges". A journey to Gloucester, a place on a haddock fisherman,—and away to the marine graveyard, from which he might return and might not, to set trawls over a bottom scattered with human bones. Cold, wet and worn out at the end of each day's work, he sought his berth to think of wife and children before nature's sweet restorer placed a finger on his eyelids. Perhaps his loved ones were pinched for food and without fuel to keep them warm, except what the boys gathered along the shore. He could not tell, away off there on Georges Bank. He was the bread-winner, and no matter what his doubts or fears he must stick to his post, and draw money from the sea for them.

Amid such stern conditions, interspersed at times with some of life's tenderer and pleasanter phases, the New England fisherman worked on until within a decade of the present time. Then the adverse influences which had been threatening him and his calling seemed to come together, and he saw the beginning of the end. The firms he had sailed for failed or went out of business, the vessels were sold, and the fisherman, now well along in years, found himself without a ready means of employment at the work he knew how to do best. His sons had drifted into different callings—had become skippers of coasting vessels, or were employed in the work of landsmen, from the peaceful occupation of building boats at home to the more exciting labors of the "cow puncher" on the western plains. There was no young blood to supplement the old and build up what had gone down in disaster. To be sure, there were fishermen; but they were not a class, numerous and distinctive, as formerly. They "tended" lobster pots or herring traps along shore, fished for cod and hake in the coast waters, or went to Gloucester, a few of them, and secured employment there; but all seemed ready to get out of the business, and let the ancient calling of their fathers fall into other hands.

"THE BIG HOUSE STOOD ONLY A LITTLE WAY BACK."

The sons of fishermen take readily to the habits of city-bred people, with whom many of them seek association, the marks of individuality are soon lost, the young men become unlike their fathers, and the effacement of a class whose sturdy virtues made their mark on New England character is swift, certain and abiding.

When these facts are considered, the personality of the old fisherman has a peculiar interest. Like the old soldier, he lives in the past. His day dreams are taken up with the brave fleets now scattered, and he compares the merits of all the vessels in which he ever made a trip. One sailed well before the wind, another made better time to windward, a third was a great sail-carrier, a fourth was noted for seagoing qualities in a storm; and so on through the list, as the old man sits in the sun before his door and lives in the days when he was in his prime. Life is monotonous to him now. He rows around the harbor in an old green dory, placidly, visiting the grocery and the post office,—for letters, newspapers and magazines come often from absent sons and daughters; and

"A SQUARE-RIGGER CAME BOWLING OUT OF THE FOG."

FROM THE PAINTING, "THE LIFTING OF THE FOG," BY MARSHALL JOHNSON.

A REMNANT OF THE OLD INDUSTRY. "PITCHING OUT A TRIP" AT A MAINE FISH WHARF.

as a diversion he "tends" a few lobster pots that are set within easy rowing distance of his home. At night the dory swings at a mooring in sight of the house, the light in the old-fashioned kitchen burns brightly in the early evening and then is quenched, and the old fisherman goes to bed knowing that he will not be called to stand watch or shorten sail. All that is over, and to the end of his days he is assured of peaceful quiet in the company of his faithful wife, the mother of his children, who toiled at home while he was on the sea, and who with her little flock around her managed to "make both ends meet" when times were hard and the bottom of the flour barrel was very near the top.

Their children are men and women now, and are making places for themselves. Summer usually brings one or more to the old home, with bright little ones ready for a vacation frolic. The old man forgets to dream of the past. He plays with his favorite grandson among the daisies of the fields, makes him boats out of shingles with sails of birch bark, takes him rowing in the old green dory, or tells him stories of shipwreck escapes, and rescue on the Grand Banks, when a square-rigger came bowling out of the fog upon his craft, and it seemed the supreme moment had come; or when an ocean liner cut the best vessel in the fleet in two, and the old man's white fiddle, long his heart's solace and known throughout the home fleet for its sweet tone, went down with the wreck.

He does not play the violin now, though he is often urged to do so by visitors to the village. He is shy in the presence of "summer people." He sees the whole town given up to them in July and August, and it disturbs him. Not a cove into which some screaming steam launch does not come with gaily clad strangers on board; not a shady nook along the banks from which some lounging couple does not watch him as he hauls his lobster pots; not a road in the woods in which strollers may not be met; and even at the old fish wharf, deserted long ago by owners and men, he finds two artists camping out in the ancient store, and cooking their meals over an oil stove placed on the very counter where he received his money on settling day.

Of course the village is picturesque —things that are old and dropping to pieces usually are,— but he can hardly reconcile the laughing, sight-seeing crowds of to-day with the scenes which are still sacred to him from memories of his strength and labors.

With his passing the question arises, Will his loss ever be felt by New England or the nation? It is a question which cannot be answered now. Perhaps the new forces will become as virile as the old; perhaps the standard of citizenship will not suffer; perhaps if another war shall come hundreds of skilled, brave seamen will be found ready to man the country's ships and carry the flag to victory as in the sixties and in 1812. Whether so or not, the old fisherman in his green dory, rowing to the post office for his newspaper, is a dark and pathetic figure that seems to stand for something which is with us to-day but may be lost to view forever to-morrow.

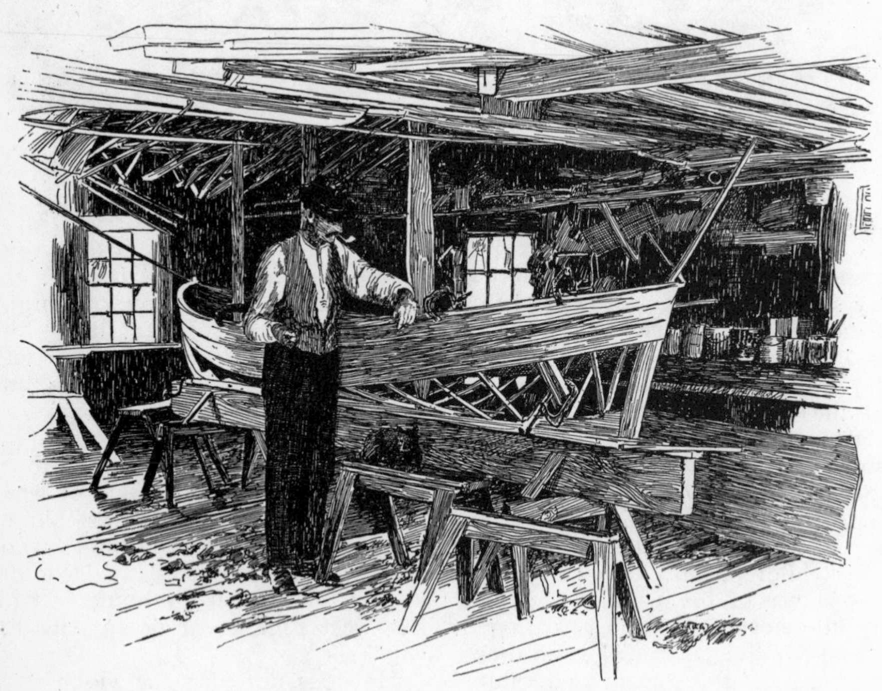

"THE PEACEFUL OCCUPATION OF BUILDING BOATS."

Old-Time Drinking Habits (1895)

OLD-TIME DRINKING HABITS.

By Charles Northend.

HOUGH there is a lamentable amount of intemperance at the present day in New England as well as elsewhere, the evil is less prevalent than it was in the early part of the present century. The number of those who are strictly temperate is very much greater than formerly. The writer can well remember when the habit of drinking intoxicating liquors was not only fashionable and reputable, but was regarded as essential to health. In most houses the sideboard was to be found liberally furnished with well-filled decanters, and almost every one imbibed more or less freely and frequently. The morning, mid-day and evening callers were invited to "take a drink," and no urging was necessary. The minister and the people deemed it right, and honestly thought they were justified in taking a little, not only for "their stomach's sake and often infirmities," but for strength to perform daily duties. At weddings and funerals, at church-raisings and ordinations, at house-raisings and social-gatherings, at huskings, in the fields, in the store and in the workshop, a liberal supply of intoxicating drinks was considered proper and helpful. In cold weather liquors were drunk to promote warmth, and in warm weather to help people keep cool. The illustrations here given of the old-time practices are taken almost at random. Hundreds like them could be gleaned from the old records.

At the ordination of the Rev. Mr. Edwards, in Windsor, Connecticut, in 1695, the people contributed money or various articles for the entertainment of ministers and others who composed the council. Among the articles thus contributed were "one and one half bushels of malt, with hops, one gallon of rum, two gallons of wine and a quantity of sidar." The ordination was followed by a ball, with the approval of the newly settled minister; it was called the "Ordination Ball."

In South Reading, now Wakefield, Massachusetts, in 1800, on the occasion of erecting the frame of the Baptist meeting-house, the society appointed a special committee "to provide for the workmen, good beef, well baked potatoes, bread and cheese, and cider and grog enough for each person."

About the year 1825, the people of Wrentham, Massachusetts, turned out to work in improving the public park. The schools were dismissed, and there was a general gathering for work; and at about eleven o'clock the minister, the Rev. Dr. Fiske, passed around among the workers, carrying in one hand a tin pail and in the other a small tin dipper. He was followed by a layman of his church bearing a larger pail and dipper. The minister's pail contained New England rum, and that of the layman cold water.

In 1770, the town of Alfred, Maine, voted "To purchase one barrel of rum, one barrel of pork, four bushels of beans, ten gallons of molasses, ten pounds of coffee, and twenty-eight pounds of sugar, to raise the meeting-house."

About one hundred years ago, the town of Milton, New Hampshire, passed the following: "Voted, That the town provide one barrel of West India rum, five barrels of New England rum, one barrel of good brown sugar, and half a box of good lemons, for framing and raising the meeting-house."

In 1692, the following order was passed in Salem, Massachusetts: "Voted, That Nathaniel Ingersoll be allowed to sell beer and syder by the quart for the tyme while the farmers are building their meeting-house and on Lord's day afterwards."

In 1740, when the people of New Hartford, Connecticut, were about to build a meeting-house, it was "Voted, That the committee make a sutabel preparation of liquor for the raising of the meeting-house."

The following is a correct copy of a bill rendered by the landlord of a public house in Hartford, Connecticut, for entertaining clergymen and others composing the council for the ordination of the Rev. B. Boardman over the Second Church in 1784: —

"1784 — The South Society in Hartford to I. Seymour Dr.

May 4th To keeping ministers etc. as follows:

			£	s	d
"	"	2 mugs tody	0	2	4
"	"	5 segars	0	5	10
"	"	1 pint of wine	0	3	0
"	"	3 lodgings	0	0	9
May 5th		3 bitters	0	0	9
"	"	3 breakfasts	0	3	6
"	"	15 boles punch	1	10	0
"	"	24 dinners	1	16	0
"	"	11 bottles wine	3	6	0
		5 mugs flip	0	5	10
		3 boles punch	0	6	0
		3 boles tody	0	3	6

Received by me
Israel Seymour."

Yet while dram-drinking was so common, drunkenness was treated as a crime and often punished severely by the fathers. The following record could probably be matched in a score of places: —

"At a cort held at Farmington In hartford county Janerary the 13: 1762 presant Jared Lee Just peace for said county whereas David Culver of Farmington In sd county was atached and brought befouer Jared Lee Just peace to answer unto one sertin Complaint Given In the Name and behalf of our Lord the king by obadiah Andrus Constabel to the sd Jared Lee Just peace the complainant saith that the sd Culver was in the hous of Jonathan Root in Southington on the 20 of october Last past and Did ther Drink Strong licker to Exses that he was Found Drunk in the Lane near Aaron websters and at his one place of abode being bereaved of the eyes of *his Reason and understanding and Lims* the sd David Culver pleads Gilty In cort therefour Find that the said Culver shall pay as a fine to the town tresuar of this town the sum of £0 8*s* 0*d* Lawful Money as Fine and Cost alowed £0 3*s* 6*d* money whearof execution Remains to be don £0 8*s* 0*d*. Fine Febuary the 6 1762 then Execution Granted on £0 3*s* 6*d* cost the above Judgment."

The following extracts from a published history of the town of Weare, New Hampshire, will confirm what has been said about the general use of ardent spirits in the early part of the present century, and also show the favorable results of the temperance reform at a later day. Mr. Little, the historian, says: —

"At the commencement of the present century New England rum was the common drink. No man could run a grocery store without keeping a barrel 'on tap' in the back room, where all customers could help themselves. At all trainings and musters, bridge building and the like, the town furnished the rum. At all ordinations, installations, councils and other great religious meetings, the church provided it. Ministers treated all who called upon them, and apologized for not having more and better liquors. Church members and others treated the minister when he called, and he often went home at night very boozy. The odor of rum was sure to be present at all town meetings, raisings, sheep washings and shearings, huskings and log rollings. It was common at funerals, and the decanter and glasses were often placed on the coffin as a token of the liberality of the mourners. In those old days it was highly commendable to get gloriously 'tight;' as now it is regarded as a great sin, to be repented of in sackcloth and ashes."

In 1784, or a little later, efforts were made to check the evils of intemperance, and by perseverance they proved largely successful. In 1888, Mr. Little says: —

"The temperance agitation has been productive of great good to Weare. It is estimated that at the beginning of the present century the yearly cost of the rum drunk was twenty dollars to each inhabitant, while at the present time it is not more than sixteen cents per individual; and as another good result of the temperance agitation it may be said that for the last forty years the town of Weare has had as few criminals and paupers as any other town of the same size in the state."

The following is quoted from "The Story of Vermont" by Mr. John Heaton: —

"In the early years of the present century the United States was a drunken and dissolute nation. This fact is so enforced upon us by unimpeachable testimony that escape is impossible, no matter how reluctant we may be to give it credit. It was a time of vigorous physical activity, but of low moral standards in many ways. Liquor was plentiful and cheap. Almost every man drank, nor was it accounted shameful to indulge to excess. The host of evil consequences which always follow in the train of drunken habits were everywhere lamented by the few and accepted by the many as inevitable. Brutal and degrading sports flourished, political controversies were waged upon a low level, and the most sordid vices were probably more common, certainly less concealed in the gratification, than is now the case. Nor was Vermont or the United States alone in this unfortunate condition, nor the reformatory impulse which dignified the second quarter of the present century confined to any one country."

It may be added that Vermont was one of the earliest and most active states in efforts to check the evils of intemperance and advocate the cause of total abstinence. The Rev. Mr. Sanford, in his very faithful and interesting history of Connecticut, says: —

"The sale and use of intoxicating drinks was the source of trouble from the founding of the colony. Drunkenness was a crime punished at the discretion of the court by stocking, fining or, more generally, whipping. Laws were passed forbidding sales to incapable or irresponsible persons, as Indians, minors and drunkards. Such a resort as the modern saloon was unknown. Tavernkeepers were allowed to sell to their guests, and the inhabitants of the town might buy liquor of them for use elsewhere; but they were forbidden to 'sit drinking and tippling' in these public houses. The number of taverns was limited to the needs of travel, and there were seldom more than one or two in a village. At the time of the Revolution, and for many years afterward, the usages of society permitted the general use of ardent spirits in the homes of the people and on festive occasions. Cider and New England rum distilled from molasses were the favorite beverages. Early in this century the disastrous effects of this custom began to attract attention, and well it might. The appetite kindled by the use of intoxicating drink had already brought poverty and misery into multitudes of homes. In many cases the sons of honored sires had become miserable drunkards and their ancestral acres had fallen into the hands of strangers."

In 1818, it is stated that fifty-two hogsheads of new rum were sold in the town of East Haddam, Connecticut, where now the amount of sales would not exceed one tenth as much. At that time the minister, the Rev. Dr. Marsh, being about to build a house, announced that no liquors would be furnished at the raising, as was then customary. He was told that the people would not "turn out" to do the work if this inducement was removed; but the house was well raised notwithstanding the absence of liquors.

In 1684, a new prison was built in Salem, Massachusetts. For a long time it was the custom to allow the keeper of the prison to have the profits for liquor sold to the prisoners. If the revenue from this amounted to much, the class of criminals confined must certainly have had a more liberal supply of funds than the same class have at the present day.

In Orcutt's history of Dorchester, Massachusetts, we find the following: —

"In the days that antedated railroads it was the custom of country ministers from the interior who came to Boston, especially on anniversary week, to put up with the Dorchester minister, who had ample room and was reputed wealthy. Not only did they put themselves up in the house, but they put their horses up in the barn. . . . They were always made welcome, although they frequently abused their privileges. . . . Before the total abstinence period the clergy made large demands for liquor and tobacco. They did not care much for wine and cigars, but their tastes ran to rum and pipes, of which an abundant supply was always kept on hand. The result of this ministerial debauch was anything but agreeable to the pastor's wife. That excellent woman, who was indeed a mother in Israel, was made to be the slave of Israel likewise. When the swarm had passed away there was a grand cleaning up: carpets were taken up and shaken; the fireplace 'jams' were scrubbed with brick-dust solution to efface the tobacco stains."

"In early times," says the historian of Wallingford, Connecticut, "rum was largely consumed. A half pint was given to every day laborer. In all families, rich or poor, it was offered to male visitors as an essential part of hospitality, or even good manners. Women took their schnapps, then called 'Hopkins's Elixir,' which was the most delicious and seductive means of getting tipsy that had been invented. Crying babies were silenced with hot toddy, then esteemed an infallible remedy for wind in the stomach. Every man imbibed his morning dram; and this was regarded as temperance. It is said that a minister talked to his people as follows: 'I say nothing, my beloved brethren, against taking a little bitters before breakfast. What I contend against is this dramming, dramming, dramming, at all hours of the day.' Tavern haunting, especially in winter, was common even with respectable farmers."

In 1804, Dr. Benjamin Rush of Philadelphia published a tract entitled, "An Inquiry into the Effects of Ardent Spirits upon the Human Body and Mind." This tract was extensively circulated, and though no immediate results followed, it undoubtedly had a favorable influence. It awakened thought on the subject in the minds of many clergymen; and yet they hesitated about taking a decided stand, and the people felt that their ministers had no right to meddle with the subject. They thought that they had a right to eat and drink what they pleased and as they pleased.

In November, 1811, at a meeting of the New York Synod, a sermon was preached in which the doctrine of total abstinence from intoxicating drinks was strongly advocated. A letter was read from Dr. Lyman Beecher, then settled at Litchfield, Connecticut, in which he took a very decided stand in favor of action in the cause of temperance. After some earnest discussion, the following resolution was passed: —

> "Resolved, That hereafter ardent spirits and wine shall constitute no part of our entertainment at any of our public meetings, and that it be recommended to churches not to treat Christian brethren or others with alcoholic drink as a part of hospitality in friendly visits."

It was also voted to send a copy of the resolution to all the churches under the care of the synod. The clergyman appointed to perform this duty remarked that, after all, he had very little faith in total abstinence. He said he did not believe there was any great harm in his taking a little when he was exhausted by the labors of the Sabbath, nor did he think it improper to invite a parishioner who called with some token of regard to take some refreshment. But he had occasion soon after to modify his views. One of his parishioners brought him a piece of meat, and took so much of the proffered refreshment that he became intoxicated. This induced the clergyman to resolve never again to offer alcoholic drinks to any one. Another clergyman, who had banished intoxicating drinks from his house, said his feelings were sorely tried by having one of his brethren refuse to dine with him on the ground that no brandy would be on the table. In 1812, the clergymen in Fairfield County, Connecticut, resolved not to use strong drinks as a beverage at their future meetings. A committee was appointed to prepare an address to the people on the subject. The Rev. Heman Humphrey, D. D., afterward president of Amherst College, was a member of the committee.

The earliest modern temperance society was organized in 1789 by two hundred farmers of Litchfield, Connecticut, who pledged themselves not to use any intoxicating drinks in their farm work during the ensuing year.

In 1813, the General Association of Connecticut recommended to the trustees of Yale College not to furnish spirits at the public dinner on Commencement Day, and to the state authorities not to furnish them for the public dinner given to the clergy on election day. The Rev. Lyman Beecher and Dr. Humphrey labored faithfully with voice and pen to promote the temperance reformation, and their influence was extensively felt for good.

A little before 1830, the custom of treating visitors with wine, cordials and brandy began to disappear. The sideboards of the rich and influential, which had previously groaned under a load of decanters, were relieved of their burden, and a very great change in the customs of society became apparent. In 1828, Dr. Hewitt was appointed for three years to an agency for the promotion of temperance in Connecticut, and he labored earnestly and successfully. At the close of 1829, there were more than one thousand temperance societies, with more than a hundred thousand members pledged to total abstinence; fifty distilleries had stopped, four hundred merchants had abandoned the traffic in liquors, and twelve hundred drunkards had been reformed. On the first of May, 1831, it appeared that more than three hundred thousand persons had signed the pledge, and not less than fifty thousand were estimated to have been saved from a drunkard's grave.

While the efforts made by individuals and organizations to suppress the evils of intemperance have not accomplished all that was to be desired, they certainly have been effectual in awakening the public mind and securing highly gratifying results. The work of Neal Dow, of John B. Gough and others is well known. While ministers were at one time in the habit of using intoxicating drinks, they were among the first to realize its evils and to take active part in efforts to check the vicious custom.

The Glouscester Fishermen (1902)

SCRIBNER'S MAGAZINE

APRIL, 1902

THE GLOUCESTER FISHERMEN

NIGHT-SEINING AND WINTER TRAWLING

By James B. Connolly

ILLUSTRATIONS BY M. J. BURNS

NIGHT-SEINING

WE were one of a fleet of Gloucester seiners, cruising lazily in the twilight of a soft September evening off the Cape Cod shore. Out toward where the shoals of Middle Bank should lie, crescent moon, brick red in the reflected after-glow of a setting summer sun, had sunk a segment behind the edge of a gently rippling sea. Around and about us the sails of our consorts were fading into the settling dark, red and green side-lights were beginning to take point, and the first whisperings of the awakening night-breeze were bursting softly from the bubbles in our wake.

Down in the fo'c's'le of our schooner the forward gang were engaged in the usual diversions of seiners at leisure. Four were playing whist at the table under tne lamp; two were lying half in and half out of opposite upper bunks, striving to get more of the light on the pages of their books; one, in a lower bunk nearer the peak, was humming something sentimental, and two were in a knot on the lockers, arguing fiercely over nothing in particular. Only the cook, just done with mixing bread, seemed to have had any serious object in life, and he was now standing by the galley fire, rolling the dough off his fingers, plainly with a desire to rest from his labors.

Down the companion-way and into the thick of this dropped the skipper. "I think," said the skipper, as his boot-heels hit the floor, "I'll have a mug-up." From the boiler on the galley-stove he poured out a mug of coffee, and from the grub-locker he took a thin slice of bread and two thick slices of cold beef. He buried the bread among the beef and leaned against the foremast while he ate.

In heavy jack-boots and summer sou'-wester, with a black jersey of fine quality sticking up above the neck of his oil-jacket, with a face that won you at sight; cheeks a uniform pink; damp, storm-beaten, and healthful; with mouth, eyes, and jaw bespeaking humor, sympathy, and courage; shoulders that seemed made for butting to windward—an attractive, inspiring, magnetic man altogether—the skipper, holding the mug of coffee in one hand and the sandwich of bread and meat in the other, leaned easily up against the butt of the foremast, and, between gulps and bites, took notice of his crew.

The Cook.

"Give me," he said genially to the cook, as the proper man for an audience, "a seiner's crew for elegant gentlemen of leisure. Look at 'em now—you'd think they were all near-sighted, with their cards up to their chins. And above them, look—Kipling to starboard, and the Duchess to port. Mulvaney, I'll bet, filled full of whiskey and keeping the heathen on the jump, and Airy Fairy Lillian, or some other daisy with winnin' ways, disturbin' the peace of mind of half a dozen dukes. Mulvaney's all right, but the Duchess! They'll be taking them kind of books to the masthead next. What d'y s'pose I found back aft the other day? What d'y s'pose? I'll bet you'd never guess. No, no. Well, it was 'He Loved, but was Lured Away.' Yes. Ain't that fine stuff for a fisherman to be feedin' on? And who d'y s'pose owned it but the Cape Island lad. Yes, sir. It was down where he came from—Cape Island, they say—that they once rigged side-lights on the lame horse and walked him around a hay-stack, and the cattle steamers out of Portland, thinking they was a little too much off-shore, used to come in closer. Yes, sir; they never have to buy any beef on Cape Island—nor coal, no. 'Well, who owns this?' says I, picking up the lured-away lad. 'Nobody,' speaks up the Cape Island boy. 'Are you sure?' I asks him. 'Sure,' says he. 'Well, then,' I said, 'over the rail he goes—being nobody's, nobody c'n kick.' And over he went, with Violet Vance and Wilful Winnie, and they floats off in a bunch to the east'ard, with maybe Winnie a foot to loo'ard.

"Violet Vance," went on the skipper, reminiscently, "Violet Vance and Wilful Winnie, and a whole holdful of airy creatures, couldn't help a fisherman when there's anything stirrin'. I waded through a whole bunch of 'em once"—he reached over and took a wedge of pie from the grub-locker—"I went through a whole bunch of 'em once—pretty good pie this, cook, though gen'rally them artificial apples that swings on strings ain't in it with the natural tree apples for pie—once when we was layin' to somewhere to the s'uth'ard of Sable Island, in a blow and a thick fog—fresh halibuting—and right in the way of the liners. And I expect I was goin' 'round the deck in my watch like a man asleep, because the skipper comes up and begins to call me down good and hard. It was my first trip with him, and I was a young lad. 'Young fellow,' says the skipper, Matt Dawson—this was in the Lorelei—'young fellow,' says Matt, 'you look tired. Let me call up the crew and swing a hammock for you, from the fore-rigging to the jumbo boom. How'll that do for you? When the jumbo slats it'll keep the hammock rockin'. Let me,' he says. 'Perhaps,' he goes on, 'you wouldn't mind wakin' up long enough to give that music-box a turn or two every now and then while the fog lasts.' We had a patent horn aboard, the first I ever

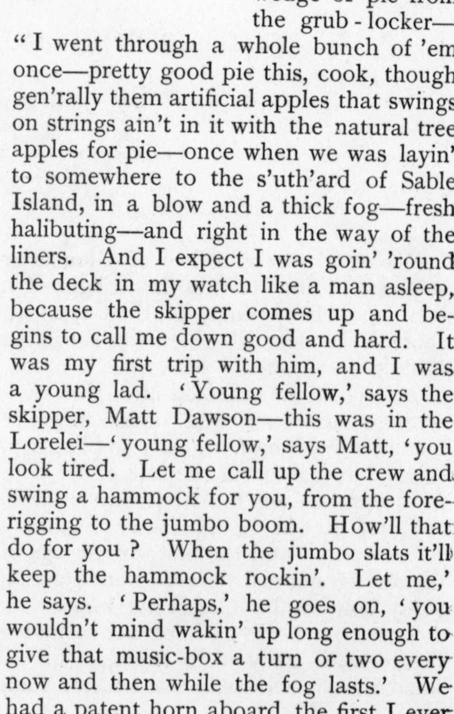

Drawn by M. J. Burns.

Seining—"Can't be sure yet, but things look all right so far!"

(Pursing-up the seine.)

saw, and I'd clear forgot it—warn't used to patent horns.

"However, I s'pose when there's nothin' doin' there's no very great harm. But we'll try to get it out of your heads for to-night. Four days now and only fifty barrels in the hold. But, praise the Lord, the moon's well down by this time and its looking black already and the sea ought to fire up fine later on. And there's a nice little breeze beginning to stir. If any of you are thinking of getting in a kink of sleep then you'd better turn in now, for you're liable to be out afore a great while. I'm going aloft."

Trawling—Looking for a Lost Dory.

The skipper climbed up the companion-way. Then followed the scraping of his boot-heels across the deck. A minute later, had anybody cared to go up and hunt, he would have been discovered astraddle the highest block above the fore-gaff, watching out sharply for the lights of the many other vessels about him, but more particularly straining his eyes for the phosphorescent trails of mackerel.

The men below knew their skipper too well to imagine that they were to be long left in peace. And then, too, the very first man off watch reported a proper night for mackerel. "Not a blessed star out—and black! It's like digging a hole in the ground and looking into it. And the skipper's getting nervous, I know. I could hear him stirring 'round up there when I was for'ard just now, and he hollered to the wheel that up to the nor'ard it looked like jibs down and to hold her up. 'Torches burnin',' he said. And I calate we ain't the only vessel got eyes for it—it's nothin' but side-lights all 'round and some of us'd do well to get into oil-skins."

Fore and aft, in cabin and fo'c's'le, the men made ready. They put away cards, novels, and acrimonious discussions, had a mug-up all, slid into oilclothes, boots, and sou'westers, and then, puffing at a last pipeful, they lay around on lockers and on the floor, backs to the butt of the mast and backs to the stove; wherever there was space for a broad back and a pair of stout legs they dropped themselves, discussing all the while the things that interest virile men—fish, fishing, gales, skippers, fast vessels, big shares, South Africa, China, the Philippines, Bob Fitzsimmons, Carrie Nation, and the awful price of real estate in Gloucester.

By and by, ringing as clearly as if the man himself stood at the companion-way, came the skipper's voice from the masthead: "On deck everybody." Stopped was all discussion, pipes were smothered in flannel bosoms, and up the companionway crowded oil-skins and jack-boots.

Then came: "It looks like vessels toward the Maine shore dressing down. Haul the boat alongside and drop the dory over."

Seining—Red and green lights were beginning to take point.

The men jumped. Four laid hands on the dory in the waist and ten or a dozen heaved away on the stiff painter of the seine-boat that was towing astern. Into the air and over the starboard rail went the dory, while ploughing up to the vessel's boom at the port fore-rigging came the bow of the seine-boat.

Followed then: "Put the tops'ls to her. Sharp now."

The halliards could be heard whirring through the blocks aloft, while two bunches of men sagged and lifted on deck below. Among them it was: "Now then, o-ho—sway away, good," until topsails were flat as boards and the schooner, close-hauled, had heeled to her scuppers.

"Slap the stays'l to her and up with the balloon. Half the fleet's driving to the no'th'ard. Lively."

She liked that rarely. With the seventy-odd foot main-boom sheeted in to her rail, with the thirty-three-foot spike bowsprit poking a lane in the sea when she dove and picking a path among the stars when she lifted, with her midship rail all but flush with the sea and the night-breeze to sing to her—of course she liked it, and she showed her liking. She'd tear herself apart now before she'd let any other creature by. And red and green lights were racing to both quarters of her.

"Into the boat and drop astern. Drop astern boat and dory." It is the master's voice again, and fifteen men go over the rail at the word. Two drop into the dory and thirteen leap from the vessel's rail onto thwarts or netting or into the bottom of the seine-boat—anywhere at all so they get in quickly. The extra hand on deck stands by to pay out the painter, and then into the schooner's boiling wake they go, the thirty-eight-foot seine-boat hardly a dozen fathoms astern, and the little dory just astern of her again. The two men in the dory fend off desperately as they slide by the boat.

On the deck of the vessel now are only the cook, who has the wheel, and the extra hand, who is to stand by the head-sheets. There will be stirring scenes soon, for occasional flashes of light, denoting small "pods" of mackerel, may be discerned on the surface of the sea. Our skipper, we know, is noting these indications, and with them a multiplicity of other things. At the mast-heads of other vessels out in the night are rival skippers, all with skill and nerve and a great will to get fish.

Our vessel may be making from ten to eleven knots now, and the painter of the seine-boat chafes and groans with every jerk in the taffrail chock. The men in the boat call for more line. "Slack away a bit, cook—slack away. We're not porpoises. She's half buried every jump, and every blessed sou'wester aboard bailin' out. And the dory might's well be hove-down altogether. Here's Sam climbed aboard us from the dory—says both of 'em couldn't live in her. Slack away for the Lord's sake, cook—that line's too short."

The cook is about to help them out, but the skipper breaks in:

"Swing her off about two points, ease your main sheet and keep an eye on that light to loo'ard. Off, off—that's good—hold her. For'ard there, slack stays'l and then foretops'l halliards. Be ready to let go balloon halliards and stand by down-haul. Look alive."

Without leaving the wheel the cook paid out some sheet from the bitt by the wheel-box and then unbuttoned the after staysail tack. Forward, the spare hand loosed up halliards until her kites dropped limp.

"Down with your balloon there for'-ard—and at the wheel there, jibe her over. Watch out for that fellow astern—he's pretty handy to our boat. Watch out in boat and dory." The last warning was a roar.

The big gossamer came rattling down the long stay and the jaws of booms ratched, fore and main, as they swung over. From astern came the voices of the men in boat and dory, warning each other to hang on when they felt her jibbing. Some of them must have come near to being jerked overboard. "Why in God's name, cook, don't you slack that painter?" came in the voice of the big seine-heaver.

"'Tain't wuth while now—in a minute now you'll be cast off," called back the cook.

"Draw away your jib—draw away your jumbo," came from aloft. Sheets are barely fast again when it is:

"Steady at the wheel—steady her, cook, ste-a-dy—Great God! man, if you can't see, can't you feel that fellow just ahead? Close your jaws astern there and mind me—water won't hurt you. Ready all!" roared the skipper.

"Ready all!" roared back the seine-heaver.

"All right. Down with your wheel a bit now, cook. Down—more yet. Hold her there."

The vessels that we had dodged by this bit of luffing were now dropping by us; one red light was slowly sliding past our quarter to port and one green shooting past our bow to starboard. Evidently our skipper had been only waiting to work clear of these two neighbors, for there was plenty of fish in sight now. The sea was flashing with trails of them. Our skipper now begins to bite out his commands.

"Stand ready everybody. In the boat and dory there — is everything ready, Pat?"

"All ready—boat and dory."

Out came his orders—rapid fire—and as he ripped them out, no whistling wind could smother his voice, no swash of the sea drown it. In boat, dory, and on deck, every brain glowed to understand, and every heart pumped to obey.

"Up with your wheel, cook, and let her swing off. Ste-a-dy. Ready in the boat. Steady your wheel. Are you ready in the boat? Let her swing off a little more, cook. Steady—hold her there. Stand by in the boat. Now then, now! Cast off your painter, cast off and pull to the west'ard, Pat. To the west'ard—to wind-'ard, Pat. And drive her! Down with the wheel, more yet—that's good. Drive her, I say, Pat. Where's that dory? I don't see the dory. The dory, the dory—where in hell's that dory—show that lantern in the dory! All right the dory. Hold her up, cook—don't let her swing off an inch now. Drive her, boys, drive her! Look out now! Stand by the seine, Pat. Stand by—now—now! Over with the seine, over with it. Give her the twine—the twine, do your hear!—the twine! Drive her—drive her—Blessed Lord, drive her. That's the boy, Pat—drive her! Let her come up, cook. Down with your wheel—down with your wheel—ste-a-dy. Drive her, Pat, drive her! Turn in now—in—in—shorter yet. Drive her now!—where's that dory!—Hold her up—not you, cook—you're all right—ste-a-dy. Hold that

Drawn by M. J. Burns.

Trawling.

The dory mate is in the waist, re-coiling and re-baiting the trawl.

dory up to the wind!—that's it, boys—you're all right—straight ahead now! That's the boy, Pat. Turn her in now again, Pat — in the dory there!—show your lantern in the dory and be ready for the seine-boat. Good enough, boys. Now cover your lantern in the dory and haul away when you're ready."

into it—and their wake alive with smoke and fire to tell them they were moving! Fancy the flatness of regattas in smooth creeks beside that!

It is in the middle of a black night out on the Atlantic, this—and the big seine-heaver is throwing the seine over the side in great armfuls. And there

Trawling—Looking at the "bottom" brought up by the lead.

is the little dory tossing behind, gamely trying to keep up! Doubtless they were glad enough in the dory to get hold of the buoy, and doubtless, too, there was some lively action aboard of her when the skipper called so fiercely to them to hold her up to the wind, so that the efforts of the crew of the seine-boat, racing to get their ten or twelve hundred foot fence around the flying school, might not go for naught.

To have experienced the strain and drive of that rush, to have held an oar in the boat during that and to have shared with them in the confidence they gathered—theirs was a skipper who knew his business—and the soul that rang in his voice!—why, merely to have stood on deck and listened to it—it was like living.

During this dash neither boat nor dory was to be made out from deck, but the splashes of light raised by the oars at every stroke were plainly to be seen in that phosphorescent sea. Certainly they were making that boat hop along—ten good men, with every man a long broad blade, and double-banked, so that every man might encourage his mate and be himself spurred on by desperate effort. Legs, arms, shoulders, back—all went

With his "Haul away now when you're ready," the skipper came down from aloft. He was sliding down, evidently, by way of the jib halliards, for there was the sound of a chafing whiz that could be nothing else than the friction of oil-skins against taut manila rope; a sudden check, as of a block met on the way; an impatient, soft

Trawling—The gunnels of their loaded dories almost flush with the sea.

little, forgivable oath, and then a plump! that meant that he must have dropped the last twelve or fifteen feet to the deck. Immediately came the scurry of his boot-heels as he hurried aft, and in another moment he stood in the glow of the binnacle light. Reaching back toward the shadow of the cook, but never turning his head from that spot out in the dark where he had last seen the boat, he signified his intention of taking the wheel.

"All right, cook, I've got you. My soul, but that's a raft of fish if they got 'em, and I think they have. Did you see that boat ahead we near ran into—the last time we put the wheel down? Man, but for a second I thought they were gone. I hope no blessed vessel comes as close to our fellows. And they were so busy rowing and heaving twine, they never saw us, and myself nearly cross-eyed trying to watch them and our own boat and the fish all at once. Go below, cook, she's all right now. Tell the lad for'ard to go below, too, and have a mug-up for himself—he must be soaked through taking the swash that must have been coming over her bows for the last hour. But tell him to come right up so 's to keep a watch out ahead."

The skipper himself stood to the wheel with his head ever turned over one shoulder, until he saw the flare of a torch from the seine-boat. "Good!" he exclaimed. "What there is is safe now, anyway."

Thereafter his work was easy. He had only to dodge the lights of other vessels now, the old red and green lights that had been his neighbors all that evening, and a few new yellow flares from other seine-boats. So his keen eyes ranged the blackness, and in rings around his own seine-boat he sailed his vessel. That his crew were an unusually long time pursing up only gave him satisfaction. "A jeesly big school, if they got it all," he mur-

Trawling—Over a "gurdy" in the bow one man hauls the stubborn line.

Cutting frozen herring and baiting trawls.

mured, "a jeesly school of 'em." And after a pause, "I think I'll stand down and have a look."

He ran down, luffed, and hailed "What's it look like, Pat?"

From the row of figures that were seen to be crowding gunwale and thwarts and hauling on the seine, one huge shadow straightened up beside a smoky torch and spoke.

"Can't be sure yet, but things look all right so far. A nice little school if we don't lose 'em."

"Well, don't lose 'em. You've got 'em fast enough now. I c'n hear 'em flippin' inside the corks as nach'l as can be. Hurry 'em, boys, it's getting along in the night."

The skipper, very well satisfied, stood away again, and continued to sail triangles around boat and dory. Being now clear of the greater part of a commander's mental strain his spirits began to lighten. Merely by way of being sociable with himself he hummed old ditties. He was possessed of the average fisherman's weakness for anything humorous. There was that about the old coaster, the Eliza Jane. He liked that and he danced an irregular one-footed jig-step by the wheel box as he bumped it out:

Oh, the 'Liza Jane with a blue foremast
And a load of hay came drifting past.
Her skipper stood aft and he says, "How do!
We're the 'Liza Jane and who be you?"
He stood by the wheel and he says, "How do!"
We're from Bangor, Maine, from where be you?"

The 'Liza Jane got a new main truck—
A darn fine thing, but wouldn't stay stuck.
Came a breeze one day from the no'no'west
And the gosh darned truck came down with the rest.

Oh, hi-diddle-di, a breeze from the west;
Who'd think the truck wouldn't stuck with the rest?

Oh, the 'Liza Jane left her wharf one day,
A fine flood tide and the day Friday,
But the darned old tide sent her bow askew
And the 'Liza Jane began for to slew.

Oh, hi-diddle-di, she'd a-fairly flew,
If she only could sail the other end to.

Oh, the 'Liza Jane left port one day,
With her hold full of squash and her deck all hay.
Two years back with her sails all set
She put from Bath—she's sailing yet.

Oh, hi-diddle-di, for a good old craft
She'd a-sailed very well with her bow on aft.

There was a long story to the Eliza Jane, but the skipper did not finish it. Possibly he felt that it was not entirely in harmony with this lowering sky or that flashing sea. Possibly, too, in the waters that boomed and the wake that smoked was the inspiration for something more stirring. At any rate, he began, in a voice that carried far, an old war ballad:

Heaving the Trawl.

'Twas the eighth day of May about ten in the morning,
The sky it was clear and bright shone the sun,
The hail of the Britisher sounded a warning
For every brave seaman to stand by his gun.

That was the preliminary, and the skipper delighted to dwell upon it. And after it:

'Twas then spoke our captain with brave resolution,
Saying: "Boys, at this monster do not be dismayed.
We've sworn to defend our beloved Constitution
And to die for our country we are not afraid."

Then the fight began. And you would think the skipper was in it, except only that now and then he would halt to see how they were getting on in the seine-boat. He laid every mast and yard over the side of her, he made her decks run with blood, and at the last, in a noble effort, he caused her to strike her flag.

By the time he had finished it happened that the skipper was running before the wind, and, going so, it was very quiet aboard the vessel. There was none of the close-hauled wash through her scuppers, nor was there much play of wind through stays and halliards. It was, in brief, unusually quiet, and it needed only that to set the skipper off on a more melancholy tack. So in a subdued voice he began the recitation of one of the incidents that have helped to make orphans of Gloucester children:

Twelve good vessels fighting through the night,
Fighting, fighting that no'th-east gale—
Every man, be sure, did his might,
But never sign of a single sail
Was there in the morning when the sun showed red,
But a hundred and seventy fine men—dead—
Was settling somewhere into the sand
On Georges shoals, which is drowned men's land.

Seventy widows kneeling——

A long hail came over the water and a torch was raised and lowered. "Hi-i-i," hallooed the voice.

"Hi-i-i," hallooed back the skipper as he put up his wheel. You might have thought he intended to run over them. But not that—at the very last moment he threw her up deftly and let her settle beside the boat, from which most of the men came tumbling immediately over the side of the vessel. Of those who stayed, one shackled the boat's bow onto the iron that hung from the boom at the fore-rigging, and, having done that, braced an oar between himself and the vessel's run to hold the boat away and steady, while another in the stern of the boat did the same thing with his oar. In the boat's waist two men hung onto the seine.

Trawling—Coming Along side.

A section of the cork edge of the seine being now gathered inboard and clamped down over the vessel's rail the mackerel were crowded into the middle part—the bunt—of the seine and thus held safely between boat and vessel. Into this space the sea swashed and slapped after a fashion that kept all in the boat completely drenched and made it rather difficult for the men in bow and stern to fend off and with it retain their balance.

Now began the bailing in. Over the rail and among the kicking fish dropped the skipper's huge dip-net. A twist and a turn and "He-yew!" he yelled. "Oy-hoo!" grunted the two gangs at the halliards, and into the air and over the rail swung the big dip-net, swimming full. Down it sagged quickly to the two men at the rail. "Hi-oh!" they called cheerfully and turned the dipper inside out. Out and down it went again, "He-yew," and up and in it came again. "Oy-hoo! Hi-oh!" and flop! it was turned upside down and another barrel of fat lusty fish flipped their lengths against the hard deck. Head and tail they flipped, each head and tail ten times a second seemingly, until it sounded—that frantic beating of flesh and bone on the bare deck—as if a battalion of gentle little drummer boys were tapping a low but marvellously quick-sounding roll. Scales flew. Some were found next morning glued to the mast-head.

"He-yew," called the skipper—"Oy-hoo," responded the halliards gang—"Hi-oh," said cheerily the pair at the rail—"Fine fat fish," commented the men in the boat, the only men who had time to draw an extra breath.

Blazing torches encircled them. Arms worked up and down, big boots stamped, while in-board and out swung the dip-net

Drawn by M. J. Burns.

Trawling—The men fork the fish over the rail.

Seining—Around the keelers the men gathered and dressing began.

and onto the deck flopped the mackerel. " Drive her," called the skipper, and " He-yew," " Oy-hoo," and " Hi-oh," it went. Drenched oil-skins steamed, wet faces glowed, and glad eyes shone through the smoke and flare. The pitching vessel, left to herself, plunged up and down to the lift and fall of every sea.

" Hold ! " said the skipper, when the deck amidships was pretty well filled, " that's enough for now, I callelate." Barrels were tossed out of the hold, "keelers " were set up, sharp-edged knives were drawn from ditty-boxes below, and the work of dressing began. Four gangs of four men each took corners in the waist. Each gang had two keelers—yard-square boxes, eight inches or so in depth—set up on two or three barrels. Into these were bailed the mackerel to be dressed, and around these the men gathered, with a long-handled torch set up amidst them.

All hands now came into it, skipper and cook too, and the work began. It was one gang against the other, each jealously counting barrels when they were filled, that full credit might be given for speed. Sixteen men were accounted for thus. The seventeenth and eighteenth were of general utility—to keep keelers filled, draw water for pickle from over the side, roll filled barrels out of the way—to help out generally.

The busiest man there was the skipper. At splitting the mackerel, or at gibbing them afterward—that is, pulling out gills and intestines—he held the pace of any man aboard. At splitting he would have made a rare record, but that he had to keep an eye out for the course of the vessel also. Vessels that are dressing fish, vessels whereon the entire crew is immersed in blood, gills, intestines, and swashing brine, might be allowed privileges, one might think. But it is assumed that they will keep a lookout just the same. On this dark night, the schooner, though making noble efforts, considering that she had jibs down and wheel in the becket, to stay as she was put, yet she would fall away or come-to, particularly when the wind shifted two or three points at a jump. Then would the alert skipper, quickly noticing, dart aft and set her right. Generally, to shift the wheel a few spokes would set her right, but occasionally he would have to give the wheel a good round whirl. Then he would sing out a warning, the torches would be lowered, the men would duck, the boom would go swinging by and the vessel would be off on the other tack. The men would brace their legs to a new angle, the skipper would hop back to his knife, and the work would go humming on again.

At top speed they raced thus through the night. Once in a while a man might drop his knife or snap off his gibbing mitt, rinse his hand in the brine barrel by his side, slap his hand impatiently across the hoops, and condemn the luck of a split finger or a thumb with a bone in it. Another might pull up for a moment, glance up at the stars or down at the white froth under the rail, draw his hand across his forehead, spit ten yards across the wind, mutter, "My soul, but I'm dry," take a full dipper from the water-pail, drink it dry, pass dipper and pail along to the next and go back to his work.

Until the morning they stood to it in that fashion, with the air around them full of the insides of mackerel. Keelers, deck, rail, their own hands, faces, and clothing, were viscid with blood, gills, and intestines. There were 150 barrels of mackerel washing in barrels when the first table gang, at the cook's call of breakfast, stopped long enough to draw full breaths.

"Oh, but the blessed day's coming on," said the skipper before disappearing below. "Smother those torches, we've done with 'em for this night."

Throughout all that day the men worked—dressing, salting, and putting all in pickle. It was a drive all through without withdrawal by any, except when it was time to relieve lookouts at the mast-head. Had the inspiring call of "School-O!" been heard aloft the men on deck would have dropped everything, jumped into the boat and been after that school most cheerfully. But at this particular time mackerel were rarely rising, except at sunset or in the early night.

Not until late in the afternoon, when the last mackerel was flattened out in the last barrel, did a good seiner feel that he could step back in his own time, stand erect and take a good look at his own handiwork. The men surveyed the oozing barrels with great satisfaction, even while they were massaging their heavy wrists with their aching fingers. It was a good bit of work that, well and quickly done, and it was good to get a halt like this, even if it should be for but a little while. Even though they had to do it all over again—to stay half-drowned in the seine-boat for half the night and then dress down for eighteen or twenty hours on top of it—what mattered a little fast work? And think of the hundred-dollar bill, maybe, to be carried home and laid in the wife's lap, or the roaring night ashore if a fellow was not a family man-m-m-!

On this evening, when the skipper descended from the misty deck to the beaming fo'c's'le, he noted, even as he scaled his sou'wester onto the floor and helped himself to his mug of coffee and handful of beef, that the forward gang were in a different mood from what they had been at this hour on the previous evening. There was no whist at the table, no reading out of upper bunks, no love-song from the peak, and no fierce debate on the lockers. The cook, as usual, was finishing up a batch of dough, but that he was not the only man who had been working lately was made plain by the wet oil-clothes hanging up to dry, and the general overhauling of change suits by the men. Every man, to be sure, except the cook, who never smoked while at work, was puffing away as if he doubted he would ever get another chance for a pipeful in this life. Altogether, it was an air of exquisite harmony that was dwelling over the fo'c's'le, and it seemed to be merely in keeping with the heavenly order of things that the atmosphere showed pale blue wherever the rays of the lamp could get a chance to strike through.

To the poetic skipper the beatitude of the scene was bound to appeal. He gazed about him as he leaned characteristically against the foremast. "My soul," said he, "but it's as if the blessed angels was fanning their wings over this forehold. There's Pat and there's George double-banked on the same locker, and not a whisper of the Boer War. There's the lad that sleeps in the peak, and not a single hallelujah of praise for his darlin' Lucille. And Bill and John no longer spoilin' their good eyesight on bad print. I expect it's that deck-load of fish. The work's made you tired, and the prospect's making you look pleased. Well, it ought. Thirteen dollars for them mackerel, or I don't know. As fine fish as ever I bailed over the rail—yes, as fine as ever I bailed in. And some of you readyreckoners c'n easy figure what's comin' to you—even if we don't head up another barrel this trip. They're an awful good thing, them mackerel. Just needed them to ballast her proper. Last thing I said to the owner as I was leaving the dock was—I'd been speaking about the vessel—'She's tender, don't you think?' says I. 'Twenty-five or thirty tons ballast wouldn't do her no harm.' 'No,' says the old man, lookin' over his shoulder and startin' up the dock—you know his way—'mebbe not. But what's the matter with two or three hundred barrels of fine fat mackerel for ballast?' Well, there's the ballast. And she certainly do seem to be in better trim since we put sail on her again. T'night, if it breezes up, and it looks now as if 'twill, we'll see the difference in her. I'll bet she don't go to the rail so easy as she did last night. One time there last night, did you notice it, cook?—that time that crazy lad started to cross our bow, and we gave her a full—why, man, she went over as if a squall hit her. I was near shook overboard. 'My lady,' says I to myself, 'I've been out in more than one breeze that would have laid your spars flat out on the sea, if that much'll put you down that far.' However, she got us to where the mackerel was, and that's what counts. She c'n sail, God bless her—with all her faults, she c'n sail. And I callelate that if there's fish showin' t'night she'll put us there as quick as the next, and that's worth all the rest in a seiner. Of course, we mayn't get a smell of 'em t'night, but then again maybe we will. Anyway, you all want to be ready for it, for it's coming on to another fine black night. And, cook," the skipper shouldered away from the foremast, "would you mind cutting out a wedge or two of one of them blueberry pies you got cooling there? A little wedge, yes—but you don't need to be too close-hauled with your knife, though. Sailing by the wind is all right when we're cruising' round in the fleet, and nothin' partic'lar doin'. But it's safe to give her a full always—always, cook, when you're cuttin' pie. That's the lad—a beam wind. Now lay one atop o' the other. There, that's what they might call a blueberry pie sandwich ashore, I callelate. M—m—, but look at the juice squish through her scuppers!" He held it aloft that all might see. "Now another little wash of coffee in the wake of that, and I'm to the masthead. Be ready for an early call, boys."

He jammed his sou'wester hard down, heroically waved away the remainder of the pie when the cook held it up, with a very determined, "No, no. First thing I know I'll be having dyspepsy. I never had it, but I might;" and heaved himself up the companion-way, humming, as he went, his old favorite:

Oh, the 'Liza Jane and the Maria Louise
Sailed a race one day for a peck of peas.
You'd hardly believe the way them two
Carried sail that day—they fairly flew.

The people ashore they said, "Gee whiz!
The 'Liza Jane the fastest is."

He scrambled, still humming, over the barrels on deck, halted long enough by the rail to pass a cheerful greeting to the forward watch, and then, blithe and buoyant, swung himself up the rigging. A school-boy might have climbed an apple-tree so, but this man, once aloft, had to face hours of strain on brain and nerve.

WINTER TRAWLING

THIS seining, or mackerel catching, as described above, whether by night or day, is the easiest of all the ways by which Gloucester fishermen drag a living from the deep. It is really only pleasure fishing to them. To get a truer idea of what these men have to endure year in and year out let us take the record of a mild little winter trawling trip. This trip was to Georges Bank. A trip to Quero, Le Have, St. Peters, or to any of the big ocean shoals to which fishermen go for quick fares, would have answered the purpose equally well. But Georges, possibly, has had more fame in song:

And eight score souls
On Georges shoals
Went down in that wintry gale.

That may not impress you at first. But if you ever heard a fisherman's wife cradle a baby to sleep with it you would get a notion of what bank fishing in winter means.

This able "haddocker," the Horace B. Parker, of Gloucester, working clear of Eastern Point at noon of one day, was by noon of the next nearly 200 miles away, in thirty fathoms of water on the slopes that lie to the westerly edge of Georges Bank. She had come 135 miles on one tack and then hauled up southerly and westerly for fifty miles or so farther before they threw her into the wind to lay-to while this rising southeaster should be passing by.

The good fishing on Georges is found on the shoals that bound its westerly edge. It is here that so many fishermen are lost. Vessels are caught with these shoals to leeward and they are gone. In places here there are only two fathoms of water. That gives a vessel no show in a gale. There is just enough water to batter her hull to pieces on the sand of the bottom, to smother the men before it batters them, too. Give him room, and let the wind blow and the sea pile up—it is a storm indeed when your Gloucester skipper fails to bring his vessel home. But here he sometimes gets no living chance.

While the Parker was trying to hang on to a favorite fishing spot, the wind was making and hauling and the glass was falling. Thirty fathoms of water was no place to be in during an easterly blow, and she was worked off the bank. By morning she was half way to the Gulf Stream, from where she was driven back, then out, and back again, in the hope that the weather would soon moderate.

It did not moderate that day or the next, and so, the Horace B. was jogged and sailed, jibed and tacked, put head-to and stern-to—handled in every conceivable way to further the main idea. It blew harder, so her mainsail was taken in altogether, her jib triced up, and under foresail and jumbo she was hove-to. For two days and three nights she hung on so. It was not a blow to mind much, except that it delayed fishing, and this was in Lent when the market was good.

The wind blew, the rain fell, and the sea arose and pounded the Horace B. On deck the watch held eternal vigilance in pairs. Watching these seas from deck you, a landsman, might wonder how the vessel lived. The seas come racing on by way of the bow, and run from clear forward to clear aft. Some come broadside on, give her an awful slap flat-handed, and then tumble on, straining the lashings of the dories in the waist and heeling her over till her lee-rail goes well under. The worst of them seem to break over her quarter. These fill the gangway between house and rail, wash the house clear of all loose stuff, and swamp wheel-box and taffrail as they go.

She was a buoyant thing and minded it as little as anybody of her size possibly could, but, even so, she was tossed about as you may have seen a soap-box tossed in the surf of an Atlantic beach when the wind is northeast. Every time she pointed up she buried her bowsprit, and every time she fell away her rails went out of sight. Her sail, you were made to understand, kept her from rolling much, and the swirl of her wake, as she fell off to leeward, caused the worst seas to break before they could strike her fairly. Otherwise it would be uncomfortable aboard of her. Indeed, yes. But now, you see, she rode like a duck. There are some vessels that would drown you here, but not this one! For her tonnage—let the watch tell it—there was no abler vessel sailing out of Gloucester—which was true.

Through all of this imagine the rain sweeping, and the deck and house and rails of the Parker dripping, bright and clean and beautiful, for a vessel never shines as in a storm. Under the lee of Joe Lecost (a protective piece of canvas made fast to the fore rigging) are the two bulky men on watch, their oil-skins bulging with the flannels and sweaters inside. They wear, also, the one leather and the other big rubber boots, large woollen mitts and sou'westers. They watch warily for the big seas. To ordinary combers they simply turn a shoulder. But when they spy a particularly able-looking gentleman—one with a white collar, starched and ironed flat, wide and thick also in breast—these two men on watch hook elbows, hug up to Joe Lecost, grip the rigging and hang on till the gentleman has passed. There they stand their watch out, trying to be sociable with each other, and dodging the seas that come aboard. To the wheel, which is in the becket, they have only to cast an eye now and again.

Safely stowed away in your bunk below while the vessel is hove-to, down in the cabin taking comfort, gives you only a smothered conception of what it is outside. Of course it was nearer the real thing than if you were buried in an inside stateroom on an ocean liner. By snugging up to her planking you could get your shoulder to within three inches of the swirling sea beneath her and early catch the premonitory heave of every sea. In advance, the side of the vessel would sag away from you so that you would be rolled to the locker side of your bunk. She would go up, up, up, and away to leeward. She would poise there a moment waiting, shivering with fear. Then the sea itself would come. You could hear the roaring of it for some little time before it struck. Then over your head on deck would be a rumbling, swashing, a pounding and thumping the whole length and breadth of her. A barrel of it would dart under the hatch and come down the companion-way. The little vessel would resist, struggle, fight to hold back. You could imagine her nerves tightening with its dread and strain, but after it she would be drawn. She was only sixty tons—remember—a little thing. She would be flung, rolled away and away, and then, suddenly, brought up with a jolt. She would quiver to her very keel after that and you could almost imagine her heart thumping against her ribs; then she would gamely pull herself together and brace for the next one.

Into the cabin came, at regular intervals, one of the drenched watch. In yellow oil-skins, rubber boots, black sou'wester and roomy woollen mitts, he would stand on the last step of the companion-way, study the clock, look around, point a finger at somebody or other, hail: "Your watch, Bill," or Mike, or Henry, or whatever it might be. The man indicated would look up reproachfully, check up the time on the clock, take half a dozen last regretful puffs, stifle the fire in the bowl, poke the pipe itself somewhere under the mattress of his bunk, and take down his storm-clothes. Laboriously he would haul on his jack-boots, over them his oil-skins, set firmly his sou'wester, draw on his mitts, take a lingering look at the clock, and then climb slowly up the companion-way. Then the old watch would come down, cast off his sou'wester and mitts, slide out of his dripping oil-skins, force off his boots, and hang all up somewhere to dry. He would then take an easy position on a locker, poke his feet into "slip-shods," dig out his pipe, slowly fill it, tamp it down, light it—puff—puff—puff—stretch his feet luxuriously toward the stove—puff—puff—and then ease himself of the weight that had been on his mind throughout his whole watch. "For the amount of wind that's going, there's a jeesly big sea on, let me tell you."—Puff—puff—"I wouldn't want to be on any old coaster that's got to beat to wind'ard to-day." —Puff—puff—a glance at the clock—"Twelve hours to another watch, thank the Lord." Puff—puff—puff.

In the fore'c's'le they would be playing seven-up, forty-five, whist, or a mild little game of "draw," until the cook, making ready for dinner, would drive them all out. Aft they would come then, dodging seas and whooping as they came, tumbling down the cabin gangway and piling in on the lockers.

Before this onslaught most of the cabin bunkers would take to their bunks, and, maybe, "When the For'ard Gang Comes Aft" would be softly hummed by way of greeting from the depths of a port berth, or caustic comment would be uttered to nobody in particular.

"Every morning—one—two—three—four—five." (This seems to issue from the shades that lie under the overhang) "every morning I goes for'ard and fills a coal-hod—give them for'ard loafers a look at the size of it, John—and brings it aft, and that ain't any saloon deck promenard this weather, and I loads the stove up to the hatches, and Lonergan he wiggles the ashes out of her hold, and Henry he sweeps up the floor nice and heaves all over the rail, and the cabin is looking fit for gentlemen, when down pitches the whole forehold, druv out by cookie, and soaks the heat all up and scoops all the locker room there is, and forgets—Lord bless us, would you believe it?—forgets to haul the hatch to behind 'em—yes. And down comes a cask or two of water, and bimeby the skipper begins to wonder why the cabin ain't dry and clean."

"There's an owner in Gloucester," says one of the invaders, ignoring entirely the premises, "and he says to me last trip in, 'Paddie, me boy, what partic'lar model of a vessel will we build for you this spring comin'? And will it please you to go seinin' or shackin' durin' the fine warm summer?' And I says, 'I'll think it over.' And I've been thinking it over, and I've a fancy of a Rob Roy bow, and a Preceptor beam, and one of those Mone-ark sterns, an' a Harry Belden style of standing up to a breeze when reaching, and a Mary Whalen way of goin' to wind'ard in a gale. But the main thing is going to be the revolution of authority from aft forard. Yes, sir, I'm going to put the cabin in the fo'c's'le. I'll be the first skipper out of Gloucester that ever bunked in the forehold for choice——"

"With electric bells from the wheel to your stateroom, I s'pose?"

"With Bruss'ls carpet and Ottermans—" goes on Paddie.

"What?"

"Ottermans — for the lockers — and brass spittoons, an' the very first cabin loafer—the very first—that comes for'ard, except to eat, I'll hand the cook the hatchet and say, 'Cut his toes off, cookie!' Yes, sir, just as soon as he sticks his feet down the gangway, it'll be, 'Cookie, cut the lobster's toes off,' and I'll bet he'll hop back on deck some lively."

"You didn't say whether you was goin' seinin' or shackin'."

"Or Mediterranean yachtin', Paddie, darlin'. If it's yachtin', maybe I'd like to speak fer a chance with——"

"Dinner!" roars the watch down the gangway, and first table gang dash for the steps, with the man of new ideas first up.

In the cabin, at about nine o'clock, on the night of the fifth day of this battering, the skipper, who had been studying the glass and the sky alternately for hours, suddenly said, "I guess we'll bait up, boys. It looks half-way good for the morning. Two tubs will do for a start." The word was passed above, and the watch on deck could be heard calling out to the fo'c's'le gang, "Below there—bait up!" In five minutes the crew were cutting frozen herring and baiting trawls down in the freezing hold.

It seemed to be yet in the middle of the night when the crew turned out for breakfast. It was certainly some time to daybreak when the men were standing by ready to drop the dories over. Into each dory as it was dropped over the side dove two men. The sea at this time was what any landsman would view with vast respect. No shore-going man, bundled up as these men were, would have made that dive over the rail for the owner's share of the trip. Were one of them to fall overboard he would go down like a lump of ballast. The dories were tossed a dozen feet away from the vessel's side when the painters were slacked and to the height of a man's head above the rail. When they settled into the hollows they fell to somewhere down near her keelson. They were then dropped astern, where swirling, jumping, sagging under the vessel's overhang and away again, they were towed by a short painter in the boiling wake of the schooner, and she tearing along by the wind under four lower sails.

The first dory was cast loose, and the man in the bow, after coiling the painter tightly over her stem, seized the oars and began to row, heaving his body well into every stroke. The man aft, at the same time threw over the buoy line. The ground line, with gangings and hooks attached, was whirled dexterously from its coils in the tub by the aid of a stick, and sent after the buoy line. One dory followed another with a quarter mile between. Some of these old trawlers kept the air full of line and hooks until their tubs were empty.

All strong, tough men were these—only such can stand trawling. Conceive a man hauling a mile and a half of trawls off the bottom on a cold winter's day! Sometimes the trawl catches on the rough bottom—gets "hung up"—and the men have to discard mitts, and grip with only a pair of "nippers," bracelets of cloth held in the palm of the hand, creased to allow of a better hold of the line. And imagine the little dory pitching to the top of every wave, and then dropping down into the hollow until, watching from the vessel's deck, you wonder if it is ever coming up again!

It is not really rough weather this day, and it is only now and then that one man has to stop and bail the dory. Sometimes so much water comes inboard that both have to bail. It might be much worse. Suppose it is really cold weather, when the spray freezes almost as fast as it comes aboard. The spray flies over the men, too, until hair and beard is iced up except where their steaming breath keeps it melted, though that is a small matter. It may be that they have to keep pounding ice to keep her gunnels out of water. Their hands and fingers begin to freeze up until there is danger that they will drop off—sometimes they do drop off—but they must go on hauling trawls. Nothing of that happened this trip. In early March the weather is not cold enough for that. But that has happened, and it will happen again. Just so long as men trawl on the banks will that happen.

When our skipper thought the trawls had been allowed to set long enough he hoisted the hauling signal to the main peak. In the nearest dory the men can be seen starting to action. Over a "gurdy" in the bow one man hauls the stubborn line. He is a hardened expert, this one, and hauls it in barehanded, stopping only now and then to slap heat into his fingers. When there appears a hook with a fish on it, he grasps the "ganging" low down, gives a forward and then an easy backward swing, which combines with a professional flirt of the wrist to free the hook and land the fish in the bottom of the dory. If it is a large fellow—a big steak cod, say—then the trawler holds him half clear of the water with one hand, while he gaffs him with the other. His dory mate, during all this, is in the waist, taking the trawl, as it comes in over the bow, re-baiting and coiling it back in the tub to be ready for the next set.

All this time the skipper is standing in and out among the dories. He has a wary eye out for signs of squalls, particularly for snow-squalls and fogs, which are the dread of trawlers, and which account for most of the trawlers lost in dories. The skipper keeps an eye out to see how the fish are coming, and when the men are ready to come aboard he shoots the vessel from one to the other when he can, to save them all the rowing possible. But wind and tide scatter them widely, and some have a long, hard row with the gunnels of their loaded dories almost flush with the sea.

Coming alongside, the men fork the fish over the rail into the compartments on her deck. It is a hard matter for them to hold their feet while pitching fish in this sea. After the first set the men stay aboard just about long enough to get a fresh pipeful—most fishermen smoke nearly all the time except when they are asleep or on watch. After their second set they stop just long enough to eat a quick dinner. They are driving things now during this good fishing. Two more sets and trawling is done for the day. After the last set three of the dories had to be picked up by torchlight.

The very last dory to be picked up caused some anxiety. It was quite dark, and the men went into the rigging to hail for her. It was a long time before the flare of her torch could be made out. It was a man to the mast-head who finally saw the little light rising and falling in the sea.

Before any further work is attempted comes the blessed supper. The men wash-up on deck, and joyfully drop into the forec's'le, where they discard oil-jackets, heave their sou'westers into the nearest bunks, and sit down to a performance that is worth a trip to see. This has been a fine day's work. Twenty-five thousand of haddock and 10,000 of cod, fine fish all, is up in the pens. The way the grub goes! The cook is up on his toes from start to finish. They steam up as they eat. Their faces begin to take on a warm glow and their tongues loosen up. All day long they have had but little to say, but now they joke and roar as they pile in the food. One dory had a string of gear caught in the tide and had to cut it away. Another dory was "hung up" for so long in the morning that the two men in her had to rush all the rest of the day to catch up. "Look at the pair of them," is the way in which attention was called their way, "they're breathing yet."

From the table the men go to dress down the fish, taking along, of course, the beloved pipe, fresh-filled. Half a dozen torches with big wicks are set around the deck and the men divide into a gang to leeward and a gang to windward. Two men of each gang rip the fish up the stomach, and three "gut," that is remove the intestines. Two men rinse them in a tub of salt water and two pitch them below. The two gangs race to see which shall get its side cleaned up first. It is drive, drive, drive. Down in the hold two men chop ice and two others pack the fish in pens and the vapor comes from off them while they work.

Four hours of this slashing work and the fish were in the hold. The decks were running fish-blood and gurry, and the oil-skins of the men dripped gore under the light of the smoking torches. Gurry, blood and salt water dripped from neck to boot heel, and streams of sweat ran down their smoked faces. There was an uproarious washing down of decks and selves. They swished buckets of water over one another almost as freely as they heaved them into the scuppers. With horse-play and some really funny talk they crowded down the forec's'le gangway. A "mug-up," and then ten minutes, possibly twenty for those who took their last pipe sedately, and the crew of the Parker had turned in. Five minutes more and it was a very quiet vessel. In the forec's'le not a sound; in the cabin only the skipper rustling a chart. On deck the watch trod softly and, when they came together, spoke in whispers.

By daybreak the next morning they were out and doing it all over again. It is bait up, into dories, drop astern, heave over trawls, let them set, haul in, come alongside and pitch fish over the rail. Four times of that in the day, with the last dory coming aboard in the dark again by the light of the torches, with the anxious watchers in the rigging. And then the drive of dressing down, with the glorious finish to it all—the "mug-up," the blissful pipe, and heavenly sleep. Two days more of it and the Parker had her load. They held her up, 'no'the no'the east' for forty-five miles by the log. Then it was—this from the skipper—"Swing her off, boom her out, west by no'the and drive her." The Horace B. Parker of Gloucester, with 70,000 pounds of haddock and twenty-odd thousand of cod was running for the Boston market. Her able crew, feeling pretty fine, overhauled trawls and other gear, or sat around and wove the dream carpets whereon to disport themselves when they should get ashore. It was down in the cabin that they gave free play to their fancies.

"Two dollars for them haddock and $3 for them market cod, and there'll be about a $70 share comin' round. This is the trip, people, when I telegraphs for the wife and we go to the theatre." He was a big lusty man, an able trawler, with hair that seemed to wave as the brain beneath it worked, and eyes that said more than his tongue.

"What show, John?"

"'Ben-Hur.' Yes, sir. They say there's a chariot race in that to fairly make your hair curl. Bill—Bill for'ard—tells me that he felt like gettin' up and hollerin'. Yes, sir, I want to see that chariot race."

He weighed about 200 pounds, this man, and the blood was ready to burst his skin. He could probably have picked up Ben-Hur and the chariot together and hove them into the wings. He was warming his toes and blowing puffs of smoke toward the skylight in extreme contentment at the prospect. He had put in twenty years at trawling. He had lived through winters on Georges. His experience in his last big blow, "The Portland breeze," when the Portland steamer went down with all on board, one hundred and fifty-odd souls, had been described by him in four sentences: "Let me tell you, people, but there was some wind and snow in the bay that night. We lay-to, misdoubting the Maggie would ride it out. The wind jumped to the no'west—oh, man, but it screeched—and we took it all night long. Next day we bucked her home—a good vessel, the old Maggie." This man regarded a chariot race on the stage as an exciting experience to look forward to.

The Parker got in. The dreams of the men were not realized. They did not get $2 for haddock, nor $3 for cod. Forty other vessels had also found good fishing after the gale, and had come home with full holds, and so the market was down. The men shared $35 apiece. John did not send for his wife, nor did he see "Ben-Hur." He contented himself with a glass of ale up on Atlantic Avenue. He treated a ship-mate and a dock loafer, and he took a small glass of ale on the return treat. "But next trip, maybe—Lent 'll be still here—the wife and me'll go to see 'Ben-Hur,'" he said.

Of abiding faith is the able fisherman—and of courage everlasting.

Collecting Salmon Spawn in Maine (1874)

COLLECTING SALMON SPAWN IN MAINE

FISH-WEIR AT BUCKSPORT NARROWS.

NOT far beyond the memory of men now living salmon abounded in nearly every New England river north of the Connecticut, which appears to have been their southern limit, and in all the tributaries of the St. Lawrence below Niagara, with rare exceptions. Under provident management the salmon fishery of these rivers might have continued for an indefinite number of years to yield a large supply of nutritious food for the sustenance of our teeming population; but the greed of the few and the indifference of the many have resulted in the extermination of this noble fish in nearly all those waters. Of the tributaries of the St. Lawrence within the limits of the United States, Salmon River, in New York, is the only one now annually frequented by salmon, and on the Atlantic coast they are constant visitors only in the Kennebec, Penobscot, Muscongus, East Machias, Dennys, and St. Croix. Of these, the Penobscot furnishes more than all the others, and its ordinary annual yield may be put at from five to ten thousand salmon. This does not exceed the twentieth part of its capacity, if the latter may be measured by the product of some Irish salmon rivers, and certainly bears a small proportion to the former actual yield of the Penobscot itself.

When the work of restoring the migratory fishes to their barren rivers was first undertaken by the New England States, the salmon naturally received a large share of attention, and from that time till the present persistent efforts have been made to re-establish him in his old haunts. It is a well-known habit of migratory fishes, such as the shad and salmon, to return, when full-grown, from the sea to the rivers where they were reared, and there deposit their spawn. In order, therefore, to restock an exhausted salmon river, it is only necessary to place in its upper waters very young salmon, in sufficient numbers to insure the growth of a considerable number to full size, after allowing for all losses by the ordinary perils incident to fish life. The only practicable way of securing an ample supply of the young fish is to obtain the eggs and hatch them.

The importance of restoring salmon rivers to the fullest possible yield will be better understood by our citizens when they learn the almost incredible growth of the fish. This is asserted by some close observers to be nearly a pound a month. The experiments thus far made in this country are not sufficiently complete to give perfect information on this point, but they do not vary greatly from facts which have been gathered by persons in Scotland and elsewhere, who seem to agree that spawn deposited in November is hatched in the following March; in May the "smolts" have attained two or three inches in length, and take their course toward salt-water, from which they return in the fall greatly increased in size. Shaw, in his *Zoology*, mentions that a salmon of seven and three-quarter pounds was marked with scissors on the back fin and tail, and turned out on the 7th of February, and being retaken in March of the following year, was found to have increased to a weight of seventeen and a half pounds. Mr. Michael Carroll, of Newfoundland, gives instances nearly as remarkable.

The first attempts at collecting the spawn were made in New Brunswick, whose rivers still abound with salmon. New Hampshire had the honor of sending out the pioneer expedition, under charge of Dr. W. W. Fletcher, who succeeded in bringing back a lot of healthy eggs. The same gentleman made a second expedition, and subsequently Mr. Livingston Stone, under the patronage of several States, erected a large hatching house on the Miramichi River, and prepared to collect eggs on a large scale. But, for reasons that it is unnecessary to discuss here, it was found impracticable to carry on these operations, and they had to be abandoned. The only remaining way of obtaining salmon eggs was to buy them at the Canadian governmental establishment in Ontario, where they were sold at forty dollars in gold per thousand, a price which would have placed the purchase of an adequate supply entirely beyond the means at the command of the State Commissioners, even had the establishment been on a sufficiently large scale to furnish them, which was not the case. Thus, before any thing adequate to the situation had been done, the cultivation of salmon was brought to a stand-still. At this juncture an enterprise was inaugurated on the Penobscot River, the success of which has put a new aspect on the matter.

The Penobscot, being the most productive salmon river at the present day on the Atlantic coast of the United States, offered better facilities than any other for the collection of spawn. It was proposed to buy a number of living salmon in the month of June, when they are ascending the river and are caught in weirs near Bucksport, and confine them in a small pond or inclosure, in fresh-water, until the maturity of their eggs, which occurs about the 1st of November. This scheme appeared to possess important advantages over the plan of capturing the fish on the upper waters of the river, at or near the spawning season, as had been commonly done in previous operations, and the Commissioners of Maine, Massachusetts, and Connecticut united in its execution. The first experiment was tried in Orland; and though the conditions under which the salmon were confined were so singularly unfortunate as to cause the loss of more than eighty per cent. of the salmon bought, yet seventy thousand eggs were obtained at a cost less than half the price asked in Canada. The result was so encouraging that in the following year the same parties, joined by the United States Commissioner of Fish and Fisheries and the Commissioners of Rhode Island, founded the establishment at Bucksport which is the subject of the present sketch.

The majority of travelers obtain their first view of Bucksport from the deck of one of the Portland or Boston steamers, and there is not another village of its size on the Penobscot River that makes a show so imposing. Four or five miles below the town the voyager leaves the broad Penobscot Bay, on which he has been sailing for five or six hours, and enters the river. If of an observant turn, particularly if it be near low water, he discerns along the shore numerous fish weirs, built of stakes, brush, and netting, running from high-water mark straight out into deep water. The part near shore always consists of a straight hedge, called the "leader," which, as its name indicates, serves to *lead* the fish into a large inclosure or "pound" at its outer end. This inclosure opens into a smaller one, and this into a third, all these being so ingeniously constructed that the fish readily pass forward into the last pound, but rarely find their way out into freedom. In the third pound the captured fish are left by the retreating tide on a floor, from which they are gathered by the fisherman at low water. Salmon are the principal fish caught in the weirs on the Penobscot; but many other kinds, such as shad, alewives, herring, menhaden, etc., are caught with them.

The average yield of the fifty-pound nets in the immediate vicinity of Bucksport is not less than four thousand salmon per annum. Quite two-thirds of this number could be secured by purchase for the hatching works, if such a vast number could be handled. At present the catch of salmon from a few nets is quite sufficient to furnish all the eggs which can be conveniently handled. Fortunately, too, the salmon delivered at the hatching house, and the average catch of the nets, will not vary much from three females to the single male, and with this run the eggs may be perfectly impregnated.

Almost any day during the latter part of June there may be seen a number of novel-shaped boats, covered with old duck or some coarse cloth, sunk deep in the water, and in tow of other boats propelled by oars, or by the wind if it be fair, gliding on the flood-tide through the narrows toward Bucksport. The covered boats in tow contain living salmon, which were carefully dipped out of the weirs just before the last ebb-tide left them high and dry. There are large holes opened in each side, near the bow and stern, below the water-line when the boat is loaded, so that when in motion the water passes freely in at one end and out at the other; iron gratings prevent the escape of the fish. The boat is of the size of a common fisherman's dory, and carries from a dozen to twenty, and sometimes as many as thirty, salmon at a single load. At a landing between two of the wharves stands a dray, backed down into the edge of the water, and on it is a large wooden box partly filled with water. As soon as a salmon boat arrives it is drawn up to the dray, and its living freight is transferred by heavy duck bags to the box. From five to seven only are put into one box, and three or four drays are hardly enough to haul away the salmon as fast as they can be dipped out. On a good fish day several hours are occupied in unloading the boats. As soon as the proper number of salmon are in a box it is filled with water, its cover is shut, and away it goes through the village streets to a fresh-water pond that lies about a mile distant over the hills.

This pond has an area of sixty acres, is fifteen feet deep in the spring, and ten feet in midsummer. It receives the drainage of an extensive tract of marsh and bog land, which has colored its water dark brown, and has covered its bottom with a deep deposit of soft mud, in which the roots of water-lilies and various other aquatic plants find generous nourishment, but which is not the kind of bottom most persons would select for a salmon pond. But since this enterprise was started salmon have been confined experimentally in several places under varying conditions of water and bottom, but nowhere have they survived the season's confinement in any better condition than here.

The muddy bottom is found in the fall to be of positive advantage. Salmon will not lay their eggs on it, and in seeking for gravel and for running water, which they much prefer, they come in large numbers into the brook by which the pond discharges its water into the Penobscot, and here they can be easily caught and deprived of their spawn.

During June and July the salmon in the pond are constantly jumping, and their agility is remarkable. On two occasions they have been seen to jump clear over a hedge five and a half feet high above the water. It is not supposed they did this with the design of passing the hedge, but accidentally, it being quite common to see them jump to an equal height in the middle of their inclosure, as though the leap were entirely aimless. During the early days of their confinement they are frequently seen swimming in great schools about the shores of the pond. As the summer advances they become more quiet, retreating to the deep water—not very deep, however, for in the drought of August and September the greatest depth in the pond is twelve feet, and in the inclosure where the salmon were kept the past season only nine feet. In such a shallow pond, with such dark water and bottom, the sun's

UNLOADING THE SALMON BOAT.

TURNING SALMON INTO THE POND.

rays exert a powerful influence in midsummer. At one time the temperature of the water at the bottom reached 72° F. Yet this excessive heat has no perceptible effect on the health of the salmon.

During all this time the salmon eat nothing. In fact, there is little room for doubt that their stay in the rivers is one long fast, lasting from six to twelve months. They do seize the sportsman's fly, but it is probably not for the purpose of food, but rather akin to the action of a turkey or a bull rushing after a red rag. It is a common opinion among sportsmen that salmon will not rise to a fly in still water, but this has been plainly disproved at Bucksport. On several occasions in May, September, and October the trial was made for the purpose of testing the matter, and the salmon in the pond were found to take the fly with as much eagerness as in the favorite pools of the Canadian salmon rivers. These were, so far as known, the first instances of salmon being caught with the fly in the Penobscot River, not because their habits are unlike those of their brethren in other rivers, but probably because they have not been fished for enough in the right places.

The salmon are not allowed to range over the whole pond, which has an area of sixty acres, but are confined in a cove containing about ten acres by a strong net, whose top is attached to stakes and whose bottom is held down by a heavy chain. Out of this cove runs the brook where the hatching house and spawning shed and other fixtures are situated. When October comes, and the salmon exhibit the uneasy, roving disposition that presages the spawning season, a new and smaller inclosure is made near the outlet, with a passage into it from the large inclosure, so contrived that the salmon readily pass through from the larger into the smaller, but can not find their way back. Thus, by the last week in October, a considerable part of the salmon are already collected within a space of about an acre, in close proximity to the brook. A dam and gate regulate the flow of water, and the fall rains have now raised the pond to such a level that when the gate is open a plentiful supply of water rushes out. Until this time a grating has been kept in front of the gate to prevent the salmon from entering the brook prematurely, but this is now removed, and the fish allowed to pass through the gate at their pleasure.

Having once passed the gate, the salmon fall over a drop which effectually prevents their returning to the pond, and are then in a long narrow sluice, which leads them some two hundred feet down the stream into a small pen, from which they are dipped when wanted. Here the whole breadth of the stream is occupied by similar pens, used for assorting and keeping the salmon during the spawning season; and close at hand is a rude shed built to shelter the operators while at work. It is during the last week in October that the first salmon enter the

GENERAL VIEW OF THE POND, SPAWNING SHED, AND SLUICE.

FEMALE SALMON AFTER SPAWNING.

THE MALE SALMON IN NOVEMBER.

brook. After the 1st of November the occurrence there of an immature fish is very rare. By this fortunate circumstance the labor attending the taking of spawn is much simplified; for each female salmon can be relieved of her spawn as soon as she comes in hand, thus avoiding the repeated handling that would be necessary were part of the fish coming down the sluice to be immature. Both sexes come together. They are now as easily distinguished as are the cock and hen of the common fowl. The male has very bright colors, has long jaws, the lower one furnished with a hook that shuts into a cavity in the roof of the mouth—characteristics that he has assumed since June, when there was very little difference between the sexes. By the middle of November the spawning season is nearly at an end. Probably all the salmon are mature by that time; but under some circumstances the eggs are retained by the female for several weeks after they are ready to be laid, and they have been taken here as late as December.

The taking of spawn commonly proceeds from day to day as fast as the fish come down the sluice. When they are plenty the spawning shed is a busy place. As many as six hundred thousand eggs have been taken in a single day. A female salmon of the smallest size weighs at this season eight pounds, and yields about six thousand eggs. The largest thus far handled weighed twenty-two pounds, and yielded sixteen thousand eggs, which measured nearly four quarts, and subtracted six pounds from the weight of the fish.

From four to six men form a convenient working party. The fish are dipped out of the pens one by one, and brought to the principal operator, who sits on a stool with a shallow tin pan before him. First a female salmon is taken in hand, and her eggs pressed out into the pan without any water other than that contained in the viscid fluid that comes with them from the fish. In clear water the eggs would soon lose the capacity of fecundation, but in their natural fluid they retain it for a long time. As soon as the fish has yielded all her eggs she is slipped into a bag and weighed, placed on a bench and measured, marked by attaching a small stamped metal tag to the back fin, and placed in one of the pens, where she soon recovers from her exhaustion, and whence in due course of time she is turned out into the brook or carted down to the river. The eggs are also weighed, and then replaced before the operator, who now takes a male salmon and presses his milt into the same pan. This is the most important part of the whole process, for without the fecundating influence of the milt the eggs would never develop into fish. It was formerly the practice to let eggs and milt fall from the fish into a dish of water; but the milt, when in water, loses the power of acting upon the eggs even quicker than the eggs lose the capacity of being acted upon, and it thus often happened that the intimate contact essential was not effected soon enough to insure fecundation. From this cause a large percentage of eggs commonly failed. A Russian gentleman made the discovery that if water were kept away from the eggs until fresh milt had come in contact with them, nearly all were fecundated. This is the method pursued at Bucksport, and with such success that, on the average, not more than two or three per cent. of the eggs fail to be fecundated. The rate of fecundation is obtained by very careful observation. At a certain stage of the development of a fecund egg the germ begins to expand laterally, sending out a thin fold, which at last completely incloses the yolk. At any time during the growth of this fold the position of its advancing margin can be traced by a line of colored oil globules, arranged in a circle on the surface of the yolk. This circle is at first quite small, and surrounds the colored disk so plainly visible on the upper side of the yolk. It enlarges day by day, until it divides the surface of the yolk into two equal parts. As it progresses beyond this point it becomes smaller, and finally it closes entirely. This process begins, in water of the temperature of 43° F., at about the thirtieth day, and is completed in seven or eight days. As it never takes place in an unfecund egg, its occurrence is positive proof of fecundation. To observe it a strong light should be thrown up through the egg, and the most convenient way of effecting this is to place the egg over a hole in a piece of sheet metal, and hold it up to a window. To obtain the ratio of fecundation a definite number of eggs is examined from each lot, and the result made the basis of a strict calculation. After they have been treated with milt the pan is partly filled with water, and placed on a shelf in the spawning shed, where it is allowed to stand half an hour or longer, before it is carried to the hatching house.

As may be supposed, the salmon do not willingly submit to manipulation. They are very strong, particularly the males, and occasionally offer the most violent resistance, struggling and squirming until the patience and strength of the operators are overtaxed, and their clothes well smeared with odorous slime. But if the weather be mild, and the fish come into the brook as fast as they are wanted, the work proceeds not only rapidly, but even merrily. Hard times come with cold weather, especially if at the same time the salmon are backward about running. Then every thing about the spawning shed is covered with ice, clothes are stiff with it, the wet fingers freeze to the utensils, and it is only with great care that the eggs themselves are kept from freezing. The pond is covered with ice. This must be broken up and got out of the way, or the seine must be drawn under it; at any rate, the seine must be drawn, and the salmon driven into the brook or swept ashore.

At last the out-door work is done, the salmon sent away, and all the eggs safely deposited in the hatching house. This is the principal building of the establishment, and is a few rods down stream from the spawning shed. Here is a large room, seventy feet by twenty-eight, whose floor is closely covered with wooden troughs. The distributing trough traverses the whole length of the building, standing close against the wall on one side. Into it are brought spring water and filtered and unfiltered brook water, the last in much greater volume than the others. Forty hatching troughs, each one foot wide, run across the room, having their

TAKING THE SPAWN.

THE HATCHING HOUSE.

heads against the distributing trough, from which they receive a constant supply of water, amounting in the aggregate to about ten thousand gallons per hour. The eggs lie in these troughs on trays made of wire-cloth smeared with a water-proof varnish, and tacked to a light wooden frame. A tray one foot wide and two feet long holds 4000 eggs. There are in most of these troughs two or three tiers of trays, one on top of another, so arranged that the water circulates freely among them. The eggs are as large as pease, or, to be more exact, an egg of average size measures a little less than a quarter of an inch in diameter. They are semi-transparent, and of a color varying from pink to salmon-color, or sometimes a deep orange-red. Very pretty objects they are.

From the time the eggs are deposited in the water a constant development goes on. On coming from the fish the outer shell is relaxed, and feels soft to the touch. After being impregnated and in the water a short time the eggs expand by absorbing water, until the shell is distended and feels very firm. After this there is no further change in size, but the embryo is steadily developing within. In spring water the eyes would become visible through the shell in about a month. But the water used here is so cold that the same stage of growth is not reached under two or three months, and the young fish hatched here, for the most part, leave the shell in April and May, about six months after the eggs are laid.

The water used for hatching is very cold, though not quite as cold as that used by Mr. Leonard at the Sebec Salmon-breeding Works, where the temperature has been above 33° but three days since November 15. At the Bucksport hatching house the temperature of the water ranges from 32½° to 34° F. through most of the winter. When the earliest eggs are first deposited it is about 44° F., and before the last of those kept here hatch out, early in May, it rises again to the same point. The lowest temperature of the whole season is experienced in April, when the snow and ice are melting.

Development goes on very slowly, and the eggs are not generally in the proper state for transportation, according to the common standard—the coloring of the eyes—until February, at which time they are divided among the several patrons of the enterprise. Of those falling to the share of Maine in 1873 a portion were kept and hatched at Bucksport. The most forward of them began to hatch in March, but only a few individuals came out then, the fall of temperature that accompanied the opening of spring appearing to almost suspend growth. The hatching proceeded very slowly until the last week in April, when the ice was all thawed in the pond above, and the temperature began to rise. I do not know that there is any disadvantage connected with this low temperature. On the contrary, I think it quite likely that the delay of hatching until April and May is rather advantageous to young fish that are to be turned out to seek their own food. Fish hatched out in January, and grown to the feeding stage in February or early in March, must either be turned out into streams that are so cold as to arrest their growth and keep them a long time small and weak, besides being perhaps lacking in natural food, or they must be fed artificially. If the latter course be adopted, I fear the fish will be unfitted, to a certain extent, to take care of themselves. The natural date of hatching in these waters must correspond closely with that of those hatched artificially. Only a small part of the eggs are hatched here, however, all of those belonging to other States, and part of those belonging to Maine, being sent away during the winter and hatched elsewhere.

The present patrons of the enterprise are the Commissioners of Fisheries of all the New England States and of Michigan, and the United States Commissioner of Fish and Fisheries. The latter, besides distributing large numbers of eggs among the rivers known to have been the natural homes of salmon, is trying the experiment of introducing them into the rivers of the Middle States, and into the tributaries of the great lakes. The eggs collected in 1872 were distributed as far south as Pennsylvania, and as far west as Wisconsin. In the month of February they are in a proper state for shipment, having attained that stage of development at which they can be handled without harm. For transportation they are packed up in wet bog-moss in boxes that are protected from the effects of extreme cold by an envelope of sawdust or some other non-conductor of heat, and in this way can be kept packed up for weeks, and sent hundreds of miles.

Though the aim of this establishment is the collection of salmon eggs on as large a scale as the funds at command will admit, the opportunities presented for the study of the natural history of the species are not neglected, it being wisely held that no sort of knowledge on the subject can come amiss, and that some of the new facts learned may prove of immense importance in the future prosecution of the art of fish-culture. At the present time the natural history of the salmon is involved in much obscurity, and it is hoped that the observations made here will contribute something toward clearing it up. It is with this view that pains are taken, after spawning, to mark each fish before it is set at liberty in such a way that if it be ever caught again it can be identified. The mode of marking now employed is the attachment of a small aluminum tag by means of fine platinum wire to the rear margin of the first dorsal fin. Each tag is stamped with a number, which is recorded, together with the sex, length, and weight of the fish, the date when liberated, and other facts. When, therefore, one of these fish is caught again, a reference to the record will show the length of time intervening between the liberation and recapture of the fish, its rate of growth meanwhile, and various other facts. A reward is offered to all fishermen in Penobscot bay and river and adjacent waters for the delivery of any tagged salmon; and even if none should ever be caught, that fact will afford negative evidence of some value.

During the last session of the American Fish-culturists' Association, held in New York, February 10, Mr. Samuel Wilmot, of the Dominion government hatching house, situated at Newcastle, Ontario, stated that he had at different times marked salmon in various ways, principally by clipping their fins, and some of these marked fish had returned considerably increased in weight to their early play-ground. To which Mr. Seth Green responded, heartily, "That's so; I saw some of those marked ones, and it reminds me how I stood some long hours of watching, for several days, from among the branches of a tree into which I had climbed to get out of sight of two salmon—that was away back in 1835—that were working their spawn in the natural way. They would come to the trench which they had prepared, and, rubbing side by side, deposit their spawn. When they had finished, they covered it up and went off—so did I. That was in Wilmot's Creek." Mr. Green subsequently stated that the percentage of fish hatched in the natural way was almost insignificant as compared with that of those hatched by artificial means.

That the mature salmon returns to the waters in which it is hatched is attested by many competent observers, and it is also known that it returns, season after season, to its early spawning ground. M. De Lande fastened a copper ring round a salmon's tail, and found that for three successive seasons it returned to the same place. In some of

INTERIOR OF THE HATCHING HOUSE.

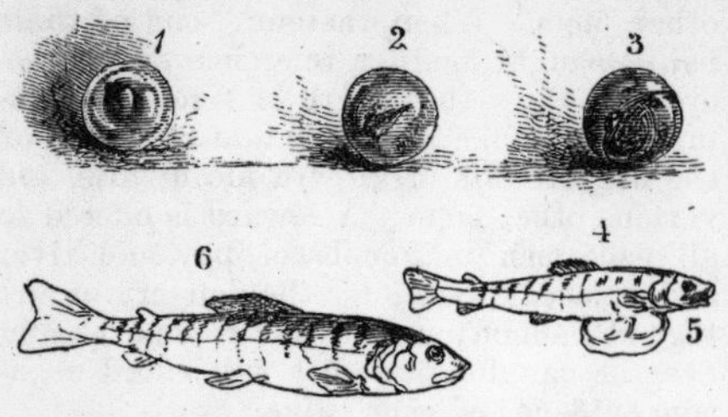

1. An unfecund Egg.—2. 103 Days; Water 34°.—3. 117 Days; Water 34°.—4. Parr at two Weeks.—5. Sac.—6. Five or six Weeks.

OVA AND PARR.

the rivers of the British Islands the salmon are marked annually, and some specimens have become so familiar that they are known by name.

The number of eggs collected at Bucksport during the first season was a million and a half. The second season was still more prosperous, and two millions and a quarter of eggs were obtained, at a cost of about $3 50 per thousand, a very gratifying reduction from the old price. When it is mentioned that a considerable expenditure for permanent fixtures enters into the cost of these eggs, it appears by no means improbable that in future spawn will be collected at a still lower cost. As it is already, with proper facilities for hatching, and with good success therein, living salmon can be put into the rivers at the rate of two for a cent. Were all the young to grow, the two salmon would be worth say five dollars in four years. But as the majority of them will perish before reaching full size, let it be stated in another way. To put two thousand young salmon into a river costs ten dollars. If one out of a hundred survives, there will in four years be twenty adult salmon, worth fifty dollars, which may be regarded as the return from the investment of ten dollars. Truly the fish-culturist has a wide margin.

Although the establishment is now conducted on such a scale that it quite eclipses all other collections of spawn of sea-going salmon in America, except those of Mr. Stone in California, the superintendent of the works does not think it wise to rest contented with its present development status, but to enlarge until the eggs annually collected shall be counted by tens of millions. Then when the commissioners wish to restock a river with salmon, they can put in a million young at once, and a proper stream thus stocked, and reasonably protected by laws which are generally enforced, will quickly develop an abundant food supply. It is not expected—having in view the increased population—that salmon will ever swarm so thickly in our rivers as to require the insertion of the old clause which may be found in some of the apprentice papers of colonial date, "and y[e] lad may not be feed y[e] salmon fishe but twice the week."

Simple laws well enforced will, it is believed, afford quite sufficient protection to any suitable stream that may be each season supplied with any considerable number of parr (newly hatched salmon). Such water should be entirely free from nets from Saturday sundown until daybreak on the following Monday. This will permit the fish to ascend the river to chosen spawning grounds near the source of the stream.

The early Scotch laws have the Sabbath close time written, "Satterdaye's sloppe," and in those days the fish laws were not fractured without personal peril or great cost. Alexander I. enacted this weekly freedom from nets forever. "The streame of the water sal be in all parts swa free that ane swine of the age of three years, well feed, may turn himself within the streame round about, swa that his snowte nor taile sal not tuch the bank of the water." James IV. made things still more uncomfortable for the breaker of fish laws, for he enacted that a third offense should receive capital punishment.

It is believed by many persons wise in piscatorial lore that the Hudson River, the Delaware, Susquehanna, Potomac, and possibly the James rivers, may be successfully stocked with salmon—not those from the Bucksport hatching house probably. Experiments now going rapidly forward with spawn from the Pacific coast are expected to confirm this theory, and eventually furnish our tables with fresh salmon which shall not be for the rich alone.

That the Hudson River ever abounded with salmon seems improbable, and the fact that any considerable number was ever taken therefrom is more than questioned by our best-informed scientists. Hendrick Hudson told a fish story when he wrote that he "tooke y[e] salmon" in this water, and showed that he did not know a big river trout from a salmon.

The eggs distributed in 1873, numbering 1,241,800, were sent to every State in New England, and also to New York, New Jersey, Pennsylvania, Ohio, Michigan, and Wisconsin. The young fish hatched were in every instance set at liberty as soon as the yolk sac was absorbed. The whole number thus turned out was 876,000. The present season the number of eggs distributed will probably exceed 2,200,000, and, unless some extraordinary mishap interferes, the number of young fish will be more than double that of last year. The distribution is so wide that hardly any river receives an adequate stock, but in some instances the number will be sufficient to produce a decided impression.

Block Island's Story
(1904)

NEW ENGLAND MAGAZINE

July, 1904

Block Island's Story

By CHARLES E. PERRY

FROM Eastport, Maine to Cape Hatteras every promontory, every long, low sand spit projecting out into the ocean has more or less of a local reputation as a danger point, at which mariners look askance, and concerning which song and story repeat and perpetuate its uncanny record. Of these, Point Judith, the southeastern extremity of the main land of Rhode Island, is by no means the least famous, and yet, in the open sea, ten miles southwest of it, lies a little green hummock, containing only ten square miles, upon which the ocean surges beat with a continuous, restless violence unequaled by any point or rocky headland, for these are sheltered, in some directions at least, by the land of which they form a part, while Block Island, located in the open ocean, is the battle ground of the angry sea, blow the wind from whatever quarter it may. Ten miles from the nearest land, which partially encircles it from northeast to northwest, it lies more unprotected from the west to the south, while to the southeast the broad expanse of the Western Ocean stretches out, with no land nearer than Spain and the Dark Continent. When the deep, heavy swells, driven before a fierce southeast gale, come tumbling in at the foot of Mohegan Bluffs on its south shore, vast walls of green water, breaking at their foot with the boom of a thousand cannon and rushing up their concave face, dash the spray in a blinding whirl over their summit, a hundred and fifty feet above, the power of the mighty waters and of Him who holds them in the hollow of His hand, is wonderfully impressive.

The average individual who has never visited Block Island seems to be pervaded by the impression that it is sandy, barren and desolate, where a few hardy fishermen by industry and privation manage to wring a scant sustenance from the waters that surround it. The facts are that the soil is, for the most part, unusually good, the crops abundant, the people enterprising and well-todo, and the Island a veritable paradise from June to November, albeit bleak and forbidding much of the time during the rest of the year.

"Dreary the land when gust and sleet
At its doors and windows howl and beat,
And winter laughs at its fires of peat;

But in summer time, when pool and pond
Held in the laps of valleys fond
Are blue as the glimpses of sea beyond,

When the hills are sweet with the briar rose
And hid in the warm, soft dells, unclose
Flowers the mainland rarely knows,

When boats to their morning fishing go,
And held to the wind and slanting low,
Whitening and darkening the small sails show,

Then is that lonely Island fair,
And the pale health seeker findeth there
The wine of life in its pleasant air."

—*Whittier.*

Block Island is situated at the entrance to Narragansett Bay on the north, and to Long Island Sound on the west; it is shaped much like a pear, the stem being represented by Sandy Point, its northern extremity; it is, approximately, six miles long and from one to three and a half miles wide. Its surface is very irregular, being a series of hills and valleys, resembling, in no small degree, the ocean by which it is surrounded, when that ocean is in an angry mood. Its highest point is Beacon Hill, an elevation of less than three hundred feet, but from whose summit, on a clear day, portions of four states, New York, Connecticut, Rhode Island and Massachusetts can be seen.

In its valleys are countless ponds, from those only a few rods in area to the Great Salt Pond of a thousand acres, which has been connected with the sea by a 600 foot channel, forming one of the finest harbors and yacht rendezvous on the coast.

The Island has been practically denuded of trees and it is so exposed to the fierce winds of winter that only the hardiest varieties can be made to thrive or even to live by constant care; it is also practically free from boulders—there were never any outcroppings of ledge formation, but the miles upon miles of stone fences that intersect the fields and make the surface, viewed from an eminence, to resemble a vast seine or net, bear indisputable evidence to the original character of the surface and to the patience and industry of its early settlers.

VIEW FROM BEACON HILL.

The Island was first discovered, so far as we have any reliable historical evidence, in 1524, by Verrazano (or Verrazani), a Portuguese navigator sailing under the flag of Francis I, King of France. Apparently he did not land, although he refers to it in his log-book as a "small island, triangular in form, about three leagues from the main land and covered with trees," and adds that it was inhabited as he "saw fires along the coast." He calls it Claudia, in honor of the mother of King Francis; the Indian name of the Island was Manisses, its meaning being "Island of the Little God."

Ninety years later, Adrian Blok, a Dutch explorer and fur trader, rediscovered it; his vessel had been burned in what is now New York harbor, the previous winter of 1613-14 and he built another, a "yacht" as he called it, which he named the Onrust (Unrest) and went sailing along the coast. He does not say, in the record of his trip, that he landed on the Island but there is strong inferential evidence that he did, and at any rate it has ever since borne his name—on the old Dutch maps as Adrian's Eyland—and later, as Block Island.

CRESCENT BEACH.

The Island was first settled by colonists from Massachusetts in 1661, having been purchased by sixteen men who divided it into seventeen shares, setting aside one of these shares for the support of an "orthodox minister." These purchasers set themselves to the task of subduing the wilderness, cutting down the forest, removing the boulders from the surface of the soil, at the same time holding in check the savages which outnumbered them twenty to one. Gradually the land was brought under cultivation and at the same time the rich harvests of the sea were not neglected.

Through a species of "natural selection" and "survival of the fittest," the hardy Islanders evolved a style of fishing boats which, for more than two centuries, served them well. This type was unique in its way, and was well adapted to the peculiar conditions which existed. The cod fishing banks lie at from six to more than twenty miles from the Island and it was necessary to have boats which could survive rough seas and heavy gales; at the same time, as there was no harbor, the boats had to be small and light, so that in bad weather they could be hauled up on the shore.

The typical Block Island boat has almost gone out of existence; a few only are left and it is improbable that any more will ever be built. The construction of harbors, where larger craft can lie in safety, has rendered this peculiar type obsolete. They were lapstreaked, open cedar boats from twelve to twenty-five feet in length, though a few were slightly larger. The cedar was fastened with copper nails to strong but light oak ribs; the boats were deep and sharp and were rigged with two masts, carrying a foresail and a mainsail. The foremast was stepped well forward and furnished all the head sail necessary, having no boom, but double sheets leading aft of the mainmast. The masts had no shrouds or stays and so were springy, easing the boat in seaway. They were "wet" boats, the spray flying over them in clouds when they were "on a wind," but, handled by the hardy Island fishermen, they were exceedingly seaworthy as is evidenced by the fact that not one has ever been lost by any accident due to bad weather. When a large Block Island boat, unprotected though they are by any deck, cannot beat to windward when it is properly handled and has a good working crew on board, it is next to impossible for anything afloat to do so.

Farming and fishing were practically the sole industries of the people up to the middle of the last century, when the beauty of the place and its unparalleled hygienic attractions began to draw attention to it as a summer resort and it is now celebrated all over the world, and the thirty or more hotels, and the cottages of summer residents, add an important factor to the old industries.

For a century or more after the forests had disappeared, the inhabitants depended upon peat for their fuel, but although large beds still exist, coal has almost wholly superseded it.

PART OF EAST HARBOR VILLAGE AND THE BAY.

Large quantities of seaweed drive ashore and this is not only valuable as a fertilizer, but that species known as "sea curl" or "Irish moss" is bleached and sold for commercial purposes.

Formerly the fishing industry was almost exclusively dependent upon the catch of cod which were salted and cured, and the excellence of Block Island codfish made them bring a higher price in the market than the best Bank cod.

The advent of a different type of fishing vessels, however, has served to make the fresh-fish catch more important, and at the present time, scarcely any fish are salted and dried.

The principal fish taken by the regular fishermen as a business, are cod, haddock, bluefish, swordfish, flounders, sea-bass and that denizen of the deep which, under the different aliases of yellowfin, chiquit, squeteague, sea-trout and succoteeg, furnishes an important article of food through the summer and fall months.

Block Island, albeit it has furnished no great military or naval heroes to history, has not been unknown to fame in the record of some of its sons and daughters.

Among its first settlers, Simon Ray and James Sands were the most prominent and their descendants through several generations were not only the leading men in local matters but were well and honorably known elsewhere.

Simon Ray, Sr., who was one of the original settlers, was born in Massachusetts, probably in Braintree, in 1635; his father, of the same name, having come from England. The latter died in 1641, leaving a large estate in Braintree. The son was twenty-five when he became one of the sixteen original purchasers of Block Island. He was a man of great physical endurance, of even temper, mild disposition, sound judgement and deep religious convictions. He lived to be one hundred and one years of age and is buried in the Island cemetery which crowns a hill near to and overlooking the new harbor, as it is called.

For nearly half a century he was Chief Warden of the town and for about thirty years its representative in the General Assembly.

He was succeeded in his local affairs, and in the love and respect of his fellow townsmen, by his son, Simon Ray, who had a large estate and whose daughters were noted for their beauty and high character. He was born April 9, 1672, was twice married, and died at the age of eighty-six, outliving his father but eighteen years.

His children were Judith, born October 4, 1726, married Thomas Hubbard of Boston; Anna, born September 27, 1728, married Governor Samuel Ward of Rhode Island; Catherine, born July 10, 1731, married Governor William Greene of Rhode Island; and Phebe, born September 10, 1733, married William Littlefield of Block Island. The latter and her husband both died at an early age, leaving a daughter Catherine, who was adopted by her aunt for whom she was named, the wife of Governor William Greene and subsequently married Major General Nathaniel Greene of Revolutionary fame. After his death she married Phineas Miller and resided in Georgia until her death She was an intimate friend of Mrs. Washington and of Benjamin Franklin and his wife. Franklin frequently refers to her in his letters.

James Sands, another of the first settlers, was born in Reading, England, in 1622; he was the son of Henry Sands, the first of the name in New England, who was admitted freeman of Boston in 1640. He was a descendant of James Sands of Staffordshire, England, who died in 1670 at the age of one hundred and forty years, his wife living to the age of one hundred and twenty. The family can be traced back in English history for about eight centuries and one of its members, Sir William Sands or Sandys, was conspicuous during the reigns of Henry VII and Henry VIII and had much to do with securing the downfall of Cardinal Wolsey and in sustaining charges against Pope Clement VII.

Capt. James Sands, who was one of the sixteen purchasers of Block Island, was, during his life, one of the foremost of its citizens and stood shoulder to shoulder with Simon Ray as typical representatives of the best blood that settled New England. He and Simon Ray, Sr., were intimate friends of Roger Williams and their descendants intermarried. He died in 1695 and he, too, is buried in the Island cemetery.

His descendants have been numerous and have been, almost without exception, recognized as men of high character and of unblemished honor.

The name of "Ray" as a surname has died out in the Island, but the innumerable families of other surnames, who have christened their sons with the "Simon Ray" prefix, bear evidence to the fact that the blood of the old settler descended through many channels on the female side, and also to the high respect in which he was held.

MOHEGAN BLUFFS ON SOUTH SHORE.

Rev. Samuel Niles, the first Rhode Island graduate of Harvard College, was a grandson of James Sands.

The sixteen first settlers of Block Island were John Ackurs, William Barker, William Billings, William Cahoone, Samuel Dering, Trustarum Dodge, Thomas Faxun, David Kimball, John Rathbone, Simon Ray, Thormut (Thomas) Rose, Thomas Terry, William Tosh, Edward Vorse, Nicholas White and Duncan Williamson. But two of the descendants of these families in the male line are now represented on the Island, but the Dodges and the Roses are among the most numerous of the family names that are still found there. James Sands appears to have been one of the first purchasers though not one of the first bona fide settlers, coming to the Island with his family a little later. Only three of his descendants in the male line now reside on the Island.

One can scarcely think of Block Island without recalling the innumerable wrecks that have occured there. Only a few of these can be alluded to, but among these are the *Mars*, an English merchantman stranded here in 1781, while endeavoring to escape from an American crusier; the Ann and Hope, an East Indian ship, belonging to Brown & Ives of Providence, and named for their wives. She struck under Mohegan Bluffs in a snow storm in the year 1806 and her captain, whose name was Lang, and several of the crew were lost. The ship went to pieces and the cargo of coffee, spices, etc., was almost a

CARTING SEAWEED.

total loss. The *Warrior*, a schooner packet, plying between Boston and New York, was lost on Sandy Point, the northern extremity of the Island, in a northeast gale in the spring of 1831. The crew and passengers, numbering twenty-one in all, were drowned and but little of the cargo was saved, The steamer *Palmetto*, bound from Philadelphia to Boston, struck Black Rock off Mohegan Bluffs in 1857 and, with a valuable cargo, sank to the bottom a few minutes later, the crew escaping in their boats. In the spring of 1876 there was a strange coincidence or series of coincidences. In the month of May of that year the Catherine May, Capt. Davis, a two-masted schooner, and the Henry J. May, Capt. Blackmar, a three-masted schooner, sailed from the same port on the same day for the same destination, and on the 21st of the month the former came ashore at Block Island at 7.30 p. m., and half an hour later the other struck only a few yards from her. They were both got off and towed into port by the Island wrecking companies. Twice at least, during the last half century, six vessels have come ashore in a single day, but the stories which might be told of these wrecks, many of them very interesting, must give place to one which, owing to the mystery which surrounds it, the strange legend which has been connected with it, and to the fact that the poet Whittier has embalmed it in verse, stands out from all the rest with startling distinctness.

MOSS GATHERER.

It is the irony of fate, that of the

story of this wreck, so interesting and so weird in many of its surroundings and in its sequel, so little is actually known.

About the year 1750, a ship came ashore on Sandy Point, the northern extremity of the Island. It was a beautiful Sunday morning in the holiday week between Christmas and New Year's, and there was scarcely a ripple on the waters that surrounded the Island.

MOSS BLEACHING.

The vessel simply drifted ashore, with all sails set; the Islanders went off to her in boats and found a few famine stricken passengers, speaking a foreign language, the crew having deserted the ship on the previous day.

They were in the last stages of starvation but were taken ashore and carried to the homes of the Islanders, most of them being taken to the houses of Simon Ray (2) and Edward Sands, grandson of James Sands previously referred to. Most of them were too far gone to be saved, even by the tender ministrations of the hospitable Islanders; they died and were buried near the house of Simon Ray, and their graves may still be seen. One of them, a woman servant of one of the passengers, recovered, however, and subsequently married a negro slave belonging to one of the Island families, and some of her descendants still reside on the Island.

The ship was the *Palatine*, and tradition says that the passengers were well-to-do Dutch emigrants, who were coming to settle near Philadelphia, having been driven from their homes by the ravages of

Marshall Turenne through the region known as the Palatinate. They brought with them much wealth in a portable form, and the officers and crew of the ship conspired to rob and then desert them. They put them on a short allowance of bread and water though there were plenty of provisions on board, and compelled them to pay the most exorbitant rates for such a miserable pittance as would support life.

When they had, at last, secured their last florin and the ship, which had been standing "off and on" for several weeks near the coast, had reached the vicinity of Block Island, the officers and crew deserted in the boats.

To go back to the story of the wrecked ship, if indeed that term is applicable, the Islanders towed her off the point on which she first stranded, in their boats, and beached her in a cove a mile or two farther south, near to the present entrance to the new harbor.

One of the passengers, a woman, who had become insane through her sufferings and her losses, refused to leave the wreck, and the first night after the ship came ashore, in some unknown manner, she took fire and was burned, with the woman on board.

For perhaps a hundred years a peculiar light, which no scientist has yet been able to explain satisfactorily, was seen from time to time in the vicinity of Block Island, and the credulous and superstitious believed that it was an apparition of the burning ship, and scores of reputable men, whose word in ordinary matters would be beyond question, have declared that they have sailed close enough to this supposed apparition to see masts, sails and ropes and even persons in the flaming rigging.

Such an apparition needed something to explain its origin, and so a story of the ship's having been lured ashore by false lights was invented and Whittier, with poetic license, enlarged upon and emphasized it to the great injustice of the Islanders, though it served to make the place known to thousands who had never before heard of it, and every summer hundreds of visitors go to visit the Palatine graves and hunt among the old farm houses for Palatine relics.

But the Island no longer needs the aid of legend or of poetry to bring people to its shores; it is indeed, in its delightful climate, its freedom from heat, from mosquitoes and from malaria, its cool winds which come from the ocean blow they from whatever quarter they may, its accessibility from New York, New London and Newport or Providence, its telegraphic and telephonic cables, its two mails a day and its world-famed Crescent Beach with its delightful surf bathing, a Mecca for the invalid in mind or body, and a delightful summer home for those who would recuperate from the maddening whirl of modern life.

The Sinking of the Bark *Kathleen* (1909)

THE SINKING OF THE BARK *KATHLEEN*

BY FREDERICK BOOTH

HIS is the story as Captain Jenkins himself told , though not in his exact words, and a strange le it is. Yet it is a true story, and is another lustration of the old adage that fact is stranger an fiction.

Captain Jenkins became master of the *Kathleen* her fifty-eighth year of service, and with a ew of thirty-odd men, his wife, and a green African parrot for company, sailed from New Bedford port on the 22d of October, 1901. Mrs. Jenkins was listed on the bark's books as assistant navigator.

Now your average sailorman everywhere is as superstitious as an Indian, and thinks there is no more certain sign of bad luck than to have a woman on a whaler outward-bound. Never did a whaling-vessel leave port with a lady in the cabin, but that there were mutterings down in the fo'c's'le and many a dark prediction of ill winds and a poor catch for the cruise.

Now, whether there is anything in sailors' superstitions or not, sure enough, the *Kathleen* had hardly stuck her forefoot outside of Buzzard's Bay when she ran into a terrific southwest gale of wind and rain. For twenty days and nights she ran under short canvas with her hatches battened down, but the bark—which was only one hundred and ninety-five tons' burden—rode the heavy seas like a duck, and when the weather cleared she was in the Gulf of Mexico with no more damage done than a weakened foretopmast. Captain Jenkins now headed for the Cape Verd Islands of the West India group, with fair weather; but in all that distance not a whale was sighted. At the Cape Verd Islands a number of Portuguese were shipped, making the crew forty in all.

The *Kathleen* then stood out to sea, to the southeast of the West India Islands. Ten days out she met another whaling-vessel and "gammed" her,—that is, the captain and officers of each vessel took turns in visiting each other; a very pleasant business, ordinarily, but there must have been something galling in it for the crew of the bark, for the other vessel had part of a cargo of oil, and the *Kathleen* had not even seen the color of a whale.

The winter months passed without a single good day. At the end of every twenty-four hours the entry made in the bark's log was, "No whales," until the days became long and monotonous. Every day the lookout in the crow's-nest searched the horizon in vain, while the crew became restive and quarrelsome under enforced and profitless idleness.

But about the 1st of March, 1902, the lookout in the crow's-nest sighted a large whale, and the bark gave chase. All day the anxious crew followed that solitary whale, but they could n't get close enough to lower the boats. At last they lost him in a rain squall. A few days later, however, on the 17th of March, the morning broke bright and clear—an ideal day for the business. As the crew were going out to masthead after breakfast, Captain Jenkins, in his habitual good-humor, called out, "Look sharp to-day, boys, for we 're going to raise a whale before night."

During the morning the men in the crow's-nest kept a keen lookout toward all points of the compass for a "blower"; for the crew of a whaler share in the season's catch—and, besides, the man who sights the first whale, or the most whales, is sure of a generous reward from the master of the craft. About one o'clock one of the men aloft sighted "white water," as they call the fine mist which the whale spouts into the air.

"There she blows! *there she blows!* off to wind'ard!" sang out a jubilant voice from the crosstrees. It proved to be sperm-whale, and there appeared to be a great number of them, some of them going one way and some another, their great hulks gleaming in the sunlight. First Mate Nichols ran aloft to take a look, and, coming down, reported it to be the greatest school of whales he had seen in all his experience, whereupon Captain Jenkins helped his wife into the shrouds to witness the unusual and welcome spectacle. Had the bark had forty boats to her davits instead of four, she could have utilized every one of them.

All was now eagerness and activity aboard the *Kathleen*. The seamen manned the davits in readiness to lower, the boat steerers stood to their steering oars, the boat header, or harpooner, looked to his iron; while the captain, sitting in the crosstrees, directed through his megaphone the approach of the bark upon the nearest of the quarry. "When we got within a mile of them," said Captain Jenkins, "we lowered the four boats, and soon afterward, Mr. Nichols, the first mate, struck a whale. The other whales went off to leeward and I followed them with the bark until I was sure the other boats saw them. Mr. Nichols then had his whale dead, about a mile to windward, so I came to the wind on the port tack; but it took us some time to get up to the mate, as we could n't carry any foretops'l or flying jib, as the topmast had given out; well, I stood on the port tack a while and then tacked. When we got braced up, Mr. Nichols was off the lee bow. I saw we were going to fetch him all right. Mr. Nichols had waffed his whale and was chasing some more. By that time the lookout aloft called that the three boats to leeward were all fast.

"Of course we were all glad of that. I ran the bark alongside of the whale and after darting at him two or three times managed to get him alongside."

Just at that moment the lookout reported the boats to leeward out of sight. The captain, who was anxious for the safety of his men, was somewhat worried at that, for the whale boats had no way of getting the bearings of the *Kathleen*, and, with night but a few hours distant, they ran a perilous chance of being lost. Leaving the cooper to get the fluke-chain on the dead whale, the master of the bark ran aloft to get the bearings of the three boats. All this time Mr. Nichols had given up chasing his second whale and was observing the bark.

It was just then that the strange thing happened which may sound incredible to landsmen, but was coolly accepted by these veterans of

THE BARK *KATHLEEN*. PHOTOGRAPHED IN NEW BEDFORD HARBOR.

salt-water adventures as an unlucky turn in their perilous lives.

The mate came alongside, and was getting ready to hoist his boat. The captain had just reached the crosstrees and had sat down when he heard a whale spout, right off the weather beam. He looked in that direction and saw, not more than five hundred feet distant, an immense bull-whale advancing directly upon the bark, flinging his giant flukes into the air and moving with a deliberate assurance that indicated his utter contempt for anything afloat.

"Hi, there, Mr. Nichols!" yelled the captain; "there 's a big fellow, trying to get alongside! Go and help him along."

The mate and his men tumbled back into the boat and bent to the oars with a will. They met the advancing monster half-way, and the mate gave him the iron "head and head." But for some reason he failed to get fast; and the whale, instead of sounding or going to windward as they usually do when struck, suddenly gave a ferocious toss with his flukes that nearly capsized the whale boat, and, churning the water to foam in his fury, rushed head-on for the bark at terrific speed. Astounded, the captain leaned out from the crow's-nest to see what would happen. Thirty feet from the vessel the whale seemed to foresee the impending collision and tried to dive; but too late! He struck the *Kathleen* just forward of the mizzen-rigging. with a crash that shook her from stem to stern. Then he passed under the vessel, lifting her two or three feet out of the water, so that when she came down her counters made a big splash.

"Is she stove in?" called out the captain.

"Everything all right," was the answer; "did n't hear anything crack."

The whale had come out on the other side and was rolling about in the water, dazed and apparently helpless. The mate, seeing this, again put his boat at him, but Captain Jenkins was wary of another encounter with the monster.

"Come aboard, Mr. Nichols!" he ordered. "We don't want that whale."

"Why not?" responded the mate; "he 's lying there waiting for us."

"Never mind the whale," answered the captain. "Come alongside and hoist that boat up as soon as you can. It 's getting dark."

At this moment a startling cry was raised from the forecastle: "She 's sprung a leak!" The cooper ran below and, coming up, reported the bark to be filling rapidly.

The captain immediately ordered flags set at all three mastheads, a signal for the boats to come in.

"But it was of no use," said the captain. "De Viera, one of the boat headers, was then not more than a mile distant, and I knew he could not help but see the flags. But he would not let go the whale that he was fast to. I set two gangs to work right away, one getting water and the other getting bread. Then I went into the cabin and found Mrs. Jenkins reading. I told her to get some warm clothing as soon as she could, but not to try to save anything else.

"Well, the first thing she did was to go for the parrot and take him on deck. Then she got a warm jacket and an old shawl. By that time it was time to take to the boat, which we did without any confusion whatever.

"The bark rolled over to windward and sank five minutes after we got clear of her.

"Well, we got to Mr. De Viera at last and divided the men and gave his boat its share of the bread and water we had taken from the bark. Then it was dark, and very necessary that we should find the other boats, for I knew they did not see the bark capsize and they would be looking for her for a day or so, with no water to drink. Well, we set our sails and steered as nearly as we could to where we thought they ought to be and at nine o'clock we found them."

The captain divided the food and water again; then he lighted a lantern and put it in the stern of his boat.

"Keep close together," he ordered, "and in the morning we will see about being rescued."

It was a terrifying situation which now confronted these unfortunates. They had five gal-

"THE WHALE RUSHED HEAD-ON FOR THE BARK AT TERRIFIC SPEED."

lons of water and several loaves of bread to each boat, and they were 1060 miles from Barbados—surely not a cheerful prospect to go to sleep over.

When the sun came up the next morning, no one boat was in sight of the others, but Third Mate Reynolds found himself in a more terrible predicament than that of being alone. When he dipped out a ration of water for the crew, he found it was salt! It had been in an open keg all night and had been splashed with brine. There was only one thing for him to do: that was to make for Barbados, so he stood away north by west, with no expectation of anything but starvation unless he could find the other boats. But the captain had been laying to since daylight looking for the others, and at about eight o'clock sighted Reynolds to windward; so they divided the captain's supply of water once more and started again.

Then, about nine o'clock in the morning, that which none had dared to expect happened. Some one in the captain's boat saw the smoke of a steamer off the port bow, which a little later proved to be the *Borderer* of Glasgow, Captain Ernest Dalton. Within half an hour the occupants of the three boats, including Captain and Mrs. Jenkins, the parrot, and the three first officers, were safely aboard, bound for Pernambuco. In three weeks they were in Philadelphia.

Eleven days and nights after the sinking of the *Kathleen,* ten gaunt, half-famished men sailed a leaky whale boat into Barbados. De Viera and his men, of the fourth boat, had had a rough and hungry voyage; but on the last day out, after having lived for ten days on a gill of water a day for each man, there was a heavy shower and they came into port with a quart of drinking water left

Rutland, Vermont
(1898)

THE OTTER CREEK VALLEY AND KILLINGTON PEAK.

RUTLAND, VERMONT.

By Julia C. R. Dorr.

MANY years ago—so many that the boys who were playing in the streets of Rutland that summer evening are the busy fathers of to-day—I stood with a friend on a hill-top overlooking the town. He had traveled in many lands, and knew well the varied beauties of earth and sea and sky; but this fair scene was quite new to him. At last, "As the mountains are round about Jerusalem!" he said under his breath—and then was silent, gazing from north to south, from east to west, in speechless admiration. Far to the south Mount Tabor lifted its rounded head like a gray shadow, and White Rock gleamed like ivory in the sunset light. Then in long and stately procession came low-browed Saltash, Bald Mountain, Round Hill and Medway, with the loftier heights soaring beyond them—Shrewsbury in the middle distance, and Killington and Pico towering to the stars, with clouds about their foreheads and the splendor of purple and gold clothing them like unto Solomon in all his glory. Farther to the north beautiful Nickwacket lifted its proud head above the hills that clustered around it; while at the west rose Belgo and Bird's Eye and the blue mists of the Taconic range.

In the heart of this majestic cordon, at the feet of Killington and Pico, nestled the village of Rutland. For this was in the early sixties, long before the unpretentious country town thought of putting on airs and

HOUSE OCCUPIED BY THE VERMONT LEGISLATURE A HUNDRED YEARS AGO.

calling itself a city. Perhaps some of us wish it had never grown worldly-wise and aspired to new dignities. Perhaps some of us, if we could have had our way, would have chosen to live in one of New England's largest villages rather than in one of its smaller cities. But never mind that! It has extended its borders since then. There are more tapering spires, more turrets and towers and rounded domes, more stately mansions and more quiet, comfortable homes catching and reflecting the golden light as the sun goes down. But the town still lies in the embrace of the mountains, bearing its humble part:

. . . "in all the pomp that fills
The circuit of the summer hills."

Fortunately, or unfortunately, one cannot be original in writing history. Facts are facts, not to be altered or gainsaid. Few of us can delve for ourselves in the dust and *debris* of the past, uncovering for the first time the priceless nuggets of truth that may be hidden there. We can only reap where others have sown. Let me say, once for all, that for a great part of the historical matter in this paper I am indebted to the researches of Mr. Henry Hall, an old resident of Rutland, to whom historic study was at once the delight and the labor of a lifetime.

On the 7th of September, 1761, Col. Josiah Willard of Winchester, N. H., procured the charter of Rutland. The document is still extant. It is stated that its original price was £20. Long previous to the granting of this charter, however, long before Rutland existed even as the day-dream of a pioneer, its site was the centre of Indian travel, Vermont water-courses furnishing the most direct and convenient route to Lake Champlain. In 1730 James Coss and twelve Caughnawaga Indians encamped here, coming from Fort Dummer, on the southern border, by way of Black River, Plymouth Pond, and Cold River. In his journal Coss alluded to the two waterfalls he found here, and to the nature of the soil. This is the first recorded visit of any white man to this vicinity. Only one hundred and sixty-eight years ago — a period of time that in the history of European nations seems but as a day! Yet when our beautiful Otter first caught the accents of the English tongue, the French fleur-de-lis floated supreme over Lake Champlain and claimed jurisdiction over all its tributaries. Years came and went, and by the fortunes of war the early settlers of Rutland owed allegiance to England, and proudly bore the lion and the unicorn on their banners. Loyal subjects they were, moreover, if we may judge from the closing stanzas of a "copy of verses" by a local poet, one Thomas Rowley, who is a somewhat conspicuous figure in the annals of the day. After urging all the world to come hither and settle in Rutland, he sings:

"The pope's supremacy
We utterly defy—
And Louis we deny,
We're George's men.
In George we will rejoice,
He is our King:
We will obey his voice
In everything.
There we his servants stand
Upon his conquered land—
Good Lord, may he defend
Our property!"

Notwithstanding this burst of loyalty, which no doubt found an echo in all hearts, it was not very long before Vermont stood solitary and alone with enemies on the right hand and on the left. For thirteen years the Green Mountain Boys rendered fealty to her only, and to the pine tree emblazoned on her shield.

THE OLD MEAD BIBLE.

DR. SAMUEL WILLIAMS.

Though Rutland obtained her charter in 1761, it was not until 1770 that her first white settler, James Mead, built him a log cabin and removed thither with his household goods, his wife, and ten children. They were three days on the weary journey from Manchester, and it is related that two of the girls, riding on one horse, and one of the boys who was driving the cows lagged behind and lost their way. Luckily they at length found the house of one Simeon Jenny, a Yorker and a Tory, who put them on the right road. But alas! when, on a stormy night in March, the tired wayfarers reached their destination, they found the cabin roofless and filled with ice and snow. Imagine how their hearts sank—the pathless forest around them, and their sole refuge from the night and the Arctic cold untenantable! Yet the fates were not utterly unkind; erelong Mead saw smoke ascending from a wigwam not far off, where a group of Caughnawagas were gathered around a blazing fire. He cautiously approached them. Would they give shelter to the women and children? There was much gesticulating and shaking of heads. Then one who

THE HOME OF DR. WILLIAMS.

SHREWSBURY POND.

seemed to be in authority arose with outstretched hands, crying, "Welcome! Welcome!" and with true knightly courtesy the red men gathered up their belongings and departed, leaving the wigwam to the occupancy of the pale-faces. Mrs. Mead was a devout woman, and Indians or no Indians, in wigwam or cabin, family prayer was never omitted. The Bible from which she read that night is still in good preservation.

In that year three children were born in the settlement, and at the close of the year its population numbered twenty-four. There were no roads, no bridges, no wagons. Whoever wished to cross Otter Creek at Centre Rutland was "ferried over the ferry" by Mead in his row-boat. Grain was scarce and there was no grist mill nearer than Skenesborough, now Whitehall. Corn was ground for samp in an iron hand mill. Still there was no fear of empty larders. Game abounded. The children whose merry voices made music in the rude log-cabins rejoiced in the finding of treasure trove in the forests and on the hills — berries, wild plums, butternuts by the bushel, to be cracked beside the great fireplaces, and musky fox grapes in the late autumn. And was there not a whole army of stately maple trees waiting to yield up their honeyed sweets? It is pleasant, too, to know that the children had brought with them from their old home two most dear companions, a cat and a little dog, which answered to the name of Fancy.

Three years later the children had other playmates. In 1773 thirty-five families had found — or made — homes in Rutland. And now its ecclesiastical history began. As in most New England communities, while distinctly repudiating any connection between church and state, the town officials made haste to build a log church, or "Meeting-house," just below Pine Hill at Centre Rutland, on or near the site of what has long been known as the old Gookin house; and the first Congregational church and society was formed, with just fourteen members. On the other side of the road ground was bought for £2 and set apart for a graveyard. In 1775 one lone sleeper rested there, probably the first person who died in the town. No doubt there was a schoolhouse, also; for here as elsewhere church and school went hand in hand. I have failed, however, to find any record thereof.

The long strife between Vermont and her neighbors on the right hand and on the left colored the early life of Rutland, and was felt as deeply there as elsewhere. In 1777, dropping the ridiculous name of the New Hampshire Grants, which it had borne for some years, the young commonwealth assumed the name of Vermont, after her own Green Mountains, and declared herself free and independent. She elected a legislature, and made Thomas Chittenden her first governor. Of the Vermont legislature Robinson says it wandered from town to town, a homeless vagrant, until 1808, when it found rest for its feet in the new state house at Montpelier. Several of its sessions were held in Rutland in the old red gambrel-roofed house that still maintains its ground near the head of West street.

Rutland bore her part in the Revolutionary war. Her soldiers were with Ethan Allen at the capture of Ticonderoga, and played their part in the siege of Quebec. She had two forts, and two militia companies, though only a trifle over eighty taxpayers. The first fort

CENTRE STREET AND MERCHANTS ROW.

built was near the present junction of North and South Main streets, and consisted chiefly of stout maple pickets planted close together. Within the enclosure thus formed there was a small building for the storing of ammunition and provisions. But this soon became of small account, and the pickets were found by the thrifty housewives of that day very convenient for firewood.

In March, 1778, it was resolved to make Rutland the headquarters of the state troops, and a large, substantial fort of unhewn hemlock logs, sunk in a deep trench, was built on the hill just east of the waterfall at Centre Rutland, and christened Fort Ranger. It was the lucky possessor of one cannon of nine pounds calibre, and twelve cannon cartridges. Under the circumstances it is perhaps fortunate that while serving its purpose as headquarters and giving some sense of protection to the townspeople, who were often alarmed by threatened inroads of Indians, it was never actually attacked. Situated near the geographical centre of the town, it seems to have been also a sort of local club-house, the rendezvous of "all sorts and conditions of men" who wished to talk over the newest bit of gossip, the price of pork and potatoes, Parson Roots' last sermon, or the latest news from the army.

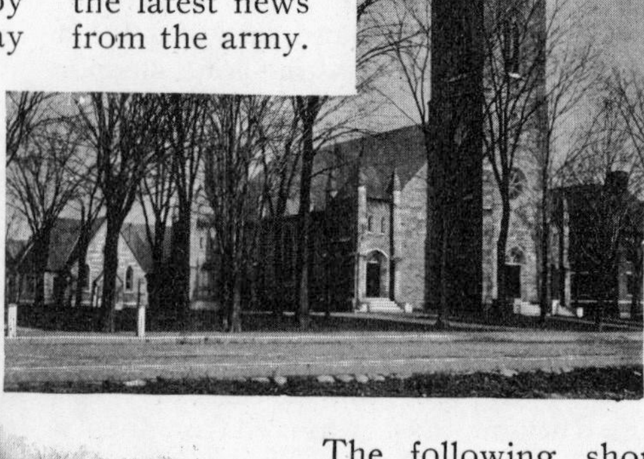

SOME OF RUTLAND'S CHURCHES.

The following short letter from the redoubtable Ethan Allen may be read with a smile, but it shows the interest the great man took in the fire-arms of his "warriors."

Sir:— The bearer, Mr. Wm. Stewart, one of the old Green Mountain *Core,* having an action at Rutland Superior Court in June instant, respecting the title of his Gun, which I am very certain he has a right to, and as he is a poor man, I desire you to plead his case and charge it to me. My Warriors must not be cheated out of their Fire-arms.

I am in haste your Friend and very Humble servant

Ethan Allen.

Stephen R. Bradley, 8th June, 1778."

The Rev. Benajah Roots, the first settled minister, lived in a log house near the site of the brick "Avery Billings house" on the Creek road, about a mile above Dorr Bridge. One evening in September, 1776, a weary traveler, pallid with sickness and half fainting with fatigue, pulled the latch string of the Rev. Benajah, and received cordial welcome. The unexpected guest was the Rev. William Emerson of Concord, Massachusetts, the grandfather of Ralph Waldo Emerson. He was a young man, only thirty-four, with a young wife and children. But when "the shot heard round the world" was fired

REV. LELAND HOWARD.

from Concord bridge, he left his pulpit and entered the army as chaplain under General Gates at Ticonderoga, where he soon became so ill that he was ordered home by his physician, and had got as far as Rutland when he grew worse and was unable to go on. He was faithfully nursed by the pastor and his family, but to no avail; he died on Sunday morning, October 20. The next day the funeral service was performed by Mr. Roots at his own house, and soldiers with muffled music led the way to a grave in that first graveyard under the hill, and fired a volley over it. Fourteen years afterward the grave was opened

REV. SILAS AIKEN.

by Mr. Emerson's son William, who identified the remains and re-interred them.

On the day of the funeral Mr. Roots wrote to the church in Concord a very long letter couched in the stilted phraseology of his time. This letter was in the possession of Mr. Emerson's illustrious grandson, who kindly loaned it that a copy might be made; and from that copy I extract the first paragraph and the postscript:

"To the Church and people of God at Concord—Men and Brethren;—

"Having with mine own hand at five o'clock in the morning, Oct. 20, closed the eyes of your dear and greatly beloved pastor (who I trust has fallen asleep in

REV. JOHN A. HICKS.

RUTLAND AND THE GREEN MOUNTAINS.

Jesus) after a long illness with ye billious fever attended with a tedious diarrhea of which he died. And Divine Providence so ordered it that he took his flight from this world of sin and sorrow to the realms of light and Regions of Eternal Day on the same day of the week that the Sun of Righteousness arose from the dark mansions of the grave; and probably the same hour of the day, too—yea, the same day in which he ascended to his meridian (I mean the highest heavens) where this bright star (or little Sun) we trust has followed his glorious head and begun his eternal sabbath early on the Lord's Day Morning."

Then followed several pages of pious condolence and instruction. Signed:

"BENAJAH ROOTS.

"Rutland, on Otter Creek, Oct. 21, 1776.

"P. S.—This 21st Oct., 1776, the Rev. Wm. Emerson of Concord was decently interred in this place with the honors of war by a detachment from Col. Vandyke's Regimint commanded by Major Shepherdson, who died of a billious on Lord's Day Morning 5 o'clock, Oct. 20, in ye 34th year of his age, after a long illness of about five weeks."

HON. SOLOMON FOOTE.

One may be pardoned for wondering whether it was Mr. Emerson or Major Shepherdson who "died of a billious." We can but hope that the good man's pulpit utterances were less involved than his correspondence. It would seem that no stone was raised; for when Mr. R. W. Emerson was a guest at The Maples about 1867, he was unable to identify the grave.

In this same "town-acre," or God's acre, is the unmarked grave also of Capt. Joseph Bowker, perhaps the most notable man in Rutland during the Revolutionary period and the years immediately following. Judge, captain, president of most of the state conventions, justice of the peace, and assistant treasurer, he seems to have been a many-sided public functionary, and, to quote from one of his many business partners, "the most considerable man in town." Henry Hall styles him the "John Hancock of Vermont." Yet, alas for the brevity of human fame, "no man knoweth his sepulchre."

In 1787 the town was divided into two parishes—the west parish and the east. In fact, the town itself was now known as East Rutland, Mead's Falls, now Centre Rutland, and West Rutland, and its inhabitants were too widely scattered to form one church family. The little log church under the hill was set off to the west parish; and during the next year a new church in the east parish was established with thirty-four members. Before the regular organization, however, the Rev. Augustine Hibbard was engaged to preach by the society, and it was voted "to raise £50 lawful money for his compensation, to be paid in beef, pork, butter, cheese, flour, or any sort of merchantable grain." But at the end of the year the Rev. Samuel Williams, LL. D., Harvard professor, scholar and gentleman, was employed, and filled the pulpit for seven years, though for some reason that has not come down to us he was never regularly installed as pastor. The new church building was on the west side of Main street, now *North* Main, just south of the old burial ground where, to the reproach of their descendants be it said, so many of early Rutland's worthiest children sleep in neglected graves. It was a plain, barn-like structure, with no bell to call the people together, nor stove to make them comfortable if they obeyed. But we read that, happily, the parish was mindful of deaf ears. Else why should it have voted that "the two fore seats in front of the square body in the lower part of the meeting-house be reserved and appropriated to the use and benefit of elderly gentlemen and ladies and they are hereby desired to make use of them accordingly." Poor souls! What benighted creatures these early fathers were, to be sure! They actually spoke of ladies and gentlemen and were appallingly ignorant of the fact that is being impressed on this generation —that it is "bad form" to use those good old words. But, whatever they were called, it is to be hoped that the elderly churchgoers availed themselves of this courtesy, for it must have removed them to a goodly distance from the front door, under which the winter snows were wont to drift when the east winds blew down from the mountains.

MEMORIAL HALL AND FREE LIBRARY.

BAXTER MEMORIAL LIBRARY.

Dr. Williams, in his wig and knee breeches, would have been a notable man anywhere. He had been part and parcel of the most cultivated society that the new world afforded. He was known, too, in the old world. The University of Edinburgh had made him an LL. D. at a time when such honors were seldom conferred on Americans; and he was a member of important scientific societies on both sides of the Atlantic. Just what induced him to take up his abode in the Rutland of that day will probably never be known. His letters to his wife show vividly the striking contrast he must have been perpetually drawing between the old life and the new — scholarly ease, refinement and even luxury on the one hand, and toil and privation on the other. It is certain he did not confine his labors wholly to the pulpit, but was a man of affairs; for in 1794 he founded the *Rutland Herald*, a journal that has kept the even tenor of its way from that day to this, and is still young and flourishing. The doctor died suddenly as late as 1817 and was buried in the North Main street burial ground, where his wife lies by his side. His son, Charles Kilbourne Williams, was governor of the state in 1850-2,

POST OFFICE.

COURT HOUSE.

and at his retirement closed an honorable public career of forty years. It was he who built the old Williams mansion, still in fine preservation and owned by F. G. Swinington, Esq. Dr. Samuel Williams lived further down the street, in the house now occupied by Mrs. Kilburn.

We are told that Rutland was not renowned for piety or virtue in those days. Only one name was added to the church roll during the ministry of Dr. Williams. During the reign of his successor, the first regularly installed pastor, Dr. Heman Ball, there was a large increase in the membership, and the old house of worship was found to have outlived its usefulness. A large brick church was built a little lower down on the other side of the street. This, too, was outgrown after the lapse of forty years, and during the ministry of the Rev. Dr. Aiken, of blessed memory, the present church with its beautiful spire, a landmark for all the country side, became the permanent home of the Congregational church of Rutland. The church prides itself not a little that during its long life of one hundred and nine years, it has had but seven pastors.

CLARENDON GORGE.

The Rutland *Herald* of September 30, 1794, had this item of news: "A Protestant Episcopal Church is formed in Rutland and vicinity under the pastoral care of Rev. Mr. Ogden." From that time on there appeared occasionally other items referring to the existence of an Episcopal church; but the parish registers do not confirm them. Church conventions were held in Rutland in 1795, 1802, and 1807, and in the *Convention Journal* of 1818 three baptisms of adults and sixteen of children are recorded. John A. Graham, a man who seems to have been most strangely compounded of opposite qualities— "half dandy, half humbug, yet with talent enough to attain notoriety in London and eminence in New York" —went to the mother country in pursuit of a bishop, and held a long correspondence with his grace, the Archbishop of Canterbury, touching the matter. It is even said that he built, or caused to be built,—whoever may have footed the bills, — a four-story house on the east side of the village green for the residence of the Bishop of Vermont — when there should be one. It would certainly seem that there must have been the inchoate beginnings of an Episcopal church here; but the formal and legal organiza-

OTTER CREEK AT HIGH WATER.

tion did not take place till 1832. The Rev. Dr. John A. Hicks was the first rector. The church stood on the west side of North Main street, opposite the present residence of John A. Sheldon, and was built of wood with a square tower. With its gallery and organ, its closed pews and its high pulpit, it was much finer in effect than the first church of the Congregationalists. Forty-four years had not only added to the wealth, but expanded the ideas of the community. Dr. Hicks was greatly beloved, not only by his own people, but by those of other churches. Tall and dignified, yet genial and tender hearted, earnest and scholarly, he moved among the people for more than a quarter of a century, the observed of all observers. There was a strong brotherly intimacy and affection between him, the Rev. Dr. Aiken, and the Rev. Leland Howard of the Baptist church. The presence of three such men was a benediction to the town.

The time came on apace when new conditions required new surroundings. In 1865 the new Trinity church, a beautiful stone building,

THE RAILROAD YARD.

was consecrated by Bishop Hopkins. One of the last services in the old church, whose bell still calls the faithful to prayer, was held on Easter even, the day of President Lincoln's death.

The Baptists, Methodists, and Universalists of Rutland all have flourishing organizations. The Irish Catholics have a strikingly beautiful stone church — the life-work, so to speak, of the Rev. Father Boylan, who was loved and honored of all men; and the lately erected church of the French Catholics adds still another to the clusters of turrets and spires that stand out in bold relief against the dark background of the mountains.

THE GATE AT "THE MAPLES."

The earlier life of Rutland, — by which is meant not so much the life of the pioneer period, as that of the closing years of the last century and the first third of the present,—is a fascinating study. The first sharp struggle for mere existence had passed, the wilderness was giving way before the march of fertile fields. The log cabin had given place to comelier and more convenient dwellings, and in many cases stately and elegant mansions had supplanted both. The village had, strictly speaking, no business centre, though its stores, the court house, the bank, a tavern or two, — including the famous old Franklin House, formerly known as Gould's tavern, — together with sundry smithies and saddlers' shops, clustered about the village green. Early in the century stocks and a whipping-post stood in convenient proximity to the court house, to the dismay of all offenders. The jail, a sombre stone building, was farther down the street. The village, in fact, consisted of Main street, not then divided into north and south, and the upper end of West street. The busy, far-reaching streets lying to-day below or west of these points, were then only a stretch of swampy pasturage. The old West street burial ground, which is now in the heart of the business district, was far out of town. All the social life of the village was on Main street or in its close neighborhood; and if the testimony of the few—alas, the very few—who are let to tell the story of those days is to be believed, the life was very delightful. Every one knew every one else; it was all like one great family, and open-handed hospitality reigned from Temple House at the head of the street to the Strong mansion at the southern end. It was a time of comparative leisure, when gentlemen wore ruffled shirts on state occasions, and had time to call on the ladies. If one of them had business in Albany, he did not fly thither on the wings of steam. A great lumbering stage coach, drawn by four strong steeds, drew up before the Franklin House, where he was in waiting, or picked him up at his own door if he had so directed. This was at six o'clock in the evening, and after prolonged adieus to wife, children and friends, he seated himself in the snuggest available corner, adjusted the strap, drew his cap down over his ears and his coat collar up to meet it, and with a sigh prepared to spend the night on the road, counting himself especially fortunate if he reached his destination in time for next day's dinner.

There was then no hurrying to catch the morning mail, or to run one's eye over the headlines of a dozen daily papers. No heart beat heavily at the sound of the postman's knock. The quiet yet spirited dames who held sway in those old houses — not old then — had no clubs, and knew nothing of federations. They had leisure for long, neighborly chats, while shining needles flew in and out, setting innumerable tiny stitches in dainty little garments — stitches that are the despair of their great-granddaughters to-day. They had time to read, and re-read, ponder over and digest the books in each other's libraries. Good books they were, too. A new Waverley was the delight of a whole winter. They had time to write long letters, that are vivid pictures of the life of the day, and are still treasured in their yellow mustiness. Letters counted when postage was twenty-five cents a sheet!

THE OLD SHELDON QUARRY.

The writer of this sketch was a mere child when she slept in Rutland for the first time — in the old Franklin House, where handsome Landlord Beaman graciously welcomed the new-comers. Let it not be thought that she makes invidious distinctions if she ventures to call the roll of Main street as it was then, naming only those of whom she has herself some personal memory, or association. Beginning at the head of the street, there were the Temples, the Williams, the Daniels, the Foots, the Hodges, the Pierpoints, the Butlers, the Halls, the Barretts, the Fays, the Goves, the Edgertons, the Cheneys,

THE MARBLE VALLEY.

the Burts, the Pages, the Porters, the Hopkins, the Ormsbees, the Royces, the Strongs, — and no doubt many other households concerning which her memory has grown cloudy. Some of these honored names are with us still; but for the most part they can be found only on tombstones — and in our hearts. The "oldest inhabitant" is fast vanishing; but there are still some left who recall with pride and loving admiration the group of noble, intellectual, dignified and graceful women who made the social life of Rutland beautiful more than half a century ago.

Main street is rich in relics of that and a much remoter life. At a luncheon given not long ago in one of these same old houses, a Copley looked down on us from the wall of the dining-room — the portrait of a fair-haired young naval officer in a blue uniform, who was drowned in Boston Harbor about the time of the famous tea-party. The ebony and gilt frame was made by one Paul Revere; and we sipped our coffee from teaspoons bearing the hall-mark (if that is the proper term) of the same skilled artisan. There was not a cup nor a plate nor a bit of glass that was not more than a century old, and the whole outfit belonged to our hostess.

In this connection it may not be amiss to say that when the families named above might have answered *adsum* to the roll-call, at the Centre there were the Gookins, the Baileys, the Ripleys, the Hosfords, the Ralph Pages, the Wells Brothers, the Griggs, the Chattertons, the Smiths, the Kelleys, the Thralls, the Graves, and the Billings. At West Rutland were the Meads, the Blanchards, the Sheldons, the Harmons, the Gilmours, the Boardmans, the Smiths, the Liscombs, and, at a later day, the Clements. But time and memory fail me. I have only attempted to put on record some of the names that were most familiar to my ears in that far-away time; and it will not be strange if I have forgotten or overlooked some that should be added to the roster.

As years went on, the marble quarries were developed, Rutland became a railroad centre; new enterprises and

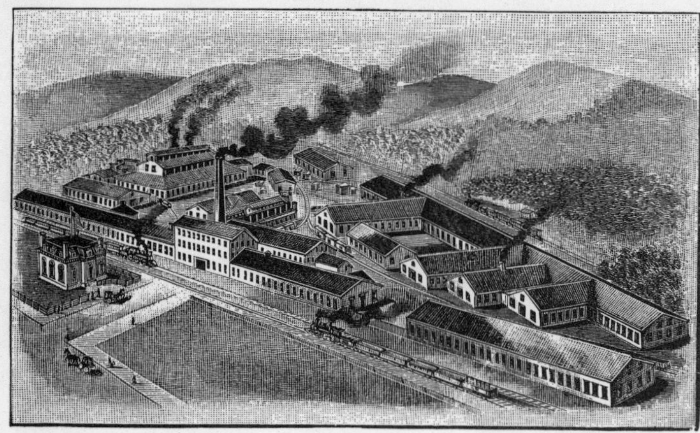

THE HOWE SCALE COMPANY'S WORKS.

new interests sprang into being; the old repose changed to modern stir and bustle; the town crept slowly down the hill by way of Centre and Washington streets, and spread hither and yon in all directions till it bore small resemblance to the village of its youth. West Rutland and Sutherland's Falls, places that had been mainly farming communities, found themselves possessors of mines of wealth that were hidden in the heart of their mountains, and sent their marbles to the ends of the earth.

Then came the low muttering thunder that preceded the outbreak of the civil war and the swift uprising of the North when the crash came. It was young Rutland that rushed to the field, *instanter*. Old Rutland cheered and raised flags, smiling proudly the while, till the drums ceased to beat and its soldiers departed, leaving the hills and valleys to breathless silence. Then it turned to its work again, to dig and delve, and raise money to supply the sinews of war, to scrape lint and roll bandages, to knit stockings, and dry fruit, and make barrels of blackberry jelly to send to the "948" boys who had gone to the front. How many of them went forth gaily as to a banquet, and came not back — or were brought back on their shields — I have not been able to ascertain. But of these last were Col. George T. Roberts, who fell at Baton Rouge, Lieut. Col. Charles P. Dudley, Capt. Edward F. Reynolds, and Lieut. John T. Sennott. Among those who returned bringing their sheaves with them—sometimes in the shape of honorable scars—were Brig. Gen. Benjamin F. Alvord, Admiral William G. Temple, Col. William T. Nichols, Lieut. Col. William Y. W. Ripley, who was so severely wounded at Malvern Hill that he was unable to remain in service, though in recognition of his gallantry on that bloody field he was offered a brigadier general's commission, which he was compelled to decline,—Lieut. Col. Charles H. Joyce, Bvt. Brig. Gen. Edward H. Ripley, and Maj. Levi G. Kingsley. The latter was in command of the first brigade of Union troops that entered Richmond, and was military commandant for many weeks. In the fine

EX-GOVERNOR JOHN B. PAGE.

memorial hall erected a few years ago as a monument to Rutland soldiers may be seen the great key of Libby Prison, which he brought thence, together with the flag of the prison, its order book, and one of the very few copies extant of the great seal of the Confederacy.

While for many years immediately following the war they were residents of Rutland, neither Col. W. G. Veazey of Gettysburg fame, Capt. S. E. Burnham, nor Col. Redfield Proctor, late Secretary of War, went from this town to the front. They were enrolled elsewhere.

After the close of the contest there followed a long season of business prosperity, and the population of Rutland increased steadily, if not rapidly. Indeed, the remark was often made that it was more like a Western than a New England town, in that it was still growing, still enlarging its borders. In 1878 the Howe Scale Company's shops were removed from Brandon, Vt., to Rutland, where large buildings were erected, covering nearly ten acres, and giving employment to a small army of men. This company, with its fourteen distributing stores, constitutes by far the largest single industry of the city, and is one of the most successful corporations of its kind in the country.

Yet it was the marble quarries that gave the town a unique position and earned for it, long before it put on civic dignities, the cognomen of The Marble City.

"Such extravagance I never saw in all my life," remarked a stranger who was taking a drive through the town. "Marble gate posts, marble doorsteps, marble sidewalks, and even marble underpinning to your houses — to say nothing of marble tombstones and monuments." It did not seem necessary to explain to this good-natured cynic that the marble sidewalks proved anything but acceptable in their dazzling whiteness, and were being exchanged as fast as possible for humble concrete. But it is true that, if it had not been for the cost of working, Rutland could have "dwelt in marble halls" as cheaply as in frame houses.

The Rutland Institute and Business College is a young but very successful school occupying a large building on North Main street, and having a yearly enrollment of over two hundred pupils. In the academic department young men and women are fitted for college or professional schools. The business college department is the largest and most complete in the state.

It is needless to say the town has its graded schools, its water works, its trolley cars, its electric lights, and other concomitants of modern civilization. But in one respect it has been less fortunate than some of its smaller neighbors, to say nothing of its beautiful sister city, Burlington. Very many Vermont towns have had gift after gift, endowment after endowment, from some who, having drifted out into the great world and made their fortunes, have tenderly remembered their old homes and showered benefactions upon them in the shape of libraries, hospitals, art galleries, theatres, school buildings, parks and fountains. I doubt whether Rutland has ever received a penny from any such source. Whatever it possesses it has earned by the sweat of its brow. Neither has it had resident citizens of great wealth to "remember it" in their wills—or during their lifetimes, for the matter of that. The wealth of the town is rather evenly distributed, the great majority of its inhabitants having neither poverty nor riches. A happy state of things, surely, yet, perhaps, not conducive to the rearing of exceptionally fine public buildings.

For a long time Rutland had been talking about one great need of the town—a public library. Once in a while somebody would "call a meeting," and after the usual preambles and whereases, it would be "resolved" that we must, could, would and should have a library. There would be a little stir and talk for a time, a trifling sum of money would be raised and deposited in the savings bank, and—that would be the end of it. Meanwhile the need was growing greater year by year. In January, 1886, sixty of the leading women of the town met at the house of Miss Mary Daniels to see what could be done. What *was* done was this: The Rutland Free Library Association was formed on the spot, and officers chosen, most of whom have served ever since. A loan exhibition was planned and held within a fortnight.

RUTLAND INSTITUTE AND BUSINESS COLLEGE.

A goodly sum was raised thereby, to which some personal gifts were added. Five thousand books were selected with great care; convenient rooms were hired and shelved; a thoroughly skilled and devoted librarian was found, and on the following Fourth of July the Rutland Free Library was declared open. From that moment its success has been beyond all hope and expectation. Its circulation is shown by actual statistics to be larger than of any other library on record in proportion to the number of books and the size of the town. Last year it reached 63,243. Two years after its establishment the library was in one sense adopted by the town. Rooms were offered it in the then new Memorial Hall, and a tax voted for its support and enlargement. It is a steadily growing power in the community, and Rutland is justly proud of it.

A very beautiful building is the H. H. Baxter Memorial Library, the building of which was completed in 1892 by the widow and son of Gen. Baxter, with its collection of choice books, some of them rare specimens of the arts of printing, binding and engraving. This is not a public library, though it is open to the public under certain conditions. The books are for reference solely, not for circulation; and it and the Free Library supplement each other.

Long before the club epidemic broke out, Rutland had her clubs which, with one exception, to be spoken of hereafter, she did not call clubs, but societies. No one thought of referring to women's clubs, unless it might be in the case of Sorosis, or the New England Women's Club. Friends in Council and the Fortnightly led the way, but were followed by the St. Theresa Society, the Unity, the Progressives, the Isabella, the Philharmonic and circle after circle of Chautauquans. The Daughters of the American Revolution have a large chapter, and a convenient room in Memorial Hall is set apart for their use. These clubs, if we must call them so, have added very greatly to the culture and higher life of the town. The only possible fault to be found with them is that they do lessen in a very appreciable degree the occasions on which, in the older life of the town, men and women met in friendly and companionable social intercourse. Being a so-called "club woman" myself, I can venture to say this. There is less time for hospitality since we women have given so much strength, thought and nervous force to club work and study and it is greatly to be regretted.

But Rutland had for many years one club to which this slight criticism does not apply. In 1873—twenty-five years ago—a Shakespeare Club was organized by Mr. Edward Lowe Temple, and it lived and flourished continuously, without a change of leadership, until two years ago. Never was there such a harmonious autocracy, never was a club conducted with less regard for red tape, and never was there more loyal cordiality. It was really what it professed to be, a club for the study of the great master, and of him alone; and of his spirit and genius, rather than his grammar. If it were still alive, how it would exult in John Fiske's "Forty Years of the Bacon-Shakespeare Folly" in the recent *Atlantic!*

Its membership numbered seventy-five. There were no dues. There was no vice-president, no board of directors, no formula of admission. "How can one get into the Shakespeare Club?" was often asked; and the answer was invariably—"Wait till the president asks you."

The president made out the casts and the rest of us obeyed, reading Hamlet or Imogene, if we were bidden, at one meeting, and at the next taking the role of clown or messenger. The reading was slightly dramatic, i. e., instead of sitting round a table there were entrances and exits, and on some occasions a little costuming; as to the latter one could do precisely as one chose. After the reading there was a social hour, with slight refreshments. For nearly a quarter of a century the Shakespeare Club was, perhaps, the most delightful feature of the literary and social life of Rutland.

But as the years went on, inevitable changes came. There were marriages, and removals and deaths. It was found impossible to create a new club out of the remains of the old one; and at length on one April evening we were called together to attend its obsequies. Peace to its ashes!

The time came at last when the large town of entire Rutland found the machinery by which its affairs were conducted, growing unwieldy. Both East and West Rutland had each their separate interests. Still another quarter of the town, Sutherland Falls, with its immense marble business, had aspirations of its own. An amicable separation was brought about, and in 1887 the twin brothers who had held the homestead in common, divided their goods and chattels and each set up housekeeping for himself. At the same time, a new town, to which was given the name of Proctor, was formed from Sutherland's Falls and a slice from the adjoining town of Pittsford. In 1893 Rutland became a city.

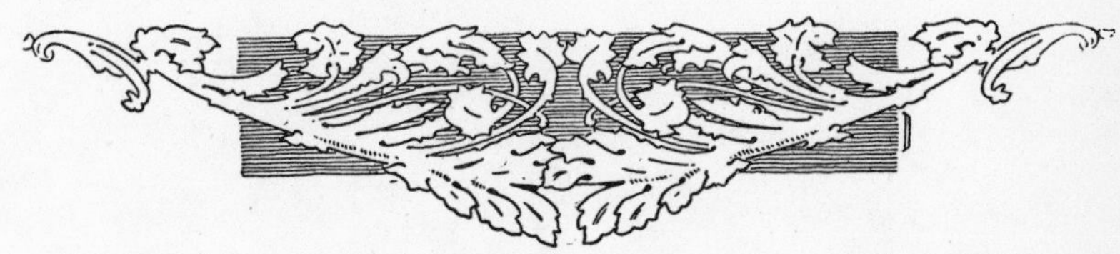

Old Dover, New Hampshire (1897)

FROM THE SITE OF THE OLD MEETINGHOUSE.

OLD DOVER, NEW HAMPSHIRE.

By Caroline Harwood Garland.

THE Cocheco river has its birth up among the foothills of the White Mountains, and wanders thence, like a country lad, down through the fields, sheltering trout, watering cattle and loitering under willows. At Farmington it floats a boat or two and gets a bridge over itself. At Rochester it has become industrious and turns wheels and pulls belts. By the time it reaches Dover it has grown to goodly proportions, and makes its final leap,—meeting tidewater at the foot of the rocks. Further down, it receives other waters, changing its name to Newichawannick and then Pascataqua; and become now a really noble river, it leaves Portsmouth on its south bank, Kittery on its north, and pours itself out into the open sea.

This river divides the city of Dover into two parts, each of which thinks the other will bear watching. The town may be a unit to outsiders, but within its borders it reserves the right to do a little quarrelling. From time immemorial the two sides have alternated in filling all electoral offices, and the city has never had a government building, partly because neither side is willing the other should have it. The present mayor, who has twice been elected with no opposing candidate in the field, when he was running for the office roomed on the south side, boarded on the north, and had his office in the building which then spanned the river.

Plymouth was but three years old, and Boston and Salem had not been thought of, when the first permanent settlement was made at Dover. Twenty years before that, Martin Pring had sailed up the Pascataqua, finding there, as he tells in his narrative, "goodly groves and woods and * * * sundry sorts of beasts. * * * But meeting with no sassafras he left those waters." Two centuries ago sassafras was the newly discovered remedy which was to do away with illness in the world. In 1614 Captain John Smith came up the river, but like Pring he sailed away again, leaving the shores to their loneliness. But in the spring of 1623 Edward Hilton, an English gentleman, and his brother William established themselves upon the neck of land now called Dover Point, built there two houses—and thus begun the first permanent settlement in New Hampshire.

"BLOODY POINT."

The little settlement did not grow rapidly. In 1630 there were but three houses in all this part of the country. But three years later, in the good ship James, "which was but eight weeks between Gravesend and Salem," there came, under the patronage of Lords Say and Brooke, a substantial emigration to the little colony. Governor Winthrop of Boston records that the ship "brought Captain Wiggin and about thirty, with one Mr. Leverich, a godly minister, to Pascataquack (which the Lord Say and the Lord Brooke had purchased of the Bristol men), and about forty for Virginia and about twenty for this place and about sixty cattle."

The place was evidently as difficult to name as a first child. Pascataqua, or Pascataquack as Winthrop wrote it, was the Indian name of the river; and Cochecho, "foaming water," of the falls in what is now the central part of the city. In the Swamscot patent, Dover Point was called Wecanacohunt; but while Hilton controlled it, it was known in English as Hilton's Point. One old map names the settlement Bristow, from Bristol, the town in England where its principal owners lived. Before 1639 it had been called Dover, but within two years had become Northam, only to change in two years more back to Dover again. The point of land opposite Dover Point, now a part of Newington, was called Bloody Point, because being included in the grants to both Portsmouth and Dover it became a ground of contention to the two plantations. In a dispute regarding its possession, the captains of the two here drew their swords. No blood was shed. "But," says the old chronicler, "in respect not of what did, but what might have fallen out, the place to this day retains the formidable name of 'Bloody Point.' "

When after eighteen years of independent life, New Hampshire for purposes of common defence entered into a union with Massachusetts, a difference of religious standpoint gave rise to numerous contests of argument, in the course of which the little state stood up vigorously against the dominance of the larger. Dr. Quint says that "to obtain the consent of the New Hampshire towns in 1641 to a union with Massachusetts that province was forced to relieve these towns from its law that none but church members could be voters in the state." Though public opinion was strong enough thus to force concessions for the right of suffrage, it did not wholly resist the influence of the larger and dominating state in matters of conscience. In December, 1662, by order of the Massachusetts government, three Quaker women were tied to a cart's tail and publicly whipped through these streets; but this severity was not long lived, and our annals are wholly free from the stain of the witchcraft delusion.

Widely known names appear in the history of the little town. Hanserd Knollys, who in December, 1638, formally organized the First Church here—though for five years previous there had been preaching by Leverich and Burdett,—was a learned scholar and

OLD GARRISON HOUSES.

author. Of his autobiography, only two copies are known to be in America, one in the library of Harvard College, the other in a private library in Dover.

Of Captain John Underhill, the friend of Sir Henry Vane, Whittier, who has sung many of the legends of this region, tells the story. Banished from Massachusetts on account of charges in which "a pipe of tobacco" figured along with reports of a graver nature, Underhill, Whittier says,

"Left three-hilled Boston and wandered down
East by north to Cochecho town."

It was more nearly north by east, but that is no matter. Dover received Underhill gladly, made him her governor, and throughout his later career of ambitious scheming and humble confession of grave sins, treated him always as befitted a man who had drawn his sword bravely in his country's service.

But of all those early names, none became the centre of so many associations as did that of Major Richard Waldron, or Walderne, as the name used to be written. Born in Alcester, England, he brought the first strength of his young manhood over to the vicissitudes of the newly opened country. Here he spent fifty years of his life, and here he met his tragic death. He was the first to build sawmills and utilize the natural facilities of the place for trade. Before that there had been uncertainties of business interests. The first comers expected to find in a new country unexhausted supplies of silver and gold. In the first grants of land a certain proportion is reserved to the crown of the "oares" found

Rev. Hanserd Knollys.

thereon. When no gold appeared, the settlers tried the planting of vineyards, only to find that New Hampshire is not a grape-growing country. But there were ever fish at their feet and forests at their very doors; and gradually grew up the industries of curing fish for the English markets and preparing lumber for West Indian trade. Then the practical eye of Waldron saw his opportunity, and saw-mills began to cluster round the falls of Cochecho. Waldron himself became chief magistrate, deputy to the assembly at Boston, Speaker of the House there, and commander of the militia, no mean position in those days. In the early part of his life, the settlement, except for religious and political disturbances, was at peace; but with the passing of the years, the Indians who had been accustomed to roam these fields and hills, seeing their hunting grounds planted with grain and their rivers forced to turn wheels for grist, grew morose and watched the steady encroachment with a menacing eye.

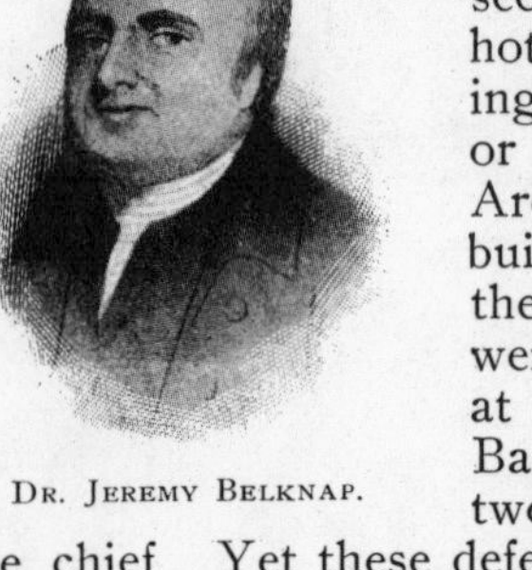

Dr. Jeremy Belknap.

By 1667 the settlers deemed it prudent to erect a bulwark around their beloved little meeting house. Garrison-houses for themselves, too, were thought wise. Into these garrison-houses the little town, consisting then of about forty families, retired every night. Looking back, one wonders how they could have stowed themselves, half a dozen families each perhaps with half a dozen children, into the tiny houses with two rooms on the ground floor and the long, low-roofed, undivided room in the half-story overhead. But here they met and slept and dreamed, and here too they fought. The only garrison-house now standing has still in its timbers bullets from those early conflicts, and from the ground near by the plough has turned up weapons, stout in spite of the rust of two hundred years.

These garrison-houses were sturdy timber structures with portholes for guns and with the second story projecting over the first in order that persons in the second might pour down hot water on foes attempting to force an entrance or to fire the building. Around the house was built a stout stockade. Of these fortifications there were six at Cochecho, one at Bellamy, one or two at Back River, and about twelve at Oyster River. Yet these defences were not sufficient to provide safety against the foe, malignant and crafty, that was rising

John P. Hale.

against them. Hope Hood, son of Robin Hood, hereditary sagamore of all the lands in this region, was only waiting his opportunity. Kankamaugus, sachem of the Pennacooks, himself sullenly hostile to the whites, fanned the desire in the neighboring Indians for revenge. The opportunity came as it always does to

"The patient search and vigil long
Of him who treasures up a wrong."

ON LOCUST STREET.

On the outbreak of King Philip's war, in 1675, the Massachusetts government at once prepared for general defence. The care of these Pascataqua towns was confided to Waldron, who was appointed commander of the militia with the rank of Major. He was powerless, however, to bring the force at his command into any effective warfare, and could only defend as best he could, the places most seriously threatened. In the early part of September, in the outlying districts of the town, grain was destroyed, houses were burnt, men were killed. By the last of the month the whole country was aroused. The 7th of October was observed as a day of fasting and prayer. On the 16th Roger Plaisted of Salmon Falls wrote to Major Waldron and Lieutenant Coffin at Dover, begging for military aid; "and let them that cannot fight, pray," he added to the appeal. But neither fighting nor prayer availed for poor Plaisted. He was killed by the Indians the very day he wrote the letter.

HOME OF JOHN P. HALE.

This border warfare continued throughout the fall, but the severity of winter bore hard on the improvident red men, and by spring they were suing for peace and begging for aid from Major Waldron. A treaty was concluded in July; but the death of Philip the following August caused many of the Southern Indians to make their way north, and as these refugees incited the tribes to renewed hostilities danger was again imminent. At this crisis came orders from the government to Major Waldron to seize all southern Indians wherever they might be found. The Major with reluctance obeyed the order. The Indians were invited to a sham fight, were surrounded, captured without bloodshed, and the southern Indians, about two hundred in number, sent to Boston. Of these, Boston hanged five or six and sold the others into slavery.

For this act Dover paid, thirteen years later, a terrible price. The Indians had regarded themselves safe under Major Waldron. They could not understand why military orders from Massachusetts should invade the peace of Pascataqua. Some of those who were sold into slavery escaped and, intent on revenge, made their way back to these regions. Here was the opportunity desired by the hostile sachems. A descent upon Cocheco was determined upon. It was a pleasant June night in 1689. The settlers and their families had as usual retired for the night to the garrison-houses. There had been flying reports for days that all was not right with the Indians, and friendly braves had given vague warnings. Yet the settlers paid little attention, and by neither friend nor foe could old Major Waldron be stirred. Mesandowit, a guest at his table, said to him the day before the treachery: "Brother Walderne, what would you do if the strange Indians should come?" "I could assemble a hundred men by lifting my finger," replied he, carelessly.

To each of the five garrison-houses there came at nightfall two squaws asking for permission to rest there over night. At Waldron's, Heard's, Otis's and the elder Coffin's they were admitted and kindly treated, even being shown how to open the doors in case they should want to go out during the night. The younger Coffin alone declined them entrance. In the dead of the night these treacherous squaws opened the gates, and the Indians waiting without rushed in. At Otis's and the elder Coffin's they killed and captured the inmates and burned the houses. At Heard's, Elder Wentworth, awakened by the barking of a dog, sprang to the door and held it till others were aroused, and so saved the garrison. At the younger Coffin's, where the squaws had been refused admission, and where, therefore, the whites were in a position to defend themselves, the Indians danced outside the stockade, jeered and hooted from a safe distance until at last, with fiendish glee, they set the captured elder Coffin out before the eyes of the safely intrenched son and threatened terrible torture unless the gates of the garrison were opened. The younger man delayed only long enough to demand promises of safety for his people and threw open his doors. As the inmates filed out they were one by one made captive, but in the darkness and the struggle many made their escape.

SOME OF DOVER'S CHURCHES.

At Waldron's the strife was hottest and the bloodshed most cruel. The Major, aroused from sleep, rushed out and, single-handed, drove back his enemies until, turning for his sword, he was struck on the back and

CENTRAL SQUARE.

stunned. Then the Indians mounted him on a chair set on a table in mock state and danced and shrieked derisively, "Who shall judge Indians now?" After feasting and drinking they each gave him a savage knife-thrust, saying, "Thus I cross out my account." When his life at last ended, they burned his house.

The early light of that June morning dawned on sad desolation and heart-breaking distress. Besides the garrisons, five or six houses had been burned, wanton destruction of property was everywhere evident, and bodies of murdered victims, from children of a few weeks to gray-haired men, lay prostrate by the roadside. Twenty-three persons were killed and twenty-nine carried into captivity that terrible night; and the fate of the dead was thought less dreadful than that of the living.

Desperate as was their condition the settlers set themselves at once with sturdy courage to repair their losses. Before noon of the next day the men had assembled and outlined their plans for rebuilding. Military aid was promised from Massachusetts, and, wasting no time in sorrow or repining, the brave little town pulled itself together and again set a stern face to the foe.

It was needed, for during nearly fifty years the place was never free from the danger of attack; yet itself growing stronger, expeditions were carried out into Indian villages until the enemy had no permanent home this side of Canada. Dr. Quint says, "In time, every man without exception save among the Friends became a trained soldier of the woods, a keen marksman, a tireless ranger. A man of forty-six had spent half his years in the field. They fought to defend their dwellings, their wives, their children. They succeeded; but in that fearful fifty years the suffering was great. They mourned for children seized from their agonized parents and, if not slain, reared by aliens in an alien faith. Dover blood was perpetuated in Canada in the descendants of these captives. Scarcely a family but had its history of inhuman torture or bloody deaths. When the end of Indian wars came, it was fated that, as Dover had been the scene of the first slaughter, that of 1675, so it was the scene of the last bloodshed, fifty years later. The Indian wars of Maine, New Hampshire and Canada began and ended in this parish."

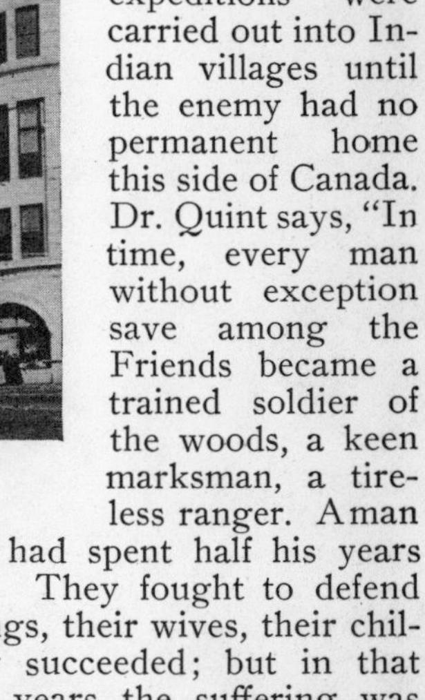

In that last bloodshed, two men were killed and one wounded, scalped and left for dead. This one was John Evans, brother of Joseph Evans, whose granddaughter, Abigail Hussey, born at Cochecho Point, was the mother of Whittier, the poet. Hence the lines in Snow-Bound:

"Our mother, while she turned her wheel,
Or run the new-knit stocking heel,

THE COCHECHO RIVER.

THE SAWYER MILLS.

Told how the Indian hordes came down
At midnight on Cocheco town,
And how her own great-uncle bore
His cruel scalp-mark to four-score."

The journal of Rev. John Pike, minister at Dover, a man to whom Cotton Mather in his *Magnalia* says he "was much beholden" for furnishing material for that work, records of those days many notes which we, sitting quiet in safe homes, read with a sense of remoteness and unreality.

May 7, 1696. John Church, sen., slain by the Indians as he traveled to seek his horse, upon a little hill betwixt Cochecho and Tole-end.

July 26, 1696. Being sacrament day. An ambush of Indians laid between Capt. Gove's field and Tobias Hanson's orchard; shot upon the people returning from meeting.

May 10, 1693. Tobias Hanson killed by the Indians as he traveled the path near the west corner of Thomas Down's field

July 18, 1684. The Indians fell suddenly and unexpectedly upon Oyster River about break of day, took the garrison (being deserted or not defended), killed and carried away 94 persons and burnt 13 houses.

This journal is a record of casualties. We read: Jan. 3, Col. Waldron's mills burnt down in a very Rainey night. Feb. 14, Mrs. Hannah Waldron died and was inhumed 16, which was the Revolution of her marriage-day.

Dec. 23. Old sister Downs died with Illness, age and suffering.

A serious combination surely. And we read the names of their maladies with a smile. One had "Meazells"; another was "grievously afflicted with snuffles"; "peripneumonia," ' 'grippings," "dry gripes," all found victims.

But our smile suddenly changes at the close of the next entry. The parson's hand, dust now these many years, added here a touch which makes us know that human hearts, however separated by miles of centuries, have ever been the same.

"My Dear son Samuel was born 1695, Ap. 1 betwixt two & 3 of the clock afternoon Monday. Lived seven years seven months, twenty-eight days. Died Nov 29 1702, Sab- morning, after two daysRelapse into a fever his principal malady was sore throat and caput-dolor. The joy of my heart."

After the cessation of Indian warfares the little town was long in recovering. Slowly industries grew and trade habits were formed. The ground was tilled, saw-mills were run, lumber was cut. The road known to this day as the Mast road received its name from the masts that were cut as early as 1665 on the lands of Robert Mason and shipped home to

Ex-Governor Charles H. Sawyer.

His Majesty for use in the Royal Navy. This lumber business and agriculture became the chief source of revenue. Hardships lessened and the little town grew. Then came the Revolution.

Historians tell us that in the hundred years preceding the Revolution emigration was stronger from this country to England than from England to us. This drifting homeward of many who preferred the settled English life to the conditions of a young country was a process naturally tending to the evolution of an American population that could think clearly, endure cheerfully, and protest vigorously. In this sifting process Dover had its share. Our settlers had been kindly and tolerant, but courageous. In 1675 they had sent a document home to His Majesty, beginning, "We protest." Their sons were also, or perhaps therefore, men in whom prevailed a strong sense of justice and a sturdy respect for their own as well as others' rights. Valiant service was done by the pulpit toward fitting men to take stands demanding purpose and steadfast courage. Dr. Jeremy Belknap, minister then of the old First Parish, stood up before his congregation and preached a sermon which he boldly named, "On account of the Difficulties of the King," and took for his text 1st Samuel, viii., 18: "And ye shall cry out in that day because of your king which ye shall have chosen you; and the Lord will not hear you in that day."

COCHECHO FALLS.

AFTER THE FLOOD.

The seed fell on good ground. The town records show that, November 7, 1774, a town meeting was called to see if the inhabitants would raise anything in "Money, Fat Cattle or Sheep," for the relief of the poor in Boston, then suffering from the operations of the Port Bill; and it was voted that the town would "give something." At the rumors of impending strife the town made ready to spring to arms. When the news of the Concord fight came, men gathered here from twenty miles around prepared to act. Companies were raised, drilled and promptly marched away. There were then, in the six towns which made up ancient Dover, 1,070 men, including the aged, the sick and the sailors at sea. By early autumn one-seventh of the whole number were under arms in the field. This alacrity prevailed throughout the state. Less than a

COCHECO MILLS.

month after the news of the first bloodshed, New Hampshire held at Exeter a convention of the Sons of Liberty and voted to raise two thousand men and accept those who had already hurried to the front. Three regiments were raised. Stark's and Reid's regiments and one company of the Second fought at Bunker Hill. Another company of the Second made a forced march of sixty-two miles, arriving in Chelsea the morning of the battle. They could not cross the river on account of the enemy, so went round by Medford.

Belknap, the scholar, the historian, the minister, and also the staunch and fearless patriot, was returning to Dover from Portsmouth when the news of the Concord fight reached him. He wheeled his horse and made straight for Boston. He wrote to his wife from the Point that he found it "absolutely necessary that I should proceed immediately to Boston, if it is not in ashes before I get there. I shall try and get a chaise at Greenland. As necessity has no law, the people must excuse my absence next Sabbath if I should not return before it." The people probably had occasion to excuse it, for on Sunday Belknap was preaching on the streets of Cambridge to the Provincial army. He soon returned to Dover to speed with stirring words the departure of Dover soldiers for the war. The brave parson must have had a heart in sympathy with them as they marched away. He himself knew how to shoulder a rifle. "Don't let my gun and munition get out of the house if you can help it," he had written his wife from Cambridge. All through the varying fortunes of the war he counselled courage and persistence, and when the end came welcomed the result with fervent gratitude and righteous exultation. Dr. Quint says: "It is a matter of known tradition that Dr. Belknap, when news arrived of the Declaration of Independence, went to the one town school at Pine Hill, then kept by Master Wigglesworth, announced that America was now a nation; and himself and the master at the head, stopping to take up a drummer by the way, the whole school marched through town as far as the Col. John Walderne mansion, and returned. At the schoolhouse Dr. Belknap offered prayer, and a holiday was then given."

When the war was over and New Hampshire ratified the Constitution, the town celebrated the event by public rejoicing and a grand procession. An old Salem newspaper thus ends its somewhat flowery account of the event:

"After passing the town, animated by the approving smiles of the ladies present, a semi-circle was formed near the meeting-house, where Nine Cannon were again discharged, and nine toasts were publickly given. After repeated cheers and expressions of unaffected joy, the Company received an invitation to the Hall-Chamber where nine flowing bowls, and four empty ones stood prepared for their reception, and Nine social songs were sung, which closed the evening in harmony."

New Hampshire was the ninth state to enter the Union. The nine flowing bowls and the four empty ones respectively represented the states which had and which had not ratified the Constitution.

During these years of struggle most of the slaves owned here had been emancipated. There had not been many. A census taken in 1775 gives, in the total population of 1666, 26 who were "negroes and slaves for life." Thomas Westbrook Walderne in his will, dated 1779, bequeathed to his heirs his "negro Dinah and her two children, Chloe and Plato." This retention was, however, merely nominal, and slavery as an institution was extinguished on the adoption of the State Constitution.

A second time the town was slow to recover from the depression consequent on war. Yet it must have been a pleasant place to live in. Its houses were comfortable and good looking, but not especially pretentious. Gardens with sweet old-fashioned flowers stretched back from the street, and tall elm trees shaded the road. Besides things good to look at they had things good to think of. Books were to be had. A social library was in existence before the Revolution and was chartered by the State Legislature in 1792, the only year the Legislature ever convened at Dover. The books belonging to this library were bound uniformly in leather and kept at some central store. There is now in the possession of one of our citizens a little, yellow, time-stained document, entitled: Catalogue of Books belonging to the Social Libery in Dover.

ST. THOMAS CHURCH AND LOW HOUSE.

THE CITY BUILDING.

It is a written list of 199 volumes, classified, three of its groups being as follows: Divinity, 40; Moral and Philosophical, 29; Entertainment, 17; from which it will be seen that the reading was forced to be of an eminently solid character. The list provided for frivolous minds runs as follows: "Devil on Crutches, 2 vols.; Terra Fillis, or the Secret History of the University of Oxford, 2 vols.; Fielding's Tom Jones, 4 vols.; Goldsmith's Vicar of Wakefield; Boyle's Voyage; Sterne's Works, 5 vols.; Plays and Skates Ballads, 2 vols.; total, 17." The novel reader of today, who expects to find, and finds, all the best fiction of the day in the Public Library about as soon as it is published, should drop a tear for the privations of those seeking "entertainment" in this lugubrious list.

The town had good schools too, to which the reluctant feet of children were started at the goodly hour of

THE COURT HOUSE.

eight, and where they remained, with the exception of the noon hour, until five at night. Business centered around the Landing, whence the Boston packets sailed, laden with lumber, and to which they returned bringing rum and other necessaries of life.

In 1812 the business men of the town found their mercantile interests embarrassed by the Embargo and the Second War with England. The Dover Cotton Factory was therefore incorporated, with a capital of $50,000. The first mill was built about two miles up the river, for it was supposed these lower falls were fully occupied with saw and grist mills. Nine years later the corporation obtained possession of this property, so long in the hands of the Waldron family, and built the mill now known as Number Two. The capital was twice enlarged and the name changed to the Dover Manufacturing Company. But its affairs were not prosperous, and in June, 1827, a new company, the present one, the Cocheco Manufacturing Company, was incorporated, with a capital of $1,500,000. By an error of the engrossing clerk in the act of incorporation, the old Indian name, Cochecho, became Cocheco. In the decade following the establishment of these mills the number of the population and the taxable property both about doubled. New streets were laid out, new houses built, the Strafford Bank was chartered, an aqueduct company incorporated, and five or six religious societies were organized.

In addition to these mills, which cluster around the falls of the Cochecho, there are a large belt factory and several shoeshops in this part of the city. In the southern part of the town, the Bellamy river affords other excellent water power, which is utilized by the Sawyer Woolen Mills. This water privilege on the Bellamy, like that at Cochecho, was once owned by Major Waldron, who gave it as a marriage portion to his two daughters, both of whom married Gerrishes.

In 1824 Alfred I. Sawyer began here the business of cloth dressing. From this grew the present large woolen industry of the city, the managers being second and third generations from the original owner. To the name of Sawyer the city of Dover owes a large

ON THE ROAD TO THE POINT.

debt. Honor and high standards bring forth results less tangible possibly, but certainly not less real than those of a large pay-roll.

Perhaps the most memorable night in our history after that of the massacre was March 1, 1896, the night of the flood. It had been raining for several days, — not furiously, but rather steadily. The ice was breaking up, too; patches of the upper river were open and big blocks of ice came floating down with the current. The ground was frozen and the surface drainage poured down into the river for miles back in the country. It was this combination of causes rather than any one of them that brought about the flood. The river rose a little all day Saturday, and rapidly Saturday night. Sunday forenoon it reached and passed the highest point it had ever made on the mill-gauge. By afternoon half the people of the town were out under umbrellas to see the sight. Everybody expected the Fourth street bridge to go. It was an old wooden thing, many times repaired, and not thought at its best to be very strong. The ice piled up above it and around it

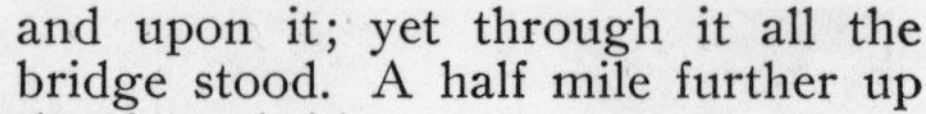

and upon it; yet through it all the bridge stood. A half mile further up the iron bridge over Whittier's Falls snapped away from its piers and went bodily down stream. The lower Washington Street bridge went out like wicker work. About the middle of Sunday afternoon, uneasiness began to be felt concerning the bridge over which is carried on most of the traffic of the city, the Central Avenue bridge, and the City Marshall gave the order to clear it. The order had not been fully obeyed before there was a tremendous thump from a submerged ice-cake, a crash of splitting timbers, and the middle of the bridge slumped. The slump threw timbers up against the doors and windows of the southerly end of the Bracewell block, making entrance to these stores difficult and dangerous. But from the others owners at once began to remove goods. Merchants further along the avenue opened their stores for the relief of their neighbors, a file of willing helpers was quickly formed, and the work of removal began. Back and forth under a long overhead arch of umbrellas held by bystanders hurried the quickly extemporized relief corps. The scene would have been ludicrous, — for some of the helpers were

MR. ARIOCH WENTWORTH.

LOCUST STREET AND CENTRAL AVENUE.

bunglers, letting long, delicate, white fabrics trail in the mud of the street, while others carried proudly aloft a single hat-box,—had there not been so many elements of the tragic. The gathering darkness, the falling rain, the rushing river, the quivering bridge, the booming ice blocks, — all these intensified the consciousness of impending calamity.

At seven the river was still steadily rising. At eight the rise was less rapid, but the water was more turbulent. Half an hour later came a big booming crash, followed by the splitting of timbers, and the little store adjoin-

ing the southern end of the Bracewell block went down stream like a bundle of jackstraws. In a few minutes more there was a bigger boom, a furious crash, a tottering of walls, a collapse, and the whole southern end of the Bracewell block and half the bridge went out. A hoarse cry went up from the crowd as a new element of danger became apparent. The electric light pole with its burden of wires swayed and reeled and finally broke and fell, snapping its living wires in every direction and tossing the arc light like a ball of fire down into the running water. For an instant the trolley wire which had been broken by the falling pole lit up the whole sky with a spitting, fiendish flame, running like lightning both ways from the break. Then the current was cut off and the whole place left to the blackness of absolute darkness. About midnight the fire alarm sounded. The flood had set fire to the barrels of lime on the river bank and the lumber yard of Converse & Hammond was all ablaze. For the rest of the night the fire department fought fire and the police and night watchmen guarded ruined buildings and watched the river.

When morning came it was found that eight bridges within the city limits had been swept away. Private losses were also large. Four stores with all their stock had gone down the river, and the loss by fire had been great. Many are the tales told of that flood. Outside of the town, just beyond the long Eliot bridge, the old toll-keeper of the bridge lay in his home very ill. To his ears there came the sound of a low, booming crash. He turned enquiring eyes toward the daughter sitting by his bedside. "It must be the bridge going out," she answered. The old man turned away. It was his last knowledge of earth.

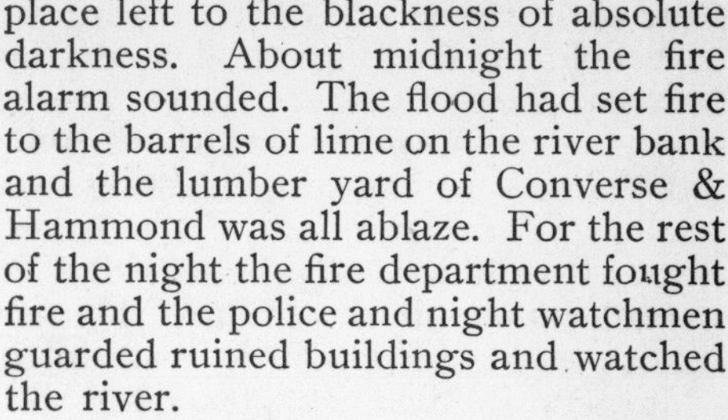

OFTEN SEEN ON THE STREET.

Dover does not begin to make the most of itself. A Western town with half its historic wealth would make itself heard all over the land and pilgrimages would be made to it from far and near. With us not a spot is labeled, not a site marked. We do not even sustain a historical society. There is an organization named the Dover Historical Society, under the auspices of which a valuable reprint of some of the early records has been made. But we hold no meetings, and at the last annual meeting there were present only a vice-president and the member at whose rooms the meeting was called. The Daughters of the American Revolution do better, but in smaller places in the country there are more energetic chapters than is the Margery Sullivan chapter here. Still it is pleasant to have ancestors and anniversaries and sites even if we do not use them much.

Nor do clubs flourish here. The one club for men, the Bellamy Club, is a purely social one,—delightful, men say,—where in well-appointed rooms members meet and smoke and do not gossip,—just talk things over. There are one or two smaller clubs, but the usual literary organization is lacking, and the town has not a Shakespeare club to its name. Once a year everybody goes to the May breakfast, an annual institution which each year puts four or five hundred dollars into the treasury of the Children's Home, the one charity upon which the whole town unites. Yet not quite the whole town either; the Roman Catholics support a home of their own in which children of their own faith are carefully reared. This division of forces is perhaps not to be regretted, since concord is often most real when differences of opinion are openly recognized and mutually respected. There is, however, one institution sorely needed, for which the whole city should with reason unite — a hospital, to which entrance and support should be conditioned not on the basis of creed or church, but on the common ground of human pain. The Home for Aged People, for which a fund was started years ago, has now become a possibility by reason of a recent gift of $10,000 from a former resident of Dover now living in Boston, Mr. Arioch Wentworth.

CENTRAL AVENUE AND FRANKLIN SQUARE.

Easy-going as the place is, it is a nice old town. If it does not make the most of itself, neither does it worry about trifles. It looks calmly on while its neighbor down the Pascataqua puts on more pretentious styles of living, and does not greatly bestir itself when an ambitious young city further up the Cochecho tries to lay violent hands on its court house and thereby become the county seat. But our people read as many books from their public library as these two cities combined, and with a cheerful indifference to fashion are united in a closeness of friendship that comes not only from sharing our neighbor's rejoicing, but even more from sorrowing in his griefs.

The life of the town is two-fold. There is the old life,—with ancestors in the past, a comfortable income for the present, and a provident outlook for the future; and there is the new life,—floating down from Canada, with many brothers and sisters, enough money to buy a gay gown, and no special thought for the future. In comparison with this Canadian element, the Irish portion of the population are old citizens,—first settlers, as it were. The problem of this intermixture is a serious one for this and many another New England town, for before the new life the old retreats as surely as did the aboriginal from the early emigrant.

In all the country round, there is no lovelier view than that from our Garrison Hill, which rises in the northern part of the city. From the observatory here may be seen the ocean, the Shoals, the spires of Portsmouth, the hills of Deerfield, Strafford, Nottingham, Blue Job at Farmington, and in a clear day the outlines of the White Mountains. Directly below lies the city, almost lost in shade trees. Coming down the hill, one passes just at the foot the oldest house in town, the Ham house, formerly the Varney house, built as early as 1696, when there were not men enough in the city to raise the frame, and help had to be summoned from Portsmouth. Just opposite is the site of the old Heard garrison, the only house saved in the massacre of 1689. A little to the north lie the open fields where camped the soldiers before they marched away to the Revolution. Coming down toward the city, one passes near Milk Street the site of the Otis garrison, whence was carried into captivity little Christine Otis, then but three months old, but who, reared by the nuns of Montreal, lived to refuse to take the veil and to marry a soldier and return to Dover, where under stress of adversity she kept for many years a tavern, "on the contry Rhoade from Dover Meeting House to Cochecho Boome." A little further on stood in Revolutionary times the mansion of Thomas Westbrook Waldrone, the soldier of Louisburg. At Franklin Square two streets diverge, one of which, Main Street, was formerly the main business thoroughfare, leading down to the Landing, but the other of which, Central Avenue, is now the trade centre. On the right of the avenue, just back of where the National Block now stands, stood two centuries ago the Waldron garrison, and where now tower big brick factories were then only grist and sawmills. Just after crossing the river, the road went up over a little rise of ground now cut entirely away, and on this knoll, just back of the present Varney's Block, the Coffin garrison was sacked and burned. Here now to the right, up past the big belt factory, turns Orchard Street, its name being the only reminder that Tristram Coffin's orchard once extended down there. The next street is Washington Street, once a gully down which Coffin's brook wandered. From the open square one looks toward the Landing again, and tries a little to think how it looked when stores and business offices filled the places that mills and crowded tenement houses now occupy, or picture it in even earlier days when trees grew to the river's edge and salmon and alewives swarmed in the water. There was an early law that the first salmon that came up the river should be given to the minister. Hungry indeed would the man in these days be who waited for salmon caught down at the Landing. From Central Square, past the Masonic Block, where the old City Hall, twice burned, stood, past the Belknap Church, named for Jeremy Belknap, the historian of New Hampshire, now one of the honored dead in the old Granary burying ground, Boston, the street goes on, curving like a country road, past the ancient residence of John Wentworth, now perched up on stores built out underneath, giving it the appearance of a crown on a four-cornered hat, — to the present City Building, big, ambitious, comprehensive, over which with pride we show our country cousins. On this spot stood until within a few years the old St. Thomas Church and the Dr. Low mansion, under the roof of which Lafayette once spent the night. The hill that slopes off sharply down to the left, Swazey's Hill, is sometimes still called Gallows Hill, because a century ago here was hanged a negro murderer. The gallows was at the foot of the hill in order that interested spectators might stand above and look down upon the death agony. Still following the curving avenue, we come to the old Dover Hotel, now a tenement house, once a flourishing hostelry, known as Peggy Gage's Inn. Next is a carriage shop, whose dignified architecture recalls the fact that it was once Bellevue Hall, where Dover's youth danced happy hours away. On the corner of Court Street stands the old court house, built in 1791. It is safe to say that not one person in fifty could point it out, yet within its walls Jeremiah Mason and Daniel Webster have often spoken. Opposite is the convent, on the verandah of which Sisters of Mercy sometimes pace for exercise. Years ago this too was a hotel, the famous New Hampshire House, in front of which stages noisily drew up, and in which Abraham Lincoln was entertained.

Then comes the Corner, a simple junction of two streets, with a peaceful-looking old store on one side and an ancient church hard by. Yet the name is as distinctive as that of a Highland clan. The "Corner boys," the "Corner girls," — these and the dwellers on "the other side of the river," — oil and water are quite as unitable. This is a mistifying matter to the unwary new-comer to the city, who looks forward to making friends without regard to the river. He at first laughs at the delusion, then ruefully accepts it, and usually ends by choosing his side and vigorously adopting its principles.

From the corner on are pleasant homes under arching trees. A few steps along on the right is the old home of John P. Hale, United States Senator and Minister to Spain, a man who, in the early days of the slavery struggle

> "Dared to be
> In the right with two or three"

If we follow the road along past the school house and Pine Hill Cemetery away out of town, it will take us down several miles to the site of the first settlers and the little Meeting-House. Standing there on the spot where, it is recorded, the pioneers expected to "build a compact city," one is tempted to ask, as perhaps they too coming from their homes in England asked: What, then, endures? Surely not buildings framed by men's hands, nor individual plans, nor the purpose of a few. For around us stretch open fields, and at our feet the very earthmarks that outlined the site of that ancient church are almost obliterated. Over the ground is a low tangle of five-finger and blackberry. Along the grass-covered ridge which outlines the length of the side, sumachs flourish. In the depression of the rifle-pit is a spreading juniper bush. Over the ground which once an armed sentinel paced, a slender slip of an elm leaning against the fence is now the only guard; and where amid peril once fervently ascended the Psalms of David, now peacefully rises the sweet hymn of the song sparrow.

Yet lifting our eyes, we look abroad

upon just what our fathers saw. To the north and west the distant hills; to the east, wooded slopes; directly before us, beautiful contours of river, bay and islands with curving shores. Above us now as then the white clouds float in blue ether; and twice a day, to-day as for many years, the tide ebbs and flows in all these waters.

But not only the forces of Nature endure. Behind us lies the "compact city" that our fathers thought to build, — not where they planned, nor as they expected, but in a place better suited for itself and in a way which its own interests have developed. The welfare of the whole, — this is evidently the abiding principle.

Along a Brook Trout Stream of Vermont (1908)

MAY, 1908

ALONG A BROOK-TROUT STREAM OF VERMONT

BY A. E. MARR

PHOTOGRAPHS BY T. E. MARR

TROUT fishing, as usually practised, is regarded as a costly sport, and undoubtedly there are few others which exceed it in point of expense, all things taken into consideration. And yet it is perfectly possible for one to enjoy this glorious sport at a moderate outlay if the matter is but judiciously planned. It is the purpose of this article to show what and what not to take and do that one may receive the maximum amount of pleasure with the minimum amount of cost.

The first consideration is the destination, where fish are to be found. There are many desirable localities where one is reasonably sure of a good catch, and this article is based on a trip to the brooks of Vermont.

If you have no preference and are a stranger to that state, select, with the aid of a map, one of the hilly backwoods towns and drop a line to the postmaster requesting him to give you information concerning the fishing and the address of some farmer who would put you up for a few days. The usual result is that the letter is passed on to the right party and the hearty response assures you that the matter of accommodation need cause no further anxiety. Be explicit in stating the number in party and about the amount of baggage. To be met at the station by a one-seater for a party of perhaps three or four, with the usual quantity of dunnage, and most likely a two hours' ride into the back country to be accomplished, is rather a disconcerting beginning.

It is always prudent to adjust the rates in advance and have it understood that they include the use of horse and team; though it has been my experience in the majority of cases, in fact with rarely an exception, when the matter of charge has been left to the farmer, the item was found to be very reasonable, frequently much less than anticipated. The usual price is from three dollars and a half to five dollars a week, each person. Occasionally, it is as high as seven; though the latter sum is the exception. These figures generally include everything from being called in the

Always try the quiet deep water below falls.

Difficult for casting. Better use shortened line and live bait.

Such places are good but care must be used about the dead wood.

Always an ideal spot below an old dam but one needs a long-handled net.

It generally pays, even though difficult, to go up stream first so as to fish down.

morning, to the putting up of the team the last thing at night, and in many cases when the host is not over-rushed with work, his presence with the party in the capacity of guide and genial helper, for the average backwoodsman delights in a day's trip to the streams in the company of city sportsmen.

Concerning the outfit, if one is a novice and requires a complete rig, it will be wisest to visit any of the large sporting goods stores and place the matter in the hands of the experienced men who have charge of the fishing departments. However, if one must rely upon a personal selection, choose a rod of split bamboo from seven to nine feet long and weighing from four to seven ounces, one that is neither too stiff nor too limber, but well balanced, and, above all, a rod which, when held in the hand, feels well, that is, seems to fit the user. Scan the cracks, or edges, where the strips of wood join, and reject those whose seams are open and the strips of wood do not seem to have been brought firmly together.

It is not my intention to attempt to tell the old angler what he needs, every angler has his own ideas on the subject, nor would it be practical to go into all the fine points for the beginners. Rod culture comes only with years of practice. The first rod is but the beginning, and suffice it to say that it is not the highest cost outfit necessarily which gets the best catch.

Such a rod as one should have in the beginning needn't cost over five dollars. When one has learned more as to his personal needs, and the proper method to care for an expensive affair, it will be plenty soon enough to procure one. There is, however, one luxury, I might almost say necessity, you should permit, if possible get a rod with agate guides and tip, even though it does advance the cost somewhat. If that is prohibitive, at least allow yourself the comfort of an agate first guide and tip. The ease of line manipulation, not to mention saving of the wear upon it, will amply repay you for the slight additional cost.

A satisfactory reel with a capacity of from eighty to a hundred yards of line can be bought for as low as two or three dollars, and, for the latter figure, a very serviceable article may be had.

Choose a braided silk waterproof line, size about No. 5. Lines perfectly good enough for brook trout fishing can be bought for as little as two or three cents a yard. Seventy-five yards will be ample, in fact more than really needed, but it is always better to have rather more, than not quite enough. The extra quantity in the first place builds up the core, or spool of the reel, thereby keeping the line in better condition than when it is tightly wound around a small spindle. It is also well to be able at times to allow, in swiftly running water, considerable line to run down in the rapids, perhaps in such places where one cannot very well wade down, and yet a likely spot to fish. Of course it is imperative to have still plenty of line left upon the reel in case of a strike which may require much playing.

The matter of flies is a deep one and therein lies the pitfall for the green angler. There is such an endless variety on the market, at from fifty cents to many dollars per dozen, it seems, to the beginner, an almost hopeless task to make a wise selection. However, the following list will be found to answer about all requirements for brook trout and is, I consider, about the very best small assortment one can procure. Silver Doctor, Parmachenee Belle, Professor, Montreal Dark, Brown Hackle, Coachman and Red Ibis. These should be mounted on a number eight hook for the larger trout, though I have better success with number ten or even the small twelve. It must be remembered the small fish cannot always take the large fly into the mouth but, on the contrary, the big fellow can always readily take the small hook and for that reason is frequently well hooked in the bargain. It is a good rule when in doubt to always choose the smaller. It pays to get the best quality fly, for it is economy in the end. If you must curtail somewhere don't let it be on the flies. These which I have mentioned, and of good grade, should cost about one dollar and a half per dozen.

It is also necessary to have some gut leaders of the best quality, dyed mist color, and about six feet long, but be sure to see that they are well moistened before using, otherwise they are very apt to crack or break. They are made in various styles and cost from ten cents up. Forty to sixty cents will give one a very excellent leader.

The subject of creel and landing net is

In the small exposed pools let the line drift down with the current.

Do not neglect a supply for the inner man.

The deep holes are the trout's favorite lurking places.

Great care must be exercised when landing in the rapids.

A good place to fish if one doesn't mind getting wet.

a small matter easily covered for about three dollars.

One now has all the necessary outfit, and if care has been exercised in picking it out, a very good one.

Vermont, being generally hilly, there are many watersheds and the brooks are therefore numerous. It is wise to plan your start so that whether the stream picked out for the day's sport be one or ten miles from the house, you will reach it prepared to do your best by daylight. I can recall very distinctly on my last trip, pulling out of the barn at half past two, although we sat up unwisely until eleven o'clock the night before talking it over, bound for a favorite brook sixteen miles away. It was cold. We were tired, yes, there was no doubt of that, but the satisfaction we had as we got the first rise, just as the day was dawning, more than repaid us for the hardship.

Don't forget, when going in the team on an all-day trip, to put in a lantern. The roads are rough in that section, steep, and in places with nothing but an old fence between one and a sheer drop of many feet. Once, on the way home, with a green horse, we got stuck without a light, and for three miles over the worst part of the road our guide walked ahead, while one of us led the horse.

Although flies are quite correct, never depend wholly upon them. I do not believe there ever has been, or ever will be found a lure to quite take the place, under all conditions, of the common worm.

Fish are past understanding. What they will take one day they may absolutely refuse on the next, even though the conditions appear to be identical. The best one can do is to try, try and then try some more, using all the variety of both artificial and live bait at one's disposal. Patience and variety I consider the two very best killers ever fished with.

In the mountain streams the trout will not rise to fly until the snow-water is out of the streams, but since the law in Vermont is not off trout until May fifteenth, that problem does not arise there.

When the day is dark, I have better luck using a light colored lure, and when the light is strong, a dark one; in other words, working a bait which seems to show up best under whatever conditions may be prevailing. For this same reason in rough water and in rapids, a larger fly is more desirable, since it shows up more than a smaller one. Occasionally, neither artificial flies nor worms will draw a response, and in those cases I have resorted to putting on a very small hook and fastening upon it a fly, miller or other insect, such as is about the brook at the time. Owing to the soft nature of this bait, the novice will have better success to gently toss it out upon the water with the underhand swing or motion, allowing it to float down with the current, giving it plenty of slack line as it works off.

In this particular country, Vermont, and for that matter the rule applies elsewhere, the angler will find it to his advantage to work down-stream. When convenient, cut across country to the head of the stream first, and then work down. If, owing to the nature of the country, it is quite impracticable to attempt that, as it was in our case on Roaring Brook, the section being well nigh impassable in places, forcing us to follow the bed of the stream up the mountain, one might stop at some of the best pools on the way up, but really it will be wiser to plod right along, hard though it may be to pass them, contenting yourself with the thought that if you fish every inch of the way on the return, your creel will be pounds heavier by doing so, and you will very likely barely reach open country then before dark.

A subject, which perhaps is one of the most vital in connection with the outfit and least likely to be properly understood, is that of footwear. It is a matter upon which the success of the whole trip really hinges, for, since walking constitutes the greater portion of the hard exercise during the day, it behooves one to give due consideration to the comfort of the feet. I have tried wading the streams in a great variety of rigs including the rawhide moccasin, heavy hip rubber-boot and the high wading pants, and only after repeated experiments which always left something to be desired, I tried wearing a combination of short golf pants, preferably of wool, heavy, long woolen stockings, and a pair of strong leather shoes.

To be successful in fishing, the first requisite is to go where the fish are. In the country in question, and in fact in

A good spot to cast where the stream widens out.

practically all mountainous sections, owing to the formation of the land, it is necessary to follow the stream closely. Usually locomotion in any other direction is generally most difficult, if not actually impractical. This means that one covers most of the distance, whether fishing or traveling from one pool to another on the same stream, by walking in the bed of the brook. The wading pants, which are much recommended, and, with the exception of the method I have advocated above, perhaps the best, have three very serious drawbacks. The high cost, the almost complete lack of air circulation producing much perspiration, this discomfort being especially marked in warm weather, and the most important point, the almost certain prospect of filling them full of water before the day is ended. The beds of the streams are more or less strewn with rocks of all shapes and sizes, uniform in nothing but a most remarkable slipperiness. When walking over such a surface, perhaps in swiftly moving water nearly to the waist, and unable to see the footing, is it strange that slips are frequent? It is needless to say the first slip fills the waders with water and there is nothing to do but go ashore, remove and empty them, and for the rest of the day one is pretty uncomfortable. Then, again, no matter how high the pants may be, one will always venture to the limit, and an unexpected hole, perhaps, but a few inches deeper, will send quarts of water scurrying down the boots.

With the golf waders there is really no set limit to the depth one may venture. The water drains off naturally, and the wool, with the heat of the body, keeps one warm and comfortable. In connection with this outfit, a short coat, made specially for wading and for sale by the sporting goods dealers, is very desirable. The pockets are all high up out of the water and there are no coat ends to be continually dragging in the wet. With this coat on, one is quite sure to have a dry warm jacket with the contents of the pockets safe unless one takes a dip all over.

It is unwise to carry a valuable timepiece with one while on the brook. The cheap ones which are sold around a dollar are very good and there is much satisfaction in the thought that if one should become soaked there will be but little loss.

As I have stated, the early morning is the best time to be right there with the bait, patience and determination to fish every likely bit of water, and some of the unlikely ones until your day is finished. I have tramped for hours with indifferent success, and, when about discouraged, struck the pool which paid me for my entire day.

Do not neglect to work down through the rapids carefully and slowly. There is pretty sure to be something there to repay one. Do not think just because the water is rough and noisy, the trout are stupid enough to allow a large, fast-moving, stumbling object to approach closely. And if one must be careful there, how much more careful must one be in still water where every movement is plainly seen and the woods are quiet with a profound stillness.

In water, where the force of the stream will rush your line down, do not be afraid to pay out plenty of it. Fish always lie with their heads upstream, watching for just such things as your bait seems to be to come floating down to them, and the farther off you are from him the more secure he will feel in darting at the bait and rushing off with it. Work patiently around old brush heaps, half submerged rocks and similar things, for it is in such places the trout loves to lie hidden while waiting and watching for his food. Should you feel a strike in the rapids be prepared to give him, at the first necessity, the needed line, for, the instant he feels the hook, he will rush down stream and the strain will be doubly hard on both line and rod with the force of the water aiding him. If he seems big, or pulls very strongly, take plenty of time, play him slowly and carefully, keeping your line only tight enough to tire him in his struggles. Use all your skill in steering him from brush, tree stumps, roots and such obstructions as he will surely rush to for safety. Carefulness and patience, coupled with his struggles, will do more to land him than anything else. Too great hurry, with strong fish in swiftly running water, results in the loss of more hooked trout than anything else I believe.

If you are a stranger in the region and haven't the services of an experienced guide, search out the difficult spots, those that seem almost hopeless of access. It is just such places as those that the average angler, tired with a day's tramp perhaps, will pass by, thinking the exertion to fish it far greater than the chance of success, and therein lies your opportunity, for in these places the trout will remain, being seldom disturbed. If you are not well repaid for all your labor it will be strange indeed. The streams in Vermont are generally small, very crooked and well overhung with vegetation, affording many such desirable places.

I have left the matter of fly casting until last because it is an art in itself and nothing but practice, and lots of it, will make one proficient. It is something one has not got to know perfectly in order to catch fish, but a method which can be used at every opportunity, until you can place the little feathered thing just when and where you want to with that ease which gives the experienced angler such confidence.

The whole gist of the matter is that trout live upon, among other things, insects which come down close to the water or on it. The angler is furnishing that feed, or what is apparently the same thing, only it happens to be attached to a line. The bait is simply to drop upon the water in the same natural manner that the live insect would. The nearer to nature you can do that, and with the least slashing and splashing of the line upon the water, the better fly-fisherman you are.

Of course, in thickly wooded places, where the open space is much limited, it will be found difficult, if not quite impossible, to make a cast. In such places it is good to work through the brush carefully to the edge of the water, taking care not to disturb the fish or be seen by them, for, owing to the cramped quarters, you will necessarily have to be very near to them. Shove the pole gently through the bushes and let the bait rest naturally upon the water. Live insects which you may find about the stream are specially good and are very successful when used in this manner

In open country, where there is room to swing a line, it should be paid out on the water for about twenty feet, allowing it to work away somewhat, then, with a quick movement of the hand, wrist and forearm, the pole is swung back while the line is switched behind the angler. Then quickly the action is reversed, with the result that the fly drops upon the surface of the water as far away as there were feet of free line. By elevating the tip of the rod and twitching the line, a very lifelike movement is imparted to the bait.

Do not be discouraged at first. You will acquire the necessary skill with perseverance, and, after a while, be able to cast such a distance, and with such accuracy, that it will be a joy to you forever after, for most certainly fly fishing is the method par excellence.

The Charcoal Burners of the Green Mountains (1885)

THE CHARCOAL BURNERS OF THE GREEN MOUNTAINS.

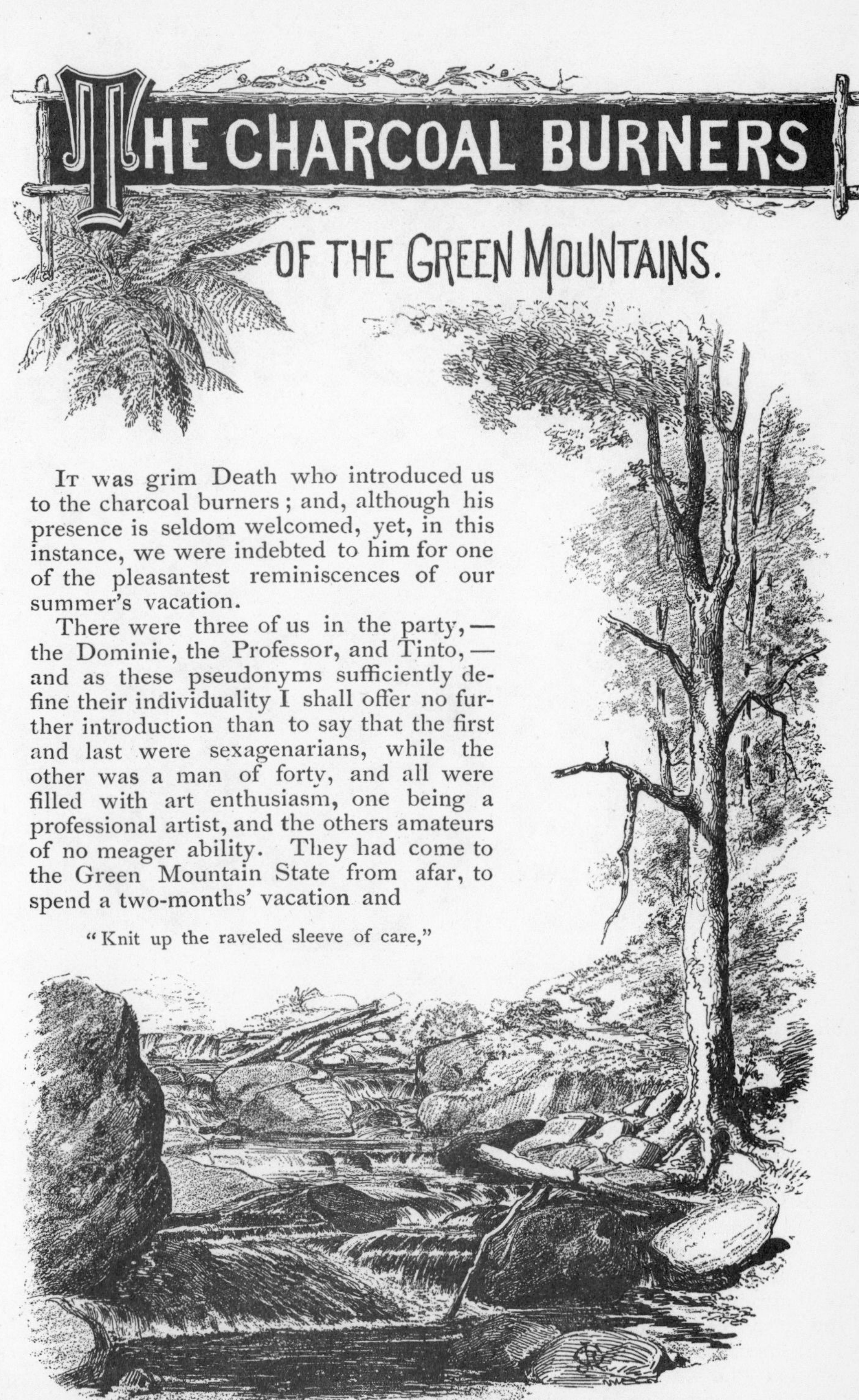

It was grim Death who introduced us to the charcoal burners; and, although his presence is seldom welcomed, yet, in this instance, we were indebted to him for one of the pleasantest reminiscences of our summer's vacation.

There were three of us in the party, — the Dominie, the Professor, and Tinto, — and as these pseudonyms sufficiently define their individuality I shall offer no further introduction than to say that the first and last were sexagenarians, while the other was a man of forty, and all were filled with art enthusiasm, one being a professional artist, and the others amateurs of no meager ability. They had come to the Green Mountain State from afar, to spend a two-months' vacation and

"Knit up the raveled sleeve of care,"

THE BLACK BRANCH JOB.

by climbing its mountains, threading its valleys, following up its streams, and in filling their portfolios with sketches from nature in this artist's paradise.

This was the third year that the trio had spent their vacation in the mountains, and when they stepped off the train at "Danby and Mt. Tabor station," the charming scene around them was neither novel nor strange, and they knew just what to expect. It is always the unexpected, however, that happens; and, as they passed around the corner of the station on the way to their inn, they found the way barred by a group of men who were tenderly placing in a wagon an oblong pine box, evidently containing a coffin, with the intent to transfer it to one of the houses in the village.

Reverently raising their hats in the presence of that foe whom the bravest dread to meet, Tinto inquired of a looker-on the personality of the deceased, and was told that it was a man "named Eli Moore, a sawyer, who was killed yesterday at the *charcoal job on the mountain*, by a log rolling onto him."

"Was he killed instantly?"

"Yes, as far as I know, he must ha' been. He had sent all his men off somewher' else, and, as he wanted a log for some purpose, he went out to the pile, and must have started it while standing in front of it, for when his wife went out to look for and call him to dinner, she found him with a log some sixteen feet long and two foot through lying across his chest, and he stone dead. It must ha' crushed the life right out of him."

Waiting until the little procession moved on its way, our trio gathered up their *impedimenta* and followed the marble sidewalk to the village inn, where they proposed to stay for a few days as a base of operations in spying out the land thereabouts.

Little was said during the short walk; but through Tinto's sensorium that phrase "The charcoal job on the mountain" was ringing its changes, and he had not reached the inn before making up his mind to know more of its meaning and purpose.

The artist is nothing if not observant; and our friend Tinto, in addition to this usual trait, was possessed of a full measure of curiosity, added to a persistency of purpose that had often stood him in good stead; and after an early supper, while the Dominie and Professor took a stroll in another direction in pursuit of objects of artistic interest, he followed the marble pathway back to the depot in search of some one who could post him on the "charcoal job." He was not long in finding the office of the institution, in close proximity to the station, and in introducing himself to Messrs. Griffith & McIntyre, the proprietors thereof, explaining to them his desire to know more of their processes and *modus operandi*. Four kilns, situated on a knoll just back of some sheds, which serve as a freight depot, afforded the opportunity, and in the course of half an hour the artist was deep in the mysteries of burning hard and soft wood in kilns, "knee vents," "waist vents," "ankle vents," "draughts," "sinks," and all the nomenclature which goes to designate and explain a "charcoal job." Before leaving, he accepted a pressing invitation for himself and friends to drive up to the "job on the mountain" at their earliest opportunity.

SHIPPING COAL AT DANBY.

"The State of Vermont has been justly called "the artist's paradise," remarked the Dominie, as Tinto rejoined his companions on the veranda of the tavern in the late twilight of the summer evening. "I know of no State in the Union, and no portion of any State, that presents such a diversity of charming scenery as this favored portion of the earth's surface. From the most expansive view over vast and continuous mountain ranges, to the close pastoral scene, and the multitudinous and charming 'bits' that surround us on every hand, this section is replete with pictures that would honor the easel of any painter."

"I wonder," said the Professor, "that these rich artistic placers have not been discovered and utilized long ago by the artists of New York, Boston, and nearer cities. They seem, however, to have been overlooked in the *furor* for the more *fashionable* White Mountains, Coast of Maine, Yellowstone, or the Rockies; and this favored land is given the go-by by artists, who continue to paint the old scenes *ad nauseam*, while directly in their pathway lies a region whose every acre is a mine of artistic wealth, and every mile is filled with æsthetic rapture."

"Well," replied Tinto, to whom these remarks were addressed, "'sufficient for the day is the evil thereof'" (at the same time holding up two fingers to indicate quotation marks, a habit he had acquired when quoting scripture in presence of the Dominie, to deprecate criticism and to intimate the lack of originality). "When other artists shall have made the discovery of this charming Switzerland, and shall have found how cheaply they can live and travel in it, they will come in crowds; the fashionable world will follow, and then adieu to the charming simplicity of its people, its reasonable rates, and unadulterated honesty. Let us enjoy it while we may, and leave the other fellows to find it out for themselves."

"By-the-way," said the Dominie, "in our tramp after supper we followed up this little stream that crosses the road here by the hotel, and found some charming cascades and falls, and I propose that in the morning we go out and see them."

This being readily acquiesced in, the conversation drifted to ordinary topics until bedtime, when the trio sought their respective dormitories, and slept the sleep of the just.

It was the third day after their arrival before they were ready to accept the invitation to "do" the "charcoal job on the mountain."

"Come, arouse thee! arouse thee! my merry Swiss boy,"

warbled the Dominie, as he rapped at Tinto's door in the morning; "it's a long day before us, and we want an early start."

"What an unearthly hour for a Christian

THE CHARCOAL BURNER AND HIS HOME.

man to get out of bed!" said Tinto, *sotto voce*, as he looked at his time-piece, which noted half-past five o'clock; "however, as we are in Turkey, I suppose we must do as the Turkeys do;" and in the course of twenty minutes he had joined his companions at the breakfast-table.

It was a lovely July morning, and all animate and inanimate nature seemed to rejoice and pay homage to the god of day as he ascended his pathway in the east, and, peeping over the mountain, looked through a lovely pink haze down into the valley. His rays seemed to kiss into life and activity all moving things, from the robin on the hillside to the superannuated old horse down in the pasture; the trees and flowers seemed to rejoice in his coming; and even the staid and sober Dominie felt the exhilarating effects of the delightful atmosphere, filled with ozone from recent showers, and was as playful as a motherly tabby with her first kitten. Tinto and he had been intimate friends for more than a quarter of a century, and the artist and his doings formed excellent butts for the shafts of his sarcastic criticism, which he would not have dared to aim at a less good-natured man.

The little hamlet of Danby, made up of not more than twenty or thirty houses, is situated in a valley between two ranges of the Green Mountains that rise some three thousand feet on either side, and extend north and south for many miles. The range on the west is composed of limestone, and in it is found marble of purest quality, which is worked to advantage, the quarries at Rutland being noted for their extent and the fineness of the material. The eastern range is granitic, and, like all the other ranges, is covered to its top with a dense growth of hemlock, spruce, beech, pine, poplar, birch, and other evergreen and deciduous trees, the former preponderating, thus giving them the right to the title of *Green* Mountains. Along the faces of the ranges, gorges and ravines are formed by the action of water, and are the only means of ingress and egress to and from the interior valleys, for the sides are generally so steep that nothing short of a goat — and he a very sober one — could climb them. Through these gorges there is barely room for the road and the stream, and the former is frequently blasted out of the solid side of the mountain, while the latter — in spring a raging torrent, carrying with and before it massive boulders, logs, and all the débris of a vernal freshet, — makes frequent and strenuous efforts to wash the highway out of existence.

It was up one of these gorges that our trio were to take their devious way to the top of the mountain, and thence over to Weston, a hamlet on West river, where they had spent their previous summer's vacation.

After considerable fussiness on the part of the Dominie, and numerous commands and countermands from Tinto, who, from his having served a term in the Home Guards during "the late unpleasantness," was honored with the command of the party, they were ready to start. The order "Forward!" was given to the driver, a pert lad of fifteen summers, the son of the landlord; and with a cheery good-by to Boniface and several villagers who had gathered on the veranda, they were off for Weston "and a market." Driving through the one street of the place to the depot, they halted long enough to appoint to meet Mr. G—— on the mountain in time for dinner, and to inspect his new stables recently erected by him for the accommodation of such of his horses as may be needed in the valley, or such as may not be able to get back to "the job" before nightfall.

In answer to a question of Tinto's, they were told that the company owned one hundred horses, sixteen yoke of oxen, and frequently were compelled to hire as many more during the busy season.

"Come, gentlemen," said Mr. G—— "before you go up the mountain let me show you how we ship our coal; there's a wagon coming in, and you can see it unloaded."

Walking along a little beyond the group of kilns, the party came to a platform, attached to and in front of a freight-shed, by the side of which stood a derrick and its attachments.

"The track is below the platform, so that the top of a freight-car comes about on a level with it, and for convenience the top of the car is open, with hinged covers, as you see," said Mr. G——.

"What is the capacity of one of these cars?" asked the Professor.

"Well, from 1,150 to 1,300 bushels; we own about fifty cars, and could use many more; we frequently have to wait for the return of our cars, causing serious delays. Nevertheless we manage to ship an average of 100,000 bushels per month, which is about the capacity of the four 'jobs;' this one here; the one on the mountain; the Black branch job, and the three kilns

by side-boards eight inches higher. They ordinarily carry 250 bushels to a wagon, and have hinged bottoms, which are kept in place by a simple mechanical contrivance until it is required to dump them. Straps of iron extend up the sides of the boxes, with an eye at the top, into which the hooks of the derrick chain are inserted, the windlass put in operation, one box lifted from the gear, swung over the car, the bolt drawn, and the contents dumped into the car, when it is swung back to its place, and the other box goes through the same process.

over by the large boarding-house on the other side of the mountain."

At this juncture the coal-wagon drove up to the platform, and the driver made preparations to unload his cargo, while the party stepped to windward to avoid the dust.

These wagons consist of a running gear about ten feet long, and four feet two inches wide, on which are mounted two large boxes, say three feet two inches wide on the bottom, by six feet long, and flaring upward to five feet wide by seven feet long, their capacity being sometimes extended

Such was the operation which our trio witnessed; and, as the dust arose in clouds and blew away to leeward, Tinto remarked:—

"'Dust thou art, and to dust shalt thou return;' I wonder if that is the kind of dust that darkies are made of?"

"*Dust* think so?" queried the Dominie.

"Perhaps it is," remarked the Professor; for if the Darwinian theory is correct, the darkey must be first cousin to our great progenitor the ape; and 'thereby hangs a tale.'"

A volley of ohs greeted this sally, the party proceeded to climb into their vehicle, and, after bidding Mr. G—— *au revoir*, started up the gorge. Before entering it, however, they had to pass through the little hamlet of Mt. Tabor, named for the mountain above it, and consisting of a store and post-office, with some half-dozen neat cottages, all with door-yards in front, in which summer flowers were blooming, and all betokening the thrift and comfort so common to the New England villages. Facing mostly to the south and west, their windows commanded charming views down the valley, and across to Dorset mountain, which at a distance of a little over a quarter of a mile rose to an altitude of 3,300 feet.

"Give me a cot in the valley I love,"

hummed Tinto. What a lovely spot to spend the remnant of one's days, dreaming life away in the enjoyment of such delightful scenery and drinking in the rich tones of the sunsets behind yon distant range"—

"Do you suppose for a moment that, with your towering intellect and vaulting ambition, you would be content to settle down in such a quiet spot as this; or do you suppose that the world would allow of it?" said the Dominie. "There are duties one owes to society as well as to one's self, and duties never clash."

"There's a little cottage with half an acre of ground, and a nice barn that you can hire for a dollar a month," said the boy driver, pointing out a neat five-room house they were passing, and evidently wishing to have his part in the conversation, which he took for gospel.

That settled the matter, and the conversation dropped, for the time being.

A hundred yards farther on they entered upon the wild beauties of the gorge, at a point where once had been a massive dam, which, having been swept away during the last spring freshet, the timbers and logs, mixed in the most inextricable confusion with the immense boulders that had caused the destruction, formed, with the rushing waters that roared and swirled through and among the débris, a wild and attractive picture. In a moment the trio were on their feet and out of the wagon; scrambling about on the rocks and broken timbers; calling upon each other to admire now this view, now that vista. Crossing the stream on the slippery stones, at the risk of wet feet and broken limbs, they behaved rather like school-boys out for a vacation, or college-boys on a lark, than three elderly professional men, who would have smiled at their own enthusiasm could they have seen it with their ordinary vision.

It was evident that the boy driver had his doubts as to the sanity of his passengers, as with half-open mouth and staring eyes he watched their antics and wondered what there was in so familiar a scene to call forth such demonstrations.

"Oh, that's nothing!" said he, as they returned to the vehicle, "to what it is in the spring; you should see it then if you want to hear roaring. There's no water on now of any consequence."

"What is there in the sight of falling water that should fill the artistic mind with such rapture?" asked the Professor, as the trio resumed their seats and the upward journey.

"I think," said the Dominie, who was always ready with his theory, before Tinto had formulated the thought with which to express his idea, "it is because of the untrammeled grace of its movements. Now look at that little fall yonder as it pours over the immense boulder and scatters its volume on the smaller rocks below; here it sweeps boldly to the right under the pile of driftwood which it has erstwhile brought down with it, and then swirls gracefully into that eddy to the left, to plunge again and again in bow-like curves over and among the rounded stones and the débris of its former rage and fury, ever singing its song of freedom. What does Solomon say in his"—

What Solomon said remains unknown, for Tinto ejaculated in a stage whisper to the Professor, "He's got 'em again; we *must* find some antidote for this, or we shall be preached to death;" and the Dominie subsided. A moment later, however, the preacher had his revenge, for his friend exclaimed, "Oh! look there! what a charming picture that is! Stop, driver! I must have that;" and, without waiting for the team to check its headway, he leaped to the ground, and was soon seated on a rock in mid-stream, sketching the scene before him, undisturbed by the Dominie's remark anent the lunatic having escaped his keepers.

They were traveling along the bottom

In the Woods

obliged to yield the right of way, or the frequent halts to "get" this or that charming bit. Ere they reached the mountain top they found their stock of expletives exhausted; and, as they realized the beauty and extent of the scenes through which they had passed, silence seemed the only way of expressing the rapture which filled them.

About half-way up they passed a spot where another mountain stream came in from the left, and were told by their driver that the rugged road along its banks "led up to the Black branch job."

of a V-shaped ravine, in which there was barely room for the stream. The road had been blasted out of the mountain side, and a fringe of trees, left at the water's edge, threw a deep shadow across the bed of the stream, while, beyond the vista thus formed, the sunlight brought out in strong relief the rustic bridge where the road made an abrupt turn and crossed to the other bank; this was the scene which the artist was trying to get for a picture.

It would be tedious to attempt to describe the beauties of this charming gorge, which in every rod of its devious ascent presented a new and attractive feature that brought forth some exclamation of surprise, admiration, or wonder, or to narrate the several incidents of passing the heavily loaded coal-carts, to which they were

Kiln ready for firing—showing the fire arch

Continuing on their course, after another hour's climbing, they found themselves passing between two rows of buildings, and emerging into a cleared and level space of about fifteen acres, which, from the kilns on the one hand, and the large saw-mill on the other, with the commodious boarding-house beyond, they recognized as "the job on the mountain."

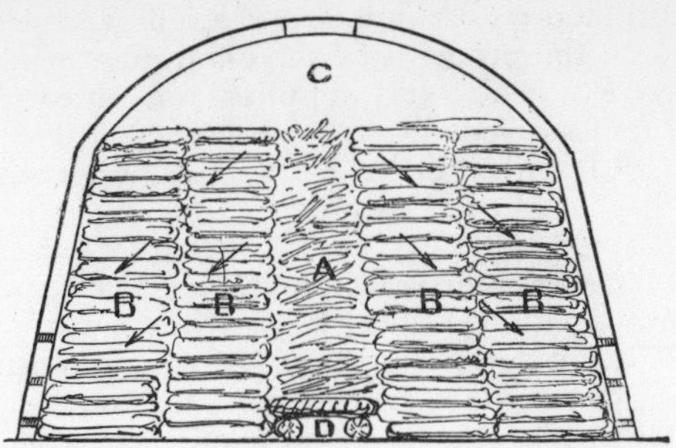

This unique settlement consisted of about forty or fifty structures, embracing a large steam saw-mill, forty by eighty feet, with all the appliances for converting the choicest hard-wood logs into lumber, which is mainly used by a mowing-machine manufactory in Hoosick Falls, N.Y.; a large boarding-house for the single men among the employés; a general store and office, with an adjoining residence for the chief clerk or manager; a harness shop; a wagon shop; blacksmith shop, and a number of cottages for the employés, besides stables for the animals, sheds for the wagons, sleds, etc.; and last, though not least, four large kilns for burning the coal. The houses are furnished the men rent free; the supplies at as near cost as possible; and everything within its capacity is manufactured on the spot by the company.

Stopping at the office, our trio were welcomed by the manager, who had been telephoned of their coming.

Their first objective point was the group of kilns, and towards these they leisurely made their way, exhilarated by the bracing atmosphere of this elevated region, made more pungent by the pyroligneous vapor arising from two of the kilns which were in full heat.

Arrived before one, which, by its open door and the wagon in front, was evidently being emptied, they were on the point of entering when they were startled by the apparition of a tall, gaunt, Italian brigand, which stalked out of the opening, and with the stride of a giant mounted the plank, one end of which was supported on a tripod at the side of the wagon, emptied the shell-like basket which he carried, and, turning upon his heel, stalked back again without giving even a look of curiosity to the trio of strangers, whom he might have touched as he passed. He was a splendid specimen of a man, and better fitted for the wild fastnesses of the Abruzzi, whence he probably came, than the peaceful scenes by which he was surrounded. The surprise of the party was somewhat allayed when they learned that quite a large proportion of the employés were natives of sunny Italy, — a fact which they soon realized in the chattering of the black-haired and black-eyed little picturesque ragamuffins, who congregated about most of the laborers' cottages and ran riot about the place. This brigand was too good a subject to lose, and Tinto subsequently made a sketch of him, which he promised to copy for the Dominie.

They did not enter the kiln, for, upon looking within, they discovered that the coal, now thoroughly charred and cooled, was being raked down, and the whole interior was filled with a fine charcoal dust, in which it seemed impossible to breathe. Three or four men, who looked more like imps than human beings, were breathing it, however, for they were engaged with long iron rakes in tearing down the serried ranks of charred logs, which, as they fell, crumbled and sent up showers of dust, through which the sunlight, entering at the opening above, sent athwart the picture a ray that produced a very weird and startling effect.

While admiring this interesting scene Mr. G—— drove up, and, as it was past noon, he invited his guests to dine with him at the boarding-house opposite the kilns, promising after dinner to explain the *modus operandi* of burning coal.

Now, if the Dominie has one weakness which dominates all his other weaknesses, it is a fondness for the pleasures of the table; and, although his personal appearance would scarcely warrant such a conclusion — for he is lean and gaunt to a degree — the sound of the breakfast or dinner bell has frequently been known to put an end to some of his finest lucubrations, and to check the flow of his most elaborate rhetorical efforts. Knowing his failing in this respect, his companions yielded a ready acquiescence to the call, and in a few moments they were seated at one of the tables in the long dining-room of the boarding-house, doing ample justice to the plain but really attractive food set before them.

An hour later, with cigars between their lips, they returned to the kilns, and their host proceeded, in his matter-of-fact way, to illuminate their minds regarding the mysteries of burning charcoal, as carried on in the precincts of the Green Mountains.

As they walked leisurely towards the kilns, Mr. G—— began by saying: "We own about thirteen thousand acres in this immediate section, and thirteen hundred in the Black branch job. The wood is mostly spruce, which is the soft timber. Birch is hard timber, and is the hard coal, used in the manufacture of barbed wire.

"The larger logs of spruce are sawed up into lumber, and the smaller ones are burned for coal. There are a hundred men employed in chopping at all seasons, but about the first of October we start all hands into the timber, where they remain until the first of April. They are divided into gangs of twelve to fifteen men each, with a boss for each gang."

"Do they remain in the woods at night?" queried Tinto.

"That depends," replied Mr. G——. "Some who are near the mill come in at night to their families or to the boarding-house, while those who are far away build shanties of logs, covered with boards, many of these improvised houses being constructed with runners, and are moved about with the progress of the chopping. They have a cook, and supplies are drawn to them on sleds."

"It must be a hard and monotonous life," said the Dominie.

"On the contrary, the men look forward to the winter season with a great deal of anticipation; although our winters are ordinarily severe, and there is frequently from eight to twelve feet of snow on the mountains, they lead a life of excitement and, to them, one of pleasure. They go to work as early as it is light enough for them to see, and chop until dark, when they repair to their shanties and spend their evenings — and many days together, too, for that matter, when it is too stormy to work — in singing, dancing, card-playing, and thrumming musical instruments of some kind."

"How are they paid?" asked Tinto.

"Some by the day, and some by the cord; and the bosses are held responsible for their proper attention to business. They

Carting Coal down the Mountain.

are paid off on the 30th of each month, when they come in to get their money and have a quiet spree."

"Do they get intoxicated on ginger pop and birch beer?" queried the Professor; "for those, I understand, are the only beverages to be had in this land of steady habits."

"Well, no," replied Mr. G——; "but they mix those liquors with the water from our mountain springs, and that, you know, is very exhilarating, especially in winter."

By this time they stood before the group of kilns, and Mr. G—— continued: "Our choice of location depends, of course, upon the preponderance of the kind of wood we want; and, having chosen a site, we proceed to cut a road to civilization, to haul our supplies and materials. We next build our houses for the accommodation of our workmen, and then proceed to build our kilns, which, you see, are of hard brick. The walls are twelve inches thick, and the kilns from twenty-five to thirty feet in diameter; twelve feet high to the crown, and about seven feet crown, with a circular opening in the crown of five feet diameter. The only other opening (except the vents) is the door, which is closed by a heavy slab of No. 8 iron. The floor is of clay and well tamped, and the foundations are thoroughly grouted before the structure is commenced, as the kilns expand with the heat, and contract while cooling. There are three tiers of vents, or openings, the size of a brick, left in the walls for the purpose of drawing the fire back and forth,—one hundred and twenty vents to each kiln; and they are called 'waist, knee, and ankle vents.' Now, if you will step this way," continued Mr. G——, "I will show you a kiln almost ready for firing, in which you can see the construction of the pile."

Climbing a steep stair-case, our friends found themselves upon a platform level with the tops of all the kilns, and looking down into one of these they saw the wood piled in two tiers, filling the kiln to within, say, three feet of the top of the crown, the logs radiating from the centre, leaving an interior space of about four feet, which was filled with soft and light wood for kindling. A foundation of logs is first laid upon and covering the floor, except a fire arch from the door to the centre. Then the logs are piled as above described, until the kiln is full, when the centre is filled with kindling, and the pile is ready for firing. A rag saturated with kerosene is attached to a pole, and, being lighted, is thrust under the fire arch to the centre, igniting the soft kindling; the door is closed and hermetically sealed; the thimble, or iron circular plate, placed over the opening at the top, and for ten or twelve days the process of charring goes on, being regulated by the vents around the base of the kiln. It is necessary that the fire should begin at the top and burn downward, and for this purpose two openings are left in the thimble at the top, each of which is easily covered with a brick. These are left open or closed, as emergency requires, and the vents are opened as needed, to draw the fire downward through the pile. When the wood is sufficiently charred above these vents, which is ascertained by the smell of the smoke, or by thrusting a bar into the vents, to *feel* whether it is wood or coal; the knee, or middle row of vents, and the ankle vents, are opened in succession, although the lower vents, as a general thing, are not opened; the collier preferring to burn the lower tier of logs in another kiln, rather than run the risk of over-firing.

Mr. G—— having been called away for a few moments, Tinto turned to the Professor for an explanation of the chemical process in the charring operation.

"Wood," said he, "is composed of carbon, hydrogen, and oxygen gases, the latter in proportions sufficient to form water. When fired in the open air it burns with a flame, freely, the carbon being consumed, leaving only a residuum of ashes, or the earthy portion. But when burned in confinement, where the oxygen of the atmosphere cannot reach it in sufficient quantity to unite with the oxygen of the wood, and cause flame, the intense heat liberates the hydrogen and oxygen gases, which go off in pyroligneous acid, which is the thin, vaporous smoke that you see rising from the kiln yonder, and issuing from the vents. The woody fiber, in the form of carbon, remains, and is the wood charcoal of commerce.

While awaiting the return of their host, our trio watched the operations of the men about them on the platform and in the kilns.

The vehicle which brought the logs from the adjacent woods to the kilns was of a peculiar construction, necessitated by the circumstances. It was an ordinary rack, mounted at the front upon runners, but at the back upon skids, which are meant to retard rather than to facilitate the progress of the vehicle, as it has to descend the steep wood-roads of the mountains, where it would seem impossible for anything but a goat to retain its footing. Yet, habit has become so far second nature with these hardy horses that they manage to handle their loads with an *élan* that is very interesting to behold. The most difficult hauling is on the level ground where the roads are much cut up, and upon the platforms where the wood is unloaded.

Mr. G——, on his return to his guests, conducted them to the interior of an open kiln, where he gave them further incidental information regarding the operations.

"You will understand," said he, "that the process is one of charring, and not of combustion, and the converting of the woody fibre into carbon; hence flame is very undesirable, as it consumes the wood. If, through the carelessness of the collier in "tending vent," as they say in the artillery, flame should once get headway, the kiln would explode, endangering many lives. The presence of flame is indicated by that white spot on the wall there; that is an infallible detective, and tells of the carelessness of the collier.

"How," asked the Professor, "do you judge of the progress of the charring, not being able to gain access to the interior?"

"Well," replied Mr. G—— "we have no means of judging, except by the smell of the smoke, the heat on the door and thimble, and by prodding the vents, as I before explained. Nevertheless, although the period of ten or twelve days, during which the charring is going on, is a time of constant watchfulness and attention to business on the part of the collier, continued every-day experience renders him so expert that we seldom have an accident or lose a firing.

"I wish," said the Dominie, "that you would explain more fully the process of drawing the fire down, as I do not fully comprehend it."

Taking a piece of coal from the ground, Mr. G—— drew the diagram of a section of a kiln ready for firing. "This," said he, "represents the wall of the kiln. A is the kindling, and BB the wood to be charred. C is the space left for the gases, and D is the fire arch. Now when the center kindling has been thoroughly ignited and the flame extinguished by closing the door and putting on the thimble at the top, the pile of kindling is reduced to a mass of red-hot embers, and this fire is drawn back and forth, now in this direction, now in that, as shown by the arrows, by opening the vents."

"Yes," said the Dominie, "but *how?* that is what I do not understand."

"Well, the fire works *against* the wind. Why, I cannot explain. I leave that to more scientific men. You will see that these kilns have a northern exposure, and, when the wind is from that direction, great care is necessary not to burn too fast. When it is from other quarters the burning is more regular. Sometimes a *sink* occurs, which means that the fire is drawn down too rapidly, leaving a middle portion uncharred. This is to be avoided, and can only occur through the carelessness of the collier. After the charring operation is complete the vents are stopped, the body of the kiln is thoroughly whitewashed, and the crown covered liberally with coal tar, to make everything air-tight, and the kiln left for two days to cool off. It is then opened, and the coal can be taken out immediately. Thus you see that it requires fourteen days at least to burn a kiln; two to fill, ten to burn, and two to cool. The secret of good coal, however, is to *take time*, and we prefer to give it twelve days to char, unless we are behind our orders, which, I am sorry to say, is generally the case."

Turning to his companions, the Dominie

A BIT NEAR DANBY.

found that Tinto was missing, and, as he was nothing without his friend, who was his *alter ego*, the party walked out into the sunlight to see what had become of him.

It was not until after an hour's wandering about the precincts of the "job," during which they stumbled upon many delightful little bits of scenery, that, in crossing a rustic bridge they discovered his genial face through the attic window of a tenantless house where he was engaged in sketching one of the numerous homes of the charcoal-burners.

"Oh, you renegade!" exclaimed the Dominie, shaking his alpen-stock in a threatening manner at the artist; "here we have been hunting you for an hour or more, while you have been perched in an attic, redolent, I have no doubt, of onions and potatoes, having us in view all the time."

"Well, I knew," said Tinto, as he rejoined his companions on the bridge, "that I could safely rely upon you to absorb the information communicated by our friend, and that all it was necessary for me to do was to squeeze the sponge and gather the residuum." He placated the Dominie's anger by showing the sketches he had got, and then added: "It is time for us to start if we expect to reach Weston for supper," which fact being acquiesced in, the driver was hunted up, the team gotten ready and farewell said to their host, whose pressing invitation to spend a day or two longer with him they were reluctantly compelled to decline.

Weston, the little hamlet where our trio had spent their previous summer's vacation, and to which their attention was now directed, is situated in a depression of the mountains about five miles from "the job;" and although the road was less rough than that from Danby up the mountain gorge, it was wild and romantic enough to satisfy the most enthusiastic artist, and to fill the party with delightful emotions, to which they were continually giving vent in exclamations both loud and deep.

The horses in this section of country are trained to take the most precipitous hill at a gallop, and to keep their gait when going down hill, so that, what with the exciting drive, the bracing mountain air, the wild and rugged scenery, which was now lighted by the declining rays of the setting sun, now shadowed by fleeting clouds; the pleasant companionship and the frequent interchange of repartee, the ride was one long to be remembered by even the boy driver.

"I often wonder," said Tinto, while the three friends were admiring the tints in the sky as the sun sank behind a bank of clouds, lighting up their edges with all the hues of the rainbow, "how these men whom we meet feel, and what they think, surrounded as they are continually by scenes which excite in us emotions that *will* vent themselves in words. They seem so stolid that one can hardly believe they see the beauty which encompasses them, and which we have come so far to enjoy."

"Men see with what they have to see with,"

quoted the Dominie.

"That's Kingsley," said the Professor, *sotto voce*, as his friend had failed to hold up his fingers indicating quotation marks.

"Two men shall stand upon the slope of a mountain looking toward the western horizon," continued the preacher, without noticing the interruption, "where the sun is lighting up with his departing rays a rich bank of clouds sweeping grandly up to the zenith, while broken fragments of vapor catch and reflect the glow of the setting orb, their edges gilded with golden light, which shades off into cooler purple and aerial grays, until the whole atmosphere is filled with gorgeous color, making the appreciative soul leap for joy that God has made the world so beautiful. Between the observers and the sun range after range of mountains catch the glowing light, while the intervening valleys are filled with that warm purple haze which floats and glimmers in the sunlight; and the foreground is made up of such glorious scenery as that round about us, thrown into shadow as the sun goes down, betokening the gloom of night.

"One of the observers shall be a farmer, born and bred near the spot where they stand; and he looks upon the scene with utilitarian eyes, seeing only the promise of fine weather to-morrow, and a chance to 'cut that grass down in the meadow.' The other shall be an artist, who, like yourself, is accustomed to prairie-like surroundings, where a hill ten feet high is a mountain, and who has traveled a thousand miles to witness and enjoy the scene before them, which his companion values so lightly. Their feelings, expressed in words, would be:—

"'What a magnificent picture! How

grandly beautiful; can anything be more charming and complete in picturesqueness? I envy you a life in such a land, — a land replete with all the charms which go to make up an artist's paradise.'

"'Humph! I reckon if you had to make a living out of this paradise, as you call it, you wouldn't think it so beautiful.'

"That expresses it to a certain degree," said the Professor, "but you leave out the element of training and culture. Now, I doubt if even Tinto would be so eloquent in the description, or enthusiastic in his admiration, were it not that he has cultivated his tastes to the point of appreciation."

Approaching a spot vernacularly known as "the Devil's Den," they took a short tramp into the woods until they came to a ledge of bold, overhanging rocks, covered with the primeval forest growth, whence, looking down into a chasm several hundred feet in depth, they could see the tops of trees which had never heard the sound of woodman's axe; and thence up and away across a wide expanse of landscape, embracing extensive mountain ranges, bathed in all the glorious tints of the setting sun. It was a scene to fill the soul with rapture, and so apposite to the Dominie's recent and eloquent description, that Tinto and the Professor exclaimed with one accord, "The Dominie's picture!" It was indeed a wild and romantic spot, and one — were it better known — that would become a favorite resort for the artist, the tourist, and the leisure traveler.

After taking a hearty drink at a clear spring, whose waters percolated through a crevice in the overhanging rock by the roadside, they drove on in the fast deepening twilight, silent now in the presence of that calm, still, mournful beauty, which settles down upon the face of nature as she draws the veil of night across her features. Each was storing away in his sensorium bright reminiscences of a delightful day well spent, whose close found them domiciled at the little inn at Weston, where they received a warm and hearty welcome from simple but honest hosts.

For four weeks our trio of artist friends remained in this delightful retreat in the heart of the Green Mountains. enjoying to the fullest extent the charming scenery, filling their books and portfolios with sketches, taking in large draughts of the pure mountain air, and laying up great stores of health with which to combat the malarial influences of their urban homes. Separated by twelve miles of mountainous country from the nearest railroad station, located seventeen hundred feet above tide water, and surrounded by mountains from two to three thousand feet in height, with no opportunity of spending money beyond the mere pittance paid for board and the hire of a team occasionally to drive to distant points, the days were spent in rambling among the glens and water-courses, the evenings in dreamy discourse or mild discussion on the veranda, and the nights in sound, refreshing, and dreamless sleep.

Sitting on the veranda on the evening previous to the day of their contemplated departure from this elysium, watching fair Cynthia as she rose from behind the mountain before them, it was proposed that on the morrow they should climb to the top of the aforesaid mountain, if peradventure they might discover where the moon came from.

Morning came, cool, bright, and bracing, and after an early breakfast, with alpen-stocks in hand, and with spirits as buoyant as those of boys let out of school, they started. Younger and less experienced men would have dashed boldly at the face of the mountain and carried the ascent by storm, but our sexagenarians chose a more circuitous, if longer route, and, following a gradually ascending road which ran around its base, found themselves, after an hour's pleasant ramble, with only about one-third of the height to master. Taking this very leisurely, stopping now to explore the inmost recesses of a sugar-house, now to "get this bit" of a fence corner, or that group of trees; perchance a quiescent ruminant (cattle being Tinto's specialty); they found only the last fifty feet of climbing at all fatiguing or tiresome. Arrived at last upon the summit, they gathered upon the bare surface of a large rock, which was voted to be "tip-top," and looked about them.

If one can imagine himself upon the top of an immense wave in mid-ocean, surrounded upon all sides by the swelling forms of storm-vexed billows, — and if those forms could be suddenly congealed or rendered motionless, — he would have an adequate conception of the scene upon which our trio admiringly gazed. Away off to the north the range, upon one of the spurs of which they stood, trended away in ever-changing and varied shapes, until the more distant peaks melted tenderly into the cool grays of the clouds, and it became a matter of discussion which was vapor and which solid earth. To the east the undulations were less abrupt, but the eye wandered over the contour of the billowy ranges, resting at last upon the far distant horizon, where the peaks of the White Mountains cut the sky-line and stood plainly revealed against the azure of the heaven above. Looking southward, the landscape gradually assumed a more pastoral appearance, the extreme distance being bounded by the Holyoke range, sixty miles away; while, westward, the Green Mountains surged and swelled in rocky waves, peak rising above peak, range above range, culminating in the shadowy Adirondacks, whose rugged outlines alone separated them from the blue ether about them. The middle distance in each view was made up of

> " Hills rock-ribbed and ancient as the sun,
> With vales stretching in pensive quietness between,
> Venerable woods, — rivers that
> Moved in majesty, and complaining brooks
> That made the meadows green," —

with here and there the bright sheen of a silver lake, the taper spire of a village church, or the lazily ascending smoke of a rustic factory, making altogether a scene so mindful of Bryant's grand Psalm of Nature that Tinto felt in his enthusiasm that no more fitting rostrum could be found, and voiced its sonorous words, while his companions drank in the gorgeous beauties of the scene which had called them forth.

" Verily, our last day has been our best day," sighed the Dominie, as the friends, after two hours of quiet converse with nature and with each other, picked their way through the woods and followed their devious pathway back to the little inn. " Could we take this to our homes, or were we able to visit it occasionally under such bright auspices, we should have no need of the Sabbath in which to worship God, for his praises would be continually upon our lips, and adoration forever welling up in our hearts for the Creator of so much beauty, of so much grandeur."

And Tinto and the Professor cried " Amen ! "

J. R. Chapin.

Old School Street
(1895)

THE

NEW ENGLAND MAGAZINE.

NOVEMBER, 1895.

OLD SCHOOL STREET.

By Henry F. Jenks.

NO street in Boston possesses greater interest in proportion to its length than School Street. It has been the witness of the events that have marked the history of Boston from the earliest times. On Washington Street, opposite its lower end, "dwelt the notables of the town — the governor, the elder of the church, the captain of the artillery company, and the most needful of the craftsmen and artificers of the humble plantation; and at a short distance from it were the meeting-house, the market-house, the town-house, the schoolhouse, and the ever-flowing spring of pure water." The direct way from the precincts of business, where the merchants have congregated and the traffic has been conducted, to the State House and the Common, it has formed part of the route of nearly every procession that has celebrated events of note to Boston as it passed from one quarter to the other, taking in its way, for over half a century, the headquarters of the city government. Through it passed the procession to celebrate the introduction of Cochituate water; that at the establishment of the Franklin statue; that on the two hundred and fiftieth anniversary of the founding of the city; that to welcome Daniel Webster, not long before his death; as well as the annual Fourth of July processions in the days when they were part of the accustomed programme, and those of the Ancient and Honorable Artillery Company as it has "meandered" from its armory in Faneuil Hall to the election on the Common. Its pavements were pressed by the feet of the regiments hastening in 1861 to the defence of the Republic, and by those of the remnants of the same regiments as in later years, returning from faithful service, they carried the tattered remnants of the flags under which they had marched to victory to deposit them in the State House, and to receive for themselves the expression of the gratitude of the Commonwealth.

Up this street Governor Winthrop often walked; and for Judge Sewall it was the natural way from his home near the corner of the present Tremont and Beacon Streets to the Old South Meeting-House, or to the residence of his pastor almost directly opposite the eastern end of the street, on Marlborough, now Washington Street. In early days it was trodden by the boys who were to occupy high places in the councils of city and state; and in later days it has been the natural course of the literati of Boston as they wended their way to the Old Corner Bookstore, and of the politicians as they betook themselves to Parker's. Franklin the schoolboy, Harrison Gray Otis as boy

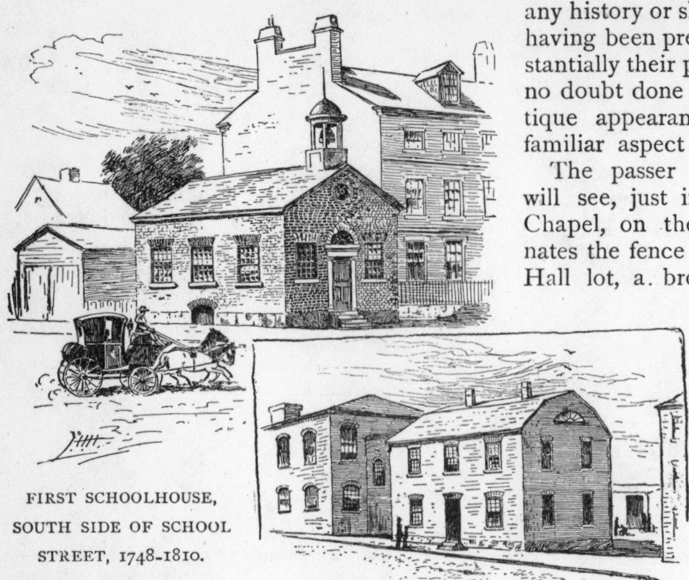

FIRST SCHOOLHOUSE, SOUTH SIDE OF SCHOOL STREET, 1748-1810.

FIRST LATIN SCHOOL, NORTH SIDE OF SCHOOL STREET.

and as mayor, Emerson as the Latin School scholar and then as the philosopher, Holmes, Hawthorne, Whittier, Longfellow, Lowell, Sumner, Henry Wilson, Frank Bird, Governor Andrew, Banks, and thousands of Boston's best known citizens have been familiar figures here. For many years it was the common thoroughfare for the "solid men of Boston" from their homes to their business. Any well-known citizen could almost surely be met at some time of the day in School Street; and even to-day there is no street in the city in which, in half an hour, one can see more of his acquaintances or more persons of distinction among the passers. No street is fuller of memories and associations, none more redolent of the past, nor more alive in the present.

For nearly fifty years School Street has undergone comparatively little outward change. Many of the old buildings that saw the funeral of the victims of the Boston Massacre still survive; and many others show that they belong to the close of the last or the early part of the present century. The street possesses two noted corner buildings which, though facing on other streets, are so associated with it as to seem properly to belong to it and to have a right to be included in any history or sketch of it; and these having been preserved so long in substantially their present condition have no doubt done much to keep the antique appearance and the present familiar aspect of the street.

The passer down School Street will see, just in the rear of King's Chapel, on the pillar which terminates the fence surrounding the City Hall lot, a bronze tablet with the following inscription:

> "On this spot stood the
> First House
> Erected for the use of
> the Boston Public
> Latin School.
> This School has been constantly maintained since it was established by the following vote of the Town:
> At a General Meeting upon Public Notice it was agreed upon that our brother
> Philemon Pormort
> shall be entreated to become Schoolmaster for the teaching and nurturing of children with us.
> April 13, 1635."

From this school, which from 1635 to 1844, more than two hundred years,—unless a recently discovered deed which appears to fix its location for the earliest years of its history somewhat farther north and nearer the present Cornhill is correct,— stood on one side or the other of the street, has come the name by which the street has been known for now nearly two centuries. Dr. Shurtleff says: "School Street was early known as the lane leading to Centry Hill, and very early received its present name, on account of the building anciently erected and used as the first schoolhouse." From the same authority we learn that "it was originally laid out as a public highway on the thirtieth of March, 1640." At one time it was called Schoolhouse Lane, at another, South Latin Grammar School Street, and later, Latin Grammar School Street; still later, all the old designations being discarded, at a meeting of the selectmen, May 3, 1708, it was ordered that "the way from Haugh's Corner leading northwesterly by the Lattin Free School extending as far as Mrs. Whatcomb's Corner be called School Street," and so for one hundred and eighty-seven years it has been known.

Haugh's corner, as we learn from the report on Bounds and Valuations, was the southeast corner of School Street and Washington Street, now occupied by the Richard Briggs Company as a crockery store; and Whatcomb's corner was the southwest corner on Tremont Street, on which a part of the Parker House now stands.

On the north side of the street, in the first century of the town, as we learn from Dr. Shurtleff, there were only three estates, those of Mr. Hutchinson and Thomas Scottow and the old burying-place. In 1798, at the end of the second century, as nearly as we can make out from the Book of Bounds, this land had been divided between Herman Brimmer, Martha Freeman, the heirs of Joseph Green, John Warren, Arnold Welles and John Lowell; while on the south side it was owned by Jane Haugh, Samuel Brown, David Greenough, John Warren, Arnold Welles, the Romish Church, the Widow Badger, Richard Saltonstall, Moses Gill, Widow Scott, Mrs. Dillaway, Giles Alexander and Joseph Foster.

William Hutchinson came into possession of the estate upon the corner extending to City Hall Square about September, 1634; and in July, 1639, his son Edward is granted leave in his behalf to sell the estate to Mr. Richard Hutchinson of London, "lynning draper." At this time it contained about half an acre, and was bounded on the west by the land belonging to Mr. Thomas Scottow, afterward purchased by the town, March 31, 1645, and called the Schoolhouse estate, and later City Hall Square. Mr. Richard Hutchinson sold the property on the eighth of March, 1657–8, to Mr. John Evered, who sold a portion measuring one hundred and fifty feet upon Schoolhouse Lane to Mr. Henry Shrimpton, who fenced it in as a garden and erected a garden-house on it. At his death, in July, 1666, Mr. Shrimpton devised the estate to his daughter Abigail, with three hundred pounds with which to build a house. After her death the property was conveyed to Mr. Thomas Crease, an apothecary, April 31, 1707. In 1711 the buildings on the lot, which were probably those erected by Mrs. Bourne (Abigail Shrimpton) under her father's will, were destroyed in a great fire; and the building now standing on the corner was erected by Mr. Crease, and completed in 1712, which date it bears. Dr. Shurtleff thus describes this building:

"The original building was constructed of brick, and was two stories in height, the roof having a double pitch towards Cornhill (Washington Street) and backwards, with two attic windows in the easterly side. From the main building projected backward the portion of the house that originally served the residents for family purposes. In front of this last mentioned part, and extending on School Street westerly from the old building, is another portion of somewhat modern construction, which has accommodated within its walls many tenants of very various occupations."

THIRD LATIN SCHOOLHOUSE, SOUTH SIDE OF SCHOOL STREET.

Mr. Crease probably used the house as a dwelling-house, and had a small shop on the Cornhill side. From Mr. Crease the property passed through various hands, until it came into those of the Brimmer and Inches families, where it remains. Though used for a dwelling-house as late as 1800, a shop was kept in it as early as 1796. In 1817 the front room of the building was used for an apothecary's shop by Dr. Samuel Clarke, the father of the Rev. Dr. James Freeman Clarke, who for a time occupied the whole building as a dwelling-house, the entrance being through a gateway and yard on School Street, the front door being in a portion of the house that ran back from the main building. In 1828 Mr. Clarke gave up his shop, and was succeeded by the various publishing and book-selling firms that have held it successively to the present day: Carter and Hendee, Allen and Ticknor, William D. Ticknor and Co., Ticknor and Fields, E. P. Dutton and Co., Alexander Williams and Co., Cupples and Upham, and Damrell and Upham. There is no more venerable and honored landmark in Boston than the "Old Corner Bookstore." Its fame has gone forth to the ends of the earth. It has been the favorite trysting place of authors young and old; and there are few of our native writers, or English writers who have visited this country, who have not been welcomed there.

In one of the upper stories of the old building Isaac Butts had for a long time a printing-office; and for many years William Dudley, the veteran haircutter, who died in September, 1893, who had cut the hair of nearly every noted resident of Boston in the middle of this century, and always told you dolefully, as you seated yourself in his chair, how many of his numerous customers had joined the silent majority since you last occupied it, had the corner room on the second story. For certainly half a century he must have had a room on one side or the other of the street, the last being in Niles Block.

CITY HALL IN 1856. FROM AN OLD PRINT.

At the other end of the street, on the Tremont Street corner, stands King's Chapel, which, as the burial-ground in which it was erected is included in School Street, may properly be regarded as belonging here, though facing on Tremont Street, and, while worthy of an entire article to itself, may yet receive a brief notice in an account of the street. The late Hon. Robert C. Winthrop once said: "I never pass the corner of School Street without rejoicing that King's Chapel has survived the ravages of time and chance. *Esto perpetua.*"

About the year 1688 the first Episcopal church was built in Boston, under the direction of Sir Edmund Andros, who took for its site a portion of the old burying-ground. The building, a wooden one, was erected about the time the "tyrant" was sent back to England. About 1710 it was so much enlarged as practically to be rebuilt. It had a square tower surmounted by a four-sided pyramid, upon the top of which was a tall staff, half way up on which was a wooden crown and on the top a weather-cock. In 1748 the wooden church was taken down and the present church begun. It was built of hammered granite from the Quincy quarries, and finished in 1749. It is told that it was so much feared that the building would exhaust the quarry, that an agreement was made that no stone should be taken from it for any other purpose until the church edifice was completed.

The old tower of King's Chapel is a familiar and beloved object to all old Bostonians, and all unite with Mr. Winthrop in wishing that the chapel may long continue to be preserved intact. The interior of the building is dignified and impressive. The roof is supported by Corinthian columns. In the chancel are beautiful stained-glass windows, the gift of John A. Lowell, and near by are marble busts of the Rev. Drs. Freeman, Francis W. P. Greenwood and Ephraim Peabody and Rev. Henry W. Foote, pastors of the church since it became Unitarian in faith; for this first Episcopal church in Boston became, in 1787, the first Unitarian church in America. Memorial tablets on the walls and the ancient high pulpit with its sounding-board give the edifice a decidedly foreign aspect.

THE CITY HALL.

Just east of the rear of the burying-ground, not far from where the statue of Franklin now stands, was the site of the first school, from which the street derives its name, destined in later times to an honorable distinction as the Boston Public Latin School. Founded in 1635, its first master was Philemon Pormort. Mr. Pormort's land was not far from this place, being about where the present building of the Boston *Herald* stands. It is uncertain that he kept school upon this spot, the recently discovered deed already referred to making it possible that his schoolhouse was nearer his dwelling; but in that case it was soon removed here, for Mr. Woodmansey, who became "schole-master" in or before 1650, is found living in a house not far from this site, which was then the property of the town and stood near the schoolhouse, there being but a single lot between them; and twenty years later we find Mr. Ezekiel Cheever keeping the school on this place and living in the schoolhouse.

The lot on which Mr. Woodmansey's house stood must have been that described by "Gleaner" (N. I. Bowditch), who says: "In 1645, on the thirty-first March, there was purchased of Thomas Scotto for the use of the town, his dwelling-house, yard and garden. This is the School Street estate on which now stands the City Hall. Of the original land, portions were subsequently sold off, on which were erected the brick buildings owned by the late John Lowell, William Sullivan, etc., and again purchased, at a much later day, by the city, being now laid out as ornamental enclosures in front of the City Hall."

The history of the Boston Latin School has been so well epitomized in the ora-

SCHOOL STREET IN 1860.

tion of Phillips Brooks commemorating its two hundred and fiftieth anniversary (republished in this magazine, August, 1893), that it need not now be dwelt upon at any great length. No school in the country has had a more distinguished list of graduates. Of the masters of the school while it was in School Street, the best known were Ezekiel Cheever, John Lovell, Benjamin Apthorp Gould and Epes S. Dixwell.

The old schoolhouse in which Cheever originally lived and taught was during his lifetime superseded by another used only for the school, probably about 1704; and this served until 1748, when, King's Chapel proving to be in a ruinous condition and too small for the uses of the congregation, it was desired to enlarge it, and application was made to the town to grant a portion of the town's land for the purpose. Mr. Lovell, the master, strenuously opposed granting the request; but it was finally agreed that it should be done in consideration of the King's Chapel congregation building a new schoolhouse; and a lot having been secured on the opposite side of the street, on the corner of Cook's Court (now Chapman Place), the school was transferred thither. This was not accomplished without many tempestuous town-meetings.

At much expense, and after many vexatious delays, the new schoolhouse was at last completed on the spot where it was to remain, in part at least, for more than a century. Men now living have seen and conversed with the boys who attended school in that building, yet it has been impossible to get any representation of it which could be accepted generally as correct. From the descriptions given by the late Eben Thayer of Brooklyn and the Rev. John L. Watson of Orange, New Jersey, a conjectural representation was made for the history of the Latin School, which is given herewith.

Mr. Lovell was a rigid loyalist, reputed to have been a personal friend of Governor Gage, and after the evacuation of Boston retired with the British to Halifax, where he remained to the end of his life. Harrison Gray Otis, the third mayor of Boston, one of his pupils, tells that as he, a little boy, eight and a half years old, was on his way to school, at seven o'clock in the morning, on the nineteenth of April, 1775, he found Percy's brigade drawn up along Tremont Street, extending from Scollay Square nearly to the Mall, only a few yards from the schoolhouse. He was obliged to go to school round the brigade, down Court and up School Streets, and as he entered the schoolhouse heard the master say: "War's begun and school's done; *deponite libros*."

It was Lovell's boys, instructed in this schoolhouse, who had the memorable interview with the British general about the destruction of their coast, of which this is the true story: The coast was not on the Common, it was not destroyed by the British soldiers, the boys did not complain to General Gage, but with these exceptions the story is literally true. The coast extended from about what is now the corner of Beacon and Somerset Streets, down Beacon, across Tremont, and down School Street past the school. General Haldimand, who commanded under Gage, lived in a house standing in the lot where the City Hall afterward stood. It may have been the Scottow house, or one that succeeded it. He had a Hessian servant, who became irritated with the boys and put ashes on their coast. The boys chose a committee to call upon the general and make a complaint. He heard them patiently and, calling the servant in, reprimanded him and sent him to sweep the coast clean. Later in the day, dining with General Gage, he related the incident to him. Two contemporary letters published in the Proceedings and Collections of the Massachusetts Historical Society confirm this story, as it was told to Rev. Edward Everett Hale, about fifty years ago, by Jonathan Darby Robins, one of the boys who participated in the interview.

In 1810 the county Court House was built of granite, at a cost of $90,000 or over, on the lot from which the schoolhouse had been removed. The main building was octagonal, with wings at each side. It was occupied by the probate office, registry of deeds, and the county courts, and was located on the traditional site of the house of Isaac Johnson, the early settler of Boston, and was early known as Johnson Hall, but more frequently spoken of as the Court House. This old Court House was converted into a City Hall in 1840; and all the offices of the city which had previously been in the Old State House were moved there during the mayoralty of Jonathan Chapman in that year. But it proved too small for the necessary uses, the offices were small and crowded; and as early as 1860 the need of a new building was recognized. The requisite orders were passed in 1862, and on the twenty-second of December of that year the corner stone of the present structure was laid, and the building was completed and dedicated September 18, 1865. It is nearly a copy of a portion of the Louvre.

In front of the old City Hall the statue of Benjamin Franklin was originally placed. This was inaugurated with much ceremony on the seventeenth of September, 1856. A long procession marched through the streets, and an oration was delivered by

FROM AN OLD PRINT.

THE FIRST KING'S CHAPEL.

Hon. Robert C. Winthrop. The statue is the work of Richard S. Greenough. It is eight feet high, and stands on a pedestal of verd-antique marble resting on a base of Quincy granite. In the die are bas-reliefs of bronze representing events in the life of Franklin. After the completion of the new City Hall, the statue was removed to its present site; and in 1879 the statue of Josiah Quincy, the second mayor of the city, and subsequently president of Harvard College, by Thomas Ball, was put in a corresponding place on the opposite side of the enclosure before the building.

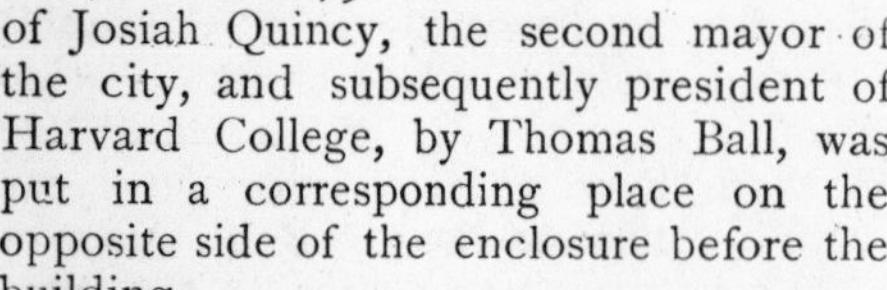

On the north side of this area, not far from the location of the Franklin statue, in the early part of this century, was a line of low buildings occupied in front by the grocery store of Asa Richardson, where the Latin School boys used to wait for the opening of the schoolhouse. In the rear of this, nearly in front of Johnson Hall, on land belonging to John Lowell, about where the statue of Quincy stands, was Barrister's Hall, a small two-story building, and next to it the engine house of Tiger No. 7, a company composed in the days of the volunteer fire department of some of the well-known citizens of Boston, such as Thomas C. Amory, Elbridge Gerry Austin and John Brooks Parker. When the voluntary fire department was changed and each engine had forty men, to each of whom the city paid $50 a year, the young members of the four Baptist churches secured this engine and used the $2000 they received to help build the Bowdoin Square Baptist Church.

Below City Hall stands Niles Block, on the site of the residence of Dr. John Warren. In the entry-way, set into the wall as a tablet, is an ancient fireback of iron, which once did service in the old house. Here, thirty or more years ago, used to be one of the best known and most popular stables in Boston, kept first by the Niles Brothers, then by William J. Niles, and later by George C. Ward, one of the most celebrated whips of his day. The stable was somewhat in the rear of the present main building. The entrance was by a passage a little lower than the present avenue to Court Square. This stable had a great reputation for its large party-sleighs, which were much used to carry parties on evening rides, about the middle of this century, when snow-storms were more severe and the street railroads did not destroy all opportunities for sleighing by carting off the snow as soon as it fell. Many a party has gone to Brighton or Lexington in one of these great sleighs, of which the best known were "Cleopatra's Barge," drawn by eight white or gray horses, usually driven by Ward himself, the "Mayflower," the "Maid of Athens" and the "Constitution," each drawn by four or six bay or black horses.

A little farther down the street, where Marston and Cunio's restaurant now is, used to be, thirty or forty years ago, the grocery store of J. P. and D. R. Palmer, where the choicest fruits, the earliest new vegetables, and the delicious Phillips Beach dun-fish were to be had; and on or very near the same site, in the forties, was the coffee-house of a Mrs. Waterman, who was very popular and patronized by the best people. Her tables were the resort of the literary men of the day. Just below were the coffee-rooms and confectionery store of Mrs. Haven, who was succeeded by Mrs. Harrington. This was a resort of politicians and literary men. Many still living can remember Mrs. Haven's coffee and cream cakes. There was nothing pretentious about her rooms, — everything was simple; but there was about them an attractiveness to the frequenters which retained their custom.

This building stood on the site of a still earlier tavern, familiar in pre-Revolutionary times to the dwellers in Boston, a house which sheltered Washington when he first visited the town, when he came, after Braddock's defeat, to report to Governor Shirley, then commander-in-chief of the forces of the Colonies. It is thus described by S. A. Drake: "Another old inn of assured celebrity was the 'Cromwell's Head' in School Street. This was a two-story wooden building of venerable appearance, conspicuously displaying over the footway a grim likeness of the Lord Protector, it is said much to the disgust of the ultra royalists, who, rather than pass underneath it, habitually took the other side of the way. . . . So when the town came under martial law, mine host Brackett, whose family kept the house for half a century or more, had to take down his sign and conceal it. . . . Colonel Washington took up his quarters at Brackett's, little imagining, perhaps, that twenty years later he would enter Boston at the head of a victorious army, after having quartered his troops in Governor Shirley's splendid mansion."

A little lower down the street, nearer the old corner, stood, about the forties, a small blacksmith's shop, which did jobs in iron work for the neighboring shop-keepers. This has disappeared, but in the remaining buildings to the corner there have been few alterations for nearly two generations, and not many changes of tenants. In one of them, forty or fifty years ago, was a small circulating library kept by Charles Callender; and in another the famous firm of Wells and Knott, which later moved across the street, kept the fashionable ladies' shoe store of Boston.

Crossing the street now, and retracing our steps, we find on the corner opposite the old bookstore the store which for nearly a century has been occupied as a china store, first by the Sumners and afterward by Richard Briggs. In the second story of this building was for many years the tailoring establishment of John Earle and Son, where the uniforms of many of the old military companies of Boston were made; and on the story above was Comer's Commercial College.

The houses above, in 1830, were kept as a boarding house by Mrs. Cecil C. Williams. Later they were occupied by M. Regally, French clock-maker, the shoe store of Thomas Knott, the trunk and saddlery store of McBurney or Holmes, and others. Above the boarding house of Mrs. Williams was the boot and shoe store of B. W. and C. C. Kingsbury; and in the building in which was McBurney's store was the studio of Chester Harding, who painted the full-length portrait of Daniel Webster belonging to the Boston Athenæum and pictures of many other Boston notabilities, men and women. Where is now the tailoring store of Charles A. Smith and Co. was a brick building, a part of which was occupied as

KING'S CHAPEL, CORNER TREMONT AND SCHOOL STREETS.

a printing-office, where the *Christian Register*, the *Youth's Companion* and other papers were printed.

This lot has been one of the most interesting in the street, for it was the site of the French church. At the time of the great persecution of the Protestants in France, many of the refugees emigrated to this country, and before the close of the seventeenth century there were many Huguenot families in Boston. The names of some have been preserved to our own times. What would the history of Boston have been without Faneuil, Bowdoin, Chardon, Sigourney and Revere? Dr. Palfrey says that about a hundred and fifty families of French Huguenots came to Massachusetts after the revocation of the Edict of Nantes in 1685. The estimate is probably too low. The French church in Boston existed as early as this year, and was probably gathered by Pierre Daillé. November 24, 1687, leave was granted to the French congregation to meet in the Latin Schoolhouse. When the new schoolhouse was done, the permission was transferred to that; and for twenty-nine or thirty years this was the meeting place of the French Protestants. In 1704 the congregation asked permission to erect a building of their own for a church, but were refused by the selectmen on the ground that they could hold their meetings in the schoolhouse, which was sufficient for a far larger number than composed the congregation. They were therefore obliged to defer action, and it was not till 1715 that they were able to erect a house of worship on the plot of ground which they had purchased ten years before.

The first minister was Laurentius Van den Bosch, who was here but a little while. He was succeeded by David de Bonrepos for a few months. For eight years then the church was without a pastor, though the pulpit was supplied by French ministers from the colonies of the exiles and by the Rev. Nehemiah Walter, Eliot's successor at Roxbury. In 1696 Pierre Daillé came from New York to Boston, and remained as pastor till his death, nineteen years later. This was the period of the church's greatest prosperity. Daillé was popular with the other ministers of Boston; he was one of the bearers at the funeral of Cotton Mather's wife. The services of his church were liturgical, and the congregation observed Christmas and Easter, so that Judge Sewall could not entirely approve them, as will be seen by referring to his journal, where he records himself as remonstrating with one of his friends "about his partaking with the French church."

Pierre Daillé died May 20, 1715, about the time of the building of the church, and was succeeded by André LeMercier, a native of Caen in Normandy. He served the society thirty-four years, during which its numbers dwindled greatly. He was not a brilliant preacher, but was an industrious worker, yet he could not stem the tide which finally resulted in the dissolution of his society in 1748. The house of worship passed into the hands of a new Congregational society, gathered under Rev. Andrew Croswell, with the proviso that the building was to be kept for the sole use of a Protestant sanctuary forever. In spite of this condition the "temple" was sold, after Mr. Croswell's death and the dissolution of his society, to the Roman Catholics, and mass was said there by a Romish priest, the Abbé de la Poterie, on the second of November, 1788. For a time the church was carried on by missionaries; but they were suc-

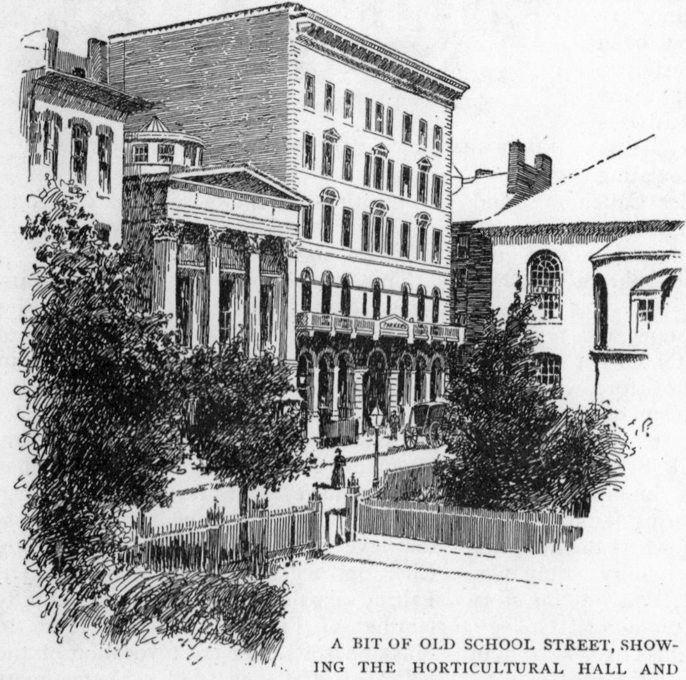

A BIT OF OLD SCHOOL STREET, SHOWING THE HORTICULTURAL HALL AND THE PARKER HOUSE BEFORE THE CORNER BUILDING WAS ERECTED.

THE PARKER HOUSE, CORNER SCHOOL AND TREMONT STREETS.

ceeded by a native Bostonian, the Rev. John Thayer, who is supposed to have been the same as a graduate of the Latin School who had been a Congregational minister and converted to the Catholic faith, who came to the town January 4, 1790, and found the Catholics using as a place of worship this small chapel, which they retained until the building of the church in Franklin Street.

On the next lot above, the Second Universalist Church erected in the summer of 1817 a meeting-house, which was dedicated in October of that year. The minister was the Rev. Hosea Ballou, who remained pastor till his death, in 1852, in the eighty-first year of his age. During his later ministry he had for colleagues two of the most eminent expounders of the Universalist faith, Edwin H. Chapin, subsequently of New York, and Alonzo Ames Miner, who, at the time of his death in 1895, was still senior pastor of the church, which had been removed to Columbus Avenue. In 1851 the old building was greatly modernized externally and internally, raised up and moved back several feet from the street, and a vestry put in the basement.

Next above this lot and forming the corner of Province Street, known in old times as Governor's Alley, were two dwelling houses, which, with but little alteration, became subsequently a provision store and an oyster saloon in the lower stories and a book-binder's establishment in the upper, and which gave place about 1855 to the elegant substantial building erected as a banking house, with offices above, by the Boston Five Cents Savings Bank.

On the opposite corner of Province Street is a building once occupied by Dr. Samuel Bemis, a celebrated dentist, who afterward removed to the Crawford Notch, in New Hampshire, and lived there. In 1830 this building was occupied by Nathaniel Bryant, a well-known cabinet-maker, and Charles Dupee, a carpenter of prominence. For half a century it has been a popular grocery. Above this store was a room frequented by many of the choice spirits who ruled the politics of Massachusetts in the years before the war; here they consulted about measures and men, and arranged political schemes and combinations. This building, King's Chapel and the Old Corner Bookstore share the distinction of being the chief old-time structures now remaining in the street. In the days of the old Tremont Theatre the upper portion of the building was a genteel place of residence and subsequently a first-class boarding house, and on the first floor, unless he who tells the tale has confounded it in his memory with the opposite corner, an oyster room was kept by one of the Atwoods. Writing in the Boston *Transcript*, this boy of the olden time says: "When a hungry boy . . . I used to pass down School Street after a late evening's enjoyment in the pit of the Tremont, with a craving stomach and an irresistible yearning for one of Atwood's incomparable stews or roasts. If after the investment of ninepence at the oyster-room I had a fourpence left in my pocket, I proceeded on my way to Mrs. Haven's and absorbed a cup of her delicious coffee. Then indeed was the cup of my enjoyment full to overflowing."

In the next building above, Bogle, the hairdresser, of Hyperion Fluid fame, with whom the veteran Dudley was once associated, had his establishment. Then we come to Dr. Cooke's estate, which was on both sides of Cooke's Court, to which it gave the name, now Chapman Place. The upper, or western, corner became the site of the Latin School after it was removed from the other side of the street, while the lower, or eastern, was the mansion of Dr. Samuel Adams, who graduated at the Harvard Medical School in 1794. Behind the house, extending up Cooke's Court to the Mears estate, was a long garden. Here Dr. Adams kept two sheep, which, when in sight, were the constant targets for missiles of wood and coal thrown at them by the boys from the upper windows of the Latin School. The large building on this corner, covering a hundred feet on the court side, is owned even yet in the Cooke family, by a Saltonstall of Salem, a relative by marriage. The land on which the Latin Schoolhouse stood once belonged to one Hollway or Holloway, a Tory, who was expelled from the town and went to England.

Cooke's Court received the name of Chapman Place from Jonathan Chapman, who was mayor of the city at the time the City Hall in School Street was first occupied. It was about twenty feet wide, and ran back to the rear of the houses in the present Bosworth Street or Montgomery Place. Through one of these houses was an arched passage from one place to the other. Within a few years these houses have been taken down and the court extended to Bosworth Street. There were several fine residences in the court. One was a large double house, shaded by elms, occupied in one part by Elijah Mears, a tailor, and in the other by Jonathan Kilham, his partner. William H. Smith, the actor, Franklin Loring, a well-known bookseller, and Daniel Morrill, the messenger at the Court House, resided in this court.

The old Latin School was taken down about 1810, and a substantial three-story edifice — which must be well remembered by some of the oldest citizens of Boston, certainly by Master E. S. Dixwell, still living at Cambridge, who taught in it — erected in its place. This again gave place in 1845 to the building of the Massachusetts Horticultural Society, in which was a fine hall for its own and other exhibitions. A part of the old Latin School walls was retained in this building, which was taken down about 1860, to make room for an extension to the Parker House, which had been built a few years before. The late Harvey D. Parker used to tell that Nathaniel P. Willis, the poet and author, on his visits to Boston, used to like to eat a beefsteak in the ladies' café in this part of the hotel, in memory of his frequent thrashings on the spot.

The lot above the schoolhouse was variously occupied. About 1800 it was the residence of Lieutenant-Governor Moses Gill, who died in May of that year. Rev. Dr. John L. Watson says that, as he remembers it, it was a two-story house with an attic. It had a long covered piazza, which in winter time was entirely closed in. The description of

MODERN SCHOOL STREET.

Mr. Eben Thayer of Brooklyn, who when a boy lived in Cooke's Court, is probably more accurate. He says: "It was situated about fifty feet west of Cooke's Court, with a front of forty feet and a door in the centre. It was three stories high, with dormer windows in the roof. On the westerly or upper side of the house was a passageway twenty or twenty-five feet wide leading to the stable and garden. This garden extended to Madame De Blois's house on Bromfield Street."

Mr. Thayer writes in 1883: "I well recollect Lieutenant Governor (at the time of his death acting Governor) Gill's funeral, for I was on my knees on a sofa, looking out of a window opening on the garden, to which the Governor's coachman came to ask for vinegar with which to bathe the horses' legs, the weather being extremely hot."

After Governor Gill's death the house fell into the hands of his relative, Ward Nicholas Boylston, through whom it came ultimately to Mr. Parker. At one time it became a hotel, under the name of the Boylston House, kept by Henry L. Bascom, and was the resort of the minor actors connected with the Tremont Theatre. This, or a house higher up the street, was the home of Jacob Wendell, the grandfather of Oliver Wendell Holmes. The Parker House at first occupied only a portion of its present site; later it was extended to Chapman Place.

Above the Parker House, on the corner of Tremont Street, but fronting on School street, was a large brick dwelling-house, which in 1830 was the residence of Dr. Jonathan Greely Stevenson, of the class of 1816 at Harvard College, then one of Boston's famous physicians, who died in 1835. Later it was the residence of T. O. H. P. Burnham, the antiquarian bookseller, who for many years had his store in a smaller building between that and the Parker House. Below this house was a stable once belonging to the Boylston House, which was at the rear of the estate and remained until about the time of the erection of the Parker House. There was a passageway between the stable and the Stevenson house, which communicated with the rear of the Tremont Theatre, which then stood on the site of the present Tremont Temple, and through which the actors reached the stage door; and it was very common for the Latin School boys to linger about this entrance, to see Finn, Johnson, Mr. and Mrs. Smith and Mr. and Mrs. George H. Barrett pass in for rehearsals. All these estates were finally embraced in the elegant marble Parker House, established by the late Harvey D. Parker, who for many years had been the proprietor of a popular restaurant on the corner of Court Street and Court Square, where part of Young's Hotel now stands.

Charles Dickens, on his visit to Boston, was a guest at Parker's, and a long line of distinguished foreigners as well as natives have enjoyed its hospitalities. At Parker's meet many of the social, literary and dining clubs which are a feature of Boston life; at Commencement time its corridors resound with the songs and merry voices of the graduates of Harvard who assemble there for their class dinners; annually, on the site of the old school, the alumni of the Boston Public Latin School at its table keep alive the memories of "the oldest school in America;" while the city fathers have found its proximity to the City Hall convenient for the refreshment which they crave when committee meetings or the sessions of the different branches of the government have been long protracted.

THE OLD CORNER BOOKSTORE IN 1865.

A New Hampshire Log-Jam (1904)

A New Hampshire Log-Jam

By WALTER DEANE

IN the picturesque valley of the Androscoggin River, in the town of Shelburne, New Hampshire, nestled at the foot of a heavily-wooded ridge with a broad outlook over the wide-spreading intervale backed by the masses of Mount Moriah, stands the spacious house of the Philbrook Farm. Here we agreed to settle for rest and pleasure during the month of June when the early spring plants are still lingering and the resident birds are in full song. All our anticipations were fully realized. We were on old and familiar ground, but we had never been there earlier than the month of July. The beautiful *Linnaea borealis* carpeted the woods, the noble Pileated Woodpecker, the wildest and grandest among its northern New England relatives, screamed as it flew over the high trees, the Banded Purple *(Basilarchia arthemis)* that exquisitely tinted White Mountain butterfly, flew past, displaying its snow-white bow as it sailed along, while in the meadow on a sunny day every stalk of the Golden Ragwort *(Senecio Robbinsii)* seemed to have, poised daintily on the rich yellow flowers, the Mountain Silver-Spot *(Argynnis atlantis)*. Bad weather, however prolonged, cannot entirely break up the attractions offered by these gifts of Nature, but on this particular month of June the fates seemed to vie with each other to render each day worse than the preceding. Dense smoke, the result of forest fires, followed by continual rains, gave us very few chances of seeing the genial sun, but there is a compensation in all things, and what we lost in one way, we gained in another, for we were treated to a wonderful spectacle which fair and sunny days would have denied us.

The Androscoggin River is the highway along which float the logs that form the immense drives that every spring are sent down from the wooded regions along its upper sources. The second great drive was in progress when we reached Shelburne during the last week in May, and we loved to sit on the river bank or lean against the railing of the bridge and watch the logs as they glided silently by either singly or in groups. It was with a feeling of sadness that my mind reverted to the barren stretches in the valleys and on the mountain slopes, left by the woodsman's axe. It is more profitable, as far as immediate gain is concerned, to strip the forest of every tree rather than to leave the small ones. This I was told by one long used to lumbering in New Hampshire. As we gazed at these messengers from the northern woods, we were occasionally attracted by a fine large relic of primeval days, but as a rule the logs were not more than six inches to a foot and a quarter in diameter. They were cut in the neighborhood of Lake Umbagog, the source of the Androscoggin River, and were on their way to Rumford Falls on the same river in Maine, there to be ground to pulp for the manufacture of paper or cut into boards, in the immense mills of the International Paper Company, the Rumford Falls Paper Company, and the Dunton Lumber Company. Each log bears the private mark of the owner cut upon it, generally at each end, with an axe, so that they are readily separated into their respective booms when they reach their final destination.

LOG-JAM AT SHELBURNE BRIDGE

During early June everything proceeded quietly, most of the logs keeping on an even course down the stream. As always happens, many were stranded along the banks, owing either to some sharp turn in the river or to the fall of the water as the season advances. These are all removed later by the rivermen. On the night of June 12, however, without the slightest warning, the river rose eight feet. It had been raining for a few days previously, but no rise in the Androscoggin was perceptible. In fact long continued rains may produce but little effect on the river. The

BREAKING UP THE JAM

cause of this tremendous flood was doubtless due to a cloud burst in the valley of the Peabody River, a tributary of the Androscoggin and flowing into it a few miles above the center of Shelburne, and in the valleys of the main streams near by. No rise was noticeable above the mouth of the Peabody River, but much damage was done to the bridges over that river. The effect of this accession of water was remarkable. By ten o'clock in the evening the wide intervale before our house was submerged, in some places to a depth of three feet, and though the waters receded very rapidly in the night, their effects were seen the next morning in the tell-tale logs quietly resting here and there over the broad meadow far from the river bed whither the floods had retreated. It was, however, on the immense drive of logs in the river itself, that the storm had shown its power. In the hands of this mighty rush of water, the huge logs were but as jack straws in the hands of a child. They were tossed up on the river banks in wild disorder and in places lay in great piles along the shore or on the small islands. Immense log-jams were formed both at Shelburne Bridge and farther up stream, a short distance below Lead Mine Bridge—from which one obtains that view of the White Mountains that Starr King has rendered famous. At Shelburne Bridge the logs were piled in gigantic confusion against two of the iron piers, extending several hundred feet up the stream, and in height reaching from the bed of the river to several feet, in some places, above the level of the bridge, making a total elevation of at least fifteen feet. These are called "centre jams" and they were estimated to contain a million feet of lumber.

LOG-JAM BELOW LEAD MINE BRIDGE

It was here that we had our first experience in witnessing the exciting work of jam breaking. On the very morning following the storm we found a gang of rivermen hard at work. They are a set of noble fellows full of brawn, muscle and courage, and always excelling in courtesy as we experienced on many occasions. Each man was armed with his cant-dog, consisting of a stout maple handle furnished with a square iron point. A piece of curved iron or "dog," as it is called, with a sharp point at one end, is hinged to the iron base of the handle. The efficiency of this weapon in the skilled hands of a riverman is marvellous. The huge logs are "canted," that is, pushed, pulled, rolled forward or backward, or pried out from under overlying masses, and I saw one man work a small log up perpendicularly from the jam by a sort of twisting process with his cant-dog. The extraction of this log caused the easier removal of others adjoining. Indeed, it was astonishing to note how quickly the men attacked the important or "key" log on every occasion. Of course where the jam rests heavily on the river bottom, it cannot be broken up by the removal of any one log.

LARRY HOWARD, A TYPICAL RIVERMAN

As the men urged on their mighty efforts, the logs rolled into the water one after another and at times a large section of the jam would "haul" or settle, often with the men on it, and frequently they were carried down stream on the floating mass. Then the batteau would follow and take them back. The batteau is a large, long-pointed dory worked by two rivermen with oars, paddles or pick-poles as the occasion requires. The pick-pole is a long pole furnished with a square iron point. This square point, both in the cant-dog and the pick-pole, enables one to thrust it into a log and then pull hard without releasing the weapon. A slight twist in either case readily frees it. As in all things, there is a knack in doing this. The batteau is a very important adjunct to the work of a riverman, especially when the water is swift and deep and there are falls in the vicinity. Often the axe must be used where a refractory log refuses to budge and yet must be removed, and here again it was a pleasure to see the axe wielded in the hands of one who had used it from boyhood and never missed his aim.

Another point upon which the rivermen pride themselves is their firm footing on the unstable foundation that they work upon. This is acquired by long practice and the use of heavily calked boots, the sharp spikes furnishing a ready hold. The boots are hand-made and are sold to the men by the companies employing them. Clad in these they run about with perfect ease over wet, floating logs that are often too small to bear them up, but they step nimbly from one sinking log to another and rarely make a misstep. Their skill in riding a single log is

RIVERMAN'S OUTFIT

very great and it was a beautiful sight to see a man standing erect as a statue on a log as it sped down the current. These calked boots, with the cant-dog, pick-pole and axe, constitute the working outfit of a riverman.

After breaking up one of the center jams and a portion of the other, a work which took but little more than two days, the men were sent back up stream nearer the end of the drive where there was more pressing need. A single riverman, Larry (Lawrence) Howard by name, was left to watch the bridge and report any fresh accumulation of logs. He was a Canadian by birth and in every way a typical riverman, strong, active and well-informed on the leading questions of the day. I had many interesting talks with him and he took me over the jam and the floating logs. The drive consisted of the following species:—Pine *(Pinus Strobus)* which is classified as Pine and Pasture Pine; the former, the typical tree of the woods with long, straight branchless trunk; the latter, the scrubby pasture form, branching low down and hence much inferior in quality; Spruce (*Picea rubra*) the timber spruce of the New England mountains; Fir (*Abies balsamea*); Hemlock (*Tsuga canadensis*) with the bark always removed; Cedar or Arbor Vitae (*Thuya occidentalis*); Poplar or "Pople" (*Populus grandidentata*) with the bark removed as in the case of the Hemlock. The bulk of the logs consisted of Spruce and "Pople."

The jam below Lead Mine Bridge a few miles up the river, was very extensive. At this point there are three islands lying at intervals across the river and making four channels. Three of these channels were "plugged" or completely closed by an unbroken mass of logs that extended far and wide in every direction. It reminded one of Kipling's

"Do you know the blackened timber? Do you know that racing stream,
With the raw right-angled log-jam at the end?"

We walked over the logs with perfect freedom, enjoying this new experience, and drew close to the men at work. Here was the greatest activity. It was the rear of the drive when we visited it and all the men to the number of fifty-five were concentrated at this point. The picturesqueness of the scene was greatly enhanced by the addition of eight pairs of horses that were employed in the shallow water in pulling out logs where there was little or no current, and we often saw them working up to their middle, a driver on the back of one of each pair. Chains attached to the horses are furnished at the ends with iron dogs which are driven into the floating logs by a few strokes of a mallet. A single blow of a cant-dog on a raised projection of the dog readily releases it.

THE BATTEAU

The great jam melted away visibly as we watched. There was almost no noise, the men needed their strength for their work, and at it they went tooth and nail, gathered in groups here and there, many of them up to their knees in water, a boss superintending the whole. In no undertaking is perfect unanimity of action more important, and it was truly thrilling to see a row of men drive their cant-dogs into a giant log with a precision almost military and send it tumbling down into the water. It is a life of continual excitement and the dangers attending it are not few. Still such is the skill of the men, and they are ever so on the alert, that I heard of no accident during our visit.

THE WANGAN

The working hours of these rivermen, which include Sundays as well as week days, would stagger the city workman. Rising at half past four in the morning they wash, dress, eat a hurried breakfast and are off to their labors by five o'clock. Lunch is served at ten and dinner at two o'clock. These are taken to the men if they are at a distance from the wangan, or camp, that no time may be wasted. At seven o'clock they stop work and walk back to headquarters which, on one occasion during our visit in Shelburne, were three miles off. Here they enjoy a hearty supper and a long rest. If any man earns his two dollars a day, food and lodging, it is a riverman. They work hard, eat heartily of the best of food, and sleep soundly. One fellow, a strong, muscular specimen, told me that he had worked consecutively, Sundays included, for sixty-five days, and had been wet above his knees during almost the whole time, and yet was in perfect physical condition. They often do not stop even to dry themselves before turning in at night. One man informed me that on the evening before, as he was returning to camp, he slipped into the water "all over," but went to bed just as he was, slept hard and woke up "steaming!"

The wangan, as the camp is always called, is moved along from time to time to keep pace with the men. On the occasion of our visit, it lay in a lovely stretch of meadow close by the cool waters of the river. Four sleeping tents extended in a row near the water. Within each tent on either side for its entire length, stretched a long heavy blanket lying on the fresh meadow grass, each sleeper's place being designated by a large number on the canvas of the tent. These blankets were broad enough to wrap over the men, thus making, as it were, a huge sleeping-bag in which twelve men could pass the night in well-earned slumber. A cook tent contained the provisions, large dishes of tempting hot custard, bread, hot biscuits, barrels of crackers, cakes and doughnuts, and meats of various kinds. I saw a loaf of gingerbread three feet long. The fact that Charlie Tidswell, well known to Maine campers, presided over the cooking, was sufficient guarantee for its quality. A large vessel was steaming over an open fire near the cook tent and we saw the cook bury a large pot of beans in a hole in the ground and cover it over with hot embers and burning sticks that had been keeping the place warm for its reception. A long table protected by a canvas covering was used to serve the meals upon and near by stood a horse and wagon ready to take the lunch and dinner to the rivermen.

One cannot but admire the endurance and courage of these hardy men whom no dangers can daunt. Many of them spend the entire winter in the woods, chopping down trees for the spring drives and, before the ice has left the rivers, are at work in the chilling water driving the logs down stream. I consider it a great privilege to have been in Shelburne last June and to have seen the noble work performed in river driving by the bold and picturesque rivermen.

The Development of Steam Navigation: Connecticut (1906)

THE DEVELOPMENT OF STEAM NAVIGATION

STORY OF THE FIRST STEAMBOATS TO SAIL THE CONNECTICUT RIVER—UNITED STATES SUPREME COURT DISCOURAGED MONOPOLY AND DECLARED THE WATERS OF THE NATION TO BE FREE FOR NAVIGATION—OLD RIVER CAPTAINS AND THEIR EXPERIENCES

BY

C. SEYMOUR BULLOCK

The notable articles by Mr. Bullock have been widely recognized as permanent contributions to history and are being accepted by the public libraries throughout the country as authoritative records in their reference departments. Although his narratives are as entertaining as romance they record the very foundation of America's greatness—the beginning of shipping and the evolution of the commerce that is fast making the United States a world power. The story herewith is more local in its color than the three that have preceded it, being confined to the historic Connecticut River. It is interesting to note that Mr. Bullock's anecdotes are being widely quoted by contemporary periodicals. His vast knowledge of his fascinating subject is also being supplemented by voluntary contributions from old steamboat captains who kindly offer to relate their experiences, some of which are important historical records and will be presented later. This opportunity is taken to express the cordial appreciation of the author and the publishers to those who have contributed data and in several instances valuable manuscripts. Much of this material is being prepared for use in future instalments.—EDITOR

THE era of steam navigation may be said to have really opened with the decision of Chief Justice Marshall declaring that the waters of the United States were free to be navigated by all citizens and that no state could grant exclusive privileges to any company or individual for the use of a navigable body of water or stream. As an illustration of the far reaching effect of this decision we may note that steamboat lines in Connecticut were at once projected for Derby, with the "La Fayette," having stage connections for Hartford and other points to the east and north, and soon afterward new lines were opened to points farther to the east along the sound.

Prior to the decision opening the waters of the whole country to whoever might care to engage in the transportation of persons or goods there had been no incentive for either capital or genius but the Connecticut General Assembly had granted two charters to steamboat companies, the Connecticut Steamboat Company, chartered in October, 1818 and the Connecticut River Steamboat Company, chartered May 23, 1819. There is but little data remaining of the organization of these two pioneer companies but the leading spirit seems to have been Col. C. H. Northam, whose name is so prominently identified with the later steamboat interests of the river and sound. Philip Ripley, who afterward became Mayor of the city, was the Hartford representative of all the early steamboat enterprises.

The first steamboat of which we have any record was a small boat built by a Mr. Kelsey, of Middletown, and the second a little "stern-wheeler," patterned after the boats on the Ohio river of the type that has prevailed so generally on western streams even down to this day. This second boat was built at New York and had two "20 H. P." engines capable of developing a speed of six miles an hour against the stream. On her first trip up the river she went as far as Barnet, Vermont, and from that little town lying at the lower end of the "fifteen miles falls" she received her name. No steamboat had been seen on the river since Samuel Morey had sailed his diminutive craft from Orford to Fairlee and thence to Hartford and to New York. This was more than thirty years before and the memories of it lingered with the old men who had watched the strange thing glide past their doors without the help of either wind or sail. The new boat brought out crowds of people and one from among them wrote a rollicking song to commemorate the event of which two stanzas yet remain:

"This is the day that Captain Nutt
Sailed up the fair Connecticut."

The next report that we have of the "Barnet" is for November 28, 1826, when she sailed up the river as far as Bellows Falls, where she lay for a few days, and returned to Springfield on the 18th of December, sailing thence to Hartford where she was laid up for the winter. At this time she was under the command of Captain Roderick Palmer, of West Springfield, who was one of the best known and most popular men on the river.

During the next year Thomas Blanchard, an inventive genius employed in the United States Armory at Springfield, built a small side-wheel boat to which he gave his own name. The "Blanchard" was built at Springfield and made her first trip on July 30, 1828, when she ran as far as South Hadley. In September she carried a party of sixty from Springfield to Hartford and return and at that time the following "ad" appeared in the Hartford and Springfield papers:

STEAMBOAT BLANCHARD

Being conveniently fitted up for the purpose, and the subscribers having been charged with the command of her, will accommodate individuals or parties on excursions of pleasure or business.

T. BLANCHARD.

SPRINGFIELD, Sept. 17, 1828.

This is probably the first steamboat "ad" in the world wherein a boat is offered for charter to excursion parties for pleasure. The "ad" of John Fitch's boat (printed in the CONNECTICUT MAGAZINE Vol. IX. No. 3) was for a regularly scheduled run established on the Delaware in 1787. Twenty years before Fulton appeared on the Hudson with his "Clermont."

Blanchard was not satisfied, however, with what the side-wheeler could do and during the next winter he built at the corner of Main street and Sutton avenue, in Springfield, another boat which was seventy-five feet long, fifteen feet wide and three feet deep; with wrought iron boilers and engine instead of cast-iron as then generally used. This was a wheel-barrow boat and was "the first steamboat with engine complete ever built in town, and if we are not mistaken, the first ever built in the state or on the borders of the Connecticut river. She is intended to ply between Hartford and Bellows Falls and elsewhere." Small as she was the "Vermont" supported a promenade deck and carried two cabins forward of the engine. The wheel was set away aft on arms or supports so that it might work to its full power in the "dead water." When the Enfield canal was formally opened, November 11, 1829, the "Vermont" was chartered to carry a large party down through the locks to Hartford and back and was then announced as having been built for regular service between Springfield and Hartford which service would be inaugurated on the fifteenth of the next May and maintained throughout the season. In the CONNECTICUT MAGAZINE, Volume IX. Number 3, there may be seen (page 566), a picture of the old "Vermont" steaming up the river from her wharf at Hartford; by mistake she is there referred to as the "Oliver Ellsworth" which was a much larger boat of which we shall speak later.

At about his time there were two other boats built to which were given the names of two members of the Valley Steamboat Company, "William Hall" and "John Cooley." These boats both had "high-pressure engines" so that their approach on the river was as clearly heralded as the approach on the road of a horse that has the heaves or an old man with the asthma, running. The "William Hall" was built at Hartford and the "John Cooley," at Springfield. Both proved good boats for the purpose for which they were intended but the company could not get a hold on the business of the river and in 1832 it passed out of existence.

In 1831 a new boat that was larger and finer than anything on the river was built for Chapin and Deming who had bought out the steamboat business of Thomas Blanchard and for fifteen years thereafter controlled the freight and passenger traffic between Springfield and Hartford. This newest boat was launched April 14, 1831, and made her first trip on June 4th of that year. She was called the "Massachusetts" in honor of the state in which she was built. This was probably the boat upon which "Cousin Boz" made the trip in 1842 so delightfully described in his "American Notes." The roads were exceptionally bad between the two cities that spring and John Sargent, the representative of Chapin-Sargent stage line, asked "Kit" Stevens, one of the original John Cooley company, to captain the "Massachusetts" down to Hartford with Adin Allen as her pilot. She was too big to go through the canal but none of the other boats available could go through the ice or hold to the course in such a current as was running in the river. Everything was made ready and the boat with its notable guest started out on its twenty-five mile sail down stream. As she "shot the rapids" Captain "Ad" stood out on the bow, but during the rest of the trip he was in the cabin with his guest. When they arrived at Hartford, Dickens asked him if he used tobacco and in answer to the affirmative reply he grasped Captain "Ad's" hand with a peculiarly warm grip and said: "It seems to be a general habit in this country." And, notwithstanding all that he afterward wrote about the filthiness of the habit, he later sent to the genial captain a silver tobacco box which is to-day one of the treasured heirlooms in the family. One of the active boatmen of those days, B. M. Douglass, has given us this description of Dickens: "The light-weight Englishman wore a swallow-tail snuff colored coat, short red and white figured vest that was not long enough to reach his pantaloons, which latter were of the true Yankee check and looked as though they had been bought from a North street Jew shop in Boston. Another thing I remember and that was his short, bell crowned hat."

The "Massachusetts" carried two engines, one on either side of the boat, supported on two arches of peculiar construction running the whole length of the hull. The cranks at the ends of the wheel-shaft were set at right angles to each other so as to avoid any dead-point or slacking of the wheel, while making a revolution. She carried a high "ladies cabin," built at the stern, and on top of this elevated room the steersman had his place. It was this arrangement that gave Dickens the idea of insecurity which he so cleverly works out in the description of his trip. The whole story as told by him is so delightfully told that we must insert it here for fear that it should be missed if left only in the "Notes" and posterity be thus left in ignorance of what we had as steamboats on the upper Connecticut when steamboating there was at its very zenith of glory.

The captain of a small steam-boat was going to make his first trip for the season that day (the second February trip, I believe, within the memory of man), and only waited for us to go on board. Accordingly, we went on board, with as little delay as might be. He was as good as his word, and started directly.

It certainly was not called a small steam-boat without reason. I omitted to ask the question, but I should think it must have been of about half a pony power. Mr. Paap, the celebrated Dwarf, might have lived and died happily in the cabin, which was fitted with common sash-windows, like an ordinary dwelling-house. These windows had bright-red curtains, too, hung on slack strings across the lower panes; so that it looked like the parlour of a Lilliputian public-house, which had got afloat in a flood or some other water accident, and was drifting nobody knew where. But even in this chamber there was a rocking-chair. It would be impossible to get on anywhere, in America, without a rocking-chair.

I am afraid to tell how many feet short this vessel was, or how many feet narrow; to apply the words length and width to such measurement would be a contradiction in terms. But I may state that we all kept the middle of the deck, lest the boat should unexpectedly tip over, and that the machinery, by some surprising process of condensation, worked between it and the keel; the whole forming a warm sandwich, about three feet thick.

It rained all day as I once thought it never did rain anywhere, but in the Highlands of Scotland. The river was full of floating blocks of ice, which were constantly crunching and cracking under us; and the depth of water, in the course we took to avoid the larger masses, carried down the middle of the river by the current, did not exceed a few inches. Nevertheless, we moved onward, dexterously; and being well wrapped up, bade defiance to the weather, and enjoyed the journey.

The older citizens of the two cities have always cherished the choicest memories of this boat and of her genial Captain, "Ad" Allen. For twelve years "Captain Ad" piloted her up and down the river with never a loss of life or an accident of any moment and during all this time she was invariably used to open navigation as soon as she could be pushed through the floating cakes of ice. In 1842 she was burned at her wharf in Hartford and became a total loss. Speaking of this incident the *Hartford Times* of May 20th, says:

"The steamboat 'Massachusetts,' one of the Hartford and Springfield line of boats, took fire between 10 and 11 o'clock on Thursday evening and was so burned as to render her forever useless. She arrived at our wharves at 4 o'clock in the afternoon from Springfield, and when the fire broke out we understand no one was on board her. It is not known what caused the fire."

The next boat after the advent of the "Massachusetts" seems to have been the "Adam Duncan," from which, on July 4, 1832, Dr. Dean, of Bath, New Hampshire, was drowned, and this was followed by the "John Ledyard" which ran from Springfield to Bellows Falls. South of Springfield the next new comer was the little boat bearing the name of that city, but this boat was probably the old "Blanchard" rebuilt and given a new name. Following her came the "James Dwight," built by Charles Stearns at the foot of State street in Springfield, and then the "Phoenix" to which some have given the honor of having been used to carry the illustrious "Boz" on that memorable trip and of furnishing him with the inspiration for the inimitable description quoted above, and this in spite of the fact that has been already mentioned that there are yet among the treasured heirlooms in the family of Captain "Ad" Allen the souvenirs given to him by his distinguished passenger on that early February trip. The "Phoenix" was burned sometime during 1860 just above Springfield where she had been used for a number of years as a boat-house. Later on came the "Franklin" which remained in commission till the railroad was opened between the two cities when she was taken to Philadelphia and used for some time on the Delaware. Three other boats, possibly four, if we include the "Holyoke," a diminutive stern-wheeler, complete the list—the little "Agawam,"built in 1837 for Frink and Chapin, which has also been accredited with having carried our cousin "Boz" from Springfield to Hartford, and the ill-fated "Greenfield" a little boat 90 x 18 feet, formerly the "Ariel Cooley," whose boiler exploded at South Hadley in May, 1840, killing three men, among them being Mr. Lancy who built the boiler at Mill river, and damaging property to the extent of $10,000, the only serious accident during the whole fifteen years that steam navigation was maintained on the upper river, and the "C. H. Dexter," the last of the wheel-barrow boats on the Connecticut, of which Captain Edward O. Douglass was the master. Captain Douglass' father had been fireman on the "William Hall" when Mr. Mulligan who afterward became president of the Connecticut River Railroad, now part of the Boston and Maine system, was engineer and Captain Asa Manchester was master. The boilers in those early days were simply iron tubes set on a foundation of brick work with flues running directly from the firebox to the chimney or smoke-stack. There were no glass water gauges and no gauges to show at a glance the pressure of the steam. When a boat or a lot of logs had to be towed above the dam, the fireman or engineer "sat on the safety-valve till the thing went." The only test as to whether there was steam enough on the boiler was that something should move. After the explosion of the boiler on the "Greenfield" some of the boat owners became "a little anxious or nervous like" and it was decided to make a trial as to how much a boiler could stand. The "Massachusetts" was then lying at Springfield and after chaining down the safety-valve the fire-box was filled with all the resinous wood it would hold and everyone stood off to watch the results. As the boiler did not explode it was thought forever afterward safe and above danger.

Those early days have left imperishable memories of never-failing interest to the families that trace their ancestry back to the men who built up an honest sustenance by daring to lead where but few cared to follow. There was Captain Increase Mosely, the best singer anywhere along the river, and Captain Hoyt, the most complete story-teller that ever spun a seaman's yarn, and Captain Peck who sailed the diminutive "Agawam" with a dignity that gave an air of aristocracy to steamboating that could have been in nowise enhanced by all the gold lace and shining buttons that characterized the days of "Jim" Fiske, when the songsters sang:

> **Six Thousand Dollars Cost the Uniform**
> **To Keep the Hero Warm**

Nor would the story be complete without some mention of Captain Jonathan Kentfield, generally known as "Captain Don't," whose pomposity was his chief title to a place in history, unless there might be an additional claim to such a place in the fact that he was blissfully unconscious that he differed in anywise from the men with whom he was daily associated.

There is a rich story told of how the body of a deceased member of Congress was sent up the river from Hartford by a play upon the failings of "Captain Don't." This body had been sent from Washington with instructions that it be forwarded by the first steamboat going up the river, but none of the up-river men would receive it and its presence was becoming quite pronounced. Finally one of the clerks, who knew the vulnerable place, approached "Captain Don't" with a story of a congressman who had died in Washington and whose body had been sent north with directions that it should be forwarded to its destination by the oldest, most experienced steamboat man on the river. It was a fatal shot, finding and piercing the undipped spot of "Captain Don't" who cried out to his crew: "Do you hear that, boys? How the people in Washington knew that I was the oldest and most experienced man on the river, God only knows, I don't, but it's God Almighty's truth, so we'll just drop down and take the old fellow on board." Thus by guile was the distinguished Congressman gotten onto the windward side of the little boat and the crew for the whole voyage drank to the health of "Captain Don't" in a vain effort to forget that there was on board with them a man that had been a long time dead.

Steamboating south of the Capitol City was begun at nearly the same time that the first attempts were made to inaugurate the small lines of which we have just spoken. The "Fulton," under Captain Bunker, had sailed up the river some ten years earlier (see Vol. X. No. 1), and some other boats had made excursion trips from New Haven, but it was not until the "Oliver Ellsworth" was built in New York in 1824, by Webb and Allen, for the Connecticut River Steamboat Company, that anything like a regular line of communication between New York and Hartford was attempted. Her first trip from New York to Hartford was made on May 6, 1824. The "Oliver Ellsworth" which was one of the first steamboats to have a cast-iron boiler was one hundred and twenty-seven feet long and thirty-six feet wide and eight feet deep. She had a "gents cabin forward with sixteen births (*sic*) and a dining cabin fifty-four feet in length, containing thirty births, a ladies' cabin on deck, twenty-six feet long, with sixteen births." Altogether she was a well-finished, well-furnished, schooner-rigged vessel of about 230 tons, with a shapely-set bowsprit, a finely-carved figure-head and a mass of scroll-work, all across the stern. The New York *Evening Post* says of her: "On the whole, she is a beautiful and well-fastened vessel, with a covered promenade." She was commanded at first by Captain Daniel Havens, of Norwich, who had formerly run the "Experiment" (a small boat that made a few trips between Hartford and New York, and later connected with the "Oliver Ellsworth" at Saybrook for new London), still later by Captain Stow of Middletown and then by Captain Henry Waterman, Jr. Stage connections were made at Calve's Wharf, in Lyme, for New London and the East and at Ely's Landing for Norwich. At Hartford stages were lined up waiting for the arrival of the boat and these were rushed off with the mails and passengers for points north and east in direct connection with coaches that touched almost every

"CHIEF JUSTICE MARSHALL" STEAMED UP CONNECTICUT RIVER IN 1833 AND RECEIVED AN OVATION FROM THE PEOPLE AT HARTFORD

"WATER-WITCH"—CAPTAINED BY ONE OF THE VANDERBILTS AND IN THE CONNECTICUT RIVER SERVICE IN 1834

"SPLENDID" — LARGEST AND FASTEST BOAT ON THE SOUND IN EARLY THIRTIES—BUILT IN 1832

WITH WIND AND CURRENT—JUST OFF THE CONNECTICUT RIVER

place of any size in the upper part of the state except such places as could be more easily reached by taking the smaller boats to Springfield and travelling from there in coaches to one's destination. In the best days of this service the stage-coach time to Boston from Hartford was advertised as being but five hours.

On her regular trip to New York on August 18, 1826, the "Oliver Ellsworth" carried four hundred passengers who were landed at the other end of the route in less than eighteen hours from the time the lines were cast off at Hartford. The trip of March 22, 1827, was one of the most memorable in the early history of navigation on the Sound. Just after passing Saybrook light on her way to New York the boiler exploded and many of the passengers were scalded by the escaping steam. Mr. Stephen Lockwood, of New York City, who had been to Hartford as a delegate from the Brick Church to the installation of the Reverend Henry Spring, died from the effects of his burns as did also one of the deck hands, William Rich, who was buried at Saybrook. A strong wind was blowing at the time which caused the boat to roll uncomfortably but after quiet had been restored, the Reverend Gardiner Spring, D. D., gathered the remaining passengers together and offered prayers of thanksgiving for their escape from a watery grave. This was the first steamboat disaster on the waters of Long Island Sound. The "Oliver Ellsworth" was afterward towed to New York by the steamboat "McDonough," a sister boat that had come from the ways a year before and ran on the Connecticut for several seasons and was then sold in 1834 for service on the coast of Maine. It is said that the legislature was in session in Hartford at the time of this terrible accident and that with the first notes of the news the next morning after the accident a post-rider rode up on his lathered horse and leaped from his saddle so full of excitement that he broke into the assembly hall with the cry: "Sister Meaker, the Elliver Ollsworth biled her buster! biled her buster!"

The "McDonough," which cared temporarily for all the business of the company, was named for Commodore Thomas McDonough, the hero of Lake Champlain, whose good judgment had led him into Connecticut to find a wife. He married into one of Middletown's best families and at his death was brought back there and buried in the old cemetery overlooking the river.

When Captain McDonough, whose father had been a major in the Continental Army, knelt on the deck of the "Saratoga" and asked the blessing of Heaven upon the arms of his men, there was a young man in his fleet who in after years had much to do with revolutionizing the navies of the world. At the meeting of the board that finally authorized the building of the "Monitor," a triumph of Connecticut perseverance and skill of which we shall write later, the chairman was Commodore Joseph Smith who was in the fight on Lake Champlain with Commodore McDonough. From him we have a most beautiful story of the unflinching valor of womanhood which, even though it has nothing to do with steamboats, must be given a place here that it may be handed down to the generations yet unborn as a holy heritage. As Commodore Smith tells the story there was on board the "Eagle," one of the ships in the American fleet on which there were thirteen killed and twenty wounded, a sailor who was accompanied by his wife. Early in the fight the husband was killed and his bleeding body was laid on the "berth-deck" where the wife found it and tried to wipe away some of the blood. One by one in the fight that lasted two hours and a half, the cabin boys were killed or so wounded as to be unfitted for duty and this little Connecticut woman stepped into the breach and began passing powder from the magazine to the guns, stepping each time over the mangled, bleeding corpse of her husband. Her name is lost to history and even to tradition but the act itself is one of the priceless gems that the Present has inherited from the Past.

But we must get back to the "Oliver Ellsworth" which we left with an exploded boiler and out of service waiting for repairs. When the "Oliver Ellsworth" came back onto her run with the "McDonough," she was like a new boat. Fare by either boat to New York was placed at $4.50, meals not included. On one of her very first trips, when she had a full list of passengers, the "Oliver Ellsworth" was run onto Coot Bar, just north of the present Stratford light (there was no light there then), and the citizens of that quaint old town rallied with scoops and shovels of all kinds and dug a "ship-canal" through which she sailed into deep water at the next high tide. Among those who worked hardest on this canal was a deaf and dumb lad to whom the predicament of a steamboat so far off her course and in such a plight appealed as if it were some injured living thing. When the captain offered him, in com mon with the others, a silver dollar for his work, he at first refused the proffer but later went back and in his sign language asked for the dollar which he carried home as a memento of the day's experience.

In 1830 the "Victory," a small boat with boilers on her guards, on the Steven's plans, which had been built at Albany two years before, came onto the Connecticut to open an opposition line from Hartford. She was only a hundred and thirty-nine feet long, twenty-five feet wide and nine feet deep, but her coming threw everything into a turmoil and precipitated a rate war that culminated in a threat to carry passengers to New York for nothing if the old line did not come to terms. There was at this time a rate of twenty-five cents with meals included and the purser tells us that a lean, lanky Yankee came up to the office window and asked how much would be thrown off from the fare if he furnished his own meals. The story goes farther and tells us that when he learned there would be no rebate he sat down to the table and ate enough for three ordinary men. But such a warfare could not be kept up forever and in a short time the little interloper left the river and returned to the Hudson where she ran with the "General Jackson," an old boat on which Captain W. Coit of Norwich had begun steamboating in 1820 and which in 1835 was running from Saybrook to Sag Harbor, New London and Norwich in connection with the Hartford boats. In 1838, after having run for a few years as a towboat, the "Victory" was broken up and her engine taken out and placed in the "Red

WHERE THE RIVER ENTERS LONG ISLAND SOUND

"LEXINGTON"—ANOTHER VANDERBILT STEAMBOAT THAT BROKE INTO THE KEEN RIVALRY OF 1834—DESTROYED BY FIRE, 1840, WITH ITS PASSENGERS—PAINTED FOR CAPT. JOHN BROOKS, 1838

Jacket," a small boat of 158 tons built at Grand Island for service on the Niagara river.

When the season of 1833 opened three boats, the "Oliver Ellsworth," the "Chief Justice Marshall" and the McDonough" were running from Hartford to New York as one line. Later the "Oliver Ellsworth" went to the Hudson river as part of the Swiftsure Line, an innovation brought about by the frequency of boiler explosions and of which we shall have something to say when we come to the part that Connecticut had in the development of steamboating on that most magnificent of all the navigable waters of the world.

A Government report on steam engines in 1838 states that the "Oliver Ellsworth" was running as a towboat on the Hudson and as late as 1851 Tredgold gives her a place there, still serving as a towboat but after that she disappears.

When the "Chief Justice Marshall" came into Hartford harbor, under the command of Captain Jabes Howes, she was given a welcome that amounted almost to an ovation. She had established a "record-run" on the Hudson of fourteen hours and a half to Albany and everyone was curious to see the "race horse of the North river." In the great naval parade on the Hudson that was arranged for La Fayette, who had just visited Hartford and sailed thence to New York on the "Oliver Ellsworth," this boat was given the place of honor at the right of the line. She was at this time under the command of the Captain Sherman whose boat, the "Burlington," on Lake Champlain, called forth such a warm testimonial from Dickens when he visited us in 1842. At the time of this parade a set of dishes was made for the "Troy Line" and from one of these the illustration of the boat given herein was taken. To the person who can read history in steamboat pictures there is a whole volume in this dish. There are no masts setting the date when the boat was built, for steamboats were all built with masts until 1831, but the "sky-covered pilot house," which was the only known kind till after Captain Beecher had rigged up a "suspended chicken coop" on the "United States," when the enclosed pilot house came into being for all boats in this country, though in the Old World the man at the wheel is yet exposed to the inclemencies of the weather, sets the date for the early thirties Finally, there is the name of the captain worked into the pennant, fully as important a feature in those days when people did not care what boat they had to travel on if they only knew the captain, and the "landing-line" with the small boat by which passengers were set ashore under certain restrictions of the state laws until a party was dumped into the river at Poughkeepsie and drowned when the regulations, which read as follows, were repealed:

> When a passenger is to be landed from a steamboat not so near the shore that he can pass from the boat to the shore, he is not suffered to go into a small boat for the purpose of being landed, until such small boat be immediately afloat and wholly disengaged from the steamboat, except by a painter; while getting into the small boat, and from the steamboat, the engine of the steamboat is stopped; and also when taken on board a small boat, belonging to a steamboat, while such small boat is at the shore, and until the passenger be on board the steamboat; except when the motion of the engine is necessary to give sufficient force to carry the small boat to the shore; or to keep the steamboat in proper direction, or to prevent her from drifting, or being driven on shore.

Passengers may be landed in a small boat, by means of a line, and boats on the shore, with passengers, may be drawn to a steamboat, by means of a line, hauled in by hand; but in no case may the line be attached to, or hauled in, by the machinery of the steamboat.

In every small boat, while landing or receiving a passenger, there is kept a pair of suitable oars, and in the night, a signal is given, from the small boat, at the shore, by horn or trumpet, to apprise those having charge of the steamboat, that the small boat having landed, or received her passengers, is ready to leave the shore.

If a line used for the purpose of landing or receiving passengers be attached, in any way, to the machinery of a steamboat, or the small boat be hauled in by means of such machinery, the master is guilty of misdemeanor, punishable by fine not exceeding $250, or imprisonment of not more than three months, or both, at the discretion of the court.

The "Chief Justice Marshall" continued on the Hartford run until she was lost on her way from New York in the awful gale of April 28, 1835. From a contemporary chronicler we learn that "she had lost her smoke stack and steam pipes and had cast anchor in the mouth of the Connecticut river, with eighteen fathoms of chain, and hoped to ride out the gale; but having sprung a leak, and the water in the hold gaining on them, they got up a gib and veered about in the hope of reaching New Haven Harbor. This however was found impossible, the wind having shifted to the S. W. She drifted about nearly unmanageable till nearly 12 o'clock when she struck shore one mile east of New Haven lighthouse, at high tide. The pilot, Hascall, cut himself adrift in a small boat fifty yards from shore with a view to affect his own safety, but when about two rods from the shore his boat was swamped and he was drowned. All the passengers and the rest of the crew got to shore safely." In the daily paper during July there is an announcement that the "hull of the 'Chief Justice Marshall,' with or without the boiler, will be sold at public auction on Wednesday, August 5, 1835, on the shore one-half mile east of New Haven Light." The "New England" had dragged her anchors in the heavy seas, but finally got a good hold off Sands Point and successfully weathered the gale.

The advent of the "Chief Justice Marshall" had opened up the old

"CLEOPATRA"—ONE OF THE FASTEST AND MOST POPULAR VANDERBILT STEAMBOATS IN THE TRAFFIC WAR OF 1836

scores and soon Captain Jacob Vanderbilt, a brother of the greater "Commodore," appeared with the "Water Witch." Connected with this little boat is a story of a people's attempt to free themselves from the grasp of a growing monopoly,—a story worth telling. Commodore Vanderbilt was at that time running his "Westchester," which later came onto the sound, on a route that had been started between Peekskill and New York. He had monopolized everything in the way of available boats and shipping facilities and one of the leading citizens of the town proposed that an association should be organized to build and run rival boats in the interest of the farmer and shippers. Subscribers were found all along the river and the "Water Witch" was the result of the agitation. This was in 1832 and the little craft ran on that run between New York and Peekskill until she was bought up and sent to the Connecticut in 1834. When she left the Hudson her place was temporarily taken by the "General Jackson," which, as we have stated, was in 1835 running from Saybrook to Sag Harbor, New London and Norwich in connection with the "New England" of the Hartford line. After the "General Jackson" returned to the Hudson, for she seems to have run upon every short

"TRAVELLER"—BUILT IN 1845 FOR COMMODORE VANDERBILT AND CARRIED THE MAILS UNTIL BEATEN BY RAILROAD COMPETITION

route that was ever opened, she was put onto the Peekskill run again and in going up the river one of her boilers exploded while lying at the wharf at Grassy Point, killing twelve persons and injuring some fourteen or fifteen more and Daniel Drew sent at once for the "Water Witch" to take her place. This seems to be the first of Drew's ventures in the steamboat world and the last of the "Water Witch" on the Connecticut, though she is said to have run for a little while to New Haven. As late as 1849 she ran with the "Cinderella" on the run between New York and Elizabeth, New Jersey.

At first the "Water Witch" and the "New England" were announced for day trips to New York but later the two companies seem to have come to some kind of an understanding for the announcement is made that the "Water Witch" will run at night and the "New England" will maintain a day schedule. Both boats are then represented by the same agents and all fighting stops. But this arrangement did not hold long and before the season closed the "Water Witch" was leaving Hartford three times a week at 5 o'clock and the "New England" was leaving on the same days at 2 o'clock. In September Vanderbilt comes out with a card headed "No Monopoly" and adds the "Lexington" to the service given by the "Water Witch," dropping the fare to two dollars which rate is met by the other boat.

The "New England" was a new boat with two copper boilers and was considered one of the best on the sound and called forth a great deal of praise as she steamed down the river on her initial trip. On the evening of October 9, 1833, when just off Essex, both boilers exploded, almost at the same instant, causing the death of fifteen passengers and the serious scalding of ten or twelve more. A rigid investigation was made and it was reported that no one was to blame for the catastrophe. After repairs had been made she came onto the route again for a short time, under Captain Memenon Sanford, and in 1837 she was sold "down East" for service on the Boston-Portland route.

In 1834 at the annual meeting of the stockholders of the Connecticut River Steamboat Company, and of the the Hartford Steamboat Company, owners of the steamboats "New England" and "Chief Justice Marshall," the following votes were passed:

Voted: That in the opinion of this meeting it is inexpedient to keep, or to allow to be kept, any ardent spirits on board the boat belonging to this company.

Voted: That the directors of this company be and they are hereby requested not to allow any ardent spirits to be kept for sale or use on board of the boat." Hartford, January 25, 1834.

The next new boat on the line was the "Bunker Hill," built by Post and Griswold at New Haven in 1835. When she first came from the ways she was a hundred and ninety-two feet long, twenty-two and a half feet wide and eight and a half feet deep. She had a beam engine, built by William Kemble of the West Point Foundry, that had a cylinder forty-four inches in diameter and an eleven foot stroke of piston and developed "145

H. P." When she first came onto the water she proved to be so "crank," the sailor's term for a boat that does not stand up well, that she had to be put back onto the ways, cut in two and lengthened. Her re-appearance in 1836 found Captain Memenon Sanford in command, under whom she made a few trips to and from Hartford and then ran as an opposition boat on the Providence route cutting the fare to $8.00. She was on this run only a very short time and then came back onto the river where she ran under Captain Harrison against the "Lexington." In 1842 she ran onto Cow Neck, in Oyster Bay, and became a complete wreck. Her engine and fittings were taken out and placed in the rebuilt "Globe" which came onto the river the next season.

The coming onto the sound of the "Lexington," which had been built by Bishop and Simonson in 1834, was really Vanderbilt's first tossing of the gauntlet into the steamboat circles, although he had owned the "Nimrod" and the "Westchester," of which more anon, when they first came over this way. At the time of the "Lexington's" appearance there were four boats running between New York and Providence. The "President" and the "Ben Franklin," looking after the interests of one company and the "Boston" and the "Providence," caring for the business of the opposition. (The "Connecticut" seems to have left the sound in 1833 and, like the "Chancellor Livingston," to have been taken east to run between Portland and Boston. When the latter sank in Boston harbor, in 1834, her boilers and engine were recovered and the engine was placed in the new steamer "Portland," her successor on the route that had taken so many of the successful Connecticut river boats). For the first four months after her appearance on the Providence run, the "Lexington" ran as a day boat, leaving New York on Tuesday, Thursday and Saturday, with direct connections by rail for Boston and the East, and Providence on the alternate days. The fare was fixed at four dollars with meals extra. The old lines at once lowered their rate to five dollars and furnished meals. But the new comer could not be frightened from her position and Vanderbilt instead of withdrawing his rate announced a round-trip ticket for the one-way fare. This was the beginning of excursion rates for regular service.

"STATE OF NEW YORK"—CAME ONTO THE CONNECTICUT RIVER IN 1866—SUNK IN 1881, AND LATER RAISED

During the little while that the "Lexington" was running on the Connecticut there still rankled the memory that she was faster than anything that the opposition companies had to pit against her and an order was given to William Brown, of New York, to build a boat that could beat her, regardless of cost. As a result there came out the "Narragansett," but she was a disappointment as either he "Lexington" or the "Cleopatra," another Vanderbilt boat, could easily run away from her and a second boat was ordered which was named the "John W. Richmond." So confident were her builders and owners that she was the fastest thing afloat that they offered to give Vanderbilt $60,000 for his boat if she should prove to be the faster of the two vessels. After months of "big talk" and little real "fight" the Providence people took the "Lexington," which had been fitted at this time with staterooms, for a fig-

"COLUMBIA"—ON THE RIVER IN 1882, DURING A PERIOD WHEN THE RIVALRY OF STEAMBOAT NAVIGATION HAD SUBSIDED-

ure somewhere near to $72,000 and two years later the boat was lost. She had started from New York for Stonington with a full list of passengers and a large cargo of freight, including a lot of silver bullion and a consignment of cotton. When off Eaton's Neck, about seven-thirty in the evening, there was an alarm of fire and before any help could reach the doomed craft, whose outlines could be clearly seen from the shore in the awful glare, nearly all on board had perished. The last survivor of the three or four who were rescued died recently at his home in Providence, but as the story belongs to another chapter we shall leave it just as it is for the present and get back again to our text.

The fare at the time the "Lexington" came onto the river was cut to a dollar for through passengers and fifty cents for passengers to Saybrook and way landings, and this latter rate was afterward cut in half. May 28, 1836, the "Cleopatra," another Vanderbilt boat, is announced under command of Captain Reynolds, and the "Lexington" is running under Captain Vanderbilt, with a dollar fare to New York, afterward raised to two dollars on the day the "Bunker Hill" is on the other end of the line. The new line announces that their boats will sail promptly at two o'clock and the old line comes out with an announcement that the "Bunker Hill" "will leave from two to five minutes after 2 o'clock to prevent the reckless destruction of their property and protect their passengers from unnecessary dangers." Later the "Bunker Hill" changes its time to 12 o'clock, and the new line announces that the "Cleopatra" will leave "precisely at 12 o'clock." In September the "Emerald," which in 1838 is on the Poughkeepsie route, came onto the river for a few trips but when the season closes the "Bunker Hill" and the "Lexington" are there alone to close the fight.

When navigation opens in 1837 the "Bunker Hill" is there with the "Cleopatra" and the fight is renewed. The "Clifton," a new boat, is now announced as making connection at Saybrook for points farther east and this arrangement continues throughout the season and until November when it is announced that the "Thorn" will carry passengers from Hartford to Saybrook where they will be taken on board the "Norwich" for New York. The hatchet seems to have been now buried, even if the handle stuck up a little above the ground, for when the next year opens the "Bunker Hill" and the "Cleopatra" appear on the same line and the two agencies are

"CITY OF LAWRENCE"—REPLACED THE "GRANITE STATE" WHICH WAS DESTROYED BY FIRE AT GOODSPEED'S LANDING IN 1883—BUILT IN 1867

consolidated with both the old agents in active service. On the fifth of November, 1841, the "Bunker Hill," which was valued at $30,000, ran onto the rocks opposite Cornfield Point, three miles from Saybrook Light, but was afterward floated and put in commission.

The "Cleopatra" was built by Bishop and Simonson especially for this run. She had an extreme length of one hundred and ninety-three feet and was laid out on very graceful lines. Her hull was twenty-three feet wide and nine feet deep. The engine was built by the West Point Foundry and had a forty-four inch cylinder with an eleven foot stroke. Her wheels were twenty-three feet in diamater, eleven and a half feet wide with blades thirty-two inches deep on the face. The cylinder was forward of the engine, a peculiarity of the Hudson river boats, which gave her a distinct personality. Old men say that she was so regular in her running, sometimes at the rate of twenty miles an hour, that it was possible to time one's watch by her passing.

While the "Cleopatra" ran on this run she was the general favorite. As one of the links in the chain of connections for a daylight trip from New York to Boston, she was everywhere spoken about with praise. There was an early start from New York with a morning sail through the Sound and up the Connecticut river, then a further daylight sail in one of the "wheelbarrow" boats up the river twenty-five miles to Springfield and a brief rail journey to Boston over one of the first railroads built in this country. She continued to run on the river till 1842 when she was transferred to the Norwich route where Captain Sanford had already established the "Charter Oak."

"CITY OF SPRINGFIELD"—THE OLD "STATE OF NEW YORK" RE-CHRISTENED AFTER HER DISASTER AND PUT INTO SERVICE ON THE CONNECTICUT RIVER

"CITY OF RICHMOND"—BURNED TO THE WATER'S EDGE WHILE WAITING FOR HER COMMISSION TO RUN ON THE LINE TO HARTFORD.

The "Charter Oak" was a new boat when she came onto the Hartford-New York run. In fact, she was built for that run by Matthew Hubbard who the next year launched at East Haddam a ship for Captain C. R. Dean. Captain Dean always said that the "Charter Oak" cost him $500 for all his men stopped their work whenever she went by that they might get a look at "Boss Hubbard's boat." She had staterooms on the promenade deck, an innovation in steamboat architecture, but as it was a Connecticut "skipper," Captain E. S. Bunker, who first advertised to furnish bedding to the passengers who travelled on his packet sloop between Albany and New York, it was right that the credit of taking the sleeping accommodations out onto the open deck, rather

"CAPITOL CITY"—RAN AGROUND AT RYE NECK IN A DENSE FOG AND WAS COMPLETELY WRECKED

than clustering them about a stuffy cabin as had been general since they were taken from the stuffier hold, should come to Connecticut. On February 19, 1842 the "Charter Oak," then on the Norwich run, struck on Fisher's Island rocks but no lives were lost and the boat was afterward floated.

In 1839 the railroad between New Haven and Hartford was formally opened, the first public announcement having appeared on April 29th, together with the announcement of the steamboat service between New York and New Haven. The year was uneventful in steamboat circles. The "Cleopatra" and the "Charter Oak" were caring for the passenger business on the regular line and connection was made at Lyme with the steamboat "Flushing" for New London. In 1840 the "Cleopatra," under Captain Dunstan, who was afterward lost on the "Atlantic" when she went ashore on Fisher's Island, had as a running mate the "Bunker Hill," under command of Captain Huntington.

There was nothing exciting on the river that year nor the next, nor for that matter, at any time afterward. The railroad had cut so into the earnings of the steamboats that no one would venture to start a fight.

There were no steamboats on the Connecticut in the spring of 1842. The "Splendid" had been running every month during the winter when navigation was possible but had been taken off in the early spring for the usual renovating. This accounts for the trip by rail from Hartford to New Haven of which Dickens speaks in his "Notes," and the sail from New Haven to New York on the "New York" which he likens to a floating bath-house, saying:

> This was the first American steamboat of any size that I had seen; and certainly to an English eye it was infinitely less like a steamboat than a huge floating bath. I could hardly persuade myself, indeed, but that the bathing establishment off Westminister Bridge, which I left a baby, had not suddenly grown to an enormous size; run away from home; and set up in foreign parts as a steamer. Being in America, too, which our vagabonds do so particularly favour, it seemed the more probable.
>
> The great difference in appearance between these packets and ours, is, that there is so much of them out of the water; the main-deck being enclosed on all sides, and filled with casks and goods, like any second or third floor in a stack of warehouses; and the promenade or hurricane-deck being a-top of that again. A part of the machinery is always above this deck; where the connecting-rod, in a strong and lofty frame, is seen working away like an iron top-sawyer. There is seldom any mast or tackle; nothing aloft but two [*sic*] tall black chimneys. The man at the helm is shut up in a little house in the fore part of the boat (the wheel being connected with the rudder by iron chains, working the whole length of the deck); and the passengers, unless the weather be very fine indeed, usually congregate below. Directly you have left the wharf, all the life, and stir, and bustle of a packet cease. You wonder for a long time how she goes on, for there seems to be nobody in charge of her; and when another of those dull machines comes splashing by, you feel quite indignant with it, as a sullen, cumbrous, ungraceful, unshiplike leviathan; quite forgetting that the vessel you are on board of, is its very counterpart.
>
> There is always a clerk's office on the lower deck, where you pay your fare; a ladies' cabin; baggage and storage rooms; engineer's room; and in short a great variety of perplexities which render the discovery of the gentleman's cabin, a matter of some difficulty. It often occupies the whole length of the boat (as it did in this case), and has three or four tiers of berths on each side. When I first descended into the cabin of the "New York," it looked, in my unaccustomed eyes, about as long as the Burlington Arcade.

The "Splendid," which was the largest and fastest boat on the sound in the early "thirties" and which Dickens probably expected to find running between Hartford and New York, for the New Haven trip seems to have no place in his itinerary, was built in 1832 by Smith, Dimon and Comstock for the New Haven route, where she had as a mate the "Superior," built two years before with the enviable record of 651 trips to and from New York without a single break or an extra cent of expense for repairs or loss. These two boats were without question the finest then on the Sound and gave complete satisfaction to both owners and public. The "Superior" was later sold for service on the Hudson, her place being taken by the new "New Haven," and the "Splendid" was run as her mate till the appearance of the "New York" when she was laid aside as a "reserve boat." When the "New York" was burned in 1839 the entire steamboat property of the New Haven company was sold to Cornelius Vanderbilt, and the Connecticut Steamboat Company, the latter being the New York and Hartford line that had run the "Oliver Ellsworth," the "New England" the "McDonough" etc. of which we have been reading.

About May 1, 1842, the "Kosiusko," under the command of Captain Van Pelt, came onto the river from the Hudson where she had been engaged in a never settled trial of speed with the "Telegraph," and ran here till her place was taken by the "New Champion" in 1846. The "Kosiusko" was an old-timer when she came onto this run but she did good service, especially during the busiest part of the season. It is said that in those days of battle on the Hudson the "Kosiusko," in order to hold down her rival, the "Telegraph," which later came onto the New Haven route, would skip her landings and send any passengers on board back from the next town beyond. On one occasion fully fifty passengers were left standing on the wharf at Peekskill. What they thought has never been put in print.

The "New Champion," which succeeded the "Kosiusko," was at first in charge of Captain Van Pelt, but later passed to the command of Captain Tinklepaugh. She was a most fortunate boat and ran on this run till 1853 when she gave way to the "Granite State" and went onto the Hudson. In 1872-4 she was on the Catskill line, running at times with the "Andrew Harder," a propeller, and at times with the "Walter Brett," formerly the "Mary Benton," which had seen considerable service as a transport during the Civil War. As late as 1878 the "New Champion" was still running, and was even then quite a favorite, but when the "Minnie Cornell" was built in 1880 she was given the engine of the "New Champion" and it was in her when she burned at Keyport, N. J., a few years later.

There was an earlier "Champion" on the river, sometime in the early 30's, running occasionally between New York and Hartford and this accounts for the use of the adjective "New" in connection with this later boat. The first boat was one hundred and sixty feet long and was equipped with a beam engine built by the West Point Foundry. She belonged to Commodore Vanderbilt and was always ready for a "scrap" of any kind. During the summer of 1838 this little midget went down the coast to measure lengths with anything that might be afloat. On the Potomac there was a boat named the "Sidney" that was thought to be very fast but the Champion had no trouble in getting away from her and after picking up some of the money deposited by her backers the triumphant broom-bearer started for New Orleans. Here a match was arranged with one of the speediest high-pressure boats on the river. The race was to be from New Orleans to Louisville for a good sized purse. The "Yank" who had taken the boat south was superseded by one of the "high-pressure-fellows" who at once changed the set of the safety valve with the result that when she had gone but a few miles there was a "sprung" lifting-rod and a consequent delay of several hours for repairs. While the repairs were being made the contesting boat went by but the actual running time between the two points made by the "Champion" showed that her boasting antagonist would have been no match for her had there been standing at her engine the man who had run her in the race on the Potomac. She was afterward sold to parties in Florida who took her that same fall to Pensacola where she saw several years more of service.

About the first of June, 1842, the rebuilt "Globe" came onto the river under the command of Captain E. D. Routh, of Norwich. The "Globe" as built in 1830 was a "cross-head engine boat," one hundred and eighty-five feet long, twenty-eight feet and seven inches wide. When rebuilt and given the fittings of the "Bunker Hill" she was a very fine boat and did excellent service for several years. At the close of the Mexican War she was sold to parties in the South and taken for service on the coast of Texas where she is said to have become as popular as she had been on the Connecticut.

After the "Globe" came the little two-pipe "Hero," with boilers on the guards, and she did service until the advent of the "City of Hartford" in 1852. This was a new boat brought out by a new company and was under the command of Captain Daniel Mills. In 1886, March 31st, the "City of Hartford," which had been renamed the "Capitol City," was under the command of Captain Russell and was sailing slowly under one bell through a dense fog, ran aground at Rye Neck and was a complete loss.

In the latter part of July, or the early part of August, of this year, 1842, an iron steam freight boat, named "Ironsides," under Captain Marshman, arrived after a fifty-six hour run from Philadelphia with a load of coal. The "Ironsides" was "100 x 23 x 7" and drew five and a half feet of water when loaded to her full capacity of one-hundred and eighty tons. She was schooner-rigged and equipped with two of Ericsson's propellers which gave her a speed of some six or eight miles an hour. According to the *Hartford Courant* she was the first of the regular line of such boats to be established on the river for carrying coal.

In "Geer's Directory" for 1848 the steam-schooners "Josephine," Capt. E. M. Simpson; "E. J. Dupont" Capt. J. H. Morrison; "Rough and Ready," Capt. William Pitt; are advertised as sailing regularly between Hartford and Philadelphia via the Delaware and Raritan Canal.

During 1850 Captain Curtis Peck was running the "Connecticut" from Hartford on the day scheduled for the "New Champion" and the "Traveller" was run on the day scheduled for the "Hero." The "Connecticut" was built in 1847 and had a reputation for great speed. The "Traveller" was built in 1845 for Commodore Vanderbilt and was one of the most popular boats that ever ran on the river. She was two hundred and twenty-five feet long, twenty-nine feet wide and nine and a half feet deep. There were two iron boilers on the guards furnishing steam for a powerful beam engine with a fifty-two inch cylinder and an eleven foot stroke. The paddle-wheels were twenty-four feet in diameter with a face of eleven feet. It is said that on Saturday, June 20, 1846, the "Traveller" and the "Oregon," one of the fastest steamboats ever built, ran side by side for twenty-five miles, covering the distance in fifty-seven minutes. In 1850 she was bought by Chester W. Chapin, of Springfield, who also bought the "New Champion," and was used as a night boat on the New Haven line, the "New Champion" serving as a link between Hartford and New Haven. At first the "Traveller" ran as a day boat between New Haven and New York, carrying the United States mail, but later an arrangement was made by which the day boat between the two cities was discontinued to force passengers to patronize the railroad and for this consideration the railroad company agreed to pay $20,000 annually for the term of five years.

Not to be outdone by its rival which

had brought out the "City of Hartford," the old company brought out the "Granite State," under the command of Captain King, and for thirty years, barring a few months that she ran on the Hudson at the close of the Civil War, she was one of the favorites on the river. In June 1883, after passing into the river she was making ready for her stop at Goodspeed's Landing when a fire broke out that spread so rapidly that the passengers had to slide down from the upper decks in an awning. Three persons lost their lives and the boat drifted down the stream like so much burning timber,—a total wreck.

The place of the "Granite State" was temporarily filled by the "City of Lawrence," an iron hull boat which had been built for the Norwich and New York Transportation Company in 1867 and which is yet in service on the Sound.

When the "Capitol City" went ashore below Stamford arrangements were made for strengthening the hull of the "City of Richmond," which had been running on the New York and Sandy Hook route, and placing her on the Hartford run. While lying at the company's wharf in New York waiting for her commission she was burned to the water's edge but subsequently rebuilt as the"William G. Edgerton," one of the John H Starin fleet of excursion steamers and later was renamed the "Glen Island," under which name she was burned while running on the Starin line from New Haven.

In 1866 the "State of New York" came onto the river under command of Captain Mills, who was superseded by Captain Dibble, and in 1881 she was sunk but was later raised and named "City of Springfield" under which name she ran up to the year 1895.

For a few years prior to 1882 the old company had suffered a good many losses and in January of that year they withdrew from the route. In February the "Columbia," which had been laid aside after her summer season on the New York and Rockaway route, was put onto this run to make three trips a week which arrangement was continued till the beginning of the season of 1893 when the old company was reorganized and put their old boats on the route once more.

In 1892 they had built for them a propeller which was named "City of Hartford." In 1896 they ordered another boat, also a propeller, which was named "Middletown." The "City of Hartford" was sold to the United States Quartermaster's Department at the outbreak of the Spanish-American War and renamed the "Terry" under which name she did service in Cuban waters. At the close of the war she was sold for service on the Great Lakes. The "Middletown" continues still in service running on alternate days with the new "City of Hartford."

Looking back over the records we find that these boats, with the "Middletown" of 1838 built to look after the business of the local river landings; the "Sachem," "Seneca," and the "Uncas," all small propellers that ran to New York between 1847 and 1852, carrying freight only; the "Island Belle," the "Mary Benton," the "S. B. Camp" and the "Sunshine," that ran to New London and Long Island ports, on a route established by the "Cricket" in 1850; the "Laurence" and the "Alice" that ran to Norwich between 1846 and 1850; and the "Silver Star" that ran between local landings along the river from 1865 till the advent of the Connecticut Valley Railroad, and later went to the Delaware under the name "Florence" comprise the complete list of all the boats that have run on the river long enough to have gained for themselves any permanent place in its history.

Black Bass Fishing in Maine (1893)

BLACK-BASS FISHING IN MAINE.

BY ARTHUR PIERRE.

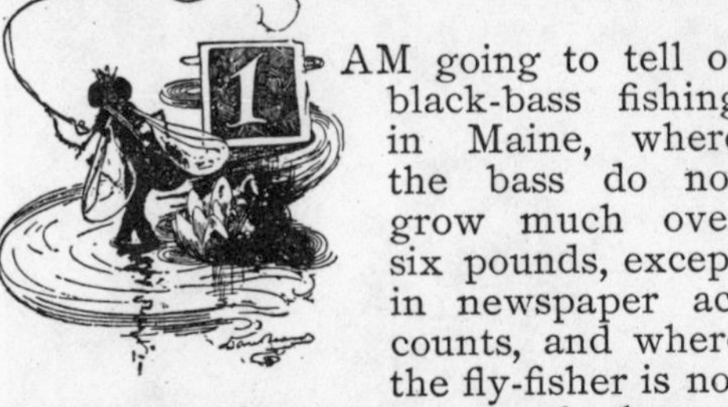

I AM going to tell of black-bass fishing in Maine, where the bass do not grow much over six pounds, except in newspaper accounts, and where the fly-fisher is not sufficiently numerous to teach the natives to look down on the humble troller. Yes, I confess it with shame, in trolling for black-bass I have passed many delightful hours and procured many a string of fish that have been a source of secret envy to less fortunate companions.

Early one morning in July I walked rapidly along a country road on my way to fulfill an appointment to "go a-fishin'" with no less a personage than Jack Pike, the blacksmith and general factotum of a little Maine village. I had long been a secret admirer of this worthy, for I had heard prodigious tales of "Jack's luck" and had gazed with unconcealed admiration at the trim lancewood rod and dainty tackle that ornamented a chosen corner of the dingy smithy.

Decidedly a blacksmith who so far defied the traditions of the place as to fish for bass with a seven-ounce lancewood instead of yanking out pickerel with a fifteen-foot pole, was a *rara avis* whom it was well worth while to cultivate. Since then, in numberless tramps through the backwoods, and in expeditions over secluded lakes and along unknown streams, I have often proved the value of the wit and wisdom that came from one of the kindest hearts that man was ever blessed with. He was not without learning also, and his occasional discussions of the topics of the day showed a keen insight into public affairs and human nature.

As I approached the shop the rhythmic blows of the hammer told me that Jack was evidently improving his time while waiting for me. As I came up to the open door, however, he stopped and threw the hammer away with a sigh of relief.

"I'd 'bout given you up," he said "an' started in to fix Mose Harper's mowin' machine, but I guess it's just as well I didn't." Then, on my half-hearted request that he keep right on working and we wait until another day, he continued:

"No; I sot out to go a-fishin' to-day, and I'm a-goin.' Besides, I'll be doin' that durn fool a real kindness not to fix his ol' machine. If he gits that done to-day, he won't know any better 'n to go an' mow down a lot o' hay, an' we're goin' to hev rain 'fore night just as sure as my name's Jack Pike. But, I reckon, we better be a-movin', fer it won't be long 'fore every durn fool in the village will be here with a hoss to shoe. They allus come when I want to go a-fishin'."

With this naïve bit of philosophy, he started through the fields to the lake, and I obediently followed. We soon reached the lake, but just as we were pushing off, a hoarse voice from the direction of the village came floating over the trees.

"J-a-a-ck! Oh, Ja-a-a-a-a-ck!" Jack looked at me with a dry smile.

"There, that fool jest knowed I wanted to go a-fishin' to-day, and he came 'round early so I'd have to fix his blamed ol' mowin'-machine, but I ruther guess we fooled him."

Just then a pensive bull-calf in the next pasture answered the persistent seeker after "J-a-a-a-ck!" with a plaintive "Pa-a-a-a!" ending in that divine guttural trill that only a healthy bull-calf can successfully accomplish.

The situation was not without humor, and as Jack rowed silently but rapidly away, he murmured partly to himself:

"Two of a kind. Two of a kind, an', I reckon, the young un has got the most sense."

As the last, lingering echoes of the bull-calf died away, I got out my line and began to troll for black-bass. Now, don't think you know all about trolling, my friend learned in piscatorial sport, for perhaps you don't. Trolling for black-bass is a science. I thought I knew it all, but when I had rigged my tackle, under Jack's direction, I felt like

"THEY ALLUS COME WHEN I WANT TO GO A-FISHIN'."

a novice. In the first place, I took a three-yard double leader and fastened to it four flies, selected by Jack from my fairly well-filled book. If I remember rightly, he chose a "Furguson," two "polkas" and a "grizzly king." At any rate, subsequent experience has taught me that these are among the best for trolling in that region. Fastening the leader to a light oiled-silk line (size F), which ran smoothly from a multiplying Hendryx click reel, fastened firmly on a seven-ounce lance-wood, which Jack had pronounced a "purty good pole," I was ready for business. I dropped the cast overboard, and let it run out behind the boat until fifteen or twenty yards were missing from the reel. I wanted to stop then, but Jack wouldn't hear of it, until over a hundred feet were trailing along behind us.

I had caught bass before, but I must say that I felt a little scared when I thought of the "gleaming eight-pound warrior" of the newspapers at the end of that delicate contrivance. However, I will warn every one that, in spite of the veracity of a truthful and unprejudiced press, eight-pounders were never quite in my line, or rather on my line.

Jack was now rowing very slowly along the shore, keeping the boat out far enough for my flies to just escape the occasional lily-pads that frequently grow along rocky and sandy shores. Pretty soon a series of little twitches told me that something was fooling with the cast. Then the twitches became sharper, and every now and then they were strong enough to run a foot or so of line off the reel. A look of disgust had gradually spread over Jack's face.

"We've run through a herd of them good fer nothin' perch, and you've got one on every hook."

Upon reeling in I found he was indeed a true prophet, for on the first three hooks were three perch gasping with astonishment at their sudden introduction into polite society. The fourth hook, however, held a small bass not more than four inches long. As he seemed thoroughly ashamed of himself, and looked duly penitent at being caught in such company, I tossed him overboard, but the perch were consigned to an old starch-box with the following rather enigmatical remark from Jack:

"'Round here folks think them's good enough fer hogs. Shouldn't wonder if you caught some more." I fancied there was a slight emphasis on the "you," but as Jack seemed as solemn as the occasion demanded, I concluded I was mistaken.

I let out my line and we went on near the shore in perfect silence, excepting the faint cawing of crows in a distant pine, and the shrill peep of an occasional snipe that was picking up his breakfast along the sand flats we passed. The water was still, and the trees and rocks on the shore were caught and held in perfect reflection. The morning sun, just rising over the tops of the pines that stood along the shore in dark array, cheered me and robbed the air of its chill. The subdued ripple of the oars as Jack silently and slowly forced the boat through the pictured woods, lulled me into a dreamy reverie in which every thought was of peace and pleasure. The magic charm of the woods was upon me, and everything seemed to happen with the delightful irrationality of a dream. I realized then as never before that all the charm of a day's fishing is not in the sport itself.

But my dreaming came to an abrupt end as I suddenly felt a sharp tug, and then my reel began to shriek its sharp warning. The change from repose to action was instantaneous. There was no need of Jack's quick "Look out!" I was looking out, and, standing up in that little boat, was engaged in a battle royal with that glittering flash of silver that now and again showed itself so very far away.

Well, yes, I suppose, Mister Cynic, that any fool *can* catch a fish, and that it is a little thing to make a fuss about; but let me put you into a combination with a light rod, a long line, and a three-pound chunk of perversity called a black bass, and if there are not times when you are willing to back the bass for all you are worth, call me no fisherman. And if you do not feel every nerve in your body tingle with excitement as the fish plunges in every direction and never seems to be coming nearer the boat, then you are indeed a cynic, and really very much to be pitied.

Slowly I reeled the bass in, but not without considerable reluctance on his part, and with no little firm persuasion on mine. Jack had meantime set the boat with steady, easy strokes, away from the shore, and soon I had the fish in deep water and away from all obstructions. For the next fifteen minutes I think I experienced nearly every feeling that the human soul can know, from the ecstasy of delight when the excited fish flashed into the air before my very eyes, to the dull anguish of utter despair as the line slackened and I thought I had lost him.

Of course I didn't lose him. If I had, he would have weighed more than three pounds. No man ever loses a fish as small as that. It is against the unwritten rules of the brotherhood, and it is worthy of note that we all observe those unwritten rules, even if the decalogue suffers a little. I presume that Jonah exaggerated the size of his *companion du voyage* when he was safe on dry land. But then Jonah had good reason to speak well of that fish. It would take a mighty mean man to undervalue a fish under such circumstances.

Finally the rushes grew less frequent and shorter, and then as the bass passed slowly by, too much exhausted to make more than a feeble protest, Jack slipped the landing net under him and soon he lay on the bottom of the boat. I sank back into the seat with a sigh of delight, and then with an attempt to look as though I was in the habit of catching three-pound bass every day in the Frog-pond, I observed, as carelessly as possible, "Hum! Not quite as big as I thought he was. Weigh about two pounds, or two and a half, perhaps?"

"Oh, he'll weigh more'n that," said Jack; "good deal nearer three an' a half. But I'll weigh him as soon's you git your line out agin."

"How are you going to weigh him?" said I, as indifferently as possible.

Now right there Jack gave additional proof that he was not an angler, but simply a fisherman, by taking a pair of balances from his pocket and weighing my bass. "Jest a shade under three an' a half," he announced, with a magisterial air, and I received the verdict with much the same air as a sweet girl graduate receives her blue ribboned diploma.

My line had soon run out again, but it hardly reached the limit when another vicious tug and whirr of the reel brought me to my feet again. This time it was two smaller ones, and they made a very pretty fight, at times leaving the line almost slack when they were pulling against each other, and then making the rod bend as they started off together.

I continued to troll, with more or less success, until eleven bass had been transferred from the lake to the box in the bow of the boat.

After a while I took the oars and Jack trolled. His first capture was a gigantic chub, that came in with all the grace of an amateur hippopotamus, and looked pretty nearly all mouth as he lay on the bottom of the boat.

"That 'ere fish reminds me a good deal of Mose Harper," said Jack. "If he'd only keep his mouth shet he'd look a blame sight purtier an' git into less trouble. Mose Harper allus has his mouth open and it often gits him inter trouble. Why, one day las' summer Mose came in to Deacon Jim Lawrence's store where the boys was all tergether a-waitin' fer the noon mail to be in. Wall, Mose has got the biggest mouth in town, an' jest as he come in the Deacon's boy, Bill, took up a molasses cookie an' took a thunderin' big bite. Wall, the boys all laughed and Mose thought he'd go the young feller one better, so he up an' opens his mouth till he looked a good deal like that chub down there. Wall, the boys all laughed agin and Mose strained his mouth wider still. Pritty soon he began to look scart and put both han's up ter his mouth as if ter push it to. But he couldn't do it. The pesky idjut had slipped his jaw back an' it had stuck, an' he stood there jest like that bull-calf we heard with his mouth wide open. Then he started on the dead run down to the Corners to ol' Dr. Child's bare-headed an' with his mouth wide open. Wall, the boys all started after him an' pritty soon half the village was going down the road tight as they could git, so that ol' Aunt Sallie Butterworth went over into Pelham an' tol' all the folks over there that Mose Harper had gone crazy and run into the woods an' all the men in town was out a chasin' him with pitchforks. Mose was mad as blazes when he heard of it.

"Wall, Mose come to the Doctor's an' flung the door open an' run right in where the doctor was eatin' dinner. The crowd came right in an' stood there behind Mose and those that couldn't git in tramped down all Mis' Child's flower beds tryin' ter peak in the winder. The ol' doctor is a pritty putchiky old chap, an he was riled, but he tried not to show it an' said as calm as he could:

"'Mornin', Mose. Can I do anythin' for you?'

"Mose stood there an' pointed to his mouth and sort of gurgled a good deal like that chub is doin' now. Then the doctor spoke up again rather short-like, 'What's the matter, Mose? Can I help you any?' Mose never said a word but stood there a pointin' to his mouth an' rolling his eyes, an' some of the fellers began to laugh. The ol' doctor thought they was laughin' at him, an' he flared right up and roared to Mose:

"'Shet yer mouth, you d— fool,' and with that he hit Mose a slap side the jaw and Mose's mouth snapped to like a snuff-box. Then the fellers stepped in an' explained matters an' it all ended up in a laugh, but I don't think the doctor ever quite forgive Mose. At any rate he sent him a bill of two dollars fer performin' an operation."

By this time Jack was fishing again and was soon rewarded with a lively bass that weighed just two pounds.

We fished by turns all day except when we landed and boiled our coffee and broiled a couple of fresh bass over the coals. Talk about epicures. The man who hasn't eaten a bass fresh from the water and broiled over the coals doesn't know the meaning of good living. Of course the sun is hot and the smoke gets into your eyes when you are near the fire, and the wood-flies when you are not, but after all a smoking black bass spread out on a flat rock is a temptation worth enduring.

Night came all too soon and we rowed slowly down the lake in the gathering dusk, tired, hungry and happy. We climbed wearily up the hill to the shop and divided the spoils in the twilight and as I turned away down the road I heard Jack murmur to himself:

"I might a-fixed that mowin' machine fer Mose Harper, an' it didn't rain after all; but then, I guess it's jest as well."

Yes, it was just as well. We had brought home two dozen bass, weighing from half a pound to three and a half. Not a big catch, surely, my brothers from the South and West, where bass grow so big that they cannot turn around in the rivers. No, not a big catch nor very big fish, but they were caught up amidst the gray New England hills where the mountain-tops are photographed on the water, and the silent pines look on with majestic approval. They were caught in the land where the surroundings, rugged and hard, make men that are in keeping with themselves, and it seems to me that even the fish partook of the grim New England character and came up to the boat with that obstinacy and resistance characteristic of New England.

"JACK WAS SOON REWARDED WITH A LIVELY BASS."

974. Oppel, F. ed.
O
Tales of New Eng
past

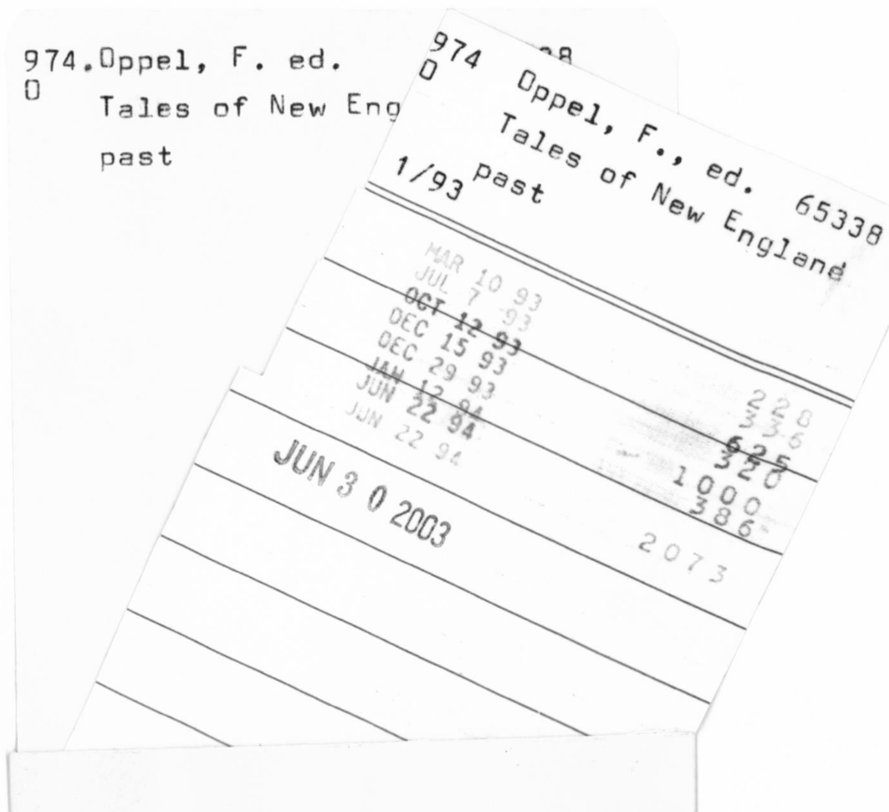

MONSON FREE LIBRARY
MONSON, MA 01057
DEMCO